Powhat

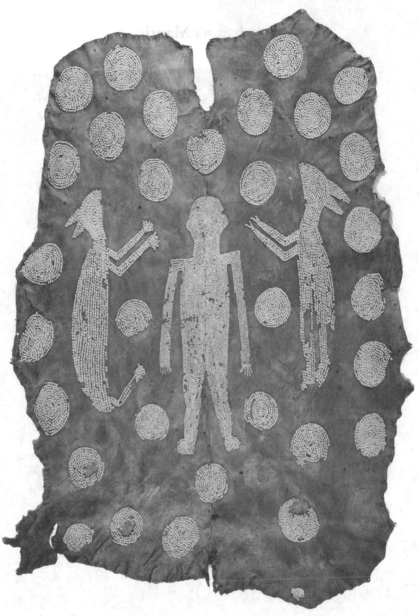

Powhatan's Mantle, circa 1608 (courtesy of the Ashmolean Museum, Oxford).

Powhatan's Mantle

Indians in the Colonial Southeast

Edited & with an introduction by Gregory A. Waselkov, Peter H. Wood, and Tom Hatley

REVISED AND EXPANDED EDITION

UNIVERSITY OF NEBRASKA PRESS • LINCOLN AND LONDON

Tom Hatley's chapter "Cherokee
Women Farmers Hold Their Ground" is
adapted from the original publication in
Appalachian Frontiers, ed. Robert Mitchell (Lexington: University Press of Kentucky, 1991, 37–51). Reprinted by permission of the University Press of Kentucky.

Ian W. Brown's chapter "The Calumet
Ceremony in the Southeast as Observed
Archaeologically" is adapted from the
original publication in *American Antiquity* 54, no. 2 (1989): 311–31. Reproduced
by permission of the Society for American Archaeology.

Set in Adobe Garamond by Kim Essman.
Designed by R. W. Boeche.

Library of Congress Cataloging-in-
Publication Data
Powhatan's mantle : Indians in the colonial Southeast / edited and with an
introduction by Gregory A. Waselkov,
Peter H. Wood, and Tom Hatley.—Rev.
and expanded ed.
p. cm.
Includes bibliographical references and
index.
ISBN-13: 978-0-8032-9861-3 (pbk. : alk.
paper)
ISBN-10: 0-8032-9861-7 (pbk. : alk.
paper)
1. Indians of North America—Southern
States—History—Colonial period, ca.
1600–1775.   2. Indians of North America—Southern States—Social life and
customs.
I. Waselkov, Gregory A.
II. Wood, Peter H., 1943–
III. Hatley, M. Thomas, 1951–
E78.S65P69 2006
975.004'97—dc22
2006014921

Contents

General Introduction to the Revised Edition

Scholars of the Americas have long been engaged in speculation and research regarding the peoples who inhabited this hemisphere in so-called pre-Columbian times, before AD 1500, and during the subsequent colonial era, up to roughly 1800.[1] Such researchers have faced numerous and basic questions. Which continents did these people come from, when did they first arrive, and what were their numbers? How did they live, and how did they respond to drastic change? Despite its esoteric language and deliberate pace, this many-sided discussion constitutes more than a remote academic discourse. It contains a deep and often hidden significance for our present and future self-understanding.

In Latin America, where intensive contact between Indians and non-Indians began earliest and occurred on the largest scale, work has proceeded actively for generations. As early as 1950, much fresh knowledge had been consolidated in the Smithsonian Institution's seven-volume *Handbook of South American Indians*. And research has progressed steadily since then, down to the impressive new studies of the present day.[2] Regarding North America, in contrast, modern research has proceeded more slowly. Only in recent decades—and particularly since the publication of *Powhatan's Mantle*—has a sizable contingent of North American scholars begun systematically to sift through the work of their historian and anthropologist forebears, crossing the persistent geographical and disciplinary boundaries that have impeded general understanding. Beginning from many different quarters, these diverse scholars have slowly started to formulate a clearer picture of the Indians, Africans, and Europeans who peopled America by 1800, at the start of the demographic explosion that shaped our modern world.[3]

Underlying much of this work has been the gradual emergence of ethnohistory. This approach combines techniques from history and anthropology to study change over time in societies that did not write their own histories. The establishment of the Indian Claims Commission by the United States government in 1946 is often cited as sparking initial efforts in ethnohistory. Suddenly scores of anthropologists, called as expert witnesses, were obliged to interact with historians in making use of written documents to legitimate specific land claims. In the 1950s, regional meetings between anthropologists and historians led to the formation of the American Indian Ethnohistorical Conference, which later expanded into the American Society for Ethnohistory and began publication of the journal *Ethnohistory*.[4]

Predictably, the greatest North American advances in Indian ethnohistory initially involved the Southwest (with a sizable Native American population, a long tradition of anthropological study, and a climate suited to archaeology) and the Northeast (with its rich historical resources, its well-endowed and prestigious university centers, and its international scholarly community on both sides of the St. Lawrence). So it is not surprising that several of the earliest completed volumes of the Smithsonian Institution's new *Handbook of North American Indians* have covered these two separate areas. But interdisciplinary work in other regions has also proceeded at an encouraging pace, aided by improved field techniques, expanded research tools, and well-run resource centers.[5]

No single North American region has gained more from this renewed groundswell of scholarly interest than the Southeast, where scholarship arguably had further to come. Important overviews by anthropologist Charles Hudson and historian J. Leitch Wright Jr. (published in 1976 and 1981, respectively) have been followed in recent years by several important collected works that summarize current knowledge and raise fresh questions.[6] The long-awaited *Southeast* volume of the *Handbook of North American Indians* repeats this process on a broader scale. Current students therefore can still return to such pioneering authors as John Swanton, James Mooney, Frank G. Speck, and Verner W. Crane, but from now on they will have many more diverse and up-to-date monographic materials available to shape—and no doubt complicate—their endeavors (see postscript).[7]

These fresh southern materials derive not only from history and anthropology but from archaeology as well.[8] Careful fieldwork in the region got an early boost during the Great Depression, when shovels and trowels became tools of survival as well as research. In succeeding decades publicly funded archaeology continued to concentrate on "salvage digs" near large construction projects, where the basic research materials were soon destroyed or covered over forever, after only a brief sampling of the site. In the 1970s and 1980s, construction of the Tellico Dam on the Little Tennessee River resulted in the loss of habitat for the endangered snail darter and in massive destruction of the Cherokee archaeological record. The accompanying public outcry helped bring an end to massive federal projects started during the New Deal that seemed intent on damming or diverting every free-flowing river in the Southeast. As a consequence of national legislation meant to protect the country's archaeological resources from destruction during any sort of federally funded development, archaeologists and tribes, now more than ever, intervene to protect threatened sites or excavate those that cannot be saved. In some areas archaeological consciousness is moving faster than the bulldozers of Sunbelt developers, and funds for basic excavation and analysis are available in certain states. We are now learning more about the South through scientific fieldwork than we have at any time since Thomas Jefferson dug his first trench through an Indian mound near Monticello. And we can hope to learn a good deal more before every last coastal dune and riverfront acre is platted, flattened, and improved.

After three hundred years of analysis, criticism, and investigation by outsiders, Native American tribal peoples are offering their own "inside" views.[9] Tribal perspectives focus on traditions and values in ways that are often opposed to the traditions and values of Western scholarship. Several trends are at work, more compelling since this book first appeared. Federal and state laws and regulations have strengthened tribal authority over human remains, sacred places, and even such issues as hydropower re-licensing in multistate areas. New revenue sources for tribes—casino gambling, for instance—are giving Native Americans seats at the political table, and control over their own "stories." Native American Studies programs, though conspicuously missing (with a few exceptions) in the South, have incubated new perspectives and injected new thinking into disciplines from history to religious studies. Several southeastern tribes have set up their own Tribal Historic Preservation Offices, and the National Museum of the American Indian rises obliquely across the Mall from the National Museum of American History.

The earliest Southerners lived by their rivers. And this assertion contains more than one layer of truth, for over thousands of years these diverse people regularly lived beside, from, and through the myriad streams that shaped the southern environment. The incomparable Mississippi system, descending from the north, has divided and nurtured the South for eons. But even the Father of Waters—Walt Whitman's "spinal column" of the continent—

can hardly overshadow the scores of smaller waterways that descend from interior slopes to the Gulf of Mexico and the Atlantic Ocean. From the Brazos and the Trinity in Texas to the Potomac and the Rappahannock on the Chesapeake, these numerous rivers follow relatively brief courses from the interior to the sea. All of them, long or short, derive from a series of confluences along the way, where several smaller branches come together to form the larger stream. For countless generations, the region's inhabitants regularly chose to locate their villages at these rich intersections.

In a sense this book is located at such an intersection, since it concerns several sets of convergences—disciplinary, chronological, and geographic. The most important confluence involves separate disciplines. This is reflected even in the backgrounds of the three editors, Tom Hatley, Peter Wood, and Greg Waselkov, for we have all pursued the study of the southern past in different ways—as forester and historian, social historian, and archaeological anthropologist, respectively. The other contributors to this volume also vary markedly in background and training, and all have suffered from the general tendencies inhibiting work across disciplinary lines. Hence all have hopes that a volume like this can help make amends.

Who is to say whether history or anthropology has been more recalcitrant about incorporating the insights of the other field? We do know, according to a broad survey of nearly four thousand scholars by the American Council of Learned Societies, that historians have been particularly "unlikely to collaborate with other members of their profession or even to exchange information," and that they "are also less likely to co-author articles or books than other scholars."[10] As editors, we have requested historical, rather than anthropological, notation throughout the book in a small concession to these conservative tendencies. In selecting and arranging these essays, we have tried to remind ourselves, our fellow contributors, and our readers of the potential insights to be gained from communication across disciplinary lines.

This collection also represents important convergences over time and space. Chronologically, it focuses for the most part upon the seventeenth and eighteenth centuries AD. This era is more distant and less populous than the familiar "Antebellum" and "Civil War" periods, so inviting to historians, or than the subsequent parade of "New Souths." But it is not as remote and difficult to document as the many generations preceding Columbus, plus the first crucial hundred years of Spanish and French intervention, which have long absorbed many of the region's best anthropologists. Situated between a less tangible "prehistory" and a too familiar recent history, it constitutes a moment of enormous change, as the ensuing essays testify, and also an era of surprising continuity with what had gone before and what was still to follow.

Geographically, our focus here includes the whole southeastern section of North America, from the Ohio River to the Gulf of Mexico and the Florida Keys, from the East Texas pinelands country to the Sea Islands and the Outer Banks. Several essays extend over virtually the entire forest; others examine in greater detail some separate aspect or single portion of the whole. For many people working outside the region, who probably know well the different nations of the Iroquois League or the separate mesa settlements of Pueblo culture, this presentation, on the one hand, may help clarify both the parts and the whole of southeastern Indian life, reducing important aspects to manageable size. On the other hand, for the increasing numbers within the region working on some local aspect of Indian life in the colonial era, this collection may help broaden their horizons beyond a specific excavation or archive, giving them a wider context for their ongoing work.

Whatever an initial glance at the title might suggest, this book concerns the entire geographic South. In fact, the title *Powhatan's Mantle* has been chosen consciously on the assumption that many readers, both laypersons and scholars, begin from a limited set of inherited images. For most of us, mention of Indians in the colonial Southeast still conjures up immediate recollections of Powhatan and Pocahontas on the Chesapeake; all else remains hazy. In a literal sense, Powhatan's mantle is a fascinating artifact, pictured in the frontispiece and discussed in Greg Waselkov's essay. But in a figurative sense it is much larger, an emblem for the Indian inheritance of the entire region, of which Powhatan's chiefdom, even at its height, embraced only a very small corner.[11]

Indeed, the word "mantle" can be read to mean the land itself, the earth's surface and subsurface, which had one significance for the South's original inhabitants and quite another for the newcomers who gradually took control of the region, piece by piece, decade by decade. The same forces that removed Powhatan's literal mantle to the Ashmolean Museum eventually seized the inheritance of numerous chiefdoms larger than his. The

southern land and its resources, "Powhatan's Mantle" in the largest metaphorical sense, passed swiftly from Indian to intruder in the course of a
few short generations.

This book, then, concentrates upon that momentous period of transition
known as the "colonial" era. The first edition brought together original studies by scholars actively at work in the field, to suggest the complexity and
importance of this portion of southern history when viewed from a fresh
perspective. With this revised edition, the significance of the topic no longer needs defense. After the passage of some fifteen to twenty years, southeastern ethnohistorical research is more lively and diverse than ever before.
In the essays that follow, the twelve original authors take the opportunity to
reflect, in textual additions and postscripts, on developments in their subject. Some have opted to leave their original chapter contents untouched.
Others have corrected, rephrased, and updated their chapters as necessary;
a few have revised extensively, and one of us—Tom Hatley—has replaced
his original contribution with another addressing the topic of gender and
agriculture. Three other colleagues accepted invitations to join the cast of
this revised, expanded production. Ian Brown's chapter on calumet ceremonialism first appeared in print in the journal *American Antiquity*. Originally
intended for the initial edition of *Powhatan's Mantle*, it appears here in an
extensively revised version. Two other essays have been written especially for
this volume. Kathleen DuVal dissects the intricate social relations created
by the diverse and intertwined peoples of "French" Louisiana, and Claudio
Saunt considers how Creek Indians came to adopt an ideology of race.

We have not arranged these chapters in any linear manner but instead
have grouped them, to borrow an Indian image, around three separate fires.
Talk at the initial fire concerns geography and population, the diverse land
and its changing peoples. Around the second fire, politics and economics
are the underlying matters of discussion. At the third fire, broad themes of
social change and cultural continuity emerge from a series of case studies.
We are grateful to our fellow contributors for their part in helping to kin-
dle these council fires.

Gregory A. Waselkov, Peter H. Wood, and Tom Hatley

Postscript: Some Recent References
on Indians of the Colonial Southeast

Proponents of indigenous history and Native Studies are challenging the fundamental basis of ethnohistory as previously conceived. Some influential critiques of traditional Indian history, anthropology, and ethnohistory include Donald L. Fixico, *The American Indian Mind in a Linear World: American Indian Studies and Traditional Knowledge* (New York: Routledge, 2003); Lisa J. Lefler and Frederic W. Gleach, eds., *Southern Indians and Anthropologists: Culture, Politics, and Identity* (Athens: University of Georgia Press, 2002); Devon A. Mihesuah, ed., *Natives and Academics: Researching and Writing about American Indians* (Lincoln: University of Nebraska Press, 1998); Russell Thornton, ed., *Studying Native America: Problems and Prospects* (Madison: University of Wisconsin Press, 1998).

Among the essay collections to appear recently on focused topics are Charles Hudson and Carmen Chaves Tesser, eds., *The Forgotten Centuries: Indians and Europeans in the American South, 1521–1704* (Athens: University of Georgia Press, 1994); Patricia B. Kwachka, ed., *Perspectives on the Southeast: Linguistics, Archaeology, and Ethnohistory*, Southern Anthropological Society Proceedings 27 (Athens: University of Georgia Press, 1994); Jeannie Whayne, ed., *Cultural Encounters in the Early South: Indians and Europeans in Arkansas* (Fayetteville: University of Arkansas Press, 1995); Linda Barrington, ed., *The Other Side of the Frontier: Economic Explorations into Native American History* (Boulder CO: Westview Press, 1999); Dennis B. Blanton and Julia A. King, eds., *Indian and European Contact in Context: The Mid-Atlantic Region* (Gainesville: University Press of Florida, 2004); and Thomas J. Pluckhahn and Robbie Ethridge, eds., *Light on the Path: The Anthropology and History of the Southeastern Indians* (Tuscaloosa: University of Alabama Press, 2006).

The impressive number of recent monographs in southeastern ethnohistory testifies to an expansion in the ranks of scholars active in the field. A growing array of publishers is distributing these studies to a historically engaged audience that now stretches well beyond the academy. The imposing shelf of works released since the original publication of *Powhatan's Mantle* includes Morris S. Arnold, *The Rumble of a Distant Drum: The Quapaws and Old World Newcomers, 1673–1804* (Fayetteville: University of

Arkansas Press, 2000); James R. Atkinson, *Splendid Land, Splendid People: The Chickasaw Indians to Removal* (Tuscaloosa: University of Alabama Press, 2004); James Axtell, *The Indians' New South: Cultural Change in the Colonial Southeast* (Baton Rouge: Louisiana State University Press, 1997); John H. Blitz and Karl G. Lorenz, *The Chattahoochee Chiefdoms* (Tuscaloosa: University of Alabama Press, 2006); Thomas John Blumer, *Catawba Indian Pottery: The Survival of a Folk Tradition* (Tuscaloosa: University of Alabama Press, 2004); Kathryn E. Holland Braund, *Deerskins and Duffels: Creek Indian Trade with Anglo-America, 1685–1815* (Lincoln: University of Nebraska Press, 1993); James Taylor Carson, *Searching for the Bright Path: The Mississippi Choctaws from Prehistory to Removal* (Lincoln: University of Nebraska Press, 1999); Kathleen L. Ehrhardt, *European Metals in Native Hands: Rethinking Technological Change, 1640–1683* (Tuscaloosa: University of Alabama Press, 2005); Robbie Ethridge, *Creek Country: The Creek Indians and Their World* (Chapel Hill: University of North Carolina Press, 2003); Andrew K. Frank, *Creeks and Southerners: Biculturalism on the Early American Frontier* (Lincoln: University of Nebraska Press, 2005); Allan Gallay, *The Indian Slave Trade: The Rise of the English Empire in the American South, 1670–1717* (New Haven CT: Yale University Press, 2002); Patricia Galloway, *Choctaw Genesis, 1500–1700* (Lincoln: University of Nebraska Press, 1995); Frederic W. Gleach, *Powhatan's World and Colonial Virginia: A Conflict of Cultures* (Lincoln: University of Nebraska Press, 1997); Robert L. Hall, *An Archaeology of the Soul: North American Indian Belief and Ritual* (Urbana: University of Illinois Press, 1997); Tom Hatley, *The Dividing Paths: Cherokees and South Carolinians through the Era of Revolution* (Oxford: Oxford University Press, 1993); Paul E. Hoffman, *Florida's Frontiers* (Bloomington: Indiana University Press, 2002); Heather A. Lapham, *Hunting for Hides: Deerskins, Status, and Cultural Change in the Protohistoric Appalachians* (Tuscaloosa: University of Alabama Press, 2005); David La Vere, *The Caddo Chiefdoms: Caddo Economics and Politics, 700–1835* (Lincoln: University of Nebraska Press, 1998); Seth Mallios, *The Deadly Politics of Giving: Exchange and Violence at Ajacan, Roanoke, and Jamestown* (Tuscaloosa: University of Alabama Press, 2006); Joel W. Martin, *Sacred Revolt: The Muskogees' Struggle for a New World* (Boston: Beacon Press, 1991); Michael N. McConnell, *A Country Between: The Upper Ohio Valley and Its Peoples, 1724–1774* (Lincoln: University of Nebraska Press, 1992);

James H. Merrell, *The Indians' New World: Catawbas and Their Neighbors from European Contact through the Era of Removal* (Chapel Hill: University of North Carolina Press, 1989), and *Into the American Woods: Negotiators on the Pennsylvania Frontier* (New York: W. W. Norton, 1999); Jane T. Merritt, *At the Crossroads: Indians and Empires on a Mid-Atlantic Frontier, 1700–1763* (Chapel Hill: University of North Carolina Press, 2003); Susan A. Miller, *Coacoochee's Bones: A Seminole Saga* (Lawrence: University Press of Kansas, 2003); Michael P. Morris, *The Bringing of Wonder: Trade and the Indians of the Southeast, 1700–1783* (Westport CT: Greenwood Press, 1999); Greg O'Brien, *Choctaws in a Revolutionary Age, 1750–1830* (Lincoln: University of Nebraska Press, 2002); Theda Perdue, *"Mixed Blood" Indians: Racial Construction in the Early South* (Athens: University of Georgia Press, 2003); Stephen R. Potter, *Commoners, Tribute, and Chiefs: The Development of Algonquian Culture in the Potomac Valley* (Charlottesville: University of Virginia Press, 1993); Helen C. Rountree, *Pocahontas's People: The Powhatan Indians of Virginia through Four Centuries* (Norman: University of Oklahoma Press, 1990), and *Pocahontas, Powhatan, Opechancanough: Three Indian Lives Changed by Jamestown* (Charlottesville: University of Virginia Press, 2005); Claudio Saunt, *A New Order of Things: Property, Power, and the Transformation of the Creek Indians, 1733–1816* (Cambridge: Cambridge University Press, 1999), and *Black, White, and Indian: Race and the Unmaking of an American Family* (Oxford: Oxford University Press, 2005); Nancy Shoemaker, *A Strange Likeness: Becoming Red and White in Eighteenth-Century North America* (Oxford: Oxford University Press, 2004); Marvin T. Smith, *Coosa: The Rise and Fall of a Southeastern Mississippian Chiefdom* (Gainesville: University Press of Florida, 2000); F. Todd Smith, *The Caddo Indians: Tribes at the Convergence of Empires, 1542–1854* (College Station: Texas A&M University Press, 1995), and *From Dominance to Disappearance: The Indians of Texas and the Near Southwest, 1786–1859* (Lincoln: University of Nebraska Press, 2005); Daniel H. Usner Jr., *Indians, Settlers, and Slaves in a Frontier Exchange Economy: The Lower Mississippi Valley before 1783* (Chapel Hill: University of North Carolina Press, 1992), and *American Indians in the Lower Mississippi Valley: Social and Economic Histories* (Lincoln: University of Nebraska Press, 1998); Patricia Riles Wickman, *The Tree That Bends: Discourse, Power, and the Survival of the Maskókî People* (Tuscaloosa: University of Alabama Press, 1999); Margaret Holmes Williamson, *Pow-*

hatan Lords of Life and Death: Command and Consent in Seventeenth-Century Virginia (Lincoln: University of Nebraska Press, 2003).

American Indian impacts on European philosophy, literature, art, and museums are considered in six volumes: Christian F. Feest, ed., *Indians in Europe: An Interdisciplinary Collection of Essays* (Lincoln: University of Nebraska Press, 1999); Karen Ordahl Kupperman, ed., *America in European Consciousness, 1493–1750* (Chapel Hill: University of North Carolina Press, 1995); Gordon M. Sayre, *Les Sauvages Américains: Representations of Native Americans in French and English Colonial Literature* (Chapel Hill: University of North Carolina Press, 1997), and *The Indian Chief as Tragic Hero: Native Resistance and the Literatures of America from Moctezuma to Tecumseh* (Chapel Hill: University of North Carolina Press, 2005); Roger Schlesinger, *In the Wake of Columbus: The Impact of the New World on Europe, 1492–1650* (Wheeling IL: Harlan Davidson, 1996); and Stuart B. Schwartz, ed., *Implicit Understandings: Observing, Reporting, and Reflecting on the Encounters between Europeans and Other Peoples in the Early Modern Era* (New York: Cambridge University Press, 1994).

The Columbian Quincentenary and the 350th anniversary of de Soto's march across the Southeast both prompted important reconsiderations of Spanish colonial interaction with the Indians of the region: Charles R. Ewen and John H. Hann, *Hernando de Soto among the Apalachee: The Archaeology of the First Winter Encampment* (Gainesville: University Press of Florida, 1998); Patricia Galloway, ed., *The Hernando de Soto Expedition: History, Historiography, and "Discovery" in the Southeast* (Lincoln: University of Nebraska Press, 1997); John H. Hann, *Indians of Central and South Florida, 1513–1763* (Gainesville: University Press of Florida, 2003); John H. Hann and Bonnie G. McEwan, eds., *The Apalachee Indians and Mission San Luis* (Gainesville: University Press of Florida, 1998); Charles Hudson, *Knights of Spain, Warriors of the Sun: Hernando de Soto and the South's Ancient Chiefdoms* (Athens: University of Georgia Press, 1997); Jerald T. Milanich, *Florida Indians and the Invasion from Europe* (Gainesville: University Press of Florida, 1995), and *Laboring in the Fields of the Lord: Spanish Missions and Southeastern Indians* (Washington DC: Smithsonian Institution Press, 1999); Jerald T. Milanich and Charles Hudson, *Hernando de Soto and the Indians of Florida* (Gainesville: University Press of Florida, 1993); Jerald T. Milanich and Susan Milbrath, eds., *First Encounters: Spanish Explorations in the*

Caribbean and the United States, 1492–1570 (Gainesville: University Press of Florida, 1989); David Hurst Thomas, ed., *Columbian Consequences*, 3 vols. (Washington DC: Smithsonian Institution Press, 1989–1991); Herman J. Viola and Carolyn Margolis, eds., *Seeds of Change: A Quincentennial Commemoration* (Washington DC: Smithsonian Institution Press, 1991); David J. Weber, *The Spanish Frontier in North America* (New Haven: Yale University Press, 1992); John E. Worth, *The Struggle for the Georgia Coast: An Eighteenth-Century Spanish Retrospective on Guale and Mocama*, Anthropological Papers 75 (New York: American Museum of Natural History, 1995), and *Timucuan Chiefdoms of Spanish Florida*, 2 vols. (Gainesville: University Press of Florida, 1998).

Linguists and native speakers have made great strides lately in documenting southeastern Indian grammars and lexicons, partly as a result of language revitalization efforts: David J. Costa, *The Miami-Illinois Language* (Lincoln: University of Nebraska Press, 2003); Emanuel J. Drechsel, *Mobilian Jargon: Linguistic and Sociohistorical Aspects of a Native American Pidgin* (Oxford: Clarendon Press, 1997); Julian Granberry, *A Grammar and Dictionary of the Timucua Language* (Tuscaloosa: University of Alabama Press, 1993); Marcia Haag and Loretta Fowler, *Chahta Anumpa: A Grammar of the Choctaw Language*, CD-ROM edition (Norman: University of Oklahoma Press, 2001); Marcia Haag and Henry Willis, *Choctaw Language and Culture: Chahta Anumpa* (Norman: University of Oklahoma Press, 2001); Geoffrey D. Kimball, *Koasati Dictionary* (Lincoln: University of Nebraska Press, 1994), and *Koasati Grammar* (Lincoln: University of Nebraska Press, 1991); Jack B. Martin and Margaret McKane Mauldin, *A Dictionary of Creek/Muskogee, with Notes on the Florida and Oklahoma Seminole Dialects of Creek* (Lincoln: University of Nebraska Press, 2000); Pamela Munro and Catherine Willmond, *Chickasaw: An Analytical Dictionary* (Norman: University of Oklahoma Press, 1994); Cora Sylestine, Heather K. Hardy, and Timothy Montler, *Dictionary of the Alabama Language* (Austin: University of Texas Press, 1993); Martha Young and Frank Siebert, *Catawba Onomastics*, Algonquian and Iroquoian Linguistics Memoir 16 (Winnipeg MB: 2003). For the first reinterpretation of the southeastern indigenous linguistic landscape in over a century, see Ives Goddard, "The Indigenous Languages of the Southeast," *Anthropological Linguistics* 47 (2005): 1–60.

A number of important publication projects have reintroduced students and scholars to classic texts newly translated (when necessary), edited to modern standards, and accompanied by interpretive annotations: Rolena Adorno and Patrick Charles Pautz, eds., *Álvar Núñez Cabeza de Vaca: His Account, His Life, and the Expedition of Pánfilo de Narváez*, 3 vols. (Lincoln: University of Nebraska Press, 1999); Fray Ramón Pané, *An Account of the Antiquities of the Indians*, ed. José Juan Arrom (Durham NC: Duke University Press, 1998); James Adair, *The History of the American Indians*, ed. Kathryn E. Holland Braund (Tuscaloosa: University of Alabama Press, 2005); Bernard Romans, *A Concise Natural History of East and West Florida*, ed. Kathryn E. Holland Braund (Tuscaloosa: University of Alabama Press, 1999); Lawrence A. Clayton, Vernon James Knight Jr., and Edward C. Moore, eds., *The De Soto Chronicles: The Expedition of Hernando de Soto to North America in 1539–1543*, 2 vols. (Tuscaloosa: University of Alabama Press, 1993); William C. Foster, ed., *The La Salle Expedition to Texas: The Journal of Henri Joutel, 1684–1687* (Austin: Texas State Historical Commission, 1998); John H. Hann, ed., *Missions to the Calusa* (Gainesville: University Press of Florida, 1991); Charles Hudson and Paul E. Hoffman, eds., *The Juan Pardo Expeditions: Exploration of the Carolinas and Tennessee, 1566–1568* (Washington DC: Smithsonian Institution Press, 1990); José de Acosta, *Natural and Moral History of the Indies*, ed. Jane E. Mangan (Durham NC: Duke University Press, 2002); Theda Perdue and Michael D. Green, eds., *The Cherokee Removal: A Brief History with Documents* (Boston: Bedford Books, 1995); Gregory A. Waselkov and Kathryn E. Holland Braund, eds., *William Bartram on the Southeastern Indians* (Lincoln: University of Nebraska Press, 1995). New editions of the writings of Antoine Le Page du Pratz and Jean François Benjamin Dumont de Montigny are expected soon.

Notes

1. For basic overviews, see Michael Coe, Dean Snow, and Elizabeth Benson, *Atlas of Ancient America* (New York: Facts on File, 1986); Brian M. Fagan, *The Great Journey: The Peopling of Ancient America* (New York: Thames and Hudson, 1987); Stuart J. Fiedel, *Prehistory of the Americas* (Cambridge: Cambridge University Press, 1987); Frederick E. Hoxie, ed., *Encyclopedia of North American Indians: Native American History, Culture, and Life from Paleo-Indians to the Present* (Boston: Houghton Mifflin, 1996); Guy E. Gibbon, ed., *Archaeology of Prehistoric Native America*, 2 vols. (New York: Garland, 1998); Alvin M. Josephy Jr., ed., *America in 1492: The World of the Indian Peoples before the Arrival of Columbus*

(New York: Knopf, 1992); Alice Beck Kehoe, *America before the European Invasions* (New York: Longman, 2002). Two recent volumes place into modern social context the controversial ongoing scientific debate over the origins of Native Americans: David Hurst Thomas, *Skull Wars: Kennewick Man, Archaeology, and the Battle for Native American Identity* (New York: Basic Books, 2000); James C. Chatters, *Ancient Encounters: Kennewick Man and the First Americans* (New York: Simon and Schuster, 2001).

Judith A. Bense presents a useful regional summary in *Archaeology of the Southeastern United States: Paleoindian to World War I* (New York: Academic Press, 1994). Several essay collections offer more detailed considerations of specific periods and regional prehistories: David G. Anderson and Kenneth E. Sassaman, eds., *The Paleoindian and Early Archaic Southeast* (Tuscaloosa: University of Alabama Press, 1996); Kenneth E. Sassaman and David G. Anderson, eds., *Archaeology of the Mid-Holocene Southeast* (Gainesville: University Press of Florida, 1996); David G. Anderson and Robert C. Mainfort Jr., eds., *The Woodland Southeast* (Tuscaloosa: University of Alabama Press, 2002); R. Barry Lewis and Charles Stout, eds., *Mississippian Towns and Sacred Spaces: Searching for an Architectural Grammar* (Tuscaloosa: University of Alabama Press, 1998); Lynne P. Sullivan and Susan C. Prezzano, eds., *Archaeology of the Appalachian Highlands* (Knoxville: University of Tennessee Press, 2001); and Robert V. Sharp, ed., *Hero, Hawk, and Open Hand: American Indian Art of the Ancient Midwest and South* (Chicago IL: Art Institute of Chicago, 2004).

2. Julian H. Steward, *Handbook of South American Indians*, 7 vols., Bureau of American Ethnology Bulletin 143 (Washington DC: Government Printing Office, 1946–59); also see Elman R. Service, "Indian-European Relations in Colonial Latin America," *American Anthropologist* 57 (1955): 411–25; Karen Spalding, "The Colonial Indian: Past and Future Research Perspectives," *Latin American Research Review* 7 (1972): 47–76. For review summaries from more recent decades, see Richard E. W. Adams and Murdo J. MacLeod, *The Cambridge History of the Native Peoples of the Americas*, vol. 2, *Mesoamerica* (Cambridge: Cambridge University Press, 2000); Frank Salomon and Stuart B. Schwartz, *The Cambridge History of the Native Peoples of the Americas*, vol. 3, *South America* (Cambridge: Cambridge University Press, 1999). For outstanding examples of modern ethnohistorical research, see Louise M. Burkhart's study, *The Slippery Earth: Nahua-Christian Moral Dialogue in Sixteenth-Century Mexico* (Tucson: University of Arizona Press, 1989); R. Brian Ferguson, *Yanomami Warfare: A Political History* (Santa Fe NM: School of American Research Press, 1995); Greg Grandin, *The Blood of Guatemala: A History of Race and Nation* (Durham NC: Duke University Press, 2000); Laura M. Rival, *Trekking through History: The Huaorani of Amazonian Ecuador* (New York: Columbia University Press, 2002).

3. Concerning Native Americans, see Francis Jennings, *The Founders of America* (New York: Norton, 1993); J. C. H. King, *First Peoples, First Contacts: Native Peoples of North America* (Cambridge MA: Harvard University Press, 1999); Peter C. Mancall and James H. Merrell, eds., *American Encounters: Natives and Newcomers from European Contact to Indian Removal, 1500–1850* (New York: Routledge, 2000); and Roger L. Nichols, *American Indians in U.S. History* (Norman: University of Oklahoma Press, 2003). On the East, see Daniel K. Richter, *Facing East from Indian Country: A Native History of Early Amer-*

ica (Cambridge MA: Harvard University Press, 1999). On the West, see Colin Calloway, *One Vast Winter Count: The Native American West before Lewis and Clark* (Lincoln: University of Nebraska Press, 2003).

On Africans, see Ira Berlin's broad study, *Generations of Captivity: A History of African-American Slaves* (Cambridge MA: Harvard University Press, 2003), including the population tables on pages 272–79. Other general studies include Peter Kolchin, *American Slavery, 1619–1877*, 10th anniversary edition (New York: Hill and Wang, 2003), and Michael A. Gomez, *Exchanging Our Country Marks: The Transformation of African Identities in the Colonial and Antebellum South* (Chapel Hill: University of North Carolina Press, 1998). For a brief overview of the era before 1776, see Peter H. Wood, *Strange New Land: Africans in Colonial America* (New York: Oxford University Press, 2003).

Regarding Europeans in North America, see John Logan Allen, ed., *North American Exploration*, vol. 1, *A New World Disclosed* and vol. 2, *A Continent Defined* (Lincoln: University of Nebraska Press, 1997); Marilyn C. Baseler, *"Asylum for Mankind": America, 1607–1800* (Ithaca NY: Cornell University Press, 1998); D. W. Meinig, *The Shaping of America: A Geographical Perspective on 500 Years of History*, vol. 1, *Atlantic America, 1492–1800* (New Haven CT: Yale University Press, 1986); and David J. Weber, *The Spanish Frontier in North America* (New Haven CT: Yale University Press, 1992), and *Bárbaros: Spaniards and Their Savages in the Age of Enlightenment* (New Haven CT: Yale University Press, 2005).

For an early attempt at a short environmental synthesis on the colonial Southeast, see Timothy Silver, *A New Face on the Countryside: Indians, Colonists, and Slaves in South Atlantic Forests, 1500–1800* (New York: Cambridge University Press, 1990). For a global perspective, see Alfred W. Crosby, *Ecological Imperialism: The Biological Expansion of Europe, 900–1900* (New York: Cambridge University Press, 1986), and Dirk Hoerder, *Cultures in Contact: World Migrations in the Second Millennium* (Durham NC: Duke University Press, 2002). For general references, see Jacob Ernest Cooke, editor in chief, *Encyclopedia of the North American Colonies*, 3 vols. (New York: Charles Scribner's Sons, 1993).

4. Robert M. Carmack, "Ethnohistory: A Review of Its Development, Definitions, Methods, and Aims," *Annual Review of Anthropology* 1 (1972): 227–46; James Axtell, "The Ethnohistory of Early America: A Review Essay," *William and Mary Quarterly*, 3d ser., 35 (January 1978): 110–44; Axtell, "Ethnohistory: An Historian's Viewpoint," *Ethnohistory* 26 (1979): 1–13; Bruce Trigger, "Ethnohistory: Problems and Prospects," *Ethnohistory* 29 (1982): 1–19; Francis Jennings, "A Growing Partnership: Historians, Anthropologists, and American Indian History," *Ethnohistory* 29 (1982): 21–41; Donald L. Fixico, ed., *Rethinking American Indian History* (Albuquerque: University of New Mexico Press, 1997); James Axtell, "The Ethnohistory of Native America," in Axtell, *Natives and Newcomers: The Cultural Origins of North America* (Oxford: Oxford University Press, 2001), 1–12.

5. In the 1980s, the best index of progress in this area was the steady appearance of volumes in the American Indian Bibliographical Series from Indiana University Press, Francis Jennings, general editor, such as the thirteenth volume: W. R. Swagerty, ed., *Scholars and the Indian Experience: Critical Reviews of Recent Writing in the Social Sciences* (Bloomington: Indiana University Press, 1984). The series was sponsored by the D'Arcy McNickle

Center for the History of the American Indian at The Newberry Library in Chicago, which played a crucial role in encouraging this scholarly resurgence. See, for example, the papers from a 1985 Washington conference in the Center's Occasional Papers in Curriculum Series, number 4, *The Impact of Indian History on the Teaching of United States History* (Chicago: The Newberry Library, 1986). Fulfilling the recurrent need for updated critical bibliographies is the new seven-volume series, Columbia Guides to American Indian History and Culture, including its inaugural volume: Theda Perdue and Michael D. Green, *The Columbia Guide to American Indians of the Southeast* (New York: Columbia University Press, 2001).

For evidence of the Smithsonian's continuing contribution, beyond publication of the multivolume *Handbook of North American Indians,* see William W. Fitzhugh, ed., *Cultures in Contact: The Impact of European Contacts on Native American Cultural Institutions,* AD *1000–1800* (Washington DC: Smithsonian Institution Press, 1985). Three decades after volume planning began, the Southeast volume of the *Handbook* finally appeared in print: Raymond D. Fogelson, ed., *Handbook of North American Indians,* vol. 14, *Southeast* (Washington DC: Smithsonian Institution, 2004).

6. Charles Hudson, *The Southeastern Indians* (Knoxville: University of Tennessee Press, 1976); J. Leitch Wright Jr., *The Only Land They Knew: The Tragic Story of the American Indians in the Old South* (New York: Free Press, 1981); Bruce G. Trigger and Wilcomb E. Washburn, eds., *The Cambridge History of the Native Peoples of the Americas,* vol. 1, *North America* (Cambridge: Cambridge University Press, 1996); Peter C. Mancall and James H. Merrell, eds., *American Encounters: Natives and Newcomers from European Contact to Indian Removal, 1500–1850* (New York: Routledge, 2000); Robbie Ethridge and Charles Hudson, eds., *The Transformation of the Southeastern Indians, 1540–1760* (Jackson: University Press of Mississippi, 2002).

7. J. Norman Heard, *Handbook of the American Frontier: Four Centuries of Indian-White Relationships,* vol. 1, *The Southeastern Woodlands,* Native American Resources Series 1 (Metuchen NJ: Scarecrow Press, 1987).

8. For example, see Alex W. Barker and Timothy R. Pauketat, eds., *Lords of the Southeast: Social Inequality and the Native Elites of Southeastern North America,* Archaeological Papers 3 (Washington DC: American Anthropological Association, 1992); David S. Brose, C. Wesley Cowan, and Robert C. Mainfort Jr., eds., *Societies in Eclipse: Archaeology of the Eastern Woodland Indians,* AD *1400–1700* (Washington DC: Smithsonian Institution Press, 2001); Patricia M. Lambert, ed., *Bioarchaeological Studies of Life in the Age of Agriculture* (Tuscaloosa: University of Alabama Press, 2000); Bonnie G. McEwan, ed., *The Spanish Missions of La Florida* (Gainesville: University Press of Florida, 1993), and *Indians of the Greater Southeast: Historical Archaeology and Ethnohistory* (Gainesville: University Press of Florida, 2000); Michael S. Nassaney and Eric S. Johnson, eds., *Interpretations of Native North American Life: Material Contributions to Ethnohistory* (Gainesville: University Press of Florida, 2000); Jill E. Neitzel, *Great Towns and Regional Polities in the Prehistoric American Southwest and Southeast* (Albuquerque: University of New Mexico Press, 1999); Evan Peacock and Timothy Schauwecker, eds., *Blackland Prairies of the Gulf Coastal Plain: Nature,*

Culture, and Stability (Tuscaloosa: University of Alabama Press, 2003); J. Daniel Rogers and Samuel M. Wilson, eds., *Ethnohistory and Archaeology: Approaches to Postcontact Change in the Americas* (New York: Plenum Press, 1993); John A. Walthall and Thomas E. Emerson, eds., *Calumet and Fleur-de-Lys: Archaeology of Indian and French Contact in the Midcontinent* (Washington DC: Smithsonian Institution Press, 1992); Cameron B. Wesson and Mark A. Rees, eds., *Between Contacts and Colonists: Archaeological Perspectives on the Protohistoric Southeast* (Tuscaloosa: University of Alabama Press, 2002).

9. For three recent book-length examples, see Jean Chaudhuri and Joyotpaul Chaudhuri, *A Sacred Path: The Way of the Muscogee Creeks* (Los Angeles: UCLA American Indian Studies Center, 2001); David Lewis Jr. and Ann T. Jordan, *Creek Indian Medicine Ways: The Enduring Power of Mvskoke Religion* (Albuquerque: University of New Mexico Press, 2002); Alice Micco Snow and Susan Enns Stans, *Healing Plants: Medicine of the Florida Seminole Indians* (Gainesville: University Press of Florida, 2001).

10. *Perspectives* (American Historical Association), January 1987, 8.

11. Also see Jon Muller and David R. Wilcox, "Powhatan's Mantle as Metaphor: Comparing Macroregional Integration in the Southwest and Southeast," in Neitzel, *Great Towns and Regional Polities*, 159.

Geography and Population

1
2
3
4
5
6
7
8
9
10
11
12
13
14
15
16
17
18
19
20
21
22
23
24
25
26
27
28
29
30
31
32
33
34
35
36

Introduction

PETER H. WOOD

Up until at least the time when Alaska and Hawaii received statehood in the middle of the last century, general United States history texts—and even specialized demographic surveys—had a peculiar way of portraying American "expansion." A chronological series of blank maps showed a few population dots along the eastern seaboard in 1650, and they multiplied steadily, migrating across an otherwise empty continent as time progressed. The dots would stop mysteriously at any political border, only to burst out across a new region like a rash of measles when "territorial acquisition" occurred.[1] So generations of students received the strong subliminal message that no one inhabited Appalachia or the Ohio valley until English-speaking settlers arrived. They were shown the Louisiana Territory as a huge void, an empty funnel in the center of the continent, before President Jefferson purchased it from the French. Accompanying text might suggest the story's greater complexity, but a picture—even a partially vacant outline map—can outweigh a great many words.

In creating such demographic pictures, did these textbook cartographers ignore the presence of Native Americans through ignorance, accident, or some conspiracy of silence? Had anyone asked them, and apparently few did, the responses would no doubt have varied. Some would invoke precedent: "We've always done it this way." Others would plead lack of hard evidence: "I'd like to show everyone, but I don't think reliable data exist." However plausible such excuses seemed at the time, these empty expanses stretching across historical population maps diminished to zero the significance of whole Indian societies and precluded the discussion of interaction between natives and newcomers. Moreover, whether inadvertently or not, they avoided the unsettling questions of Indian decimation and removal associated with the European colonization and conquest of North America.[2]

But the fiction could not be maintained forever, and after midcentury the picture began to change as two competing influences came to bear. One model for population reconstruction came from farther south and west,

where historical demographers, spurred on by anthropologists and archaeologists studying Latin America and the Southwest and inspired by ecological modeling, had been asking questions about the resource productivity
and "carrying capacity" of specific environments, using elaborate models
for broad areas. Meanwhile, an alternative approach to population issues
came from the north and east, where colonial historians began to apply the
tools of localized historical demography developed in Europe to early English villages in the New World. Working with excellent written records at
the parish level, they soon became sophisticated and precise about demographic processes, though for the most part they remained less interested
in reconstructing whole populations over time.

Both perspectives are beginning to make valid contributions toward understanding the postcontact Southeast, though reconciling these different
approaches cannot be swift for a region where demographic study regarding
the colonial era has been slow to take hold. If black dots marching across
an empty map are a thing of the past, more realistic population pictures
have been slow to evolve. An atlas for the era of the American Revolution
that appeared in 1976, for example, combined state-of-the-art cartography
with segregation concepts from an earlier time. On maps of settlement the
editors inserted a small disclaimer in parentheses: "(Indian population not
included)." Then on other pages they introduced separate maps of some—
by no means all—of the documented Indian towns of the East (although,
as is customary with treatments of the Revolutionary era, they omitted Indians of the Mississippi valley and the Great West altogether). The map ti-
tled "Southern Indian Villages, 1760–94" was carefully prepared by Adele
Hast and Helen Hornbeck Tanner. Despite its necessarily small scale, this
summary overview approached again, after two centuries, the level of detail with regard to the names and locations of Native American towns that
had appeared on the large-scale chart of the region drawn up before the
Revolution by Joseph Purcell, under the direction of John Stuart, superintendent of Indian affairs for the Southern District.[3]

Helen Tanner has continued to pioneer in linking Indian history to geography through maps. Her *Atlas of Great Lakes Indian History* (published
in 1987) provides a model of what can be accomplished through painstak-
ing research and innovative cartography.[4] As yet, the diverse region below
the Ohio River has not been subjected to such careful scrutiny. But the ma-

terials now exist for such an undertaking, whenever the right match can be arranged between dedicated researchers, a supportive press, and an enlightened funding agency.[5] Meanwhile, the chapters in this section, focusing on the geography and demography of the postcontact South, offer some hint of what an *Atlas of Southeastern Indians* might portray in its presentation of the colonial era.

Fittingly, the initial essay is by Helen Tanner, providing a brief introduction to the system of communication that linked southeastern Indians by land and water. Tanner does not attempt to chart the whole elaborate network in all its complexity over time. Instead, she surveys the major patterns of communication and the dominant arteries of contact that shaped the societies of the South.[6] Her chapter not only summarizes current knowledge and offers an introductory overview but also opens the door to ethnographers with an interest in mental mapping. For as Gregory Waselkov demonstrates near the end of this volume, we are only beginning to understand Indian perceptions of the geographic world in which they lived.

However stationary it may appear from the early twenty-first century, there was nothing static about this world, as Tanner's lines of communication make clear. And more was in motion than warbelts and trade goods, crop gatherers and hunting parties. Shifts from shoreline to hillside as seasons changed, from old field to new field as soil became depleted, from townsite to townsite as a community grew or dwindled—all these local movements were a regular feature of southern life in the era before European contact. But so was large-scale migration, as numerous tribal myths of origin suggest.[7]

The arrival of Europeans spurred further relocations, some of which are sketched in Marvin Smith's essay on the southern interior. It is important to remember that the widespread social and political reorganization that began after de Soto, and continued until Removal some three hundred years later, affected the entire Southeast, not just the area and time span Smith focuses on here. Indeed, all the major tribal entities of the historic period (Creeks, Choctaws, Chickasaws, Catawbas, Cherokees, and later the Seminoles) were amalgams, to a greater or lesser degree, of numerous local and refugee groups that coalesced from the population remnants left after the ravages of virgin soil epidemics and the English-inspired slave wars of the late seventeenth and eighteenth centuries.[8]

Not long ago, Smith's propositions might have seemed pure conjecture. But recent historical research into early Spanish documents, on one hand, and increasingly extensive and precise archaeological evidence, on the other, make it possible to suggest specific patterns of change.[9] Physically and linguistically diverse groups moved to form loosely organized confederacies, unions of mutual convenience, that effectively restrained interethnic hostilities in the absence of the hierarchical social controls characteristic of prehistoric southeastern chiefdoms. Further research will test and modify these patterns, adding details for areas not covered in Smith's case study. But his hypothesis that population decline brought on by foreign diseases played a role in opening new prospects for relocation and reorganization seems likely to find support in future studies.

The population decline mentioned by Smith and subsequent authors becomes a central focus for Peter Wood's long chapter on the demography of the South during the final century of the colonial era. The causes and consequences, the extent and duration, of this overall decline—in the South and elsewhere—have absorbed and divided scholars for some time. This first attempt at a systematic survey of change over time for the entire southern region estimates arriving Europeans and Africans alongside the established Indian groups they would eventually displace. By focusing on the late colonial period, when the records are most complete, Wood creates a framework that registers change from one decade to the next and from one subregion to another.

The results of this comparative overview are startling, to say the least, especially when transposed into a series of revealing tables and graphs. It is precisely in this century, from the 1680s to the 1780s, that the population of the South undergoes its most dramatic transformation. Before 1700 the region is inhabited almost entirely by Native Americans, and their numbers are continuing to decline at a rate that more than offsets the growing influx of newcomers; the southern population as a whole—generations of colonial historians notwithstanding—is actually growing smaller year by year. Two generations later, on the eve of the American Revolution, all this has changed. The decline among Indian groups has slowed and even begun to reverse itself in places, Wood shows, but this severely diminished population is now heavily outnumbered, in one area after another, by the rapidly expanding and migrating population of whites and blacks from overseas.

The interactions of these three groups—Indians, Europeans, and Africans—are the focus of the chapter by Kathleen DuVal, one of the new contributors to this volume. Her essay begins to tease apart the countless intertwined narratives that emerged from the colony the French called *La Louisiane*, where "Choctaws, Natchez, Chickasaws, Tunicas, Osages, Quapaws, Bambaras, Mobilians, Caddoans, Britons, Spaniards, and other groups and individuals" met, traded with, intermarried, fought, resisted, manipulated, cajoled, and, in some instances, even persuaded the colonizing French. DuVal portrays the Mississippi valley of the eighteenth century as "largely an Indian-defined and Indian-controlled place" through her exploration of the myriad ways diverse populations interconnected in this native world.

Daniel Usner's essay on the Indians of colonial New Orleans, which concludes this initial section, zeros in on one small and little-known piece of the large demographic quilt displayed by Wood and DuVal. By delving into the complex interracial origins of his home city in Louisiana, Usner reminds readers that there is nothing new about the people sociologists call "urban Indians." His detailed reconstruction of which native people were present in the French colonial port, and why, provides a suggestive reminder about the sheer diversity of the Indian experience in the long colonial era and the extent to which careful research can restore forgotten people to their complex world in a meaningful way.

Together, these five very different essays serve to introduce the varied landscapes and differing peoples who are the subject of this volume. Like the essays to follow, they draw upon generations of intriguing scholarship in long-separated fields and point the way toward more integrated research in the future. They attempt, so to speak, to "put southern Indians back on the map." This having been done, it will be possible in parts 2 and 3 to focus upon the changing worlds—political, economic, social, and philosophical—in which these indigenous Southerners lived out their lives during the first three centuries after steady transatlantic contact began.

Notes

1. John Noyes has remarked on the "real inability of the European eye to look at the world and see anything other than European space—a space which is by definition empty where it is not inhabited by Europeans." John K. Noyes, *Colonial Space: Spatiality in the*

Discourse of German South West Africa, 1884–1915 (Philadelphia: Harwood Academic Publishers, 1992), 196. See also David E. Nye, "Technology, Nature, and American Origin Stories," *Environmental History* 8 (January 2003): 8–24.

2. Even in 2003, editors at the Center for Great Plains Studies in Lincoln, Nebraska, working on *The Atlas of the Great Plains*, were still debating whether to acknowledge any Native American presence in their maps of population density on the Great Plains in the era of the early republic.

3. Lester J. Cappon, ed., *Atlas of Early American History: The Revolutionary Era, 1760–1790* (Princeton NJ: Princeton University Press, 1976), 19–21, 95–96; cf. disclaimer on p. 78. For details of the Stuart-Purcell map of about 1773 in the Ayer Collection of The Newberry Library in Chicago, see William P. Cumming, *The Southeast in Early Maps*, 3rd ed., revised and enlarged by Louis De Vorsey Jr. (Chapel Hill: University of North Carolina Press, 1998), 323–25.

4. Helen Hornbeck Tanner, ed., *Atlas of Great Lakes Indian History* (Norman: University of Oklahoma Press, 1987); also see William H. Goetzmann and Glyndwr Williams, *The Atlas of North American Exploration: From the Norse Voyages to the Race to the Pole* (New York: Prentice Hall, 1992); Helen Hornbeck Tanner, ed., *The Settling of North America: The Atlas of the Great Migrations into North America from the Ice Age to the Present* (New York: Macmillan, 1995).

5. A century of archaeological fieldwork forms the basis of some remarkable maps of native population centers in eastern North America for the periods AD 1400–1450, 1500–1550, and 1600–1650. George R. Milner, David G. Anderson, and Marvin T. Smith, "The Distribution of Eastern Woodlands Peoples at the Prehistoric and Historic Interface," in *Societies in Eclipse: Archaeology of the Eastern Woodland Indians, AD 1400–1700*, ed. David S. Brose, C. Wesley Cowan, and Robert C. Mainfort Jr. (Washington DC: Smithsonian Institution Press, 2001), 11–13.

6. For comparison, see the innovative study by Kenneth Banks of early eighteenth-century, transatlantic communication systems exploring the multifaceted nature of information exchange in French colonial North America. Kenneth J. Banks, *Chasing Empire across the Sea: Communications and the State in the French Atlantic, 1713–1763* (Montreal: McGill-Queen's University Press, 2002).

7. Indian travel, communication, and trade between the Southeast and points west in the centuries immediately preceding and following contact with Europeans are discussed in several recent articles by archaeologists: Joni L. Manson, "Transmississippi Trade and Travel: The Buffalo Plains and Beyond," *Plains Anthropologist* 43 (November 1998): 385–400; Ian W. Brown, "Contact, Communication, and Exchange: Some Thoughts on the Rapid Movement of Ideas and Objects," in *Raw Materials and Exchange in the Mid-South*, Archaeological Report 29, ed. Evan Peacock and Samuel O. Brookes (Jackson: Mississippi Department of Archives and History, 1999), 132–41; Frank F. Schambach, "Osage Orange Bows, Indian Horses, and the Blackland Prairie of Northeastern Texas," in *Blackland Prairies of the Gulf Coastal Plain: Nature, Culture, and Sustainability* (Tuscaloosa: University of Alabama Press, 2003), 212–36. Trade and other contacts on the northern periphery are

documented by Penelope Ballard Drooker, *The View from Madisonville: Protohistoric West-ern Fort Ancient Interaction Patterns*, Memoirs of the Museum of Anthropology (Ann Arbor: University of Michigan, 1997).

8. For a recent overview of the contentious topic of population decline caused by introduced epidemic diseases, see Russell Thornton, "Health, Disease, and Demography," in *A Companion to American Indian History*, ed. Philip J. Deloria and Neal Salisbury (Malden MA: Blackwell, 2002), 68–84. Elizabeth A. Fenn details the devastating impact of a continent-wide epidemic and its circuitous course across North America in *Pox Americana: The Great Smallpox Epidemic of 1775–82* (New York: Hill and Wang, 2001). On Native American enslavement, see two recent prize-winning books: Alan Gallay, *The Indian Slave Trade: The Rise of the English Empire in the American South* (New Haven CT: Yale University Press, 2002); James F. Brooks, *Captives and Cousins: Slavery, Kinship, and Community in the Southwest Borderlands* (Chapel Hill: University of North Carolina Press, 2002).

9. Collaborative teams of archaeologists and physical anthropologists have used in-depth analyses of human skeletal remains to study the impact of European contact upon the health of Native Americans. See Brenda J. Baker and Lisa Kealhofer, eds., *Bioarchaeology of Native American Adaptation in the Spanish Borderlands* (Gainesville: University Press of Florida, 1996); Clark Spencer Larsen, *Skeletons in Our Closet: Revealing Our Past through Bioarchaeology* (Princeton NJ: Princeton University Press, 2000); Patricia M. Lambert, ed., *Bioarchaeological Studies of Life in the Age of Agriculture* (Tuscaloosa: University of Alabama Press, 2000).

Much recent research has been spurred by deadlines imposed on further study of burials excavated years ago—in some cases, many decades ago—with implementation in 1990 of the Native American Graves Protection and Repatriation Act. This legislation, known as NAGPRA, enjoins archaeologists to confer with Indian peoples, whose ancestors the scholars elect to study. Institutions such as universities and museums must negotiate with descendant Native Americans concerning the disposition of human remains, funerary goods, sacred objects, or objects of cultural patrimony in their collections. See Nina Swidler et al., eds., *Native Americans and Archaeologists: Stepping Stones to Common Ground* (Walnut Creek CA: Altamira Press, 1997); Joe Watkins, *Indigenous Archaeology* (Walnut Creek CA: Altamira Press, 2001); Kathleen S. Fine-Dare, *Grave Injustice: The American Indian Repatriation Movement and NAGPRA* (Lincoln: University of Nebraska Press, 2002).

The Land and Water Communication Systems of the Southeastern Indians

HELEN HORNBECK TANNER

The vitality of Indian community life in the southeastern section of the present United States was enhanced by a maze of intervillage contacts. The frequency of interaction depended upon the distance between townsites. Descriptions of southern Indian society include accounts of intertown ball games, itinerant peddling of goods in a barter economy, diplomatic councils, and gatherings for seasonal festivals. These lines of contact were engraved in the earth as pathways connecting associated towns.

But there were also intertribal contacts utilizing trails and canoe routes over distances of several hundred miles, extending in the case of war parties and diplomatic missions to 1,000 or 1,500 miles. These longer routes formed a network that also had a bearing on life in the individual villages. The entire communication system, composed of local subsystems, hubs, or intermediate terminals, and connections with other networks, can be roughly outlined with the view of demonstrating the wide range of contacts accessible to southeastern Indians (fig. 1).

This outline deals primarily with the major population groups of the eighteenth century, the Cherokees, Creeks, Seminoles, Choctaws, and Chickasaws east of the Mississippi River and the Caddos of Louisiana and east Texas.[1] The overall area involved in this treatment of the Southeast is the region south of the Ohio River and southwest of the Great Kanawha River, a major southern tributary of the Ohio River flowing through West Virginia, and also southwest of the James River entering the Atlantic Ocean at the southern end of Chesapeake Bay. West of the Mississippi, the Arkansas River is a reasonable north-south dividing line. The Arkansas River marks the traditional northern border of the country of the Caddos, a people more similar to their eastern neighbors across the Mississippi River than to those living in any other direction. The western border of this definition of the Southeast is the Cross Timbers, originally a belt of forest that extended north and south in central Oklahoma, reaching into northern Texas.[2] Geographically, the Southeast ends near modern Dallas at the head of the Trinity River.

Most of the information about the details of traditional transportation routes in the southland comes from eighteenth-century sources, though some references date from both the early seventeenth century and the early nineteenth. Yet the persistence of the same transportation routes, in some cases evident from the time of the mastodon to the present highway and railroad era, makes it possible to use reports from different time periods in forming a coherent picture of a communications system for the Southeast.

Turning attention first to the trail system in the southeastern United States, it is important to distinguish between pathways chiefly used for local purposes, any series of short links, and the lengthy thoroughfares of interregional communication that are the ultimate concern of this discussion.[3] From maps already published, it is apparent that there were a number of trails developed solely to serve local population concentrations. Notable are the networks connecting fifty Choctaw towns in southeastern Mississippi and Alabama, the local pattern reflecting the tight formation of seven Chickasaw towns near modern Tupelo in northeastern Mississippi, and the intricate maze crisscrossing the southern Appalachian Highlands in the Cherokee country of eastern Tennessee and adjacent sections of North Carolina and Georgia.[4]

In the total communication system of the Southeast, there are also hubs where important trails going in different directions crossed and branched. Significant examples of this feature of the communication system are present in Nashville and Chattanooga, Tennessee, and in Montgomery, Alabama—places that have always been geographic focal points. The Hiwassee River valley near Murphy, Tennessee, close to the Georgia–North Carolina border, was another focal point of aboriginal travel.[5] These townsites are all in the interior heartland of the Southeast, but the trail system spread out to touch points on both the Gulf and Atlantic coasts, frequently following paths from the highlands to the coastal plain along river valleys such as the Santee, Savannah, Chattahoochee, and Coosa.

The most comprehensive work on regional land trails is the monograph of William E. Myer, edited by John R. Swanton and published in 1928.[6] In his summary of thirty-five years of research into the trail system of the south-

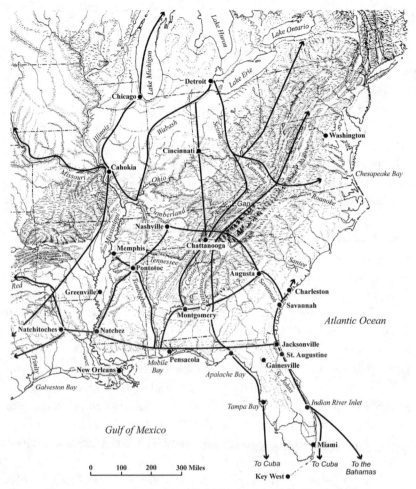

Figure 1. Communications network of the colonial Southeast, by Helen Hornbeck Tanner.

eastern United States, Myer identified 125 separate trails. His investigation of Tennessee and Kentucky was exceptionally thorough; the coverage of southern Georgia, Florida, and Louisiana was less complete. The more recent work of Utley and Hemperly augments Myer's original contribution.[7]

Myer became firmly convinced that Indian people throughout eastern North America, including the Southeast, often traveled well over a thousand miles on war and trading expeditions. He gave particular attention to the principal north-south artery "Great Indian Warpath" that extended southward from the Kanawha River of West Virginia. The main prong of the Great Warrior Path led southeast up the Kanawha to the New River, then west to the Holston River's north fork and present Kingsport, Tennessee. One branch diverted east, to the Catawba country near Roanoke, Virginia, and followed the valley of the Shenandoah River. The main route continued through the east Tennessee Cherokee settlements, including the ancient capital of Echota, to present Chattanooga, Tennessee, and on south to the Upper Creek villages around present Montgomery, Alabama. A Pennsylvania branch of the Great Warrior Path was the route of Iroquois parties raiding southern Indian villages. In the opposite direction, it was the route of the Tuscaroras seeking refuge with the Iroquois in 1715.[8]

The Kanawha River mouth was actually the easternmost of three trails crossing the Ohio River within the boundaries of the present state of Ohio. They were all important in interregional relations between northeastern and southeastern Indians. The second notable crossing was at the mouth of the Scioto River, where a trail ran southeast through the Kentucky bluegrass district to the Cumberland Gap, there intersecting the main branch of the Great Warrior Path in the Holston valley of Tennessee.[9] The geological formation of the southern Appalachian Range offered a number of parallel routes running through valleys in a northeast to southwesterly direction.[10] The third important crossing in this section of the Ohio River was at the mouth of the Licking River opposite modern Cincinnati, an alternative route to present Chattanooga. Trails joining at that point led south to the country of the Creeks and Cherokees in Alabama and Georgia. North of the Ohio River, trails converged toward Detroit and the Upper Great Lakes crossroads at the Straits of Mackinac.

While the Great Warrior Path, with spreading prongs and feeder routes throughout its length, was probably used for war and trade in earlier eras, the documents of colonial times show that warriors, messengers, and tribal delegations traveled this path regularly in the eighteenth century. This trail system was used by Wyandots from Detroit in warfare against the Catawbas, and by Cherokees coming to the mouth of the Scioto River for conferences with the Shawnees in 1751 and 1752.[11] Chippewas from the Straits of Mackinac were also among the tribes that met for intertribal councils with the Shawnees of the Scioto valley, a significant point of interregional contact. Delawares living in the Muskingum valley of eastern Ohio in the 1770s sent a delegation to live with the Cherokees for several years; they returned home in 1779 with Cherokee representatives who brought articles to trade.[12]

Following the American Revolution, Creek and Cherokee leaders traveled north to Detroit to join Great Lakes tribes in councils with British authorities.[13] These are examples of use of the communication system for interchange between southeastern Indians and Indian peoples living north of the Ohio River in the eighteenth century. Indian leaders and runners spending considerable time on intertribal business learned several languages.

Continuing with an examination of the transportation routes in the upper section of the Southeast, it is next important to observe the course of the Cumberland and Tennessee rivers. Both have their headwaters near the all-important Cumberland Gap through the Appalachian Range, where the southwestern tip of Virginia meets the Kentucky-Tennessee border. Their middle courses diverge widely, the Cumberland keeping to the north along both sides of the Kentucky-Tennessee border while the Tennessee River dips into northern Alabama. But downstream both rivers turn north to follow parallel courses, entering the Ohio River only about twenty miles apart near Paducah, Kentucky. Dam construction has obscured the original watercourses, but the relative position of the two rivers is still plain on a modern map.

From headwaters to river mouth, the Cumberland and Tennessee were channels of east-west communication, but segments of the Tennessee in particular also served as part of a north-south communication line. At the bend of the Tennessee River in the extreme northwestern corner of Alabama, near Muscle Shoals, a main trail ran south to the Chickasaw towns.[14] On the Illinois shore of the Ohio River, opposite the mouths of the Cumberland and Tennessee rivers, were the trails north to Cahokia, a location strategically situated to tap trade up the Missouri, Mississippi, and Illinois rivers. Recognizing the Cherokees' use of the entire course of the Cumberland and Tennessee rivers, the French in 1757 built the "Cherokee Fort" on the lower Ohio by these river mouths.[15]

For traveling northeast from the mouths of the Cumberland and Tennessee rivers, water transportation was available all the way to Detroit except for a short portage at present Fort Wayne. This route ascended the Ohio for a short distance to the Wabash, continuing up the Wabash and down the Maumee to Lake Erie at present Toledo, Ohio, then north to the entrance to the Detroit River. The Wabash, Ohio, Tennessee river route was probably the one used by the Miamis in their raids on the Chickasaws, and by the Chickasaws in attacks on French Vincennes in the 1730s.[16] The stretch of the Ohio River between the entrances of the Tennessee and the Wabash also was crossed by several land trails from southern Illinois converging at Nashville.

The east-west lines of communication across the lower southland were land trails. The most enterprising British trader in Charlestown, South Carolina, founded in 1670, had reached the Mississippi before 1690, traveling more than eight hundred miles westward from his home base.[17] The British Indian trade also pushed across the Mississippi River very early in the colonial era. In 1698 a trader went beyond the Chickasaws to establish trade with the Quapaws near the mouth of the Arkansas River.[18] It is interesting that when the first French explorer with trade in mind penetrated the Indian country of central Oklahoma by way of the Red River in 1719, he found the inhabitants of a Wichita village already trading with a Chickasaw, who soon returned to the Yazoo River.[19] At that time Charlestown was the center of English colonial trade with the southern Indians, challenging the French trade based at Mobile beginning in 1702 as well as the less competitive Spanish traders from St. Augustine. Merchants from Savannah and Augusta later entered the system of existing Indian trails to trade with the Creeks and Choctaws east of the Mississippi. Although the Mississippi River was a formidable barrier during seasons of high water, the southeastern communication system crossed the river at present Memphis, Vicksburg, and Natchez. The main trail from present Birmingham, Alabama, to Greenville, Mississippi, had a branch looping north specifically to connect with the mouth of the Arkansas River.[20]

British traders began developing east-west trade routes through the interior country of the Southeast in the late seventeenth century. In 1685 a large convoy of traders with English goods arrived at Coweta, center of the Lower Creeks near the falls of the Chattahoochee River. The following spring, 150 Indian burdeners laden with deerskin packs returned to Charlestown, beginning an expanding trade network.[21] By the mid-eighteenth century, trains of packhorses replaced the Indian burdeners, creating a well-beaten trail pattern. The main path and a number of alternate routes to Oakfuskee, Upper Creek trade center on the Tallapoosa River, have been worked out by John Goff. The Upper Creek path had an important branch to the Cherokees of northwest Georgia and northeast Alabama, and on the Coosa River it connected with trails leading westward to the Chickasaws and Choctaws.[22]

The most southerly east-west route originated on the Atlantic coast at St. Augustine, Florida. It headed toward the fording point at the bend in the lower St. Johns River (present Jacksonville), then continued by way of present Tallahassee to Mobile and on to the Mississippi River opposite the mouth of the Red River. Either ascending the Red River from its mouth, or crossing farther north at Natchez, the traveler arrived at Natchitoches, Louisiana, the gateway to the Caddo country. From Natchitoches the overland trail westward ran through the Caddo (or Hasinai) settlements in the Neches and Angelina valleys of east Texas to San Antonio, and through Presidio on the Rio Grande at the mouth of the Rio Conchos. The juncture of the two rivers was the sixteenth-century homeland of the Jumanos Indians, noted intermediaries in the regional trade network.[23] Here, on the present Mexican border, trails led southwest to Chihuahua in the direction of Casas Grandes, a thirteenth-century trade center, and to Mexico City. Early in the eighteenth century, the major route to Mexico City from San Antonio shifted southwest to cross the Rio Grande at several points near present Eagle Pass–Piedras Negras, a roadway that became the "Camino Real." A delegation of Texas Cherokees followed this route in 1833 to Monclava, at the time provincial capital of Coahuila and Texas, seeking a land grant in east Texas. In 1850 the Seminole leader Coacoochee [Wild Cat] led his followers along this roadway into Coahuila where he died encamped near Muzquiz.[24]

The long overland route from the Atlantic coast of Florida eventually reaching Mexico City was primarily used in sections, with concentrated local traffic between the east coast of Florida and the Apalachee Bay area and also from Apalachee to Pensacola and Mobile bays.[25] Mobile to Natchez, Mississippi, and Natchitoches, Louisiana, was another intermediate link. But the first ambitious French trader to locate in Mobile, before the founding of New Orleans in 1718, went back and forth over this land trail from Mobile beyond Natchitoches to the Texas border carrying on lucrative illegal trade with the Spaniards.[26] East-west contact across the Mississippi River between the Creeks and the Caddos continued into the early nineteenth century. The Creeks sought military aid from the Caddos at the time they were threatened by General Andrew Jackson's army.[27]

Natchitoches was also an important terminal in two other long-distance lines of communication besides the trans-Texas land route. Trading and exploring parties went up the Red River from Natchitoches or from the cluster of Caddo towns at the river bend near present Texarkana and continued to Santa Fe, New Mexico.[28] The last lap of course was overland. The Arkansas River by way of the Canadian River was another largely water route from the Mississippi valley to Santa Fe.

From both modern Texarkana, Texas, and Natchitoches, trails headed northeast, meeting in southern Arkansas, with Cahokia as the ultimate destination. The route the Caddos used to take horses to the Illinois country is on an early map of Louisiana; and from documentary evidence it is apparent that this trade was well established before 1700.[29] By the late eighteenth century, of course, the marketing center on the upper Mississippi was St. Louis, across the river from Cahokia, the ancient Indian population center much diminished in comparison with its peak development about AD 1200. At this point it is probably important to interject the observation that the route from the Caddo country to Cahokia was undoubtedly used for other kinds of trade and interchange before the horse-trading era.

Considered as a whole, the land passage traced from present Jacksonville, Florida, to the Mexican border was essentially an inland circuit of the Gulf coast following the most geographically feasible line of travel just north of the numerous bays and marshes.[30] Crossing this east-west route were several north-south lines of communication. The points of intersection between the north-south and the east-west communication lines formed significant transportation terminals. East of the Mississippi River, three of these interchanges or terminals deserve special attention. These are Mobile Bay, Apalachee Bay, and the bay at the mouth of the St. Johns River that extends inland to present Jacksonville. The routes of travel outlined for the upper section of the Southeast all connected with those three southern terminals. First of all, there is a natural drainage along the Tombigbee and Coosa-Alabama rivers funneling into Mobile Bay. The trail system northwest of Mobile Bay, passing through the Choctaw and Chickasaw towns, extended to the Mississippi River at present Memphis. Similarly, direct trails connected the Upper Creek towns near the junction of the Tallapoosa and Coosa rivers with Mobile. As a terminal in the total network, Mobile Bay offered many transportation alternatives, including coastal waterways around the Gulf of Mexico.

Apalachee Bay to the east of Mobile Bay also offered diversified transportation opportunities. From St. Marks Creek at the head of Apalachee Bay, a trail led straight north through the Lower Creek country to the eastern Cherokee towns. Apalachee Bay was also a port of embarkation for coastal canoe traffic south to Tampa Bay. Northwest of the bay, the trail pattern led to the meeting ground where the Chattahoochee and Flint rivers converge to form the Apalachicola River, on the Georgia-Florida state boundary. In the late eighteenth century the main Lower Creek towns were situated along the Chattahoochee about a hundred miles north of this junction. East of Apalachee Bay, the trail pattern included alternative paths, one swinging south through the Seminole settlements in the Alachua prairie (present Gainesville, Florida) to St. Augustine. This section of northern Florida had been a more populous region in the sixteenth century.

Jacksonville, at the fording point on the St. Johns River, is the easternmost point of intersection between main east-west and north-south routes forming part of the basic southeastern communication system. West of Jacksonville the long overland route to the Mississippi River and beyond has already been traced. But this fording point at Jacksonville was also near the southern end of the inland roadway along the south Atlantic coast terminating on the ocean shore at present St. Augustine.[31] Beyond St. Augustine the sandy beach was available for foot travel but was not a principal transportation route. From Jacksonville south, the course of the St. Johns River was the main artery for travel throughout the interior of the Florida peninsula. The river is exceptional because it flows not south but northward from headwaters nearly two hundred miles away near Melbourne, Florida. From its upper waters, branches provided access via portages to both the Tampa and Miami regions.[32] The second important fording point on the St. Johns River, at Picolata directly west of St. Augustine, gave access to the fertile Alachua prairie region, in the eighteenth century a Seminole stronghold.[33]

Among the evidence of use of the north-south routes of Florida in the late seventeenth and eighteenth centuries is the narrative of Gabriel Arthur. As a prisoner of Indians in the region of the French Broad River of North Carolina between 1673 and 1675, he accompanied a contingent carrying warfare into Spanish Florida and also made a trip north to the Ohio River by way of the Kanawha. According to a contemporary French map, the Shawnees living in Tennessee in the 1680s, probably near Nashville, went to St.

Augustine to trade with the Spaniards.[34] In the early eighteenth century, raids from South Carolina against the Florida Indians extended into the Kissimmee River region north of Lake Okeechobee. Raids of Yuchi Indians from the north forced abandonment of an attempted mission on St. Lucie Inlet in 1743.[35] In 1785 ambassadors of the Northern Indian Confederacy attended spring councils of the Creek Nation in Alabama. A Creek delegation relayed their news to departing British officials and the incoming Spanish governor of East Florida.[36] Corresponding delegations of Creeks and Cherokees using the Great Warrior Path for more peaceful missions were present in both the Ohio country and Iroquois councils in New York in the late eighteenth century.

From the point of view of a communications network, Florida divides into two subsystems, one along the Atlantic coast and the other along the Gulf coast. Except for the trail already described across the northern neck of the peninsula and a water route along the Caloosahatchee River from the southern Gulf coast through Lake Okeechobee, there was little east-west travel across Florida. Finding good drinking water along the interior ridges was apparently a problem.[37]

Geographically, the Florida peninsula as a whole appears as an appendage to the southeastern United States, but for this very reason the area provides unique extensions to the total communications network. The southeast coast of Florida was connected with the Bahama Islands by canoe travel. Indian people congregated on the coast near the Indian River to gather turtle eggs in the proper season. People came from Providence Island in the Bahamas for turtle hunting as well. In the 1780s, when the adventurer William Augustus Bowles wanted to get from Providence Island to his Creek relatives, he and his followers landed near the Indian River inlet, went overland to the St. Johns River, and descended the river with the objective of reaching the Flint River by way of the Alachua prairie.[38] In the early nineteenth century, Seminoles from southern Florida fled in their cypress canoes to Andros Island, nearest of the Bahamas.

On the west side of the Florida peninsula, dugout canoes regularly carried Indian people from Tampa Bay back and forth to the island of Cuba by way of Key West. Feathers and birds wings were lightweight but valuable items of commerce exported from Florida to Cuba.[39] There were also connections with the sparse population of the Keys. Matacumbe Key was particularly important for its fresh water supply.[40]

Tampa Bay served as a principal trading terminal with connections north and south along the Gulf coast and an entry into the interior of the peninsula. An allied channel was the Suwannee River entering the Gulf coast near Cedar Key. Spanish *hacendados* from the Apalachee and St. Johns river districts used the mouth of the Suwannee as a port of embarkation for shipping beef to Cuba before 1700.[41] In the early years of the American Revolution, Spanish guns and ammunition reached the Creek and Cherokee towns by way of Tampa, Apalachee Bay, and the Chattahoochee River.[42] Independent Indian voyages by cypress canoe continued between Florida and Cuba until the time of the Second Seminole War in 1840. All in all, the Florida peninsula should be considered a special subsystem furnishing two-way communication with the South Atlantic and Caribbean Islands.

The foregoing brief overview of a large communications network gives special emphasis to canoe routes because there is a tendency to overlook the importance of watercourses. Dugout canoes were not the only watercraft in use. On the Kanawha, Cumberland, and Tennessee river systems, canoes were constructed of a framework covered with elm or hickory bark. Sometimes these were used for only part of a long expedition and were hidden or buried in the water to be picked up on the return trip. Bark canoes were also built exclusively for one-way trips downriver and then discarded in favor of returning upstream on foot. While streams undoubtedly aided transportation in some directions, for overland travel in other directions they created time-consuming and hazardous problems. For example, stream crossings were a major impediment in traveling from the Upper Creek towns to St. Augustine, a trip that often required three weeks to accomplish.

A vivid description of triumph over natural difficulties in this part of the Southeast was recorded by an American agent returning in 1790 with a Creek delegation following negotiations for the Treaty of New York. Proceeding south on board ship, the Creeks asked to be let off at the mouth of St. Mary's River, the present Georgia-Florida border, to take a shortcut to their home communities. The party of travelers advanced upstream well past the first big bend, then followed a trail skirting the Okefenokee Swamp. Along the way they encountered one stream swollen and turbulent from fall rains. Confronted with this challenge, the Indians shot wild cattle and stretched the green hides over sapling hoops to form a bowl-shaped watercraft that was then used to ferry the American agent and the baggage across the stream. The power was supplied by Indian swimmers, who held the tow strings in their teeth and at intervals gave war whoops to frighten off the alligators, at the same time evading the tangled vines and branches being swept along by the current.[43]

A summary of the communication system of the southeastern Indians focuses first on the primary network consisting of interior trails and watercourses. On the perimeter of the interior networks are terminals supplying connections with other networks. Selected locations cited in this discussion were points on the Ohio River; Cahokia, Illinois; Natchitoches, Louisiana; Mobile, Alabama; and four places on the long shoreline of Florida: Apalachee Bay, Tampa Bay, St. Johns River near the mouth, and the Indian River Inlet.

In the late eighteenth century, the communications network served a southeastern population east of the Mississippi estimated at well over 50,000 Indians living in more than one hundred towns.[44] Two centuries earlier, before penetration by Europeans, the population of the Southeast was much larger and included additional Indian provinces along the Atlantic coast south of Chesapeake Bay. Although the data used in this discussion are from the late colonial period, the same routes of travel had probably been in use for centuries. Indian people living in the highlands of the interior Southeast were not restricted to knowledge of their immediate areas; all made use of access to the seacoast. Those living along the coast were certainly not landlocked. The geographic panorama for a well-informed southeastern Indian extended north to the Great Lakes region, westward to the Great Plains, southwest to the Mexican border, and southeast to islands in the Atlantic and Caribbean.

Postscript

Since the original publication of *Powhatan's Mantle* in 1989, no publication specifically devoted to communication networks in the Southeast has come to my attention. However, three articles have appeared contributing additional information and interpretations. With a nineteenth-century emphasis, William Dollaride summarized data on "Roads to the Old South

West," for the *American Genealogical Lending Library Newsletter*, Bulletin 28 (July–August 1995): 1–7. Of particular interest is his map, page 4, showing the route from Washington DC to New Orleans in 1806 using a horse path through the Creek Towns, provided for in the Creek Treaty of 1805. More recently, Joshua Piker published "White & Clean & Contested: Creek Towns and Trading Paths in the Aftermath of the Seven Years' War," *Ethnohistory* 50, no. 2 (Spring 2003): 315–47. He points out the shifting use of travel routes in the Southeast as alliances changed between Indian groups and European traders. Historic trail locations in northern Georgia provide Thomas G. Whitley and Lacey M. Hicks a means of assessing environmental constraints on prehistoric travel routes in "A Geographic Information Systems Approach to Understanding Potential Prehistoric and Historic Travel Corridors," *Southeastern Archaeology* 22, no. 1 (Summer 2003): 77–91. Current interest in travel routes was apparent in papers presented by Robbie Ethridge and Wendy St. Jean during the day-long symposium on the Southeast at the annual meeting of the American Society for Ethnohistory held November 5–8, 2003, at the University of California, Riverside. Contemporary research uses knowledge of travel routes as an aid to the study of population movements during the colonial era.

Notes

1. See Adele Hast and Helen Hornbeck Tanner, "Southern Indian Villages, 1760–1794" in *Atlas of Early American History*, ed. Lester J. Cappon (Princeton NJ: Princeton University Press, 1976), 19, and explanatory text, 95.

2. The significance of the Cross Timbers as a boundary zone is discussed in Helen Hornbeck Tanner, "The Territory of the Caddo Tribe of Oklahoma," in *Caddoan Indians*, vol. 4 (New York: Garland, 1974), 70–74.

3. See fig. 1, "Communications network of the colonial Southeast." To clarify geographical locations, present city names are used. It should be noted, however, that Cahokia in southwestern Illinois was supplanted in importance in the early nineteenth century by St. Louis, established across the Mississippi River on the west bank in 1764.

4. See map in Henry T. Malone, *Cherokees of the Old South; A People in Transition* (Athens: University of Georgia Press, 1956). See also William T. Myer, "Indian Trails of the Southeast," in *Forty-Second Annual Report of the Bureau of American Ethnology for 1924–1925* (Washington DC: Government Printing Office, 1928), pl. 15. The city of Tupelo, incorporated 1870, is a more accurate geographical reference point for the late eighteenth-century Chickasaw towns than the more frequently cited historic Pontotoc, established in 1836 at a site about fifteen miles farther west. See maps in James R. Atkinson, *Splendid*

Land, Splendid People: The Chickasaw Indians to Removal (Tuscaloosa: University of Alabama Press, 2003), 12–13.

5. Frank M. Setzler and Jesse D. Jennings, *Peachtree Mound and Village Site, Cherokee County, North Carolina*, Bureau of American Ethnology Bulletin 131 (Washington DC: Government Printing Office, 1941), 7–10.

6. Myer, "Indian Trails."

7. Francis Lee Utley and Marion R. Hemperly, *Place Names in Georgia* (Athens: University of Georgia Press, 1975).

8. Myer, "Indian Trails," 765.

9. For discussion of the Great Warrior Path, see Myer, "Indian Trails," 749–57. The trade route from Petersburg in southwestern Virginia through the highlands to Augusta can be traced on a modern highway map. See Douglas L. Rights, "The Trading Path to the Indians," *North Carolina Historical Review* 8 (1931): 404.

10. See Erwin Raisz, *Landforms of the United States*, 6th ed., rev. (Cambridge MA: Erwin Raisz, 1957). Every American historian should have this map at hand.

11. Helen Hornbeck Tanner, "Cherokees in the Ohio Country," *Journal of Cherokee Studies* 3, no. 2 (1978): 94–95.

12. John Heckewelder, *A Narrative of a Mission to the United Brethren among the Delaware and Mohegan Indians* (Philadelphia: McCarty and Davis, 1820), 179–203.

13. Tanner, "Cherokees," 99. See also James G. Simcoe, Speech to the Indians, October 9, 1792, in *Collections and Researches Made by the Michigan Pioneer and Historical Society*, 40 vols. (Lansing MI: Thorp and Godfrey and others, 1874–1949), 24:499–500.

14. During the mid-nineteenth century slaves from Mississippi used a similar trail to escape up the Tombigbee and down the lower Tennessee River to the Ohio River and freedom. (Peter Wood kindly provided this additional information.)

15. That is, Fort Massac. Reuben Gold Thwaites and Louise P. Kellogg, *Frontier Defense on the Upper Ohio* (Madison: Wisconsin Historical Society, 1912), 202–3.

16. Ermine Wheeler Voegelin, *Miami, Wea and Eel-River Indians of Southern Indiana* (New York: Garland, 1974), 85–86.

17. Wilbur R. Jacobs, ed., *The Appalachian Indian Frontier: The Edmund Atkin Report and Plan of 1755* (Lincoln: University of Nebraska Press, 1941), 16.

18. Verner W. Crane, "The Tennessee River as the Road to Carolina: The Beginnings of Exploration and Trade," *Mississippi Valley Historical Review* 3 (June 1916): 8.

19. Ralph A. Smith, ed. and trans., "Account of the Journey of Bénard de la Harpe," *Southwest Historical Quarterly* 62 (1959): 533.

20. Myer, "Indian Trails," pl. 15.

21. David H. Corkran, *The Creek Frontier, 1540–1783* (Norman: University of Oklahoma Press, 1967), 50–51.

22. See map in John H. Goff, "The Path to Oakfuskee: Upper Trading Route in Georgia to the Creek Indians," *Georgia Historical Quarterly* 39 (1955). To coordinate this detailed

map with the system map, fig. 1, note the position of Augusta, Georgia, on both maps. The site of Fort Toulouse in the southwestern corner of Goff's map is about ten miles north of present Montgomery, Alabama, shown on fig. 1.

23. J. Charles Kelly, "Juan Sabeata and Diffusion," *American Anthropologist* 57 (1955): 55.

24. Susan A. Miller, *Coacoochee's Bones: A Seminole Saga* (Lawrence: University Press of Kansas, 2003), 149.

25. Joseph Purcell, "A Map of the Southern Indian District of North America, 1773," original in The Newberry Library, Chicago.

26. Herbert E. Bolton, *Athanase de Mézières and the Louisiana-Texas Frontier, 1768–1780*, 2 vols. (Cleveland: Arthur Clark, 1914), 1:36–37.

27. William C. C. Claiborne, *Official Letterbooks of W. C. C. Claiborne, 1801–1816*, ed. Dunbar Rowland, 6 vols. (Jackson: Mississippi Department of Archives and History, 1917), 6:293.

28. Carlos E. Castaneda, ed., "Map of Texas, 1761–1810," in *The End of the Spanish Regime, 1780–1810*, vol. 5 of *Our Catholic Heritage in Texas*, 7 vols. (Austin: Von Boeckman-Jones, 1936–58), facing p. 514. For accounts of route up the Red River, see Noel H. Loomis and Abraham P. Nasatir, *Pedro Vial and the Roads to Santa Fe* (Norman: University of Oklahoma Press, 1967). For a detailed description of the river course to the vicinity of the "great bend" near present Texarkana, Texas, see Dan L. Flores, ed., *Jefferson and Southwestern Exploration: The Freeman and Custis Accounts of the Red River Expedition of 1806* (Norman: University of Oklahoma Press, 1984).

29. William Darby, *A Map of the State of Louisiana . . . from Actual Survey* (Philadelphia: John Melish, 1816). See also Charles Claude du Tisné, "Du Tisné chez les Missouri," in *Découvertes et établissements des Français dans l'ouest et dans le sud de l'Amérique Septentrionale* (1614–1754), ed. Pierre Margry, 6 vols. (Paris: Imprimérie D. Jouast, 1876–86), 6:312–15.

30. Myer, "Indian Trails," 831–32.

31. Charles L. Mowat, *East Florida as a British Province* (Berkeley: University of California Press, 1943), 123.

32. James Adair, *Adair's History of the American Indians*, ed. Samuel Cole Williams (1775; Johnson City TN: Watauga Press, 1930), 439.

33. Lester J. Cappon, "Travels of John and William Bartram," in *Atlas of Early American History*, ed. Lester J. Cappon (Princeton NJ: Princeton University Press, 1976), 33, 108. See also Mowat, *East Florida*, 25, 67–68.

34. Myer, "Indian Trails," 736. Jean Baptiste Franquelin, "Carte de Louisiana, ou des voyages du Sr. de la Salle, 1684," in *The Jesuit Relations and Allied Documents, 1610–1791*, ed. Reuben Gold Thwaites, 73 vols. (Cleveland: Burrows Brothers, 1896–1901), 70:63.

35. John M. Goggin, "The Indians and the History of the Matacumbe Region," in *Indian and Spanish Selected Writings*, ed. John M. Goggin (Coral Gables FL: University of Miami Press, 1964).

36. Vicente Manuel de Zéspedes to Bernardo de Gálvez, June 12, 1785, in Joseph B. Lockey, *East Florida, 1783–1785* (Berkeley: University of California Press, 1949), 557.

37. Bernard Romans, *A Concise Natural History of East and West Florida* (New York: R. Aitkin, 1775), 38, 187–88.

38. Helen Hornbeck Tanner, *Zéspedes in East Florida, 1784–1790* (Coral Gables FL: University of Miami Press, 1963), 189–95.

39. James W. Covington, "Trade Relations between Southwestern Florida and Cuba," *Florida Historical Quarterly* 39 (1959): 114–28.

40. Goggin, "Indians."

41. Charles Arnade, "Cattle Raising in Spanish Florida, 1573–1763," *Agricultural History* 35 (July 1961): 116–24.

42. Helen Hornbeck Tanner, "Pipesmoke and Muskets: Florida Indian Intrigues of the Revolutionary Era," in *Eighteenth-Century Florida and Its Borderlands*, ed. Samuel Proctor (Gainesville: University Press of Florida, 1975), 18–19.

43. Henry Rowe Schoolcraft, *Archives of Aboriginal Knowledge*, 6 vols. (Philadelphia: J. B. Lippincott, 1868), 5:253–61.

44. See table 1 in Peter Wood's essay, this volume. For a more expansive contemporary estimate made during wartime, see Lachlan McIntosh, Letter to General George Washington, Savannah, April 12, 1777, "The Letter Book of Lachlan McIntosh, 1776–1777," *Georgia Historical Quarterly* 38 (1954): 367. McIntosh reports the estimate of 20,000 gunmen for the combined southern tribes. At the usual ratio of five to one, this number of gunmen would imply a total population of 100,000, exclusive of the Caddos west of the Mississippi, estimated at about 5,000 at the time of the American Revolution.

Aboriginal Population Movements in the Early Historic Period Interior Southeast

MARVIN T. SMITH

Spanish exploration was particularly hard on southeastern Indians. Natives were killed or conscripted for forced labor, stored food supplies were stolen, and new diseases were introduced by the Spanish explorers, particularly Hernando de Soto (1540) and his men. Later English settlers established an organized slave trade using Indian middlemen.[1] The trauma of contact between Indians and Europeans during the sixteenth and seventeenth centuries set in motion complex population movements. Using historical and archaeological data, this brief essay seeks to describe and explain these movements in the interior Southeast. The area to be considered includes the Valley and Ridge and piedmont portions of Alabama, Georgia, Tennessee, and South Carolina, as well as portions of the Appalachian Summit of North Carolina. Chronologically, the period covered here stretches from the mid-sixteenth to the late seventeenth century.

This span of more than 150 years can be divided into three time segments, each with its own sources of data. Population movements that took place during the second half of the sixteenth century can be traced by two methods. Towns located by a reconstruction of the route of Hernando de Soto can be compared with towns visited a generation later by the Juan Pardo and Tristán de Luna expeditions.[2] Other sixteenth-century movements can be demonstrated archaeologically. During the first three-quarters of the seventeenth century, there were virtually no Europeans residing in the study area, and the lack of written records obliges scholars to rely solely on archaeological data in tracking possible population shifts.

Finally, European explorers again penetrated the interior in the late seventeenth century and left us valuable records of population movements. Besides giving firsthand accounts of contemporary shifts, they also reported new locations of towns mentioned by de Soto and Luna. The sources do not suggest when these moves occurred or whether they took place in gradual stages or as single episodes. However, archaeological data allow us to construct some inferences that can be tested by further archaeological research. Many of the reconstructed population movements presented here should be considered as testable hypotheses to be investigated further.

The baseline knowledge of the location of aboriginal groups in the study area comes from the recent reconstruction of the routes of Hernando de Soto, Tristán de Luna, and Juan Pardo by Charles Hudson and his associates.[3] Population centers include the upper Coosa drainage, the Oconee drainage, the Santee-Wateree drainage, the upper Tennessee River, the Little Tennessee River, the middle Coosa River, the upper Alabama River, and many other areas. Archaeological knowledge suggests many other areas of dense population, among them the lower Tallapoosa valley, the central Chattahoochee, the upper Savannah, and the Appalachian Summit area for a few examples.[4]

The expeditions of Luna and Pardo during the 1560s give us a further glimpse of the interior a few years after the de Soto *entrada*. Luna and Pardo visited many of the same towns as de Soto. Thus we know that Cofitachequi, Xuala, Chiaha, Coosa, Ulibahali, and probably Apica and Piachi remained in the same locations where de Soto had found them.[5] The Luna expedition also allows us to locate the Napochie villages at the Citico and Audubon Acres sites near Chattanooga, Tennessee (fig. 1). Conspicuously absent, however, are the Tascaloosa towns of the upper Alabama River and the Talisi towns of the middle Coosa. Apparently the Tascaloosa chiefdom collapsed after the battle of Mabila in 1540, perhaps moving down the Alabama River. Archaeological research by Knight and Wilson suggests that the Talisi towns moved away from the Coosa River up Talladega Creek to such sites as Hightower village.[6]

By the beginning of the seventeenth century, archaeological data demonstrate more radical movements of people (see fig. 2). The Coosa chiefdom abandoned the upper Coosa drainage, moving downriver to the present Lake Weiss area of Alabama and later farther downstream.[7] Similarly, the Mouse Creek towns along the Hiwassee River were abandoned, and I have suggested that these groups moved north to the Tennessee River proper, to such sites as Upper Hampton and De Armond that were occupied during the seventeenth century, based on the presence of diagnostic European trade goods.[8] Later these people may have moved south to Hiwassee Island, where there is evidence of mid- to late seventeenth-century burials placed

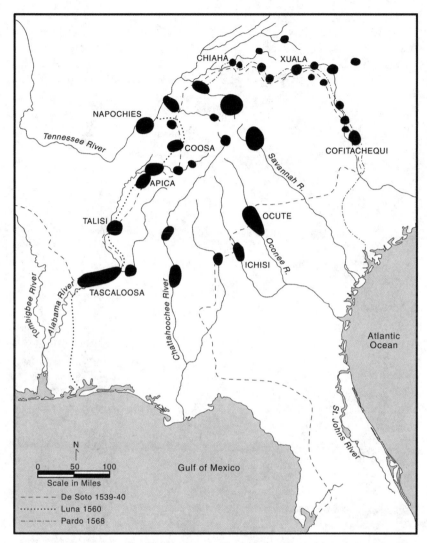

Figure 1. Sixteenth-century populations encountered by Spanish explorers or known through archae-ological research.

into earlier Woodland period burial mounds, which were constructed in the first millennium AD.[9]

The Little Tennessee River drainage also underwent demographic changes. The large Citico, McMurray, and Toqua mound sites appear to have been abandoned during the sixteenth century. Probable late sixteenth-century components are known from the Stratton, Brakebill, and McMahon sites

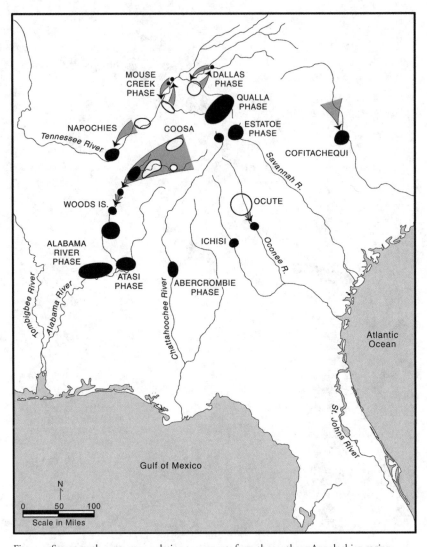

Figure 2. Seventeenth-century population movements from the southern Appalachian region.

on the Tennessee River proper, perhaps indicating a movement to the main river valley paralleling that hypothesized for the Hiwassee River groups. Early seventeenth-century materials have been reported from the Bussel Island and Tomotley sites on the Little Tennessee and the Post Oak Island site on the Tennessee River proper. That none of these sites contains the quantity of European goods seen on contemporary sites in Alabama may indicate that they were abandoned early in the seventeenth century or that access to European goods proved more difficult in this more northerly region. Late in the seventeenth century there appears to have been a sudden influx of people, based on the abundance of late seventeenth-century European trade material at such sites as Tallassee, Toqua, and Citico. I interpret this influx as a movement of Cherokee-speaking peoples into the valley.[10]

Archaeological evidence from the Chattanooga, Tennessee, area can be interpreted as follows. The Audubon Acres and Citico sites have been identified as two towns of the Napochies attacked by members of the Luna expedition and Coosa warriors in 1560.[11] Archaeological evidence suggests that Audubon Acres was abandoned before about 1575 and that Citico was abandoned shortly thereafter. Major late sixteenth/early seventeenth-century components are present on Williams Island and the Hampton Place site on Moccasin Bend across from Chattanooga, and it seems reasonable to interpret these sites as Napochie towns that had moved north across the Tennessee River to put that barrier between them and the Coosa chiefdom and its apparent Spanish allies to the south.[12] All sites in the Chattanooga area appear to have been abandoned by the mid-seventeenth century, just when several sites in the Guntersville Reservoir area appear to have been first settled. I have therefore suggested that the Napochies moved downstream southwest into Alabama, but this hypothesis needs additional testing.

The Oconee River valley (particularly the Wallace Reservoir area south to the fall line), part of the Ocute chiefdom described in the de Soto narratives, shows some population decline and settlement redistribution but remains occupied into the seventeenth century. Major mound centers all appear to have been abandoned by the beginning of the seventeenth century, and population apparently became dispersed into smaller sites.[13] By approximately 1630, the Wallace Reservoir area of the piedmont appears to have been abandoned. The population was concentrated on the Fall Line at the Shinholser site, known to the Spaniards as Altamaha or Tama.[14] These people later moved south to the Atlantic coast, were they became the core of the Yamassee.[15]

Both de Soto and Pardo recorded a thriving population at Cofitachequi on the fall line of the Wateree River near present Camden, South Carolina. Pedro de Torres visited Cofitachequi again in 1628, and it was still important and apparently still in the same location when English explorers reached the area in 1670.[16] All references to Cofitachequi seem to relate to the same location, and archaeological research at the Mulberry site suggests occupation well into the seventeenth century.[17] I strongly suspect, although I do not have the data to demonstrate, that this area received a great population influx from the north during the sixteenth and seventeenth centuries, comparable to that recorded historically for the Tallapoosa valley.

The Tallapoosa valley was not visited by any of the three sixteenth-century Spanish expeditions, but archaeological research demonstrates that this area was a population center in the sixteenth and seventeenth centuries. Both the sixteenth-century Shine II phase and the seventeenth-century Atasi phase sites are known to be concentrated along the lower valley.[18]

The fall line area of the Chattahoochee River was also important throughout the period in question. Resurvey and analysis of the Walter F. George Reservoir have yielded an excellent picture of the population dynamics of the region.[19] Sixteenth-century Bull Creek phase population levels dropped dramatically during the subsequent Abercrombie phase, probably following the introduction of European diseases. By the late seventeenth century, a population recovery is noted. It is not clear whether this is a natural population recovery or simply an influx of other people. The presence of the Taskigis in the area in 1686 suggests that some in-migration occurred.[20]

The fall line area of the Ocmulgee River near present Macon, Georgia, was also an important population center during de Soto's day. Here he found the Province of Ichisi, consisting of several towns, with the capital probably at the Lamar archaeological site.[21] It is suggested that this site continued to be an important location up to the time Chattahoochee River groups moved east to the Ocmulgee in 1690. Three forms of evidence suggest this stability: the presence of late seventeenth-century European trade materials at the site; that the Creek groups of the area were known to the English by the name Ochese Creeks, an obvious corruption of the name Ichisi recorded by the Spaniards; and probable ceramic continuity.[22]

The upper Savannah River valley also appears to have been a major population center during the Mississippi and early historic periods (ca. 1000–1670). Current research indicates that this area may not have been continuously occupied throughout the Lamar period (sixteenth- and seventeenth-century Tugalo phase) into the historic eighteenth-century Cherokees (Estatoe phase).[23] There may have been a gap in occupation at the major sites during the seventeenth century. It is not at present known whether the entire region was depopulated or only the major centers were abandoned. The abandonment of mound centers has been documented for other areas of the Southeast during the late sixteenth century.[24]

The Appalachian Summit area of North Carolina appears to have maintained population stability from the prehistoric Qualla phase to the historically documented eighteenth-century Cherokee presence.[25] Changes occurred in settlement pattern and location, but these were relatively minor shifts. In general there was a movement away from the French Broad River westward toward the Little Tennessee. Sites became smaller and more dispersed, but a large population was maintained. These villages became known to history as the Middle Towns of the Cherokees, and their numbers diminished steadily after 1700.

Late in the seventeenth century Europeans began to reenter the area, leaving records of actual movements of people and giving new locations for groups found by sixteenth-century Spanish exploratory expeditions. The slave trade out of Charlestown became an important factor in population movements. Early maps provide much information. These relocations are illustrated in figure 3.

During the late seventeenth century, numerous groups from the north are known to have moved into the lower Coosa and Tallapoosa valleys. In 1675 Bishop Calderón reported that the Tuasis were in this area, whereas their location during the de Soto period was in northeastern Alabama.[26] In 1686 Marcos Delgado reported that several northern groups had moved to the area around the junction of the Coosa and Tallapoosa rivers. For example, inhabitants of Qusate, the Coste of de Soto and Koasati of the eighteenth century, had moved from their sixteenth-century location at the mouth of the Little Tennessee River, fleeing English explorers and warlike Indians.[27] The Alabamas (Aymamu) were also reported to have fled to this area because of warfare. This group can be identified with the Alimamus of the de Soto period, when they had been situated in northern Mississippi. The Alabamas may have been responsible for some or all of the Alabama River phase sites on the Alabama River during the seventeenth century.[28] By 1700 the Napochies were situated in this area (having moved from the Tennessee River), and by 1733 the Taskigis were also here—long removed from their north Georgia home documented by Pardo in 1568.[29] They did not move directly, however, since they are known to have been on the Chatta-

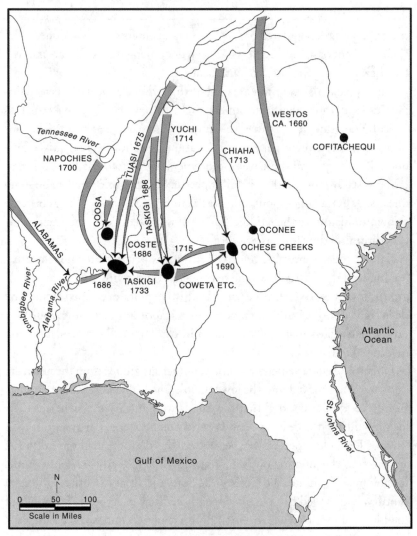

Figure 3. Documented Indian movements after the establishment of the Carolina colony, circa 1675–1715.

hoochee River in 1686.[30] It is apparent that this fall line region of Alabama along the lower Coosa and Tallapoosa rivers was an important focal point for population resettlement.

Other seventeenth-century movements were recorded. Problems with Spanish belligerence and the lure of English trade prompted several towns to abandon the Chattahoochee River area about 1690 to move to the fall line area of the Ocmulgee River near present Macon, Georgia. After the Yamasee War of 1715 these groups, joined by other refugees, moved back to the Chattahoochee.[31]

In 1712 the Yuchis were reported to be situated on the Hiwassee River at the Chestowe site. These may have been the same people who had previously inhabited the Mouse Creek sites and Hiwassee Island. This town was abandoned in 1714 when the Yuchis moved to the Chattahoochee River to join the Lower Creeks.[32] Before 1715 Chiaha, whose sixteenth-century location is believed to have been on Zimmerman's Island in eastern Tennessee, was on the fall line of the Ocmulgee, again demonstrating the attraction of this zone.[33]

By the early eighteenth century, Coosas and Abihkas are known to have been situated on the middle reaches of the Coosa River, considerably downstream from their sixteenth-century home in northern Georgia.[34] It has been suggested that this was a gradual movement that took place in several stages.[35]

Several points can be made from these attempts to portray population movements. Warfare, famine, and disease brought about by the de Soto expedition did have effects on population. From the Luna accounts only twenty years later, we know that the powerful chiefdom of Tascaloosa was destroyed, or at least relocated, and the chiefdom of Talisi was also moved or possibly temporarily abandoned. Effects of disease and other disruptive factors seen archaeologically suggest that by the end of the sixteenth century dramatic changes in population centers had taken place. Thus northwestern Georgia, the lower Hiwassee River, and perhaps the Little Tennessee River in Tennessee were abandoned. Dramatic losses of population can be demonstrated for the central Chattahoochee and the central Oconee, where new diseases had an enormous impact.

Archaeological evidence suggests possible areas of migration during the seventeenth century that need to be tested by future research. Groups from northwestern Georgia apparently moved down the Coosa River; Little Tennessee and Hiwassee River groups may have moved to the main Tennessee River valley; the Napochies in the Chattanooga area apparently moved to the north side of the river, then later moved downriver to the southwest; Oconee River groups may have concentrated on the fall line; and Alabama River phase groups reoccupied the upper Alabama River.

By the late seventeenth and early eighteenth centuries, historical documentation is again available. Eastern Tennessee groups now appeared on the fall
line area of the Coosa and Tallapoosa rivers. Chattahoochee River and Tennessee groups appeared on the fall line area of the Ocmulgee River. Groups
were appearing on the long-abandoned middle Savannah River near the fall
line. The fall line areas of the Wateree River and the Oconee River were documented as important centers, and the fall line of the Chattahoochee River
was reoccupied by groups following the Yamasee War of 1715.

What was the draw of this fall line zone from central Alabama to central South Carolina? Certainly it is an area rich in natural resources suitable for aboriginal farming, hunting, and gathering. These areas of most
southeastern rivers had been important population centers throughout the
Mississippi period. With decreasing population density brought about by
the introduction of European diseases, more groups were able to settle these
choice locations. They were also closer to sources of European trade goods,
a factor that became important at least as early as the first half of the seventeenth century. Later in the seventeenth century, Indian trails along the
fall line became important routes for English traders out of Charlestown,
and more aboriginal groups appeared to take advantage of this trade. The
fall line was no doubt important in prehistoric trade routes as well.

It also seems apparent from the writings of Marcos Delgado in 1686 that
many northern (mostly eastern Tennessee) groups were moving south to
flee English slave raiders and Indians armed with European weapons. Elsewhere I have argued that the fur trade wars of the Northeast set in motion a
chain reaction of population movements that pushed other groups farther
south.[36] Groups of northern Indians, already armed with firearms, were entering the Southeast before 1670, especially the Westos, who may have been
an Erie Iroquois group.[37] These movements of well-armed Indians, some
of whom participated in the English slave trade, caused many other population displacements.

Another important point can be made. It seems likely that the natives
of areas that were spared direct European contact in the sixteenth century
emerged by the beginning of the eighteenth century as the most important
and powerful groups. Thus the lower Tallapoosa and Chattahoochee river
valleys, bypassed by de Soto and Luna, became the important core areas
of the Creek Confederacy—the Upper and Lower Creeks, respectively.[38]

These areas are historically documented as having received many refugee groups from farther north. The upper Savannah River was the center for the Lower Cherokee towns, and the Appalachian Summit of North Carolina was the center for the Middle towns of the Cherokees. These groups appear much stronger in eighteenth-century historical records than would have been expected given the simple chiefdoms seen archaeologically for the fifteenth and sixteenth centuries. Major chiefdoms—such as Coosa, Ocute, and Ichisi—documented by de Soto, had virtually disappeared or become relatively minor towns (or groups of towns) in the Creek Confederacy by the eighteenth century. Thus northwestern Georgia and much of eastern Tennessee were depopulated, allowing the movement of Cherokee speakers into the area during the late seventeenth, eighteenth, and nineteenth centuries.

One major exception is Cofitachequi, which apparently maintained its power in spite of repeated visits by Europeans. However, Cofitachequi was already situated on the favored fall line, and I suspect that further research will show that large groups of refugees amalgamated with the Cofitachequi core to maintain its importance. I suspect that the important complex chiefdom of the sixteenth century devolved into basically one town by about 1670. Within a few years the name Cofitachequi disappears from the colonial records, and Catawbas, Esaws, Waterees, and Waxhaws are the recorded inhabitants of the area.

I hope that this brief attempt to describe aboriginal population movements will stimulate further research. Many of the hypothesized population movements described in this chapter require archaeological confirmation. The dramatic population changes that took place following European contact are still poorly known, but they must be understood if we are to unravel the complexities of the contact-period Southeast.[39]

Postscript

This chapter is based on a paper originally delivered at the 1986 Southeastern Archaeological Conference. It has benefited greatly by comments from Charles Hudson, Gregory Waselkov, Vernon Knight, David Hally, David Anderson, Peter Wood, and Tom Hatley. I am grateful for their assistance. This chapter has been updated to include more recent references and to cor-

rect some faults in the original draft. I am grateful to Gregory Waselkov for
many useful suggestions.

Notes

1. J. Leitch Wright Jr., *The Only Land They Knew* (New York: Free Press, 1981).

2. On de Soto see Charles Hudson, Marvin T. Smith, and Chester DePratter, "The Hernando de Soto Expedition: From Apalachee to Chiaha," *Southeastern Archaeology* 3 (Summer 1984): 65–77; Chester DePratter, Charles Hudson, and Marvin T. Smith, "The De Soto
Expedition: From Chiaha to Mabila," in *Alabama and the Borderlands, from Prehistory to
Statehood*, ed. Reid Badger and Lawrence Clayton (Tuscaloosa: University of Alabama Press,
1985), 108–27; Charles Hudson, *Knights of Spain, Warriors of the Sun* (Athens: University
of Georgia Press, 1997). On Pardo see Chester DePratter, Charles Hudson, and Marvin T.
Smith, "The Route of Juan Pardo's Explorations in the Interior Southeast, 1566–1568," *Florida Historical Quarterly* 62 (October 1983): 125–58; Charles Hudson, *The Juan Pardo Expeditions* (Washington DC: Smithsonian Institution Press, 1990); Robin Beck, "From Joara
to Chiaha: Spanish Exploration of the Appalachian Summit Area, 1540–1568," *Southeastern
Archaeology* 16 (Winter 1997): 162–68. On Luna see Charles Hudson et al., "The Tristan de
Luna Expedition, 1559–1561," *Southeastern Archaeology* 8 (Summer 1989): 31–45.

3. Hudson, Smith, and DePratter, "De Soto"; DePratter, Hudson, and Smith, "Juan
Pardo's Explorations"; DePratter, Hudson, and Smith, "De Soto Expedition"; Marvin T.
Smith, *Archaeology of Aboriginal Culture Change in the Interior Southeast: Depopulation
during the Early Historic Period* (Gainesville: University Press of Florida, 1987); Hudson,
Pardo Expeditions; Hudson, *Knights of Spain*.

4. On the lower Tallapoosa valley see Vernon J. Knight Jr., *Tukabatchee: Archaeological
Investigations at an Historic Creek Town, Elmore County, Alabama, 1984*, Report of Investi-
gations 45 (Moundville: University of Alabama, Office of Archaeological Research, 1985);
Gregory A. Waselkov, "Lower Tallapoosa River Cultural Resources Survey: Phase 1 Report"
(Alabama Historical Commission, Montgomery, 1981). On the central Chattahoochee see
Vernon J. Knight Jr., and Tim S. Mistovich, *Walter F. George Lake: Archaeological Survey
of Fee Owned Lands, Alabama and Georgia*, Report of Investigations 42 (Moundville: Uni-
versity of Alabama, Office of Archaeological Research, 1984). On the upper Savannah see
David J. Hally, "The Cherokee Archaeology of Georgia," in *The Conference on Cherokee
Prehistory*, ed. David Moore (Swannanoa NC: Warren Wilson College, 1986). On the Ap-
palachian Summit area see Bennie Keel, *Cherokee Archaeology* (Knoxville: University of
Tennessee Press, 1976); Roy S. Dickens Jr., *Cherokee Prehistory* (Knoxville: University of
Tennessee Press, 1976); Dickens, "Settlement Patterns in the Appalachian Summit Area:
The Pisgah and Qualla Phases," in *Mississippian Settlement Patterns*, ed. Bruce D. Smith
(New York: Academic Press, 1978), 115–40.

5. Charles Hudson et al., "Coosa: A Chiefdom in the Sixteenth Century Southeastern
United States," *American Antiquity* 50 (October 1985): 723–37.

6. Vernon J. Knight Jr., Gloria Cole, and Richard Walling, *An Archaeological Recon-*

naissance of the Coosa and Tallapoosa River Valleys, East Alabama: 1983, Report of Investigations 43 (Moundville: University of Alabama, Office of Archaeological Research, 1984); Robert C. Wilson, personal communication, 1986.

7. Marvin T. Smith, *Coosa: The Rise and Fall of a Southeastern Mississippian Chiefdom* (Gainesville: University Press of Florida, 2000).

8. Smith, *Aboriginal Culture Change*.

9. T. M. N. Lewis and Madeline Kneberg, *Hiwassee Island* (Knoxville: University of Tennessee Press, 1946).

10. Smith, *Aboriginal Culture Change*.

11. Marvin T. Smith, "Depopulation and Culture Change in the Early Historic Period Interior Southeast" (PhD diss., University of Florida, 1984); Hudson et al., "Tristan de Luna Expedition."

12. Marvin T. Smith, "The Route of De Soto through Tennessee, Georgia, and Alabama: The Evidence from Material Culture," *Early Georgia* 4 (1976): 27–48; Smith, "Depopulation and Culture Change."

13. Marvin T. Smith, *Archaeological Investigations at the Dyar Site, 9Ge5*, University of Georgia Laboratory of Archaeology Series Report Number 32 (Athens: University of Georgia, Department of Anthropology, 1994); J. Mark Williams, "Archaeological Excavations at Scull Shoals Mounds (9Ge4), 1983 and 1985," *Lamar Institute Report* 1 (Athens: University of Georgia, 1992); Williams, "Growth and Decline of the Oconee Province" in *The Forgotten Centuries*, ed. Charles Hudson and Carmen Chaves Tesser (Athens: University of Georgia Press, 1994), 179–96.

14. John Worth, "Prelude to Abandonment: The Interior Provinces of Early 17th-Century Georgia," *Early Georgia* 21 (1993): 24–58.

15. John Worth, *The Struggle for the Georgia Coast* (New York: American Museum of Natural History, 1995).

16. John R. Swanton, *Early History of the Creek Indians and Their Neighbors*, Bureau of American Ethnology Bulletin 73 (Washington DC: Government Printing Office, 1922), 217–20; John Worth, "Late Spanish Military Expeditions in the Interior Southeast, 1597–1628," in Hudson and Tesser, *Forgotten Centuries*, 104–22.

17. Chester DePratter, "The Chiefdom of Cofitachequi," in Hudson and Tesser, *Forgotten Centuries*, 197–226.

18. Knight, *Tukabatchee*; Vernon J. Knight Jr. and Marvin T. Smith, "Big Tallassee: A Contribution to Upper Creek Site Archaeology," *Early Georgia* 8 (1980): 59–74; Waselkov, "Lower Tallapoosa River." The term "phase" is used by archaeologists to describe a group of archaeological sites that have similar material culture, are found in a restricted area, and appear to date to a relatively restricted period (usually about a century or less). This term is used by prehistorians when precise tribal identifications are unknown.

19. Knight and Mistovich, *Walter F. George Lake*.

20. Manuel Serrano y Sanz, *Documentos históricos de la Florida y la Luisiana, siglos XVI al XVIII* (Madrid: Libreria General de Victoriano Suarez, 1912), 194.

21. Hudson, Smith, and DePratter, "De Soto."

22. The ceramic continuity was recognized by David Hally, personal communication, 1986.

23. Hally, "Cherokee Archaeology."

24. Smith, "Depopulation and Culture Change."

25. Dickens, "Appalachian Summit"; Christopher Rodning, "Reconstructing the Coalescence of Cherokee Communities in Southern Appalachia," in *The Transformation of the Southeastern Indians, 1540–1760*, ed. Robbie Ethridge and Charles Hudson (Jackson: University Press of Mississippi, 2002), 155–75.

26. Lucy Wenhold, *A Seventeenth Century Letter of Gabriel Diaz Vara Calderón. Bishop of Cuba, Describing the Indians and Indian Missions of Florida*, Smithsonian Miscellaneous Collections 95, pt. 16 (Washington DC: Government Printing Office, 1936), 1–15; DePratter, Hudson, and Smith, "De Soto Expedition."

27. Mark F. Boyd, "Expedition of Marcos Delgado, 1686," *Florida Historical Quarterly* 16 (July 1937): 26.

28. Craig T. Sheldon Jr., "The Mississippian-Historic Transition in Central Alabama" (PhD diss., University of Oregon, 1974), 54–65.

29. John Barnwell's map of ca. 1721, illustrated in William P. Cumming, *The Southeast in Early Maps*, 3rd ed., revised and enlarged by Louis De Vorsey Jr. (Chapel Hill: University of North Carolina Press, 1998), pl. 48; Smith, *Aboriginal Culture Change*.

30. Knight, *Tukabatchee*, 24; Serrano y Sanz, *Documentos históricos*, 194.

31. Verner W. Crane, *The Southern Frontier, 1670–1732*, ed. Peter H. Wood (New York: W. W. Norton, 1981); Carol I. Mason, *The Archaeology of Ocmulgee Old Fields, Macon, Georgia* (Tuscaloosa: University of Alabama Press, 2005).

32. Lewis and Kneberg, *Hiwassee Island*, 14.

33. DePratter, Hudson, and Smith, "De Soto Expedition"; Swanton, *Creek Indians*, 169.

34. Knight, Cole, and Walling, *Archaeological Reconnaissance*.

35. Smith, *Coosa: Rise and Fall*.

36. Smith, "Depopulation and Culture Change"; Smith, *Aboriginal Culture Change*.

37. Crane, *Southern Frontier*; Carol I. Mason, "A Reconsideration of Westo Yuchi Identification," *American Anthropologist* 65 (December 1963): 1342–46; Smith, "Depopulation and Culture Change"; Eric Bowne, "The Rise and Fall of the Westo Indians: An Evaluation of the Documentary Evidence," *Early Georgia* 28 (2000): 56–78, and *The Westo Indians: Slave Traders of the Early Colonial South* (Tuscaloosa: University of Alabama Press, 2005).

38. Vernon James Knight Jr., "The Formation of the Creeks," in Hudson and Tesser, *Forgotten Centuries*, 373–92.

39. For a recent discussion of forces that prompted movements, see Marvin T. Smith, "Aboriginal Population Movements in the Postcontact Southeast," in *Transformation of the Southeastern Indians*, ed. Ethridge and Hudson, 3–20. Patricia Galloway, *Choctaw Genesis, 1500–1700* (Lincoln: University of Nebraska Press, 1995) discusses population movements just to the west of the present area of consideration.

The Changing Population of the Colonial South

An Overview by Race and Region, 1685–1790

PETER H. WOOD

It is hard to fathom the historical and cultural patterns of a region, especially in times of great demographic change, without understanding the basic size and distribution of the whole population. This may be one reason the overall history of the South in the eighteenth century has remained elusive and incomplete for so many generations. Surprisingly, almost no one has ever posed the basic question: How many people lived in the southern geographic region during the century before the formation of the United States? And nobody has tried, even in rough terms, to find the answer to this many-sided problem in any systematic and sustained way. In recent years, with help from others, I have explored numerical changes in the population of southeastern North America in the late colonial period. This chapter presents the picture that emerges from such an extended demographic survey.[1]

My goal has been to seek out and combine population data on Indians, Africans, and Europeans from the late seventeenth century through the late eighteenth century. Specifically, I took 1790, the year of the first federal census, as a final date and, more arbitrarily, 1685 as the starting point. Much of the most dramatic change in the Indian populations of the region had already occurred by that time, as is now well known. But written records covering the preceding century and a half of intermittent foreign intrusion do not touch all parts of the South and are neither frequent nor reliable. By examining the most accessible, and lowest, part of the downward demographic curve among southern Indians, I hoped to assist, indirectly, in the discussion of earlier and less well documented population change. At the same time, I wanted to integrate data concerning Indians with figures for the rapidly changing white and black populations of the region. Only then would it be possible for demographic maps to show for the first time, at least roughly, the actual distribution of people across the South over the course of the eighteenth century. To establish this distribution meaningfully, it proved necessary to divide the region into a set of logical subregions.

I began, therefore, by separating the entire domain east of the Great Plains and south of the Ohio and Potomac rivers into a workable number of distinct subregions. Some of these ten zones might be combined, such as North and South Carolina, while others could be further divided, such as the Choctaw/Chickasaw area. Plausibly, a "Maryland" subregion could be added on the periphery.[2] But as they stand here, each of the ten districts had a geographical, political, or social identity during the colonial era that was separate enough to distinguish it from the rest of the region. Within each broad district the settlements, both Indian and colonial, generally occurred in rather concentrated locales, separated by considerable open space or "hunting land" between different ethnic and economic clusters. These communities were by no means stationary, and occasionally families, villages, or whole groups relocated within the district or migrated from one subregion to another, temporarily or permanently. Only with the largest shifts, as when the Seminoles moved into Florida, have I noted these movements, for they generally had more social and political than demographic significance.

As treated successively in separate sections and as shown on the accompanying figures and tables, the ten subregions include (I) Virginia, (II) North Carolina, and (III) South Carolina—all to the eastern edge of the mountains. Farther south lies (IV) Florida, following the boundary of the present state rather than the shifting borders imposed by eighteenth-century treaties. Touching the Atlantic coast between the Savannah and the St. Mary's rivers but extending inland to include all of modern Georgia and Alabama below the Appalachian chain and east of the Tombigbee River is (V) the Creek Confederacy. To its north, (VI) the Cherokee Nation occupies southern Appalachia. Still farther to the west lie (VII) the Choctaw and Chickasaw homelands in Mississippi and (VIII) the rich lowcountry of the greater Mississippi Delta in Louisiana, dominated first by the Natchez and their neighbors, later by the French and the Spanish. At the western edge of the geographic South, reaching to the Balcones Fault near modern San Antonio, stands the sparsely inhabited trans-Mississippi area of East Texas and Arkansas (IX). Finally, stretching across the north lies (X) the vast interior crescent below the Ohio, frequently traversed by Shawnee Indians and others, that would become West Virginia, trans-Appalachian Kentucky, and Tennessee.

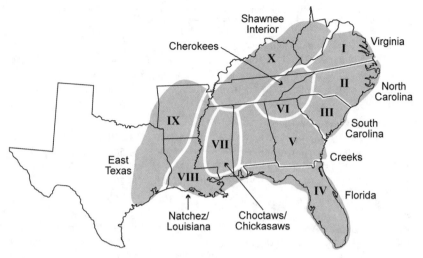

Figure 1.The ten population regions of the colonial Southeast.

With these convenient boundaries in mind, I then sought out population figures for each area by race—red, white, and black. I used racial categories not only because the numbers that survive were recorded that way, but also because these divisions represent the three interdependent cultural worlds that made up the early South. From the time colonization began, these worlds were not isolated genetically, any more than they were in terms of trade or disease; considerable miscegenation had occurred before 1685, and a great deal more would follow.[3] Since on the surface these simple categories obscure that fact, it is necessary to keep in mind the more complex underlying reality. This is especially important because intervening generations of racist thought and practice in the South have made such interactions difficult for many to accept.[4] Needless to say, the simplified picture presented here does not single out the numerous offspring of French traders and their Choctaw wives, of Virginia planters and their African workers, or of black men and Indian women enslaved on Carolina plantations, but all these persons are incorporated in the statistics compiled here.

To avoid undue simplification on the one hand and unjustified precision on the other proved no easy matter. Beginning at 1685 and ending at 1790, I divided the period into fifteen-year intervals at 1700, 1715, 1730, 1745, 1760, and 1775. I then set out to determine population estimates for all three races, in all ten subregions, for each of these eight years—240 sep-

Table 1. Estimated Southern Population by Race and Region, 1685–1790

	1685	1700	1715	1730	1745	1760	1775	1790
I. Virginia (east of the mountains)								
Red	2,900	1,900	1,300	900	600	400	200	200
White	38,100	56,100	74,100	103,300	148,300	196,300	279,500	442,100
Black	2,600	5,500	20,900	49,700	85,300	130,900	186,400	305,500
Total	43,600	63,500	96,300	153,900	234,200	327,600	466,200	747,800
II. North Carolina (east of the mountains)								
Red	10,000	7,200	3,000	2,000	1,500	1,000	500	300
White	5,700	9,400	14,800	27,300	42,700	84,500	156,800	288,200
Black	200	400	1,800	5,500	14,000	28,200	52,300	105,500
Total	15,900	17,000	19,600	34,800	58,200	113,700	209,600	394,000
III. South Carolina (east of the mountains)								
Red	10,000	7,500	5,100	2,000	1,500	1,000	500	300
White	1,400	3,800	5,500	9,800	20,300	38,600	71,600	140,200
Black	500	2,800	8,600	21,600	40,600	57,900	107,300	108,900
Total	11,900	14,100	19,200	33,400	62,400	97,500	179,400	249,400
IV. Florida								
Red	16,000	10,000	3,700	2,800	1,700	700	1,500	2,000
White	1,500	1,500	1,500	1,700	2,100	2,700	1,800	1,400
Black	—	—	—	100	300	500	3,000	500
Total	17,500	11,500	5,200	4,600	4,100	3,900	6,300	3,900
V. Creeks/Georgia/Alabama								
Red	15,000	9,000	10,000	11,000	12,000	13,000	14,000	15,000
White	—	—	—	100	1,400	6,000	18,000	52,900
Black	—	—	—	—	100	3,600	15,000	29,700
Total	15,000	9,000	10,000	11,100	13,500	22,600	47,000	97,600
VI. Cherokees								
Red	32,000	16,000	11,200	10,500	9,000	7,200	8,500	7,500
White	—	—	—	—	—	300	2,000	26,100
Black	—	—	—	—	—	—	200	2,500
Total	32,000	16,000	11,200	10,500	9,000	7,500	10,700	36,100
VII. Choctaws/Chickasaws								
Red	35,000	26,000	20,800	14,300	14,500	14,900	16,300	17,800
White	—	—	—	100	100	100	100	500
Black	—	—	—	—	—	—	—	300
Total	35,000	26,000	20,800	14,400	14,600	15,000	16,400	18,600
VIII. Natchez/Louisiana								
Red	42,000	27,000	15,000	8,000	5,000	3,600	3,700	4,000
White	—	100	300	1,700	3,900	4,000	10,900	19,400
Black	—	—	100	3,600	4,100	5,300	9,600	23,200
Total	42,000	27,100	15,400	13,300	13,000	12,900	24,200	46,600

continued

	1685	1700	1715	1730	1745	1760	1775	1790
IX. East Texas								
Red	28,000	21,000	17,000	14,000	12,000	10,000	8,300	7,000
White	200	—	300	600	900	1,200	1,500	1,800
Black	—	—	—	100	200	300	600	600
Total	28,200	21,000	17,300	14,700	13,100	11,500	10,400	9,400
X. Shawnee Interior								
Red	8,500	5,000	3,000	1,200	1,500	1,800	2,000	1,800
White	—	—	—	—	—	—	300	67,000
Black	—	—	—	—	—	—	—	13,800
Total	8,500	5,000	3,000	1,200	1,500	1,800	2,300	82,600
Totals for Regions I–X								
Red	199,400	130,600	90,100	66,700	59,300	53,600	55,600	55,900
White	46,900	70,900	96,500	144,600	219,700	333,700	542,500	1,039,600
Black	3,300	8,700	31,400	80,600	144,600	226,700	374,400	590,500
Total	249,600	210,200	218,000	291,900	423,600	614,000	972,500	1,686,000

arate numbers in all. Knowing that credible data for such a regular and detailed grid would not be easily available, I started to dig in official and unofficial sources from the Spanish, French, and English colonies, using for guidance works by John R. Swanton and scores of other researchers, past and present. Eventually I recovered hundreds of figures (only a small portion are cited in this summary) that varied greatly in completeness, precision, and reliability. I discovered that for a variety of reasons—military, economic, religious, and scientific—plausible statistics still exist, or can be extrapolated with varying degrees of accuracy, on each group in every region over four generations.

Table 1 presents this general overview. Completing such a large grid proved rather like doing a crossword puzzle; once I could fill in certain items with confidence, it became more plausible to evaluate differing evidence for the empty squares. Missing numbers between two known numbers could be projected. Divergent contemporary estimates could be weighed against established figures. When some source yielded an obvious mistake, involving a clerical error or wild guess in the past, the misleading number could be spotted and discarded. In reconciling conflicting estimates, I have tried to steer an informed middle course, but given the intricacy of the topic and the condensed nature of this survey, numerous adjustments remain ahead.

Even more than most historical statistics, these population figures will continue to demand revision and to invite interpretation.

Both the geographical and the racial boundaries employed are by definition indistinct. Moreover, the separate numbers used here vary in accuracy from precise firsthand head counts to rough secondhand "guesstimates." So all primary-source figures, including those given down to the last significant digit, have been rounded off on the grid to the nearest hundred. Even that suggests much more precision than the records actually allow in many cases, for the statistical quilt presented here has been stitched together from hundreds of scraps of partial and conflicting evidence, few of which conformed neatly to the geographic, racial, and chronological lines laid out in table 1. Inevitably, therefore, this new quilt contains distortions owing to the inaccuracies of certain original records or of my own calculations and projections for any one group in any one year. I hope such limits are more than counterbalanced by the opportunity to obtain, for the first time, an overview of the demography of the entire southern region during a crucial transitional century.

I. Virginia

The Native American population of coastal and piedmont Virginia during the late colonial period consisted of small communities of Indian "tributaries" living on assigned lands and paying annual tribute to the local English government. They had been reduced to little more than reservation status by the early and extensive colonial invasion of the Chesapeake Tidewater region. Although not so old as Spanish Florida, Virginia had become the first successful settler colony in the South, owing to Europe's infatuation with American tobacco. By 1685 more than 38,000 whites and roughly 2,600 blacks already lived in coastal Virginia. Although small compared with English colonies farther north that had grown more quickly, the Virginia settlement was by far the largest contingent of non-Indians in the seventeenth-century South. As this population base finally became more stable and healthy, its size began to increase rapidly through new births, longer lives, and increased migration. With the expanding slave trade, the number of blacks grew at an even faster rate than the figure for whites, reaching 5,500 (or perhaps exceeding 6,000) by 1700. Although African Americans

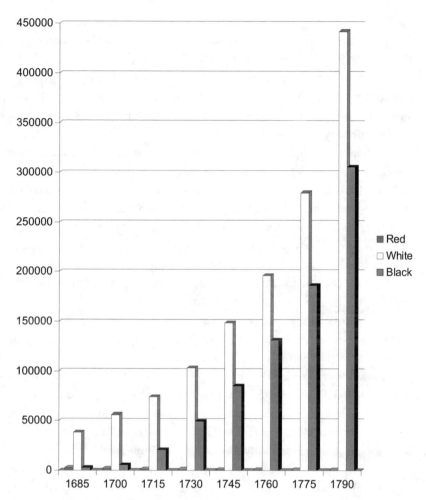

Figure 2. Region I, Virginia (east of the mountains).

made up less than a quarter of Virginia's population in 1715, by 1760 they made up 40 percent. By 1790 only Virginia and the two Carolinas among the South's ten subregions contained 250,000 persons or more, and Virginia—with nearly 750,000—was almost twice as populous as North Carolina and three times more than South Carolina.

Within Virginia's expansive tobacco society, the recognizable Indian presence became small indeed. As the pressure for farmland intensified, colonial warfare destroyed some native inhabitants and forced others to flee. The Occaneechees, for example, who resided on an island in the Roanoke

River, suffered heavy losses during Bacon's Rebellion in 1676 and withdrew south to the Eno River in North Carolina. Moreover, in Virginia, as in the later coastal colonies, innumerable individuals found themselves absorbed into the ranks of enslaved blacks and free whites, where their original racial and cultural identity often became obscured within several generations.[5] In 1669 the Virginia Assembly had listed eighteen groups of "Indian tributaries" that were to deliver so many wolves' heads annually in exchange for the right to remain in the region under colonial protection. Together they had 725 "bowmen," according to authorities. James Mooney accepted a ratio of 4:1 between total population and warriors among southern Indians near the Atlantic coast, and recent archaeological evidence seems to confirm this ratio, so we can estimate a Virginia Indian population of 2,900 in 1669. Several groups seem to have been missed, but their numbers would be roughly offset by the attrition of the next sixteen years, so we can put the Virginia Indian population of 1685 at 2,900 as well.[6]

Although the rate of decline over the next century varied from group to group and decade to decade, the overall reduction amounted to roughly one-third of the existing Indian population every fifteen years. Prominent colonial authors recorded this demise. "The Indians of Virginia are almost wasted," wrote Robert Beverley at the start of the eighteenth century. He listed "such Towns, or People as retain their Names, and live in Bodies," but he estimated that all these communities "together can't raise five hundred fighting men. They live poorly," he added, "and much in fear of neighboring Indians." At most, therefore, they must have totaled fewer than 2,000 in 1700, and a sampling of Beverley's comments upon individual towns makes clear their steadily declining condition:

> Matomkin *is much decreased of late by the Small Pox, that was carried thither.*
>
> Gingoteque. *The few remains of this Town are joyn'd with a Nation of the* Maryland Indians.
>
> Kiequotank, *is reduc'd to very few Men.*
>
> Matchopungo, *has a small number yet living.* . . .
>
> Chiconessex, *has very few, who just keep the name.* . . .
>
> Wyanoke, *is almost wasted, and now gone to live among other* Indians. . . .

Appamattox. *These Live in Collonel Byrd's Pasture, not being*
    above seven Families. . . .
Rappahannock, *is reduc'd to a few Families, and live scatter'd*
    upon the English *Seats. . . .*
Wiccocomoco, *has but three men living, which yet keep up their*
    Kingdom, and retain their Fashion; they live by themselves,
    separate from all other Indians, *and from the* English.[7]

Even those groups that prospered for a generation or two and gained
from the attrition of their neighbors could not endure indefinitely. Just after 1700 Beverley said that the Nottoways (listed in 1669 as including ninety
bowmen in two towns) "are about a hundred Bow men, of late a thriving
and increasing People." But by 1764 a report of the Indian Superintendent
for the South added Virginia's Nottoway and Sapony groups together for a
total of "60 gun-men."[8] In his *Notes on the State of Virginia*, written at the
end of the Revolutionary War and published in 1787, Thomas Jefferson recorded, "Of the *Nottoways*, not a male is left. A few women constitute the
remains of that tribe." According to Jefferson, the Mattaponys and the Pamunkeys (who had had twenty and fifty hunters, respectively, in the statute
of 1669) each absorbed remnants of the Chickahominys early in the eighteenth century. But by the 1780s, Jefferson stated:

> *There remain of the Mattaponies three or four men only, and have*
> *more negro than Indian blood in them. They have lost their lan-*
> *guage, have reduced themselves, by voluntary sales, to about fifty*
> *acres of land, which lie on the river of their own name, and have*
> *from time to time, been joining the Pamunkies, from whom they*
> *are distant but ten miles. The Pamunkies are reduced to about ten*
> *or twelve men, tolerably pure from mixture with other colors. The*
> *older ones among them preserve their language in a small degree,*
> *which are the last vestiges on earth, as far as we know, of the Pow-*
> *hatan language. They have about three hundred acres of very fer-*
> *tile land on Pamunkey River.*[9]

Hence, if identifiable Indians living apart from the Virginia settlers included no more than 2,000 at the start of the century, they probably numbered fewer than 200 by 1790. Nowhere else in the South had the native

population been reduced so low, in either relative or absolute terms. By this time President Washington, grown wealthy upon lands once occupied by native Virginians, was concerned with suppressing Indians farther west: the strong alliance in the Ohio valley and the so-called Chickamaugas in south-central Tennessee, under the leadership of Dragging Canoe. Meanwhile Washington's secretary of state, the fellow planter from Monticello, had plunged into the debate about Indian origins and undertaken some of the first systematic excavations of Indian remains. Elsewhere in the South such abstract speculation and research would gain ground in the following century, after procedures for destruction and Removal of Indian people became sanctioned elements of state and federal policy.

II. North Carolina

In contrast to Virginia, with its enormous bay and accessible rivers, North Carolina was protected from overseas colonization by the treacherous Outer Banks and the lack of suitable harbors. Separate contacts during the sixteenth century by the French (Verrazzano), the Spanish (de Soto and Pardo), and the English (Barlowe and White) had introduced foreign goods and diseases into the region, but lasting colonization did not occur until the second half of the seventeenth century, as land-hungry English settlers pushed south from the Chesapeake Tidewater into the region of Albemarle Sound. The dynamics experienced by Powhatan's Virginia in the seventeenth century of a foreign influx, a strong and protracted resistance from the dominant Indians near the coast, and an eventual decline and dispersal of the native population would recur farther south in the early eighteenth century.

In 1586 English colonists at Roanoke Island had heard about the powerful Tuscaroras, a large Iroquoian-speaking group living to the west, between the Roanoke and Neuse rivers. The smaller Algonquian-speaking tribes along the coast referred to these rivals as the Rattlesnakes ("Mangoak"), "whose name and multitude besides their valor is terrible to all the rest of the provinces." During the ensuing generations the Tuscaroras extended their power through war and trade, so that the English who settled at Jamestown heard stories of a chief to the south who was "a greater weroance" than Powhatan. Dealing first with the Spanish and later with the English, the Tuscaroras established themselves as effective middlemen, occasionally carrying European goods as far as the Mississippi during the seventeenth century. In the 1660s and 1670s they tolerated the movement of several thousand whites

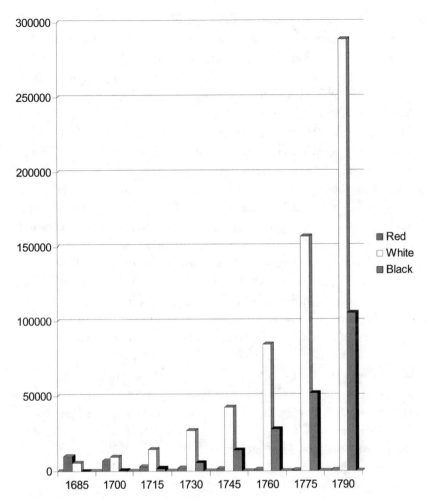

Figure 3. Region II, North Carolina (east of the mountains).

and a few hundred blacks into the area north of Albemarle Sound and east of the Chowan River, taking advantage of trade possibilities while preventing any further advance. In 1683 Lord Culpeper put the Tuscarora population at between 6,000 and 8,000 persons. Several thousand more Indians were dispersed nearer the coast in more than a dozen small groups, some of which had moved southward from the Chesapeake.[10]

Considering the Cape Fear and Catawba Indians with South Carolina and regarding the Cherokees in the mountains as inhabitants of a separate geographic region, the Indian population of North Carolina's piedmont and coastal plain must have come to roughly 10,000 persons in 1685, nearly twice the non-Indian population. But this ratio was shifting rapidly. In England in 1689, the proprietors of Carolina named a separate governor for the region stretching from Albemarle to Cape Fear, marking the beginnings of North Carolina as a distinct colonial entity, and migration from the north continued. When an epidemic devastated the Pamlico Indians in 1695, white settlers moved south to occupy the peninsula between Albemarle Sound and the Pamlico River. Modern estimates that this colonial population had reached 10,000 by 1700 may be somewhat too high, and the contemporary enumeration of Indian residents by John Lawson may have been too low, but by the start of the eighteenth century white and black newcomers probably outnumbered native inhabitants for the first time.[11]

John Lawson explored North Carolina soon after 1700, and his description of the region published in London in 1709 included a detailed account of the local Indian tribes and a summary of their numbers in terms of "Fighting Men." For the dominant Tuscaroras he named fifteen villages with a total of 1,200 men. Their neighbors included three smaller Iroquoian tribes: the Meherrins to the north, with 50 men in a town along the Meherrin River, and the Neusiocs and Corees to the south, with a total of 40 men in four villages on the Neuse River and Core Sound. Just south of the Tuscaroras a Siouan tribe, the Woccons, had two villages with 120 fighting men. Farther east, a series of small Algonquian-language tribes lined the coast from north to south, each reduced to a single village. North of Albemarle Sound lived the Chowanocs, Pasquotanks, and Poteskeets, with a total of 55 fighting men (plus the surviving Yeopims with only 6 persons in all). Below the sound lived the Pamlico, Hatteras, Matchapunga, and Bay (or Bear) River tribes, with a total of 111 fighting men. Lawson noted one village of Nottoway Indians from Virginia, with 30 men, and added that "five Nations of the Totero's, Sapona's, Keiauwee's, Aconechos, and Schoccories, are lately come amongst us, and may contain, in all, about 750 Men, Women and Children."[12]

From this summary Lawson put the total Indian population soon after the turn of the century at 4,780, but this estimate may be low on several counts. First of all, in dealing with the dominant Tuscaroras, Lawson's list of fifteen towns omits half a dozen in the north that show up several years later in other documents, so it appears, according to the best recent study, "that he underestimated Tuscarora strength." He also underestimated all the Indian women and children by guessing that they "probably" numbered three for every two fighting men, whereas it is likely that they made up about 75 percent, rather than 60 percent, of every village. In addition, Lawson seems to have reached his totals "not including Old Men." Perhaps he minimized Indian numbers because his book was intended to promote further migration from Europe. Or perhaps he simply wished to emphasize their drastic decline within two generations. "The Small-Pox and Rum have made such a Destruction amongst them," he wrote, "that, on good grounds, I do believe, there is not the sixth Savage living within two hundred Miles of all our Settlements, as there were fifty Years ago. These poor Creatures have so many Enemies to destroy them, that it's a wonder one of them is left alive near us."[13]

As was often the case elsewhere, such devastation helped prompt a desperate anticolonial war. Smallpox was spreading among the Tuscaroras by 1707, perhaps for the first time, and over the next few years, according to a later account, it "destroyed most of those Savages that were seized with it." When southern Tuscarora villages attacked the Pamlico settlers in 1711, colonial forces struck back with aid from their South Carolina neighbors. South Carolinians, eager to obtain Indian slaves and eyeing the prospect of plantations in the Cape Fear region, sent expeditions that made heavy use of Yamasee and Cherokee allies. By 1713 they had crushed the Tuscaroras, killing some 1,400 in battle and enslaving nearly 1,000 more. In 1717 the survivors were removed to a reservation on the north bank of the Roanoke River, and many abandoned North Carolina altogether, moving north to affirm their links to the Iroquois League. By 1715, therefore, the area's Indian population was scarcely 3,000, and a generation later it appeared little more than half that. "The Indians in North Carolina that live near the Planters, are few," John Brickell reported in the 1730s, "not exceeding *Fifteen* or *Sixteen* hundred Men, Women and Children, and those in good harmony with the *English*, with whom they constantly trade."[14]

By then the region's non-Indian population, according to the slightly optimistic estimate of Governor Burrington in 1732, had reached 30,000 whites and 6,000 blacks, and not all of the latter were consigned to slavery. "It is clear," William Byrd wrote in 1728, that "many Slaves Shelter themselves in this Obscure part of the World, nor will any of their righteous Neighbors discover them." As plantation agriculture expanded over the next half century, particularly near the coast, the proportion of blacks to whites in North Carolina increased somewhat, but the rapid migration of white farmers from England and Scotland, Virginia and Pennsylvania kept the white population two or three times as large as the black. The transition of the native hunting lands and "old fields" into colonial farms, whether slave or free, ensured that North Carolina's unassimilated Indians would fall to statistical insignificance, probably fewer than 400 persons in a total population east of the mountains that was rapidly approaching 400,000 by 1790.[15]

III. South Carolina

The colony of South Carolina evolved rather differently from its sister province to the north. Significantly, the Sea Islands provided protection from ocean storms without hindering transatlantic shipping. Indeed, the harbor formed by the convergence of the Ashley and Cooper rivers provided the best Atlantic port south of Chesapeake Bay, and within a decade of their arrival in 1670, English settlers had begun to lay out the village of Charlestown on the peninsula between the two rivers. By 1685 there were almost 1,400 whites and nearly 500 blacks in the area, and fifteen years later, as would-be planters continued to arrive from overcrowded Barbados with their slaves, whites numbered roughly 3,800 and blacks 2,800. By 1700 it was becoming clear that with sufficient labor rice could be grown commercially in the lowcountry's freshwater swamps. Whites who initially made money by raising cattle and pigs in the woods and selling the meat to the West Indies could now invest their profits in workers to grow rice.

Some of the initial laborers were Indians captured in tribal wars or on deliberate slaving raids. Between 1703 and 1708, the number of Indian slaves in the English colony (not to be confused with the total number of Indians in the South Carolina region) jumped from 350 to 1,400, while the white population rose by less than 300, from 3,800 to 4,080. But the regional supply of enslaved Indians could not keep up with escalating demand for unfree labor, and besides, colonial aggression was creating diplomatic and strategic problems on the frontier. Africans, on the other hand, could be obtained in great numbers without local repercussions, especially since the monopoly of England's Royal African Company had given way to "inde-

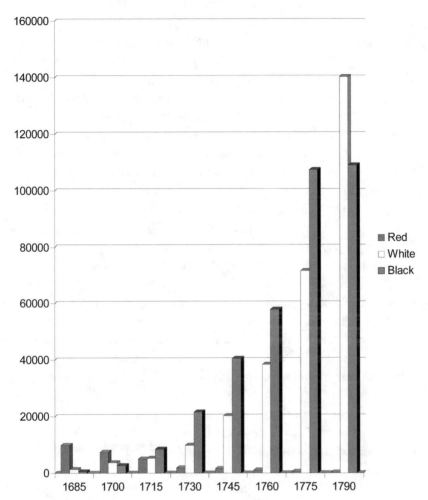

Figure 4. Region III, South Carolina (east of the mountains).

pendent" trade. Unlike indentured servants from Europe, West Africans and their offspring could be exploited in perpetuity, with little chance of escape. Moreover, they were less vulnerable to malaria than the Europeans, and many of them already had a valuable familiarity with rice cultivation. In the same five-year span before 1708, the enslaved black population rose from 3,000 to 4,100. Since men outnumbered women among the black newcomers and women exceeded men among the Indian slaves, miscegenation between these two races produced a considerable mixed-blood population. But in succeeding generations these "mustees" were, for the most part, absorbed back into the rapidly expanding African American slave commu-nity, while the number of discernable Indian slaves—never more than a few thousand—gradually declined.[16]

By 1715 blacks in the colony numbered 8,600 and exceeded whites by more than 3,000. By 1730 (with the smaller ports of Georgetown and Port Royal now actively buying slaves via Charlestown and shipping back produce in return) the ratio had grown to more than two to one, and the sizable black majority continued in South Carolina through the American Revolution. In 1775 there were twice as many blacks in South Carolina as in North Carolina (107,300 to 52,300) and fewer than half as many whites (71,600 to 156,800). Over the next fifteen years the number of black South Carolinians increased very little. War interrupted the trade from Africa; rich loyalists emigrated with their slaves; and adventuresome planters began transporting human property to the Georgia frontier. The census of 1790 showed 107,094 slaves in South Carolina, along with 1,801 free blacks, bringing the total recorded African American population to 108,895. In contrast, the white population had virtually doubled since Independence, reaching 140,178 according to the 1790 census. Most of these newcomers had arrived from farther north, taking up land in the backcountry once controlled by Indians. But as had been true for more than a century, South Carolina's total white population still did not equal half that of its northern neighbor.[17]

Despite the contrasts in their non-Indian populations during the eigh-teenth century, the demographic histories of the Indian occupants in the two Carolinas have much in common. As in North Carolina, the small tribes near the South Carolina coast were decimated within several genera-tions after foreign colonization. An exhaustive study by Gene Waddell has reconstructed this demise in unique detail. Already reduced by sickness and slave raiding during the era of Spanish dominance, they numbered scarcely 1,000 by 1685. In 1686, St. Helena and Edisto Indians in the vicinity of Port Royal died during a Spanish raid on the colony. Sometime during the next decade a party of Sewee Indians put out to sea in canoes, hoping to avoid colonial middlemen by establishing direct contact with England somewhere beyond the horizon; most drowned in a storm and others were taken up by an English ship and sold into slavery in the Caribbean.[18] But as usual, dis-ease caused the greatest destruction. Afra Coming probably referred to the Wando tribe northeast of Charlestown when she wrote in 1699 that smallpox was "said to have swept away a whole neighboring nation, all to 5 or 6 which ran away and left their dead unburied, lying on the ground for the vultures to devouer." In the righteous words of Governor Archdale, "the Hand of God was eminently seen in Thinning the Indians, to make room for the English."[19]

Numbering perhaps 800 at the outbreak of the Yamasee War in 1715, most of these coastal Indians sided with the colonists and suffered because of it. The Wimbee, Combahee, Kussah, and Ashepoo tribes (all of whom resided south of Edisto Island in the Port Royal area, where the warfare was most intense) never appear again in the records, and the groups that survived were now so dependent as to be called "Indians residing within the Settlement." By 1730 they numbered scarcely 500 in all, and the St. Helena, Edisto, Kiawah, and Kussoe tribes are last mentioned in 1743. An Anglican minister in St. Paul's Parish west of Charlestown, where the Kussoes resided, reported in that year that they numbered "about 65 Men Women and Children in all; though formerly they consisted of about 1000, as they say." By 1751 only the Etiwans appear by name in English records, and by 1760 the coastal survivors numbered 250 or fewer, though some still held together in groups. "There are among our Settlements several small Tribes of *Indians*, consisting only of some few Families each," reported Governor Glen in 1761.[20]

Groups that resided to the north or farther inland fared only slightly better, as can be seen from a list prepared at the beginning of 1715 to document the "Strength of all the Indian Nations that were subject to the Government of South Carolina, and solely traded with them." This "Exact Account" listed more than half a dozen Siouan tribes of various sizes living north of Charlestown. Some 57 Sewees survived following the effort to cross the Atlantic; 106 Winyahs remained after a generation of slaving raids. The Santee and Congaree tribes, situated in three towns near the fall line on the Santee River, numbered only 125 persons together, while the Cape Fears totaled 206 people in five small towns near the Cape Fear River. Two larger groups had recently moved southward as a result of disruptions farther north. The Saras, or Cheraws, who had earlier moved north to the Dan River to avoid the Spanish, now inhabited a single large town of 510 near the Pedee River. The Waccomassees, or Waccamaws, totaling 610 persons in four villages, were new arrivals who—several years earlier as the Woccon Indians—had been neighbors of the Tuscaroras.[21]

This census had scarcely been compiled before a new conflict erupted in April 1715. Just as the Tuscaroras, linked to the Iroquois, lost a desperate war in North Carolina and then eventually withdrew to the north, so the Yamasees, tied to the Creeks, launched a major campaign against South Carolina. When they failed, just barely, in their efforts to dislodge the English and African newcomers, they removed to the south and took up residence near the Spanish in Florida, but the struggle changed the face of South Carolina. In June 1715, for example, a combined force of Siouan warriors raided plantation outposts and captured the colonial garrison on the Santee River, but the English launched an immediate counterattack, enslaving captives where possible, and gradually regained the upper hand. By the end of 1716 a Charlestown official could report of the "Northward Indians" that "several Slaughters and Blood Sheddings" had "lessened their numbers and utterly Extirpated some little tribes as the Congarees, Santees, Seawees," and others.[22] But the largest of these Siouan tribes remained intact, and for the rest of the eighteenth century by far the most numerous native group between the edge of the Cherokee hunting domain and the Atlantic Coast would be the Catawba Indians.

Adair's assertion that the Catawbas had "mustered fifteen hundred fighting men" when South Carolina "was in its infancy" seems well founded, for in 1682 the English had estimated Catawba warriors at 1,500—"or about 4,600 souls," according to Swanton's extrapolation.[23] The "Exact Account" of 1715 put the Catawba population at only 1,470, with 570 men in seven villages. But the dislocations of the Yamasee War added to their total, so that two years later on a visit to Charlestown "the Catawba Chief King" could claim 700 gunmen.[24] This unique piedmont nation was centered on a nucleus of towns near the confluence of Sugar Creek and the Catawba River. These villages, 200 miles north-northwest of Charlestown, had their own "eastern Siouan" language. But they were joined over time by a score of smaller groups drawn from all directions, the remnants of other tribes, who spoke a variety of languages and took up residence nearby.

To foster trade with this considerable nation, Carolina arranged in 1717 "for a garrison to be built at Congarees," near the site of modern Columbia. For several years Congaree Fort served as a government trading post, securing the northern trail between Charlestown and the Cherokees and guarding the fork where the path to the Catawbas (now U.S. 21) branched off to the north.[25] When he surveyed the Catawbas' homeland a decade later, Virginian William Byrd took note of their antagonisms with the Tuscaroras and the other members of the Iroquois Confederacy, saying the Catawbas had formerly been "a very Numerous Powerful People. But the frequent Slaughters made upon them by the Northern Indians, and, what has been still more destructive by far, the Intemperence and Foul Distempers introduc'd amongst them by the Carolina Traders, have now reduc'd their Numbers to little More than 400 Fighting Men, besides Women and Children."[26] According to James Adair, "About the year 1743, their nation consisted of almost 400 warriors, of above twenty different dialects."[27]

Catawba numbers continued to decline, and by midcentury a debate, sparked by the Cheraw desire to withdraw and relocate, led to bloodshed. Outbreaks of smallpox, one in 1738 and another in 1760, added to the destruction. Noting their "bitter war" with the Iroquois League since "time immemorial," James Adair wrote before the Revolution that "the Katahba are now reduced to very few above one hundred fighting men—the smallpox, and intemperate drinking, have contributed however more than their wars to their great decay."[28] But he noted that unlike other coastal and piedmont tribes that had suffered even greater decimation, the Catawbas still maintained a distinct territory of their own, "bounded on the north and northeast, by North-Carolina—on the east and south, by South Carolina—and about west-south-west by the Cheerake nation."[29] During the Revolution the Catawbas remained loyal to the Patriot cause, providing men at Fort Moultrie in 1776 and Guilford Court House in 1781. Yet their land base and their population continued to diminish, and by the 1790s whites claimed the Catawbas once had been "numerous but were now a very small and despised nation" of several hundred inhabitants.[30]

Overall, the sharp decline in the Indian population of coastal and piedmont South Carolina since the late 1600s had run a course comparable to that of North Carolina, though no doubt less similar than indicated by the rounded estimates of table 1. In the northern district the impact of the Tuscarora War preceded 1715, and to the south the disruptions of the Yamasee conflict came several years later. But in each of these similar and adjoining regions the number of Indian inhabitants dropped from at least 10,000 to only a few hundred in the course of a century.

IV. Florida

Closest to the Caribbean, Florida became the first portion of North America to be invaded by the Spanish, beginning in 1513. During the initial five or six generations of contact with slave raiders, European viruses, and Christian missionaries, Florida's native population declined enormously. The most extended study of this decline, by Henry Dobyns, is also the most expansive in estimating its horrendous scope. But even if one modifies Dobyns's upper-limit calculations, a more conservative reading of the evidence still suggests that during the first 170 years after Spanish arrival, Florida's population may have fallen by a factor of ten, from several hundred thousand to fewer than 20,000. The debate sparked by Dobyns's projections belongs, of course, to the larger controversy over the size of America's entire pre-Columbian population and over the causes, timing, and extent of its subsequent decline. Regardless of where that broader argument may lead, no one disputes that in the Southeast Florida sustained the earliest severe losses owing to the arrival of outsiders.[31]

The seventeenth century marked the height of Spanish missionary activity in northern Florida, but death outstripped conversions. A letter of February 2, 1635, claimed 30,000 Christian Indians associated with forty-four missions, but within forty years this number would be only half as great. In October 1655 Governor Rebolledo described "a high mortality rate" in Timucua province as a result of a "series of small-pox plagues which have affected the country for the last ten months . . . and of the trials and hunger which these unfortunate people have suffered." These conditions brought on a major rebellion in Timucua the following year that Rebolledo brutally suppressed, compounding the destruction. In 1657 he reported that Timucua and the province of Guale farther north had been annihilated— "wiped out with the sickness of the plague and smallpox which has overtaken them in the past years."[32]

Two decades later, in 1675, Bishop Calderón of Cuba made a lengthy expedition through the region. He asserted that nearly all of the surviving Indians of northern Florida had been nominally Christianized, but they now

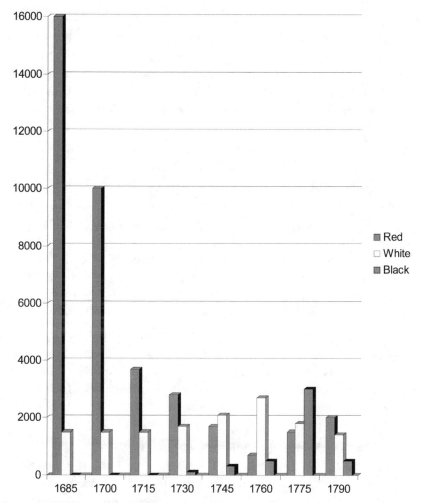

Figure 5. Region IV, Florida.

totaled scarcely 13,000 in all. Along the Atlantic coast north of St. Augustine the province of Guale had eight missions, and just west of St. Augustine the smaller province of Timucua included eleven missions. Farther west the Apalaches, with a population of about 6,000 people, inhabited thirteen missions. In the northwestern province of Apalachicola, Calderón reported that the 130 residents in two Chatot villages near Pensacola Bay had received baptism in 1674, and the bishop himself claimed to have "converted to our holy faith" several leaders of the neighboring Lower Creeks, setting up a mission at their southernmost town of Sabacola el Menor. In all, Bishop

Calderón reported 13,152 Christian Indians in these four provinces, an inclusive census that appears to some scholars to represent an actual enumeration.[33] Since the Spanish presence in north Florida at this time totaled 1,500 at most, primarily in the vicinity of St. Augustine, these priests and soldiers were outnumbered nearly ten to one by their native allies.[34]

Estimating the population for 1685 we can assume that those not counted in 1675 offset those lost in the intervening decade. And while roughly 13,000 Indians remained in northern Florida, another several thousand persons inhabited the coastlines of the peninsula farther south. Less familiar to the Spanish, they constituted more than a dozen small nonagricultural tribes, such as the Ais and the Tequestas along the Atlantic coast. In 1675 Bishop Calderón had characterized these coastal groups as "savage heathen Carib Indians, in camps, having no fixed abodes, living only on fish and roots of trees." Both culturally and numerically the dominant group in south Florida remained the once-powerful Calusas, living between Lake Okeechobee and the Gulf of Mexico. A report from an expedition through five Calusa villages in 1680 counted 960 persons, representing a persons/town ratio of 192:1. Since they had other villages as well, the Calusas still numbered more than 1,000, but all the inhabitants of southern Florida probably constituted no more than 3,000 persons. This would bring the total Florida Indian population in 1685 to roughly 16,000 persons.[35]

Although documentation is scarce, that population clearly continued to drop. According to William Sturtevant, another "period of depopulation—perhaps better called disintegration and annihilation—begins about 1680," as slave-seeking Englishmen start trading guns to their Indian allies. For southern Florida, we can apply a crude average rate of decline of 500 persons every fifteen years. Before 1715 raiders from Carolina had probably reduced the Calusas and their neighbors to 2,000, including refugees from the north, and thirty years later the number was perhaps half that. In 1763 about eighty Calusa families evacuated Florida with the Spanish, and remnants of the southernmost tribes were seeking refuge on the Florida Keys from the Lower Creek newcomers who became known as Seminoles.[36]

In northern Florida, where native inhabitants had allied with the Spanish, the latest round of devastation arrived abruptly and can be closely documented. After a Spanish effort to dislodge the English from Charlestown failed in 1686, the Guale Indians withdrew southward from their exposed mission towns on the Georgia coast, taking up residence below the St. Mary's River by 1692. Between 1702 and 1713, during the War of the Spanish Succession, repeated assaults by Englishmen from Carolina and their Indian allies destroyed almost all of northern Florida's remaining Indian missions. These raids, mounted to disrupt the Spanish borderland and obtain profitable slaves, forced Indian survivors in the Timucua and Apalache provinces to take permanent refuge near St. Augustine. The largest attack, a brutal thrust into western Florida by the English and their Creek allies in 1704, resulted in death for hundreds of Apalache Indians and enslavement for hundreds more. To avoid slavery another 1,300 agreed to resettle near the English (at the falls of the Savannah River), 400 more sought protection near the French at Mobile Bay, while another 100 formed a new town near Pensacola. A Spanish report claimed that by 1705 Carolina forces had destroyed thirty-two Indian towns in all.[37]

And the devastation continued. Thomas Nairne, at the center of Carolina's aggressive policy, could boast in 1709 that "the garrison of Saint Augustine is by this warr reduced to the bare walls, their castle and Indian towns all consumed either by us in our invasion of that place or by the Indian subjects since who in quest of booty are now obliged to goe down as far as the point of Florida as the firm land will permitt." The Indian raiding parties, Nairne concluded, "have drove the Floridians to the islands of the Cape, have brought in and sold many hundreds of them and daily now continue that trade." When these same Yamasee and Lower Creek raiders turned against the English in 1715, the Spanish sought to claim them as allies, and the Indian population of northern Florida was slightly renewed by the dislocations of the Yamasee War. A census of the ten remaining missions near St. Augustine in 1717 counted 1,591 Indians, including Apalache, Timucua, and Yamasee refugees. But even this number, plus the 100 Apalaches at Pensacola, suggests a total of fewer than 1,700 Indians in northern Florida, a drop of 87 percent in thirty years. They scarcely outnumbered the Spanish, who had added a small garrison at Pensacola in 1698 and who continued to average roughly 1,500 inhabitants (though the main population center at St. Augustine may have been slightly reduced).[38]

During the next generation Florida's small Spanish population showed an upward turn, to roughly 1,700 in 1730, 2,100 in 1745, and 2,700 by 1760. The total of black residents, enslaved and free, rose over the same time, from scarcely 100 in 1730 to nearly 500 in 1760, as new migrants brought Negroes from Cuba and as the number of runaways escaping from the neighboring English slave colonies increased. In contrast, the small Indian population continued to decline. If we estimate the Calusas and others in southern Florida as shrinking from 1,500 in 1730 to 500 in 1760, we can add more detailed data for the northern regions. At Pensacola the Apalache refugee village established in 1715 apparently persisted, for evacuation figures from that Gulf coast port in 1763 indicate that 108 Christian Indians left with the Spanish. Farther east, at San Marcos de Apalache, the Indian inhabitants dropped from 160 in 1730 to 25 three decades later. But the largest decline was in the St. Augustine region, where the number of Indians—by Spanish count—fell from 1,011 in 1729 to 79 in 1760. All told, Florida's Native Americans decreased from nearly 2,800 in 1730 to scarcely 700 thirty years later. (An estimated middle figure for 1745 would be 1,700).[39]

After the British acquired Florida in 1763 the non-Indian population rose to nearly 5,000 before the American Revolution, as white immigrants brought some 3,000 slaves to the new colony in hopes of establishing plantations. But many of these endeavors failed, and by 1790, following the departure of British loyalists and their slaves and the reimposition of Spanish colonial rule, only 1,400 whites and 500 blacks remained. The young naturalist William Bartram was among those who attempted to use slaves to start a frontier plantation in the mid-1760s, but he soon gave up, returning to explore the South a decade later. In Florida, as elsewhere, he observed clear signs of the diminished native population, and he illustrated the decline of Spanish power through his description of the road that had once connected St. Augustine to St. Mark's on Apalache Bay. Traveling across northern Florida in the summer of 1774, Bartram noted that the historic route had been "unfrequented for many years past, since the Creeks subdued the remnant tribes of ancient Floridans, and drove the Spaniards from their settlements in East Florida into St. Augustine, which effectually cut off their communication between that Garrison and St. Mark's." Therefore, he reported, "this ancient highway is grown up in many places with trees and shrubs; but yet has left so deep a track on the surface of the earth, that it may be traced for ages yet to come."[40]

This portion of Bartram's extensive travels put him in an excellent position to observe the expansion of the Seminoles, Lower Creek Indians who had been gradually drifting into Florida and filling the void left by previous tribes. "The Siminoles are but a weak people with respect to numbers," Bartram wrote after his journey in the 1770s. "All of them, I suppose, would not be sufficient to people one of the towns in the Muscogulge; for instance, the Uches on the main branch of the Apalachucla river, which alone contains near two thousand inhabitants. Yet this handful of people possesses a vast territory; all East Florida and the greatest part of West Florida." The Seminoles, who assimilated the remnants of local groups and added runaway slaves to their number, may have included 1,500 by 1775 and 2,000 by 1790. They continued to spread out after the turn of the century, and we know that by 1822 Florida's Indian population, dispersed among some thirty-five towns, had again reached 5,000 persons, the highest total in more than a century.[41]

V. Creeks/Georgia/Alabama

The broad inland domain just above the eastern Gulf coast differed markedly from neighboring Florida in its eighteenth-century population profile. Geographically, it included most of what is now Alabama and Georgia, minus the Appalachian foothills in the north, the Choctaw hunting grounds beyond the Tombigbee River in the west, and the Mobile Bay area to the south, which became associated with French Louisiana. The Muskogee Indians, later known as the Creeks, had dominated this region for hundreds of years when the first Europeans arrived in the sixteenth century. After surviving the incursions of de Soto (1540) and Luna (1559), the Muskogees consolidated their enviable position between southern Appalachia and the sea, much as other Indian nations were attempting to do farther east. Like the Tuscaroras, they proved astute traders and aggressive warriors, and like the Catawbas, they maintained a loose confederacy of towns that readily absorbed refugees from other areas. But unlike the eastern piedmont tribes, they found themselves one step removed from the colonizing pressures of the English and strategically situated between two, then three, rival European forces. Taking advantage of this unique location through aggressive military and diplomatic policies, they managed to enhance both their power and their population during the late colonial period, in the face of dramatic demographic and political shifts taking place around them.

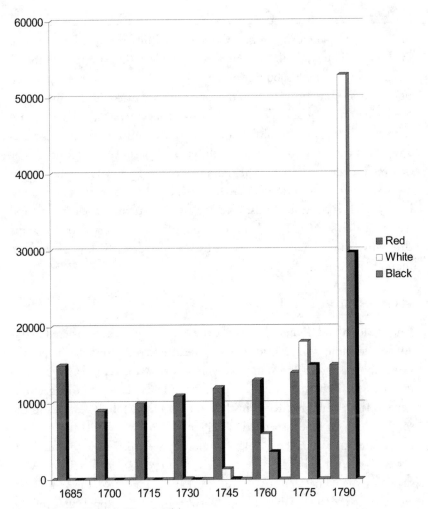

Figure 6. Region V, Creeks/Georgia/Alabama.

By the late seventeenth century, the numerous villages on the Tallapoosa and Coosa, near where these rivers combine to make the Alabama, were being pressured from the west by the more numerous Choctaws and by the Mobilian tribes near the coast. Farther east, along the Chattahoochee (the modern border between southern Georgia and Alabama) north of where it joins the Flint River to form the Apalachicola, similar communities found themselves vulnerable to the Westo Indians of Carolina, newly armed with guns from Charlestown. As a last resort some of these towns sought aid and protection from the Spanish in Florida. But others objected strenuously, and in 1685 pro-English factions helped Henry Woodward erect a stockade near the falls of the Chattahoochee so they could begin direct trade with Carolina. Within five years a number of towns had moved east to the Altamaha and settled along its western branch, the Ocmulgee River, the upper portion of which was known to the English as Ochese Creek. Soon the English were calling these Ochese Creek Indians simply Creeks, and the name quickly came to include the entire confederation. The eastern portion, living in the valleys of the Chattahoochee, Flint, and Ocmulgee rivers in Georgia, became known as Lower Creeks. Those residing farther "up" the trading path from Charlestown, on the Coosa, Tallapoosa, and Alabama rivers in central Alabama, were designated Upper Creeks.[42]

Long resentful of Choctaw incursions from the west and Spanish intimidation from the south, the Creeks, now armed and encouraged by English traders, struck back. They took Choctaw captives for sale in Charlestown's growing slave trade, and they stole horses from Spanish missions to sell to Carolina traders. With the arrival of the French in Mobile at the turn of the century, regional politics became increasingly complex. Agents from Charlestown failed in their efforts to move additional Creek allies eastward to help Carolina resist her Spanish and French enemies. But the English did convince Creek warriors to spearhead attacks on St. Augustine (1703), the Apalache missions (1704), and the Spanish fort at Pensacola (1707 and 1708). These raids were followed by forays against French Mobile (1709) and France's Choctaw allies (1711) before the Creek-English alliance broke down.[43]

A gradual increase (less steady than suggested in table 1) in the region's Indian population during the eighteenth century can be established from numerous sources. But it is harder to estimate seventeenth-century numbers; just how sharply native towns had been reduced by initial Spanish contacts, and how fully they had recovered after several generations, remains uncertain. The few European reports surviving from the late seventeenth century, such as Bishop Calderón's 1675 letter, give evidence for the interior that is secondhand or incomplete.[44] Moreover, as previously noted, whole towns occasionally relocated—often preserving their names—when new pressures prevailed. So the few estimates made by competing European empires conflict, omitting some groups and exaggerating or double-counting others. In table 1, I have put the region's Indian population at 15,000 persons for 1685, but this figure is even more speculative than most. The actual number may have been nearly half again as high but declining rapidly owing to increased English contact. Or it may have been scarcely half that number but already rising slowly as it would continue to do over the next century.

By 1700 the Indian population probably hovered somewhere around 9,000 persons. In 1708 the governor of South Carolina wrote that 150 miles west from Charlestown "are settled on ochasee River eleven Towns of Indians consisting of six hundred men." Highly pleased by his allies, Nathaniel Johnson added: "These people are great Hunters & Warriors & consume great quantity of English goods." Farther west, on the Chattahoochee River, Johnson noted another community that provided a "very serviceable" stopping point for English traders on their way to the Upper Creek settlements "of the Tallabousees & the Alabamees." He noted vaguely that these more western groups reside in "many Towns," and their 1,300 men "are Great Warriors & Trade with this Government for a great quantity of goods."[45] Johnson seems to suggest a sum of 1,900 Creek men, which, if multiplied by the accepted figure of 3.5, gives a total population of 6,650. To this number can be added several thousand people from the smaller adjacent groups noted in the next paragraph.

Johnson's numbers are similar to, though slightly smaller than, the figures submitted in 1715 as part of a South Carolina census of neighboring Indians that had been in preparation for several years. The document listed ten villages of the Ochese Creeks, containing 731 men and 2,406 persons in all. (As with Johnson's 1708 figures, a contingent of Lower Creeks remaining on the Chattahoochee may have been overlooked in the calculations.) The census recorded 1,352 adult men among the three divisions of the Upper Creeks, giving the following breakdown of their overall population: 1,773 Abeikas in fifteen towns, 2,343 Tallapoosas in thirteen towns, and 770 Alabamas in four towns. So the census offers totals of 2,083 men and 7,292 inhabitants living in forty-two villages. Although the towns obviously varied considerably in size and composition, according to these figures the average Creek townsite in 1715 had 50 men and 174 residents. (This confirms a total population/warrior ratio of 3.5:1, which I have applied to other Creek data as well.) Additional precise figures were given for villages of the Yamasees (10), Apalachicolas (2), Apalaches (4), Savannahs (3), and Yuchis (2), total-

ing another 2,700 inhabitants. This would mean some 10,000 Indians resided in the region in 1715, on the eve of the Yamasee War.[46]

If the Creek population had fallen below 10,000 persons in the decades
before 1715, it began to rise again in succeeding generations. As a new phase
of diplomacy began, refugees from power struggles elsewhere sought protection in Creek territory. The nation that had assimilated Apalachicola Indians from Florida added Taensas from Louisiana; after 1730 Natchez survivors arrived from the Mississippi. Creek scholar David Corkran notes that
by the 1740s, "Several score Chickasaws, faltering under the pounding that
nation had taken from the French and Choctaws, had settled in the upper
reaches of the Abeika country at a town to be known as the Breed Camp
and had become part of the Creek confederacy . . . and in 1744 a village of
Shawnees from the Ohio country came to settle among the Upper Creeks."[47]
An English estimate made in 1749 and published in 1755 put the number of
Creek fighting men at 1,200 in the "Lower Nation" and 1,365 in the "Upper Nation," a total of 2,565 warriors, or nearly 9,000 Creeks in all. At the
same time, non-Creeks in the area had diminished somewhat, having migrated, died out, or been absorbed.[48]

Meanwhile, James Oglethorpe's small Georgia colony was establishing
a foothold near the Atlantic coast, aided by a local village of several hundred Yamacraw Indians, who had been banished by the Creeks during the
1720s and had settled near the Savannah River shortly before Oglethorpe
arrived. By 1745 there were nearly 1,400 whites in the colony, plus some runaway blacks from South Carolina and some illegally enslaved black workers—probably fewer than 100 in all. By 1760, with steady immigration, improved living conditions, and decreased mortality, the white population had
risen to roughly 6,000 persons. In addition, following the legalization of
slavery in 1751, several thousand blacks had been imported to clear coastal
plantation sites. But farther west the Creek population also continued to
grow, and it still remained the dominant numerical presence in the region
as a whole. One English estimate from 1764 put the number of Creek fighting men at 3,655, while another census report from the same year showed an
equivalent figure of 3,683 gunmen in fifty-nine villages. So the total Creek
population may have approached 13,000 by 1760, and it probably continued to expand somewhat despite the turbulence of the ensuing decades.[49]
James Adair wrote of the Creeks in 1775, "This nation is generally com-

puted to consist of about 3500 men fit to bear arms; and has fifty towns, or villages." His appraisal may have been slightly dated, secondhand, and incomplete, though Bernard Romans published the same rough estimate in the same year.[50]

Even if the region's Indian population had risen slightly, to perhaps 14,000, by 1775, the non-Indian populations had grown much more rapidly. Migration into the expanding English colony—both free and forced, by land and sea—had brought the number of black and white Georgians to 15,000 and 18,000 respectively. According to the census of 1790, the new state of Georgia included 52,886 whites, plus 29,264 slaves and 398 free blacks. Creek numbers too increased during the fifteen years after American Independence, though at nowhere near the same rate. An estimate from 1780 (which included the roughly 1,500 Seminoles in Florida) put the Creek total at 17,280, of whom 5,860 were said to be gunmen.[51] Five years later a report to Richard Henry Lee put the gunmen of the "Upper and Lower Creek nation" (excluding the Seminoles) at 5,400, and in 1791 Creek leader Alexander McGillivray was said to estimate "the number of gun-men to be between 5000 and 6000, exclusive of the Seminolies."[52] A report to the governor of West Florida and Louisiana for the Spanish in 1793 recorded 8,715 people in thirty-one Upper Creek towns and 6,445 persons in twenty-five Lower Creek towns, for a total of 15,160 within the Creek Nation, roughly double the number that had lived there eighty years before.[53]

Although this upward trend seems clear, individual estimates remain uncertain, for the ratio of total population to warriors varied depending on conditions and methods of counting, and whole communities shifted in size, location, and importance over time. Whereas the English census of 1715 shows a ratio of 3.5:1, a report to the secretary of war in 1789 put the "number of old men, women, and children, in the proportion as four to one of the warriors." As for villages, the same report conceded, "The number of towns in each district, could not be ascertained, probably about eighty in the whole, of which about forty-five are in the upper country. The towns are very different in magnitude; and a few, of what are called the mother towns, have the principle direction of national affairs."[54]

Caleb Swan, writing two years later, reported a similar number of towns, varying in size from twenty houses to two hundred. He put the number of whites in the nation at 300, and with regard to the overall population, he

expressed what earlier observers had also felt. "From their roving and un-
steady manner of living," Swan wrote, "it is impossible to determine, with
much precision, the number of Indians that compose the Creek nation."
But he added a succinct explanation for their demographic rise. "It appears
long to have been a maxim of their policy, to give equal liberty and protection to tribes conquered by themselves, as well as those vanquished by others," he observed, briefly rehearsing the nation's history. "The Alabamas and
Coosades are said to be the first who adopted the ceremonies and customs
of the Creeks, and became part of the nation. The Natchez, or Sunset Indians, from the Mississippi, joined the Creeks about fifty years since, after being driven out of Louisiana, and added considerably to their confed-
erative body. And now," he noted in 1791, "the Shawanese, called by them
Sawanes, are joining them in large numbers every year, having already four
towns on the Tallapoosee river, that contain near 300 war men, and more
are soon expected." In short, Swan concluded, "Their numbers have increased faster by acquisition of foreign subjects, than by the increase of the
original stock."[55]

VI. Cherokees

According to "An Exact Account of the Number and Strength of all the Indian Nations that were subject to the Government of South Carolina" in
1715, the Cherokee Nation at that time contained 11,210 persons living in
sixty villages. (This would be an average of 187 persons per village, though
scholars believe the median town size not long before had been twice as
great, suggesting a much larger overall population.)[56] Broken down by locality, the census—clearly using slightly rounded numbers—lists 2,100
people in eleven Lower towns, 6,350 people in thirty Middle towns, and
2,760 people in nineteen Upper towns. Divided by age and sex, this document shows 7,600 adults plus 3,610 children; 5,750 men and boys plus 5,460
women and girls. Since it records 4,000 adult men in all, the ratio of total
population to male warriors in this census comes to 2.8:1. This approaches
the ratio of 3:1 that emerges from later records and that I have applied to
counts of Cherokee warriors from other years.[57]

    The first such military count by the English had appeared seven years
earlier, in 1708, when South Carolina governor Nathaniel Johnson reported
from Charlestown: "The Chereky Indians live about Two hundred & fifty

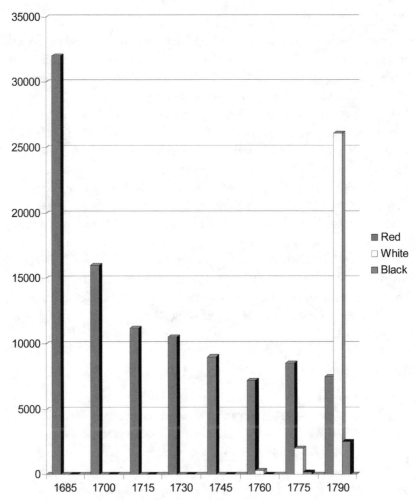

Figure 7. Region VI, Cherokees.

miles northwest from our Settlement on a Ridge of Mountains." He described them as "a numerous people . . . settled in sixty Towns," and he estimated their warriors "are at least Five thousand men." At a ratio of 3:1, this would put the total population at 15,000 (2.8:1 would yield 14,000). Johnson's figures may not have been entirely accurate or up to date, and the drop during the seven years preceding 1708 may well have differed from the decline during the seven following years. Nevertheless, a conservative extrapolation backward from these two totals would put the Cherokee population above 16,000 in 1700.[58]

Projecting further back, into the preceding century, the population size becomes even sketchier. James Mooney estimated long ago that the Cherokees numbered 22,000 in 1650, but his undocumented figure was probably too low. If sixteenth-century Spanish incursions had caused serious depopulation in the mountains, the relatively isolated Cherokees may well have recovered within a century. Their constant exposure to Europeans began only in the late seventeenth century, with the opening of the deerskin trade to Charlestown, and the first documented smallpox epidemic to reach their settlements arrived in 1697. We know from comparable situations that this dread disease often destroyed half or three-quarters of all the inhabitants in previously unexposed Indian populations. By applying a smallpox death rate of 50 percent to the post-epidemic estimate of 16,000 Cherokees in 1700, we can project backward to a much larger pre-epidemic population of between 30,000 and 35,000 in 1685.[59]

Projections forward in the generations after 1715 are scarcely easier, for though the documentary estimates become more numerous, they remain hard to reconcile. For example, in his report of 1755, Edmond Atkin estimated that the Cherokees numbered "above three Thousand Men," suggesting a total population exceeding 9,000 persons.[60] But the same year Governor Arthur Dobbs of North Carolina sent the Board of Trade an account of Cherokee warriors broken down by locality that showed a total of only 2,590 men, suggesting an overall population of 7,770. Twenty years later James Adair, publishing his *History of the American Indians* in 1775, remarked:

> *Formerly, the Cheerake were a very numerous and potent nation. Not above forty years ago, they had 64 towns and villages, populous, and full of women and children. According to the computations of the most intelligent old traders of that time, they amounted to upwards of six-thousand fighting men; a prodigious number to have so close on our settlements, defended by blue-topped ledges of inaccessible mountains.*[61]

At face value, Adair's comment leads to the often-cited figure of 18,000 Cherokees for 1735, and it fits with his recollection that in "about the year 1738, the Cheerake received a most depopulating shock, by the small pox, which reduced them almost one half, in about a year's time." Adair was correct about the date of the smallpox scourge—and perhaps about its awesome extent as well, for he had been a trader among the Cherokees as early as 1736—but his population estimate remains ambiguous.[62] If correct, this relatively high number would suggest that previous counts had missed a substantial percentage of these mountain people. Cherokee population figures at the time of English contact would be pushed higher, and the rate of decline would become even steeper (leading downward to lower estimates after midcentury, such as that of Governor Dobbs). On the other hand, Adair (or his London editor) may have conflated his own forty years among the Indians from 1735 to 1775 with the preceding forty years of contact that he heard about from "intelligent old traders," combining the devastating epidemic of 1697–98 with that of 1738–39. A population of 6,000 warriors and 18,000 inhabitants among sixty-four villages in the mid-1690s, four decades before his first arrival in the mountains, would square very well with the estimates given previously for 1708 and 1715.

The epidemic of 1738 was followed by a continued decline in population through warfare, first with Indian neighbors and then with the encroaching Europeans. Between 1759 and 1761 the Cherokees fought a destructive war against the English, made worse by the cyclical return of smallpox to strike a new generation. "We learn from the Cherokee country," wrote an informant in mid-1760, "that the People of the Lower Towns have carried smallpox into the Middle Settlement and Valley, where that disease rages with great Violence, and that the Upper Towns are in such dread of the Infection, that they will not allow a single Person from the above named places to come amongst them."[63] At the end of the Cherokee War, according to Adair, "the traders calculated the number of their warriors to consist of about two thousand three-hundred, which is a great diminution for so short a space of time."[64] This suggests a total community of about 6,900, down from an overall population in 1755 of just below 8,000, estimating from Dobbs (or at least 1,000 more, judging from Atkin). Therefore Cherokee numbers may have dropped to perhaps 7,200 by the middle of the war in 1760 and to a nadir of fewer than 7,000 persons several years later.

In the following decades the Cherokee Nation apparently rebounded somewhat, though recollections of their numbers may have been slightly exaggerated by one "Mr. Purcell, who, in the year 1780, resided among them." Fifteen years later he provided David Ramsay with the intelligence that at that time the Cherokees had numbered 8,550, of whom 2,800 "were gunmen" (a total population/warrior ratio of just over 3:1). If this was more than an inflated estimate of wartime power during the Revolution, any such demographic renewal probably derived mostly from the assimilation of traders and Indian refugees, plus a further withdrawal from expanding colonial settlements. The so-called Chickamauga Cherokees—some 500 warriors and their families who relocated to a mountain fastness in south-central Tennessee, under the leadership of Dragging Canoe, in March 1777—drew to them diverse Indians committed to waging a serious resistance struggle against mounting white encroachment.[65]

But in 1783 the Cherokees experienced yet another smallpox epidemic, and conflicts with white newcomers took an increasing toll that could not be offset by the continued assimilation of refugees or resistance fighters. In November 1785, at the time of the Hopewell Treaty, Indian commissioners put Cherokee strength "at 2,000 warriors, but they were estimated, in 1787, by Colonel Joseph Martin, who was well acquainted with them, at 2,650." In reporting these figures to President Washington in 1789, his secretary of war added, "it is probable they may be lessened since, by the depredations committed on them."[66]

While the native population of the Cherokee region oscillated somewhere between 7,000 and 8,500 persons during the last third of the century, the non-Indian population jumped dramatically. By 1760, 93 colonial soldiers were garrisoned at Fort Prince George, built in 1753 next to the Cherokee town of Keowee on a tributary of the Savannah River, and 136 men were stationed at Fort Loudoun, erected in 1757 five miles west of the Indian town of Chota. Assuming that some women and children accompanied these men and that other families and isolated traders already resided in the area, there were perhaps 300 white settlers living beyond the piedmont in the fringes of Appalachia in 1760. South Carolina laws prohibited black participation in the deerskin trade and offered bounties to Indian "slavecatchers" for the return of black runaways, dead or alive. So the number of African Americans in the region who were not passing as red or white must have remained negligible.[67]

After 1768 colonists from North Carolina and Virginia began to migrate into the Watauga valley. The Watauga, Holston, and Nolachucky settlements constituted the earliest core of white population in the Cherokee territory, and from there the newcomers spread out through northeastern Tennessee.

To avoid eviction by the Cherokees and to evade the royal proclamation of 1763 against purchasing Indian lands, the Wataugans and their neighbors leased the land they occupied from the Cherokee chief Attakullakulla in 1772. By 1776 these Appalachian settlers could muster between 700 and 800 riflemen, according to Moses Fisk, and many of these occasional soldiers helped defeat the British—particularly at King's Mountain in 1780. George Imlay, who traveled in the Watauga valley at the time of the Revolution, put the number of settlers there at about 2,000.[68] A handful may have brought black servants with them to help clear the land, and the dislocations of the decade may have contributed small bands of runaway slaves, spurred by rumors of pending freedom in the West. But the black population could hardly have exceeded several hundred.[69]

After the War of Independence the rush westward began in earnest. In the 1790 census, five counties of east Tennessee (Washington, Sullivan, Greene, Hawkins, and South of French Broad) already contained 26,100 whites. In addition, 293 "other free persons" and 2,256 slaves gave a total of 2,549 blacks. Together these non-Indians scattering through the mountains (hundreds more of whom must have gone uncounted) suddenly made up more than three-quarters of the population of southern Appalachia. And this number does not even include figures from the mountain fringes of modern Alabama, Georgia, and the Carolinas that had been a part of the Cherokee domain.[70]

VII. Choctaws/Chickasaws

West of the Alabama River and east of the Mississippi, two Indian nations dominated what is now central and eastern Mississippi and western Alabama throughout the colonial period. By the Choctaws' own account their ancestors had entered the region from the west centuries earlier, settling at Nanih Waiya near the Pearl River in central Mississippi and erecting a large temple mound at this sacred center. From the great curve of the Pearl they expanded their settlements eastward to the next two rivers that ran south to the Gulf, the Chickasawhay (or Pascagoula) and the longer Tombigbee, with its westward tributary the Noxubee. Meanwhile their genetic and cultural kinsmen, the Chickasaws, had separated themselves completely, establishing towns farther north, not far from the Mississippi, between the up-

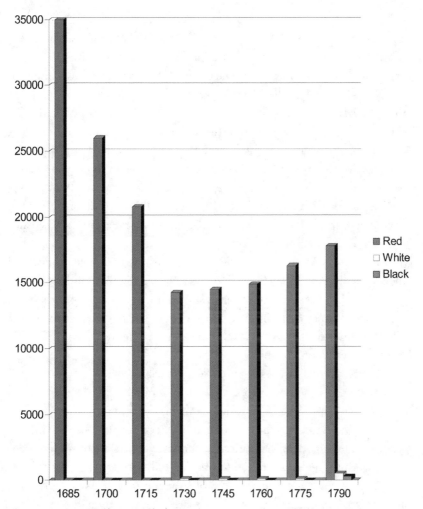

Figure 8. Region VII, Choctaws/Chickasaws.

per reaches of the Yazoo River and the headwaters of the Tombigbee. With their common heritage, adjoining hunting grounds, and mutually intelligible languages, it makes sense to associate the Choctaws and Chickasaws for demographic purposes. But throughout the colonial period they were generally bitter rivals, the allies of competing European powers, and frequently enemies in open war.

The Chickasaws were probably the smaller of the two groups from the time of their separation, and they may have suffered more heavily in the mid-sixteenth century from greater direct contact with de Soto's forces. Consid-

ering what happened to their western neighbors the Quapaws at the end of
the seventeenth century (see next section), presumably the Chickasaws also
experienced severe losses during the generation of early French and English
contact following La Salle's descent of the Mississippi. But the exact scale of
this Chickasaw decline remains unclear since the earliest population references are vague. "They seem to be the remains of a populous nation," commented a French writer, noting that the Choctaws continued to "speak the
Chickasaw language, though somewhat corrupted, and those who speak it
best value themselves upon it." Antoine Le Page du Pratz who lived among
the neighboring Natchez in the 1720s, after a full generation of Chickasaw
slaving raids inspired by English traders, believed that the Chickasaws' "warlike disposition had prompted them to invade several nations, whom they
have indeed destroyed, but not without diminishing their own numbers by
those expeditions." "Their tradition says they had ten thousand men fit for
war, when they first came from the west, and this account seems very probable," wrote James Adair in the eighteenth century, since—along with the
Choctaws and the smaller Chakchiumas—they originally "came together
from the west as one family."[71]

The first French visitors in the 1680s, associated with La Salle's exploration, varied in their estimates of Chickasaw population. "This nation is
very numerous," Father Anastasius Douay noted in 1687; "they count at
least four thousand warriors; have an abundance of peltry." Tonti, in contrast, recalled that they had "2,000 warriors" at the time of his first contact, but this may have referred to only several villages. French estimates
after 1700 remained vague. In 1702 Iberville thought the Chickasaws had
at least "2,000 families," and two years later La Vente thought they might
be "as numerous as the Choctaw," with 700 to 800 cabins.[72] But the earliest English estimates were lower. In part this is because they were made
later, at a time when the population was falling rapidly, but in part it is because the English had established themselves as trading allies and had obtained ready access to Chickasaw villages. In 1708 a report from Charlestown attributed at least 600 warriors, while another from 1715 showed 700
men and 1,200 others, for a total population of 1,900 (and a total popula-
tion/warrior ratio of 2.7:1).

Swanton, who first accumulated these figures, concluded there must have
been roughly 2,000 Chickasaws in 1715, and 3,000 to 3,500 fifteen years

earlier. Projecting back further in time at a similar rate of decline would mean the population in 1685 had been between 4,500 and 6,125 persons. But the firsthand French estimates from that time would put the number higher, no matter which figures one uses. On the low side, Tonti's 2,000 warriors at a ratio of 3.5:1 yields a total of 7,000; while at the opposite extreme, Douay's 4,000 warriors at 3.5:1 suggests 14,000 inhabitants. Applying the lower ratio of 2.7:1 that appears in the English tally of 1715 would yield between 5,400 and 10,800. While 7,000 falls inside all these limits, it is probably a conservative estimate for 1685. Round numbers of 5,000 for 1700 and 4,000 for 1715, though above the estimates from Swanton and English sources, may not be unreasonable. At the time of Chickasaw Removal back across the Mississippi 120 years later, that nation's population, with the addition of black slaves, would again exceed 6,000, but for much of the eighteenth century it was scarcely half that size.[73]

A combination of factors forced Chickasaw numbers below 4,000 for roughly a century. Recurrent disease continued to take its toll, as did bitter warfare with the French and their Choctaw allies, more bloody than the traditional boundary skirmishes of earlier times. "As long as the Chickasaws exist we shall always have to fear that they shall entice away the others from us in favor of the English," Bienville wrote to the French Ministry in 1734. "The entire destruction of this hostile nation therefore becomes every day more necessary to our interests and I am going to exert all diligence to accomplish it." Equipped with English weapons the Chickasaws managed to repulse concerted attacks in 1736, 1739, and 1752. But their alliance with the English not only incurred French animosity, it also applied significant centrifugal forces to Chickasaw society. As time passed, warriors roamed ever more widely in search of deerskins to trade with the English, along with other items obtained in the West and valued in Carolina: captive slaves and "Chickasaw" horses. Probably to maximize that trade and to protect it, one band under the Squirrel King moved all the way to the Savannah River in 1723, while another migrated to Creek territory, near the head of the Coosa River. Given these diverse pressures, the Chickasaw nucleus in northern Mississippi probably fell to 3,100 in 1730, 2,300 in 1745, and 1,600 in 1760, before rebounding—after the removal of the French— to 2,300 in 1775, and 3,100 in 1790.[74]

In contrast to the Chickasaws, their rival kinsmen to the south and east, the Choctaws appear to have been a far larger and more stable population throughout the late colonial era. Indeed, Swanton, after compiling various contrasting estimates, settled for a rough and unchanging total of 15,000 for more than a century, stating that the "numbers of Choctaw seem to have varied little from the period of first white contact, though earlier figures sometimes disagree very considerably." Like James Mooney before him, Swanton guessed at "a population of about 15,000 in 1650" and went on to speculate that "we shall not be far wrong if we assume" the same number for 1700. "The figures for the Choctaw appear to tell a simple story," Swanton wrote. "It would seem from the figures given us by travelers and officials that during the eighteenth century the tribe had a population of about 15,000. Only a few small tribes were added to it during the historic period. Toward the end of that century and during the first three decades of the nineteenth the population appears to have increased gradually."[75]

Swanton exaggerated Choctaw stability and the ease with which the nation's size can be determined across time, but his basic estimate points to the appropriate range. As with other southeastern groups, European enumerations for the Choctaws did not always include all the villages, and the total population/warrior ratio could fluctuate. For example, consider two Choctaw censuses from 1795 compiled for officials of Spanish Louisiana, not available to Swanton. These summaries, now in the Bancroft Library at Berkeley, list more than 11,200 persons living in fifty-three villages, but only two of the three Choctaw districts seem to be covered adequately. The towns named on the lists vary in size from several dozen persons to 765 inhabitants; in some locations men outnumber women while in others the reverse is true. All told, the lists report 3,230 warriors (plus 186 chiefs and captains), along with 3,500 women and 3,377 children. Since the Choctaws had "war towns" and "peace towns," the total population/warrior ratio varied from less than 3:1 to more than 4:1, averaging out to slightly below 3.5:1.[76]

Additional problems exist for determining population figures among the Choctaws. The French, their trading and military partners throughout most of the period, rarely made detailed census counts and sometimes exaggerated the numbers of their Indian allies for government and religious officials at home. To the English, with more limited firsthand knowledge of the Choctaws, such estimates often seemed like deliberate misinformation spread by the French to keep their more numerous colonial rivals at bay. According to James Adair, "The French, to intimidate the English traders by the prodigious number of their red legions in West-Florida, boasted that the Choktah consisted of nine thousand men fit to bear arms: but we find the true amount of their numbers, since West-Florida was ceded to us, to be not above half as many as the French report ascertained. And indeed," Adair added pointedly, "if the French and Spanish writers of the American Aborigines, had kept so near the truth, as to mix one half of realities, with their flourishing wild hyperboles, the literati would have owed them more thanks than is now their due."[77]

Although much work on the colonial Choctaws remains to be done, it seems likely that their population line over time was less flat than Swanton surmised and more in keeping with the downward curves of other groups. In the late seventeenth century the overall community was probably as large as or larger than the Cherokees, declining almost as far and as fast after French and English began to enter the region. Assuming a constant ratio of 3.5:1 for total population/warriors, there could have been as many as 8,000 bowmen and 28,000 inhabitants in 1685, 6,000 fighters and 21,000 persons by 1700, and 4,800 warriors and 16,800 individuals in 1715. In 1702 Iberville, with little firsthand knowledge as yet, appears to have put the number of Choctaw warriors too low, at "about 3800 to 4000 men" (though a year earlier, on the basis of discussions with coastal Indians, he had guessed "there must be more than six thousand men" in over fifty Choctaw villages).[78] On the other hand, French estimates several decades later may have ranged too high. A 1723 letter from Louisiana refers to the "the war we have stirred up between the Choctaws and the Chickasaws," suggesting the need "to maintain this war" through aid to "the Choctaws, a nation that contains nearly eight thousand men."[79]

Still later, Le Page du Pratz observed vaguely that this "great nation" was reckoned at 25,000 warriors.[80] But it is hard to say whether he was mistaking warriors for total inhabitants, referring to some earlier time, exaggerating greatly—or some combination of these. Setting such "wild hyperboles" aside, it appears that the Choctaw population may have reached its nadir in the 1730s, gradually renewing somewhat over succeeding generations, despite occasional setbacks from war and disease. A Frenchman named Lusser who compiled a census after a visit to Choctaw villages in 1730 recorded 3,010 men bearing arms, and a summary drawn up by Regis du Roullet two years later showed 2,728 warriors.[81] Both lists were undoubtedly incomplete, but the population may well have declined to some 3,200 warriors, or 11,200 inhabitants, by 1730 before leveling out in the subsequent decade.

If Choctaw numbers dipped this low at the time of the Natchez War, they had begun to recover slightly by midcentury, despite the internal conflict that flared for several years after 1746. In the winter of 1743–44, the new governor of Louisiana, Marquis Vaudreuil, "welcomed more than 3,000 members of the Choctaw tribe" to Mobile, and one of his subsequent reports to the French secretary of state, which fell into the hands of the British, contained a town-by-town census that showed 3,600 Choctaw men.[82] Louis Billouard de Kerlérec, who arrived in Louisiana in 1753 and governed the French colony in its final decade, gave various estimates of Choctaw strength, ranging from 3,000 to 4,000 men bearing arms, as he worked to retain these crucial allies. Jean-Bernard Bossu, writing from Tombigbee late in 1759, reported that the Choctaws "can muster four thousand warriors who would be happy to fight."[83] From these conflicting numbers a rough working estimate would be 3,600 fighters and 12,200 persons in 1745, rising to perhaps 3,800 warriors and 13,300 inhabitants in 1760.

Figures on the Choctaws seem no more consistent or reliable after French removal from the Gulf, and few observers were as candid as the Reverend Elam Potter in 1768, who followed his low estimate of "8 or 900 fighting men" with the warning, "I could get no certain account of their number, it being very lately that any traders have gone amongst them." In contrast, Mr. Purcell's account for 1780 implied complete, if unfounded, accuracy. "The Chactaw nation, at that time," he wrote confidently to David Ramsay fifteen years later, "consisted of 13,423 of which were gun-men . . . 4,141." Summing up conflicting intelligence on the Choctaws from the 1780s, Secretary of War Knox wrote in July 1789, "This nation of Indians were estimated by the commissioners of the United States, at 6,000 warriors; other opinions state them at 4,500 or 5,000." That same year a vague report told the secretary, "We think . . . the Choctaws about 3,000" gunmen. But twelve years later a more informed estimate for a new secretary of war claimed the Choctaw population "exceeds fifteen thousand."[84] A tentative estimate reconciling some—but not all—of the existing numbers would be 4,000 warriors and 14,000 people in 1775 (following a decade of wars with the Creeks), with 4,200 gunmen and 14,700 people in 1790.

Like the Cherokees, the Choctaws were a numerous people well situated to withstand the European invasion of the South, and they were initially more remote from the economic and military designs of the expansive English. The same relative isolation and independence that prevented foreigners from obtaining a reliable overview of Choctaw numbers also allowed the population to rebound sooner and more rapidly than smaller or less protected groups. For the Chickasaw and Choctaw region as a whole, therefore, the Indian population probably reached its lowest in the middle decades of the eighteenth century, with fewer than 15,000 people, and then rose gradually. By 1790 Indian numbers were still barely half what they had been in 1685 (though they were approaching seventeenth-century levels again by the time of forced removal in the nineteenth century). From the beginning of the eighteenth century occasional black runaways entered the region, and during generations after 1715 the number of French and English traders and agents in the area probably exceeded 50 at any given time. The other non-Indians who began to enter the region after the Revolution—perhaps 500 whites and 300 blacks by 1790—would soon transform cornfields, ball grounds, and hunting preserves into extensive cotton plantations.

VIII. Natchez/Louisiana

To the west and south of the Choctaw-Chickasaw region, well-established Indian communities of various sizes had long inhabited the fertile lands of the enormous Mississippi Delta and the adjacent shores of the central Gulf coast. During the colonial period these groups were of moderate and decreasing size; their lifestyle was mobile, their mortality rate was desperate, and the population estimates made by European colonizers were inconsistent at best. In analyzing demographic data for his *Indian Tribes of the Lower Mississippi Valley*, Swanton observed at one point that the surviving historical "figures are so fragmentary and conflicting that it is nearly impossible to base any satisfactory conclusions upon them." That situation still persists, but it is possible, using Swanton's somewhat low estimates and the research of more recent scholars, to put together a rough profile of demographic change in the region during the century after La Salle's exploration of the Mississippi in 1682.[85]

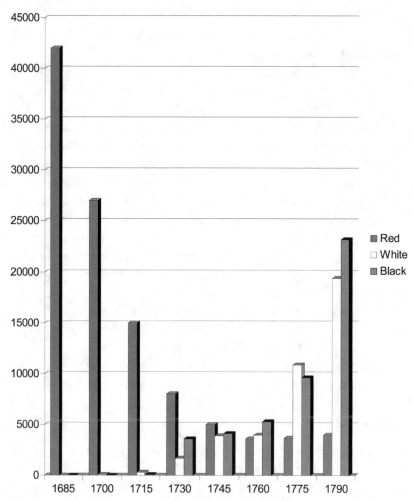

Figure 9. Region VIII, Natchez/Louisiana.

As we have seen, Indians on the eastern slope of the Appalachian chain often divided into small and vulnerable shore communities, larger groups somewhat removed from the coast, and stronger and more stable nations in the protected interior. Similarly, the Indians near the Mississippi Delta can be separated into three geographic groupings for the purpose of estimating overall native population. The location of small coastal tribes, such as the Biloxis, Pascagoulas, and once-numerous Mobilians, would prompt the French colonizers to use their names to identify bays and rivers along the Gulf. Meanwhile, the Houmas, Chitimachas, and others resided near the base of the Mississippi, where it flowed southeastward toward the Gulf (and where the French would establish the town of New Orleans between Lake Pontchartrain and the river in 1718). Farther upstream, between where the Red River and the Arkansas enter the Mississippi, lived several larger nations, particularly the Natchez and the Quapaws.

Unlike most of the South's subregions, Louisiana did not provide relative geographical isolation and protection for its sizable interior nations, delaying and blunting the impact of invasion from abroad. On the contrary, the extraordinary highway of the Mississippi meant that Louisiana was explored and colonized from the north as well as from the south, so by the start of the eighteenth century not only the native inhabitants of Biloxi Bay and Mobile Bay but also residents of the Yazoo Basin more than three hundred miles inland were experiencing foreign diseases and colonial-inspired slaving raids. The pattern was not new. When de Soto's huge expeditionary force had spread disease and destruction across the region in the 1540s, they not only massacred several thousand Mobilians near the coast but brought incalculable devastation to interior nations along the banks of the Mississippi as well. La Salle, carrying maps and chronicles of de Soto's venture with him in 1682, doubted whether he was on the same river the Spaniards had crossed, because the Indian populations he encountered seemed so much smaller than those his predecessor had described.

Having reached the mouth of the Mississippi in 1682, where it protrudes far into the Gulf, La Salle failed to locate the river again when he returned by sea in 1685. The explorer led several hundred French colonists to the latitude on the Gulf coast where he thought he would find the Mississippi. But this put him in East Texas, and he was killed by disheartened followers several years later while still struggling to rectify his error. When local Indians destroyed La Salle's colony near Matagorda Bay, French plans to occupy the Mississippi were delayed by more than a decade. Finally, in 1699, a Canadian-born adventurer found the mouth of the river by sailing along the Gulf coast. But Iberville and his younger brother Bienville chose to establish the initial French outposts near sheltered coastal bays well east of the delta—first at Biloxi, later at Mobile.[86]

When some Mobile and Tohome Indians arrived at Biloxi Bay from their towns on the Mobile River in August 1699, they were said to represent "nations together numbering more than seven hundred men," or roughly 2,500 persons. Soon after that the local Pascagoula Indians told Iberville that these two groups each had about 300 warriors, but when he visited their villages for himself in 1702 he estimated their combined total of fighting men at no more than 350. Their numbers continued to drop rapidly, so that in 1725–26 Bienville put the warrior total (including the Little Tohomes, or Naniabas) at 150, while stating that he could remember a time at the turn of the century when it had been roughly 800 men. An estimate from 1730 put the number of Mobile, Tohome, and Naniaba Indians at 140, and by 1758 Kerlérec estimated that these groups had scarcely 100 warriors. Assuming that fighting men remained a stable proportion of the population but declined in number from approximately 750 in 1700 to 150 in 1725 and 100 in 1750, this represents an 80 percent population drop during the first quarter of the eighteenth century and an additional 33 percent decline during the second quarter. The other small coastal tribes, such as the Biloxis, Pascagoulas, Moctobis, and Capinas, probably equaled in combined size the once-powerful Mobiles and their Tohome neighbors and undoubtedly diminished at a comparable rate.[87]

This steep demise of the small coastal population can be estimated over fifteen-year intervals, as shown on the first line in table 2. The second line summarizes the decline of the Lower River groups, and the third line projects the reduction of the Central River nations. The final line in table 2 offers combined totals for the native inhabitants of the Natchez/Louisiana region as a whole, situated between the Choctaws, Chickasaws, and Upper Creeks to the east and the various inhabitants of East Texas and the Red River area to the west. All told, the region's Indian population seems to have dropped by more than 90 percent in seventy-five years, recovering very slightly, at least among some of the Mississippi River communities, during the last third of the eighteenth century.

Groups along the Lower River were roughly twice as numerous as the coastal peoples when the French arrived; they included the Ouachas, Chaouchas, Mongoulachas, Bayogoulas, Chitimachas, Atakapas, Opelousas, Houmas, and Acolapissas. Here, as along the coast, scanty records suggest crushing declines in population. The informed calculations of Daniel Usner, upon which I have relied considerably for the estimates in table 2, suggest nearly 10,000 for these Lower River groups in 1700, fewer than 3,000 by 1725, well under 1,000 by midcentury, and only slightly more than that

Table 2. Indian Population of the Natchez, Louisiana, Region, 1685–1790

	1685	1700	1715	1730	1745	1760	1775	1790
Gulf coast	8,000	5,000	2,000	1,500	1,000	700	450	300
Lower River	16,000	10,000	5,000	2,500	1,300	900	1,150	1,400
Central River	18,000	12,000	8,000	4,000	2,700	2,000	2,100	2,300
Total	42,000	27,000	15,000	8,000	5,000	3,600	3,700	4,000

in 1775. (As will be noted, at least 100 Indians residing in the Lower River area in 1760 were enslaved.)[88]

The full weight of French colonization was felt slightly later along the Lower River, but foreign diseases, coupled with warfare and alcohol, took an enormous toll within several generations. Timing varied from village to village, but no group escaped. Some disappeared entirely, the survivors melting into neighboring communities. Others relocated closer to the growing town of New Orleans, which had come under Spanish control in 1763, where they managed to subsist by marketing provisions. Table 2 reflects the fact that some of these diminished groups began to increase in numbers during the last third of the century. Their resistance to foreign diseases grew, and they absorbed additional Indians from decimated towns elsewhere.

The Houmas, one of the larger and better-documented groups in the area, are apparently typical in the rate and extent of their demise. They occupied a large village on the Mississippi just south of the Bayogoulas. (A tall red stake on the east bank marked the line between Houma and Bayogoula hunting grounds; the site would become known in French as Baton Rouge.) Smallpox was already ravaging the Houma town when Iberville arrived there in 1699. Conflicting initial estimates by the French suggest more than 250 warriors at the start of the century. La Harpe reported 200 fighting men in 1718, while a 1739 report found only 90 to 100 warriors, though the dwindling Houmas had been joined by remnants of the Acolapissas and Bayogoulas. By 1758 Kerlérec noted 60 warriors in the entire group, and in 1784 Thomas Hutchins wrote that the Houmas, "once a considerable nation of Indians," were "reduced now to about 25 warriors," while their neighbors, the Chitimachas, "reckon about 27 warriors."[89]

The so-called Central River nations farther north, including the Quapaws and Taensas, the Tunicas and Natchez, and the Upper and Lower Yazoos, were the largest of the groupings in the region. But they too had been touched by the early Spanish incursion and were dramatically affected by the arrival of the French via the Great River, first from the north and then from the south. Moreover, English traders and slave-raiding parties appeared in the Central River area before the end of the seventeenth century, and they may have been responsible for the major epidemic that swept the area in 1698. Within three generations after La Salle's appearance, the number of local Indians had plummeted by nearly 90 percent, from at least 18,000 in the 1680s to scarcely 2,000 in the middle of the eighteenth century. Consolidation with other groups may have brought a slight rise of a few hundred persons over the ensuing decades.[90]

The plight of the Quapaw Indians, or "Downstream People," is representative. In 1682, according to historian David Baird, they numbered somewhere between 6,000 and 15,000 persons, settled in four large towns on the Mississippi near the mouth of the Arkansas. But the epidemic of 1698 reduced their population by two-thirds, and English-sponsored slave raids took an additional toll. When a French priest established a mission among them in 1727, they had withdrawn to three small villages along the Arkansas and numbered scarcely 1,200 persons. Further epidemics followed in 1747 and 1751. By 1763 fewer than 700 people survived, of whom only 160 were men of fighting age. "Their use as raiders and auxiliary troops by the French accounted for some of the decrease, but their reduction was mostly a consequence of European introduced disease," explains Baird. "The governmental organization of the Downstream People had reflected the four-part division" of their original towns, "hence it too was altered. Rather than four chiefs who acted in concert only when national interests required it, a great chief emerged to claim special hereditary prerogatives." Baird concludes that, as with so many southern Indian groups, the Quapaws' social structure must have been "altered in other ways by the decimation of the population."[91]

The Tunicas suffered similar heavy losses at the end of the seventeenth century and continued to decline from several thousand to only a few score. "Sickness was among them when we arrived there," wrote a French visitor in 1698. "They were dying in great numbers." The Tunicas, Thomas Hutchins stated in 1784, were "formerly a numerous nation of Indians; but their constant intercourse with the white people, and immoderate use of spirituous liquors, have reduced them to about twenty warriors." In fact, disease constituted the primary cause of decline, as it did with the Taensas as well. When Iberville visited their locale in March 1700, he reported that this nation had previously been numerous but that at present it had no more than 300 men.[92]

That same month Iberville's party visited the Natchez Indians, who possessed far more elaborate ceremonial traditions and retained strong memories of a once-formidable demographic presence. "According to the Natchez, there were formerly . . . more than two hundred thousand persons," La Harpe explained vaguely. If such numbers ever existed, they occurred generations earlier, perhaps even before the Natchez settled beside the Mississippi, but during the seventeenth century the nation remained one of the larger ones in the region. By 1704, however, a newly arrived clergyman wrote regarding the Natchez that during the past six years their "number has diminished a third." Father Charlevoix, who visited the Natchez in 1721, testified to their continuing demise, though he may have overstated their population somewhat. The French priest reported that "about six years ago they reckoned among them four thousand warriors. It appears that they were more numerous in the time of M. de la Salle, and even when M. d'Iberville discovered the mouth of the Mississippi. At present," Charlevoix continued, "the Natchez cannot raise two thousand fighting men. They attribute this decrease to some contagious diseases, which in these last years have made a great ravage of them."[93]

Soon pestilence was joined by war, for in 1729 bitter Natchez warriors attacked the French outpost of Fort Rosalie and killed 237 people, after being told by a contemptuous officer that they would have to move their villages. The French retaliated, and the next two years saw the virtual destruction of the Natchez nation. Some 450 captives were taken to New Orleans and sold into slavery in St. Domingue. Only a few hundred Natchez survived in the vicinity, taking refuge among the Chickasaws. As suggested in the third line of table 2, the Indian population of the Central River area as a whole was roughly 12,000 persons in 1700 and already declining rapidly. Over the next two generations this population was reduced by five-sixths, before increasing slightly during the era of the American Revolution.[94]

Compared with English settlements on the east coast, Louisiana's non-Indian population grew slowly. At the start of 1700 a small and sickly French vanguard of scarcely 80 men under Bienville inhabited the newly built Fort Maurepas on Biloxi Bay, awaiting the return of Iberville from France with reinforcements. They had already encountered a few Englishmen and several half-starved runaways from the rival Spanish outpost at Pensacola. But even as Canadian voyageurs and French missionaries began to appear along the Mississippi, the total number of whites in the region may not have exceeded 100 persons. By 1715, after the uphill battle to locate a settlement at Old Mobile, hardly 300 French and Canadians remained in the area, along with a few dozen African slaves (a rounded figure of 100 is no doubt too large). In contrast, the shift of colonization efforts to the Mississippi and the founding of New Orleans made the next fifteen years a period of rapid growth, creating new pressures for Indian groups along the river. By the time of the French-Natchez War the number of whites had risen at least to 1,700, and perhaps considerably higher. Through forced importation the total of blacks had climbed faster, approaching 3,600 by 1730.[95]

The defeat of the Natchez, coupled with the earlier decimation of neighboring tribes through disease, meant that during the 1730s the combined colonial population came to exceed the number of Indians in the region for the first time, though the total figure for the area probably continued to decline slightly, rising again only after the political shifts of 1763. By 1745 there were roughly 8,000 newcomers—4,100 Africans and 3,900 Europeans—in Louisiana, and by 1760 the colony still did not exceed 10,000, with an estimated 5,300 blacks and 4,000 whites plus 100 Indian slaves. While overall Indian numbers may have revived slightly after 1760, the totals for non-Indians during the subsequent generation of Spanish control approximately doubled during the first fifteen years and doubled again in the fifteen years after that. The white census had reached nearly 11,000 persons by 1775, and as Acadians continued to arrive, it was approaching 20,000 by 1790. For a brief span (after a generation of numerical dominance), African Americans represented less than 50 percent of the non-Indian population, climbing only to 9,600 by 1775. But by 1790, as the Haitian Revolution began to unfold in the Caribbean, blacks in Louisiana numbered over 23,000, roughly equaling the combined total of Native Americans and Euro-Americans residing in the region.[96]

IX. East Texas

The final two regions, though large and significant geographically, remained relatively inaccessible to European settlement until late in the eighteenth century, so records regarding the size and location of Indian groups dur-

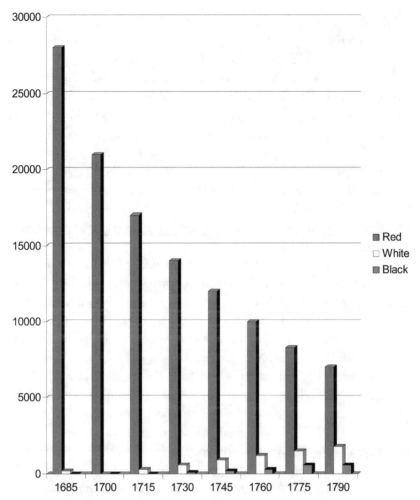

Figure 10. Region IX, East Texas.

ing earlier generations remain somewhat tentative and sketchy. Neither the timberland of western Louisiana and East Texas nor the huge swath of land stretching from the banks of the Arkansas to the headwaters of the Potomac witnessed an extended colonizing onslaught during the century before the American Revolution. However, there was enough contact, both direct and indirect, during this era to prompt Indian numbers to decrease markedly in these regions and to allow for crude estimates of that decline.

In the late seventeenth century three loose confederacies of Caddo Indians, including more than two dozen groups in all, dominated what is now western Louisiana and eastern Texas. They lived in separate clusters of towns and spoke different dialects of the same Caddo language. They were connected linguistically to the Pawnee and Wichita peoples farther north who spoke related, though very different, Caddoan languages. But culturally they had more in common with southeastern Indian nations. Like the Natchez, they were productive agriculturalists who developed substantial ceremonial centers during the centuries before de Soto's sudden arrival. And their flat-topped temple mounds, like those of the Natchez, suggest a significant population density before the colonial period. As with the Natchez, there are indications, according to W. W. Newcomb Jr., "that the culture of the historic Caddoes was in some respects the disintegrating shadow of something which had once been more spectacular."[97]

Their first major confrontation with Europeans had occurred in October 1541, with the appearance of de Soto's army, shortly before the leader's death. The next year de Soto's successor returned briefly, but further contacts were minimal until La Salle's party entered the region well over a century later. When the French encountered the Caddos in the 1680s, there were three distinct groupings, plus several independent Caddo communities (the Yatasi, the Adais, and the Eyeish—or Hais). First, along the lower reaches of the Red River in central Louisiana, resided the Natchitoches Indians, near the site of the modern town that bears their name. Second, several hundred miles upstream where the Red River flows west to east above the present city of Texarkana, stretched the towns of the Kadohadacho confederacy, which included the upper Natchitoches, the Nanatsohos, the Nasonis, and the Kadohadachos or Caddos proper. The third and largest grouping was the Hasinais, or Cenis, consisting of eight or ten neighboring groups along the streams that come together to form the Neches River in East Texas. (They called each other "teyshas," or "allies," and when they applied the same term of friendship to Spaniards arriving from the southwest, the newcomers used this word for the area, and eventually for the whole state of Texas.)[98]

"Although it is true that even as early as the seventeenth and eighteenth centuries the Caddoes appear to have passed their zenith," Newcomb writes of these groupings, "they remained, nonetheless, the most productive, advanced, and populous peoples of Texas." But their demise was imminent, he states, and "seems to have been primarily brought about by epidemics rather than by war. The collapse of these confederacies was so rapid, and their decline in numbers so great that the onrushing American frontier hardly took notice of the Caddoes, the dregs of what had been two centuries earlier rich, splendid, barbaric theocracies."[99]

To the south of the Caddos, in the valley of the Trinity River and beyond, lived the Atakapan peoples. Closest to the Caddos geographically and culturally were the Bidais and Deadoses, residing more than a hundred miles inland. The little-known Patiris lived nearer to the coast, not far north of modern Houston. The Akokisas inhabited the north side of Galveston Bay and may have been the "Hans" with whom the Spaniard Cabeza de Vaca lived in 1528. To their east, the Atakapas proper occupied the coastal littoral near Sabine Lake, between present Beaumont and the Gulf. These small groups, linked by language to the Tunicas farther east in the Yazoo River area, were much less culturally impressive than the Caddo confederacies, and they were less numerous as well. Newcomb, drawing on Swanton, estimates their total population at fewer than 3,500 persons during the colonial period. More than 200 Atakapan speakers from the interrelated Bidais, Deadoses, and Akokisas were attracted west to the new Spanish mission of San Ildefonso on the San Gabriel River in 1749. But within six years Apache raids and internal dissent had caused the demise of this and neighboring missions in the vicinity of present Rockdale, Texas.[100]

From the west side of Galveston Bay, the Karankawas occupied several hundred miles of coastline, stretching toward the southwest. These nomadic bands of tattooed hunters and fishermen resisted the arrival of several hundred would-be colonizers under La Salle who disembarked at Matagorda Bay in 1685. Within several years they had successfully destroyed the isolated French outpost of Fort St. Louis on Garcitas Creek, absorbing a few young survivors into their tribe. A generation later Europeans again met a hostile reception. Bénard de La Harpe's French expedition entered Karankawa territory briefly in 1720, and in response the Spanish attempted to set up a fort and a mission in the area two years later. But by 1726 the Spanish presidio and mission had withdrawn westward to the San Antonio River, and this small coastal group continued to resist cultural intrusion throughout the century.[101]

By the 1770s the Karankawas were being joined by remnants of the Tonkawan bands that had long been their inland neighbors to the immediate north. The Tonkawas, like the Karankawas, occupied the ecological and cultural transition area between the South and the West. Weakened in the seventeenth century, whether by rivals or disease, these Indians living between the Brazos and the Colorado rivers sought protection from Spanish newcomers, and they may have paid a high demographic price for contact with the foreign missionaries and soldiers. "The number of Tonkowas must have declined considerably during the eighteenth century," Newcomb writes, "though information is sparse on this point."[102]

The non-Indian population of East Texas had scarcely reached 1,200 persons by the mid-eighteenth century. In 1685 La Salle's settlers at Fort St. Louis numbered several hundred. But many died of smallpox, according to Spanish reports, and the rest were killed by Indians, except for a handful of deserters and children. By 1694 the first Spanish missions, designed to counteract the French intrusion, had also failed, and for two more decades non-Indians were virtually absent from East Texas for the last time. After 1715 new missions were established at San Antonio, giving Spanish clerics a forward base for carrying their message farther east. At the same time the French consolidated their hold on Natchitoches and pushed farther up the Red River. In rounded numbers, however, the combination of Spanish missionaries and soldiers, plus French traders and planters, probably amounted to no more than 300 in 1715, 600 in 1730, 900 in 1745, and 1,200 in 1760. (Several hundred black and mulatto slaves, runaways, and freedmen were also present by midcentury.) After France relinquished its land west of the Mississippi to Spain in 1763, the small non-Indian population continued to grow, as more enslaved blacks were imported to work on frontier plantations along the Red River.

Although relatively small, these colonial incursions had a devastating effect on the native population of East Texas, which may well have been between 25,000 and 30,000 in 1685. Mooney estimated the region's Indians at just below 14,000 in 1690, with 8,500 Caddoans making up more than half the total. But a modern authority, John C. Ewers, stated in 1973 that "Mooney's estimates for the Indian tribes of Texas appear to be conservative." Ewers increased some of Mooney's local estimates by 50 percent and his general totals by nearly 20 percent. (An analysis of East Texas demography for the late eighteenth century, published the following year by Alicia V. Tjarks, suggests indirectly that these early numbers should be even higher.) Ewers pointed out that Mooney cited only two "great epidemics" between 1685 and 1790: a sickness that killed some 3,000 Caddoans in 1691 and a smallpox outbreak that swept most tribes in 1778. Examining colonial records in greater detail, Ewers found evidence for more than a dozen other epidemics among East Texas Indians during these years.[103]

The scale of the decimation is suggested by a French report of 1715 that a Yatasi group had lost four-fifths of its people, reduced from 2,500 to 500 by sickness and Chickasaw raids. Even if other groups suffered less severely, it seems likely that the overall population by 1730 may have been scarcely half what it had been forty or fifty years earlier. In 1739 smallpox and measles devastated the new missions at San Antonio, and Indians who fled this destruction apparently carried the diseases eastward among the Tonkawan and Atakapan peoples. Twenty years later, in 1759, smallpox and measles were rampant among the Caddoan nations. By 1760 the region's total Indian population had probably been reduced to roughly 10,000 persons. After that, expanding interracial contact meant a further rise in persons of mixed ancestry, and uncertain geographic boundaries and crude census methods compound the problems of calculating total inhabitants by simplified racial category. Still, the frequency and accuracy of population estimates increased as the Spanish extended their colonial control over the area, and it is possible to weigh these figures both for contemporary totals and for a baseline in gauging the larger Indian population of previous times.[104]

After 1760 Indian numbers continued to decrease, though the small communities of non-Indians probably remained in the minority when all the native inhabitants are considered.[105] Unfortunately, historians have often focused only on the carefully enumerated mission Indians, a tradition Tjarks invoked when analyzing colonial census records in 1974. She took the practical but misleading position that "roaming Indian tribes cannot be included in the general estimate of the Texan population. Some information about them exists," Tjarks conceded, but available figures "are merely approximate or rough estimates, notwithstanding that they resulted from commendable efforts." Opting for precision over inclusiveness, she focused only upon some 1,000 Christianized Indians and mestizos living near the Spanish. "To proceed otherwise—that is, trying to add into the calculations a minimum of 6,000 pagan Indians (Croix mentioned 7,280 in 1778) to some 3,000 inhabitants of the three Spanish towns—would lead to extreme ambiguity and lack of precision."[106]

Taken together, the Indians of East Texas had roughly equaled the Cherokees in number during the seventeenth century. But they were more widely dispersed and farther removed from the new sicknesses of Europeans, so their population seems to have reached its lowest point at a somewhat later date. In 1764 a severe smallpox epidemic devastated a mission west of San Antonio, and in 1777, according to Elizabeth John, a "virulent epidemic ravaged the populations of eastern Texas and western Louisiana" and returned to do more damage the following summer. During the mid-1770s some 1,500 Spaniards and 600 blacks and mulattoes lived near the established missions, along with nearly 1,000 Indians and mestizos, while another 7,300 Native Americans subsisted outside Spanish control. Further outbreaks of disease occurred in the 1780s, and by 1790 there were probably no more than 7,000 Indians, Christianized or pagan, in the whole East Texas region, along with 2,400 non-Indians. For the first time in centuries the area had fewer than 10,000 total inhabitants, and its overall population would not begin to increase again until after 1800.[107]

X. The Shawnee Interior

The tenth and final southeastern region, which I have broadly termed the Shawnee Interior, was both the largest and, from the coastal perspective of intruding Europeans, the most remote. So demographic estimates are scarce for this broad arc, spreading over the South like a wide umbrella from the Arkansas River in the west to the headwaters of the Potomac in the east. But there can be little doubt that in terms of both relative density and absolute numbers, this was by far the least populous area of the entire South in the century before the American Revolution. Despite its geographic size its permanent inhabitants were few until the dramatic influx across the Appalachian chain in the decades after Independence.

For the most part, the region served as a vast buffer zone and hunting ground between the Iroquois and their dependent allies to the north and the Cherokees and other nations to the south. Numerous salt licks throughout what is now Kentucky (along the Salt River and the Licking River, for example) attracted deer and buffalo. The Indian hunters who frequented such locations found that they could nurture these herds and direct their movements by killing trees and allowing the extensive grasslands to expand, providing enhanced grazing spots to which the animals would return at

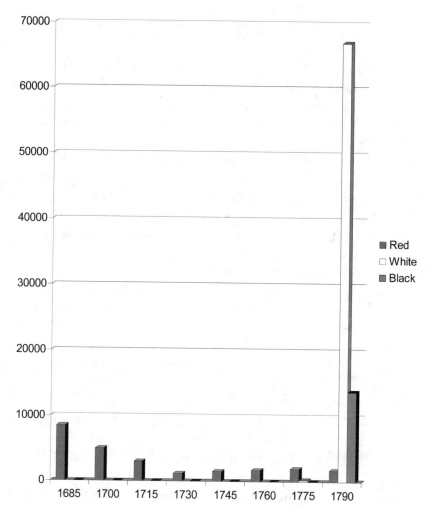

Figure 11. Region X, Shawnee Interior.

predictable times, especially when undergrowth was burned off to prompt tender new growth for browsing. As competition for skins increased during the eighteenth century, so did conflict within this arena. The trail that crossed the Ohio at what is now Maysville, Kentucky, and curved south in two branches toward Cumberland Gap and Pound Gap, was known, significantly, as the Great Warrior Path. This same name was applied to the portion of the trail on the eastern side of the Appalachian Divide, where the much-traveled route stretched along the Shenandoah River as it flows northeastward to its confluence with the Potomac.

In March 1762 Lieutenant Henry Timberlake witnessed the return of Cherokee warriors to their town of Tommotly after attacking "a party of Shawnese, hunting buffaloes" several hundred miles away near the Ohio River. Such hostile encounters in this valuable hunting region had become commonplace in recent generations, and the danger involved in seeking skins limited the resident Indian population, prompting herds to increase further. Nevertheless, those most familiar with the area appear to have been the much traveled and widely dispersed Shawnees, an Algonquian-speaking people who had moved gradually eastward from Illinois to Pennsylvania after the French appeared in the Mississippi valley. They migrated back into the Ohio region a generation later in response to English pressure, while repeatedly dispersing small contingents to reside in the Deep South. In fact, their name derived from the Algonquian words *shawan* for "south" and *shawunogi* meaning "southerner." According to Jerry E. Clark, "They probably numbered between 2,000 and 4,000 individuals during the early historic period," though that estimate may be too low for all five divisions of this peripatetic nation.[108]

Exactly when, where, and how many Shawnees—and other groups—inhabited the zone between Cherokee country and the Ohio River remains uncertain. Perhaps as early as the 1680s, and certainly by the 1730s, members of the Piqua division of the Shawnees occupied the village of Eskippakithiki, or "blue lick place," less than fifty miles south of the Ohio on the Great Warrior Path, and slightly east of modern Lexington. (A French census from 1736 recorded 200 men in the town.) At times the Shawnees also inhabited sites farther east along the various tributaries flowing northwest to the Ohio: the Big Sandy, the Kanawha, the little Kanawha, and the Monongahela. But as Clark points out, "It is not certain whether many of the settlements in eastern Kentucky were permanent or whether they were merely seasonal hunting and warring encampments."[109]

Although increased trade and protection offered by the French drew many of the Shawnee settlements to the north side of the Ohio River by the eighteenth century, this highly mobile nation, like the neighboring Delawares, maintained a presence in the southern Ohio valley. When King George's War broke out in 1744, the British navy was able to harass French shipping on the Atlantic and disrupt the trade of Canadian merchants with their Indian allies in the Ohio valley. In 1748 at Logstown, on the upper Ohio just west of modern Pittsburgh, Conrad Weiser and George Croghan convinced Shawnee, Delaware, and other chiefs to pledge allegiance to England and open the area to traders from the British colonies. The Iroquois League continued to claim control over the Ohio valley by right of conquest, but its leaders ceded the area to the British at the Treaty of Fort Stanwix in 1768, much to the dismay of the Shawnees.[110]

Notwithstanding the royal proclamation of 1763 prohibiting settlement west of the Appalachian Divide, migration westward from the English colonies began in earnest. Indian occupants of the trans-Appalachian region resisted, and mutual reprisals escalated. When white newcomers killed the family of Logan, a Cayuga or Mingo leader married to a Shawnee woman, warfare erupted in 1774. Some 300 Shawnee warriors under Cornstalk, having tried to drive the invaders out of their traditional hunting grounds, were eventually defeated by 1,100 of Lord Dunmore's Virginia militiamen at Point Pleasant near the mouth of the Kanawha River in October. (Puckeshinwa, father of Tecumseh and Tenskwatawa, was among those who died.) By the spring of 1775, the floodgates for westward migration into the interior had been opened wide. Nearly 80,000 non-Indians poured into the region over the next fifteen years. Nevertheless, the Shawnees did not relinquish their claims to land south of the Ohio until the Treaty of Greenville in 1795, following General Anthony Wayne's victory at Fallen Timbers the previous year.[111]

The demographic picture of this interior zone, therefore, is both atypical and cloudy. In the late seventeenth century, when La Salle was encountering Shawnees as far west as the Illinois, we might assume that this region below the Ohio had at least 8,500 inhabitants, many of whom were situated near the Mississippi. Since these occupants had steady contact with hunters and warriors from outside the region, it must be assumed that they did not entirely escape the dangerous diseases that were reducing Indian numbers in other areas. On the other hand, they were widely dispersed, and the rate of decline in this well-protected area was no doubt minor compared with other parts of the South. Perhaps numbers in the interior dropped to 5,000 by 1700 and to 3,000 by 1715. Out-migration by Shawnees to both north and south, plus warfare and sickness, may have reduced the total population to as low as 1,200 during the following decades. But by 1745 it was probably beginning to rise slightly with the arrival of small refugee groups from all directions, perhaps reaching 1,800 by 1760 and 2,000 again by 1775. Continuing warfare and the onslaught of non-Indian migration may have reduced this small population somewhat, to perhaps 1,800, in the years during and after the American Revolution.

Even if these tentative figures for native inhabitants of the interior region are considerably off base for some years, as they may well be, this would not change the dimensions of the extraordinary demographic shift in the eastern portion of this region during the late eighteenth century. When Daniel Boone set out from Hillsborough, North Carolina, in 1775 there were almost no African Americans and only a few hundred European Americans residing beyond the mountains. But soon the trickle became a torrent as settlers from Pennsylvania and Maryland followed those from North Carolina and Virginia. In the spring of 1780 alone, three hundred boatloads of migrants reached the Falls of the Ohio. Census figures for 1790 showed 66,946 whites and 13,773 blacks in what would become Tennessee and Kentucky. In other words, more than 80,000 persons, both free and enslaved, had poured into one segment of the vast interior region within fifteen years (not to mention thousands more who were now residing in the mountains of extreme western Virginia and North Carolina). Suddenly the total population had jumped more than twenty-five times in little over a decade, and this proved only a prologue to the influx that was still to come.[112]

Conclusion

The process of revising, confirming, and interpreting the data presented here remains an extended task to which numerous scholars will lend their expertise. A demographic foundation such as the one laid out in table 1 becomes strong and useful only when other builders test its validity and reduce its shortcomings. Various researchers will arrange and explain these numbers in different ways, using them to alter traditional narratives and open up new lines of inquiry. Treated with due care and skepticism, as a set of interlocking estimations in a field where we have had no prior overview, these population figures can provide a background and framework for much that anthropologists and historians are discovering about the colonial South. Behind these seemingly innocuous quantitative estimates lie broad expanses of history—social and cultural, economic and military—waiting to be written or rewritten.

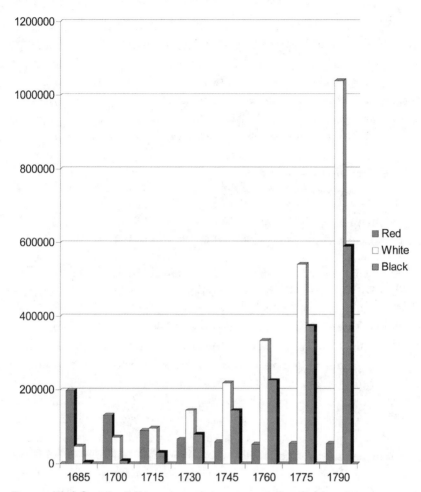

Figure 12. Totals for regions I–X.

Although the period examined here has long received only passing attention, few will deny that it marked a crucial transition and deserves more than cursory reexamination. As George Fredrickson noted in his comparative study of South Africa and the American South:

> The process of stripping the indigenes of their patrimony and reducing them to subservience or marginality was, from the historian's perspective, a complex and uneven one that cannot be fully appreciated . . . merely by looking at the final outcome as the predetermined result of white attitudes, motivations, and advantages. Not only did

the indigenous peoples put up a stiff resistance that at times seemed
capable of stalling the white advance indefinitely, but the lack of a
firm consensus of interests and attitudes within the invading com-
munity, or between the actual settlers and the agents of a metropole
or mother country, could lead to internal disagreements concerning
the character and pace of expansion and even on whether it should
continue at all. Ultimate white hegemony may have been virtually
inevitable, especially in the American case, but this outcome was less
clear to the historical actors than to future generations.[113]

The numbers themselves cannot tell this complicated and significant story. Nevertheless, in conclusion it is worth pointing out several patterns that emerge from an overview of this kind. First of all, the colony of Virginia, which has so often been used by colonial historians to represent the early South, is actually an aberration in the region as a whole. Although not as old as Spanish Florida, Virginia had been the first successful settler colony in the region, and by 1685 approximately four-fifths of all the whites (38,100 of 46,900) and blacks (2,600 of 3,300) in the entire South lived in coastal Virginia. On the eve of the American Revolution in 1775, Virginia east of the mountains still contained more than half the people with European and African ancestry in the whole region (some 465,900 of an estimated 916,900). Even in 1790, when the exodus westward via Cumberland Gap and other routes was well under way, white and black Virginians numbered nearly 750,000 within a southern non-Indian population that had reached 1,630,000. Within the geographic South as a whole, therefore, Virginia's growth after the 1680s makes it the exception rather than the rule. The long shadow cast by the world of Williamsburg has obscured our view of the wider southern world beyond.

When Virginia is removed, the figures for the rest of the region look strikingly different. The total population by race for the nine subregions south and west of Virginia over the course of the eighteenth century appears in table 3 (totals II–X). Across that whole domain in 1685, from the Outer Banks to the Texas pine forests, 95 of every 100 people were Native Americans (some 196,500 out of 206,000). Even when Virginia is put back in the balance (totals I–X), four out of every five persons (almost 200,000 of nearly 250,000 inhabitants) were Indians in 1685—not a statistic that our standard approaches to early southern history have reflected in a serious way.

Table 3. Comparison of Population Totals for Different Parts of the South, 1685–1790

	1685	1700	1715	1730	1745	1760	1775	1790
Totals for Areas I–X								
Red	199,400	130,600	90,100	66,700	59,300	53,600	55,600	55,900
White	46,900	70,900	96,500	144,600	219,700	333,700	542,500	1,039,600
Black	3,300	8,700	31,400	80,600	144,600	226,700	374,400	590,500
Total	249,600	210,200	218,000	291,900	423,600	614,000	972,500	1,686,000
Totals for Areas II–X (Excluding Virginia)								
Red	196,500	128,700	88,800	65,800	58,700	53,200	55,300	55,700
White	8,800	14,800	22,400	41,300	71,400	137,400	263,000	597,500
Black	700	3,200	10,500	30,900	59,300	95,800	188,000	285,000
Total	206,000	146,700	121,700	138,000	189,400	286,400	506,300	938,200
Totals for Areas III–X (Excluding Virginia and North Carolina)								
Red	186,500	121,500	85,800	63,800	57,200	52,200	54,800	55,400
White	3,100	5,400	7,600	14,000	28,700	52,900	106,200	309,300
Black	500	2,800	8,700	25,400	45,300	67,600	135,700	179,500
Total	190,100	129,700	102,100	103,200	131,200	172,700	296,700	544,200
Totals for Areas IV–X (Excluding Virginia and North and South Carolina)								
Red	176,500	114,000	80,700	61,800	55,700	51,200	54,300	55,100
White	1,700	1,600	2,100	4,200	8,400	14,300	34,600	169,100
Black	—	—	100	3,800	4,700	9,700	28,400	70,600
Total	178,200	115,600	82,900	69,800	68,800	75,200	117,300	294,800

But if this composite overview reveals a striking preponderance of Indians in the late seventeenth-century South, it also documents their rapid, ongoing demise. The region's Native American population had already been suffering a steep decline for nearly two centuries, particularly among the coastal tribes, though the early figures are far harder to recover and therefore much more tentative and controversial. During the generation after the 1680s, where we begin to have access to somewhat more reliable and comprehensive statistics, it is clear that disaster was again spreading inland, as it had during the Spanish incursions of the mid-sixteenth century. Between 1685 and 1730, the South's native population was further reduced by a full two-thirds, from roughly 200,000 to fewer than 67,000. Warfare, enslavement, and migration, but most of all epidemic disease, ravaged the major peoples of the Southeast.

As the smallpox virus spread along lines of broadening intercultural trade, the drop in numbers between 1685 and 1730 became cataclysmic: the Cherokees—32,000 to 10,500; the Choctaws—28,000 to 11,200; the Natchez and their neighbors—42,000 to 8,000. Since such groups dominated the

Deep South's landscape, their decimation meant that the overall population of the South beyond Virginia declined by fully one-third over these
forty-five years, despite a steady influx from Europe and Africa. Indeed,
as revealed in totals II–X of table 3, the drop during the generation before
1715 was even steeper, from 206,000 to 121,700. Contrary to popular imagery, the greater South in the early eighteenth century was a region in demographic decline.

If we have underestimated the rapidity and significance of this regional
pandemic among Native Americans, we tend to exaggerate the ease and rapidity of non-Indian expansion. By 1730 the combined white and black population of the non-Virginia South had come to slightly surpass the Indian
population of the same area—a dramatic shift from fifteen years before,
when Indians still outnumbered non-Indians more than eight to three. But
the geographic distribution of the recent arrivals remains striking. Of more
than 72,000 southern blacks and whites outside Virginia in 1730, all but
8,000 lived along a thin strip of land within one hundred miles of the coast
of North and South Carolina. In other words, if Virginia's population skews
the demography of the entire South most dramatically, the rapidly growing
colonies of North and South Carolina also have a significant effect.

This can be seen in table 3 when first one (totals III–X) and then both of
the Carolinas are removed from consideration, along with Virginia. Focusing on the rest of the South (totals IV–X), it is evident that in 1685 seven out
of eight southern Indians reside in this wide domain away from the Atlantic
coast claimed by England, and the proportion increases much further during the ensuing century. In contrast to coastal and piedmont Virginia and
the Carolinas, the overall population in this domain is far less dense, and
it is also far more indigenous. Here non-Indians do not begin to outnumber Indians until the decade before the American Revolution, and even in
1790, despite the flood of postwar migration, more than one person in six
is still a Native American. But it also follows that when the largest English
colonies are removed, the extent of population loss for the rest of the South
appears all the more dramatic. For areas IV to X, the total population did
not cease its absolute decline until the 1740s, having fallen by more than
three-fifths in scarcely two generations.

It is clear from the aggregate calculations presented here that the rate of
decline within the southern Indian population slowed during the eighteenth

century and eventually reversed itself, achieving a slight net increase in the
era of the Revolution after centuries of decline. Whether one examines the
region as a whole or the somewhat smaller portions also shown in table 3, the
number of Native Americans reaches its nadir about the time of the Cherokee War with the English in 1760, and overall numbers begin to rise again
slowly over the next generation. The timing for the shift was not uniform,
for local situations varied, but the general pattern is undeniable.

Several writers have suggested an epidemiological explanation for this pattern. When Old World disease organisms first entered the Southeast in the
sixteenth century, the effects were devastating. Sporadic exposure, perhaps
no more often than once in a generation, prevented native groups from acquiring natural immunities, so entire populations suffered equally during
repeated onslaughts. But as contacts with European traders became more
extensive in the late seventeenth century, southern Indians gradually began to adapt to the shifting disease environment. More frequent exposure
to a contagious illness such as smallpox meant that increasingly it became a
childhood disease, having its greatest impact upon the newest members of
the society. Among the Creeks, for example, research suggests that health
status improved during the eighteenth century as occasional epidemics gave
way to more common, but less devastating, endemic illnesses focused on
young children. This first slowed the rate of population decline, then led to
a gradual numerical increase, as confirmed by ethnohistorical and archaeological evidence. This upswing that appears clearly in the eighteenth-century southern data reflects a pattern found elsewhere in North America at
different times, coinciding with the inception of regular direct contact by
Indians with Europeans and Africans.[114]

Although a crucial demographic trend, this slowing and reversing of the
population decline among southern Indians did not occur soon enough or
fast enough, given the enormous influx of non-Indians into the region during the late colonial era. The overall population of the South had already
begun to rebound during the first quarter of the eighteenth century, owing to new arrivals along the Atlantic coast. Over the next several generations these newcomers would slowly, then rapidly, intrude across the entire
South, achieving both demographic and cultural hegemony. The region's
main language would become English, its dominant religion would become
Protestant Christianity, and its emergent political economy would become

tied to free-market capitalism. These multiple transformations were by no means simple or predetermined, but until we comprehend the demographic context in which they occurred, we can never begin to understand the eighteenth-century South in all its dimensions.

Postscript

Fortunately, the specific population estimates for this essay have held up well in the face of continuing scrutiny and research. Still, two facts are important to re-emphasize. First, all of the numbers presented in the tables are informed estimates and should not be treated as unduly precise or definitive totals. Second, while some individual numbers could no doubt be raised or lowered slightly, the least solid estimates are generally in regions with small overall populations, so altering one estimate by a few hundred or thousand would not disrupt the general overall picture that emerges.

It is this broad picture of change over time, both in the ten subregions and in the South as a whole, that I found most interesting and important from the start. So I appreciate the chance to bring these dramatic shifts more clearly to life through the use of graphics, prepared by Sarah Mattics. The charts (which necessarily vary in scale) underscore striking variations in population from decade to decade and from place to place—demographic changes that both reflect and explain the complexity of early Southern history. The new map sketches the rough location of the ten subregions. The geopolitical boundaries are, of course, imprecise, and they only conform occasionally to the outlines of modern states.

Notes

1. The collaboration of Janice Blinder and Daniel H. Usner Jr. in early stages of this project proved invaluable. I am indebted to them and to others who have provided references, suggestions, and criticism. A brief preview of this research, with graphs, appeared in *Southern Exposure* 16 (Summer 1988).

2. One might include Maryland separately, or along with Virginia as part of a larger Chesapeake zone. The two colonies had very similar demographic profiles. While scholars still discuss the so-called Tidewater area as "typifying" the colonial South, the Chesapeake differed markedly from the geographic South as a whole in terms of population makeup and density.

3. See, for example, David D. Smits, "'Abominable Mixture': Toward the Repudiation of Anglo-Indian Intermarriage in Seventeenth-Century Virginia," *Virginia Magazine of*

History and Biography 95 (April 1987): 157–92. This repudiation came much earlier in Virginia than throughout most of the South.

4. This can be seen in the "better-dead-than-red" approach to the disappearance of the English settlement at Roanoke in the 1580s, where the belief that the colony was "lost" persists in the face of evidence that many of the English were absorbed into local Indian populations.

5. Ben C. McCary, *Indians in Seventeenth-Century Virginia* (Charlottesville: University of Virginia Press, 1957), 81–82; Judith Reynolds, "Marriage between the English and Indians in Seventeenth-Century Virginia," Archeological Society of Virginia Quarterly Bulletin 17 (1962): 19–25. Cf. Wesley Frank Craven, *White, Red and Black: The Seventeenth-Century Virginian* (Charlottesville: University of Virginia Press, 1971); Lynn E. Kauffman, James C. O'Neill, and Patricia A. Jehle, *Bibliography of the Virginia Indians* (Fredericksburg: Archeological Society of Virginia, 1976). Also see J. Frederick Fausz, "The Invasion of Virginia: Indians, Colonialism, and the Conquest of Cant, a Review Essay on Anglo-Indian Relations in the Chesapeake," *Virginia Magazine of History and Biography* 95 (April 1987): 133–56; and Helen C. Rountree, "The Termination and Dispersal of the Nottaway Indians of Virginia," *Virginia Magazine of History and Biography* 95 (April 1987): 193–215.

6. "An Act for Destroying Wolves," October 1669, in William W. Hening, *The Statutes at Large: Being a Collection of All Laws of Virginia, from the First Session of the Legislature in the Year 1619*, 13 vols. (Richmond: Samuel Pleasants, 1809–23), 2:274–75; Douglas H. Ubelaker, *Reconstruction of Demographic Profiles from Ossuary Skeletal Samples: A Case Study from the Tidewater Potomac* (Washington DC: Smithsonian Institution Press, 1974), 69.

7. Robert Beverley, *The History and Present State of Virginia* (1705), ed. Louis B. Wright (Chapel Hill: University of North Carolina Press, 1947), 232–33. Cf. Christian F. Feest, "Virginia Algonquians," in *Handbook of North American Indians*, vol. 15, *Northeast*, ed. Bruce G. Trigger, gen. ed. William C. Sturtevant (Washington DC: Smithsonian Institution, 1978), 253–70.

8. Beverley, *History*, 232; Clarence Carter, ed., "Observations of Superintendent John Stuart and Governor James Grant of East Florida on the Proposed Plan of 1764 for the Future Management of Indian Affairs," *American Historical Review* 20 (July 1915): 825.

9. Thomas Jefferson, *Notes on the State of Virginia* (1787; New York: Harper and Row, 1964), 91–92. Cf. Rountree, "Termination and Dispersal of the Nottaway Indians of Virginia."

10. Thomas C. Parramore, "The Tuscarora Ascendancy," *North Carolina Historical Review* 59 (Autumn 1982): 307–15.

11. Parramore, "Tuscarora Ascendancy," 317; James W. Clay et al., *North Carolina Atlas: Portrait of a Changing Southern State* (Chapel Hill: University of North Carolina Press, 1975), fig. 1.2, p. 14; Feest, "North Carolina Algonquians," in Trigger, *Handbook of North American Indians, Northeast*, 271–81.

12. John Lawson, *A New Voyage to Carolina*, ed. Hugh T. Lefler (London, 1709; Chapel Hill: University of North Carolina Press, 1967), 242–43; E. Lawrence Lee, *Indian Wars in North Carolina, 1663–1763* (Raleigh: Carolina Charter Tercentenary Commission, 1963), 3–5; Clay et al., *North Carolina Atlas*, 13.

13. Parramore, "Tuscarora Ascendancy," 315; Lawson, *New Voyage*, 232, 243. On the devastating impact of the rum trade, see Peter C. Mancall, *Deadly Medicine: Indians and Alcohol in Early America* (Ithaca NY: Cornell University Press, 1995).

14. Parramore, "Tuscarora Ascendancy," 315; Thomas C. Parramore, "With Tuscarora Jack on the Back Path to Bath," *North Carolina Historical Review* 64 (April 1987): 115–38; John Brickell, *The Natural History of North-Carolina* (Dublin: James Carson, 1737; reprint, Murfreesboro NC: Johnson, 1968), 253, 282; Patrick H. Garrow, *The Mattamuskeet Documents: A Study in Social History* (Raleigh: Archaeology Branch, North Carolina Division of Archives and History, 1975).

15. Elizabeth A. Fenn and Peter H. Wood, *Natives and Newcomers: The Way We Lived in North Carolina before 1770* (Chapel Hill: University of North Carolina Press, 1983), 31; James Mooney, *The Siouan Tribes of the East*, Bureau of American Ethnology Bulletin 22 (Washington DC: Government Printing Office, 1894), 8. Ongoing research by Erin Avots suggests the estimate of 400 blacks in North Carolina in 1700 may soon need to be adjusted upward by at least several hundred.

16. Peter H. Wood, *Black Majority: Negroes in Colonial South Carolina from 1670 through the Stono Rebellion* (New York: Alfred A. Knopf, 1974), 37–42, 143–44; Wood, "Indian Slavery in the Southeast," in *Handbook of North American Indians*, vol. 4, *History of Indian-White Relations*, ed. Wilcomb E. Washburn (Washington DC: Smithsonian Institution, 1988), 407–9.

17. Wood, *Black Majority*, 145–55; Donald B. Dodd and Wynelle S. Dodd, *Historical Statistics of the South, 1790–1970* (Tuscaloosa: University of Alabama Press, 1973), 46.

18. Gene Waddell, *Indians of the South Carolina Lowcountry, 1562–1751* (Spartanburg SC: Reprint Company, 1980), 14, 292–93.

19. Afra Coming to her sister, March 6, 1698/99, in Edward McCrady, *The History of South Carolina under the Proprietary Government, 1670–1719* (1897; reprint, New York: Russell and Russell, 1969), 308; John Archdale, *A New Description of That Fertile and Pleasant Province of Carolina* (London: John Wyat, 1707), reprinted in *Narratives of Early Carolina, 1650–1708*, ed. Alexander S. Salley Jr. (New York: Charles Scribner's Sons, 1911), 285.

20. Waddell, *Indians of the Lowcountry*, 6, 14, 269; James Glen, *A Description of South Carolina: Containing Many Curious and Interesting Particulars Relating to the Civil, Natural and Commercial History of that Colony* (London: R. and J. Dodsley, 1761), 68.

21. Chapman J. Milling, *Red Carolinians*, 2nd ed. (Columbia: University of South Carolina Press, 1969), 219–20, 222; Lee, *Indian Wars*, 47.

22. Lee, *Indian Wars*, 39–45; Milling, *Red Carolinians*, 222–23.

23. Samuel Cole Williams, ed., *Adair's History of the American Indians* (London, 1775; reprint, New York: Argonaut Press, 1966), 235; John R. Swanton, *The Indians of the Southeastern United States*, Bureau of American Ethnology Bulletin 137 (Washington DC: Government Printing Office, 1946), 105.

24. Milling, *Red Carolinians*, 222, 235. See also James H. Merrell, "The Indians' New World: The Catawba Experience," *William and Mary Quarterly*, 3rd ser., 41 (October 1984): 537–65.

25. Verner W. Crane, *The Southern Frontier, 1670–1732* (Durham NC: Duke University Press, 1928; reissued with a new preface by Peter H. Wood, New York: W. W. Norton, 1981), 129, 188; Larry E. Ivers, *Colonial Forts of South Carolina, 1670–1775* (Columbia: University of South Carolina Press, 1970), 43–44.

26. William K. Boyd, ed., *William Byrd's Histories of the Dividing Line betwixt Virginia and North Carolina* (New York: Dover, 1967), 300.

27. Williams, *Adair's History*, 235.

28. Williams, *Adair's History*, 235.

29. Williams, *Adair's History*, 233.

30. Milling, *Red Carolinians*, 253–54; "Report of the Journey of the Brethren Abraham Steiner and Frederick C. De Schweinitz to the Cherokees and the Cumberland Settlements (1799)," in Samuel Cole Williams, ed., *Early Travels in the Tennessee Country, 1540–1800* (Johnson City TN: Watauga Press, 1928), 460.

31. Henry F. Dobyns, *Their Number Become Thinned: Native American Population Dynamics in Eastern North America* (Knoxville: University of Tennessee Press, 1983); William M. Denevan, ed., *The Native Population of the Americas in 1492* (Madison: University of Wisconsin Press, 1976); Douglas H. Ubelaker, "Prehistoric New World Population Size: Historical Review and Current Appraisal of North American Estimates," *American Journal of Physical Anthropology* 45 (1976): 661–66; James H. Merrell, "Playing the Indian Numbers Game," *Reviews in American History* 12 (1984): 354–58.

32. Swanton, *Indians of the Southeastern United States*, 194; John H. Hann, "Demographic Patterns and Changes in Mid-Seventeenth Century Timucua and Apalachee," *Florida Historical Quarterly* 64 (April 1986): 378–81; Kathleen A. Deagan, "Cultures in Transition: Fusion and Assimilation among the Eastern Timucua," in *Tacachale: Essays on the Indians of Florida and Southeastern Georgia during the Historic Period*, ed. Jerald T. Milanich and Samuel Proctor (Gainesville: University Press of Florida, 1978), 89–119.

33. J. G. Johnson, "The Spanish Southeast in the Seventeenth Century," *Georgia Historical Quarterly* 16 (March 1932): 23; Lucy L. Wenhold, trans., *A Seventeenth-Century Letter of Gabriel Diaz Vara Calderón, Bishop of Cuba, Describing the Indians and Indian Missions of Florida*, with an introduction by John R. Swanton, Smithsonian Miscellaneous Collections 95, no. 16 (Washington DC: Government Printing Office, 1936), 8–12; Mark F. Boyd, Hale G. Smith, and John W. Griffin, *Here They Once Stood: The Tragic End of the Apalachee Missions* (Gainesville: University Press of Florida, 1951), 8. Native resistance and English interference prevented Spanish conversion of the Creeks, so Calderón's total does not include thirteen Lower Creek villages along the Apalachicola River or fourteen Upper Creek villages farther north and west. These towns, and others not named in the bishop's initial listing, are included in the Indian population estimates for the Creek-Georgia-Alabama area. This is also true for Calderón's "more than 4,000 heathen called Chiscas," or Yuchis, "who sustain themselves with game, nuts and roots of trees" in the same area.

34. For evidence on Florida's non-Indian populations, see John R. Dunkle, "Population Change as an Element in the Historical Geography of St. Augustine," *Florida Historical Quarterly* 37 (July 1958): 3–22; Kathleen A. Deagan, "*Mestizaje* in Colonial San Au-

gustine," *Ethnohistory* 20 (1973): 55–65; Theodore G. Corbett, "Population Structure in Hispanic St. Augustine, 1629–1763," *Florida Historical Quarterly* 54 (January 1976): 263–84; W. H. Siebert, "Slavery and White Servitude in East Florida, 1726–1776," *Florida Historical Quarterly* 10 (July 1931): 5; Kenneth W. Porter, "Negroes on the Southern Frontier, 1670–1763," *Journal of Negro History* 33 (1948): 53–78; John J. TePaske, "The Fugitive Slave: Intercolonial Rivalry and Spanish Slave Policy, 1697–1764," in *Eighteenth-Century Florida and Its Borderlands*, ed. Samuel Proctor (Gainesville, University Press of Florida, 1975), 1–12; Jane Landers, "Spanish Sanctuary: Fugitives in Florida, 1687–1790," *Florida Historical Quarterly* 62 (January 1984): 296–313; Joseph B. Lockey, *East Florida, 1783–1785: A File of Documents Assembled and Many of Them Translated* (Berkeley: University of California Press, 1949), 10–11, 420–21.

35. Wenhold, *Seventeenth-Century Letter*, 11; Swanton, *Indians of the Southeastern United States*, 102; Lewis H. Larson, *Aboriginal Subsistence Technology on the Southeastern Coastal Plain during the Late Prehistoric Period* (Gainesville: University Press of Florida, 1980), 23–34; Clifford M. Lewis, "The Calusa," in Milanich and Proctor, *Tacachale*, 19–49.

36. William C. Sturtevant, "Spanish-Indian Relations in Southeastern North America," *Ethnohistory* 9 (Winter 1962): 68–71; James W. Covington, "Migration of the Seminoles into Florida, 1700–1820," *Florida Historical Quarterly* 46 (April 1968): 341–44.

37. Lewis H. Larson Jr., "Historic Guale Indians of the Georgia Coast and the Impact of the Spanish Mission Effort," in Milanich and Proctor, *Tacachale*, 120; Crane, *Southern Frontier*, 80; Milling, *Red Carolinians*, 170–74; John Jay TePaske, *The Governorship of Spanish Florida, 1700–1763* (Durham NC: Duke University Press, 1964), 197. Also see Alan Gallay, *The Indian Slave Trade: The Rise of the English Empire in the American South, 1670–1717* (New Haven CT: Yale University Press, 2002), 127–54, and Jerald T. Milanich, *Laboring in the Fields of the Lord: Spanish Missions and Southeastern Indians* (Washington DC: Smithsonian Institution Press, 1999), 157–95.

38. Thomas Nairne to the Earl of Sunderland, July 10, 1709, in Great Britain, The National Archives, Public Record Office, Colonial Office 5/382, no. 11 (hereafter cited as PRO, CO); Sturtevant, "Spanish-Indian Relations," 71.

39. Theodore G. Corbett, "Migration to a Spanish Imperial Frontier in the Seventeenth and Eighteenth Centuries: St. Augustine," *Hispanic American Historical Review* 54 (August 1974): 428–30; Robert L. Gold, *Borderland Empires in Transition: The Triple Nation Transfer of Florida* (Carbondale: Southern Illinois University Press, 1969), 76; Sturtevant, "Spanish-Indian Relations," 71; John R. Swanton, *Early History of the Creek Indians and Their Neighbors*, Bureau of American Ethnology Bulletin 73 (Washington DC: Government Printing Office, 1922), 423; Covington, "Migration of the Seminoles," 342.

40. William Bartram, *Travels through North and South Carolina, Georgia, East and West Florida* (facsimile of the 1792 London edition; Savannah: Beehive Press, 1973), 206–7.

41. Bartram, *Travels through North and South Carolina, Georgia, East and West Florida*, 209; Clarence E. Carter, ed., *The Territorial Papers of the United States*, vol. 22, *The Territory of Florida, 1821–1824* (Washington DC: Government Printing Office, 1956), 463–65; Henry A. Kersey Jr., *The Seminole and Miccosukee Tribes: A Critical Bibliography* (Bloomington:

Indiana University Press, 1987). On Seminole population, cf. Swanton, *Early History of the Creek Indians*, 400, 456, and Swanton, *Indians of the Southeastern United States*, 181.

42. Crane, *Southern Frontier*, 33–36. A convincing case for referring to these diverse peoples as the Muscogulges and to their homeland, encompassing most of the region described here, as Muskogee is made in Joel Wayne Martin, *Sacred Revolt: The Muskogee's Struggle for a New World* (Boston: Beacon Press, 1991).

43. David H. Corkran, *The Creek Frontier, 1540–1783* (Norman: University of Oklahoma Press, 1967), 48–56.

44. Wenhold, *Seventeenth-Century Letter*, 9–10; Mark F. Boyd, "Expedition of Marcos Delgado from Apalache to the Upper Creek Country in 1686," *Florida Historical Quarterly* 16 (July 1937): 3–32; Vernon J. Knight Jr., and Sherée L. Adams, "A Voyage to the Mobile and Tomeh in 1700, with Notes on the Interior of Alabama," *Ethnohistory* 28 (1981): 179–94.

45. "Letter from N. Johnson, Thomas Broughton, Robt. Gibbs, George Smith, and Richard Beresford," September 17, 1708, in A. S. Salley, indexer, *Records in the British Public Record Office Relating to South Carolina, 1701–1710* (Columbia SC, 1947), 208.

46. "An exact Account of ye Number and Strength of all the Indian Nations that were subject to the Government of South Carolina, and solely traded with them in ye beginning of ye year 1715 . . . ," in *A Chapter in the Early History of South Carolina*, ed. William J. Rivers (Charleston, 1874), 94.

47. Corkran, *Creek Frontier*, 114. Cf. Bernard Romans, *A Concise Natural History of East and West Florida* (1775), facsimile reproduction, ed. Rembert W. Patrick (Gainesville: University Press of Florida, 1962), 90–91.

48. Wilber R. Jacobs, ed., *Indians of the Southern Colonial Frontier: The Edmond Atkin Report and Plan of 1755* (Columbia: University of South Carolina Press, 1954), 43.

49. "Names of the Villages inhabited by the Creek Indians & the No in each Village. in Majr Farmar's letter of 24th Jany 1764," in *Mississippi Provincial Archives, 1763–1766: English Dominion*, vol. 1 (Nashville TN: Brandon Printing Company, 1911), 94–97; Report of Francis Ogilvie, July 8, 1764, in volume 21 of the Papers of General Thomas Gage, Clements Library, Ann Arbor, Michigan, cited in Corkran, *Creek Frontier*, 6.

50. Williams, *Adair's History*, 274; Romans, *Concise Natural History*, 90–91.

51. Dodd and Dodd, *Historical Statistics*, 18; "Observations on the Indians in the southern Parts of the United States, in a Letter from the Hon. Dr. Ramsay, corresponding Member of the Historical Society, March 10, 1795," including Mr. Purcell's 1780 estimate, *Collections of the Massachusetts Historical Society*, 1st ser., 4 (1795): 99–100.

52. "General Knox, Secretary of War, to the President of the United States," July 7, 1789, including letter from Hawkins et al., to Richard Henry Lee, December 2, 1785, in *American State Papers*, Class II, *Indian Affairs*, 1:38–39; Caleb Swan, "Position and State of Manners and Arts in the Creek, or Muscoggee Nation in 1791," in *Historical and Statistical Information Respecting the History, Condition, and Prospects of the Indian Tribes of the United States*, ed. Henry Rowe Schoolcraft, 6 vols. (Philadelphia: Lippincott, Grambo, 1851–57; reprint, New York: Paladin Press, 1969; New York: AMS, 1977), 5:263.

53. "Statement of the towns of the different tribes of Indians which today compose the

nation known under the name of Creek or Maskoke," enclosed in a letter from Pedro Ol-
ivier to Carondelet, December 1, 1793, in *Spain in the Mississippi Valley, 1765–1794*, ed. Lawrence Kinnaird (Washington DC: Government Printing Office, 1946–49), part 3, 229–
32. Cf. Albert S. Gatschet, "Towns and Villages of the Creek Confederacy in the XVIII.
and XIX. Centuries," *Publications of the Alabama Historical Society*, Miscellaneous Collections 1, part 5 (1901): 386–415. The map "Southern Indian Villages, 1760–1794," in *Atlas of Early American History: The Revolutionary Era, 1760–1790*, ed. Lester J. Cappon et al.
(Princeton NJ: Princeton University Press for The Newberry Library, 1976), 19, shows only
ten Creek towns.

54. "The Commissioners to the Secretary of War," November 20, 1789, in *American
State Papers*, Class II, *Indian Affairs*, 1:78–79. A decade later Benjamin Hawkins listed
the major "old towns" and elaborated on the system of satellite villages that made town
counts vary so greatly. Besides the seven Seminole towns in Florida, Hawkins reported,
"There are thirty-seven towns in the Creek nation, twelve on the waters of the Chat-to-
ho-che, and twenty-five on the waters of Coo-sau and Tal-la-poo-sa. The small towns or
villages belong to some one of these." Hawkins also commented upon population fluctu-
ations within individual towns. Discussing the village of "Autosse" on the Tallapoosa, he
wrote in 1799: "In the year 1766 there were forty-three gun men, and lately they were estimated at eighty. This is a much greater increase of population than is to be met with
in other towns! They appear to be stationary generally, and in some towns are on the decrease; the apparent difference here, or increase, may be greater than the real; as formerly
men grown were rated as gun men, and now boys of fifteen, who are hunters, are rated as
gun men; they have for two years past been on the decline; are very sickly, and have lost
many of their inhabitants; they are now rated at fifty gun men only." Benjamin Hawkins,
"A Sketch of the Creek Country in the Years 1798 and 1799," *Collections of the Georgia Historical Society* 3, part 1 (1848): 24–25, 32.

55. Swan, "Position and State of Manners," 259–63.

56. Gary C. Goodwin, *Cherokees in Transition: A Study of Changing Culture and Environment Prior to 1775* (Chicago: University of Chicago Department of Geography, 1977), 41.

57. "Exact Account," 94. If the breakdowns are correct, then the 11,530 given in the original
document (PRO, CO 5:1265, Q 201) is in error and should be 11,210 as presented in Rivers.

58. Letter from Governor Nathaniel Johnson and Council to Proprietors, September
17, 1708, in *Records of the British Public Record Office Relating to South Carolina, 1663–1710*,
5 vols., comp. W. Noel Sainsbury (Atlanta and Columbia, 1928–47), 5:209.

59. James Mooney, *The Aboriginal Population of America North of Mexico*, Smithsonian
Miscellaneous Collections 80, no. 7 (Washington DC: Government Printing Office, 1928),
8. On Indian smallpox death rates, see Conrad Heidenreich, *Huronia: A History and Geography of the Huron Indians, 1600–1650* (Toronto: McClelland and Stewart, 1971), 97–98.

60. Jacobs, *Indians*, 42.

61. Williams, *Adair's History*, 238.

62. Williams, *Adair's History*, 244, 327.

63. Pennsylvania *Gazette*, September 4, 1760. I am indebted to Suzanne Krebsbach

for this reference. Cf. Peter H. Wood, "The Impact of Smallpox on the Native Population of the Eighteenth-Century South," *New York State Journal of Medicine* 87 (January
1987): 30–36.

64. Williams, *Adair's History*, 239.

65. "Observations," *Collections of the Massachusetts Historical Society*, 1st ser., 4 (1795):
99–100; James Paul Pate, "The Chickamauga: A Forgotten Segment of Indian Resistance
on the Southern Frontier" (PhD diss., Mississippi State University, 1969), 80–82. For a
more recent overview, see Jon W. Parmenter, "Dragging Canoe (Tsi'yu-gûnsi'ni), Chickamauga Cherokee Patriot," in *The Human Tradition in the American Revolution*, ed. Nancy
L. Rhoden and Ian K. Steele (Wilmington DE: Scholarly Resources, 1999), 117–37.

66. "Gen. Henry Knox to the President," July 7, 1789, *American State Papers, Indian
Affairs*, 1:38.

67. Robert L. Meriwether, *The Expansion of South Carolina, 1729–1765* (Kingsport TN:
Southern Publishers, 1940), 217, 232; Larry E. Ivers, *Colonial Forts of South Carolina, 1670–
1775* (Columbia: University of South Carolina Press for the South Carolina Tricentennial
Commission, 1970), 16.

68. Max Dixon, *The Wataugans* (Nashville: Tennessee American Revolution Bicenten-
nial Commission, 1976), 26; Evarts B. Greene and Virginia D. Harrington, *American Population before the Federal Census of 1790* (New York: Columbia University Press, 1932), 193.

69. Peter H. Wood, "'Impatient of Oppression': Black Freedom Struggles on the Eve
of White Independence," *Southern Exposure* 12 (November–December 1984): 10–16; and
Theda Perdue "Red and Black in the Southern Appalachians," in "Liberating Our Past:
Four Hundred Years of Southern History," *Southern Exposure* 12 (November–December
1984): 17–24.

70. Stella H. Sutherland, *Population Distribution in Colonial America* (New York: Columbia University Press, 1936), 209.

71. Antoine Le Page du Pratz, *The History of Louisiana*, facsimile reproduction of the
1774 translated British edition, ed. Joseph Tragle Jr. (Baton Rouge: Louisiana State University Press, 1975), 310–11; Williams, *Adair's History*, 377.

72. Williams, *Early Travels in the Tennessee Country*, 62; Benjamin Franklin French,
Historical Collections of Louisiana, 5 vols. (New York: Lamport, Blakeman and Law, 1846–
53), 1:60.

73. Swanton, *Early History of the Creek Indians*, 449, 456. A roll prepared by federal officials in the mid-1830s showed a population of 6,070, made up of 4,914 Chickasaws and
1,156 slaves. Arrell M. Gibson, *The Chickasaws* (Norman: University of Oklahoma Press,
1971), 179.

74. Gibson, *Chickasaws*, 39–57, 63–64; Bienville to Maurepas, August 26, 1734, is quoted
on p. 50.

75. Swanton, *Indians of the Southeastern United States*, 123; Swanton, *Early History of the
Creek Indians*, 456, 450–51.

76. Jack D. L. Holmes, "The Choctaws in 1795," *Alabama Historical Quarterly* 30 (Spring
1968): 33–50. The totals on page 38 contain an error in addition or transcription.

77. Williams, *Adair's History*, 302–3.

78. Richebourg Gaillard McWilliams, ed. and trans., *Iberville's Gulf Journals* (Tusca-loosa: University of Alabama Press, 1981), 174, 141. In a 1702 speech to several chiefs of the warring Chickasaws and Choctaws (p. 172), Iberville repeated what he had learned of their recent attrition. "You Chicacha can observe that during the last eight to ten years when you have been at war with the Chaqueta at the instigation of the English, who gave you am-munition and thirty guns for that purpose, you have taken more than 500 prisoners and killed more than 1,800 Chaqueta. Those prisoners were sold; but taking those prisoners cost you more than 800 men, slain on various war parties."

79. Letter of August 3, 1723, by LeBlond de la Tour, in "Minutes of the Superior Coun-cil of Louisiana," in *Mississippi Provincial Archives: French Dominion*, trans. and ed. Dun-bar Rowland and Albert Sanders, 3 vols. (Jackson: Mississippi Department of Archives and History, 1927–32), 3:357–58.

80. Le Page du Pratz, *History of Louisiana*, 309.

81. Rowland and Sanders, *Mississippi Provincial Archives*, 1:115–17, 150–54.

82. Patricia Dillon Woods, *French-Indian Relations on the Southern Frontier, 1699–1762* (Ann Arbor MI: UMI Research Press, 1980), 148; Jacobs, *Indians*, 43–44. For overzealous es-timates of Choctaw strength by English colonial officials seeking to win a powerful new ally against the French in the late 1730s, see Allen D. Candler and Lucian Lamar Knight, eds., *The Colonial Records of the State of Georgia*, 24 vols. (Athens GA, 1904–16), 5:56, 190–91.

83. Woods, *French-Indian Relations*, 168; "Rapport du Chevalier de Kerlérec," *Compte Rendu du Congrès International des Américanistes*, 15th sess., 1:76n; Seymour Feiler, ed. and trans., *Jean-Bernard Bossu's Travels in the Interior of North America, 1751–1762* (Norman: University of Oklahoma Press, 1962), 163.

84. "An Account of Several Nations of Southern Indians. In a Letter From Rev. Elam Potter to Rev. Dr. Stiles, AD 1768," *Collections of the Massachusetts Historical Society*, 1st ser. 10 (1795): 119–21; "Observations on the Indians in the Southern Parts of the United States, in a Letter from the Hon. Dr. Ramsay, Corresponding Member of the Historical Society. March 10, 1795," *Collections of the Massachusetts Historical Society*, 1st ser., 4:99; *American State Papers, Indian Affairs*, 1:39, 49, 659.

85. John R. Swanton, *Indian Tribes of the Lower Mississippi Valley and Adjacent Coast of the Gulf of Mexico*, Bureau of American Ethnology Bulletin 43 (Washington DC: Govern-ment Printing Office, 1911), 43. For a later overview, see Fred B. Kniffen, Hiram F. Greg-ory, and George A. Stokes, *The Historic Indian Tribes of Louisiana from 1542 to the Present* (Baton Rouge: Louisiana State University Press, 1987).

86. Peter H. Wood, "La Salle: Discovery of a Lost Explorer," *American Historical Re-view* 89 (April 1984): 294–323.

87. Jean-Baptiste Bernard de La Harpe, *The Historical Journal of the Establishment of the French in Louisiana* (Lafayette: University of Southwestern Louisiana Press, 1971), 23; Swanton, *Indian Tribes of the Lower Mississippi Valley*, 41, Swanton, *Early History of the Creek Indians*, 425.

88. Daniel H. Usner Jr., "Frontier Exchange in the Lower Mississippi Valley: Race

Relations and Economic Life in Colonial Louisiana, 1699–1783" (PhD diss., Duke University, 1981), 69.

89. Swanton, *Indians of the Southeast*, 140; Thomas Hutchins, *An Historical Narrative and Topographical Description of Louisiana, and West-Florida*, facsimile reproduction of 1784 edition, ed. Joseph G. Tragle Jr. (Gainesville: University Press of Florida, 1968), 39.

90. Usner, "Frontier Exchange," 69.

91. W. David Baird, *The Quapaw Indians: A History of the Downstream People* (Norman: University of Oklahoma Press, 1980), 31, 37.

92. "Letter of Mr. Thaumur de la Source," in *Early Voyages Up and Down the Mississippi*, ed. John D. G. Shea (Albany NY: Joel Munsell, 1861), 81; Hutchins, *Historical Narrative*, 44; Pierre Margry, *Découvertes et établissements des Français dans l'ouest et dans le sud de l'Amérique Septentrionale (1614–1754): Mémoires et documents origineaux*, 6 vols. (Paris: Imprimerie D. Jouast, 1876–86), 4:414.

93. La Harpe, *Historical Journal*, 33–34; Letter of Roulleaux de La Vente, September 20, 1704, quoted in Swanton, *Indian Tribes of the Lower Mississippi Valley*, 39; "Historical Journal of Father Pierre François Xavier de Charlevoix," in French, *Historical Collections of Louisiana*, 3:162.

94. Woods, *French-Indian Relations*, 95–110; Usner, "Frontier Exchange," 69.

95. Marcel Giraud, *A History of French Louisiana* (Baton Rouge: Louisiana State University Press, 1974), 277–79; Daniel H. Usner Jr., "From African Captivity to American Slavery: The Introduction of Black Laborers to Colonial Louisiana," *Louisiana History* 20 (Winter 1979): 25–48.

96. Usner, "Frontier Exchange," 122, 140, 146; Andrew Walsh and Robert Wells, "Population Dynamics in the Eighteenth-Century Mississippi River Valley: Acadians in Louisiana," *Journal of Social History* 11 (Summer 1978): 521–45.

97. W. W. Newcomb Jr., *The Indians of Texas from Prehistoric to Modern Times* (Austin: University of Texas Press, 1961), 283. See also the four volumes of *Caddoan Indians* (New York: Garland, 1974) in the American Indian Ethnohistory Series, ed. David Agee Horr, containing expert testimony submitted to the Indian Claims Commission, such as Helen Hornbeck Tanner, "The Territory of the Caddo Tribe of Oklahoma," 4:9–144.

98. See Herbert Eugene Bolton, *The Hasinais: South Caddoans as Seen by the Earliest Europeans*, ed. Russell M. Magnaghi (Norman: University of Oklahoma Press, 1987).

99. Newcomb, *Indians of Texas*, 313. In addition, see Timothy K. Perttula, *"The Caddo Nation": Archaeological and Ethnohistoric Perspectives* (Austin: University of Texas Press, 1992), 84–92, and F. Todd Smith, *The Caddo Indians: Tribes at the Convergence of Empires, 1542–1854* (College Station: Texas A&M University Press, 1995).

100. Newcomb, *Indians of Texas*, 315–29; Herbert Eugene Bolton, *Texas in the Middle Eighteenth Century: Studies in Spanish Colonial History and Administration* (Austin: University of Texas Press, 1970), 196–203, 219–40. (This book was originally published in 1915 as volume 3 of the University of California Publications in History.)

101. Newcomb, *Indians of Texas*, 59–81. On the Atakapas and Karankawas, also see Lawrence E. Aten, *Indians of the Upper Texas Coast* (New York: Academic Press, 1983).

102. Newcomb, *Indians of Texas*, 136.

103. John C. Ewers, "The Influence of Epidemics on the Indian Population and Cultures of Texas," *Plains Anthropologist* 18 (May 1973): 104–15, esp. 105–7; Alicia V. Tjarks, "Comparative Demographic Analysis of Texas, 1777–1793," *Southwestern Historical Quarterly* 77 (January 1974): 291–338.

104. Elizabeth A. H. John, *Storms Brewed in Other Men's Worlds: The Confrontation of Indians, Spanish, and French in the Southwest, 1540–1795* (College Station: Texas A&M University Press, 1975), 204–5; Ewers, "Influence of Epidemics," 108.

105. Non-Indian numbers regarding East Texas before 1775 have not yet been adequately documented. For several estimates larger than those given in table 1, see Tjarks, "Comparative Demographic Analysis of Texas," 299.

106. Tjarks, "Comparative Demographic Analysis of Texas," 295–96.

107. Tjarks, "Comparative Demographic Analysis of Texas," 301, 324–25; John, *Storms*, 369, 499, 523, 540–41. For more on the devastations around 1780, see Elizabeth A. Fenn, *Pox Americana: The Great Smallpox Epidemic of 1775–82* (New York: Hill and Wang, 2001).

108. Samuel Cole Williams, ed., *Lieut. Henry Timberlake's Memoirs, 1756–1765* (1927; reprint, Marietta GA: Continental Book Company, 1948), 113–16; Charles Callender, "Shawnee," in Trigger, *Handbook of North American Indians, Northeast*, 23, 630–31; Jerry E. Clark, *The Shawnee* (Lexington: University Press of Kentucky, 977), 3.

109. Clark, *Shawnee*, 15–16, 18; Lucien Beckner, "Eskippakithiki: The Last Indian Town in Kentucky," *Filson Club History Quarterly* 6 (1932): 355–82; Ernest H. Howerton, "Logan, the Shawnee Capital of West Virginia—from 1760 to 1780," *West Virginia History* 16 (July 1955): 313–33.

110. Michael N. McConnell, "Peoples 'In Between': The Iroquois and the Ohio Indians, 1720–1768," in *Beyond the Covenant Chain: The Iroquois and Their Neighbors in Indian North America, 1675–1775*, ed. James H. Merrell and Daniel K. Richter (Syracuse NY: Syracuse University Press, 1987).

111. R. David Edmunds, *The Shawnee Prophet* (Lincoln: University of Nebraska Press, 1983), 10; Edmunds, *Tecumseh and the Quest for Indian Leadership* (Boston: Little, Brown, 1984), 20.

112. James H. Pauley, "Early North Carolina Migrations into the Tennessee Country, 1768–1782: A Study in Historical Demography" (PhD diss., Middle Tennessee State University, 1969); Patricia Watlington, "The Partisan Spirit: Kentucky Politics, 1779–1792" (PhD diss., Yale University, 1964), 49.

113. George M. Frederickson, *White Supremacy: A Comparative Study in American and South African History* (New York: Oxford University Press, 1981), 5.

114. Jeanne Kay, "The Fur Trade and Native American Population Growth," *Ethnohistory* 31 (1984): 265–87; Kenneth R. Turner, "Health, Illness, and the People of Hoithlewaulee," in *Culture Change on the Creek Indian Frontier*, ed. Gregory A. Waselkov, Final Report to the National Science Foundation, Grant Award BNS-8305437, 55–82.

Interconnectedness and Diversity in "French Louisiana"

KATHLEEN DUVAL

In 1750, after more than half a century of colonization, the French governor of Louisiana declared in exasperation, "we can do nothing by ourselves."[1] While the French called Louisiana their colony, in reality, as Governor Vaudreuil knew, officials, explorers, priests, merchants, traders, and slaves became small parts of the large, complex neighborhood of the Mississippi valley. One narrative of the late seventeenth and eighteenth centuries stars French colonial officials such as Vaudreuil forging (and losing) Louisiana, where they sought to profit and to challenge France's European rivals. But countless other intertwined narratives run through this place and time, centering on Choctaws, Natchez, Chickasaws, Tunicas, Osages, Quapaws, Bambaras, Mobilians, Caddoans, Britons, Spaniards, and other groups and individuals within them.

This is not to say that the French had no effect on Louisiana. On the contrary, European diseases and goods changed the region's history. Indians became entangled in the world economies that colonialism created, and ultimately the arrival of the French proved one of the most important events of the late seventeenth-century Mississippi valley. But emphasizing change that occurred after Europeans arrived can create the impression that Europeans *directed* change. In reality, the French had little power, and the Mississippi valley remained largely an Indian-defined and Indian-controlled place through the end of the eighteenth century.[2]

Native peoples chose how to deal with and interpret the new dangers and opportunities that resulted from foreign incursions. Most Mississippi valley people's priorities did not center on Europeans. To Indians, who constituted the vast majority of Louisiana's population, Indian rivalries, alliances, military strategies, trade networks, and ways of conducting foreign relations generally bore more relevance than Europeans. Indians sought European alliances and trade in order to gain an advantage in their rivalries with other Indians or to draw Indians into alliance by offering desired goods. Even most of the colonial population operated with little regard for French colonial interests. Seeking converts and trading partners, priests and traders focused on Indians. Runaway slaves and deserting soldiers by definition worked against the colonial establishment.

All people living in the place that Europeans called colonial Louisiana found themselves entangled in foreign relations. Any of them could have complained of their inability to do anything "by ourselves." But the ambitions of the colonial project made the French particularly dependent on others. Because they wanted a colony to rival the Spanish and English and because they sought to rule Louisiana despite lacking a large army, they had to pay attention to Indian priorities. Of the scores of diverse and intertwined peoples who populated Louisiana, the French proved one of the least independent and least successful in manipulating others.

The roots of eighteenth-century alliances and rivalries lie in the Mississippi period. Beginning around AD 800, independent groups built ceremonial centers, where they conducted planting and harvest rituals and festivals. Some provided a place for mutual defense or storing and protecting food. Eventually thousands of people settled in or near towns that rose and fell in the Mississippi valley and the Southeast, including (in the names used today) Moundville in northwestern Alabama, Etowah in the foothills of the Appalachians, Cahokia across the Mississippi from present St. Louis, and Spiro on the Arkansas River near the state border of Oklahoma and Arkansas. While centralized societies had existed previously in North America, the Mississippian chiefdoms were unprecedented in number and density. Over the centuries some chiefdoms fell and others took their places. Until the American Revolution no population centers north of Mexico would approach these towns in size or centralization.[3]

Between the mid-1500s and the mid-1600s centralized Mississippian towns ceased to exist, probably because of some combination of factors—climate change, depleted fields, drought, floods, warfare, and European diseases. Before 1492 smallpox, measles, mumps, rubella, diphtheria, whooping cough, chicken pox, influenza, malaria, typhoid fever, cholera, pneumonia, yellow fever, and scarlet fever were unknown in the Americas, and American Indians had not developed resistance to them.[4] Beginning with Spanish exploration and settlement, waves of epidemics spread across North America, directly from Europeans and through native trading networks.[5]

In response some Mississippian peoples disbanded entirely. Others adapted their social and political structures to new circumstances, many moving or combining with other peoples.[6] Choctaw origin histories suggest that some of their ancestors lived in the Mississippian chiefdom of Moundville. After 1500 they abandoned Moundville, founded dispersed settlements in what is now the state of Mississippi, and merged with allied chiefdoms and others from surrounding areas. The clear regional and ethnic divisions that remained within the Choctaw nation in the eighteenth century and beyond represented vestiges of these earlier mergings.[7] The Natchez probably changed the least. Although their territory contracted and some of their districts combined, they continued to build mounds and retained their chiefdom's hierarchical class structure with a powerful nobility and a great chief. They adopted neighboring peoples whose chiefdoms had suffered more devastating change, but it appears that, unlike the looser and more equitable affiliating of Choctaw ancestors, the Natchez incorporated others as subordinates in their society.[8]

The seventeenth century also saw the arrival of new Indian peoples, including the Osages and Quapaws. Their oral histories and tales to early European explorers suggest that they moved west from the Ohio River valley across the Mississippi River, perhaps fleeing Iroquoian-speakers armed with Dutch weapons. In turn, newcomers altered the dynamics of the Mississippi valley. The Quapaws probably drove some former Mississippians south of the Arkansas River, and the Osages established themselves as a powerful new presence below the Missouri River.[9] Counterattacks and ill will from these intrusions lingered into the eighteenth century.

The fall of the Mississippian chiefdoms changed diplomacy in the region. Chiefs or their representatives had generally negotiated Mississippian foreign relations, but it appears that Mississippian decline led some people to distrust concentrated power. Authority both within societies and over foreign relations spread more broadly across most populations. Probably building on earlier customs in which chiefs provided hospitality and gifts to visiting dignitaries, reciprocity became the central component in foreign relations.[10] By the late seventeenth century, most North American Indians saw reciprocal gift-giving and marital or fictive kinship ties as the means to establish and maintain good relations between peoples.[11] When the French arrived, Indians greeted them with the same ceremonies they used to transform any foreigners into friends and allies—calumet (peace pipe) dances and songs, speeches of welcome, and feasts to demonstrate generosity and friendship.[12]

Indians courted the French because the French had something that Indians wanted. Facing threats from others newly armed with Spanish and English weapons, Indians throughout the Mississippi valley needed French guns and ammunition. By 1700 Chickasaw bands were raiding old enemies, and making new ones, to acquire slaves to trade to the English at Charlestown for guns, ammunition, and horses.[13] In the northeast, Iroquoian peoples monopolized Dutch and British trade and regularly attacked Illinois Indians and others east of the Mississippi. In the west, Apache and Comanche bands soon blocked Spanish trade.

Mississippi valley Indians who hoped to attract French trade used established diplomatic methods to recruit the French. For example, in 1680 Quapaw, Osage, and Chickasaw delegates came together to the new French mission at Kaskaskia. There they presented deerskins and other hides to the Frenchmen, told the French that the Mississippi was navigable to the Gulf of Mexico, and invited them to come to their towns to "dance the Calumet of peace" and establish trade relations.[14] These delegates hoped to use the French to serve their own purposes in relations with other Indians. Not only would French trade strengthen each of the three peoples, but their coming together also suggests that they hoped French goods would lessen the Chickasaws' English trade and thus reduce Chickasaw slave raids, which often victimized the Quapaws. Because goods distribution within Indian societies could enhance a person's prestige, the delegates may also have sought to enhance their individual influence within their own communities.

To the south, other Indians also sought French assistance to counter the Chickasaw-English trade. In May of 1700 Tohome and Mobilian chiefs traveled to the new French capital on Biloxi Bay to request a trade alliance. They offered provisions, which the governor of Louisiana, Pierre Le Moyne d'Iberville, desperately needed. In return the Tohomes and Mobilians solicited assistance against enemy attacks. They "passionately" urged the French to move closer to them, explaining that a Spanish delegation had visited them from the new post at Pensacola several months earlier but had not re-

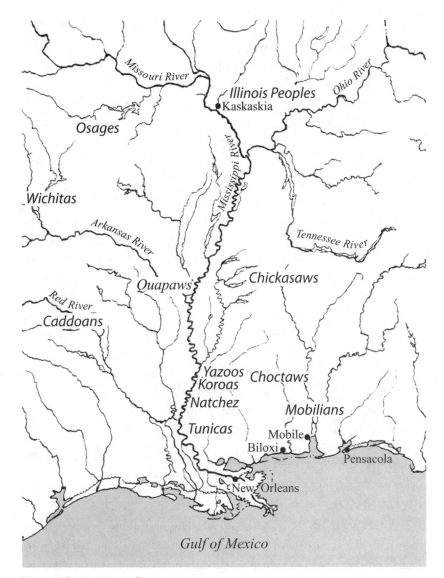

Figure 1. The Mississippi valley.

turned. The Tohomes and Mobilians succeeded. Knowing that his weak numbers would require Indian allies and supplies (and eager to move in before the Spanish did), Governor Iberville established a new French capital at Mobile.[15]

In the eighteenth century, Indians farther west sought French trade to compete with Spanish-armed rivals and Indians such as the Osages who established trade with the French earlier. In 1719 people living on the Arkansas River, probably in what is now Oklahoma, heard that a French party was approaching. By the time it drew near several thousand Tawakonis, Taovayas, Guichitas, and Iscanis (mostly ancestors of the Wichita or Kitikitish confederacy) had assembled at a Tawakoni town, with speeches prepared. The chiefs told the expedition's leader, Jean-Baptiste Bénard de La Harpe, that all the peoples of the middle Arkansas wished to ally with the French, who "would bring weapons for them to defend themselves against their enemies." In return, they promised horses, bison robes, salt, tobacco, various metals and stones, and slaves. One chief whispered to La Harpe that they also had "yellow iron," which "the Spanish value very highly."[16]

Despite their immediate popularity, the French were one of the weakest groups in a land full of people struggling to strengthen their positions in the wake of sixteenth-century change. Although colonial officials regularly requested more soldiers and arms to "intimidate the Indians," tight budgets, desertions, and recurrent French war against other European nations kept Louisiana's forces small and unstable. At times, fewer than two hundred soldiers were assigned to the entire colony, on both sides of the Mississippi. In the mid-1720s Louisiana had some 2,500 French, plus 1,500 slaves. In contrast, Louisiana Indians numbered well over 35,000. While many Indian groups were tiny, the Choctaws, Chickasaws, Natchez, Osages, and Caddoans all had populations greater than the French, and many others rivaled the French population.[17] No one people had the power to rule the others, and all found themselves entangled in webs of foreign relations and obligations.

Size was not everything. Although the largest group, Choctaws found that regional and ethnic loyalties often outweighed national interests. Some smaller groups such as the Quapaws used their relative unity to wield an influence beyond their numbers. Even more fragmented than the Choctaws, the French arrived in North America as diverse people with various goals and methods, which only occasionally combined into serving the colonial project. French men and women came to the region for many reasons besides the advancement of the colony—converting Indians to Christianity, making individual profits, escaping trouble at home, and forced removal from the streets of Paris and Marseilles.

The presence of powerful native peoples weakened French officials' control over the colonial population by broadening opportunities. The *voyageurs* (independent traders) who traversed the land held more allegiance to their own interests and often to their Indian trading partners than they did to French officials, as the French hierarchy was well aware. Etienne de Périer, Louisiana governor in 1729, petitioned his superior to strengthen the Louisiana government in order to "subdue the inhabitants of this area who are just *voyageurs* and *coureurs de bois* who work that trade only because they want to be their own masters and who would easily withdraw from their obedience to the King if we were not prepared to repress them."[18] Like the Chickasaws at Kaskaskia, these Frenchmen sought trade from multiple sources, which could help them "be their own masters." Even French soldiers did not always serve colonial interests. Desertion was a constant problem as the fur trade lured scores of soldiers away from the dangers and deprivations of the colonial army.[19] The Quapaws recruited French deserters to settle nearby in order to strengthen their own numbers on a contested Indian borderland. At times the Quapaws successfully protected and incorporated runaway slaves and soldiers accused of treason, desertion, and even murder.[20]

The extreme fragmentation of the colonial population put the French in a unique position. In some ways being fragmented made them more influential because they spread across the countryside, encountering a wider variety of people than most Indians met and offering goods that native peoples wanted. But being fragmented also meant that the French were more influenced by native peoples than they might otherwise have been. Various French people's goals and methods often conflicted, and their decentralized nature attenuated them, giving more centralized, established, and knowledgeable people opportunities to influence the newcomers. French officials quickly learned that their low numbers and fragmentation precluded dominating Indians.

In fact, Indian power and French weakness forced the French to do the opposite—attempt to persuade Indians to fight French battles. But more often than not French officials found themselves conducting foreign policy according to their Indian allies' interests. In 1730 Périer informed his superiors that using Indian allies was the least efficient way to run the colony. As he explained, he had to spend so much on gifts to allies that "it will cost the Company more to make the Indians act when they are needed" than to support the same number of troops. To make matters worse for the governor, paying Indians by no means guaranteed that they would do his bidding. As Périer put it, "the least little nation thinks itself our protector" and "that we use them only because we are not capable of making war"—which of course was true.[21] Indians knew how much the French depended on them.

How various Indians used this knowledge depended on their own history, their beliefs about themselves and the world, their current relations with neighbors, what they needed or wanted from Europeans, as well as what kind and how many Europeans they met and how often. As the French attempted to make Indians serve colonial purposes, Indians worked to shape the French into useful allies and neighbors. All Indian allies demanded French compliance with the dictates of reciprocity. As early as 1717, the Commissary General of Louisiana, Marc Antoine Hubert, could report that "all the chiefs of the Indians, even those remote from these posts," regularly traveled "to see the commandants, with the expectation of receiving some presents." Within the rubric of reciprocity, these gifts served as the obligation of those wealthy in exotic goods but short on practicalities to those able to provide guides, interpreters, warriors, food, and land. Often in fact short on goods, French officials thought of these demands as tribute. When Jean Michele de L'Epinay arrived in March of 1717 to take his place as governor he had to spend more than two months hosting calumet ceremonies from two dozen nations, including the Mobilians, Tohomes, Choctaws, Natchez, Tunicas, and Chickasaws, of course giving presents to all. Nonetheless, according to Hubert, many Indians considered Governor L'Epinay stingier than his predecessor, calling him "an old mangy dog."[22]

French officials had no choice but to comply. There was no other way to counter the English and Spanish. In fact, Indians' desire for French weapons to counter enemies armed by Spanish and especially English trade harmonized with French imperial objectives.[23] French-Indian negotiations developed a standard vocabulary that drew on the presence of other Europeans. Indians complained of attacks by European-armed foes, and French officials promised not only weapons but also a friendship more in line with Indian ideals of reciprocity and obligation than other Europeans would provide.

For example, when a delegation of seven Chickasaws and four Choctaws arrived at Mobile in March of 1702, Governor Iberville quickly prepared a generous gift—each delegate received 200 pounds of gunpowder, 200 pounds of bullets, 200 pounds of game-shot, 12 guns, 100 axes, 150 knives, and several kettles, glass beads, and gun flints. Knowing well the Chickasaws' advantageous trade with Charlestown, the governor had his anti-English speech prepared. He declared that the French desired for all Indians to live in peace and prosperity, whereas the English were inciting the Chickasaws to make war on the Choctaws so that the English could profit from the slave trade. Iberville accused the English of false friendship, saying that they would sell Chickasaws as slaves too, if they had the chance, because they cared only for profit.

Iberville portrayed the English as deviants in a world governed by Indian epistemologies, while the French were true friends, bound by local rules and relationships. Rather than inciting Indian wars and seeking Indian slaves, he declared, "skins of buffalo, deer, and bear—those are the slaves I want. . . . To get them will not cost you your lives." Still, the French were not all goodness and light either. If the Chickasaws continued to trade with the English, Iberville warned, "the French and you cannot be friends with one another, and I shall engage in no trading with you" and instead would arm the Choctaws, Mobilians, Tohomes, Natchez, Illinois, and other allies against the Chickasaws. As violent as the threat was, it complied with his listeners' notions of friendship. Allies had obligations, but if the Chickasaws chose to be the enemies of the French and their allies, attacks against them were not unreasonable.[24] The English used similar tactics, repeatedly telling the Chickasaws that the French only pretended to be true friends but in reality planned to destroy the Chickasaws and other Indians so that they could have Louisiana to themselves.[25]

Native peoples in turn used their knowledge of European rivalries to instruct Europeans in how they should act. Louisiana Indians sought trade with as many Europeans as possible, and most traded at least sporadically with the English from at least 1700.[26] Despite French, English, and Spanish admonitions that trading relationships were exclusive to one European power, their Indian partners did not agree. In 1745 Quapaw leaders warned their local commandant that if supplies did not improve they would "see the English again." They knew that mentioning the English would always agitate the French official, who quickly wrote to the governor requesting more merchandise.[27]

At times people used an alliance with one nation to attract others. The Choctaw delegates who met Iberville in 1702 surely hoped to use French trade to draw their troublesome Chickasaw neighbors into a peaceful alliance, as the Quapaws and Osages had unsuccessfully attempted at Kaskaskia twenty years before. Chickasaw and Creek raids were enslaving and killing thousands of Choctaws. The same month, other Choctaws and Chickasaws were using French officer Henri de Tonti as a mediator. Similarly the Chickasaws used English trade goods to entice Indians into trading relations.[28]

Events surrounding the Natchez war, which began in 1729, illuminate this unstable world of alliances and rivalries. Triggered by Natchez-French conflict, war spread through the complicated alliances of the Mississippi valley. Natchez-French relations began with mixed messages. In 1682 the Natchez initially received the Sieur de La Salle and his entourage well, but farther down the Mississippi La Salle's men skirmished with some Quinipissas. By the time the French party made its way back upstream, the Natchez had learned of the battle. Whether alarmed by French ferocity, sympathetic to the Quinipissas, aiming to keep the grain supplies that the French had stored at Natchez, or simply angling for battle, some 1,500 armed Natchez warriors assembled to meet the French. After seeing this display and receiving a warning from the chief, the French wisely hurried on their way.[29]

By the next French visit Natchez advocates of French usefulness appear to have prevailed. In 1700 they hosted Iberville with a three-day calumet peace ceremony and feasting, and they agreed to his proposal to send a French boy to live with them and learn their language. Indeed, André Pénicaut, who visited the Natchez again in 1704, called them "the most courteous and civil along the banks of the Missicipy." By the next decade, they had established steady French trade, exchanging food and hides for guns, powder, lead, cloth, and brandy. However, like most of their neighbors, they also found ways of acquiring English goods. In 1713 fifteen Choctaws escorted several English traders and a Welch trader to the Natchez and Tunicas. To acquire slaves to sell, a party of Natchez, Yazoos, and Chickasaws immediately set off to raid the Chaouachas, a smaller nation to the south.[30]

In coming years, distrust mounted between Natchez and French leaders, as each attempted to dominate the other. To the Natchez allowing French settlements made these French into subordinates, like previous Indian set-

tlers. When French traders and officials proved less pliable than the Natchez expected, some began to consider that pillaging French goods and recruiting English trade might be a more reliable way to maintain Natchez
security than continuing this unstable and unpredictable relationship. As
Tattooed Serpent, a military leader and brother of the Great Sun Chief, explained to settler Antoine Simon Le Page du Pratz, "before the arrival of
the French, we lived like men who can be satisfied with what they have."
The Natchez had found French goods tantalizingly useful but perhaps more
trouble than they were worth.[31]

On several occasions beginning in the 1710s Natchez killed and raided
French parties when they violated Natchez propriety. In the 1720s the Natchez's White Apple village found itself at the center of conflict. In the winter of 1723 a dispute over debt led to the death of one of that village's men.
When the French commandant only reprimanded the murderer, warriors
from the White Apple village attacked nearby French settlements. Only the
careful diplomacy of Tattooed Serpent restored peace between the village
and the French, as he had in the past. Despite the renewed and formalized
peace, Louisiana Lieutenant Governor Jean-Baptiste Le Moyne, Sieur de Bienville, led an army the following winter to punish the White Apple village.
Pressured by French violence and probably the insistence of other villages,
the White Apple village surrendered the chief whom Bienville demanded as
recompense for the previous winter's violence. In the peace terms the Natchez agreed to build a fort on their lands that the French would staff and
supply, granting the Natchez steadier access to trade and a means for settling future disputes with French traders and settlers.[32]

Still, anger lingered over Bienville's flouting of the previous peace. Tattooed Serpent asked Le Page du Pratz, "Have the French two hearts, a good
one to-day and to-morrow a bad one?" As Natchez distrust grew, they discussed with their neighbors how to handle the French. As early as 1714 three
Natchez traveled to the Tunicas to encourage them to pillage the French
and increase trade with the English, who gave better prices. The Tunicas
refused the advice and told the French of Natchez overtures, undermining
the already deteriorating Natchez-French relationship.[33]

Despite the tension more French settlers came to farm tobacco on Natchez
lands. In the 1720s these settlements grew to 200 Frenchmen, 80 French-
women, 150 French children, and 280 black slaves. Although the Natchez

had originally welcomed settlers, they seemed to be growing out of Natchez control. Indeed, in the 1723 conflict White Apple village warriors had attacked the symbols of French settlements, livestock and slaves, as well as the settlers themselves. Although the Natchez had assigned the previous land grants, in late November of 1729, the commandant of the French post, the Sieur de Chépart, ordered the White Apple village to evacuate so that French settlers could farm their land.[34]

More accustomed to giving than taking orders, the Natchez decided to get rid of these interlopers once and for all. At the urging of the White Apple village's chiefs, the Natchez again sent representatives to meet with potential allies, including Yazoos, Koroas, Illinois, Chickasaws, and Choctaws.[35] Changing tactics this time, they also reached out to African slaves held on the plantations near Natchez. According to a later report, the Natchez invited all slaves to join the Natchez side and thereby gain their freedom. But they warned that those who refused would be sold to the Chickasaws and the English when the Natchez prevailed.[36] At eight in the morning of November 28, Natchez warriors knocked at the door of each French house and asked to borrow guns for a hunting expedition. Then they turned the guns on their owners, killing nearly all the Frenchmen, including the commandant and the Jesuit priest. The Natchez captured the slaves and most of the French women and children and burned the houses and sheds, destroying thousands of pounds of tobacco. Thus they cast out the disrespectful newcomers who would not play by Natchez rules.[37]

The Natchez attack decisively placed the French on the opposite side of this conflict. But lining up the sides did not determine how the French should react. Many desired vengeance, but fear was the dominant reaction among the French population. As Governor Périer reported in 1730 of his colonists, "the least rumor makes them rush to the woods like hares."[38] Local Indians stoked these fears with reports that the powerful Chickasaws and Choctaws had joined the conspiracy and were going to kill all the French throughout the colony.[39] With frightened and outnumbered colonists, French officials knew that they would have to persuade their allies to reject Natchez overtures and instead assist the French in getting revenge.

The crisis of 1729 brought alliances into the open, forcing people who preferred to cultivate friendship broadly now to choose sides. In the conflict all Natchez neighbors felt pulled by the demands of allies, and all attempted to enforce their own notions of alliance obligations on others. Generally having the least power, Africans took opportunities when they came. Slaves at Natchez did not kill any French that November, but some apparently joined the Natchez defense later. In January of 1730 captured slaves fought off a Choctaw attack long enough to allow the Natchez to regroup within their forts. More often, Africans' wartime opportunities came in fighting for the French or laboring for the French military. Although officials feared armed slaves, they continued to use them (in small numbers) because, as Governor Périer put it, slaves seemed to fight considerably better than the French soldiers, "who seem expressly made for Louisiana, they are so bad." In addition, Périer hoped that pitting slaves against native enemies would prevent Indian-African collaboration.[40]

Most Indians' reactions to the crisis depended more on relationships with other Indians than with Europeans. The Yazoos and Koroas agreed to join the Natchez effort. Their familial and alliance ties to the Natchez and the devastation they had experienced from European disease joined to pull their loyalties to the Natchez side.[41] Following the Natchez example the Yazoos and Koroas killed their Jesuit missionary, the French who were in their post, and several ill-fated traders who happened to pass along the Mississippi. Koroa women, who apparently had the authority to determine the fate of captives, decreed that five French women and four children be taken to the Chickasaws and sold rather than killed.[42] With their decision to attack the French in November of 1729, the Yazoos and Koroas found their destinies linked with the Natchez.[43]

The Quapaws' choice was as clear as the Yazoos' and Koroas'. Since the Quapaws' move west, they had resisted these Mississippian descendants, who contested the Quapaws' right to settle on the Mississippi River. The Quapaws eagerly joined the fight against their enemies, declaring that "while there was an [Quapaw] in the world, the Natchez and the Yazoos would not be without an enemy."[44] Throughout the 1730s they conducted successful raids against the Natchez, Yazoos, and Koroas.[45] Rather than fighting *for* the French, as historians often describe Indian-European military alliances, the Quapaws were delighted to have an agitated ally who would provide troops, supplies, and encouragement.

The Quapaws' good relations with the French also contributed to their decision. In contrast to the Natchez the Quapaws built a strong friendship with their French neighbors. One reason was the smaller numbers of French—fewer than fifty—living in their midst.[46] And these French and the Quapaws both had reasons to be more adaptable than did their French and Natchez counterparts. Not only outnumbered in a strange land hundreds of miles from Louisiana's French capital, non-Indians on the Arkansas also had not come as settlers determined to build plantations. They were voyageurs, *engagés* (indentured servants) freed and stranded by John Law's 1720 financial debacle, and deserters. For the Quapaws' part, their status as newcomers on a contested land seems to have given them a flexibility that the long-powerful Natchez chiefs lacked as well as a greater desire to get along with the most recent newcomers. The French farmed fields and lived in a town surrounded by Quapaw fields and towns, and under their supervision. The French settlers provided mutual protection in a dangerous place and traded furs, food, and other material goods. Their needs coincided with those of the Quapaws, and Quapaw rituals transformed neighbors into family. Having successfully incorporated French men and women, largely on local terms, the Quapaws seized the opportunity to ally with the French against old enemies.[47]

Although not enemies of the Natchez, Yazoos, or Koroas, the Choctaws had no particular affinity for them and hoped to profit from the captives, spoils, and French supplies that would come from the war. French officials very much hoped to have this powerful people on their side, whose participation would be infinitely more valuable than the Louisiana army. In January of 1730, French soldiers established a siege on Natchez. But when the Natchez charged out of the fort to fight, the French soldiers fled "without firing a single shot," as Governor Périer despondently informed his superior. To the governor's and the Natchez's surprise, five hundred Choctaws attacked Natchez two days later. In the battle, they killed at least one hundred Natchez and recovered fifty French women and children and between fifty and one hundred African slaves. The French governor's delight was dimmed a bit by a rumor that the Choctaws had attacked rapidly because they wanted to retrieve the captives before the French or any other Indians got to them.

When the French politely asked for the captives' return, the Choctaws demanded ransoms for each, in part to make up for the hunting their warriors had forfeited in order to fight. They declared their willingness to sell the African captives to the English if they gave better prices. The French claim that the slaves belonged to them carried little weight. The Choctaws considered them justly acquired in battle. While the French might have a claim to the return of their families, they had held the Africans in bondage and had no right to prevent the Choctaws or English from doing the same. Alibamon Mingo, a Choctaw chief from the town of Concha, listed the price for each black slave: "a coat, a gun, a white blanket, four ells of limburg cloth," plus presents for each town and for individual chiefs. One Choctaw chief told French officer Régis du Roullet that his men were keeping the slaves that they had captured to serve them and that "the French ought to be content with those who had been returned to them." Without Choctaw assistance, the chief pointed out, the French "would have got nothing at all" because they "did not have enough courage to take them."[48]

The Tunicas' history with the Natchez made them more ambivalent than the Yazoos, Koroas, Quapaws, or Choctaws. They apparently had allied with the Natchez in the past, but conflict had erupted in 1723 when Tunicas killed three Natchez.[49] In early 1730 the Tunicas swore to fight the Natchez and their allies. They scouted for the French, although it is not clear that they actually engaged in battle.[50] Whatever their earlier designs, in June of 1730 the Tunicas made a mistake. One hundred Natchez men plus women and children who had fled after the Choctaw attack sought refuge among the Tunicas. They asked for Tunica mediation to make peace with the French. Whether sincerely or in hopes of capturing the Natchez to deliver to the French, the Tunicas invited the Natchez refugees to settle among them. When the Tunicas asked the Natchez men to hand over their arms, the men answered that they wanted to but they needed to hold onto them "to reassure their wives," who were naturally apprehensive about entering the town of their former enemy. Acceding to the sensibility of the women's fear, the Tunicas hosted the Natchez with a calumet ceremony and feast that lasted well into the night. After the Tunicas went to sleep, the Natchez guests killed twenty of them and drove off the rest long enough to escape with the Tunicas' guns and ammunition, of which they had a large supply due to recent French recruitment.[51] This betrayal placed the Tunicas firmly on the anti-Natchez side. They routed Natchez refugees along both sides of the Mississippi through the early 1740s, demanding provisions and armaments from the French to supply their missions.[52]

According to one account the Natchez were assisted at the Tunicas by
Koroa and Chickasaw warriors who had hidden outside the town during
the feasting.[53] Traditionally allies of the Natchez, Yazoos, and Koroas, the
Chickasaws at first hoped to play both sides in the conflict. The French had
failed to defeat them in the "First Chickasaw War" of the early 1720s, but
most Chickasaws seemed to prefer neutrality to overt war. They apparently
knew of Natchez plans in 1729 but did not join in the violence. However,
when refugees from the three nations sought protection in Chickasaw country after the Choctaws drove them from their homes in early 1730, the Chickasaws could not remain neutral.[54] The demands and plight of the Natchez
pulled the Chickasaws toward war. In the summer of 1730 they sent emissaries to the Quapaws, Choctaws, Cherokees, Miamis, and several Illinois
peoples proposing that they all join against the French with the Natchez,
Yazoos, and Koroas, armed with English weapons supplied by the Chickasaws. Apparently at least one former French slave who had been captured
by the Natchez simultaneously traveled to New Orleans to tell slaves that
"they would get their liberty" if they revolted against the French.[55]

By early 1731, after some debate, the Chickasaws escorted Natchez refugees onto Chickasaw lands, allowing them to settle near their clustered towns
to act as a barrier from Choctaw raids.[56] Although Chickasaw-Natchez relations would occasionally become strained, the Chickasaws generally fulfilled their alliance obligations. When Governor Périer demanded that the
Chickasaws surrender these refugees, the Chickasaws answered that they
"had not gone to get them in order to hand them over."[57] As they committed themselves to the Natchez coalition in the 1730s the Chickasaws continued to attempt to recruit the Choctaws, Tunicas, and Quapaws, and the
French determined to pursue a second Chickasaw war.[58]

Despite occasional disagreements the French, Choctaws, Quapaws, and
Tunicas generally agreed to fight the Natchez, Yazoos, and Koroas. When
the French attempted to include the Chickasaws among the war's targets,
the allies proved less united. Not all French officials agreed on the wisdom of
fighting the Chickasaws. Mobile Commandant Diron d'Artaguette warned
that the Chickasaws were strong enough to "bar the Mississippi to us for
more than one hundred leagues."[59] But Governor Périer determined "to destroy them without fail."[60] Not all French defined their interests in line with
those of colonial decision-makers. In 1736 Bienville discovered an apparent

plot by four French and Swiss soldiers at Fort Tombecbé to kill the rest of the garrison and seek refuge with the Chickasaws and English.[61]

Fighting the Natchez fit Quapaw, Tunica, and Choctaw alliance obligations as well as interests. Not only were the Natchez old aggressors, their attacks on the French and the Tunicas did seem to break the rules. Even a Chickasaw chief reportedly told a Natchez delegation in 1730 that the French had a right to defend themselves and avenge the killings at the Natchez post.[62] For most Indians, fighting Chickasaws was harder to justify. While often enemies of the Quapaws and Choctaws, their main offense here was harboring fugitives.[63] More importantly, the Chickasaws were more populous and better armed, and starting a war against them would decisively cut off the English trade that they brokered.

Much of the debate surrounded the nature of alliance. To all, alliances entailed obligations, within limits. As Patricia Galloway has demonstrated, Europeans and Indians often interpreted one another's vocabularies and symbols of alliance differently, a misinterpretation useful in first encounters but that could cause difficulties in determining responsibilities in times of crisis.[64] Reciprocal by nature, the alliances were under no one people's control. Having the same enemy did not necessarily make two peoples into allies. In the spring of 1734, 150 Quapaws going to fight the Natchez came across a band of Tunicas on the same mission. They instead began to argue, reviving their old animosity. Just before their warriors came to blows the Tunicas turned home, and the Quapaws did the same, both abandoning their war plans.[65] At least out in the field their old rivalry trumped their opposition to common enemies and their common alliance with the French. French officials instructed their allies to destroy the Chickasaws, but the Quapaws, Tunicas, and Choctaws fought according to their own methods and goals.

Choctaws had varying reactions to this French-Chickasaw war. The divided nature of the Choctaw polity meant that different divisions maintained ties with different neighbors, and the Choctaw western towns had in recent years found themselves drawn into Chickasaw offers of trade.[66] The history of Chickasaw and English violence against the Choctaws proved a vivid enough memory to prevent the Choctaws from joining the Chickasaws' coalition, but a unified anti-Chickasaw policy proved elusive.[67] In 1734, Choctaw chiefs sent word to Bienville that they might go against the

Chickasaws if provided with the necessary munitions. In response, Bienville sent 1,000 pounds of powder, 2,000 pounds of bullets, 20 guns, and several pounds of red war paint. But after receiving these supplies, the Choctaws said they were unwilling to fight alone. They requested 100 French soldiers. Bienville sent 15 men—all he thought he could spare from New Orleans's defenses. The Choctaws called this effort "very feeble." When the governor sent 15 more, 1,000 Choctaw men marched with them toward the Chickasaws.

But the party fell apart when it began to plan its attack. Thirty leagues from the Chickasaw towns, many Choctaws began to argue that they should not attack the Chickasaws directly but rather should pretend to make peace and have the warriors surreptitiously attack the towns while the chiefs were at the negotiation. Then other Choctaws suggested sincerely making peace, a plan that to many sounded even safer. One speaker proposed that, if "the English sell goods as cheaply as they are offering them, why should we refuse these advantages? Could we not[,] without offending the French[,] trade with both?" With the thirty French soldiers helpless to lead the party, the Choctaws decided not to fight and instead to send an embassy to a place where they had heard there might be English traders.[68]

On other occasions French-Choctaw war parties split over strategy, and Choctaw reasoning generally prevailed.[69] In contrast to their essential and decisive participation in the Natchez war, Choctaw warriors preferred small skirmishes intended to obtain spoils but not alienate English traders or Choctaws opposed to the war.[70] For example, in the 1730s, Red Shoe, who had trading and familial ties with certain Chickasaw towns, raided other Chickasaw towns in the late fall or early spring, just in time to reap rewards at the annual French present ceremonies, while trading with the English throughout much of the year.[71]

Tensions over alliance methods heightened when the French attempted to assemble their allies to defeat the Chickasaws in one decisive conflict. The war party was to include 1,000 French soldiers led by Bienville, more than 300 African slaves, Choctaws, Quapaws, Indians and French civilians from the Illinois country, and an Iroquois contingent, which the Quapaws supposedly had recruited. At first the allies heartily backed such a decisive plan. In the fall of 1737 Quapaw guides led a French party to explore the route from the Mississippi to the Chickasaw towns. Quapaws and several parties of Illinois Indians helped to build forts on both sides of the Mississippi to house the coming troops and supplies for an assault in the fall of 1739. But Bienville repeatedly postponed the attack because of delays and lack of communication among New Orleans, the forces assembled on the Mississippi, the reinforcements supposedly coming from the Illinois country, and the promised Iroquois. In addition, French officials vacillated between including the Choctaws and keeping them out of the battle for fear they would demand high prices for their services.

Frustration mounted. For months the assembled warriors urged Bienville to commence the fight. But Bienville wanted everything to be ready first, including roads built to the Chickasaw towns for his heavy artillery. His war strategy must have seemed absurd to people who believed that the best military tactic was surprise attack. Building a road to the enemy's town certainly spoiled the surprise. French soldiers were no happier with the delay and exposure to potential Chickasaw assaults and grew more mutinous as provisions ran out and illness decreased their ranks. In January of 1740 a contingent of French soldiers, acting without orders, sent a message to the Chickasaws saying that, if they surrendered the Natchez refugees and cast out the English, the French would make peace. The Indian allies began to disband, and Bienville had to accept a Chickasaw peace plan, which lasted only long enough for the Chickasaws to ascertain that the war party had dispersed.[72]

When the peace proved short-lived and Chickasaws began to inflict heavy damage on French convoys, the Quapaws persuaded the French to accept an alternative war plan for protecting the Mississippi River. The Quapaws fought the Chickasaws when they wished, in parties of 30 to 50 warriors who could strike quickly and escape without major casualties.[73] The French contributed by paying the Quapaws for Chickasaw scalps. Nor did they interfere when Quapaw attacks occasionally hit the Choctaws. Louisiana's governor in the 1740s, Vaudreuil, told his superiors that he had "engaged" the Quapaws to raid the Chickasaws; however, it is clear that the Quapaws were now in charge of their effort and that their methods were more effective.[74]

In contrast, Choctaw unity dissolved as the war dragged on. Unable to remain neutral, Choctaws disagreed over their Chickasaw, English, and French policies, arguments that devolved into violent civil strife in the 1740s. Many historians have labeled the Choctaw divisions in this civil war as "pro-English" (usually the western towns) and "pro-French" (the eastern). But European relations were less central to Choctaw decision-making than these labels imply. The conflict centered on how Choctaws as a society would decide how to handle the demands and inducements of their neighbors, including the Chickasaws, English, French, and other nations.

By the 1740s many Choctaws had wearied of the Chickasaw war. If the French had met the Choctaws' pecuniary demands, they might have simply skirmished occasionally against the Chickasaws, as Red Shoe did in the 1730s and the Quapaws and Tunicas continued to do. But the persistent temptations of trade that the Chickasaws offered prompted some Choctaws to desire a Chickasaw alliance.[75] When rumors spread that the French were trading and allying with the Chickasaws behind Choctaw backs, many Choctaws felt they had been duped into depriving themselves of Chickasaw trade. These desires and grievances pulled against both the eastern Choctaw towns' continued reliance on French trade and the Choctaws' history of alliance with the French versus the Chickasaws and English. A movement arose to make a publicized peace with all. In 1738 Red Shoe declared in front of French and Chickasaw listeners, "I have made peace with the Chickasaws whom I regard as my brothers. For too long a time the French have been causing the blood of the Indians to be shed."[76] Over the next few years more Choctaws came to agree with Red Shoe, while others resolutely opposed him. In the 1740s violence escalated and became more chaotic as groups of Choctaws, French, and Chickasaws raided and counterraided one another, some Choctaws attacked English traders, and ultimately various Choctaw factions committed violence against one another.[77]

Old alliances and animosities had expanded the Natchez-French conflict into regional, and in one case civil, war. When the Natchez used extreme violence against the French invaders, they forced their neighbors to make choices, informed by their relations with others. Pushed by their allegiance to the Natchez and conflict with the French, Choctaws, and Quapaws, the Yazoos and Koroas supported the Natchez. By the summer of 1732 most of them were dead, enslaved and shipped to the Caribbean, or refugees among the Chickasaws, Creeks, and Cherokees.[78] While some African captives fought with the Natchez, most found themselves treated like booty, captured in Choctaw and Chickasaw raids and counterraids. At least twenty

returned to French slavery. Others were sold to the English or died in captivity, and a few escaped to build lives lost to the records.[79] The Natchez
war had repercussions for other Africans, too. Participation on the French
side resulted in permanent free black participation in Louisiana militia.[80]
And the Natchez war may have inspired an attempted slave revolt. In the
summer of 1731, French officials in New Orleans uncovered an apparent
plot to kill the masters returning from mass. Even if the French exaggerated the conspiracy, clearly some New Orleans men and women had considered following the Natchez example, or at least taking advantage of the
troops' preoccupation to the north, and some were executed for the possibility.[81] The Choctaws, Tunicas, and Quapaws sought moderate policies,
which led the Tunicas to expose themselves to Natchez deception and the
Choctaws to internal discord. Still, all remained influential groups into
the nineteenth century and beyond. Despite their decision to support the
Natchez, so too did the Chickasaws, whom the French by no means succeeded in destroying.

Europeans and Africans carved out what spaces they could in this native
world. Rather than being colonized, Indians drew these newcomers into local alliances, rivalries, and ways of conducting diplomacy, trade, and war,
which held sway even as they adapted to changing circumstances. By mold-
ing colonialism to fit Indian desires and demands, French officials maintained a presence in Louisiana for nearly a century, but the colonial project
of extracting natural resources for profit failed, and Louisiana's economy
remained more Indian than colonial.[82] This is not to say that any particular
Indians ruled Louisiana, or that their world did not change. Rather, groups
and individuals used Europeans and Africans to forward their own priorities in the intricate and changing relationships of the Mississippi valley.

Acknowledgments

The author thanks Patricia Galloway, Gregory Waselkov, and Peter Wood
for their comments on this chapter. This research was funded in part by
grants from the Andrew W. Mellon Foundation through the McNeil Center for Early American Studies, The Huntington Library, and The Newberry Library.

Notes

1. Vaudreuil to Rouillé, February 1, 1750, LO 203, box 5, Vaudreuil Papers, Loudoun Collection, Huntington Library, San Marino, California. Translations throughout are mine unless an English-language edition is noted.

2. Most histories of the colonial Mississippi valley have focused on the French imperial narrative. See, for example, W. J. Eccles, *The French in North America, 1500–1765* (East Lansing: Michigan State University Press, 1998); Norman Ward Caldwell, *The French in the Mississippi Valley, 1740–1750* (Urbana: University of Illinois Press, 1941). Even historians whose interests also lie in other narratives tend to emphasize how the French changed native economies and ways of living on the land, even if they were not as effective as later colonizers would be. See, for example, Richard White, *The Roots of Dependency: Subsistence, Environment, and Social Change among the Choctaws, Pawnees, and Navajos* (Lincoln: University of Nebraska Press, 1983).

3. Bruce D. Smith, "The Archaeology of the Southeastern United States: From Dalton to De Soto, 10,500–500 BP," *Advances in World Archaeology* 5 (1986): 1–92; Brian M. Fagan, *Ancient North America: The Archaeology of a Continent*, 3rd ed. (London: Thames and Hudson, 2000), 439–68; Lynda Norene Shaffer, *Native Americans before 1492: The Moundbuilding Centers of the Eastern Woodlands* (Armonk NY: M. E. Sharpe, 1992).

4. Alfred W. Crosby, *Ecological Imperialism: The Biological Expansion of Europe, 900–1900* (New York: Cambridge University Press, 1986), 197–201.

5. Barbara A. Burnett and Katherine A. Murray, "Death, Drought, and de Soto: The Bioarcheology of Depopulation," in *The Expedition of Hernando de Soto West of the Mississippi, 1541–1543: Proceedings of the De Soto Symposia 1988 and 1990*, ed. Gloria A. Young and Michael P. Hoffman (Fayetteville: University of Arkansas Press, 1993), 232–35; Ann F. Ramenofsky and Patricia Galloway, "Disease and the Soto Entrada," in *The Hernando de Soto Expedition: History, Historiography, and "Discovery" in the Southeast*, ed. Patricia Galloway (Lincoln: University of Nebraska Press, 1997), 259–79; Elizabeth A. H. John, *Storms Brewed in Other Men's Worlds: The Confrontation of Indians, Spanish, and French in the Southwest, 1540–1795*, 2nd ed. (Norman: University of Oklahoma Press, 1996), 38–39, 63, 83, 86, 134; James F. Brooks, *Captives and Cousins: Slavery, Kinship, and Community in the Southwest Borderlands* (Chapel Hill: University of North Carolina Press for the Omohundro Institute of Early American History and Culture, 2002), 49–50; John L. Kessell, *Spain in the Southwest: A Narrative History of Colonial New Mexico, Arizona, Texas, and California* (Norman: University of Oklahoma Press, 2002), 159, 167, 297; Crosby, *Ecological Imperialism*, 266; Alfred W. Crosby, "Virgin Soil Epidemics as a Factor in the Aboriginal Depopulation in America," *William and Mary Quarterly* 33 (April 1976): 290.

6. See, for example, Daniel K. Richter, *Facing East from Indian Country: A Native History of Early America* (Cambridge MA: Harvard University Press, 2001), 34–39; Tristram R. Kidder, "Excavations at the Jordan Site (16MO1), Morehouse Parish, Louisiana," *Southeastern Archaeology* 11 (Winter 1992): 109–31.

7. Patricia Galloway, *Choctaw Genesis, 1500–1700* (Lincoln: University of Nebraska Press,

1995); Greg O'Brien, *Choctaws in a Revolutionary Age, 1750–1830* (Lincoln: University of Nebraska Press, 2002), 12–20; Clara Sue Kidwell, "Choctaw," in *Encyclopedia of North American Indians*, ed. Frederick Hoxie (Boston: Houghton Mifflin, 1996), 119; Peter H. Wood, "The Changing Population of the Colonial South: An Overview by Race and Region, 1685–1790," this volume; Patricia Galloway, "Choctaw Factionalism and Civil War, 1746–1750," *Journal of Mississippi History* 44 (1982): 294–95.

8. Jeffrey P. Brain, "La Salle at The Natchez: An Archaeological and Historical Perspective," in *La Salle and His Legacy: Frenchmen and Indians in the Lower Mississippi Valley*, ed. Patricia Galloway (Jackson: University Press of Mississippi, 1982), 53–55; Jeffrey P. Brain, "The Natchez 'Paradox,'" *Ethnology* 10 (1971): 215–22; Ian W. Brown, "Natchez Indians and the Remains of a Proud Past," in *Natchez before 1830*, ed. Noel Polk (Jackson: University Press of Mississippi, 1989), 8–28; Fagan, *Ancient North America*, 467; André Pénicaut, *Fleur de Lys and Calumet: Being the Pénicaut Narrative of French Adventure in Louisiana*, trans. and ed. Richebourg Gaillard McWilliams (Baton Rouge: Louisiana State University Press, 1953), 85, 89–96.

9. Tonti to his brother, March 4, 1700, "Tonti Letters," *Mid-America* 21 (July 1939): 230; Jacques Gravier, "Relation or Journal of the Voyage of Father Gravier, of the Society of Jesus, in 1700, from the Country of the Illinois to the Mouth of the Mississippi River," February 16, 1701, in *The Jesuit Relations and Allied Documents: Travels and Explorations of the Jesuit Missionaries in New France, 1610–1791*, trans. and ed. Reuben Gold Thwaites (New York: Pageant Book Company, 1959), 65:107; Anastasious Douay, Relation, in *First Establishment of the Faith in New France, Containing the publication of the Gospel, the history of the French colonies, and the famous discoveries from the river St. Lawrence, Louisiana, and the river Colbert, to the Gulf of Mexico, accomplished under the direction of the late Mr. de la Salle*, ed. Christian Le Clerq, trans. John Gilmary Shea (New York: John G. Shea, 1881), 2:272; Thomas Nuttall, *A Journal of Travels into the Arkansas Territory during the Year 1819*, ed. Savoie Lottinville (Norman: University of Oklahoma Press, 1980), 93; Susan C. Vehik, "Dhegiha Origins and Plains Archaeology," *Plains Anthropologist* 38 (1993): 231–52; Michael P. Hoffman, "The Terminal Mississippian Period in the Arkansas River Valley and Quapaw Ethnogenesis," in *Towns and Temples along the Mississippi*, ed. David H. Dye and Cheryl Anne Cox (Tuscaloosa: University of Alabama Press, 1990), 208–26; George Sabo III, "The Quapaw Indians of Arkansas, 1673–1803," in *Indians of the Greater Southeast: Historical Archaeology and Ethnohistory*, ed. Bonnie G. McEwan (Gainesville: University Press of Florida, 2000), 185–86; W. David Baird, *The Quapaw Indians: A History of the Downstream People* (Norman: University of Oklahoma Press, 1980), 3–8; Willard H. Rollings, *The Osage: An Ethnohistorical Study of Hegemony on the Prairie-Plains* (Columbia: University of Missouri Press, 1992), 5; John Joseph Mathews, *The Osages, Children of the Middle Waters* (Norman: University of Oklahoma Press, 1961), 341.

10. Patricia Galloway, "'The Chief Who Is Your Father': Choctaw and French Views of the Diplomatic Relation," this volume. For examples of diplomacy in the 1530s and 1540s, see A Gentleman of Elvas, "True Relation of the Hardships Suffered by Governor Don Hernando de Soto and Certain Portuguese Gentlemen in the Discovery of the Province of

Florida," trans. James Alexander Robertson, and Rodrigo Rangel, "Account of the Northern Conquest and Discovery of Hernando De Soto," trans. John E. Worth, both in *The De Soto Chronicles: The Expedition of Hernando de Soto to North America in 1539–1543*, ed. Lawrence A. Clayton, Vernon James Knight Jr., and Edward C. Moore (Tuscaloosa: University of Alabama Press, 1993), 1:119–21, 124, 303.

11. Mary Druke Becker, "Linking Arms: The Structure of Iroquois Intertribal Diplomacy," in *Beyond the Covenant Chain: The Iroquois and Their Neighbors in Indian North America, 1600–1800*, ed. Daniel K. Richter and James H. Merrell, 2nd ed. (University Park: Pennsylvania State University Press, 2003), 29–39; Robert A. Williams Jr., *Linking Arms Together: American Indian Treaty Visions of Law and Peace, 1600–1800* (New York: Oxford University Press, 1997), 62, 76–81; Cornelius J. Jaenen, "The Role of Presents in French-Amerindian Trade," in *Explorations in Canadian Economic History: Essays in Honour of Irene M. Spry*, ed. Duncan Cameron (Ottawa: University of Ottawa Press, 1985), 231; James Axtell, *Natives and Newcomers: The Cultural Origins of North America* (New York: Oxford University Press, 2001), 40; Daniel Richter, *The Ordeal of the Longhouse: The Peoples of the Iroquois League in the Era of European Colonization* (Chapel Hill: University of North Carolina Press, 1992), 22.

12. See, for example, Jacques Marquette, "Of the First Voyage Made by Father Marquette toward New Mexico," *Jesuit Relations*, 59:114.

13. Jay K. Johnson, "The Chickasaws," in *Indians of the Greater Southeast*, 85, 91, 93; Alan Gallay, *The Indian Slave Trade: The Rise of the English Empire in the American South, 1670–1717* (New Haven CT: Yale University Press, 2002); John D. Stubbs, Jr., "The Chickasaw Contact with the La Salle Expedition in 1682," in *La Salle and His Legacy*, 47. For more on Chickasaw policies and foreign relations throughout the late seventeenth and eighteenth centuries, see Wendy St. Jean, "Trading Paths: Chickasaws and Their Neighbors in the Greater Southeast, 1690s–1790s" (PhD diss., University of Connecticut, 2004).

14. R. P. Louis Hennepin, *Description de la Louisiane, Nouvellement Découverte au Sud Ouest de la Nouvelle France, par ordre du Roy* (Paris: Sebastien Huré, 1683), 180–81; R. P. Louis Hennepin, *Nouvelle Découverte d'un tres grand pays situé dans l'Amérique, entre Le Nouveau Mexique, et La Mer Glaciale* (Utrecht: Guillaume Broedelet, 1697), 234.

15. De Sauvole de la Villantray, Narrative, August 4, 1701, *Mississippi Provincial Archives: French Dominion* (MPAFD), trans. and ed. Dunbar Rowland and A. G. Sanders (vols. 1–3: Jackson: Mississippi Department of Archives and History, 1927–1932; vols. 4–5: ed. Patricia Kay Galloway, Baton Rouge: Louisiana State University Press, 1984), 2:9–10; Daniel H. Usner Jr., *Indians, Settlers, and Slaves in a Frontier Exchange Economy: The Lower Mississippi Valley before 1783* (Chapel Hill: University of North Carolina Press, 1992), 17–18. For more on Indian-English trade, see Joel W. Martin, "Southeastern Indians and the English Trade in Skins and Slaves," in *The Forgotten Centuries: Indians and Europeans in the American South, 1521–1704*, ed. Charles Hudson and Carmen Chaves Tesser (Athens: University of Georgia Press, 1994), 304–24. In 1713, Tohomes killed Welch trader Price Hughes, knowing that he bought slaves from Chickasaw and other raiders. Pénicaut, *Fleur de Lys*, 163.

16. Jean-Baptiste Bénard de la Harpe, "Relation du voyage de Bénard de la Harpe, dé-

couverte faite par lui de plusieurs nations situées a l'ouest," *Découvertes et établissements des Français dans l'ouest et dans le sud de l'Amérique septentrionale, 1614–1698: mémoires et documents inedits,* ed. Pierre Margry (New York: AMS Press, 1974), 6:289–93; La Harpe to the Directors of the Company of the Indies, December 25, 1720, folio 99, bob. 9, C13A6, Louisiana Colonial Records Project, Historic New Orleans Collection, New Orleans, Louisiana, microfilmed from the Archives Nationales, Colonies, Paris, France; George H. Odell, *La Harpe's Post: A Tale of French-Wichita Contact on the Eastern Plains* (Tuscaloosa: University of Alabama Press, 2002).

17. Pierre Le Moyne d'Iberville, *Iberville's Gulf Journals,* ed. and trans. Richebourg Gaillard McWilliams (Tuscaloosa: University of Alabama Press, 1950), 174; Tonti to his brother, March 4, 1700, "Tonti Letters," 229, 232; St. Cosme to the Bishop of Quebec, n.d. [1699], *Early Voyages Up and Down the Mississippi by Cavelier, St. Cosme, Le Sueur, Gravier, and Guignas,* ed. and trans. John Gilmary Shea (Albany NY: Joel Munsell, 1861), 74; Montigny to —, May 6, 1699, "Tonti Letters," 229n; François Le Maire, "M. Le Maire on Louisiana," January 15, 1714, ed. and trans. Jean Delanglez, *Mid-America* 19 (April 1937): 146–47; Etienne Veniard de Bourgmont, "Etienne Veniard De Bourgmont's 'Exact Description of Louisiana,'" c. 1714, trans. Mrs. Max W. Myer, ed. Marcel Giraud, *Missouri Historical Society Bulletin* 15 (October 1958): 13; Du Poisson to Father —, October 3, 1727, *Jesuit Relations,* 67:319; Wood, "Changing Population," this volume; Usner, *Indians, Settlers, and Slaves,* 44–49; Daniel H. Usner Jr., *American Indians in the Lower Mississippi Valley: Social and Economic Histories* (Lincoln: University of Nebraska Press, 1998), 35.

18. Périer to Le Pelletier, April 1, 1729, fol. 7, bob. 18, C13A12, Louisiana Colonial Records Project.

19. Vaudreuil to the Court, July 20, 1751, 2:152, LO 9, Vaudreuil Letterbook, Loudoun Collection, Huntington Library; Vaudreuil to Rouillé, October 10, 1751, *Illinois on the Eve of the Seven Years' War, 1747–1755,* ed. and trans. Theodore Calvin Pease and Ernestine Jenison (Springfield: Illinois State Historical Library, 1940), 410; Macarty to Vaudreuil, September 2, 1752, LO 376, box 7, Vaudreuil Papers; Caldwell, *French in the Mississippi Valley,* 13; Faye, "Arkansas Post of Louisiana: French Domination," 700; "Translated Excerpts from Declarations Made in Santa Fé, New Mexico, in 1749 and 1750," Appendix, Mildred Mott Wedel, *The Deer Creek Site, Oklahoma: A Wichita Village Sometimes Called Ferdinandina, An Ethnohistorian's View* (Oklahoma City: Oklahoma Historical Society, 1981), 68, 70–72.

20. See, for example, Vaudreuil to Maurepas, December 20, 1744, 1:42v, LO 9, Vaudreuil Letterbook; Le Pelletier to Vaudreuil, December 1, 1752, LO 410, box 8, Vaudreuil Papers; Guedetonguay, Speech, June 20, 1756, MPAFD, 5:173–75; De Clouet to Monsieur, August 4, 1769, folio 14, legajo 107, Papeles de Cuba, Archivo de Indias, Seville, Spain. The 1785 census showed that one-sixth of the non-Indians living on the lower Arkansas were "free people of color," by far the largest percentage in all of Louisiana or West Florida and one of the largest populations of free people of color in these colonies. Usner, *Indians, Settlers, and Slaves,* 114.

21. Périer to Ory, December 18, 1730, MPAFD, 4:39–40.

22. The Choctaws particularly received a large share. By 1733 the colonial government was giving some 150 *livres* to each of the 111 "chiefs" plus separate presents to the thirty-nine towns. Analysis of Bienville Letters, May 15, 1733, fol. 206, bob. 23, C13A16, Louisiana Colonial Records Project; Hubert to the Council, October 26, 1717, MPAFD, 2:249–50; Pénicaut, *Fleur de Lys*, 206.

23. The Bourbon alliance mitigated French-Spanish tension for a decade and a half, during and immediately after the War of Spanish Succession (1702–13).

24. *Iberville's Gulf Journals*, 171–73.

25. Diron d'Artaguette to Maurepas, October 24, 1737, MPAFD, 4:149–50.

26. See, for example, Pierre Le Moyne d'Iberville, "Journal du voyage du chevalier d'Iberville sur le vaisseau du Roi la *Renommée*, en 1699, depuis le cap Français jusqu'à la côte du Mississipi, et son retour," *Découvertes et établissements*, 4:430; Gravier, "Relation," February 16, 1701, 65:119; Verner W. Crane, "The Tennessee River as the Road to Carolina: The Beginnings of Exploration and Trade," *Mississippi Valley Historical Review* 3 (June 1916): 6–13; Verner W. Crane, "The Southern Frontier in Queen Anne's War," *American Historical Review* 24 (April 1919): 382, 390.

27. Vaudreuil to Maurepas, October 30, 1745, 1:65, LO 9, Vaudreuil Letterbook.

28. Patricia K. Galloway, "Henri de Tonti du village des Chacta, 1702: The Beginning of the French Alliance," in *La Salle and His Legacy*, 158–62; Tonti to Iberville, March 14, 1702, trans. Patricia K. Galloway, printed in "Henri de Tonti du village des Chacta," 168–72; Richard White, "Red Shoes: Warrior and Diplomat," in *Struggle and Survival in Colonial America*, ed. David G. Sweet and Gary B. Nash (Berkeley: University of California Press, 1981), 50.

29. "Memoir Sent in 1693, on the Discovery of the Mississippi and the Neighboring Nations by M. de La Salle, from the Year 1678 to the time of his death, and by the Sieur de Tonty to the Year 1691," in *Historical Collections of Louisiana*, ed. B. F. French (Baton Rouge: Louisiana State University Libraries, 1994), 1:62–65.

30. Pénicaut, *Fleur de Lys*, 28–30, 83, 159–63; Antoine Simon Le Page du Pratz, *The History of Louisiana* (Baton Rouge: Louisiana State University Press, rpt. of 1774 trans., 1975). For more on Natchez-French relations, see Usner, *American Indians in the Lower Mississippi Valley*, 15–32.

31. Le Page du Pratz, *History of Louisiana*, 44–45.

32. Le Page du Pratz, *History of Louisiana*, 36–42; Pénicaut, *Fleur de Lys*, 180–82; Usner, *American Indians in the Lower Mississippi Valley*, 21.

33. Pénicaut, *Fleur de Lys*, 167–77; Bienville to Raudot, January 20, 1716, MPAFD, 3:198; Duclos to Pontchartrain, June 7, 1716, MPAFD, 3:205–9; Le Page du Pratz, *History of Louisiana*, 43–44.

34. Le Page du Pratz, *History of Louisiana*, 28, 44, 79–80; Diron d'Artaguette to Maurepas, March 20, 1730, *Découvertes et établissements*, 1:76; Patricia Dillon Woods, *French-Indian Relations on the Southern Frontier, 1699–1762* (Ann Arbor MI: UMI Research Press, 1979), 73–74.

35. Lusser to Maurepas, journal entry for March 9, 1730, MPAFD, 1:99; Périer to Maurepas,

March 18, 1730, MPAFD, 1:64; Périer to Maurepas, April 10, 1730, fol. 300, bob. 19, C13A12, Louisiana Colonial Records Project; Le Page du Pratz, *History of Louisiana*, 84, 86.

36. Périer to Maurepas, March 18, 1730, MPAFD, 1:63; Gwendolyn Midlo Hall, *Africans in Colonial Louisiana: The Development of Afro-Creole Culture in the Eighteenth Century* (Baton Rouge: Louisiana State University Press, 1992), 100–101.

37. Diron d'Artaguette to Maurepas, February 9, 1730, *Découvertes et établissements*, 1:57–58; Périer to Maurepas, March 18, 1730, MPAFD, 1:62–63, 71; Diron d'Artaguette to Maurepas, March 20, 1730, *Découvertes et établissements*, 1:76–77; Father Philibert, Register of those massacred at Natchez, June 9, 1730, MPAFD, 1:122–26; Périer to Ory, December 18, 1730, MPAFD, 4:39; Le Page du Pratz, *History of Louisiana*, 90; Woods, *French-Indian Relations*, 96.

38. Périer to Ory, December 18, 1730, MPAFD, 4:39.

39. Périer to Maurepas, March 18, 1730, MPAFD, 1:62–64.

40. Périer to Maurepas, March 18, 1730, MPAFD, 1:64, 68, 70, 71–72; Hall, *Africans in Colonial Louisiana*, 102–4; Usner, *Indians, Settlers, and Slaves*, 86–87.

41. Bienville, Memoir on Louisiana, 1726, MPAFD, 3:531; Brain, "La Salle at The Natchez," 55.

42. Diron d'Artaguette to Maurepas, February 9, 1730, MPAFD, 1:58; Lusser to Maurepas, journal entry for March 9, 1730, MPAFD, 1:99–100; Le Page du Pratz, *History of Louisiana*, 91.

43. Périer to Maurepas, April 1, 1730, fol. 352, bob. 19, C13A12, Louisiana Colonial Records Project; Périer to Ory, December 18, 1730, MPAFD, 4:41.

44. Lepetit to D'Avagour, July 12, 1730, *Jesuit Relations*, 67:377; Watrin, "Banishment of the Jesuits from Louisiana," September 3, 1764, *Jesuit Relations*, 70:247.

45. Périer to Ory, December 18, 1730, MPAFD, 4:41; Marchand to Périer, abstract, September 15, 1732, MPAFD, 4:124; Périer to Maurepas, January 25, 1733, MPAFD, 1:167. For earlier raids on the Koroas, see, for example, Bienville to Pontchartrain, September 6, 1704, MPAFD, 3:22–23.

46. Du Poisson to Patouillet, [1726], *Jesuit Relations*, 67:261; "Recensement general des habitans establys a sotébouy Arkansas et des Ouvriers de la concession cy devans apartenant a Sr. Law," February 18, 1723, transcribed by Dorothy Core, no. 6a, box I, Small Manuscripts Collection, Arkansas Historical Commission, Little Rock, Arkansas; Usner, *Indians, Settlers, and Slaves*, 48.

47. In 1758 a French observer noted that the two communities were "more like brothers than like neighbors." Antoine Simon Le Page du Pratz, *Histoire de la Louisiane, Contenant la Découverte de ce vaste Pays; sa Description géographique; un Voyage dans les Terres; l'Histoire Naturelle; les Moeurs, Coûtumes & Religion des Naturels, avec leurs Origines; deux Voyages dans le Nord du nouveau Mexique, dont un jusqu'à la Mer du Sud; ornée de deux Cartes & de 40 Planches en Taille douce* (Paris: De Bure, 1758), 2:291; Diron d'Artaguiette, Journal, 1722–23, *Travels in the American Colonies*, ed. Newton D. Mereness (New York: Antiquarian Press, 1961), 56. For more on this relationship, see Kathleen DuVal, "'A Good

Relationship, & Commerce': The Native Political Economy of the Arkansas River Valley," *Early American Studies* 1 (Spring 2003): 61–89.

48. Diron d'Artaguette to Maurepas, February 10, 1730 (postscript to February 9), MPAFD, 1:60–61; Périer to Maurepas, March 18, 1730, MPAFD, 1:67–69; Régis du Roullet, Journal, entries for February 8, March 20, March 29, April 2, April 13, April 27, May 13, and July 5, 1730, MPAFD, 1:178–81; Le Page du Pratz, *History of Louisiana*, 92. For other instances of Choctaws and others haggling over the return of the French captives, see Lusser to Maurepas, journal entries for March 9 and 16, 1730, MPAFD, 1:101, 109–11.

49. Bienville, Representations to the Superior Council of Louisiana, August 3 and 10, 1723, MPAFD, 3:360–61, 369–70; Leblond de La Tour, Representation to the Superior Council of Louisiana, August 5, 1723, MPAFD, 3:364.

50. Périer to Maurepas, April 1, 1730, fol. 352, bob. 19, C13A12, Louisiana Colonial Records Project; Périer to Maurepas, April 10, 1730, fol. 300, bob. 19, C13A12, Louisiana Colonial Records Project.

51. Diron d'Artaguette to Maurepas, June 24, 1731, MPAFD, 4:77; Beauchamp to Maurepas, November 5, 1731, MPAFD, 4:79; Périer to Maurepas, December 10, 1731, MPAFD, 4:102–3; Le Page du Pratz, *History of Louisiana*, 93.

52. See, for example, Bienville to Maurepas, May 18, 1733, MPAFD, 3:623; Bienville to Maurepas, March 15, 1734, MPAFD, 3:635; Bienville to Maurepas, April 28, 1738, MPAFD, 3:708; Bienville to Maurepas, September 30, 1741, MPAFD, 3:756.

53. Périer to Maurepas, December 10, 1731, MPAFD, 4:103.

54. Périer to Maurepas, April 10, 1730, fol. 300, bob. 19, C13A12, Louisiana Colonial Records Project; Lepetit to D'Avagour, July 12, 1730, *Jesuit Relations*, 67:377; Bienville to Maurepas, May 18, 1733, MPAFD, 3:622.

55. Périer to Maurepas, April 1, 1730, fol. 352, bob. 19, C13A12, Louisiana Colonial Records Project; Périer to Maurepas, August 1, 1730, MPAFD, 4:35; Périer to Ory, December 18, 1730, MPAFD, 4:39, 41; Beauchamp to Maurepas, November 5, 1731, MPAFD, 4:81; Périer to Maurepas, December 10, 1731, MPAFD, 4:104–5; St. Ange to Périer, abstract, October 30, 1732, MPAFD, 4:124; Périer to Maurepas, January 25, 1733, MPAFD, 1:167; Vaudreuil to La Houssaye, November 2, 1743, 3:16, LO 9, Vaudreuil Letterbook.

56. Régis de Roullet to Périer, February 21, 1731, MPAFD, 4:62; Régis de Roullet to Périer, March 16, 1731, MPAFD, 4:70; Louboey to Maurepas, May 8, 1733, MPAFD, 1:215–16; Analysis of letters from Bienville, May 15, 1733, fol. 206, bob. 23, C13A16, Louisiana Colonial Records Project.

57. Diron d'Artaguette to Maurepas, June 24, 1731, MPAFD, 4:78.

58. See, for example, Bienville to Maurepas, February 10, 1736, MPAFD, 1:281–85.

59. Diron d'Artaguette to Maurepas, February 9, 1730, MPAFD, 1:59.

60. Périer to Ory, December 18, 1730, MPAFD, 4:41.

61. Le Page du Pratz, *History of Louisiana*, 97–98.

62. Régis du Roullet to Maurepas, journal abstract for October 9, 1730, MPAFD, 1:182–83.

63. Still, this was an offense. Choctaw War Chief Red Shoe explained that accepting

refugees could mean taking on the refugees' enemies. Régis de Roullet to Périer, March 16, 1731, MPAFD, 4:70.

64. Galloway, "The Chief Who Is Your Father," this volume. For more on the usefulness of what Richard White calls "creative misunderstandings," see Richard White, *The Middle Ground: Indians, Empires, and Republics in the Great Lakes Region, 1650–1815* (New York: Cambridge University Press, 1991).

65. Bienville to Maurepas, April 23, 1734, MPAFD, 1:228.

66. O'Brien, *Choctaws in a Revolutionary Age*, 14.

67. For Chickasaw recruitment of the Choctaws through trade, marriage, and calumet chiefs, see St. Jean, "Trading Paths," chap. 4.

68. Bienville to Maurepas, April 23, 1734, MPAFD, 1:222–24; Bienville to Maurepas, August 26, 1734, MPAFD, 1:231–33.

69. Bienville to Maurepas, June 28, 1736, MPAFD, 1:300–310.

70. Régis du Roullet, journal entry for November 20, 1730, MPAFD, 1:190; Bienville to Maurepas, April 23, 1734, MPAFD, 1:228–29; Bienville to Maurepas, August 26, 1734, MPAFD, 1:229–32.

71. Galloway, "Choctaw Factionalism," 299, 304; Régis du Roullet to Maurepas, 1729, MPAFD, 1:34; Noyan to Maurepas, November 8, 1734, MPAFD, 4:139; Louboey to Maurepas, July 11, 1738, MPAFD, 1:371. For more on Red Shoe, see also White, "Red Shoes: Warrior and Diplomat."

72. Bienville to Maurepas, February 28, 1737, MPAFD, 3:693–94; Bienville and Salmon to Maurepas, December 22, 1737, MPAFD, 1:357–59; Salmon to Maurepas, May 4, 1740, MPAFD, 1:441–45; Bienville to Maurepas, May 6, 1740, MPAFD, 1:449–61; Le Page du Pratz, *History of Louisiana*, 102–4; Usner, *Indians, Settlers, and Slaves*, 84.

73. Vaudreuil to d'Erneville, November 11, 1744, 3:144, LO 9, Vaudreuil Letterbook; Vaudreuil to Maurepas, December 24, 1744, 1:44v, LO 9, Vaudreuil Letterbook; Vaudreuil to Maurepas, October 30, 1745, 1:65, LO 9, Vaudreuil Letterbook.

74. Vaudreuil to Maurepas, March 15, 1747, LO 89, box 2, Vaudreuil Papers; Vaudreuil to Maurepas, November 5, 1748, LO 147, box 3, Vaudreuil Papers; Vaudreuil to Rouillé, September 22, 1749, LO 185, box 4, Vaudreuil Papers.

75. See, for example, Vaudreuil to Maurepas, December 28, 1744, MPAFD, 4:230; Louboey to Maurepas, November 6, 1745, MPAFD, 4:255.

76. Bienville to Maurepas, April 28, 1738, MPAFD, 3:711. Greg O'Brien, in *Choctaws in a Revolutionary Age*, points out that in the eighteenth century rival sources of authority existed within Choctaw society, an older one based on ritual and spirituality and a newer one based on access to European goods. Red Shoe drew on the latter source to build his influence.

77. One of the first victims of intra-Choctaw violence was Red Shoe himself. Bienville to Maurepas, June 28, 1736, MPAFD, 1:300–310; Beauchamp, Journal, August 1746, MPAFD, 4:269–94; Louboey to Maurepas, February 16, 1748, MPAFD, 4:312; Descloseaux to Maurepas, October 25, 1748, MPAFD, 4:329–30. For a full discussion of hostilities within the Choctaw nation, see White, "Red Shoes: Warrior and Diplomat," 49–68; Galloway, "Choctaw Factionalism," 289–327; Usner, *Indians, Settlers, and Slaves*, 78–96. For Red Shoe's

past involvement in the Chickasaw war, see for example, Bienville to Maurepas, August 23, 1734, MPAFD, 1:224.

78. Usner, *American Indians in the Lower Mississippi Valley*, 30–31.

79. Usner, *Indians, Settlers, and Slaves*, 74.

80. Hall, *Africans in Colonial Louisiana*, 103; Usner, *Indians, Settlers, and Slaves*, 86–87.

81. Beauchamp to Maurepas, November 5, 1731, MPAFD, 4:82; Périer to Maurepas, December 10, 1731, MPAFD, 4:104; Le Page du Pratz, *History of Louisiana*, 77–79; Usner, *Indians, Settlers, and Slaves*, 74–75; Hall, *Africans in Colonial Louisiana*, 106–12.

82. For more on Louisiana's economy, see Usner, *Indians, Settlers, and Slaves*.

American Indians in Colonial New Orleans

DANIEL H. USNER JR.

So much of the scholarship on American Indians in colonial North America has concentrated on the populous nations inhabiting the interior that relatively little is understood about those smaller Indian groups situated in the midst of colonial settlements and towns. The praying towns of New England and the mission reserves of Canada are the most familiar of such communities, thanks to recent investigations into the refugees and survivors of seventeenth-century wars.[1] Since so much research is needed on southeastern Indians in general, one is hard pressed to urge emphasis on any particular category of colonial-Indian relations. The large picture of geopolitical, economic, and cultural interaction demands closer attention to the Cherokees, Creeks, Choctaws, Chickasaws, and Caddos before we can afford the luxury of studying smaller, more enclosed Indian communities. Yet to ignore the latter would exclude Indian peoples living within sizable parts of the Southeast—like the Tidewater and piedmont Atlantic areas, the Florida panhandle, and the alluvial plain of the Mississippi River—who experienced colonialism differently, but no less importantly, than did interior tribespeople.[2]

Colonial towns serve as especially informative foci for examining forms of Indian adaptation and persistence different from those that occurred within Indian nations situated in the backcountry of European colonies. In diverse eighteenth-century towns across the Southeast, Indians frequently lived and visited in an array of circumstances. An inestimable number of Indians from many tribes found themselves either being shipped away as slaves from colonial ports or working as slaves in and around them. Charlestown merchants waged slave-raiding expeditions that brought captive Timucuans, Apalaches, Tuscaroras, Yamasees, and Choctaws to households in their town as well as to plantations in Virginia and Carolina. Intimate contact with Europeans and Africans and coercive labor at entirely new tasks undoubtedly changed life for Indian servants and slaves inhabiting colonized areas while channeling Indian influences to the colonial populace. The colonial capitals of Williamsburg, Charlestown, Savannah, and St. Augustine, and eventually such interior centers as Augusta, Fort Toulouse, and Natchez, became important meeting places for Indian diplomats, many of whom traveled long distances to exchange words and gifts with European officials. More regularly these emerging cities were frequented by Indian villagers who lived nearby and, though reduced to tributary or subordinate status by war or flight, participated actively in the social and economic rhythm of town life as boathands, packhorsemen, interpreters, day laborers, and peddlers.[3] All these types of activity were experienced by American Indians in another southern colonial town, named by its French founders "Nouvelle Orléans."

Traveling up the Mississippi River in early March 1699, Pierre Le Moyne d'Iberville was shown by his Bayogoula Indian guide "the place through which the Indians make their portage to this river from the back of the bay where the ships are anchored. They drag their canoes over a rather good road, at which we found several pieces of baggage owned by men that were going there or were returning."[4] Situated between a chain of lakes and the Mississippi, the crescent-shaped bend at what became New Orleans had been mainly used by Indians for transport between waterways and seasonal gathering of food sources. Yet natural conditions that made this site ideal for portage and fishing reduced its potential for permanent occupation.[5] Now a metropolis slowly sinking inside artificial levees and spillways, New Orleans sits on a natural levee, created by sediment deposited during seasonal flooding, that slopes down from a crest of fifteen feet above sea level to almost five feet below sea level. The city's vulnerability to flooding is exacerbated by Lake Pontchartrain to the north and Lake Borgne to the east.[6]

Before European contact Indians used the four-to-eight-mile-wide strip of swampland as a fishing/hunting/gathering station and as a portage between the lakes and the river. The most habitable sites were along Bayou St. John, a few miles long and about twenty feet wide when Iberville traveled it, and on the Metairie ridge, which linked that bayou with Bayou Chapitoulas. From this junction Indians reached the Mississippi by a three-mile portage.[7] Since René-Robert Cavalier de La Salle's voyage down the Mississippi in 1682, this had been a highly volatile area. A Tangipahoa village a few miles above the portage road was destroyed, perhaps by Quinipissas from upriver. By 1699 a group of Acolapissas occupied Metairie ridge, but during the first decade of the eighteenth century some Biloxis and then some Houmas moved in temporarily. English slave raids upriver to the north and French war against the Chitimachas kept the lower Mississippi Delta in turmoil until Jean-Baptiste Le Moyne de Bienville began construction of New Orleans in 1718.[8]

Largely in consequence of this early conflict, enslaved Indians constituted the core of the resident Indian population in French New Orleans, resembling the earlier presence of Native American slaves in such colonial towns as Boston, New York, and Charlestown. French and English colonies in North America allowed and periodically encouraged the enslavement of Indian people from enemy tribes or distant territories. Most captives were transported from one region to another, but many enslaved Indians remained in their locale to be joined by black and Indian slaves imported from abroad. By November 1721 fifty-one Indian slaves lived in the vicinity of New Orleans—twenty-one in town and the rest on farms at Bayou St. John, Gentilly, Chapitoulas, Cannes Bruslée, and Chaouchas. Louisiana's total slave population at the time numbered 161 Indians and 680 Africans.[9]

Indian slaves in the colony belonged to several tribes. "Panis," an epithet for Indians captured above the Arkansas River, were present, but Alibamon, Taensa, and Chitimacha slaves—captives in local wars—also lived in colonial households. Suffering more enslavement than other local tribes, the Chitimachas of Bayou Lafourche became a significant ethnic component in the early slave population of lower Louisiana. Late in 1706 some Chitimachas assassinated Jean François Buisson de Saint-Cosme, a priest of the Foreign Missions, and subsequent French and allied-Indian warfare against the tribe lasted more than a decade, with scores of captured Chitimachas being sold into slavery in Louisiana and the Caribbean. When he arrived at Bayou St. John in the winter of 1718–19, Antoine Le Page du Pratz purchased a Chitimacha woman from another settler "in order to have a person who could dress our victuals."[10]

Before New Orleans was founded, the presence of Indian slave women in Louisiana households had generated a great deal of controversy. While some marriages between Frenchmen and Indian women were blessed by priests at Mobile and Kaskaskia, where few white women lived during the early colonial period, most officials and clergymen condemned soldiers and settlers who cohabited with their female servants. Accusations of laxness toward this practice flew across factional lines in the colonial government. In a memoir written after his return to France in 1710, the former pastor of the colony's main settlement at Mobile denounced many Louisianians for preferring over legitimate marriage "to maintain scandalous concubinages with young Indian women, driven by their proclivity for the extremes of licentiousness. They have bought them under the pretext of keeping them as servants, but actually to seduce them, as they in fact have done."[11] The immigration of more European women to Louisiana after 1717 created a more balanced gender ratio within the colonial population and made intimacy with Indian women less threatening to the colony's order. The Black Code issued for Louisiana in 1724, furthermore, prohibited sexual intercourse between slaves and colonists. But interracial cohabitation, like so many other acts forbidden by that law, certainly did not end. While the census taken in January 1726 did not designate the sexual identity of the 229 Indians and 1,540 blacks in the colony's rapidly growing slave population, a large proportion were women, many of whom were obliged to live among the French as mistresses or common-law wives. Although "the number of those who maintain young Indian women or negresses to satisfy their intemperance is considerably diminished," Père Raphael reported that same year, "there still remain enough to scandalize the church and to require an effective remedy."[12]

Complaints of concubinage, although it undoubtedly existed in some cases, should not divert attention from other services rendered by Indian men and women who worked for families and artisans. Dispersed among urban households and neighboring farms by the 1720s, Indian slaves influenced material life in early New Orleans. The 1726 census showed thirty Indian slaves inside the city residing in diverse household arrangements. On the Rue Royalle two Indian and four black slaves lived with carpenter Thomas Dezery, and one slave lived in the household of a locksmith named Sulpice L'Evique with his wife and three children. Seven Indian slaves lived in another conjugal household on the Rue St. Louis, that of François St. Amand, his wife, and his two children. On the Rue du Quay a slave lived with Sieur Duval and his family, and another inhabited the house of Reboul, a hunter, perhaps as a female companion or a male assistant. At Chapitoulas, just above New Orleans along the Mississippi, eleven Indian slaves lived on four separate plantations along with eleven European servants and

302 black slaves. At Bayou St. John and Gentilly, on the northeastern out-skirts of the city, eight Indian slaves also worked beside white and black la-borers on several farms.[13]

The recalcitrance of Indian slaves intensified the colonial government's anxiety over the potential for a slave revolt in Louisiana, where enslaved blacks outnumbered the white populace by the 1730s. Given their knowl-edge of the region, runaway Indian slaves around New Orleans seriously threatened the property and security of slaveowners, even alarming officials into discouraging further enslavement of Louisiana Indians. Following re-ports of *marrons sauvages* raiding cattle and attacking the black public ex-ecutioner, a maroon camp called Natanapallé was discovered in 1727. San-cousy, an Indian slave who lost his owner's ox, fled to this makeshift village, where he met about fifteen black and Indian fugitives. These escaped slaves possessed enough guns and ammunition to defend themselves against any pursuers. The arrest of other runaways who had apparently seen this com-munity influenced Governor Etienne Boucher de Périer to request that the trade for Indian slaves be terminated. Not only did this traffic incite costly wars between tribes, but also "these Indian slaves being mixed with our ne-groes may induce them to desert with them, as has already happened, as they may maintain relations with them which might be disastrous to the colony when there are more blacks."[14]

A conjunction of circumstances that Louisiana shared with other North American colonies slowed the rate of Indian enslavement. The decimation of neighboring tribes by disease, the desire to secure stable trading relations, and the ease with which Indian captives could abscond all contributed to this decline. The increased availability of Africans by the 1720s reinforced the racial categorization of slaves as Negro and mulatto. Major conflicts with the Natchez in 1729–30 and with the Chickasaws over the following decade produced hundreds of slaves, mostly Natchez, but the abatement of warfare elsewhere in the lower Mississippi valley reduced the general in-cidence of captivity. Some of the five hundred or more men, women, and children captured in the Natchez war remained in Louisiana as slaves and others were executed, but most were shipped by the Company of the Indies to the Caribbean. The New Orleans census of January 1732 lists only six Indian women and five Indian men amid a town population of 626 Euro-

Americans and 258 African Americans, while fewer than fifty Indian slaves inhabited farms below and above the city.[15]

Fear of Indian and black cooperation combined with stable Indian-French relations to reduce the number of Indian slaves in and around the colonial capital, but the economic interests of slaveowners managed to maintain an Indian slave population of 120 persons in Louisiana by 1771. The number of Indian slaves recorded in New Orleans had actually increased to forty-two females and nineteen males of different ages. One also should conjecture that liaisons between Indian and African American slaves produced children who were ascribed by owners to Negro and mulatto identities and that some offspring of Indian women and white men grew up free. As in other early towns, therefore, a portion of the Indian population was assimilated by the colonial society through slavery.[16]

Only with its transfer to Spain in 1766 did laws prohibiting the enslavement, purchase, or transfer of Indians reach the colony. During the Spanish period the Indian slave populace in the city and the colony at large virtually disappeared. Avenues to emancipation available under Spanish law contributed slightly to this diminution, and undecided petitions by some slaves claiming Indian ancestry were inherited by the Orleans Territory courts of the United States. "It is reported to me," wrote Governor William Claiborne to Secretary of State James Madison in 1808, "that in this Territory, there are now several hundred persons held as slaves, who are descended of Indian families."[17] But by then the inhabitants of New Orleans fell into a rigid tripartite division of racial identity: free whites, enslaved blacks (some actually being mulatto), and free people of color. Nearly 20 percent of the city's 8,500 people were classified as *gens de couleur*, which was synonymous with mixed ancestry. And in the process of making blacks and slaves the same category, the Louisiana Supreme Court ruled in 1810 that "persons of color may be descended from Indians on both sides, from a white parent, or mulatto parents in possession of their freedom."[18] The fascinating legal and social ramifications of this kind of decision aside, continuing absorption into a rapidly growing non-Indian population and a tightening racial structure together caused the apparent disappearance of Indian slaves in New Orleans by the nineteenth century.

More conspicuous than the presence of Indian slaves in colonial New Orleans were diplomatic visits by chiefs and delegates from various Indian nations. The ritual protocol of Native American diplomacy created dramatic spectacles in many North American towns. The location of a port and the security of concessions along the lower Mississippi hinged upon securing peace with the Chitimachas, who were raiding newly established plantations at Chapitoulas. Upon receiving an overture from the French in 1718, the beleaguered tribe agreed to meet Bienville at the site where construction of New Orleans had just begun. Chitimacha delegates solemnly marched to the cadence of their own voices from the riverbank to Bienville's cabin. After they sat on the ground and poised their faces in their hands, the word-bearer rose to light the sacred calumet. He puffed the pipe and passed it to the governor and then to everyone assembled. After presenting Bienville with the pipe and a gift of deerskins, the elderly Chitimacha bemoaned the years of warfare with the French, when "our women wept unceasingly, our children cried with fright, the game fled far from us, our houses were abandoned, and our fields uncultivated." Then, as translated for Le Page du Pratz by his Chitimacha slave, the Indian diplomat voiced the joy of his people "to see that we will walk along the same road as you, Frenchmen."[19]

Throughout the eighteenth century, the Chitimachas and other *petites nations* sent annual delegations to New Orleans to receive gifts from French and, after 1766, Spanish governors. Other official visits involved providing military assistance to Louisiana, returning runaway slaves, and even requesting pardons for deserting soldiers. The Tunicas were the most visible allies among the small tribes in the French war against the Natchez. After the first campaign of 1730, Governor Périer permitted Tunica warriors to burn a Natchez woman at the stake in New Orleans, "before the whole city, who flocked to witness the spectacle." As she underwent a slow torture, according to one witness, the captive taunted her tormentors for their unskillfulness and threatened revenge by her tribe. Her prophecy was fulfilled a year later, when a party of Natchez struck the Tunica village by surprise, burning it down and killing its chief along with many other residents. Testifying to the Tunicas' military importance to Louisiana, Diron d'Artaguette feared that this great tragedy would expose New Orleans and the colony's most lucrative plantations to enemy attack.[20] Local Indians served regularly as scouts and soldiers to defend Louisiana colonists. In 1750 Governor Pierre François Rigault de Cavagnal et Vaudreuil persuaded a group of Indians, probably some Bayogoulas or Ouachas, to settle opposite the

German Coast for the sole purpose of guarding that settlement against attacks by rebellious Choctaws. The Tunicas and other small nations closer to New Orleans fought in later French campaigns against the Chickasaws and in the Spanish seizure of English West Florida posts during the American Revolution.[21]

While deployment of allied Indian warriors against hostile groups helped the colonial government by discouraging unified opposition among Indian nations, paying local Indians to capture runaway slaves promoted hostility between blacks and Indians. Familiarity with the countryside and the promise of rewards made Indians effective bounty hunters. A group of Indians on patrol for Governor Bienville in the spring of 1738 caught a runaway black man named La Fleur, who accused his owners of not giving him enough food. In 1748 Jean Deslandes of the German Coast hired an Indian to accompany ten of his slaves on an attack against a camp of armed runaways. The Indian fired at the planter's command and seriously wounded one of the *marrons*. For killing a black highwayman outside the city, an authorized posse of Indians received one hundred pesos from the New Orleans cabildo in 1785.[22]

Louisiana Indians did not hesitate to visit New Orleans in pursuit of their own interests and desires, as when an entourage of Quapaws under Guedelonguay met with Governor Louis Billouard de Kerlérec at the government house on June 20, 1756. Guedelonguay requested pardons for four French soldiers who had deserted from the Arkansas fort and taken refuge in the Indians' temple. He explained that anyone finding sanctuary in the sacred cabin of his people "is regarded as washed clean of his crime." He then warned with bowed head that if the soldiers "were put to death, he would not answer for the dangerous attacks and the rebellions that the chief of the sacred cabin could bring about." The Quapaw chief also reminded the governor "that his nation having lately been at war against the Chickasaws as a mark of affection for the French, his son was killed there and his daughter wounded, and it is because of this that he asks that the loss of the one and the spilled blood of the other be repaid by the pardon that he asks for the four soldiers." Kerlérec grudgingly granted Guedelonguay's request in exchange for a promise "to hand over to him in the future all deserting soldiers or malefactors or other culprits, with no restriction or condition whatever."[23]

Diplomatic journeys from the Choctaw nation, most populous and powerful Indian ally of French Louisiana, were annually made to Mobile instead of New Orleans. The proximity of the older colonial port to the Choctaw towns influenced this pattern, but French anxiety over the security of the New Orleans area made it official policy. When Governor Périer invited Choctaw chiefs to the city in 1729–30, recruiting their military services against the rebellious Natchez, he was chastised by company officials for familiarizing them with the unfortified capital and the scattered plantations along the Mississippi River. In 1748 raids just upriver from New Orleans by Choctaw rebels intensified fear of Choctaw access to the area, yet negotiations terminating the Choctaw revolt brought a delegation of fourteen leaders from the upstart western villages to New Orleans for meetings with the governor. The Choctaws periodically visited the city on their own initiative, and seven "honored men" welcomed a new governor in early March 1753 with seven Chickasaw scalps. "After two days of speeches as long as [they were] bad," an unappreciative and novice Governor Kerlérec "expressly forbade them to make a habit of coming to New Orleans, assuring them that I would not fail to go to Mobile every year." During the 1750s and 1760s complaints against delayed distributions of gifts provoked more diplomatic missions by Choctaws to the capital, causing repeated consternation among New Orleanians. News of Louisiana's transfer to Spain and of English dominion in West Florida generated further excited journeys of Choctaw chiefs to the city.[24]

New Orleans hosted a series of ceremonial visits in the autumn of 1769, when Alexandro O'Reilly summoned lower Mississippi River tribes after completing the military occupation of Louisiana for Spain. On September 30, chiefs, interpreters, and other persons from the Tunicas, Taensas, Pacanas, Houmas, Bayogoulas, Ofogoulas, Chaouchas, and Ouachas approached the general's house with song and music. Inside he greeted them under a canopy in the company of prominent residents of New Orleans. Each chief placed his weapon at O'Reilly's feet and waved a feather fan over his head. O'Reilly accepted their fans, smoked their pipes, and clasped their hands. Then the Bayogoula leader spoke for the delegation, offering loyalty to the Spanish and requesting that they "grant us the same favors and benefits as did the French." After exhorting the Indians to treat both the English in West Florida and the Spanish in Louisiana peaceably, O'Reilly placed medals hanging from scarlet ribbons around the chiefs' necks and had presents distributed. This procedure was repeated when the Chahtos, Biloxis, Pascagoulas, and Mobilians arrived on October 22, the Chitimachas on October 29, and the Quapaws on November 16.[25]

After the American Revolution, Indian diplomacy in New Orleans entered a new era. Spanish Louisiana contended against the United States for Indian allies, while the Creek, Chickasaw, and Choctaw nations maneuvered to preserve their sovereignty. Indian missions to New Orleans came frequently and in large numbers during the 1790s, including delegations of Cherokees, but the tribes avoided showing signs of exclusive allegiance and therefore refused to make visits to the Spanish governor an obligatory routine. Chiefs often excused themselves from traveling to the city because of bad weather or poor health and, whenever they did complete a junket, complained about inadequate provisions and insulting treatment. "They don't say anything in the City," reported Juan de la Villebeuvre from the Choctaw village of Boukfouca, "but in the Nation they murmur very much."[26] At the time Spain ceded Louisiana to the French Republic in 1800, the intensity of intrigue and diplomacy in the city led Pierre-Clément de Laussat, prefect charged with overseeing the transfer, to "count on there descending, after the expression of the country 2 to 3,000 Indians per year to New Orleans: others say 3 to 400 chiefs."[27]

Purchase of Louisiana by the United States in 1803 suddenly decelerated Indian political activity in New Orleans. Agencies established near the large interior nations—at Fort St. Stephens, Chickasaw Bluffs, and Natchitoches—virtually ended their diplomatic ties to the Crescent City. For another decade, the small nations in the area continued making formal visits to territorial officials. In 1806 Governor Claiborne of the Orleans Territory presented uniform coats to two representatives from the Houma tribe in Ascension Parish, and in 1811 he distributed $100 worth of articles to Chief Chac-Chouma of the Houmas and his attendants. "From the different Governors of Louisiana," Claiborne summarized their diplomatic relationship with New Orleans, "they were accustomed to receive marks of friendly attention. At the present day, the number of this Tribe is greatly diminished; it does not exceed 80 souls, but their conduct is exemplary and the late visit of the Chief being the first paid to me, I thought it a matter of policy to make him a small present." This meeting marked the beginning of the Houma Indians' struggle for official recognition by the United States government. But they and other petites nations along the lower Mississippi and Red rivers were denied the political protection needed to secure their small land bases. After a century of alliance with colonial governments in New Orleans, the Chitimachas, Houmas, Tunicas, and others were finally pressured into the backcountry of Louisiana. The federal government indifferently lost sight of them, for the time being.[28]

Neither the severance of diplomatic ties with New Orleans nor the dissipation of resident Indian slaves by the nineteenth century ended the presence of American Indians in the city. A more continuous and lasting relationship had evolved over the colonial period through an array of informal economic activities, especially the marketing of food in town by neighboring Indians. In their 1718 treaty with the French, the Chitimachas agreed to move their village from Bayou Lafourche closer to the incipient town, a few miles below the Paris brothers' plantation. Other tribes also migrated toward New Orleans. From the backcountry south of the town site, the Chaouchas settled within several miles on the east bank of the Mississippi and the Ouachas about twenty miles above New Orleans on the west bank. The Acolapissas moved from the north shore of Lake Pontchartrain to the east bank of the Mississippi some fifty miles above town. "All these nations are highly industrious," observed André Pénicaut, "and all are quite helpful in furnishing food to the French, to the troops as well as to the people on the concessions."[29]

In addition to these newly relocated Indian settlements, villages of Houmas, Tunicas, and Bayogoulas also occupied the banks of the Mississippi near New Orleans. In 1706–9 Tunica refugees from upriver drove the Houmas from their village 150 miles above the Bayou St. John portage and occupied the spacious bluff east of the river themselves. After a brief stay on Bayou St. John, the Houmas by 1718 resettled several miles below Bayou Lafourche. All these people suffered severe population loss, from epidemics more than warfare, but in 1725 they still composed a substantial percentage of the total population along the Mississippi south of the Red River. Interspersed among one thousand European settlers and another thousand African slaves within this area, seven Indian communities totaled approximately three thousand men, women, and children.[30]

Indians in the New Orleans area provided important goods and services to the colonial town. Indian men frequently visited as packhorsemen accompanying traders or as crewmen paddling or rowing boats. As already seen, French and later Spanish governors recruited auxiliaries from neighboring villages for military campaigns and paid bounties to Indians who captured and returned runaway slaves and soldiers. During the Natchez revolt, however, the Chaoucha village was virtually destroyed when Périer dispatched a group of armed black slaves against it, hoping to alleviate fear in New Orleans over local attacks and to generate black-Indian antagonism. Commending the slaves for their prompt and secret mission, the governor boasted, "If I had been willing to use our negro volunteers I should have destroyed all these little nations which are of no use to us, and which might on the contrary cause our negroes to revolt." He did not further employ these black soldiers "for fear of rendering [them] . . . too bold and of inclining them perhaps to revolt after the example of those who joined the Natchez." Defying customary practices more than once during his troublesome governorship, Périer was criticized for his genocidal assessment of local Indians, who in fact proved very useful to colonial Louisiana.[31]

Provisioning early New Orleans with food, more than any other activity, integrated Indians into the social and economic life of the colonial town. In the mid-1720s Bienville acknowledged that the farming, hunting, and fishing skills of lower Louisiana Indians produced food supplies for the colony. Estimating their population at fifty men, he reported that the Houmas "have rendered us good services in the famines that we have experienced in recent years by the abundance of provisions that they have furnished us." Bénard de La Harpe had earlier observed that the Houma village of some sixty cabins "busies itself in raising hens and in the culture of maize and beans." The one hundred men of the Acolapissas, Bienville noted, "furnish us almost all the fresh meat that is consumed at New Orleans without however their neglecting the cultivation of their lands which produce a great deal of corn."[32]

The continuous presence of Indians in New Orleans—whether as slaves, guides, boatmen, or peddlers—affected how the colonial government regulated interaction among social groups. Like their counterparts in Boston, New York, and Charlestown, New Orleans officials associated both free and enslaved Indians with blacks, free people of color, and lower-class whites in efforts to police behavior on the city's streets and behind its closed doors. In all of these towns Indians were subject during the eighteenth century to the same ordinances that prohibited slaves and free blacks from carrying firearms, congregating, owning livestock, trading without special permission, and walking the streets after curfew—ordinances intended to reduce insolence and theft aimed at white property owners. In New Orleans much insubordination was attributed to the consumption of alcohol by soldiers as well as by Indians and blacks. In 1751 the Louisiana Superior Council tried to reinforce the Black Code and a series of other regulations on drinking, gambling, and assemblies by issuing a new set of police regulations. Among articles mostly restricting the social and economic activities of slaves and free blacks, there was a prohibition against the six newly licensed taverns selling wine or liquor to soldiers, Indians, and blacks.[33]

Face-to-face contact with settlers, soldiers, and slaves posed special problems for Indians who frequented New Orleans. Trade had a debilitating effect on the petites nations, Governor Kerlérec explained, "mainly because of the quantity of drink that has been traded to them." Contagious diseases continued to strike down lower Louisiana Indians and by midcentury reduced their number to about two hundred warriors or seven hundred people. As in other colonial regions, those Indian groups experiencing the longest and most intimate contact with colonists suffered more drastically from exposure to viruses and alcohol than did the interior tribes, many becoming extinct or being absorbed by other peoples. "The Chaouchas, the Washas, [the] Acolapissas, and also the Avoyelles and the Bayogoulas were so many different nations," Kerlérec wrote in 1758, "which the proximity of the French and the trade in drink have likewise destroyed." Only through their own resilience and resourcefulness, especially in their capacity to adopt refugees and other outsiders into community life, did any Indian enclaves survive within colonial society.[34]

Attrition among the Indian populace around New Orleans was actually reversed in the mid-1760s when villagers from the Mobile Bay area and from the Choctaw Nation began resettlement on the north shore of Lake Pontchartrain and along the banks of the Mississippi River. After Great Britain occupied West Florida, the Apalaches, Taensas, Pacanas, Mobilians, Alibamons, Biloxis, Chahtos, and Pascagoulas—many of them Roman Catholic in religion—migrated to the French settlements in lower Louisi-

ana, then discovered that the colony belonged to Spain. Kerlérec realized
the benefits to be derived from the approximately eighty Apalache Indians,
"being hunters and farmers," and in September 1763 he decided to locate
them at the rapids of the Red River. "There," recorded general commissioner Jean-Jacques Blaise d'Abbadie, "they will be useful for aiding vessels
ascending the river towards Natchitoches. Moreover, through their hunting, they will be able to supply New Orleans."[35] As they extended authority over the east side of the Mississippi River, above the chain of lakes and
bayous that made New Orleans a Spanish island, the English also vied for
the services of these immigrant Indians. During the spring of 1768 Mont-
fort Browne met a group of Chahtos and Mobilians building a new village
on the Amite River and was welcomed at the palmetto-covered house of
chief Mattaha with a calumet dance. The Indians had already supplied the
English at Fort Bute with three boats and, "as I found them a great deal
disgusted against the Spaniards' late behavior," Browne persuaded them to
settle closer to Baton Rouge after the year's harvest. "As these Savages are a
good deal civilized, industrious and excellent Hunters," he wrote, "the acquisition will be the greater."[36]

By the early 1770s at least eight villages were interspersed among colonial
settlements between New Orleans and the Red River, totaling more than
one thousand Indians. The colonial population within this stretch (see fig.
1) included about 2,750 blacks and 2,300 whites (New Orleans itself containing 1,000 blacks and 1,800 whites), and the plantations below New
Orleans included 1,600 blacks and 450 whites. "The Houma, Chitimacha,
and other Indian communities that were dispersed among the plantations,"
cartographer and naturalist Bernard Romans noted, "serve as hunters, and
for some other laborious uses, something similar to subdued tribes of New
England."[37] In 1773 the main town of the Houmas, consisting of some forty
gunmen, stood on the east bank of the Mississippi sixty miles above New
Orleans. Another Houma village was situated across the river. A league below Manchac the Taensas, Pacanas, and Mobilians lived on the west bank
in a single town of about thirty gunmen. The Alibamons counted thirty-
seven gunmen and lived just above Manchac on the east side. While some
Chitimachas were moving down Bayou Plaquemine, about fifteen gunmen
and their families remained along the Mississippi. Down the bayou other
Chitimachas and some Atakapas and Opelousas totaled another fifty gun-

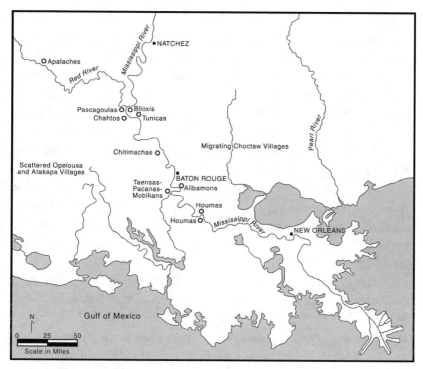

Figure 1. Indian villages on the banks of the Mississippi and Red rivers, 1773.

men. The Tunicas still occupied their town, numbering about thirty-five gunmen, on the east bluff above the Pointe Coupée plantations. Above Tunica stood a village of ten to twelve Chahto gunmen and another of fifteen Pascagoula gunmen on the west bank. The Biloxis, numbering nearly one hundred gunmen, had just moved from the west to the east bank a short distance below the Red River.[38] Over the next few decades most of these communities migrated from the Mississippi River either to the Red River habitat of the Apalaches or down Bayous Plaquemine and Lafourche. Also during the 1790s more groups of Choctaws and Coushattas were migrating west of the Mississippi River into Louisiana, though their numbers were overshadowed by the contemporaneous immigration of Anglo-American settlers and African American slaves.[39]

The migration of some Choctaws into the New Orleans area, which began during the 1760s, was more volatile than that of others. Yet in the long run their proximity proved to be the most enduring in New Orleans history. After Great Britain assumed control over West Florida's trade with interior tribes, many Choctaws—especially from the Six Towns district—attempted to maintain ties with the French. They complained of abuses committed by English traders, carried on illicit trade with inhabitants of Louisiana, and committed acts of banditry against settlers in West Florida. General Frederick Haldimand reported in 1768 to General Thomas Gage, "The continual depredations of the Choctaw Indians of the six villages, who hunt in and frequent continually the neighborhood of lakes Pontchartrain and Maurepas where they pillage the inhabitants, kill their animals, and introduce French traders in their country, require that there should be some one of confidence and authority among them who would repress their outbreaks."[40] Groups of Choctaws were then settling farther down Pearl River, around Pass Christian, and on the north shore of Lake Pontchartrain, where many French settlers also lived resentfully under British rule. As hunting and trading increased in this thickly pine-forested area, colonial residents at Spanish Galveztown and English Baton Rouge exchanged rum, ammunition, and corn for pelts, game, and bear oil produced by traveling Choctaw families. Although it perturbed merchants in Pensacola and Mobile with privileged rights over Choctaw trade and antagonized farmers and planters vulnerable to pilferage, this commerce germinated several new Indian communities across Lake Pontchartrain from New Orleans.[41]

The movement of Choctaws and other groups toward the Crescent City after 1763 discloses how some Indians relied on cities in their adjustment to new political and economic circumstances. By the late eighteenth century, New Orleans had become an important station for the seasonally varied strategies Indians devised to cope with a decline in diplomatic and commercial leverage. Faced with diminishing opportunity in the deerskin trade—manifested by falling prices for pelts and mounting debts to merchants—and with growing numbers of Anglo-American immigrants, Indians in the lower Mississippi valley resorted to a seasonal cycle of itinerant economic activities.[42] Camps of extended families, formerly the units that spent only winter hunting seasons away from their villages, sojourned more frequently along waterways and roads, trading small quantities of goods with other travelers, farmers, and slaves. While the men hunted to supply local meat markets, women sold leaves and roots, baskets and mats, and even began to pick cotton during the harvest season.[43]

On the outskirts of New Orleans, groups of Houmas, Chitimachas, and Choctaws camped along Bayou St. John and Bayou Road. Hundreds of Indians gathered in late winter to request gifts from officials and to join in the celebration of carnival.[44] On the city's streets and in the marketplace, Indian women peddled baskets, mats, sifters, plants, herbs, and firewood; their men sold venison, wildfowl, and cane blowguns and occasionally earned wages as day laborers and dockworkers. On his way to a Choctaw camp behind the city gates, Fortescue Cuming met on a March afternoon in 1799 "numbers of Indian women with large bundles of wood on their backs, first tied together and then held by a strap carried over their foreheads." A few years later Paul Alliot observed that the Indian men "kill game with great dexterity, and sell it for excellent prices" and that the women "busy themselves in making reed baskets which they sell at good prices."[45]

The impact of Indians upon the culture of New Orleans, through their diversified presence in the colonial city, is not easily measured. Many New Orleanians, identified as white, black, or free colored by the end of the eighteenth century, possessed various degrees of Indian ancestry. Inside urban households and in the marketplace, Indian women influenced cuisine not only through their uses of corn and beans but also through a knowledge of the region's wild plants and animals.[46] On the outskirts of town or around its taverns, Indians also shared music, dance, and other cultural expressions with colonists and slaves. Perhaps the most fascinating Indian contribution to New Orleans social life was the ball game called *toli* by the Choctaws and *raquettes* by the French, the city's most popular spectator sport until the arrival of baseball. Before United States acquisition of New Orleans, contests had become Sunday afternoon events behind the city gates. Spectators assembled on the "Communes de la Ville," also called Congo Plains, where players carrying short sticks in both hands tossed the small buckskin ball between two goal posts sometimes placed a half-mile apart. As described by Pierre-Clément de Laussat, two prominent black teams in 1803 were the Bayous, players from the Bayou St. John area, and the La Villes, those from the city proper. They competed against white teams as well as against each other, and some Indians reportedly belonged to the Bayous. The particular circumstances in which New Orleanians adopted this ancient Indian ball game are obscure, but its performance over the eighteenth century by Indians in and around the city must have been influential.[47]

For Indians living in the eighteenth-century Southeast, contact with colonists and slaves produced a variety of new settings in which they made decisions and had choices forced upon them.[48] Life in or around colonial settlements was filled with a multitude of challenges, and in an urban setting
different kinds of exchange and struggle converged. Colonial towns proved
to be destructive intrusions for many Indian groups. The largest tribe in
the Mississippi Delta by the early eighteenth century, the Chitimachas, suffered a protracted war as the French tried to establish a permanent base on
the river. The beginning of construction at New Orleans in 1718 marked
the end of their struggle, but not before many Chitimachas had been captured and enslaved. Colonial towns like New Orleans became hotbeds of
anxiety over Indian and slave rebellions. The Chaoucha village just below
New Orleans was destroyed in 1729, during the Natchez revolt, when the
governor decided to alleviate fear in town and avert a black-Indian coalition—which had already occurred at Natchez—by sending a small army
of black slaves against the closest community of Indians. The New Orleans
experience also shows how dangerous an alliance with colonists could be,
when the well-armed Tunica village was devastated by Natchez attackers
after it supplied vital military assistance to the French army. Small Indian
nations along the lower Mississippi, including the surviving Tunicas, continued to provide valuable defense for New Orleans and its surrounding
plantations.

Many Indian tribes found towns to be places for engaging in diplomacy
rather than warfare. Throughout the eighteenth century, Indians traveled
to New Orleans from near and far to negotiate agreements that helped them
adjust to the European presence. Issues discussed in the government house
ranged from the return of runaway slaves and soldiers to the defense of Louisiana against other European colonies and their Indian allies. Indian diplomatic protocol constituted a dramatic form of public interaction in which
colonial officials received processions of singers, smoked the calumet, and
presented gifts. These very formal displays of reciprocal alliance were as
much a part of the city's calendar as were Easter, Christmas, and the king's
birthday, and even the most ethnocentric of European observers were impressed by the dignity and importance of Indian diplomacy.[49]

At the level of daily life, Indian experiences in New Orleans varied widely.
There were some Indian men, women, and children who worked as slaves

in households and shops. Employment in long-distance trade and transportation brought Indian men regularly through the city, while the growing urban populace provided a market for foods and other goods produced by neighboring Indian villages. Even in taking advantage of this opportunity, however, Louisiana Indians faced difficulties in the city. Disease and alcohol endangered their health and took the lives of countless individuals. Government efforts to control the behavior of Indians, slaves, and soldiers created mounting vigilance against the activities of Indians inside and outside the city walls. But as the political and economic status of Indian nations continued to decay toward the end of the eighteenth century, New Orleans did not witness a declining Indian presence. Instead, many Indian families turned to the city as a useful way station in a new pattern of adjustment and survival.[50]

Notes

1. For samples of literature on New England and Canadian settlement Indians, see Laurence M. Hauptman and James D. Wherry, eds., *The Pequots in Southern New England: The Fall and Rise of an American Indian Nation* (Norman: University of Oklahoma Press, 1990); John Demos, *The Unredeemed Captive: A Family Story from Early America* (New York: Knopf, 1994); Daniel R. Mandell, *Behind the Frontier: Indians in Eighteenth-Century Eastern Massachusetts* (Lincoln: University of Nebraska Press, 1996); Robert S. Grumet, ed., *Northeastern Indian Lives, 1632–1816* (Amherst: University of Massachusetts Press, 1996); Colin G. Calloway, ed., *After King Philip's War: Presence and Persistence in Indian New England* (Hanover NH: University Press of New England, 1997); Jean M. O'Brien, *Dispossession by Degrees: Indian Land and Identity in Natick, Massachusetts, 1650–1790* (New York: Cambridge University Press, 1997); and Ann Marie Plane, *Colonial Intimacies: Indian Marriage in Early New England* (Ithaca NY: Cornell University Press, 2000).

2. For major studies of southeastern coastal communities, see James Merrell, *The Indians' New World: Catawbas and Their Neighbors from European Contact through the Era of Removal* (Chapel Hill: University of North Carolina Press, 1989); Helen C. Rountree, *Pocahontas's People: The Powhatan Indians of Virginia through Four Centuries* (Norman: University of Oklahoma Press, 1990); Daniel H. Usner Jr., *Indians, Settlers, and Slaves in a Frontier Exchange Economy: The Lower Mississippi Valley before 1783* (Chapel Hill: University of North Carolina Press, 1992); John H. Hann and Bonnie G. McEwan, *The Apalachee Indians and Mission San Luis* (Gainesville: University Press of Florida, 1998); Jerald T. Milanich, *Laboring in the Fields of the Lord: Spanish Missions and Southeastern Indians* (Washington DC: Smithsonian Institution Press, 1999); and Gregory A. Waselkov and Bonnie L. Gums, *Plantation Archaeology at Rivière aux Chiens, ca. 1725–1848* (Mobile: University of South Alabama Center for Archaeological Studies, 2000).

3. These town experiences of southeastern Indians are gleaned from Verner W. Crane, *The Southern Frontier, 1670–1732* (Durham NC: Duke University Press, 1928); Peter H. Wood, *Black Majority: Negroes in Colonial South Carolina from 1670 through the Stono Rebellion* (New York: Alfred A. Knopf, 1974); Phinizy Spalding, *Oglethorpe in America* (Chicago: University of Chicago Press, 1977); Charles H. Fairbanks, "From Missionary to Mestizo: Changing Culture of Eighteenth-Century St. Augustine," in *Eighteenth-Century Florida and the Caribbean*, ed. Samuel Proctor (Gainesville: University Press of Florida, 1976), 88–99; J. Leitch Wright Jr., *The Only Land They Knew: The Tragic Story of the American Indians in the Old South* (New York: Free Press, 1981); and Kathleen A. Deagan, *Spanish St. Augustine: The Archaeology of a Colonial Creole Community* (New York: Academic Press, 1983).

4. Richebourg Gaillard McWilliams, trans. and ed., *Iberville's Gulf Journals* (Tuscaloosa: University of Alabama Press, 1981), 57.

5. Marco J. Giardino, "Documentary Evidence for the Location of Historic Indian Villages in the Mississippi Delta," in *Perspectives on Gulf Coast Prehistory*, ed. Dave D. Davis (Gainesville: University Press of Florida, 1984), 232–57; Tristram R. Kidder, "Making the City Inevitable: Native Americans and the Geography of New Orleans," in *Transforming New Orleans and Its Environs: Centuries of Change*, ed. Craig E. Colten (Pittsburgh: University of Pittsburgh Press, 2000), 9–21.

6. Peirce F. Lewis, *New Orleans: The Making of an Urban Landscape* (Cambridge MA: Ballinger, 1976), 17–30; Rod E. Emmer and Karen Wicker, "Sedimentary Environments, Ecological Systems, and Land Use in Southwestern Louisiana," and Fredrick W. Wagner, "Development Problems in the New Orleans Coastal Zone," in *A Field Guidebook for Louisiana*, ed. Richard E. Kesel and Robert A. Sauder (Washington DC: Association of American Geographers, 1978), 48–53, 124–27.

7. McWilliams, *Gulf Journals*, 111–12; Richard J. Shenkel and Jon L. Gibson, "Big Oak Island, an Historical Perspective of Changing Site Function," *Louisiana Studies* 13 (Summer 1974): 173–86; Richard J. Shenkel, *Oak Island Archaeology: Prehistoric Estuarine Adaptations in the Mississippi River Delta* (New Orleans: Jean Lafitte National Historical Park, 1980).

8. Marc de Villiers du Terrage, "A History of the Foundation of New Orleans (1717–1722)," trans. Warrington Dawson, *Louisiana Historical Quarterly* 3 (April 1920): 157–251, at 161–79; John R. Swanton, *Indian Tribes of the Lower Mississippi Valley and Adjacent Coast of the Gulf of Mexico*, Bureau of American Ethnology Bulletin 43 (Washington DC: Government Printing Office, 1911), 274–84, 297–301. Also see Henry C. Bezou, *Metairie: A Tongue of Land to Pasture* (Gretna LA: Pelican, 1973), 35–36; and Edna B. Freiberg, *Bayou St. John in Colonial Louisiana, 1699–1803* (New Orleans: Harvey Press, 1980), 26–27.

9. Charles R. Maduell Jr., comp. and ed., *The Census Tables for the French Colony of Louisiana from 1699 through 1732* (Baltimore: Genealogical Publishing Company, 1972), 16–27. Almon Wheeler Lauber, *Indian Slavery in Colonial Times within the Present Limits of the United States* (New York: Columbia University, 1913), is still the most comprehensive treatment of enslaved Indians across North America. But for close analysis of the Indian slave trade carried out by the English in the South, see Alan Gallay, *The Indian Slave*

Trade: The Rise of the English Empire in the American South, 1670–1717 (New Haven CT: Yale University Press, 2002).

10. Richebourg Gaillard McWilliams, ed. and trans. *Fleur de Lys and Calumet: Being the Pénicaut Narrative of French Adventure in Louisiana* (Baton Rouge: Louisiana State University Press, 1953), 101–2, cited hereafter as *Pénicaut Narrative*; Antoine Le Page du Pratz, *The History of Louisiana*, facsimile reproduction of the 1774 translated British edition, ed. Joseph Tregle Jr. (Baton Rouge: Louisiana State University Press, 1975), 20–21; Marcel Giraud, *A History of French Louisiana*, vol. 1, *The Reign of Louis XIV, 1698–1715*, trans. Joseph C. Lambert (1953; reprint, Baton Rouge: Louisiana State University Press, 1974), 177–80.

11. Archives des Colonies, Paris, ser. C13A, vol. 3, fol. 390, cited hereafter as AC, C13A, volume number: folio number; Giraud, *History of French Louisiana*, 278–80; Charles Edwards O'Neill, *Church and State in French Colonial Louisiana: Policy and Politics to 1732* (New Haven CT: Yale University Press, 1966), 86–92, 248–55; Carl A. Brasseaux, "The Moral Climate of French Colonial Louisiana, 1699–1763," *Louisiana History* 27 (Winter 1986): 27–41.

12. AC, C13A, 10:46; Carl A. Brasseaux, "The Administration of Slave Regulations in French Louisiana, 1725–1766," *Louisiana History* 21 (Spring 1980): 139–58.

13. Maduell, *Census Tables*, 50–76. Our understanding of New Orleans during the eighteenth century has been recently advanced by Gwendolyn Midlo Hall, *Africans in Colonial Louisiana: The Development of Afro-Creole Culture in the Eighteenth Century* (Baton Rouge: Louisiana State University Press, 1992); Kimberly S. Hanger, *Bounded Lives, Bounded Places: Free Black Society in Colonial New Orleans, 1769–1803* (Durham NC: Duke University Press, 1997); and Thomas N. Ingersoll, *Mammon and Manon: The First Slave Society in the Deep South, 1718–1819* (Knoxville: University of Tennessee Press, 1998).

14. "Records of the Superior Council," *Louisiana Historical Quarterly* 1 (January 1918): 109, 3 (July 1920): 414, 443–44; Dunbar Rowland and Albert G. Sanders, trans. and ed., *Mississippi Provincial Archives: French Dominion*, 3 vols. (Jackson: Mississippi Department of Archives and History, 1929–32), 2:573–74, cited hereafter as MPAFD.

15. "Records of the Superior Council," *Louisiana Historical Quarterly* 13 (April 1930): 329, 14 (July 1931): 458, 14 (October 1931): 580; Maduell, *Census Tables*, 113, 123; Patricia Kay Galloway, trans. and ed., *Mississippi Provincial Archives: French Dominion*, vols. 4 and 5 (Baton Rouge: Louisiana State University Press, 1984), 4:79, 102–5; cited hereafter as MPAFD (1984).

16. Lawrence Kinnaird, trans. and ed., *Spain in the Mississippi Valley, 1765–1794*, 3 vols. (Washington DC: American Historical Association, 1946–49), 1:125–26, 196; Wright, *Only Land They Knew*, 126–50, 248–78. For discussions of Indian slavery in the Northeast, see A. Leon Higginbotham Jr., *In the Matter of Color. Race and the American Legal Process: The Colonial Period* (New York: Oxford University Press, 1978); and John A. Sainsbury, "Indian Labor in Early Rhode Island," *New England Quarterly* 48 (September 1975): 378–93.

17. Dunbar Rowland, ed., *Official Letter Books of W. C. C. Claiborne, 1801–1816*, 6 vols. (Jackson: Mississippi Department of Archives and History, 1917), 4:179–81. Hans Baade, "The Law of Slavery in Spanish Louisiana, 1769–1803," in *Louisiana's Legal Heritage*, ed. Edward F. Haas (New Orleans: Louisiana State Museum, 1983), 43–86, and Stephen We-

bre, "The Problem of Indian Slavery in Spanish Louisiana, 1769–1803," *Louisiana History* 25 (Spring 1984): 117–35, are important analyses of slavery during the Spanish period.

18. Charles L. Thompson, ed., *New Orleans in 1805: A Directory and a Census* (New Orleans: Pelican Gallery, 1936); Ira Berlin, *Slaves without Master: The Free Negro in the Antebellum South* (New York: Pantheon Books, 1974), 108–32; Virginia R. Dominguez, *White by Definition: Social Classification in Creole Louisiana* (New Brunswick NJ: Rutgers University Press, 1986), 23–26.

19. *Pénicaut Narrative*, 216–18; Antoine Le Page du Pratz, *Histoire de la Louisiane*, 3 vols. (Paris: De Bure, La Veuve et Lambert, 1758), 1:106–14.

20. MPAFD (1984) 4:37, 77; "Historical Memoirs of M. Dumont," in *Historical Collections of Louisiana*, ed. Benjamin Franklin French, 5 vols. (New York: Lamport, Blakeman and Law, 1846–53), 5:98–97.

21. MPAFD (1984) 4:40, 49; Patricia D. Woods, *French-Indian Relations on the Southern Frontier, 1699–1762* (Ann Arbor MI: UMI Research Press, 1980), 139; J. Barton Starr, *Tories, Dons, and Rebels: The American Revolution in British West Florida* (Gainesville: University Press of Florida, 1976), 142–60.

22. "Records of the Superior Council," *Louisiana Historical Quarterly* 3 (July 1920): 414, 5 (October 1922): 593–94, 19 (October 1936): 1087–88; Records and Deliberations of the Cabildo, November 25, 1785 (Louisiana Division, New Orleans Public Library).

23. MPAFD (1984) 4:187–88, 5:173–78.

24. MPAFD (1984) 4:46–47, 81–82, 5:38–44, 122, 183, 273–74.

25. Kinnaird, *Spain in the Mississippi Valley*, 1:101–2, 154–55.

26. Kinnaird, *Spain in the Mississippi Valley*, 2:185, 258, 3:141–43, 151–52; Miro to Luis de las Casas, September 10, December 26, 1790, June 28, 1791, Dispatches of the Spanish Governors of Louisiana, WPA typescript in Louisiana Historical Center, New Orleans; Villebeuvre to Carondelet, January 16, February 7, March 30, 1793, *East Tennessee Historical Society Publications* 29 (1957): 142–43, 152, 30 (1958): 101–2.

27. Laussat to Minister of Navy, September 27, 1802, Claude Perrin Victor Papers, the Historic New Orleans Collection, New Orleans; James Wilkinson to William Claiborne, Fort Adams, April 13, 1803, Indian Department Journal, Mississippi Department of History and Archives, Jackson: "I have received the following information from a confidential source in New Orleans, viz: 'Mingo poos Coos has been here, and thro the Interpreter has been invited to bring his people to meet their old friends the French, the Indians are daily comeing in, and the Interpreter has gone over the lake [Pontchartrain] to provide for their accommodation.'"

28. Rowland, *Official Letter Books of W. C. C. Claiborne*, 5:275, 322–23. For overviews of the Houmas since the eighteenth century, see Jan Curry, "A History of the Houma Indians and Their Story of Federal Nonrecognition," *American Indian Journal* 5 (February 1979): 8–28; and Dave D. Davis, "A Case of Identity: Ethnogenesis of the New Houma Indians," *Ethnohistory* 48 (Summer 2001): 473–94.

29. *Pénicaut Narrative*, 216–20; MPAFD 3:527–28, 535.

30. Jean-Baptiste Bénard de La Harpe, *The Historical Journal of the Establishment of*

the French in Louisiana, trans. Joan Cain and Virginia Koenig, ed. and annotated Glenn R. Conrad (Lafayette: University of Southwestern Louisiana Press, 1971), 60–79; MPAFD 3:526–35.

31. MPAFD 1:64–65, 71.

32. La Harpe, *Historical Journal*, 75–76; MPAFD 3:527–29, 535.

33. AC, C13A, 35:39–52. Patterns of control affecting blacks and Indians in other eighteenth-century colonial towns are best examined in Wood, *Black Majority*, and Higginbotham, *In the Matter of Color*.

34. MPAFD (1984) 5:212–13.

35. Carl A. Brasseaux, trans., ed., and annotator, *A Comparative View of French Louisiana, 1699 and 1762: The Journals of Pierre Le Moyne d'Iberville and Jean-Jacques-Blaise d'Abbadie* (Lafayette: University of Southwestern Louisiana Press, 1979), 100–102, 107, 112.

36. Browne to Hillsborough, Pensacola, July 6, 1768, English Provincial Records, Mississippi Department of Archives and History, Jackson.

37. Bernard Romans, *A Concise Natural History of East and West Florida* (1775; reprint, New Orleans: Pelican, 1961), 69–71.

38. List of the Several Tribes of Indians inhabiting the banks of the Mississippi, Between New Orleans and Red River, with their number of gun-men and places of residence, January 1, 1773, William Haldimand Papers, British Museum (microfilm in Louisiana Division, New Orleans Public Library). Other population estimates of these Indian communities for this period can be found in Jacqueline K. Voorhies, trans. and comp., *Some Late Eighteenth-Century Louisianians: Census Records of the Colony, 1758–1796* (Lafayette: University of Southwestern Louisiana Press, 1973), 164–66; Eron Dunbar Rowland, ed., "Peter Chester: Third Governor of the Province of West Florida under the British Dominion, 1770–1781," Publications of the Mississippi Historical Society: Centenary Series 5 (1925): 97; Philip Pittman, *The Present State of the European Settlements on the Mississippi*, facsimile of 1770 edition, ed. Robert Rea (Gainesville: University Press of Florida, 1973), 24, 35–36.

39. Daniel H. Usner Jr., *American Indians in the Lower Mississippi Valley: Social and Economic Histories* (Lincoln: University of Nebraska Press, 1998), 47–48, 97–100. The migration of Indians into the Atchafalaya and Red River basins can be traced in Daniel Clark, "An Account of the Indian Tribes in Louisiana, New Orleans, Sept. 29, 1803," in *The Territorial Papers of the United States*, ed. Clarence E. Carter, 26 vols. (Washington DC: Government Printing Office, 1934–62), 9:62–64; John Sibley, "Historical Sketches of the Several Indian Tribes in Louisiana, South of the Arkansas River, and between the Mississippi and River Grand," in *Annals of the Congress of the United States*, 9th Cong., 2d sess. (Washington DC: Gales and Seaton, 1852), 1076–88; Sibley, *A Report from Natchitoches in 1807*, ed. Annie Heloise Abel (New York: Museum of the American Indian, 1922). For a history of the Choctaws who settled permanently in central Louisiana, see Hiram F. Gregory, "Jena Band of Louisiana Choctaw," *American Indian Journal* 3 (February 1977): 2–16.

40. Brasseaux, *Comparative View*, 11; Clarence W. Alvord and C. E. Carter, eds., *The Critical Period, 1763–1765* (Springfield: Illinois State Historical Library, 1915), 200–201, 413–14.

41. Kinnaird, *Spain in the Mississippi Valley*, 2:382–84, 3:53–54; William Panton to Carondelet, Pensacola, April 16, 1792, *Georgia Historical Quarterly* 22 (December 1938): 393; John Forbes to Carondelet, October 31, 1792, Panton to Carondelet, November 6, 1792, *East Tennessee Historical Society Publications* 28 (1956): 131–33; James A. Robertson, ed., *Louisiana under the Rule of Spain, France, and the United States, 1785–1807*, 2 vols. (Cleveland: Arthur H. Clark, 1911), 2:103.

42. The economic strategies devised by lower Mississippi valley Indians in the late eighteenth and early nineteenth centuries are discussed in Richard White, *The Roots of Dependency: Subsistence, Environment, and Social Change among the Choctaws, Pawnees, and Navajos* (Lincoln: University of Nebraska Press, 1983); Usner, *American Indians in the Lower Mississippi Valley*; James Taylor Carson, *Searching for the Bright Path: The Mississippi Choctaws from Prehistory to Removal* (Lincoln: University of Nebraska Press, 1999); and Greg O'Brien, *Choctaws in a Revolutionary Age, 1750–1830* (Lincoln: University of Nebraska Press, 2002).

43. John A. Watkins Manuscript on Choctaw Indians, Howard-Tilton Memorial Library, Tulane University, New Orleans; Fortescue Cuming, *Sketches of a Tour to the Western Country* (1810; reprint, Cleveland: Arthur H. Clark, 1904), 351–52.

44. Berquin-Duvallon, *Travels in Louisiana and the Floridas, in the Year, 1802, Giving a Correct Picture of Those Countries*, trans. John Davis (New York: Isaac Riley, 1806), 96–99; Christian Schultz Jr., *Travels on an Inland Voyage through the States of New-York, Pennsylvania, Virginia, Ohio, Kentucky and Tennessee, and through the Territories of Indiana, Louisiana, Mississippi and New-Orleans*, 2 vols. (New York: Isaac Riley, 1810), 2:198.

45. Cuming, *Sketches of a Tour*, 365–66; Robertson, *Louisiana under the Rule of Spain, France, and the United States*, 2:81–83.

46. Indian influences on Louisiana foodways are explored in Usner, *Indians, Settlers, and Slaves*, 191–218.

47. Pierre-Clément de Laussat, *Memoirs of My Life to My Son during the Years 1803 and After*, trans. Sister Agnes-Josephine Pastwa and ed. Robert D. Bush (Baton Rouge: Louisiana State University Press, 1978), 53–54; Dominique Rouquette, "The Choctaws" (typescript of a manuscript written in 1850, Louisiana Historical Center, New Orleans), 51–54; George W. Cable, "The Dance in Place Congo," *Century Magazine* 31 (February 1886): 518–19.

48. For the broad spectrum of Indian experiences produced by contact with colonial settlers and slaves, see James Merrell, "The Indians' New World: The Catawba Experience," *William and Mary Quarterly*, 3rd ser., 41 (October 1984): 537–65; and Claudio Saunt, *A New Order of Things: Property, Power, and the Transformation of the Creek Indians, 1733–1816* (New York: Cambridge University Press, 1999).

49. Francis Jennings, William N. Fenton, Mary A. Druke, and David R. Miller, eds., *The History and Culture of Iroquois Diplomacy: An Interdisciplinary Guide to the Treaties of the Six Nations and Their League* (Syracuse NY: Syracuse University Press, 1985), offers a collection of useful approaches to the form as well as the content of Indian-European diplomacy.

50. To follow the American Indian presence in New Orleans through the nineteenth century, see Usner, *American Indians in the Lower Mississippi Valley*, 111–37.

Politics and Economics

Introduction

GREGORY A. WASELKOV

"Count the lying black marks of this one,"exclaimed Attakullakulla (Little Carpenter), paper in hand, as he detailed the hypocrisies and half-truths contained in a stack of letters the colonial governor of South Carolina had sent him. The Cherokee leader "kept them regularly piled in a bundle, according to the time he received them," James Adair recalled, "and often shewed them to the traders, in order to expose their fine promising contents." The Indian elder conceded that the earliest messages from Governor James Glen "contained a little truth," according to Adair, "and he excused the failure" of the governor's subsequent letters on the ground that "much business might have perplexed him, so as to occasion him to forget complying with his strong promise." But eventually Attakullakulla, like Adair himself, "repented of trusting to the governor's promises" and admitted that his patience was exhausted. The governor's letters, he proclaimed, "were an heap of black broad papers, and ought to be burnt in the old years fire."[1]

Adair's scene presents two contrasting forms of evidence for understanding this distant time: written—and often misleading—European documents on the one hand and pointed—but rarely preserved—opinions of native Southeasterners on the other. Unfortunately, the heaps of black broad papers that now constitute our principal source for constructing interpretive narratives of the colonial past are seldom accompanied by the first-person Indian perspectives so essential to a balanced picture of the period. Keenly aware of this bias, the authors of the following five chapters have metaphorically invoked the purifying fires of the *poskita* (or "busk") in their critical studies of documentary and archaeological evidence. They have revealed long-stilled native voices speaking to issues of political and economic interaction, the same realms that colonial agents and officials sought most eagerly to dominate.

Amy Turner Bushnell discusses the dual political systems that functioned effectively for a century in Spanish Florida. Native leaders retained much of their authority at the village level, providing a basis for long-term stability.

By means of a complex web of mutual obligations, sedentary Florida Indians managed to coexist relatively peacefully with Franciscan friars and secular Spanish colonists. This little-known experiment in Indian-European interaction deserves much more attention from ethnohistorians, who, as Bushnell correctly states, have generally regarded French and (especially) English colonization of the Southeast as "the central story."[2]

As familiar as we are with the English colonial adventure in Virginia, the next two chapters contain some startling revelations on the Native American response to that invasion. By focusing on Cockacoeske, successor to Powhatan and Opechancanough, Martha McCartney explains in the third chapter of this section how the "Queen of Pamunkey" adroitly manipulated colonial treaty negotiations in an ingenious (though ultimately unsuccessful) attempt to reestablish the dominance of her own people in a reconstituted Powhatan chiefdom. In the process, McCartney also provides us with a detailed biographical depiction of an Indian woman in the colonial era. Unfortunately, few Indian women were as frequently mentioned in colonial-era documents as Cockacoeske.[3]

McCartney's portrait of Cockacoeske clearly indicates the weakness of chiefly authority that characterized Virginia's Algonquian political scene in the late seventeenth century. How the chiefs' influence declined is the subject of Stephen Potter's essay, the second chapter in this section. Since the earliest historical sources describe nearly total control by the chiefs over the acquisition of prestige items, including newly available European trade goods, Potter looks at the changing distribution of these objects in graves to pinpoint the first signs of lessening chiefly authority. As the availability of formerly scarce, high-status items rapidly increased with an accelerating intercultural trade in corn and furs, trade goods were acquired by—and buried with—a broader cross section of Indian society. Because possession of these valued goods originally served to validate the chiefs' claims to privileged rank, Potter argues, their gradual acquisition by other elements of the population mirrored the weakening authority of the chiefs.[4]

Copper, particularly in the form of gorgets (a type of pendant), served as a symbol of rank exclusively reserved for the Virginia Algonquian chiefs. When English-made buttons, bells, and other objects of copper and brass suddenly became available through trade, these too were incorporated directly into the traditional belief system, carrying a symbolic import similar to those items produced locally of native copper.[5] In applying conventional meanings to a new empirical environment, however, the Powhatan elite discovered that the pragmatics of trade led to practical revaluations.[6] Because chiefs no longer could effectively control the source of copper, the social power they had ascribed to its possession now became accessible to anyone with English trading connections. A depreciation of the metal's symbolic content ultimately occurred, at the expense of chiefly prestige.

Changes in cultural meanings and social contexts through the pragmatics of trade are the subject of James Merrell's chapter. In his survey of intercultural exchange in the Carolina piedmont between 1650 and 1750, Merrell looks beyond the objects of trade—slaves and deerskins, cloth and guns— to the "code of conduct" that, by scrupulous observance, permitted peaceful exchange. During the first half of the eighteenth century, trading activities depended upon the establishment of formal relationships between trade partners typical of those found in native southeastern gift economies. Transactions had simultaneous economic, social, and religious implications, differing in almost every regard from the one-dimensional commodity exchanges typical of European market economies.[7] Merrell traces the decline in gift-economy transactions, which coincided with a growing dependence (and a growing awareness of dependence) on manufactured trade goods by the Catawbas and other piedmont tribes. By 1750 the old code of conduct that had once proved indispensable for productive commerce now survived only in token gift exchanges signifying patron/client relationships, which were the reality of the late colonial period. In a new introduction, Merrell reflects on the directions recent archaeological and historical scholarship on the colonial Carolina piedmont, and, more generally, on the intercultural encounters that characterized the colonial era throughout eastern North America, have taken in the years since he wrote his original essay.

English demand for deerskins affected village life in many ways, with ramifications extending far beyond the immediate trade relationship. In an essay new to this collection, Tom Hatley explores other aspects of Cherokee economic ecology—the interconnectedness of human demographics, land use, labor commitments, gender roles—and the unanticipated changes in settlement pattern and subsistence strategy that resulted from increasing pressures on domestic production. By tracing the dynamic nature of Appalachian agriculture from roots thousands of years old, Hatley replaces an outdated evaluation of Cherokee women's agriculture as conservative and unresponsive to change with his portrayal of a resilient, adaptive farming that provided a stable domestic economy for the Cherokees during the eighteenth century, when they endured repeated devastations from war and disease. He also elucidates one important aspect of Cherokee sexual politics.[8] Through their control of surplus corn, women reinforced cultural boundaries, maintained subsistence independence, and—perhaps of greatest significance for the long-term survival of Cherokee culture—defended their own central place in the village economy, providing a needed balance to the male-dominated deerskin production and trade.

Most discussions of colonial-period deer hunting by southeastern Indians end with the native economies in ruins owing to the improvident extermination of deer herds by hunters blind to their own self-interest.[9] In fact, while overhunting undoubtedly occurred locally, there are no documented instances of extirpated white-tailed deer populations until the nineteenth century. Hatley's analysis of the complexities of Cherokee village economics demonstrates how a variety of alternative subsistence strategies developed during the long decline of the increasingly unprofitable deerskin trade. The Cherokee response to the European presence was a lengthy adaptive process guided primarily by the desire to maintain biological, economic, and spiritual links with an environment they had long known intimately.[10]

Notes

1. James Adair, *The History of the American Indians*, ed. Kathryn E. Holland Braund (1775; Tuscaloosa: University of Alabama Press, 2005), 332; cf. James Axtell, "The Power of Print in the Eastern Woodlands," *William and Mary Quarterly*, 3rd ser., 44 (April 1987): 300–309.

2. For more research on Indian-Spanish relations and trade, see Kathleen A. Deagan, "Spanish-Indian Interaction in Sixteenth-Century Florida and Hispaniola," in *Cultures in Contact*, ed. William W. Fitzhugh (Washington DC: Smithsonian Institution Press, 1985); Amy Bushnell, *The King's Coffer: Proprietors of the Spanish Florida Treasury, 1565–1702* (Gainesville: University Press of Florida, 1981), passim; John Jay TePaske, *The Governorship of Spanish Florida, 1700–1763* (Durham NC: Duke University Press, 1964), 193–226; Gregory A. Waselkov, "Seventeenth-Century Trade in the Colonial Southeast," *Southeastern Archaeology* 8 (Winter 1989): 117–33; John H. Hann and Bonnie G. McEwan, *The Apalachee Indians and Mission San Luis* (Gainesville: University Press of Florida, 1998); Kathleen A. Deagan, "Colonial Origins and Colonial Transformations in Spanish America," *Historical Archaeology* 37, no. 4 (2003): 3–13.

3. For some examples of men profiled in this genre, see J. Frederick Fausz, "Opechancanough: Indian Resistance Leader," in *Struggle and Survival in Colonial America*, ed. David G. Sweet and Gary B. Nash (Berkeley: University of California Press, 1981), 21–37; James H. Merrell, "Minding the Business of the Nation: Hagler as Catawba Leader," *Ethnohistory* 33 (January 1986): 55–70.

4. Eric Wolf has pointed out how frequently chiefs "proved to be notorious collaborators of European fur traders and slave hunters on two continents. Connection with the Europeans offered chiefs access to arms and valuables, and hence to a following outside of kinship and unencumbered by it." Eric Wolf, *Europe and the People without History* (Berkeley: University of California Press, 1982), 96.

5. The interpretation of newly imported artifact forms according to traditional ideology and a priori structural categories has been frequently noted; see Christopher L. Miller and George R. Hamell, "A New Perspective on Indian-White Contact," *Journal of American History* 73 (1986): 315, 317; Gregory A. Waselkov and R. Eli Paul, "Frontiers and Archaeology," *North American Archaeologist* 2 (1981): 316. For a discussion of archaeological measures of material culture change, see Jeffrey P. Brain, *Tunica Treasure*, Papers of the Peabody Museum of Archaeology and Ethnology 71 (Cambridge MA: Harvard University, 1979), 270–82.

6. The "pragmatics of trade" is one topic dealt with by Marshall Sahlins, *Islands of History* (Chicago: University of Chicago Press, 1985), 138, 145.

7. Marshall Sahlins, *Stone Age Economics* (Chicago: Aldine, 1972), 185–314; Lewis Hyde, *The Gift* (New York: Random House, 1983); Daniel H. Usner Jr., "The Frontier Exchange Economy of the Lower Mississippi Valley in the Eighteenth Century," *William and Mary Quarterly*, 3rd ser., 44 (April 1987): 165–92.

8. Cf. Sahlins, *Islands of History*, 7.

9. Two articles that present alternative perspectives to the overhunting model are by Richard L. Haan, "'The Trade Do's Not Flourish as Formerly': The Ecological Origins of the Yamassee War of 1715," *Ethnohistory* 28 (Fall 1981): 347–51, and Charles H. Hudson Jr., "Why the Southeastern Indians Slaughtered Deer," in *Indians, Animals, and the Fur Trade*, ed. Shepard Krech III (Athens: University of Georgia Press, 1981), 155–76. More balanced economic analyses can be found in Daniel H. Usner Jr., "American Indians on the Cotton Frontier: Changing Economic Relations with Citizens and Slaves in the Mississippi Territory," *Journal of American History* 72 (September 1985): 297–317; Kathryn E. Holland Braund, *Deerskins and Duffels: Creek Indian Trade with Anglo-America, 1685–1815* (Lincoln: University of Nebraska Press, 1993); Gregory A. Waselkov, "The Eighteenth-Century Anglo-Indian Trade in Southeastern North America," in *New Faces of the Fur Trade: Selected Papers of the Seventh North American Fur Trade Conference, Halifax, Nova Scotia, 1995*, ed. Jo-Anne Fiske, Susan Sleeper-Smith, and William Wicken (East Lansing: Michigan State University Press, 1998), 202–5; Shepard Krech III, *The Ecological Indian: Myth and History* (New York: W. W. Norton, 1999), 151–71. For recent archaeological perspectives, see Barnet Pavao-Zuckerman, "Vertebrate Subsistence in the Mississippian-Historic Transition," *Southeastern Archaeology* 19 (Winter 2000): 135–44, and Heather A. Lapham, *Hunting for*

Hides: Deerskins, Status, and Cultural Change in the Protohistoric Appalachians (Tuscaloosa: University of Alabama Press, 2005).

10. Calvin Martin, "Epilogue," in *The American Indian and the Problem of History*, ed. Calvin Martin (New York: Oxford University Press, 1987), esp. 212–17; for a useful survey of this topic, see Richard White, "Native Americans and the Environment," in *Scholars and the Indian Experience*, ed. W. R. Swagerty (Bloomington: Indiana University Press, 1984). For more on Cherokee women in the early nineteenth century, see Michael C. Coleman, "American Indian School Pupils as Cultural Brokers: Cherokee Girls at Brainerd Mission, 1828–1829," in *Between Indian and White Worlds: The Cultural Broker*, ed. Margaret Connell Szasz (Norman: University of Oklahoma Press, 1994), 122–35; Sarah H. Hill, *Weaving New Worlds: Southeastern Cherokee Women and Their Basketry* (Chapel Hill: University of North Carolina Press, 1997); Carolyn Ross Johnston, *Cherokee Women in Crisis: Trail of Tears, Civil War, and Allotment, 1838–1907* (Tuscaloosa: University of Alabama Press, 2003); Theda Perdue, *Cherokee Women: Gender and Culture Change, 1700–1835* (Lincoln: University of Nebraska Press, 1998), esp. 135–84.

Ruling "the Republic of Indians" in Seventeenth-Century Florida

AMY TURNER BUSHNELL

In the literature on colonial North America, scholars commonly contrast the English colonists, who courted the Indians through trade goods while holding them at a distance, with the French, who converted the Indians to Christianity and themselves to native life. Historians and anthropologists alike tend to discount Spanish and Indian interaction, regarding it as marginal to the central story—that of the French and English. Yet the Spanish presence in eastern North America lasted more than three centuries, irrevocably altering the lives of thousands of Spanish-speaking colonists and many thousands of American Indians.

An examination of the ways Spanish and native cultures adapted to one another in the New World can provide a third model to lay against the better-known French and English ones. In the Spanish model, Indians accepted vassalage along with Christianity and were turned, through the agency of their own leaders, into a labor reserve. It was a system the Spanish applied with success throughout Central and South America wherever they encountered natives who were agricultural, sedentary, and with leaders they could co-opt. In due course they brought the system to North America to use in the self-contained polity of the provinces of Florida. This chapter introduces the native leadership of those provinces and examines the means by which Indians and Spaniards shared authority, as well as the reasons why authority could be seen as something to share.

Spaniards arrived in the Southeast with a sober respect for the formalities of conquest, developed over centuries of reconquering Spain from the Moors and generations of experience in the New World. The sweatiest of *entradas* into unknown territory was a matter of order and record, with banners flying and notaries at the ready. If the entrada resulted in the extension of the king's domains, the royal coat of arms was left as evidence in every town, mounted on the council house.[1] Religious entradas were equally formal, and more than a little military looking when the friars had an armed escort and carried the cross painted on a banner.[2] Anywhere the friars gained access they erected a cross, added a saint to the town's name, and gave directions for building a church.[3] To raise a cross was to found a *visita*, or a stop on the missionary circuit, which in the course of time could develop into a *doctrina* complete with resident friars.[4] Indians, recognizing the symbols of occupation, often signaled a rebellion by pulling down coats of arms and crosses and burning them.[5]

Besides the secular and church officials, a third power existed in the provinces of Spanish Florida, that of the region's chiefs, who survived the foreign invasion to become integral to the governmental system that developed out of it. Their underlying, continuing authority could well have been symbolized by the ball poles of their towns. Raising a ball pole in the Southeast was tantamount to founding a town, which was not so much a place as a corporate entity. Although the townsite had to be relocated periodically as the fertility of surrounding soil became exhausted and firewood gave out, the town's playing field and ball pole remained in place as a sign of ownership and continuity.[6] Aware that the Indian ball game had non-Christian significance, some of the friars would have had the natives take down their ball poles and raise crosses, but other Spaniards said that the playing leagues and the gatherings for games were necessary to the functioning of native government.[7]

As always, what the chiefs had to say on the subject remains open to question. Although some of them became literate in their own languages, they did not often resort to writing.[8] Officers and friars occasionally wrote for a chief's signature, and interpreters were used to translate their statements for recording by notaries, yet one can seldom be sure of what a native ruler really said, much less what he or she had in mind.[9] Nevertheless, we cannot allow the difficulty of the sources to make us underestimate the importance of these rulers or omit them from the provincial picture.

It had not been easy to bring them into line. In the sixteenth century the Spanish tried an array of tactics: wholesale enslavement, wars, trade alliances, conversion with and without force, and intermarriage. The first official expedition to touch Florida, that of Juan Ponce de León in 1513, was little more than a legalized slave raid. Explorers Pánfilo de Narváez and Hernando de Soto in subsequent decades, seeking other Mexicos and other

Perus, took slaves to serve their large armies as they penetrated the southern interior. The natives retaliated in kind. The Dominicans who came to
Tampa Bay in 1547 were martyred on the beach, while the castaways from
shipwrecks along the Florida coast, if not slaughtered, became slaves. The
mutual ransoming of captives, called *rescate*, evolved into a wary sort of barter similar to that between Caribbean colonists and the French and English corsairs who ventured into their ports.[10]

In 1557 Philip II decided that Florida had strategic importance for the
return route of the treasure fleet and must be occupied. After an unsuccessful attempt by the viceroy of New Spain to plant a colony at Pensacola, Pedro Menéndez de Avilés sailed directly from Spain in 1565 to surprise French Fort Caroline and establish a colony on the west coast.[11] The
king of Spain might want Spaniards in Florida, but the Indians did not.
Although Menéndez founded three settlements and put a Jesuit and a fort
at nearly every deepwater harbor, the price in Spanish lives was high. He
finally declared that one could do nothing with the "treacherous" Indians of Florida except wage a "just war" on them, transport them to the islands, and sell them.[12]

This drastic a solution the Crown forbade. Menéndez and his successors had to pull in the borders, withdrawing isolated garrisons and un-
protected missionaries. The three original settlements contracted to two,
then one: St. Augustine. From that single outpost the Spanish slowly "pac-
ified" the Indians of Florida as they had the Chichimecas of northern New
Spain, by a combination of "wars of fire and blood" on the one hand and
presents on the other.[13] One after another, as the Spanish conquered the
various tribes or maneuvered them into treaties of alliance, the rulers were
forced to agree to a monopoly of their trade, to cooperation in time of war,
to the levying of tribute upon their vassals, and not least, to the presence
in their towns of Franciscans, who had replaced Jesuits as the indoctrinat-
ing agents in Florida.

In return, the new allies received access to the royal largesse. Every year,
when the chiefs came to kiss the governor's hands, he distributed lengths of
cloth, axes, felt hats, and other gifts among them in the name of the king,
while the king's coffer outfitted their churches with altar furnishings and
bells.[14] The expense of the gifts to the chiefs rose from 1,500 ducats in 1615

to four times as much in 1650. They accepted this bounty as no more than their due, and when presents were delayed, loyalty faltered.[15]

Franciscans urged their converts to live year-round in towns "like rational beings," within reach of the sacraments. In Florida this met with varying success. The wandering Ais and Tequesta Indians of the coast south of St. Augustine, "possessionless as deer," were never Hispanicized, nor were the nonagricultural Calusas of the southwestern coast.[16] The Guales and eastern Timucuans, hunters and gatherers as well as corn growers, took to the woods seasonally, abandoning both friars and "reductions"—the new towns formed at Spanish instance through a process of aggregation. One anticlerical governor said that if he were an Indian, he would run away too.[17] Only those natives who were both agricultural and sedentary, the Apalaches and western Timucuans, were what a friar could call "Indians of sense and satisfaction."[18]

In the sixteenth century the Spanish, thinking it possible to absorb sensible Indians into their own society through Christian association, encouraged close ties. Priests performed marriages between soldiers and high-ranking native women, and Menéndez himself accepted an Indian consort. Concubinage was common—the traditional Spanish form of union with a woman of lesser rank.[19] Governors served as godfathers to chiefs, bestowing their surnames with their baptismal gifts, so that the frontier of conversions might be traced by matching names of chiefs to names of governors. Native nobles sent their children to be raised in St. Augustine. Painted warriors fought side by side with soldiers in padded cotton doublets, and at least one chief was favored with a military pension.[20] Expectations for trade were idyllic, and priests foresaw a time when happy natives would paddle downriver to the towns of Spaniards, bringing canoeloads of chickens and taking back civilization.[21]

Efforts toward an integrated polity ended at the close of the sixteenth century with the Guale Rebellion, which showed how far from idyllic Indians could be. One governor pronounced the conversion of the natives a chimera.[22] The seventeenth century saw the development of the far different system of social order known as the two republics.[23] The Republic of Spaniards and the separate Republic of Indians were to be united in allegiance to the Crown and obedience to the "law of God"; otherwise they were intended to stay strictly apart.

The two republics occupied different territories of the same country. Until the refounding of Pensacola in 1698, St. Augustine remained Florida's one authorized Spanish municipality, whereas there were up to forty towns of Christian Indians, divided by language group into the provinces of Guale (on the Georgia coast), Timucua (in central Florida), and Apalache (around present Tallahassee).[24] Indians were not to come to St. Augustine without a pass.[25] Spaniards, blacks, mestizos, and mulattoes traveling on the king's business could stay no more than three days in an Indian town and must sleep in the council house.[26]

The Franciscans would willingly have quarantined the converts they instructed in doctrine and provided with the consolations and discipline of their religion—and discipline it was, for the natives of the "lower sort" attended mass with regularity out of fear of a whipping.[27] The missionaries asked only to live peaceably in their convents, meeting in chapter at St. Augustine every three years to elect a *padre provincial* as administrator and spokesman. But the king did not intend the friars to create theocracies. Through a series of papal concessions known as the *patronato real*, the Crown had long since gained control of the Spanish church and clergy in all but matters of doctrine, and the governor represented royal authority to the friars, as he often reminded them.[28]

To show the flag and keep track of the friars, the governor eventually stationed in every province a detachment of troops under a *teniente* or deputy governor. Because married soldiers imposed less of a burden on the Indians, many of the soldiers brought along dependents, most of whom could claim descent from some native group. In the garrison town of San Luis de Apalache a rough frontier settlement emerged, far to the west of the Spanish center of order and government in St. Augustine.[29] The soldiers and Florida-born creoles, called *floridanos*, tried the patience of missionaries with their incorrigible swearing, womanizing, mass skipping, and gambling at the ball games. Yet the system itself was clearly stable, for in the seventeenth century there were never more than two or three hundred able-bodied, armed Spaniards in all Florida to hold in check up to 26,000 Christian Indians.[30]

The Republic of Indians remained less centralized than the Spanish republic. Each town had its government of chief (*cacique*) and headmen (*principales* or *mandadores*), whom the Spanish interpreted as a town council (*cabildo*).[31] Sometimes a larger town would have subsidiary or satellite towns with subchiefs or tolerate a settlement of refugees from another tribe within its jurisdiction. The chiefs of the principal towns in a province met as needed to deal with defense and other intertown problems. The Spanish governor addressed them familiarly as "my sons and cousins."[32]

The formal means of communication was the yearly *visita*, a tour of inspection by the governor or his representative. As the *visitador* traveled from place to place the chiefs spoke to him one at a time, then gathered at an appointed location in the province to address him in council. The visita notary recorded their complaints about soldiers in debt to their vassals, floridanos running cattle across their fields, friars interfering with their games and dances, deputies treating them with disrespect, and other offenses to the Republic of Indians of which they were the acknowledged rulers. In the hundreds of pages of testimony one fact becomes clear. The chiefs were a force to reckon with in the provinces; they could have deputies withdrawn and friars reassigned.[33]

They had this power because to Spaniards it was unthinkable for them not to have it. According to medieval rationale, the right way to govern a country was to obtain the allegiance of its natural lords and through them the loyalty of their vassals. In Florida those Indian nobles who accepted Christianity and paid homage to the king of Spain could not reasonably be set aside, for that would have destroyed legitimacy in government. Instead they were drawn into alliances, favored, and supported in their rights as the natural lords (*señores naturales*) of the land. The rights of such leaders before contact varied from tribe to tribe. But during the Spanish hegemony their rights, as seen through Spanish eyes, were seigneurial. Equally with a Spanish *señor*, an Indian noble had the right to inherit title and position, the right to the preeminences of rank, the right to enjoy lands and rule vassals, and the right to combine with other lords and make war.

Like most Europeans, Spaniards traced descent patrilineally, from father to son. Southeastern natives, in contrast, were matrilineal. This meant that a chief's successor would be not his son but his nephew, son of his eldest sister. At first the Spanish found this system unnatural and lent their support to the "rightful heirs," particularly when the chief was a *cacica* married to a Spanish soldier.[34] In time, however, they came to understand that the imposition of Spanish inheritance patterns would undermine chiefs and disrupt clans, and so they accepted matriliny as the norm for the Republic of Indians.[35]

Because of the impermanent nature of townsites in Florida, a native title of nobility based itself upon a body of vassals rather than a tract of land. Don Patricio de Hinachuba, for instance, held the title chief of Ivitachuco, a town in Apalache province. He retained the appellation after leading an exodus of his vassals and their cattle to a place called Abosaya, far into Timucua province.[36] Such a title could be valid even without the vassals. Owing to the fortunes of war, disease, and famine, doña María, cacica of San Francisco, no longer had vassals of her own. She and her Cuban husband entered the historical record in the 1670s by trying unsuccessfully to persuade the subjects of another cacica to join her and form a new town.[37]

From a European standpoint, chiefs and headmen formed the equivalent of a Second Estate. They did not pay head tax or tribute; they were not subject to corporal punishment; they lived off the labor of commoners. Like their Spanish counterparts, the *hidalgos*, they were entitled to wear swords and ride horses.[38] Some chiefs of Apalache traded horses to the chiefs of Apalachicola, who in turn traded them to the English for guns. Determinedly heathen, the chiefs of Apalachicola told the Spanish governor that if God ever wanted them to accept Christianity they would let the Spanish know.[39]

Government in the Republic of Indians was financed by what might be called the "*sabana* system." Once or twice a year the common people of a town cleared, dug, and planted a sabana, or field, for their chief and each of their headmen, as well as the medicine man or woman, the best ballplayers, and the interpreter. There was one large communal field to provide for widows, orphans, and travelers and to put away a reserve.[40] Church expenses were met by another sabana, although friars were not impressed by the Indians as husbandmen and said that for the things of this world they were not ones to kill themselves.[41]

Chiefs and headmen did no manual labor, and neither did their families. Common women were expected to shuck and smoke oysters, parch cassina leaves for tea, shell and grind corn, and extract hickory oil, but an outraged chief of Guale threatened in writing to abandon his post on the frontier and bring all his people to be fed in St. Augustine if his daughter was called to such tasks at the convent.[42]

A chief convicted of rebellion or another crime could forfeit his or her position but not the preeminences of rank, which were a birthright. A ruler was sentenced to a term of exile rather than to hard labor.[43] Hence Governor Rebolledo made a serious mistake in 1655 when he ordered up the Timucuan militia to reinforce St. Augustine—for who knew where the piratical English would attack after capturing Jamaica—and peremptorily told them all, including the headmen, to bring three *arrobas* of corn, a backpack load of seventy-five pounds. The Franciscans tried to enlighten him on social stratification. In the provinces, they explained, chiefs were the same as lords, sometimes absolute lords, and principales were the same as hidalgos; they were not of the "vile" or common people who carried burdens on their backs. Rebolledo ignored this wise counsel, whereupon the rulers rose in rebellion. Rebolledo executed eleven of them, and the Council of the Indies had him arrested for provoking the lords of the land to revolt and then cruelly hanging them.[44]

Unsure what to make of a system in which a chief owed his position to his mother's brother, Spaniards tended to confuse the communal lands or properties of a town with the chief's patrimony. They referred, for instance, to the old fields of the *chief* of Asile when they meant of the *town*. This was because a chief frequently did speak for his or her town in matters of land use, whether to grant hunting rights within its jurisdiction or grazing rights to its fallow fields.[45] The Laws of the Indies stipulated that no cattle ranches were to be situated nearer than three leagues from any native settlement, but in both republics there were ways to get around a law. The Crown objected to chiefs who leased their lands for money, not because the land was being alienated but because rents were a form of tribute, and tribute remained a royal prerogative.[46] In time, the depopulation of the provinces left more and more vacant lands where there had once been people, but these lands did not revert to the royal domain as long as there was an heir of the chief's line.[47]

Land was plentiful; without improvements it had little value. A town had other properties that were worth more, such as the herd of individually owned cattle (not to be confused with the cattle belonging to the chief) and the food reserve in the town's several public granaries.[48] In a good year the combined contents of all the granaries of all the towns could amount to a sizable surplus for the province and might become the subject of bitter dispute among Spaniards. The governors expected to purchase the corn and beans at low prices to feed St. Augustine. They instructed their deputies to enforce extra plantings to that end. The Franciscans, believing they were the ones who had taught double-cropping to the Indians, wanted to sell the same surplus in Havana to reduce their chapter's debts and beautify the native sanctuaries.[49] A large amount of money went into the competitive adorning of churches; the value of chrismatories, diadems, and other religious treasure in Apalache province once amounted to 2,500 pesos per town, more than a single Indian could earn in a lifetime of work at the king's wages.[50]

A town granary was double-locked, with Spanish locks and keys. Whoever might be fighting over the second of the locks, the key to the first remained in the hands of the chief, who upon the advice of his headmen might choose not to sell the town's surplus at all.[51] Officers and friars quarreled similarly over who held jurisdiction over the church confines. For the Indians this too was a moot point. The church structure they had built; the contents they had either purchased or been given by the Crown.[52] One friar who had to close down a mission was sued by his erstwhile parishioners for carrying off their church ornaments and bell. To represent them the governor appointed a "defender of the Indians," as was required when natives appeared in a Spanish court, and the decision was in their favor.[53]

Just as in Spain each kingdom preserved its ancient *fueros*, or privileges, the Republic of Indians governed itself according to established law and custom, which the Crown saw no need to alter.[54] Only the practices contrary to the "law of God," such as magical cures and multiple wives, could be forbidden. (In their innocence the Indians had imagined that sororate polygyny, in which one's wives were close relatives of each other, was no worse than Spanish concubinage.)[55] A chief retained considerable power over his or her vassals.[56] If they obeyed poorly, the governor could be called upon to help subdue them even if heathen mercenaries had to be brought in to do it. It was one of the ways the Spanish made themselves indispensable in the provinces.[57]

The relationship between chiefs and governor was symbiotic. He guaranteed their authority; they provided him with labor, and as far as the Spanish were concerned this was their principal function. Communities in the Republic of Indians were liable to a head tax based on the number of married males in the census the friars made every Lenten season. Soon this tribute was commuted to a labor levy, the *repartimiento*.[58] The Spaniards made themselves the cobeneficiaries of the sabana system described earlier by having workers sent to the city in relays to clear, dig, and plant the "king's" sabana, do the first, second, and third hoeings, and guard the ripening corn for the harvest.[59] These field hands, called *indios de cava*, were given rations only. The chiefs who sent them to St. Augustine received tools and other items needed by the town.[60]

From time to time authorities asked the chiefs to send additional workers for the king's service to unload ships, paddle canoes, cut firewood, carry messages, and be servants to important people. These *indios de servicio* got their rations plus a daily wage in trade goods originally figured to be worth one *real* per day, an eighth of a peso. The choices ran to beads, knives, and half-blankets.[61] One subset of the indios de servicio was the *indios de fábricas* assigned to public works projects, usually building fortifications such as the stone Castillo de San Marcos. When the public works were in their own province the chiefs sometimes donated their vassals' labor and paid for materials out of provincial tithes, which were apparently theirs to administer.

A second subset of the indios de servicio was the *indios de carga*, who carried heavy loads of supplies or trade goods on their backs for long distances. The Crown repeatedly prohibited this use of Indians without addressing the cause, which was the lack of mules and packhorses in Florida. The use of indios de carga became another heated issue between the friars and the governors, each side—with justification—accusing the other of abuses. Still, Spaniards believed that the Indians of Florida were not ill-treated compared with the natives in the rest of the Indies. As a contemporary compiler pointed out, in Florida there were no *encomiendas* or factories or mines in which the natives could be occupied, and they did not pay tribute.[62]

The labor quota of a town was adjusted if its inhabitants had soldiers quartered on them, operated a ferry, or moved to a new place on the frontier or along the king's highway to accommodate the Spanish.[63] The quota was not adjusted to account for the Indians who had left the town to become craftsmen or apprentices or to work for private persons (at a better wage than the Crown paid), whether by the day, by the job, or on yearly contract. This is why Spanish and Indian authorities united to oppose peonage. A peon on a ranch was likely to be a man evading his turn on the labor levy and letting his neighbors support his family.[64]

If the Spanish took advantage of the sabana system, they also profited by the native inclination to war. Again, the chiefs were the agency. The vassals they supplied were used at first for couriers and indios de carga. Later, as the Spanish learned respect for Indian archers, their allies were enjoined to keep fifty arrows in their quivers. By the middle of the seventeenth century the Christian Indians were organized into companies of militia under their chiefs. When called to service they received rations and sometimes firearms. If after King Philip's War in 1675 and the Pueblo Revolt of 1680 the Crown had reservations about putting guns in the hands of Indians, the Florida governors usually felt this was justified. The Indians fought more bravely than the Spanish did, they said, and with greater readiness.[65] Prowess in battle allowed an Indian warrior to advance through the ranks to *noroco* or *tascaya*, dancing in the council house with a fine string of scalps and exempt from the labor levy.[66]

Chiefs and Spanish officers might have joint command, as on the expeditions sent northward in the 1620s to locate de Soto's lagoon of pearls.[67] Or the chiefs might go out on their own. In 1680 the chief of Santa Fé took warriors out the Suwanee River in canoes and down the west coast to Charlotte Harbor to rescue Spaniards held captive by the powerful Calusas; two years later Timucuan chiefs rescued a floridano rancher and his people being held for ransom by French buccaneers.[68] The chiefs legalized their campaigns in the Spanish manner, meeting in junta and listing the provocations that called for retaliation and entitled them to take booty. Sometimes a few soldiers went with the Indians; more and more often toward the end of the century they were not invited because of what was called "*la mala unión.*"[69]

Relations between the Republic of Spaniards and the Republic of Indians were becoming strained, and the cause was Carolina, founded in 1670. True to the English model, the initial colonists of Charlestown wanted only to trade with the natives. Governor James Colleton ingenuously expressed their policy in these words to his counterpart, Florida governor Diego de Quiroga y Losada: "As for the Yamassees . . . they have nothing to do with our government nor do we trouble ourselves about them . . . showing no profit but of a few deerskins for which we sell them powder, guns and shot as we do to all Indians indifferently."[70]

In the 1680s, Indians equipped with English firearms and ammunition began to raid Florida towns to take slaves for the markets of Charlestown.

This onslaught intensified during Queen Anne's War, when Colonel James Moore twice led armies of Creeks and Carolinians into Florida to destroy the provinces. Martyrologist accounts of the invasion of Apalache relate how Christians were burned on their own crosses, coats of arms defaced, and ball poles uprooted.[71]

The Spanish in the provinces recognized that in addition to invasion they and the chiefs faced a vassals' rebellion. Provincial and town government broke down. Mestizos, rejecting both sides of their heritage, turned to brigandage. Native warriors demanded that soldiers dismount and fight beside them with ammunition equally divided, while officials became reluctant to issue firearms to Indians who were probably going to defect.[72] Among the several thousand Florida natives who accompanied Moore back to Carolina, many went voluntarily. Others headed for the new Spanish fort at Pensacola, for French territory, or for parts unknown, saying they would not stay to die with Spaniards.

Faced with wholesale desertion, the teniente at San Luis spiked the cannons, packed up the salvaged church treasure, and carted it to St. Augustine. In the end only one chief of importance, don Patricio de Hinachuba of the town of Ivitachuco, remained an ally. Having compounded with Moore to spare his town at the expense of its sacred treasure, he settled his vassals and their livestock on the empty savannas of Timucua, far from the Spanish capital.[73]

In the eighteenth century little was left in the provinces to remind one of the time of the two republics or of the rulers who had shared sovereignty with Spaniards. It was the English system that survived. With sadness the Spanish acknowledged that the southeastern Indians had become interested only in guns and gewgaws and that they gave their vassalage to no one. Baptism they might consent to for the sake of the presents, but once out of sight they made a mockery of it, striking their foreheads and calling, "Water, begone! I am no Christian!"[74]

Postscript

Since the mid-1980s, a growing number of archaeologists and archaeology-minded historians have directed their attention to the Southeast, and the result is an impressive, communally built mound of fresh information about southeastern chiefdoms, rich in insights about the structure and workings of native hierarchies. With the exception of Charles Hudson's masterwork, *Knights of Spain, Warriors of the Sun: Hernando de Soto and the South's Ancient Chiefdoms* (Athens: University of Georgia Press, 1997), that literature is available mainly in collections, good examples being Alex W. Barker and Timothy R. Pauketat, eds., *Lords of the Southeast: Social Inequality and the Native Elites of Southeastern North America*, Archaeological Papers of the American Anthropological Association 3 (1992); Charles Hudson and Carmen Chaves Tesser, eds., *The Forgotten Centuries: Indians and Europeans in the American South, 1521–1704* (Athens: University of Georgia Press, 1994); John F. Scarry, ed., *Political Structure and Change in the Prehistoric Southeastern United States* (Gainesville: University Press of Florida, 1996); and Cameron B. Wesson and Mark A. Rees, eds., *Between Contacts and Colonies: Archaeological Perspectives on the Protohistoric Southeast* (Tuscaloosa: University of Alabama Press, 2002). Further bibliography can be found in Amy Turner Bushnell, "The First Southerners: Indians of the Early South," in *A Companion to the American South*, ed. John B. Boles (Oxford: Blackwell Publishers, 2002), 3–23.

The chiefdoms whose leaders, having assessed their options, entered into compacts with Spaniards (promising to fight their enemies, acknowledge their king, be indoctrinated into their religion, and cease trading with other Europeans) have received special attention, much of it by scholars sensitized to native agency by the sophisticated "new Indian history." The resulting "provinces of Florida," whose inhabitants had juridical status as the Republic of Indians, have been studied both by region, in John H. Hann, *Apalachee: The Land between the Rivers* (Gainesville: University Press of Florida, 1988), and *A History of the Timucua Indians and Missions* (Gainesville: University Press of Florida, 1996); John E. Worth, *The Struggle for the Georgia Coast: An Eighteenth-Century Spanish Retrospective on Guale and Mocama* (New York: American Museum of Natural History, 1995), and *Timucuan Chiefdoms of Spanish Florida*, 2 vols. (Gainesville: University Press of Florida, 1998); and by topic, in Amy Turner Bushnell, *Situado and Sabana: Spain's Support System for the Presidio and Mission Provinces of Florida* (New York: American Museum of Natural History, 1994); and Jerald T. Milanich, *Laboring in the Fields of the Lord: Spanish Missions and Southeastern Indians* (Washington DC: Smithsonian Institution Press, 1999). The Christianized chiefdoms also figure importantly in a number of shorter studies, including

Gregory A. Waselkov, "Seventeenth-Century Trade in the Colonial Southeast," *Southeastern Archaeology* 8, no. 2 (1989): 117–33; Amy Turner Bushnell, "The Sacramental Imperative: Catholic Ritual and Indian Sedentism in the Provinces of Florida," in *Columbian Consequences*, vol. 2, *Archaeology and History of the Spanish Borderlands East*, ed. David Hurst Thomas (Washington DC: Smithsonian Institution Press, 1990), 475–90; and John H. Hann, "Political Leadership among the Natives of Spanish Florida," *Florida Historical Quarterly* 71, no. 2 (1992): 188–208; in edited collections, such as Robbie Ethridge and Charles Hudson, eds., *Transformation of the Southeastern Indians, 1540–1760* (Jackson: University Press of Mississippi, 2002), and Bonnie G. McEwan, ed., *The Spanish Missions of La Florida* (Gainesville: University Press of Florida, 1993); and in two major historical syntheses: David J. Weber, *The Spanish Frontier in North America* (New Haven CT: Yale University Press, 1992), and Paul E. Hoffman, *Florida's Frontiers* (Bloomington: Indiana University Press, 2002).

The political and economic relationship between native and European authorities is a subject that opens new lines of investigation. My own interest in it continues in essays such as "How to Fight a Pirate: Provincials, Royalists, and the Defense of Minor Ports during the Age of Buccaneers," *Gulf Coast Historical Review* 5, no. 2 (1990): 18–35; "Republic of Spaniards, Republic of Indians," in *The New History of Florida*, ed. Michael Gannon (Gainesville: University Press of Florida, 1996), 62–77; "Spain's Conquest by Contract: Pacification and the Mission System in Eastern North America," in *The World Turned Upside Down: The State of Eighteenth-Century American Studies at the Beginning of the Twenty-First Century*, ed. Michael V. Kennedy and William G. Shade (Bethlehem PA: Lehigh University Press, 2001), 289–320; "'Gastos de indios': The Crown and the Chiefdom-Presidio Compact in Florida," unpublished; "'None of these wandering nations has ever been reduced to the Faith': Missions and Mobility on the Spanish-American Frontier," in *The Spiritual Conversion of the Americas*, ed. James Muldoon (Gainesville: University Press of Florida, 2004), 142–68; and "Escape of the Nickaleers: European-Indian Relations on the Wild Coast of Florida in 1696, from Jonathan Dickinson's Journal," forthcoming in *Coastal Encounters: Accommodations and Confrontations in the Eighteenth-Century Gulf South*, ed. Richmond Brown (Lincoln: University of Nebraska Press).

Notes

1. Alonso de las Alas and Juan Menéndez Márquez to the Crown, St. Augustine, December 13, 1595, *Archivo General de Indias, ramo Gobierno: Santo Domingo, legajo 229, número 18*. (Hereafter cited as SD; unless otherwise noted, origin is St. Augustine and addressee the Crown.)

2. Fr. Francisco Pareja, January 17, 1617, SD 235.

3. Friars in chapter, Octofber 16, 1612, SD 232/61.

4. Fr. Alonso del Moral, [summary seen in Council September 18, 1676], SD 235/102.

5. Francisco Menéndez Márquez and Pedro Benedit Horruytiner, July 27, 1647, SD 235.

6. John R. Swanton, *Modern Square Grounds of the Creek Indians*, Smithsonian Miscellaneous Collections 85, no. 8 (Washington DC: Government Printing Office, 1931), 38.

7. Amy Bushnell, "'That Demonic Game': The Campaign to Stop Indian *Pelota* Playing in Spanish Florida, 1675–1684," *The Americas* 35 (July 1978): 1–19.

8. Father Luis Gerónimo de Oré, a contemporary observer, said that the Indians, men and women, learned to read easily and wrote letters to one another in their own languages. *The Martyrs of Florida, 1513–1616*, ed. and trans. Maynard Geiger, OFM, Franciscan Studies 18 (New York: Joseph F. Wagner, 1936), 103.

9. On the reliability of interested parties see Gov. Alonso de Aranguíz y Cotes, November 14, 1661, SD 225.

10. Irene Wright, "Rescates: With Special Reference to Cuba, 1599–1610," *Hispanic American Historical Review* 3 (August 1920): 336–61; Paul E. Hoffman, *The Spanish Crown and the Defense of the Caribbean, 1535–1585: Precedent, Patrimonialism and Royal Parsimony* (Baton Rouge: Louisiana State University Press, 1980), 112–22.

11. Eugene Lyon, *The Enterprise of Florida: Pedro Menéndez de Avilés and the Spanish Conquest of 1565–1568* (Gainesville: University Press of Florida, 1976), is definitive on this expedition and the first years of conquest.

12. The contemporary arguments for and against Menéndez's plan can be found in Jeannette Thurber Connor, trans. and ed., *Colonial Records of Spanish Florida*, 2 vols. (DeLand: Florida Historical Society, 1925, 1930), 1:31–37, 77–81; Cédula to Gerónimo de Montalva, Governor of Cuba, August 10, 1574, in "Registros: Reales órdenes y nombramientos dirigidos a autoridades y particulares de la Florida. Años 1570 a 1604," typescript, [1907], P. K. Yonge Library of Florida History, 70–74.

13. Juan Menéndez Márquez, March 14, 1608, SD 229/58; Gov. Juan Fernández de Olivera, October 13, 1612, SD 229/74.

14. Domingo de Leturiondo, in *Auto* on Mayaca and Enacape, March 15, 1682 to September 7, 1682, SD 226/95.

15. For a discussion of the fund for the "expense of Indians" (*gasto de indios*) see Amy Bushnell, *The King's Coffer: Proprietors of the Spanish Florida Treasury, 1565–1702* (Gainesville: University Press of Florida, 1981), 66.

16. Friars in chapter, December 5, 1693, SD 235/134, and October 16, 1612, SD 232/61; Gov. Laureano de Torres y Ayala, September 19, 1699, SD 228/155.

17. Francisco Menéndez Márquez and Pedro Benedit Horruytiner, March 18, 1647, SD 229; Informe against Gov. Juan Márquez Cabrera, Havana, August 4, 1688, SD 864/8.

18. Fr. Juan de Paiva, Pelota Manuscript, San Luis de Talimali, September 23, 1676, in the Domingo de Leturiondo Visita of Apalache and Timucua, 1677–78, Residencia of Gov. Pablo de Hita Salazar, ramo Escribanía de Cámara 156-A, fols. 568–83 (hereafter cited as EC).

19. Stephen Edward Reilly, "A Marriage of Expedience: The Calusa Indians and Their Relations with Pedro Menéndez de Avilés in Southwest Florida, 1566–1569," *Florida Historical Quarterly* 59 (April 1981): 395–421; Kathleen A. Deagan, "Mestizaje in Colonial St. Augustine," *Ethnohistory* 20, no. 1 (Winter 1973): 55–65.

20. Don Gáspar Márquez, Chief of San Sebastian and Tocoy, June 23, 1606, SD 232/47; Catalina de Valdés, 1606, SD 19; Valdés, [1616], SD 232/76; Gov. Melchor de Navarrete, November 15, 1749, SD 2541/101.

21. In Informe on St. Augustine, September 16, 1602, SD 235/10.

22. Fr. Francisco Pareja, January 17, 1617, SD 235.

23. The ordering of the two republics is described by Lyle N. McAlister in *Spain and Portugal in the New World, 1492–1700* (Minneapolis: University of Minnesota Press, 1984), 391–95.

24. Mark F. Boyd, "Enumeration of Florida Spanish Missions in 1675," *Florida Historical Quarterly* 27 (October 1948): 181–88. A *provincia* in Florida was the same as a *partido* in Honduras, according to Gov. Juan Márquez Cabrera, June 14, 1681, SD 226.

25. Junta of Guale chiefs, Santa María, February 7, 1701, and Orders for Guale and Mocama, San Juan del Puerto, February 11, 1701, Residencia of Gov. Joseph de Zúñiga y Cerda, SD 858/4, fols. 179–85; Juan de Pueyo Visita of Guale and Mocama in 1695, Residencia of Gov. Laureano de Torres y Ayala, EC 157-A.

26. Orders for Timucua, San Francisco de Potano, December 24, 1694, in the Joachin de Florencia Visita of Apalache and Timucua, 1694–95, Residencia of Gov. Laureano de Torres y Ayala, EC 157-A.

27. Fr. Juan de Pareja, January 17, 1617, SD 235; Friars in chapter to Gov. Diego de Rebolledo, May 10, 1657, in Friars in chapter to Gov. Diego de Rebolledo, September 10, 1657, SD 235; Junta de Guerra, [Spain], July 15, 1660, SD 839; Friars in chapter vs. Gov. Juan Márquez Cabrera, May 10, 1681 to May 30, 1681, SD 226. The mission beadle, a native known as a *fiscal*, administered the punishment.

28. Gov. Pedro de Ybarra to Fr. Pedro Bermejo, December 13, 1605, SD 232; Gov. Juan Márquez Cabrera, December 8, 1680, SD 226/68.

29. For discussions of Spanish settlers in the provinces see Amy Bushnell, "The Menéndez Márquez Cattle Barony at La Chua and the Determinants of Economic Expansion in Seventeenth-Century Florida," *Florida Historical Quarterly* 56 (April 1978): 407–31; Bushnell, "Patricio de Hinachuba: Defender of the Word of God, the Crown of the King, and the Little Children of Ivitachuco," *American Indian Culture and Research Journal* 3 (July 1979): 1–21; Bushnell, *King's Coffer*, 14.

30. In 1655 the Franciscans reported seventy friars, thirty-eight doctrinas, and 26,000

Christian Indians in Florida. See Michael V. Gannon, *The Cross in the Sand: The Early Catholic Church in Florida, 1513–1870* (Gainesville: University Press of Florida, 1967), 57.

31. These are terms the Spanish brought with them. In the Indian languages, words for chiefs were *mico, inija, usinjulo,* and *alayguita.*

32. Gov. Joseph de Zúñiga y Cerda to the chiefs and principales of Vitachuco and San Luis, April 24, 1704, SD 858/B.

33. For accounts of visitas see Fred Lamar Pearson Jr., "The Florencia Investigation of Spanish Timucua," *Florida Historical Quarterly* 51 (October 1972): 166–76; Pearson, "Spanish-Indian Relations in Florida, 1602–1675: Some Aspects of Selected *Visitas," Florida Historical Quarterly* 52 (January 1974): 261–73; Bushnell, "That Demonic Game"; Bushnell, "Patricio de Hinachuba," 4–5. Ecclesiastical visitas were also made, usually by the padre provincial. See Gov. Francisco de la Guerra y de la Vega, February 28, 1668, SD 233/68; Gov. Juan Márquez Cabrera, December 8, 1680, SD 226/68.

34. Kathleen A. Deagan, "Cultures in Transition: Fusion and Assimilation among the Eastern Timucua," in *Tacachale: Essays on the Indians of Florida and Southeastern Georgia during the Historic Period,* ed. Jerald T. Milanich and Samuel Proctor (Gainesville: University Press of Florida, 1978), 103–4; don Gáspar Márquez, Chief of San Sebastian and Tocoy, June 23, 1606, SD 232/47.

35. Leturiondo Visita of 1677–78, EC 156-A; Florencia Visita of 1694–95, EC 157-A; Patricio, Chief of Ybitachuco [at Abosaya], to Gov. Joseph de Zúñiga y Cerda, May 29, 1705, SD 858/4.

36. Bushnell, "Patricio de Hinachuba."

37. Reported petition of María de Jesús, Cacica of San Francisco de Potano, January 25, 1678, acted upon at Salamototo, January 30, 1678, in the Leturiondo Visita of 1677–78, EC 156-A.

38. Florencia Visita of 1694–95, EC 157-A.

39. Gov. Joseph de Zúñiga y Cerda, September 30, 1702, SD 840/58; Gov. Juan Márquez Cabrera, September 20, 1681, SD 226/95.

40. Gov. Juan Márquez Cabrera, June 14, 1681, SD 226; Florencia Visita of 1694–95, EC 157-A; Orders for Guale and Mocama, San Juan del Puerto, February 11, 1701, SD 858/4, fol. 179; Teniente Antonio Mateos to Gov. Juan Márquez Cabrera, [San Luis de Talimali], March 14, 1686, SD 839/82.

41. "Por las cosas deste mundo no se matan mucho" (Friars in chapter vs. Gov. Juan Márquez Cabrera, May 10, 1681 to May 30, 1681, SD 226).

42. Chief of Guale to Gov. Juan Márquez Cabrera, Sápala, May 5, 1681, SD 226.

43. Gov. Pablo de Hita Salazar, July 5, 1677, EC 158.

44. Fr. Juan Gómez de Engraba to Fr. Francisco Martínez, Havana, March 13, 1657 and April 4, 1657. SD 225; Investigation of Gov. Diego de Rebolledo by the Council of the Indies, July 7, 1657, included with Anon., Informe against Gov. Diego de Rebolledo, June 15, 1657, SD 6/17; Friars in chapter, September 10, 1657, SD 235.

45. Friars in chapter, September 10, 1657, SD 235; Pedro Benedit Horruytiner, November 10, 1657, SD 233/55.

46. For discussions of land grants and use in Florida see Bushnell, *King's Coffer*, 80–82, 113, and Bushnell, "Menéndez Márquez Cattle Barony."

47. Henry F. Dobyns examines Timucuan depopulation as a representative case in *Their Number Become Thinned: Native American Population Dynamics in Eastern North America* (Knoxville: University of Tennessee Press, 1983), but his conclusions on total figures should be used with care. See David Henige, in "Primary Source by Primary Source? On the Role of Epidemics in New World Depopulation," *Ethnohistory* 33 (Summer 1986): 293–312.

48. Florencia Visita of 1694–95, EC 157-A. Owners identified their stock by ear notching.

49. Bushnell, *King's Coffer*, 11–12, 24, 70, 99; Gov. Pablo de Hita Salazar, September 6, 1677, SD 839/46; Gov. Juan Márquez Cabrera to Teniente Juan Fernández de Florencia, January 20, 1681, SD 226/76; Friars in chapter vs. Gov. Juan Márquez Cabrera, May 10, 1681 to May 30, 1681, SD 226.

50. See Bushnell, "Patricio de Hinachuba," 12.

51. Orders for Guale and Mocama, San Juan del Puerto, February 11, 1701, SD 858/4, fol. 179; Florencia Visita of 1694–95, EC 157-A.

52. Gov. Juan Márquez Cabrera to Fr. Blas de Robles, May 10, 1681, SD 226/76.

53. Domingo de Leturiondo, n.d., in Auto on Mayaca and Enacape, March 15, 1682 to September 7, 1682, SD 226/95; Domingo de Leturiondo, August 26, 1682, with Gov. Juan Márquez Cabrera, October 7, 1682, SD 226/95. On the defender of the Indians in Florida see Bushnell, *King's Coffer*, 40, 111. Cf. Charles R. Cutter, *The Protector de Indios in Colonial New Mexico, 1659–1821* (Albuquerque: University of New Mexico Press, 1986).

54. Captain Antonio de Argüelles, February 24, 1688, SD 234/87; Fiscal of the Council of the Indies, July 23, 1700, with Gov. Laureano de Torres y Ayala, September 16, 1699, SD 228/151.

55. Florencia Visita of 1694–95, EC 157-A; Lewis H. Larson Jr., "Historic Guale Indians of the Georgia Coast and the Impact of the Spanish Mission Effort," in Milanich and Proctor, *Tacachale*, 120–40; Bushnell, "That Demonic Game," 8.

56. Jerald T. Milanich and William C. Sturtevant, eds., *Francisco Pareja's 1613 "Confessionario": A Documentary Source for Timucuan Ethnography*, trans. Emilio Moran (Tallahassee: Florida Department of State, 1972), 34–35.

57. Friars, Informe on St. Augustine, September 16, 1602, SD 235/10; Gov. Juan Fernández de Olivera, October 13, 1612, SD 229/74; Florencia Visita of 1694–95, EC 157-A.

58. On the tribute and repartimiento see Bushnell, *King's Coffer*, 11–13, 16–25, 37–46, 97–99, 106, 110–11; Bushnell, "Patricio de Hinachuba," 8; Florencia Visita of 1694–95, EC 157-A; Francisco Menéndez Márquez and Pedro Benedit Horruytiner, July 27, 1647, SD 235.

59. Friars to Gov. Diego de Rebolledo, May 10, 1657, with Friars in chapter, September 10, 1657, SD 235.

60. Bartolomé de Argüelles, October 31, 1598, SD 229/25; Fr. Antonio de Somoza, Commissary General of the Indies, [Spain], May 2, 1673, SD 235/97; Teniente Antonio Mateos to Gov. Juan Márquez Cabrera, February 8, 1686, SD 839/82.

61. Apparently the blanket fabric was woven on a narrow backstrap loom, and a full blanket had a seam down the middle.

62. Juan Díez de la Calle, *Memorial y noticias sacras y reales del imperio de las Indias occidentales* (Madrid, 1646).

63. Friars in chapter to Gov. Diego de Rebolledo, May 10, 1657, in Friars in chapter, September 10, 1657, SD 235; Florencia Visita of 1694–95, EC 157-A. For examples of town relocation to serve the communications network, see Leturiondo Visita of 1677–78, EC 156-A, fols. 568–83, and Bushnell, "Menéndez Márquez Cattle Barony," 420.

64. Fr. Alonso del Moral, [summary seen in Council November 5, 1676], SD 235/104; Auto on the abuses of the friars, June 28, 1683, SD 226/105; Florencia Visita of 1694–95, EC 157-A.

65. Francisco Menéndez Márquez and Pedro Benedit Horruytiner, July 27, 1647, SD 235; Fr. Miguel de Valverde and Fr. Rodrigo de la Barrera, San Nicolás de Tolentino, September 10, 1674, SD 234; Gov. Pablo de Hita Salazar, May 14, 1680, SD 839/63; Cédula, March 22, 1685, SD 852/34; Florencia Visita of 1694–95, EC 157-A; Gov. Juan Márquez Cabrera, March 30, 1686, SD 852.

66. Gov. Joseph de Zúñiga y Cerda, Orders on scalp taking, March 14, 1701, SD 858/B-252; Bushnell, "That Demonic Game," 11–12, 16; Bushnell, *King's Coffer,* 96–97.

67. Bushnell, *King's Coffer,* 92.

68. Gov. Pablo de Hita Salazar, March 6, 1680, SD 226; Bushnell, "Menéndez Márquez Cattle Barony," 428.

69. Juntas de Guerra, St. Augustine, November 3, 1694, and San Luis de Talimali, October 22, 1702, SD 858/B-14.

70. Gov. James Colleton of Carolina, Charlestown, n.d., to Gov. Diego de Quiroga y Losada, translation sent to the Crown on April 1, 1688, SD 839.

71. See Charles W. Arnade, *The Siege of St. Augustine in 1702* (Gainesville: University Press of Florida, 1959); Mark F. Boyd, Hale G. Smith, and John W. Griffin, eds., *Here They Once Stood: The Tragic End of the Apalachee Missions* (Gainesville: University Press of Florida, 1951).

72. Bushnell, "Patricio de Hinachuba," 10; Captain Francisco Romo de Uriza, San Luis de Talimali, October 22, 1702, SD 858/B-14.

73. Bushnell, "Patricio de Hinachuba," 7–14.

74. Gov. Francisco del Moral Sánchez, June 8, 1734, SD 844/28; "Florida in the Late First Spanish Period: The 1756 Griñán Report," ed. Michael C. Scardaville and trans. Jesús María Belmonte, *El Escribano* 16 (1979): 16; Francisco de Buenaventura, Bishop of Tricale, April 29, 1736, SD 863/119.

Early English Effects on Virginia Algonquian Exchange and Tribute in the Tidewater Potomac

STEPHEN R. POTTER

Not long after an unsuccessful attempt to destroy the English colonists at Jamestown, in May of 1607, the paramount chief, or *mamanatowick*, of the Virginia Algonquians and his chiefs, or *werowances*, began trading with the English. In a scene replayed countless times, Indian maize was exchanged for European goods.[1] Such exchanges were more than ritual expressions of professed friendship—they were attempts by both Europeans and Indians to control and benefit from one another through trade.

From the perspective of the Algonquian werowances, this trade was a conscious effort to incorporate the strangers, or *tassantasses*, into the native system of exchange and tribute. It is my thesis that during earliest Anglo-Indian contact in Tidewater Virginia, the Algonquian werowances sought to control the flow of European goods into aboriginal society, much as they controlled the flow of luxury and status items gathered through tribute from their own people. As Anglo-Indian contact continued, Algonquian responses to the English differed depending upon their political relations with the Powhatan chiefdom of the James-York river basins and their distance from the earliest permanent English settlements. Among groups such as the Patawomekes, farther from both the Powhatan chiefdom and the Virginia English, the process of culture change was initially different even though the end result was the same—the collapse of centralized Algonquian political authority. This is most apparent in the English effects upon native systems of tribute and exchange, especially among peripheral chiefdoms like the Patawomekes.

In the late 1500s and early 1600s, the southeastern Algonquian groups blanketed the temperate coastal plain of the mid-Atlantic from the shores of the Chesapeake Bay and the tidewater regions of Maryland and Virginia to Albemarle and Pamlico sounds in North Carolina.[2] They consisted of a series of ranked, kin-oriented societies living in semipermanent villages and hamlets composed of arborlike structures made of poles covered with bark or cane mats. The villages, situated near streams and rivers, were surrounded by extensive fields of maize and beans, maintained through slash-and-burn techniques. Smaller garden plots of squash, pumpkins, gourds, sunflowers, and tobacco were tended near the longhouses. Agricultural harvests were supplemented by communal deer hunts, solitary stalking of game, harvesting marine and estuarine fish and mollusks, and gathering a host of plant foods. Their social and political organization featured rank-differentiated roles and functions, dress, and burial customs; polygyny; matrilineal descent of chieftains; tribute systems; and trade monopolies.[3] Although the degree of social and political centralization varied among these groups, all of them manifested what Marshall Sahlins describes as "a system of chieftainship, a hierarchy of major and minor authorities holding forth over major and minor subdivisions of the tribe: a chain of command linking paramount to middle range and local level leaders."[4]

The largest and most centralized of the southeastern Algonquian polities was the Powhatan chiefdom, named for the paramount chief who ruled the majority of Virginia Algonquians at the time of English colonization in 1607. The apical status position of paramount chief was occupied by Powhatan, or Wahunsonacock, from about 1572 until 1617.[5] From this position of authority, Powhatan served as a mediator between the secular and the sacred, as both a peace-chief and priest. Subordinate to Powhatan were the werowances who ruled the local groups. If there was more than one village in a group's territory, then subchiefs, or "lesser werowances," governed the villages where the werowance did not reside. It is likely that the werowances were peace-chiefs, concerned generally with internal matters. Conversely, the English mentioned captains or war-chiefs, who probably handled certain external affairs. As Frederic Gleach observed, "the distinction between peace-chief and war-chief is common among Algonquian groups and in the Southeast; the position of war-chief was achieved by a demonstration of bravery and ability to lead, and not inherited."[6] Nonchiefly, high-status positions included advisers, priests, and distinguished warriors. Commoners and war captives occupied the bottom two positions within the social hierarchy.[7]

Although the position of werowance was hereditarily ascribed (at least by the early seventeenth century), social rank was maintained and reaffirmed by the accumulation and control of wealth.[8] Indeed, the Algonquian word *werowance* has been variously interpreted as meaning "he is rich," "he is of influence," or "he is wise."[9] Among the Virginia Algonquians, the primary means of wealth acquisition by the paramount chief and the werowances of the petty chiefdoms was through a hierarchical system of tribute. Powhatan received a diversity of tribute items from his werowances, including "skinnes, beades, copper, pearle, deare, turkies, wild beasts, and corne."[10] One of the early Virginia chroniclers, William Strachey, discussed tribute collection in some detail in an often-cited passage.

> *Every Weroance knowes his owne Meeres and lymitts to fish fowle or hunt in (as before said) but they hold all of their great Weroance Powhatan, unto whome they paie 8. parts of 10. tribute of all the Commodities which their Countrey yeildeth, as of wheat [i.e., corn], pease, beanes, 8. measures of 10. (and these measured out in little Cades or Basketts which the great king appoints) of the dying roots 8. measures of ten; of all sorts of skyns and furrs 8. of tenne, and so he robbes the poore in effect of al they have even to the deares Skyn wherewith they cover them from Could, in so much as they dare not dresse yt and put yt on untill he have seene yt and refused yt; for what he Comaundeth they dare not disobey in the least thing.[11]*

More than likely, Powhatan's assessment of eight parts out of every ten was made against the total tribute collected by each werowance from his respective local group and was not an assessment made against all the economic yields and goods produced by each group.[12]

The goods collected were usually stored in mortuary temples near the house of each werowance, although Powhatan's three mortuary temples were situated at the core of his chiefdom and not at his primary place of residence in 1607. In a society lacking locks and doors, the mortuary temple, containing the preserved remains of deceased werowances and guarded by carved images of their gods, was sacred space—the Algonquian's sanctum sanctorum—and the perfect place to keep tribute goods and luxuries. Tribute items were used to support the werowances, their families, and the priests; to entertain visiting personages; and for communal feasts and religious activities. Werowances and their immediate supporters were the principal recipients of any luxury or prestige goods. Diffusion to society at large was mainly limited to those status items easily regulated in number and size, such as strands of beads and pearls, or sheet copper in the form of small geometric pieces or rolled tubular beads. The werowances used these items to reward warriors for bravery, to repay individuals who helped plant and harvest their fields, and possibly to dispense to commoners after certain funeral rites.[13]

Of all the prestige goods, the one the werowances seem to have coveted most was copper—so much so that they strictly controlled its trade. Large gorgets, made from sheet copper cut in a variety of geometric shapes, were reserved for the werowances and other individuals of high status. They were worn either about the head or suspended from the neck. The shiny red metal was used to purchase assistance in warfare and was buried with the werowances in their mortuary temples. Indeed, it was the combination of copper's reddish color and reflective qualities that made it an item of ritual significance, identified with the spirit world.[14]

The formation of the Powhatan chiefdom began sometime during the 1570s when Powhatan inherited six to nine groups occupying territories that formed a crescent from the fall line of the James River, north-northeast to the York River (fig. 1). Urged on by his priests and their prophecy that "from the Chesapeack Bay a Nation should arise, which should dissolve and give end to his Empier," Powhatan expanded his chiefdom eastward to the coast.[15] By the end of 1608, through intimidation and warfare, Powhatan's core area consisted of almost all of the petty chiefdoms between the falls of the James and York rivers, and Chesapeake Bay.[16]

The notable exception to Powhatan's conquests were the Chickahominys, who thwarted his efforts to appoint a werowance to rule them. The Chickahominys were the only Virginia Algonquians not governed by a werowance. Instead, they were ruled by a council of eight priests or elders (or both). This different form of governance may explain why individual Chickahominy families were able to trade their baskets of maize for Captain John Smith's goods.[17] Describing his "discovery of the country of Chikhamania," Smith wrote "[I] shewed them what copper and hatchets they shuld have for corne, each family seeking to give me most content: so long they caused me to stay that 100 at least was expecting my coming by the river, with corne."[18]

When the English established Jamestown in 1607, Powhatan was preoccupied with expanding the bounds of his eponymous polity to include the remaining Tidewater Virginia Algonquians. Groups along the Rappahannock River, the southern bank of the Potomac River (such as the Patawomekes), and the Accomacs and Occohannocks of Virginia's Eastern Shore were part of Powhatan's "ethnic fringe," as Helen Rountree has described it—peripheral chiefdoms strongly influenced, though not absolutely dominated, by Powhatan. Beyond the York and James rivers, Powhatan's authority diminished as the distance from the center of his chiefdom increased, a fact not lost on the English invaders.[19]

Despite the abrupt intrusion of the English in the midst of Powhatan's James River territories, the colonists and Powhatan natives attempted to accommodate one another during the period from July 1607 to 1609. William Strachey observed that the Indians were "generally Covetous of our Commodities, as Copper, white beades for their women, Hatchetts . . . Howes to pare their Corne ground, knyves and such like."[20] Captain John Smith added "they were no lesse desirous of our commodities then we of their Corne."[21] Thus only occasional outbreaks of violence marred the trade of European goods for Indian maize.

During the early years of the Jamestown settlement, it was the paramount chief and his werowances who controlled, for the most part, the distribution of European goods among their people, particularly prestige items. On one occasion the paramount chief Powhatan told Captain Newport, "It is not agreeable to my greatnesse, in this pedling manner to trade for trifles, and I esteeme you also a great Werowance. Therefore lay me downe all your commodities together; what I like I will take, and in recompence give you what I thinke fitting their value."[22] Moreover, Powhatan attempted to "monopolize all the Copper brought into Virginia by the English: and whereas the English are now content, to receave in Exchange a few measures of Corne for a great deale of that mettell. . . . Powhatan doth againe vent some smale quantety thereof to his neighbour Nations for 100. tymes the value, reserving notwithstanding for himself a plentiful quantety."[23]

In the course of their initial trading with the Jamestown colonists, the werowances were usually the ones who conducted the trade. Even items stolen from the English were taken to the werowance for first refusal, as mentioned by Captain John Smith:

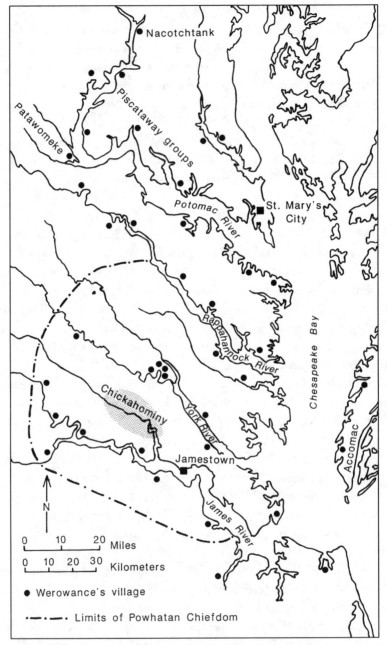

Figure 1. Map of Algonquian groups bordering Chesapeake Bay at the beginning of English occupation.

At our Fort, the tooles we had, were so ordinarily stolen by the In-
dians, as necessity inforced us to correct their braving theeverie.
. . . Their custome is to take any thing they can ceaze off . . . but
what others can steale, their King receiveth. . . . From Nansamond,
which is 30. miles from us, the King sent us a Hatchet which they
had stollen from us at our being there.[24]

Twenty-two years before the settling of Jamestown, Sir Walter Raleigh's colonists had similar experiences trading with the North Carolina Algonquians.
Regarding the Roanoke Indians, Arthur Barlowe penned the following:

The next day there came unto us divers boates, and in one of them
the Kings brother, accompanied with fortie or fiftie men. . . . When
hee came to the place, his servants spread a long matte uppon the
grounde, on which he sat downe, and at the ende of the matte, foure
others of his companie did the like. . . . After wee had presented this
his brother, with such things as we thought he liked, we likewise gave
somewhat to the other that sate with him on the matte: but presently
he arose, and tooke all from them, and put it into his owne basket,
making signes and tokens, that all things ought to be delivered unto
him, and the rest were but his servants, and followers.[25]

Given the authority of the werowances to levy tribute, it should come as no
surprise that they sought to control the flow of European goods into aboriginal society.

By 1609 private trading between English mariners (who came to the
Jamestown colony on supply ships) and members of the Powhatan chiefdom
flooded the James River chiefdoms with copper, potentially diminishing its
value among the Algonquians as well as the prestige of the werowances.[26]
With copper aplenty, Powhatan now asked for English arms in exchange
for Indian maize.[27] Unwilling to trade in arms and backed by a new charter charging the English colonists with "the conversion and reduccion of the
[native] people in those parts unto the true worshipp of God and Christian
religion," the Jamestown government launched attacks against the Powhatans to destroy their priesthood and obtain the precious corn by force.[28]

For most of the next quarter-century, members of the Powhatan chiefdom and their English neighbors engaged in "vengeful perpetual warre,"

interspersed with short-lived periods of peace.[29] The First Anglo-Powhatan War (1609–14) ended in English victory. Three years later Powhatan abdicated his position as paramount chief in favor of his brothers Opitchapam, the paramount or peace-chief, and Opechancanough, the war-chief. The following year Powhatan died. By 1622 Christian missionary fervor and forced adoption of English "Fassions" seriously threatened Powhatan culture. These factors, coupled with loss of land, led Opechancanough to launch an attack against the tassantasses in 1622. Ten years later the Second Anglo-Powhatan War officially ended, leaving the Powhatan chiefdom in a state of near collapse. Over the next dozen years, further territorial expansion by the English and Opechancanough's perception that the colony was vulnerable due to the English Civil War triggered the Third Anglo-Powhatan War in 1644. Two years later the war was over, Opechancanough was dead, the Powhatan chiefdom was destroyed, and *all* Virginia Algonquian groups were made tributary to the colony.[30]

As Anglo-Indian relations on the James and York rivers were being forged in the crucible of war, English relations took a different turn with the Virginia Algonquians farther from both the English and the Powhatans. In May 1609, before the outbreak of hostilities, members of the Virginia Company of London advised the Jamestown leaders:

> *If you make friendship with any of these nations as you must doe, choose to doe it with those that are fartherest from you and enemies unto those amonge whom you dwell, for you shall have least occasion to have differences with them and by that meanes a suerer league of amity, and you shalbe suer of their trade partely for covetousnes and to serve their owne ends, where the copper is yett in his primary estimacion which Powhatan hath hitherto engrossed.*[31]

Advice became policy and distance from English settlements the means of distinguishing Indian friend from foe.

Hastening to put policy into action, in 1610 Captain Samuel Argall established a lucrative trade with the werowance of Patawomeke, "A King as great as Powhatan" and "a Person of great Interest and Authority, throughout the whole [Potomac] River."[32] The Patawomekes were the largest and most powerful of the northern Virginia Algonquian chiefdoms and had been key players in the native trade network before the English invasion—

indeed, the name Patawomeke has been interpreted as "trading center."[33] Almost 1,000 Patawomekes lived in ten villages near the southern shore of the Potomac River, with several of the minor villages or hamlets governed by Japazaw, a lesser werowance and brother to the great werowance of Patawomeke.[34]

As the First Anglo-Powhatan War raged in the lower reaches of the James and York rivers, Captain Argall, "trading for corne, with the great king of Patawomeck [Patawomeke], from him obteyned well neere 400. bushells of wheat [i.e., corn], pease and beanes (besyde many kind of furrs) for 9. poundes of Copper, 4. bunches of beades, 8. dozen of hatchetts, 5 dozen of knives, 4 bunches of bells, 1. dozen of sizers, all not much more worth than 40s. English."[35] Capitalizing on his earlier success, Argall returned to the Patawomekes in 1612, obtained 1,100 bushels of maize, and, more important, sealed a defensive military alliance with them against Powhatan.[36]

Yet Argall's greatest coup in the maize trade with the Patawomekes occurred in 1613. To quote another Jamestown chronicler, Ralph Hamor:

> *It chaunced Powhatans delight and darling, his daughter Pocahuntas . . . tooke some pleasure . . . to be among her friends at Pataomecke . . . imploied thither, as shopkeepers to a Fare, to exchange some of her Fathers commodities for theirs, where residing some three months or longer it fortuned upon occasion either of promise or profit, Captain Argall to arrive there.*[37]

With the aid of Japazaw and the approval of the werowance of Patawomeke, Argall succeeded in kidnapping Pocahontas for the price of "a small Copper kettle and som other les valuable toies."[38] This action, plus a devastating English raid on the Pamunkeys a year later, helped force an end to the First Anglo-Powhatan War.[39]

The maize trade with the northern Virginia Algonquians and Piscataway groups along the Potomac River slackened after the end of the war in 1614, as the colonists became more self-sufficient. Viewing the cessation of hostilities as an opportunity to Christianize the Indians, the Virginia Company of London promoted the metamorphosis of Algonquians into Anglicans while the Virginia English promoted the growth of tobacco production. As the profitable tobacco market grew during the next seven years, English land acquisition and Christian missionary efforts helped precipitate the Second Anglo-Powhatan War of 1622–32.[40]

Acutely aware of the Patawomekes' invaluable services in the past and their nonparticipation in Opechancanough's attack of March 22, 1622, the Jamestown government realized the necessity of maintaining good relations with those Virginia Indians who were not in league with Opechancanough. In 1622 the English built a fort adjacent to the village of Patawomeke and the werowance of Patawomeke provided "40. or 50 choise Bow-men to conduct and assist" the English in a raid to seize maize from the Patawomekes' enemies, the Nacotchtanks.[41] Near summer's end, the beneficial alliance with the Patawomekes was severed for a time when Captain Isaac Maddison acted rashly on false information and brutally killed thirty or forty Patawomekes.[42]

The following March, Captain Henry Spelman and twenty-one Englishmen were killed somewhere on the Potomac River, within approximately thirty miles of present Washington, DC. Some thought the Nacotchtanks responsible, others the Patawomekes. Both certainly had reason to want revenge on the English, but the one man who lived to tell about the attack—Henry Fleet—blamed the Nacotchtanks. Regardless of the group responsible, Governor Wyatt sought to renew the English alliance with the Patawomekes by leading an expedition against their enemies, the Nacotchtanks and Piscataways. By the fall of 1623 the English and Patawomekes were allies once again, and the maize trade resumed.[43]

Benefiting from their experience in the maize trade of the 1620s, individuals like Henry Fleet and William Claiborne saw the profit to be had in pelts. By 1630 as the Second Anglo-Powhatan War was slowly coming to an end on the James and York rivers, the beaver trade was beginning on Chesapeake Bay. With the establishment of the Maryland English at St. Mary's City in 1634, Marylanders competed with Virginians in the ever-increasing search for pelts.[44] Although the Chesapeake beaver trade lasted only until the 1650s, as J. Frederick Fausz wrote, it "brought Englishmen and Indians together in the most direct and intense form of cultural contact short of war, and yet it . . . demanded . . . that Indians remain Indians, pursuing the skills they knew best without fear of territorial dispossession, and that Englishmen remain Englishmen, performing the services they understood without the need to become Christian crusaders."[45]

Increased Anglo-Algonquian contact brought about by the profitable fur trade on the Potomac River opened the floodgates for European trade goods to pour into the area. With increased contact, first through trade and later through English settlement, the werowances' authority diminished owing to a variety of factors including population decline, displacement or loss of land, discrediting of the priesthood through its ineffectiveness against European diseases, and loss of clear matrilineal successors to the chieftainship. By the 1650s and 1660s some werowances were being appointed by the English; other werowances governed with their "great men," and in at least one case, groups of "great men" ruled in lieu of a werowance.[46] As the centralized political power of the werowances weakened, so did their control over the tribute and exchange systems, opening up opportunities for greater individual trade and acquisition of goods.

Unfortunately for historians, after the beginning of the Second Anglo-Powhatan War in 1622, English accounts of Virginia Algonquian lifeways are sparse and provide little information about the effects of acculturation on the power and authority of the werowances.[47] If the Algonquian werowances' control over European goods, particularly prestige items, waned with time as their authority diminished (as the written record strongly indicates), then such a change should be reflected archaeologically by an increase in both number and diversity of European trade goods found in common burial sites, and by the presence there of items formerly reserved for individuals of high status. Assuming a person's status in life is manifested in death by the manner of burial, it is possible to document changes over time in the control, distribution, and acquisition of certain classes of material goods that are preserved in the archaeological record.

To investigate this possibility, an examination was made of archaeological collections from the vicinity of Potomac Creek in Stafford County, Virginia. Here, according to Thomas Jefferson, was the location of the "chief town" of the Patawomeke Indians, where the werowance resided.[48] These collections of artifacts and archival materials, now in the Smithsonian Institution, were made between 1869 and 1937, mainly by antiquarians and avocational archaeologists. Consequently there is great variation in the degree of control exercised in the collection and recording of the archaeological materials. Additional research in the same locale by late nineteenth-century professional archaeologists and twentieth-century physical anthropologists and archaeologists has helped offset some inadequacies of the data.[49] Taken together, all of this information can be used to reconstruct and interpret a remarkable series of late prehistoric/protohistoric and historic burial sites of the Patawomeke Indians.

At the Potomac Creek site, a palisaded village occupied from about AD 1300 to 1560, four ossuaries were discovered. Ossuaries are large, saucer-shaped pits, usually elliptical in outline, containing mass human reburials. The four ossuaries held at least 41, 67, 135, and 287 individuals of all ages and both sexes. Only items of native manufacture were found in association with the skeletal material in the ossuaries—a few bone awls and clay smoking pipes; a variety of disk, columella, and marginella shell beads (most found with children's skeletons); and "three small pieces" of native copper in one ossuary and "two small copper pendants" associated with the remains of two children in another.[50] The communal nature of the reburials, the relative paucity of grave goods per individual, the preponderance of shell beads associated mainly with children, and the limited number and small size of copper objects (ostensibly of native origin) fit the expected pattern of precontact Algonquian society, when the werowances and their successors controlled the distribution of tribute and prestige items. Relatively few prestige goods, particularly those made of copper, trickled down to the hands of commoners prior to English settlement in the region.

On another part of Potomac Neck, near a historic Patawomeke occupation at Indian Point, a single flexed burial was reported in 1891. Archival records indicate the skeleton had been placed in a small pit, three feet deep. Associated objects included a large crescent-shaped copper breastplate, tubular copper beads, and "numerous needles 4 or 5 inches" long. Other objects possibly included with the burial were "rough" glass beads and "pipes of clay."[51] Depending upon whether glass beads were in association and whether the copper was of North American or European origin, the isolated burial could date from late prehistoric times to the mid-seventeenth century. With no way of confirming the presence of glass beads or the origin of the copper and no data on the skeleton, further interpretation of this isolated burial is problematic.

In 1869 a most remarkable multiple burial site was discovered by a party of four antiquarians near Indian Point. Their finds were reported by Elmer Reynolds in 1880, and it is upon his account, published descriptions of some

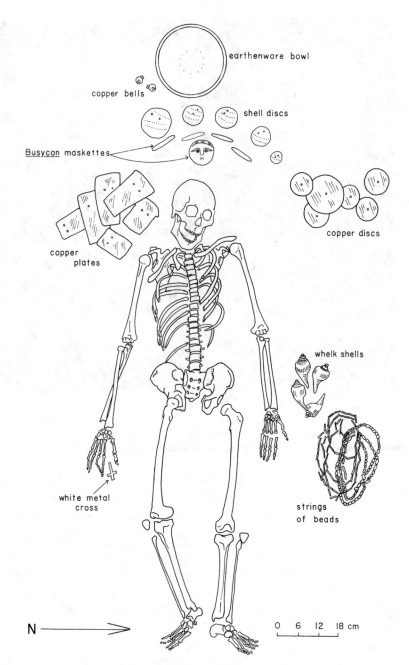

earthenware bowl

copper bells

shell discs

Busycon maskettes

copper plates

copper discs

whelk shells

white metal cross

strings of beads

N

0 6 12 18 cm

Figure 2. Artist's reconstruction of the twelfth skeleton and associated objects from the high-status multiple burial (circa 1608 to 1630) at Potomac Neck, Virginia.

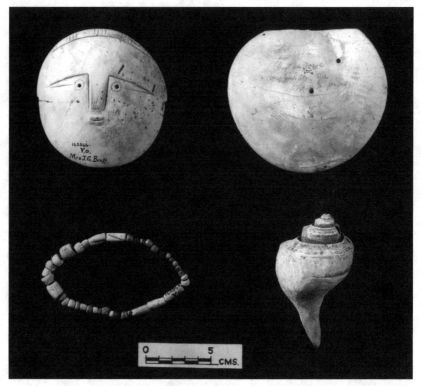

Figure 3. Artifacts from the high-status multiple burial at Potomac Neck, Virginia. *Upper left: Busycon* maskette with stylized human face; *upper right:* plain *Busycon* pendant; *lower left:* native-made shell beads and European drawn round glass beads; and *lower right:* a small whelk shell (courtesy of the Department of Anthropology, Smithsonian Institution).

of the artifacts, and an examination of the Smithsonian Institution collection that the following reconstruction is based (fig. 2).[52] The burial consisted of the extended skeletons of twelve adults, all but one in association with native-made shell beads. Associated with the twelfth skeleton was a diverse array of artifacts—five *Busycon* shell maskettes with stylized human faces in bas-relief (fig. 3); five circular shell gorgets; four small whelk shells; two flushloop brass bells; six circular copper gorgets; six quadrangular copper gorgets (fig. 4); a native-made earthenware bowl; approximately four quarts of beads made of rolled sheet copper, bone, clay, and shell; and fifteen drawn round beads of monochrome blue glass. "A cross of white metal of rude construction," wrote Reynolds, "was found in an erect position, sustained by the earth, between the thumb and forefinger of the skeleton."[53]

Figure 4. Three large gorgets or plates made from sheet copper, found with the twelfth skeleton in the high-status multiple burial at Potomac Neck, Virginia (courtesy of the Department of Anthropology, Smithsonian Institution).

The twelfth individual in this multiple grave probably represents a high-status burial dating from about 1608 to 1630, based on the presence of the *Busycon* mask gorgets, and the glass beads and brass bells that were most prevalent in the Susquehanna River/Chesapeake Bay region during this period—a time when the English periodically traded with the Patawomekes for Indian souls and maize.[54] Ethnohistorical documentation indicates that possession of large objects of sheet copper, such as those described here, were limited to the werowances and others of high status. Circular and rectangular copper gorgets have been found archaeologically with high-status burials dating to the late sixteenth and seventeenth centuries throughout other parts of the Southeast.[55] As for the "white metal" cross, it could easily have been acquired by the Patawomekes during the early years of the Jamestown colony when the Anglican settlers were instructed by the Virginia Company of London to "endeavour the conversion of the natives to the true god and their redeemer Christ Jesus." From the beginning, Jamestown colonists were erecting wooden crosses, carving crosses in trees, and leaving metal crosses behind as they trekked about the Chesapeake Tidewater region.[56]

Another ossuary excavated at the Potomac Creek site was found about 70 feet outside the palisade lines. This ossuary was an oval-shaped pit 37.5 feet long, 15 feet wide, and 5 feet deep, containing the skeletal remains of 181 individuals of all ages and both sexes. Objects associated with burials in the ossuary included thousands of shell columella and disk beads "often associated with children's skeletons," shell gorgets, aboriginal clay smoking pipes, a pair of scissors, and two small flushloop brass bells. Copper was found with twenty-eight skeletons, "usually in the form of tubular beads." More than sixty tubular copper beads were recovered, along with a few cone-shaped tinklers, a small copper band fitted to a pipestem, and four small square copper plates, at least one of which was associated with an adult male. Glass beads were found with six skeletons, and all were drawn round beads, described by T. Dale Stewart as "small, crudely spherical beads. The majority of these (19) were dark blue in color and ranged up to 4.5 mm in diameter. Other plain colored beads about the same size were violet-blue (3), light blue (2) and green [greenish blue] (45). Also, there were eight red beads with black centers and one [white with alternating red and blue] striped bead."[57]

This ossuary probably dates from the period of earliest English contact in the Potomac valley, between about 1608 and 1630. Copper objects are mainly small tubular beads, and the relatively few European glass beads are all drawn round beads typical of this period. During this time the authority of the werowance and his immediate supporters was still implicit in the relatively restricted flow of European trade material and status goods to society at large, before the inception of the Chesapeake beaver trade about 1630.

The latest aboriginal burial feature from the vicinity of the Potomac Creek site was a shallow pit, about 6 to 8 feet in diameter, containing at least ten individual burials of children and adults. Some of the objects associated with this group burial include large quantities of disk and columella shell beads, one-half of a shell gorget with a drilled-dot star pattern on the inside, a small whelk shell, a stone pipe, a fragment of a bone comb, two bone awls, a small silver English dram cup dating to about 1640, a brass spur rowel dating to the second half of the seventeenth century, a section of copper chain, six copper buttons, forty flushloop brass bells, and European glass beads. The beads consisted of both drawn tube beads (also known as straw or cane beads) and drawn round beads. The tube beads were small (about 17 mm long and 4 mm in diameter), and most were monochrome red or blue (nine black and one white were also found). The remaining drawn round beads were made of monochrome blue, red, or green glass.[58]

In the lower Susquehanna River red tube beads and some blue, black, and white ones occur most frequently at sites dating 1630 to 1680.[59] Since evidence from the historical documents suggests that no later than the 1660s the Patawomekes had abandoned their ancestral lands at Potomac Neck, owing to encroachment by English settlers, the presence of monochrome tube beads, the spur rowel, and the English dram cup help date this group burial between 1640 and the 1660s.[60] The change from mass ossuary burials to small group burials of primary interments and the presence of greater quantities of European objects per number of individuals interred is probably a reflection of the changes in aboriginal social and political organization indicative of the weakening power of the werowances.

During late prehistoric and protohistoric times, the difficulties associated with the acquisition of copper helped limit its possession to those with control over other scarce commodities—the werowances and their advisers. Since possession was controlled by the elite, it was associated with the status of the owners and in turn conferred prestige on them, serving to validate and sanctify their rank in society. The four late prehistoric/protohistoric ossuaries discovered at Potomac Neck, Virginia, reflect the werowances' control of the distribution of luxury and status goods to the general populace.

Within two years of the establishment of Jamestown, the availability of formerly scarce items such as copper created a temporary crisis within the social and political hierarchy of the James River chiefdoms. Powhatan tried to control the trade and maintain his monopoly. Those werowances farthest from the core of Powhatan's chiefdom and only nominally under his control (the Patawomekes, for instance) could most successfully circumvent this effort. Until other factors (such as depopulation, defeats in war, and discrediting of the priesthood) weakened their authority, the werowances were apparently able to limit the devaluation of copper and its widespread acquisition by the majority of society. At Potomac Neck, the multiple-status burial and an ossuary probably date to the time of earliest English contact in the Potomac valley, about 1608 to 1630. Continued control by the elites of certain luxury and status goods is evidenced by the dozen large copper gorgets and other prestige items associated with the twelfth skeleton in the high-status burial. On the other hand, the ossuary burial of at least 181 individuals contained few high-status or European items.

The beaver trade in the Potomac-Chesapeake tidewater, about 1630 to 1660, created new possibilities for ownership of copper and other European items. As the fur trade grew and the werowances' authority diminished, the economically restrictive practices formerly enforced by the werowances and their advisers also diminished. This set of circumstances brought about increased opportunities for individual Algonquians to engage in trade and acquire European goods, as exemplified by the greater number of European objects interred per person in the 1640–60s group burial from Potomac Neck.

Moreover, successful Indian trapper/traders could conceivably acquire and keep prestige items, such as copper, thereby flouting the ebbing authority of the werowances. Status achievement was now open to more people who could compete for elite positions by acquiring wealth and employing symbols previously reserved to the werowances and others of high status. Perhaps such a process allowed individuals formerly unable to become advisers or "great men" to rise to such positions, subtly contributing to the decline in power and authority of the werowances.

Postscript

For this new edition of *Powhatan's Mantle*, I updated the original text and expanded endnotes and references. Most research on this topic, since this chapter first appeared, has focused on the practice of ossuary burial and the part it may have played in reflecting people's status differences in life.

Looking at ossuaries from a secular perspective, Christine Jirikowic proposed that the large Potomac River communal reburials were one means by which the native peoples defined their distinctness from other groups, as well as a reflection of the politically stratified chiefdom-level societies responsible for their creation. The ethnohistorical sources are quite clear that the werowances or rulers and other elites received separate treatment at death, with the remains of the rulers kept in a specially constructed mortuary temple. "The whole mortuary program," Jirikowic observed, "effectively devalues individual differences among the commoners and enhances the differences between the commoners and elite. In this way the mortuary practice of these groups may have acted as an important ideological legitimation of this stratified social order."[61]

In a similar vein, but from a sacred perspective, I suggested that the difference in mortuary treatment between rulers and commoners also reinforced the hierarchical social order. Only those of very high standing, the rulers and priests, were thought to have an afterlife. "A cosmology that admitted only werowances and priests into an Algonquian paradise would not have permitted them to be placed in communal burial pits with commoners."[62]

E. Randolph Turner remarked upon the differences between the Potomac River ossuaries and those farther south in the coastal plain of Virginia. The ones from the Potomac were quite large, with the vast majority containing from forty-one to over six hundred individuals, with large numbers of shell beads associated with the remains of children. Most ossuaries from the York and James rivers held from ten to twenty individuals, and the "intentional interment of artifacts with burials was extremely rare and never in conspicuous amounts."[63]

More recently, partial excavation of an unpalisaded Paspahegh village (44JC308) dating from the 1500s to about 1611 revealed the diversity and complexity of Late Woodland/Early Contact period Algonquian mortuary practices. Located near the confluence of the Chickahominy and James rivers, the single component site included forty-eight structural post patterns, two hearth pits, and twenty-five certain or presumed human burial features.[64]

Three levels of social rank were inferred by the investigators, based on the distribution of copper ornaments, orientation of the graves, ages of the deceased, and the spatial distribution of the burial features.[65] Commoners were buried in individual grave pits with no preferred cardinal orientation and without copper grave goods.[66] Both adults and subadults were present and the graves "were clustered within a cemetery area which was spatially isolated within the settlement."[67]

Adult men and women of "achieved status" all received primary burials that faced west. They were also found in different parts of the village from the cemetery area.[68] One burial, in particular—that of a thirty-five+-year-old male—was more elaborate than the others. The burial pit was large, presumably to accommodate a litter and body wrappings. Around the man's neck were found five copper beads, two made of European copper.[69]

Two small ossuaries were excavated that are thought to represent "high status interments," based on the "high frequency of copper ornaments," their distinct manner of burial compared to the other interments identified at site 44JC308, and the presence of both adults and subadults.[70] Six people, the remains of two adults and four subadults, were found in one ossuary.

Eighty-eight copper ornaments were directly associated with the remains; all are tube beads except for three small pendants. The majority of the beads and pendants were found with two subadults. Chemical analysis of seventeen of the copper ornaments demonstrated that five were made of native copper and twelve of European.[71] The other ossuary contained remains of three adults (one an older male) and one subadult. Sixty-two copper tube beads were found and most were associated with one of the adults. Analysis of the composition of twelve beads indicated that three were made of native copper and nine of European.[72]

Because both ossuaries contained ornaments made from native and European copper, the researchers concluded that the interred individuals were of high status, as opposed to commoners with greater access to European goods, particularly copper, gained through an illicit trade with English mariners and settlers. It is their view "that such a dramatic change in traditional [Algonquian] authority over the eventual control of high status items is unlikely to have occurred so rapidly after the establishment of Jamestown." They suggest that "archaeologists might reassess the assumption that ossuaries among the Powhatan represent the remains of common folk only."[73]

However, six miles downriver from the Paspahegh village of 44JC308, ongoing archaeological excavations at Jamestown are uncovering abundant "copper scraps, the trimmings from the English manufacture of trade goods . . . [and] one of the most commonly found items at the site."[74] The greatest quantities of copper have turned up in deposits dating to the earliest years of the settlement, just when visiting merchant sailors and some of the English colonists were introducing vast amounts of copper into the local native exchange network, of which the Paspeheghs were a part. As William Kelso and his colleagues note, "Glutting Powhatan society with copper objects devalued the metal and upset the native social order. Copper no longer distinguished chiefs from their followers. In fact, this disruption in the balance of the copper trade contributed to the overall deterioration of English/Powhatan relations."[75]

The question, then, is not whether Algonquian rulers and other elites were buried in ossuaries, but whether rulers and elites were buried with commoners. The ethnohistorical sources seem pretty clear upon that point; no, they were not. Yet a host of other questions remain unanswered. What happened when the mortuary platform within a temple could hold no more

preserved remains of deceased rulers? Did they enlarge the mortuary platform, store the oldest remains in special containers, or inter the remains in
the ground? If the latter, how were the remains interred? And, how were
the deceased spouses, children, brothers, and sisters of the rulers treated?
Through kinship they were members of the ruling elite who, most likely,
were treated differently from commoners in death just as they had been
in life. How were they buried? And, finally, what happened to those commoners who achieved some degree of status by their wits or deeds? How
were they buried and how would one tell them apart from, say, the burial
of a ruler's kinsman? These questions just begin to probe the complexities
of southeastern Algonquian burial ritual and its relationship to social organization, as illustrated by Dennis Curry's recent synthesis of Maryland ossuaries.[76] The answers lie in more detailed comparative studies at sites like
the Paspahegh village.

Acknowledgments

I thank Gregory Waselkov and my wife, Carter Shields, for their comments
and assistance in revising this essay. The artist's reconstruction of the high-
status burial shown in figure 2 was drawn by Ellen Paige, to whom I am
most grateful.

Notes

1. J. Frederick Fausz, "The Powhatan Uprising of 1622: A Historical Study of Ethnocentrism and Cultural Conflict" (PhD diss., College of William and Mary, 1977), 224,
229–32.

2. Christian F. Feest, "Nanticoke and Neighboring Tribes," in *Handbook of North American Indians*, vol. 15, *Northeast*, ed. Bruce G. Trigger (Washington DC: Smithsonian Institution, 1978), 240–52; Feest, "Virginia Algonquians," in *Handbook of North American
Indians*, 253–70; Feest, "North Carolina Algonquians," in *Handbook of North American
Indians*, 271–81.

3. Helen C. Rountree, *Pocahontas's People: The Powhatan Indians of Virginia through
Four Centuries* (Norman: University of Oklahoma Press, 1990), 3–14; E. Randolph Turner,
"An Archaeological and Ethnohistorical Study on the Evolution of Rank Societies in the
Virginia Coastal Plain" (PhD diss., Pennsylvania State University, 1976), 92–126; Ste-
phen R. Potter, "An Analysis of Chicacoan Settlement Patterns" (PhD diss., University of
North Carolina, 1982), 35–46, 52–83; Lewis R. Binford, "Archaeological and Ethnohis-
torical Investigation of Cultural Diversity and Progressive Development among Aborig-

inal Cultures of Coastal Virginia and North Carolina" (PhD diss., University of Michigan, 1964), 74–118; Paul B. Cissna, "The Piscataway Indians of Southern Maryland: An Ethnohistory from Pre-European Contact to the Present" (PhD diss., American University, 1986), 53–99.

4. Marshall D. Sahlins, *Tribesmen* (Englewood Cliffs NJ Prentice-Hall, 1968), 26. This is an anthropological definition of the word "chiefdom," which denotes a society with a greater degree of political centralization than was found among most aboriginal groups in the eastern United States during the colonial period.

5. Stephen R. Potter, *Commoners, Tribute, and Chiefs: The Development of Algonquian Culture in the Potomac Valley* (Charlottesville: University of Virginia Press, 1993), 14, 179–84.

6. Frederic W. Gleach, *Powhatan's World and Colonial Virginia: A Conflict of Cultures* (Lincoln: University of Nebraska Press, 1997), 34.

7. Potter, "Chicacoan Settlement Patterns," 35–36; Turner, "Rank Societies," 123–24; Binford, "Coastal Virginia," 91–93; Gleach, *Powhatan's World*, 28–35.

8. Turner, "Rank Societies," 96–100, 105–7; Binford, "Coastal Virginia," 90–91, 93–96. For a different interpretation of the position of werowance see John H. Haynes Jr., "The Seasons of Tsenacommacoh and the Rise of Wahunsenacawh: Structure and Ecology in Social Evolution" (master's thesis, University of Virginia, 1984), 170–72.

9. William R. Gerard, "Some Virginia Indian Words," *American Anthropologist* 7, no. 2 (1905): 229–30; Philip L. Barbour, "The Earliest Reconnaissance of Chesapeake Bay Area: Captain John Smith's Map and Indian Vocabulary, Part II," *Virginia Magazine of History and Biography* 80, no. 1 (1972): 46–47; William M. Tooker, "Some More about Virginia Names," *American Anthropologist* 7, no. 3 (1905): 525.

10. John Smith, "A Map of Virginia with a Description of the Countrey, the Commodities, People, Government and Religion, 1612," in *Travels and Works of Captain John Smith, President of Virginia and Admiral of New England, 1580–1631,* ed. Edward Arber and A. G. Bradley, 2 vols. (Edinburgh: John Grant, 1910), 1:81.

11. William Strachey, *The Historie of Travell into Virginia Britania (1612),* ed. Louis B. Wright and Virginia Freund, Hakluyt Society, 2nd ser., no. 103 (London: University Press for the Society, 1953), 87.

12. Haynes, "Seasons of Tsenacommacoh," 100.

13. Potter, *Commoners,* 26; Feest, "Virginia Algonquians," 261; Binford, "Coastal Virginia," 94; Turner, "Rank Societies," 108.

14. Strachey, *Historie of Travell,* 107; Smith, "Map of Virginia," 75; Philip L. Barbour, ed., *The Jamestown Voyages under the First Charter, 1606–1609,* Hakluyt Society, 2nd ser., no. 136, vol. 1 (Cambridge: University Press for the Society, 1969), 92; David B. Quinn, ed., *The Roanoke Voyages, 1584–1590,* Hakluyt Society, 2nd ser., no. 109, vol. 1 (London: University Press for the Society, 1955), 101–2; George Percy, *Observations Gathered out of "A Discourse of the Plantation of the Southern Colony in Virginia by the English, 1606,"* ed. David B. Quinn (Charlottesville: University of Virginia Press, 1967), 13; Gleach, *Powhatan's World,* 57.

15. Strachey, *Historie of Travell,* 43–44, 57, 104; Smith, "Map of Virginia," 79. Following

Smith, the original six groups of Powhatan's inheritance were the Pamunkeys, Mattaponis, Powhatans, Arrohatecks, Appamatucks, and Youghtanunds. Strachey mentions all the groups listed by Smith and adds three more: Orapaks, Kiskiacks, and Werowocomocos.

16. Smith, "Map of Virginia," 51, 82; John Smith, "The Generall Historie of Virginia, New England, and the Summer Isles," in *Travels and Works of Captain John Smith*, 2:514–15; Strachey, *Historie of Travell*, 44, 58–59, 105–6; Potter, *Commoners*, 18–19; Helen C. Rountree, *The Powhatan Indians of Virginia: Their Traditional Culture* (Norman: University of Oklahoma Press, 1989), 14.

17. Strachey, *Historie of Travell*, 58–59; John Smith, "A True Relation of Occurrences and Accidents in Virginia, 1608," in *Travels and Works of Captain John Smith*, 1:11–13; Smith, "Generall Historie of Virginia," 514–15; Potter, "Chicacoan Settlement Patterns," 35–36, 40.

18. Smith, "True Relation," 11.

19. The limits of the Powhatan chiefdom, about 1608, are difficult to establish, owing in part to its rapid and relatively recent expansion, which caused fluctuating alliances and intergroup relations of varying stability. Depending upon the interpretation of the ethnohistorical sources, estimates of the number of petty chiefdoms controlled by Powhatan range from ten to thirty-six. See Turner, "Rank Societies," 133–35; Binford, "Coastal Virginia," 74; Feest, "Virginia Algonquians," 254–56; Potter, "Chicacoan Settlement Patterns," 40–45; Stephen R. Potter, "An Ethnohistorical Examination of Indian Groups in Northumberland County, Virginia: 1608–1719" (master's thesis, University of North Carolina, 1976), 15–24; Potter, *Commoners*, 18–19, 179–80; Rountree, *Powhatan Indians*, 13–14.

20. Strachey, *Historie of Travell*, 75.

21. Smith, "True Relation," 10.

22. William Simmonds, "The Proceedings and Accidents of the English Colony in Virginia," in *Travels and Works of Captain John Smith*, 2:406.

23. Strachey, *Historie of Travell*, 107.

24. Smith, "True Relation," 32–33.

25. Quinn, "Roanoke Voyages," 98–100.

26. Recent archaeological discoveries at Jamestown demonstrate the importance of copper as a trade item during the early years of the settlement. The greatest amount of copper comes from the oldest deposits, but declines sharply over time, reflecting the effects of the glutting of Powhatan society with copper objects. See William M. Kelso, J. Eric Deetz, Seth W. Mallios, and Beverly A. Straube, *Jamestown Rediscovery VII* (Richmond: The Association for the Preservation of Virginia Antiquities, 2001), 30–33.

27. Fausz, "Powhatan Uprising," 248–50, 270–73.

28. Samuel Bemiss, "The Three Charters of the Virginia Company of London, with Seven Related Documents, 1601–1621," in *Jamestown 350th Anniversary Historical Booklet*, no. 4 (Charlottesville: University of Virginia Press, 1957), 54.

29. Susan Myra Kingsbury, ed., *Records of the Virginia Company of London*, vol. 2 (Washington DC: Government Printing Office, 1906), 672.

30. Fausz, "Powhatan Uprising," 253, 283–85, 322–24, 338–42, 512, 582–83; Gleach, *Pow-*

hatan's World, 142–43, 146; E. Randolph Turner, "Socio-Political Organization within the Powhatan Chiefdom and the Effects of European Contact, AD 1607–1646," in *Cultures in Contact*, ed. William H. Fitzhugh (Washington DC: Smithsonian Institution Press, 1985), 212–16; William L. Shea, *The Virginia Militia in the Seventeenth Century* (Baton Rouge; Louisiana State University Press, 1983), 59. Trade with the Algonquian Indians on the James and York rivers was suspended in 1624, 1632, and 1643. See William W. Hening, ed., *The Statutes at Large; Being a Collection of All the Laws of Virginia*, vol. 1 (New York, 1823), 126, 177, 255.

31. Bemiss, "Virginia Company," 63.

32. Lyon G. Tyler, ed., *Narratives of Early Virginia, 1606–1625* (New York: Barnes and Noble, 1907), 213; William Stith, *History of the First Discovery and Settlement of Virginia* (1747; reprint, Williamsburg: Virginia State Library, 1912), 240.

33. Philip L. Barbour, "The Earliest Reconnaissance of the Chesapeake Bay Area," *Virginia Magazine of History and Biography* 79, no. 3 (1971): 296.

34. Potter, *Commoners*, 21–22, 175; Potter, "Chicacoan Settlement Patterns," 49–51, 67; Feest, "Virginia Algonquians," 258.

35. Strachey, *Historie of Travell*, 46.

36. Fausz, "Powhatan Uprising," 282.

37. Ralph Hamor, *A True Discourse of the Present Estate of Virginia* (London, 1615), 4.

38. Hamor, *True Discourse*, 5.

39. Fausz, "Powhatan Uprising," 283–84.

40. J. Frederick Fausz, "'By Warre upon Our Enemies and Kinde Usage of Our Friends': The Beaver Trade and Interest Group Rivalry in the Development of the Chesapeake, 1607–1652" (paper delivered at the Colloquium in Colonial American History, Institute of Early American History and Culture, Williamsburg, Virginia, October 1982), 6–8.

41. Smith, "Generall Historie of Virginia," 592.

42. Smith, "Generall Historie of Virginia," 596–98.

43. Smith, "Generall Historie of Virginia," 606; Fausz, "Powhatan Uprising," 504–6; Potter, *Commoners*, 187.

44. J. Frederick Fausz, "Profits, Pelts, and Power: The 'Americanization' of English Culture in the Chesapeake, 1620–1652" (paper delivered at the annual meeting of the American Historical Association, Washington DC, December 30, 1982), 2–9. The Susquehannocks were receiving trade goods in the lower Susquehanna valley after 1575, but the nature and extent of the trade system and the exact source of the goods are not known. See Barry C. Kent's *Susquehanna's Indians*, Pennsylvania Historical and Museum Commission Anthropological Series 6 (Harrisburg: Pennsylvania Historical and Museum Commission, 1984), 19–21.

45. J. Frederick Fausz, "Patterns of Anglo-Indian Aggression and Accommodation along the Mid-Atlantic Coast, 1584–1634," in *Cultures in Contact*, 252.

46. Potter, *Commoners*, 189–98; Potter, "Indian Groups," 46–47; Stephen R. Potter, "Ethnohistory and the Owings Site: A Reanalysis," *Archeological Society of Virginia Quarterly Bulletin* (June–September 1977): 172–73; Gregory A. Waselkov, "Indians of West-

moreland County," in *Westmoreland County, Virginia, 1653–1983*, ed. Walter B. Norris Jr. (Montross VA: Westmoreland County Commission for History and Archaeology, 1983), 25. Among the Piscataways of southern Maryland, clear succession to the paramount chieftainship (or *tayac*) was interrupted between 1641 and 1666 because the tayac had no brother or nephew to succeed him. See James H. Merrell, "Cultural Continuity among the Piscataway Indians of Colonial Maryland," *William and Mary Quarterly*, 3rd ser., 36 (October 1979): 559, 561–62; and Cissna, "Piscataway Indians," 140–44, 149–53.

47. Turner, "Powhatan Chiefdom," 213.

48. Thomas Jefferson, *Notes on the State of Virginia*, ed. William Peden (New York: W. W. Norton, 1972), 95.

49. Potomac Neck is a narrow strip of land in Stafford County, Virginia. The "neck" is bordered on three sides by water—Accakeek Creek, Potomac Creek, and the Potomac River. In some of the early records pertaining to archaeological discoveries at Potomac Neck, Accotink Creek (in nearby Fairfax County) is incorrectly given as one of the geographical reference points, undoubtedly because of its phonetic similarity to Accakeek Creek. Occasionally later researchers perpetuated the error. The earliest archaeological report on the area is Elmer R. Reynolds, "Ossuary at Accotink, Va.," in *Abstract of Transactions of the Anthropological Society of Washington* DC, prepared by J. W. Powell (Washington DC: Smithsonian Institution, 1881), 92–94. Other accounts include William H. Holmes, William Dinwiddie, and Gerard Fowke, "Archeological Survey of the Tidewater Maryland and Virginia Area," 1891, National Anthropological Archives manuscript 2125, Smithsonian Institution, Washington DC; T. Dale Stewart, *Archeological Exploration of Patawomeke: The Indian Town Site (44St2) Ancestral to the One (44St1) Visited in 1608 by Captain John Smith*, Smithsonian Contributions to Anthropology Number 36 (Washington DC: Smithsonian Institution Press, 1992); Karl Schmitt, "Patawomeke: An Historic Algonkian Site," *Archeological Society of Virginia Quarterly Bulletin* 20, no. 1 (1965): 1–36; Howard A. MacCord Sr., "The Indian Point Site, Stafford County, Virginia," *Archeological Society of Virginia Quarterly Bulletin* 46, no. 3 (1991): 117–40; and Dennis B. Blanton, Stevan C. Pullins, and Veronica L. Deitrick, *The Potomac Creek Site (44St2) Revisited*, Research Report Series No. 10 (Richmond: Virginia Department of Historic Resources, 1999).

50. Stewart, *Archeological Exploration*, 8–11, 17–28, 81. These were ossuaries 2, 3, 4, and 5 at the Potomac Creek site. Ossuaries 2, 3, and 4, excavated by amateur archaeologists between 1935 and 1937, contained at least 287, 67, and 41 individuals, respectively. Ossuary 5, excavated by T. Dale Stewart (a physical anthropologist with the Smithsonian Institution) in 1939–40, contained the skeletal remains of 135 individuals. Also, see Blanton, Pullins, and Deitrick, *Potomac Creek*, 92–98.

51. Holmes, Dinwiddie, and Fowke, "Archeological Survey."

52. Reynolds, "Ossuary at Accotink, Va.," 92–94; Ben C. McCary, "A Conch Shell Mask Found in Virginia," *Archeological Society of Virginia Quarterly Bulletin* 12, no. 4 (1958), n.p.; McCary, "Further Notes on the Melton Mask," *Archeological Society of Virginia Quarterly Bulletin* 13, no. 2 (1958), n.p.; Joseph D. McGuire, "Pipes and Smoking Customs of the American Aborigines, based on Material in the U.S. National Museum," in *Report of the*

U.S. National Museum under the Direction of the Smithsonian Institution for the Year 1897 (Washington DC: Government Printing Office, 1899), 428; MacCord, "Indian Point," 120–31; Potter, *Commoners*, 213–18.

53. Reynolds, "Ossuary at Accotink, Va.," 93.

54. Potter, *Commoners*, 213; Kent, *Susquehanna's Indians*, 212–13; Henry Miller, Dennis Pogue, and Michael Smolek, "Beads from the Seventeenth Century Chesapeake," in *Proceedings of the 1982 Glass Trade Bead Conference*, Rochester Museum and Science Center Research Records 16 (Rochester NY: Research Division, Rochester Museum and Science Center, 1983), 138–39; Fausz, "'By Warre upon Our Enemies,'" 6. As noted by Kent, the chronology and popularity of particular beads in the Susquehanna River/Chesapeake Bay region may not apply to areas in the southeastern United States.

55. Quinn, "Roanoke Voyages," 101–2; Quinn, *Observations*, 13; Smith, "Map of Virginia," 75; Strachey, *Historie of Travell*, 107; Barbour, *Jamestown Voyages*, 1:92; Gregory A. Waselkov, "Seventeenth-Century Trade in the Colonial Southeast," *Southeastern Archaeology* 8, no. 2 (Winter 1989): 121–24.

56. John Smith, "The General Historie of Virginia, New England, and the Summer Isles," in *The Complete Works of Captain John Smith*, ed. Philip L. Barbour, 3 vols. (Chapel Hill: University of North Carolina Press, 1986), 3:172. It has been suggested that the Patawomekes got the cross in 1642 from Father Andrew White, a Jesuit priest. See MacCord, "Indian Point," 127–28. For a discussion of alternatives to MacCord's interpretation see Potter, *Commoners*, 213–18.

57. Stewart, *Archeological Exploration*, 7–8.

58. Stewart, *Archeological Exploration*, 5–6, 68–74, 76–77.

59. Kent, *Susquehanna's Indians*, 213.

60. Stewart, *Archeological Exploration*, 68–74; Waselkov, "Indians of Westmoreland County," 20–21, 28; Rountree, *Pocahontas's People*, 121; Potter, *Commoners*, 219.

61. Christine Jirikowic, "The Political Implications of a Cultural Practice: A New Perspective on Ossuary Burial in the Potomac Valley," *North American Archaeologist* 11, no. 4 (1990): 353–74.

62. Potter, *Commoners*, 211–13.

63. E. Randolph Turner III, "The Virginia Coastal Plain during the Late Woodland Period," in *Middle and Late Woodland Research in Virginia: A Synthesis*, ed. Theodore R. Reinhart and Mary Ellen N. Hodges (Richmond: The Dietz Press, 1992), 118.

64. Mary Ellen N. Hodges and Charles T. Hodges, eds., "Paspahegh Archaeology: Data Recovery Investigations of Site 44JC308 at Governor's Land at Two Rivers, James City County, Virginia," Report submitted to Governor's Land Associates, Inc. (Williamsburg: James River Institute for Archaeology, Inc., 1994), iv.

65. Hodges and Hodges, "Paspahegh Archaeology," 307.

66. Hodges and Hodges, "Paspahegh Archaeology," 165.

67. Hodges and Hodges, "Paspahegh Archaeology," 305.

68. Hodges and Hodges, "Paspahegh Archaeology," 307.

69. Hodges and Hodges, "Paspahegh Archaeology," 106–17.

70. Hodges and Hodges, "Paspahegh Archaeology," 307.

71. Hodges and Hodges, "Paspahegh Archaeology," 125–37, 206, 222.

72. Hodges and Hodges, "Paspahegh Archaeology," 137–41, 206, 222.

73. Hodges and Hodges, "Paspahegh Archaeology," 310.

74. Kelso et al., *Jamestown*, 31.

75. Kelso et al., *Jamestown*, 33.

76. Dennis C. Curry, *Feast of the Dead: Aboriginal Ossuaries in Maryland* (Crownsville: Archeological Society of Maryland, Inc., and the Maryland Historical Trust Press, 1999), 86–91.

Cockacoeske, Queen of Pamunkey

Diplomat and Suzeraine

MARTHA W. MCCARTNEY

Cockacoeske, queen of the Pamunkey Indians, donned the mantle of Pow-hatan's chiefdom in 1656 and governed her people for some thirty years. Brit-ish archival records that have recently come to light suggest that she worked within the context of the Virginia colonial government in an attempt to recapture the power her people had wielded in the early seventeenth cen-tury, when Pamunkey leaders politically dominated the Indians of the Vir-ginia coastal plain. Although Cockacoeske was a leader of considerable in-fluence and political acumen, she has been largely overlooked by modern scholars. Yet colonial documents contain more personal detail about Cock-acoeske than is perhaps available on any other Native American woman of her day, and her attempts to reverse the long decline of the Powhatan chief-dom warrant recognition.

Cockacoeske was a relative of Powhatan, the Algonquian paramount chief who ruled the Indians of the Virginia coastal plain when English col-onists arrived in 1607. Captain John Smith called Powhatan's mode of gov-ernment monarchical and described Powhatan himself as an emperor who controlled his territory by placing his brothers, progeny, and other close kin in positions of power within the various districts he ruled.[1] According to Smith, Powhatan, a Pamunkey, governed six tribal territories through the right of inheritance and numerous others that he had acquired by con-quest. He was said to have been born at a village called Powhatan, on the upper James River, but his principal residence was at Werowocomoco on the York.[2]

The Powhatan chiefdom's leadership descended matrilineally among the sons of the eldest sister, then devolved to the progeny of younger sisters.[3] By 1618, Powhatan's brother Opitchapam assumed the leadership role, only to be replaced soon after by Opechancanough, another brother, the great war captain who masterminded the March 1622 Indian attack. This up-rising, a concerted attempt by the Indians of the coastal plain to drive the English from their soil, led to the loss of nearly one-third of the colony's population.[4]

Opechancanough's influence (if not necessarily his authority) reportedly extended north to the Potomac River and south to the lower side of the James, eastward to include Virginia's Eastern Shore, and westward to the falls of the colony's major rivers. According to at least one early explorer's account, certain tribes in the region considerably south of the James River also were under his sway.[5] Thus throughout the first half of the seventeenth century, first with Powhatan and then with Opechancanough, the Pamunkey Indians enjoyed dominance over the native groups in eastern Virginia.

In April 1644 Opechancanough, who was then said to be almost one hundred years old, led a second major Indian uprising that claimed nearly four hundred lives. The assault focused upon the upper reaches of the York River but also extended to the south side of the James. The English, who called Opechancanough "that Bloody Monster," captured him during the retaliatory expeditions that followed, and he was slain while imprisoned at Jamestown.[6]

After the death of Opechancanough, a Pamunkey warrior named Necotowance assumed leadership. Documentary evidence suggests, however, that the effects of the colonists' reprisals against the Indians and the loss of their principal leader had exacted a severe toll, precipitating the disintegration of the once-mighty Powhatan chiefdom. One writer, describing the dissolution or scattering of the tribes that had previously been under common leadership, claimed that Virginia officials had made deliberate efforts to liberate the other natives from the control of the "house of Pamunkey," employing the familiar "divide and conquer" approach in dealing with remnants of the once-powerful Powhatan chiefdom.[7]

In October 1646 Necotowance, "King of the Indians," concluded a treaty with the Virginia government whereby the natives ceded much of their territory to the English and acknowledged that their right to the possession of the remaining land was derived from the English monarch. From that moment they formally became tributaries to the English government. The implementation, or imposition, of a tributary system, which can be likened to the way Powhatan and Opechancanough ruled the tribes under their control, was in fact a tangible symbol of the Indian's political subservience to the English.[8]

In 1648 Necotowance, called "emperor," presented his people's first annual tribute to Virginia's governor. Only "five more petty kings attended him," a reflection of the extent to which the ancient Powhatan chiefdom had disintegrated. That the delicate balance of power between the Indians and the colonists had shifted in favor of the latter is evidenced in Necotowance's statement to his countrymen that "the English will kill you if you goe into their bounds." He noted that skeptical Indians called him a liar for making such a blunt observation, but in fact at least three persons already had been killed for entering the ceded territory.[9]

By 1649 Necotowance had been replaced by Totopotomoy, another Pamunkey male. The written record indicates that, unlike his predecessors, Totopotomoy represented only his own tribe when he interacted with English officials. A legislative act dated March 1649 suggests that by then unified leadership of coastal Virginia's Indians had completely deteriorated, for equal amounts of land were allocated to three Indian leaders, whose people formerly had been subordinate to Opechancanough as paramount chief. Thus the Pamunkeys probably wielded little if any power over other native groups. Totopotomoy, unlike Necotowance, was called king of the Pamunkeys, not king of the Indians.[10] This shift in power also signaled the disintegration of the Powhatan chiefdom. A staunch ally of the English, Totopotomoy was killed in 1656 while fighting at their side against an outlying Indian group, the Rickohockans, in a conflict later known as the Battle of Bloody Run.[11]

After the death of Totopotomoy his widow, Cockacoeske, became the leader or queen of the Pamunkeys, a role she occupied until her death in the 1680s. She was described by one contemporary as a descendant of Opechancanough, Powhatan's brother.[12] If Totopotomoy was also a descendant, she may have been his cousin as well as his wife. During the nearly thirty years Cockacoeske ruled, her people remained tributaries of the colonial government and, to a considerable degree, attempted to act within the framework of its legal system. Even so, she asserted her dominance in subtle ways, demonstrating that she, like her forebears, was a shrewd politician.

Meanwhile, the population of Virginia's tributary Indians declined owing to disease and loss of subsistence habitat. Pressure from stronger, outlying hostile tribes at the heads of the colony's rivers confined them within the bounds of the coastal plain, while the relentless inland expansion of the English frontier compressed them into a steadily shrinking space. Attempts by Virginia Indian leaders to cope with this crisis are mentioned

only obliquely in the historical record, which, one should recall, is chroni-
cled from the European perspective. Even so, certain seventeenth-century
Virginia documents in British repositories yield new insights on the political complexities of Anglo-American/Native American relationships during this era, particularly during the fourth quarter of the seventeenth century. Contemporary correspondence between Virginia and England during
this period also reveals that there was some collusion between colonial officials and certain Indian leaders, principal among whom was the queen
of Pamunkey.

An able and politically astute leader, Cockacoeske attempted to assert her
dominance while acting within the limits of the colony's legal system, perhaps perceiving that her people's principal hope of survival lay in reestab-
lishing the political unity of the Powhatan chiefdom. As will be seen, she
was able to turn the English political system effectively to her own people's
advantage, at least for a time. Evidence of Cockacoeske's considerable influence and her quasi-political alliances can be found in contemporary correspondence; in the provisions of the 1677 Treaty of Middle Plantation, a
monumental document that governed relations between the colonists and
Virginia Indians for nearly a hundred years; and in the fact that she was
singled out for special recognition by King Charles II.

During 1676 sporadic Indian raids alarmed the colony's frontier, sparking a popular uprising that became known as Bacon's Rebellion. Outlying
settlers rallied behind young Nathaniel Bacon and marched upon the nearest Indians rather than confronting the stronger inland tribes, such as the
Susquehannocks and Senecas, whom some high officials blamed for the incursions.[13] Early on Cockacoeske, who by then had led the Pamunkeys for
twenty years, was summoned to the statehouse at Jamestown, where she appeared before a committee of the Governor's Council. One contemporary
wrote that Cockacoeske, apparently a commanding personage, "entered
the chamber with a comportment gracefull to admiration, bringing on her
right hand an Englishmen interpreter, and on her left, her son, a stripling
twenty years of age," said to be the offspring of an English colonel. Cockacoeske's head was crowned with a braid of black-and-white wampum peake,
three inches broad, and she was clothed in a deerskin mantle that reached
from shoulders to feet, a garment whose edges had been trimmed to resemble deep, twisted fringe. Flanked by her companions, Cockacoeske, "with

grave courtlike gestures and a majestick air in her face," walked to the head of the council table and sat down. She elected to communicate only through her interpreter, though the council believed she understood the English language very well.[14]

Queried by the council committee as to the number of men she would provide to serve as guides in the wilderness and to assist the English in a campaign against hostile Indians, Cockacoeske kept silent. When pressed further, "after a little musing, with an earnest passionate countenance as if tears were ready to gush out and with a fervent sort of expression [she] made a harangue about a quarter of an hour, often interlacing with a high shrill voice and vehement passion these words, 'Tatapatamoi Chepiack,' i.e., Tatapatomoy dead," a reminder to the council that it was in identical circumstances that her husband and a hundred of his bowmen had lost their lives, for which sacrifice there had been no compensation. At length Cockacoeske agreed to provide twelve warriors from her town, though she was said to have 150 men under her command.[15]

As the rift between Bacon's followers and the supporters of Governor William Berkeley gradually widened, finally flaring into overt military conflict, officials in England who viewed the popular uprising with concern persuaded King Charles II to dispatch special commissioners to Virginia to investigate the causes and extent of the unrest. These commissioners, Sir John Berry, Colonel Francis Moryson, and Herbert Jeffreys, arrived in Virginia early in 1677. Their official correspondence sheds much light upon how Virginia's tributary Indians were affected by Bacon's Rebellion and also shows how the natives, in turn, responded to the political climate it created.[16]

According to one record, an Indian interpreter named Wilford, who was executed by Governor Berkeley for his participation in the rebellion, had allegedly "frightened the Queen of Pamunkey from the land she had been granted by the Assembly a month after the peace was concluded with her."[17] Despite the fact that a peace agreement evidently had been reached with the Pamunkeys in March 1676, in August Nathaniel Bacon led a march against the Pamunkeys, who lived on the fringe of the English settlement. The attack may have been inspired by recently enacted legislation entitling settlers to claim property that had been abandoned by the Indians.[18] Riding down upon the Indians' encampment at the edge of a swamp, Bacon's men were impeded by the mire and succeeded only in capturing a small child and killing an elderly woman. Cockacoeske, who ordered her people to refrain from firing upon the English, abandoned the encampment and all her personal belongings. In their pursuit, Bacon's followers took prisoner an old Indian woman, Cockacoeske's nurse or attendant, ordering her to guide them to the natives who had fled. Later, when they discovered she had deliberately misled them, she was put to death.[19]

A short time later Bacon came upon the Pamunkeys at another encampment. During the attack that ensued Cockacoeske escaped, but forty-five of her people were captured. Bacon's men reportedly took away three horseloads of plunder, including Indian mats, baskets, parcels of wampum peake, and pieces of linen, broadcloth, and other English goods the queen was said to value highly. According to a report filed by the king's commissioners, Cockacoeske, though fleeing from Bacon's army, decided to come back "with designe to throw herself upon the mercy of the English [but] she happened to meet with a dead Indian woman lying in the way (being one of her own nation) which struck such a terror in the Queene that fearing their cruelty by that ghastly example she went on her first intended way into the wild woods where she was lost and missing from her own People fourteen days," nearly starving.[20]

The king's commissioners, arriving in Virginia early in 1677, addressed the assembly, admonishing the burgesses to act quickly in establishing peace with the colony's natives. Speaking pragmatically, the commissioners reminded the assembly that the neighboring Indians provided the best guards on the frontier against the more hostile tribes of the continent.[21] They also pointed out that it was Governor William Berkeley who had first conquered the Indians and made peace with them, the breach of which was depriving the colony of the benefit of their trade and labors.[22] Berkeley, in turn, reported to the commissioners that the queen of the Pamunkey Indians, having been driven from her village by Nathaniel Bacon's followers, had returned home and that a good foundation for peace had been laid.[23]

On February 20, 1677, Cockacoeske petitioned Virginia's assembly for the restoration of her belongings and the land she had abandoned "through the feare of the Rebell Bacon and his accomplices."[24] The burgesses, however, granted her scant satisfaction, agreeing only to restore those items that she could prove were hers and insisting that she return any horses or goods in her possession that belonged to the English. In contrast, the king's commissioners were much more sympathetic to her plea, for they reported that she had been "driven out into the wildwoods and there almost famished, plundered of all she had, her people taken prisoners and sold, the Queen robbed of her rich watchcoat [matchcoat] for which she had great value." They added the queen of Pamunkey's name to their list of those who had suffered during Bacon's Rebellion, calling her "a faithfull friend to and lover of the English," and they recommended that she be given a gift in recompense for her sufferings and the loss of her belongings.[25]

On March 27, 1677, the commissioners wrote to England's secretary of state Henry Coventry that the kings and queens of the Nottoways, Nansemonds, Appomattocks, and Pamunkeys had met with them, signifying their willingness to conclude a treaty.[26] By the end of April Herbert Jeffreys, who was appointed to act as lieutenant governor during Governor Berkeley's recall to England, publicly expressed his firm belief that harmonious relations with the nearby Indians were essential to the colony's wellbeing.[27] Soon after Berkeley's departure from Virginia on May 5, Jeffreys set about formally concluding a peace treaty with several groups of neighboring Indians.[28] The king's commissioners' report states that they "sent to the Queene of Pamunkey who not only came in herself but brought in severall scattered nations of Indians, *whome we afterwards reduc'd (as she desired) under her subjection, as anciently they had beene.*"[29]

As a consequence of the commissioners' efforts, on May 29, 1677, King Charles II's birthday and the anniversary of his restoration to the throne, a major peace agreement was concluded between colonial officials and certain tidewater Indian groups. This landmark document, commonly known as the Treaty of Middle Plantation, ushered in peaceful relations between the colonists and the Indians of Virginia's coastal plain, governing their official interactions for nearly a century. As will be seen, Cockacoeske, queen of Pamunkey, exerted considerable influence over the treaty's architects, for some of the document's terms were greatly to her advantage.

Herbert Jeffreys, as a special commissioner, wrote to the king on June 11, 1677, describing the treaty ceremony and the protocol observed. The new guardhouse at Middle Plantation had been especially fitted out for the occasion.[30] Jeffreys wrote that,

*Silence being Proclaimed, the Articles were openly read before them
and the severall Enterpreters sworn to expound each distinct paragraph to them which they openly read to their general satisfaction.
Then the Queen of Pamunkey was invited within the Barr of the
Court to sign this Treaty on behalf of herself and Severall Nations*
now reunited under her Subjection and Government as anciently,
*who (with the rest) subscribed and delivered up the same with the
most humble Reverence (as to his Majestie) on her bended knees, all
of them publically acknowledging to hold their Crowns and Lands
of the Great King of England.*[31]

This latter sentence is especially significant, for it refers to article 12 of the
treaty, which committed several smaller, unspecified Indian nations to Cockacoeske's rule, tangible evidence of her success in manipulating the treaty
agreement to her own people's advantage.

Jeffreys continued,

*And myself having signed that part (in behalf of his Majestie) to
them they all knelt donne and with low obeysance received it, as
from his Majestie's Royall hands, at the same tyme (on their onne
free accord) kissing the most acceptable paper of peace one after another. Thus being concluded with the day the Field Pieces were dis-
charged several rounds, with volleys of small shot and Fireworks and
Loud Acclamations of Joy allover the Camp and so having Quietly
Entertained Our Indian ffriends that night, they departed the next
day to their several homes, well satisfied with this treaty.*[32]

Cockacoeske's son, called "Captain John West," endorsed the treaty along
with the leaders of three other Indian tribes: the queen of the Weyanokes,
the king of the Nottoways, and the king of the Nansemonds.[33] Peracuta, the
king of the Appomattocks, though present at the ceremony, was not allowed
to sign, for some of his people stood accused of murder. Nicholas Spencer,
who later became secretary of the colony, reported that a few Nanzattico
Indians also had attended the treaty ceremony but departed without signing.[34] Whether they were invited to participate is unknown.

A month after Herbert Jeffreys wrote to England reporting that the treaty
had been executed, Sir John Berry and Colonel Francis Moryson, as com-

missioners, sent word to the Privy Council that "even the remote Indians when they heard of [the treaty's] justice of their own accord came forward and asked to be included."[35] Thus if the commissioners' report is to be believed, the natives thought the treaty advantageous.

In early August Berry and Moryson set sail for England, leaving Jeffreys behind as lieutenant governor. The commissioners brought to England not only the report of their investigation into Bacon's Rebellion but also the original treaty document, which they delivered to the Lords of Trade and Plantations at Whitehall. Lord Baltimore, who had just presented to that body a treaty the Maryland government had concluded with the northern Indians, took exception to the fact that Virginia's peace agreement did not extend its protection to his own colony, whereas Maryland's treaty applied to Virginia as well.

In October 1677 the Lords of Trade and Plantations recommended to the king that Lieutenant Governor Jeffreys be ordered to expand the coverage of Virginia's treaty to include Maryland and his majesty's other colonies.[36] The King's Privy Council, meanwhile, issued a directive for the document then in hand to be printed and distributed.[37] On January 18, 1678, Secretary Henry Coventry was instructed to order Lieutenant Governor Jeffreys to expand the Treaty of Middle Plantation, a directive that was carried out sometime between April and June 1680.[38]

Meanwhile, in response to the recommendation Berry and Moryson had made to the king when the first treaty was newly in hand, presents were commissioned for the Indian leaders who had signed the original document. As tangible signs of goodwill and symbols of their rank, crowns and royal robes were to be made for the queens of the Pamunkeys and the Weyanokes and the kings of the Nottoways and the Nansemonds, "the Indians accompting guifts a kind of sacred pledge of friendship." But Cockacoeske, the queen of Pamunkey, "who was robbed of her rich matchcoat by the rebells," was singled out for special recognition.[39]

It was recommended that Cockacoeske receive "a crown and robe, together with a stript [striped] Indian gown of gay colours and a Bracelet of falce stones." For her son, "a scarlett coate belayered with gold and silver lace, with breeches, shoes and stockings, hatt, sword and belt suitable, and a pair of good pistoles" were deemed befitting. Bill books of the Lord Chamberlain's Department detail the nature of the gifts that were prepared for the Indian leaders. According to the bills, the tailors and clothmakers used scarlet cloth, lined with purple manto, for Cockacoeske's regal robe, and they also prepared for her a silver and gold brocade Indian gown, lined with cherry-colored sarcenet, a soft silk. They made a scarlet suit for her son, young John West, just as Berry and Moryson had recommended, plus stockings of scarlet worsted, the latter embroidered with black silk thread. A white beaver hat trimmed with a gold and silver band, a finely embroidered belt, and a sword and pistols decorated with gold and silver also were made for him. For the queen of Pamunkey's interpreter, Cornelius Dabney, a suit of gray cloth was tailored, to be worn with scarlet stockings, and her chief counselor, Seosteyn, received a purple robe lined with scarlet shalloon, a twill-woven woolen. Similar purple robes were prepared for the queen of the Weyanokes and the kings of the Nottoways and the Nansemonds, demonstrating that their rank was perceived as equal to that of Cockacoeske's chief counselor.[40]

A cap of crimson velvet trimmed with ermine fur was fashioned for each of the four Indian rulers. Royal Jewel House invoices disclose that English craftsmen made "small crowns or coronets of thinne silver plate, gilt and adorned with false stones of various colours, with the inscription 'A Carolo Secondo Magna Brittaniae Rege'" for the Indian leaders. For the queen of Pamunkey, the Royal Jewel House also created a bracelet of false stones, just as Berry and Moryson had asked, as well as an undescribed necklace, probably the silver "frontlet" that still survives (fig. 1). Twenty small silver badges bearing the king's name and the title of each tributary Indian leader were prepared.[41]

In June 1680 Governor Thomas Culpeper arrived in Virginia, to succeed Herbert Jeffreys, who had died in December 1678. Among Culpeper's instructions were orders to deliver the king's gifts to the Indian rulers who had signed the Treaty of Middle Plantation. The Executive Council, however, tried to persuade him not to do so, particularly objecting to the crowns, for they felt that jealousy and discord would result if some tributary Indian leaders were to receive gifts and others did not. This indicates that by the time the gifts had been brought to the colony, the treaty had been expanded, for when the original agreement was amended, to include Maryland within its protection, it was signed by twelve Indian leaders rather than five, who represented seven Indian groups, rather than four. Besides, the council as-

Figure 1. Silver pendant of the queen of Pamunkey, inscribed with the royal arms of King Charles II (courtesy of the Virginia Department of Historic Resources).

serted, "such Marks of Dignity as Coronets . . . must not be prostituted to such meane [inconsequential] persons."[42]

Despite the optimism sparked by the consummation of the Treaty of Middle Plantation, colonial officials soon discovered that it was not the panacea for enduring peace and friendship that its proponents had purported it to be. Two of the treaty's articles proved to be particularly troublesome to Indians and colonists alike, at least one of which, article 12, bore the mark of Cockacoeske's influence. Article 12 specified that "each Indian King and Queen have equall power to govern their owne people and none to have greater power than other except the Queen of Pamunkey to whom several scattered Indian Nations doe now againe owne their antient subjection, and are agreed to come in and plant themselves under her power . . . and are to keep and observe the same towards the said Queen in all things as her Subjects, as well as toward the English." Article 18, on the other hand, stated that "upon any discord or breach of peace happening to arise between any of the Indians in amity with the English . . . they shall repaire to his Majesties Governor by whose Justice and wisdome it is concluded such difference shall be made up and decided."[43] Thus several of the tributary Indian groups were to be placed under the rule of the Pamunkeys, and all the tributaries were to resolve their differences through arbitration before the governor.

It should be recalled that before the signing of the treaty, commissioners Berry and Moryson wrote a letter stating that certain Indian tribes had been placed under the queen of Pamunkey's aegis, "reduced (*as she desired*) under her Subjection, as anceintly they had beene," clearly revealing that article 12 was Cockacoeske's idea.[44] She may also have had a hand in the formulation of article 18, believing that colonial officials, with whom she was acquainted, might weigh justice in her favor. Moreover, the Virginia government's obligation to protect the tributary Indians, as recipients of English justice, surely would have been perceived as an advantage, given the natives' diminished strength.[45]

There are several reasons why Cockacoeske would have been able to exert some influence on colonial officials and work within their political system. During the approximately thirty years she ruled as queen of Pamunkey, she maintained close ties with the Virginia government, representing her people in an official capacity. Cockacoeske's period of leadership, which began more than twenty years before Bacon's Rebellion, would have spanned Francis Moryson's term as deputy governor, March to December 1661, at

which time Governor William Berkeley was in England. Thus she would
have had an opportunity to establish rapport with Moryson himself, a distinct advantage when he returned to Virginia as a special commissioner of
the king. Moreover, Cockacoeske's romantic liaison with the English colonel, John West, an important Virginia official, supporter of Governor Berkeley, and grandson of former Virginia governor Sir Thomas West, Lord De
La Warr, may have furthered her insight into the machinations of colonial politics, and the presence of their son as a future go-between may have
given her an added measure of influence. The account of Cockacoeske's appearance before the governor and council reveals that she was a person of
imposing dignity and that she understood the English language. Cockacoeske's appreciation of European goods is evidenced by her possession of
"pieces of Lynnen, Broad cloth, and divers sorts of English goods wch the
Queene had much value for" when Nathaniel Bacon's men raided her encampment. But there are equally strong indications that Cockacoeske remained true to her native cultural traditions.

Correspondence between officials in Virginia and England discloses that
after the 1677 treaty was signed, Cockacoeske attempted to enforce the terms
of article 12 by exacting tribute and servility from the tribes placed under
her subjection, in sum, trying to reestablish the chiefly dominance enjoyed
by the Pamunkey leaders before Opechancanough's death.[46] Although the
identity of the Indian groups placed under Cockacoeske's charge is not set
forth in either version of the 1677 treaty, the omission of the names of certain prominent Tidewater Virginia Indian groups from the list of treaty signatories provides a clue to their identity, especially when viewed in light of
the relative propinquity of these groups to the Pamunkey homeland.

Contemporary correspondence identifies the Chickahominys and Rappahannocks as two of the groups subjugated to the Pamunkey leadership,
and mention is made of a third Indian nation, perhaps the Mattaponys or
Totachus, both of whom, at the time of the 1669 census, were residing in
New Kent County, where the Pamunkeys also lived. Another tribe, the
Chiskiacks, who at the time of the census were few in number and said to be
steadily dwindling, also may have been made subservient to Cockacoeske,
though in 1677 they were living in Gloucester County, their home at least
since 1629.[47] Some or all of these groups likely constituted the "several scattered nations" subjected to the queen of Pamunkey's leadership.[48]

Even before the second version of the 1677 treaty had been signed, Virginia officials realized that some of the Indians placed under Cockacoeske's rule, notably the Chickahominys and Rappahannocks, strongly resented the attempt to force their subservience and stubbornly refused to cooperate with her, claiming that they had not intended such subjection by subscribing to the peace treaty. In a list of grievances presented by the queen of Pamunkey and her son, Captain John West, to the governor and his council on June 5, 1678, Cockacoeske alleged that the Chickahominys were unwilling to pay tribute, obey her orders, or make her village their home. She also accused them of harboring her son's wife, who had run away. Great mutual enmity is apparent in the nine grievances, for the Chickahominys were accused of poisoning one of Cockacoeske's great men and plotting revenge upon eight more, whereas she herself was alleged by the Chickahominys to have "cutt off soe many Chickahominy heads." A prior tradition of close interaction between the two Indian groups is suggested by the fact that Captain West's absconded wife had been "bred and born at Chickahominy though her Parents were Pamunkeys."[49]

At the end of June Cockacoeske described the state of affairs to Colonel Moryson in a letter, which she dictated to her interpreter. In elegant and courtly language, Cockacoeske professed her loyalty to King Charles II but expressed her dissatisfaction with the Rappahannocks and Chickahominys, "who are very disobedient to my commands." In a politically savvy move, however, she qualified her complaint by assuring Moryson that it was "not that they grudge to be under my subjection."[50]

The affection and esteem in which Cockacoeske held Colonel Moryson is evidenced by her addressing him twice as "Netop," an Algonquian word William Strachey's dictionary translates as "my good friend." At the close of the letter, within the words "Cockacoeske Queen of Pamunkey," she affixed her mark, signifying the communication's authenticity, the same W-like symbol with which she had previously endorsed both versions of the 1677 treaty (fig. 2).

The Pamunkeys' interpreter, Cornelius Dabney, dispatched a personal letter to Colonel Moryson on the same day, corroborating Cockacoeske's allegations against the Chickahominys. He alluded to his own misunderstandings with the current governor and other officials, blaming his problems on the malice of the Chickahominy Indians' interpreter, Richard Yar-

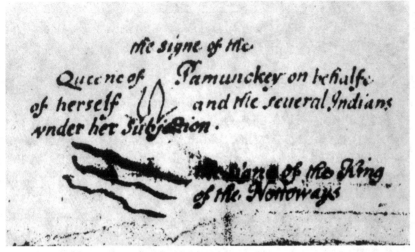

Figure 2. The queen of Pamunkey's mark, endorsing the Treaty of Middle Plantation, May 29, 1677 (courtesy of the Virginia Department of Historic Resources).

borough, who, Dabney claimed, was attempting to undermine peaceful relations with the tributary Indians by his manipulation of various government officials.[51]

Interestingly, the prose Cornelius Dabney used when writing on Cockacoeske's behalf contrasts markedly with the tone of the letter he sent personally. When acting as the queen of Pamunkey's interpreter, he addressed Moryson as a friend and an equal, whereas when writing on his own behalf, he expressed himself with humility and in far simpler language, displaying great deference to Moryson's superior social position. Dabney's letter acknowledges the plight of the tributary Indians who were caught between the colonists' spreading settlement and hostile outlying tribes; in response to Moryson's request for an elk, he replied that the "Senecas having put our Indians into a feare, dare not go so high to hunt."[52]

The colony's secretary, Thomas Ludwell, writing home to England before the second version of the treaty had been signed, claimed that the peace agreement, by reuniting several Indian groups under the queen of Pamunkey's leadership, had created turmoil. He explained that because "several Indian nations again are united under that family . . . though we are confident the Queen of Pamunkey not mistreats or harms, yet most of the young men of the several townes being dissatisfied, is contemptible at their new subjection to that Queen wch they say was consented to by . . . old men against their [the younger men's] wills." He noted that these young warriors "doe lie off in hiding in the woods and will not come in. . . . To grant them their former liberty, the Queen will take it as a breach of the peace and we cannot force them to her obedience but by hazarding another warr wch would bring on great Disorders if not another Rebellion amongst us."[53]

Ludwell recalled that "upon Governor William Berkeley's conquest of Apechancanough it was by him and the government thought the safest way by setting all the lesser nations at Liberty from that obedience they paid to the house of Pamunkey to keep them divided and indeed the effect may be more advantageous to us for they like to warr with each other and destroy themselves more in a year than we can do it." But, Ludwell said, "since this last war there are severall nations again united under that family which we since find to be troublesome and hazardous." In another letter he declared:

> *I could heartily wish those two Articles concerning that subjection and ye making us judges of their differences had been left out, for I never thought it in the interest of this Colony to hinder them from cutting each others throats so we had no hand in it and its plain that upon the conquest of Appechancaenoe and the setting all the tributary nations to that house at Liberty they have weakened themselves more by their Intestine Broyls than ever we could doe by all the Warrs wee have had with them.*[54]

The resentment generated by placing under the queen of Pamunkey's dominance certain Indian nations that had been independent since the death of Opechancanough about 1646 was very much apparent during the summer of 1678. Thomas Ludwell wrote on June 8 that "we had at last Court a great contest between the Queen of Pamunkey and a nation which lives neer her whom she takes amongst others to be subjected to her by the last articles of peace . . . upon whom she had imposed a great tax to be paid every Spring and Fall besides great servility in hunting and weeding of corn which they refused to perform." He added that the group claimed "they had never paid it [tribute] since the death of Appechancano, which is about 33 years since and that they intended no such subjection by those articles."[55]

Similarly, Ludwell informed Secretary Coventry on June 28, 1678, that "the Queen [of Pamunkey] lays a great tax to be paid every spring and fall upon a nation who lives near her and are more powerful than she and they not only deny to pay that tax but any such Subjection to her." He added that the queen "was fair to confess they had not paid such tax above these 30 years."[56] In August 1678 Ludwell reiterated that point, stating that the queen of Pamunkey was "imposing a tribute upon them such as they never paid these 33 years since the conquest of Appochankeno [Opechancanough]."[57] Thus article 12 of the treaty, which required the Indians subjected to the queen of Pamunkey to pay her tribute comparable to what she herself paid to the colonial government, was an overt attempt by Cockacoeske to reestablish Powhatan's old tributary system.

Although relatively little is known about the immediate fate of the Indian groups that article 12 of the treaty attempted to reunite under the queen of Pamunkey, government records suggest that the Chickahominys and the Rappahannocks retained their independence, though they continued to uphold their groups' commitment to the treaty itself. The Chickahominys continued to reside in a village on the Mattaponi River until at least the first decade of the eighteenth century, an indication that they never did obey the commands of Cockacoeske to seat at the Pamunkey town.[58]

The allocation of separate tracts of land to the Pamunkeys and Chickahominys during this period further implies that they continued to remain separate entities and that the latter never did come under Cockacoeske's subjection. Moreover, on subsequent occasions members of the Chickahominy tribe sought justice on their own behalf through the colony's legal system, a further indication that their group retained its autonomy. The Rappahannocks also appear to have retained their independence; throughout the last quarter of the seventeenth century they are mentioned separately by name and are documented as residing in the York-Rappahannock peninsula, having removed themselves from the Pamunkeys' territory. Cockacoeske, meanwhile, continued to lead her own people, residing in Pamunkey Neck, the landmass lying between the Pamunkey and Mattaponi rivers that had been the traditional home of her people.

On July 1, 1686, the Pamunkeys' interpreter, George Smith, informed the governor that the Pamunkey queen "was lately dead and that ye Pamunkey Indians did desire that ye late Queen's niece . . . upon [whom] ye right of Government of that Indian nation doe devolve, might succeed."[59] Virginia's governor might have expected to see the succession pass to the queen's own half-English son, but traditional ideas of inheritance still prevailed among the Pamunkeys. In 1702 the name of "Ms. Betty Queen ye Queen" of the Pamunkey Indians was mentioned in a land transaction and by 1708 that of Queen Ann began appearing in official documents. During the first quarter of the eighteenth century, Queen Ann of the Pamunkeys presented a number of petitions to the governor's council and the assembly, continuing Cockacoeske's policy of working within the framework of the colony's laws.[60] But the Pamunkeys never again attempted to reestablish their dominance over the Indians of Virginia's coastal plain.

Postscript

During the years that have elapsed since the original publication of *Powhatan's Mantle*, documentary resources have yielded very little new information about Cockacoeske, the Queen of Pamunkey. She has, however, become much more widely known and appreciated as an important Native leader. Cockacoeske was featured prominently in the Virginia Women's History Project and her silver frontlet is displayed in the National Park Service Visitor Center at Jamestown. In 1999, when the City of Williamsburg (originally Middle Plantation) celebrated its 300th anniversary, the landmark treaty that the Queen of Pamunkey and other Native leaders signed in 1677 was recognized for its significance.

In the course of my historical research for the Jamestown Archaeological Assessment (1992–99)—a cooperative project between the National Park Service, Colonial Williamsburg Foundation, and the College of William and Mary—I learned that several buildings found during earlier excavations had housed tributary Indians while visiting the capital city on official business. Other recent developments include online access to synopses of British Public Records Office documents and other overseas sources via the Library of Virginia's Web site. This is certain to fuel scholarly interest in Virginia's Native Americans during the colonial period, ultimately leading to new and important discoveries.

Notes

1. John Smith, *Travels and Works of Captain John Smith, President of Virginia and Admiral of New England, 1580–1631*, ed. Edward Arber and A. G. Bradley, 2 vols. (Edinburgh: John Grant, 1910), 1:79; E. Randolph Turner, "An Archaeological and Ethnohistorical

Study on the Evolution of Rank Societies in the Virginia Coastal Plain" (PhD diss., Pennsylvania State University, 1976), 98–99.

2. Smith, *Travels and Works of Captain John Smith*, 1:51, 79; William Strachey, *The Historie of Travell into Virginia Britania (1612)*, ed. Louis B. Wright and Virginia Freund, Hakluyt Society, 2nd ser., no. 103 (London: University Press for the Society, 1953), 56; John Smith, *Virginia Discovered and Described by Captayne John Smith, 1606* (London, 1612).

3. Smith, *Travels and Works of Captain John Smith*, 81.

4. Smith, *Travels and Works of Captain John Smith*, 539.

5. Susan M. Kingsbury, *Records of the Virginia Company of London*, 4 vols. (Washington DC: Government Printing Office, 1906–35), 3:708–10. The account of Abraham Wood, written in 1650, quotes a Nottoway Indian as referring to Opechancanough as his people's old emperor. He is mentioned similarly in connection with the Meherrins. Alexander S. Salley, *Narratives of Early Carolina, 1650–1708* (New York: Charles Scribner's Sons, 1911), 10–15.

6. Robert Beverley, *The History and Present State of Virginia (1705)*, ed. Louis B. Wright (Chapel Hill: University of North Carolina Press, 1947), 49–50.

7. Thomas Ludwell, letter to the "Right Honorable," June 30, 1678, in Henry Coventry Papers, vol. 73, Bath 65, fol. 264 (microfilm, Colonial Williamsburg Foundation, Williamsburg, Virginia). The documentary record also reveals that in August 1645 many of the Pamunkey warriors who had been taken prisoner when Governor William Berkeley stormed Opechancanough's stronghold, taking him captive, were transported by ship from the mainland to Western (now Tangier) Island in Chesapeake Bay, where they were abandoned. H. R. McIlwaine, comp., *Minutes of Council and General Court, 1622–1632, 1670–1676* (Richmond VA: Library Board, 1924), 564.

8. William W. Hening, *The Statutes at Large: Being a Collection of All the Laws of Virginia from the First Session of the Legislature in the Year 1619*, 13 vols. (Richmond VA: Samuel Pleasants, 1809–23), 1:323–29.

9. Peter Force, *Tracts and Other Papers Relating Principally to the Origin, Settlement, and Progress of the Colonies in North America*, 4 vols. (Gloucester VA: Peter Smith, 1963), vol. 2, book 8, 25, 35.

10. Warren Billings, "Some Acts Not in Hening's, April 1652, November 1652, and July 1653," *Virginia Magazine of History and Biography* 83 (1975): 65–72. Consistent with seventeenth-century Anglo-American usage, the terms "king" and "queen" have been applied throughout this chapter to Indian leaders whose titles were likened by Virginia colonists to those of the English monarchy.

11. Force, *Tracts*, vol. 1, book 8, 14; John Lederer, *The Discoveries of John Lederer with Unpublished Letters by and about Lederer to Governor John Winthrop, Jr., and an Essay on the Indians of Lederer's Discoveries*, ed. William P. Cummings (Charlottesville: University of Virginia Press, 1958), 16; Edward D. Neill, *Virginia Carolorum: The Colony under the Rule of Charles the First and Second AD 1625–AD 1685, Based upon Manuscripts and Documents of the Period* (Albany NY: Joel Munsell's Sons, 1886), 245.

12. Force, *Tracts*, vol. 1, book 8, 14–15. T. M., who wrote this account, was an eyewit-

ness; he has been identified by researchers as Thomas Mathew, a Northumberland County planter and burgess to the June 1676 assembly.

13. Wilcomb E. Washburn, *The Governor and the Rebel: A History of Bacon's Rebellion in Virginia* (New York: W. W. Norton, 1972), 20–30; Stephen Saunders Webb, *1676: The End of American Independence* (New York: Alfred A. Knopf, 1984), 21–25. Grievances, presented by county officials to the king's commissioners, who forwarded them to England, reveal that Indian attacks had occurred along the colony's frontier, that is, in the upper reaches of the Rappahannock and Potomac rivers. King's Commissioners, "A Repertory of the General County Grievances of Virginia, October 15, 1677," in Great Britain, The National Archives, Public Record Office, Colonial Office Papers (hereafter cited as PRO, CO) 5/1312, part 1, fols. 318–19 (microfilm at Colonial Williamsburg Foundation, Williamsburg, Virginia).

14. Force, *Tracts*, vol. 1, book 8, 14–15. On identity of the queen's son, see note 33.

15. Force, *Tracts*, vol. 1, book 8, 14–15.

16. Privy Council, letter to Commissioners Inquiring into Grievances in Virginia, November 9, 1676, in Samuel Wiseman's Book of Record, 1676–77, Pepysian Library 2582, Great Britain, Magdalen College, Cambridge (microfilm at Colonial Williamsburg Foundation, Williamsburg, Virginia); Privy Council, Instructions to William Berkeley, October 13, 1676, in PRO, CO 5/1355, fols. 111–14.

17. H. R. McIlwaine and J. P. Kennedy, comps., *Journals of the House of Burgesses*, 13 vols. (Richmond VA: Library Board, 1905–15), 1659/60–1693, 89.

18. Hening, *Statutes*, 2:251.

19. Charles M. Andrews, *Narratives of the Insurrections* (New York: Charles Scribner's Sons, 1915), 125–27.

20. Andrews, *Narratives*, 127–28.

21. McIlwaine and Kennedy, *House*, 1659/60–1693, 89; William Berkeley, "Names and Short Characters of those that have bin executed for Rebellion," in Samuel Wiseman's Book of Record, 1676–77.

22. John Berry, Herbert Jeffreys, and Francis Moryson, "Address of King's Commissioners to Grand Assembly, February 27, 1676/77," in Samuel Wiseman's Book of Record, 1676–77.

23. John Berry, Herbert Jeffreys, and Francis Moryson, letter of Commissioners to Principal Secretary of State, February 27, 1676/77, in Samuel Wiseman's Book of Record, 1676–77.

24. McIlwaine and Kennedy, *House*, 1659/60–1693, 89.

25. Andrews, *Narratives*, 127; Lord Chamberlain's Accounts in Jewel House Warrant Books, ser. 1, 1677–1709, January 18, 1677/78, in PRO, Lord Chamberlain's Papers (LC) 5/108, fol. 8; Lord Chamberlain's Department Wardrobe Accounts, Bill Books, ser. 1, 1675–79, November 1679 entry in PRO, LC 9/275, fols. 264ro–267ro; Virginia Colonial Records Project (VCRP) Survey Report 5736.

26. John Berry, Herbert Jeffreys, and Francis Moryson, "Commissioners to Mr. Secretary Coventry, March 27, 1677," in Samuel Wiseman's Book of Record, 1676–77.

27. Herbert Jeffreys, Declaration of Colonel Jeffreys, Governor of Virginia, April 27, 1677, in PRO, CO 5/1355 fols. 145–49.

28. John Berry, Herbert Jeffreys, and Francis Moryson, "Commissioners Instructions together with their answers how they have performed the Several Articles," n.d., in Samuel Wiseman's Book of Record, 1676–77; Thomas Notley, lieutenant governor of Maryland, letter to Lord Baltimore, proprietor of Maryland, May 22, 1677, in PRO, CO 1/40, fols. 186–87.

29. Emphasis added. John Berry, Herbert Jeffreys, and Francis Moryson, "Particular Accounts how we yr Majesties Commissioners for the affairs of Virginia have observed and Comply'd with our Instructions" in PRO, CO 5/1371, fol. 365.

30. In 1699 Middle Plantation was laid out as the site of Williamsburg and designated the capital of the colony.

31. Herbert Jeffreys, letter to Right Honorable, June 11, 1677, in Coventry Papers, vol. 73, Bath 65, fols. 64–65 (microfilm at Colonial Williamsburg Foundation, Williamsburg, Virginia; PRO, CO 5/1371 fol. 365). Emphasis added.

32. Jeffreys, letter to Right Honorable.

33. Young West, earlier described as the son of an English colonel, was likely the offspring of Captain John West, who by the time of Totopotomoy's death in 1656, owned land in Pamunkey Neck, near Cockacoeske's village. According to one descendant of the elder West, his English wife, Unity, left him because of his liaison with the queen of Pamunkey. George H. S. King, letter to J. P. Hudson, July 14, 1961.

34. Nicholas Spencer, letter to Right Honorable, June 22, 1677, in PRO, CO 1/40, fols. 249–50.

35. Herbert Jeffreys, letter to Right Honorable, June 11, 1677, in Coventry Papers, vol. 73, Bath 65, fols. 64–65; John Berry, Herbert Jeffreys, and Francis Moryson, "Letter of Commissioners to King, July 20, 1677," in Samuel Wiseman's Book of Record, 1676–77.

36. Lords of Trade and Plantations, letter to king, October 19, 1677, in PRO, CO 1/41, fol. 222.

37. Privy Council, Order to Secretary Coventry, October 19, 1677, in PRO, CO 5/1355, fols. 198–200.

38. Privy Council, Order to Secretary Henry Coventry in PRO, CO 5/1355, fols. 243–45. The second treaty agreement, also called the Treaty of Middle Plantation and back-dated to May 29, 1677, contained twenty-two articles, not twenty-one, its extra article extending treaty coverage to Maryland. The second treaty was endorsed not only by the original signatories of the earlier document but also by Peracuta, the king of the Appomattocks, who previously had not been allowed to sign; Mastegonoe, the king of the Saponis, and Tachapoake, their chief man; Shurenough, the king of the Manakins; Vnuntsquero, the chief man of the Meherrins, and Horehannah, their next chief man; and Pattanochus, who signed as king of the Nanzatticos, Nansemonds, and Portobagos. "Articles of Peace between the Most Serene and Mighty Prince Charles II . . . Concluded the 29th day of May 1677," in Miscellaneous Virginia Records 1606–92, Bland Manuscripts, Papers of Thomas Jefferson, 8th ser. 14:226–33 (microfilm at College of William and Mary, Williamsburg).

Note: the Nansemonds mentioned with the Nanzatticos and Portobagos were a Rappahannock River group and should not be confused with the Nansemonds living on the south
side of the James River.

39. From Berry and Moryson's letter requesting the presents we learn that she was "of
a meane or indifferent stature and somewhat plump of body" and that young John West,
whom they called "the Prince, her son and successor," was a "good, brave young man pretty
full of stature and slender of body, a great warr captain among the Indians and one that has
been very active in the service of the English." Lord Chamberlain's Accounts, Jewel House
Warrant Books, ser. 1, 1677–1709, January 18, 1677/78, in PRO, LC 5/108, fol. 8; Wardrobe
Accounts, Bill Books, ser. 1, 1675–79, November 1679 entry, PRO, LC 9/275, fols. 264ro-
267ro; VCRP Survey Report 5736.

40. Wardrobe Accounts, Bill Books, ser. 1, 1675–79, November 1679 entry, PRO, LC 9/275,
fols. 264ro-267ro; VCRP Survey Report 5736.

41. Wardrobe Accounts, Bill Books, ser. 1, 1675–79, November 1679 entry, PRO, LC 9/275,
fols. 264ro–267ro; VCRP Survey Report 5736. These badges should not be confused with
the ones made in the early 1660s, which did not bear the name of the English monarch. A
1662 law stipulated that any Indians entering the territory ceded to the Virginia government in 1646 had to wear a special silver or copper badge inscribed with his town's name.
These medals served as badges of safe conduct. In the 1980s C. G. Holland and Ben Mc-
Cary reported upon the discovery of three of these medals in archaeological contexts and
attributed them to the 1662 policy of controlling access to the colonized area. These artifacts have incised floral designs and the words "Ye King of" are cut into the upper half of
one side. As late as 1711 copper badges were issued to tributary Indians who needed to enter settled areas, and pewter badges were issued to nontributary Indians. Hening, *Statutes*,
2:141–42; C. G. Holland, "The Silver Frontlet," *Archeological Society of Virginia, Quarterly
Bulletin* 37, no. 1 (March 1982): 27–28; Ben C. McCary, "The Virginia Tributary Indians
and Their Metal Badges of 1661/62," *Archeological Society of Virginia, Quarterly Bulletin*
38, no. 3 (September 1982): 182–96; H. R. McIlwaine, ed., *Journals of the Executive Council*, 6 vols. (Richmond: Virginia State Library, 1925–1945), 3:286.

42. Hening, *Statutes*, 2:275–77; "Treaty," Bland Manuscripts; McIlwaine, *Executive
Council*, 1:4. In the more than three hundred years that have elapsed since King Charles II
sent gifts to some of Virginia's tributary Indian leaders, confusion has arisen over whether a
silver ornament preserved at Jamestown, which is inscribed with the name of King Charles
II and the crest of the British monarchy, is Cockacoeske's crown or her necklace. Some
nineteenth- and early twentieth-century writers have called it the Pamunkey crown, but
the crowns prepared for the queens of Pamunkey and Weyanoke and the kings of Nottoway and Nansemond were, in fact, adorned with false stones. Their maker, according to
royal Jewel House account books, submitted a bill "for making new screws and fastening
several stones in the crowns," evidence that the coronets were indeed jeweled. Moreover,
those crowns were never delivered to the Indian kings and queens but instead were lost at
sea. According to a notation made by Governor Thomas Culpeper in the margin of King
Charles's instructions to him "to deliver unto them [the Indian rulers] our Royal Presents,"

Culpeper did "exactly execute all but only the Coronets which by advice of Council there I did not deliver and which were cast away with my goods," a reference to the sinking of the ship transporting his baggage back to England. Thus the silver "frontlet" that has survived three centuries is likely to be the necklace that Jewel House Warrant Books list as being among the items made for Cockacoeske in England. Privy Council, Instructions to Thomas Lord Culpeper, December 6, 1679, in PRO, CO 5/1355, fols. 243–45.

43. "Treaty," Bland Manuscripts; Hening, *Statutes*, 2:275–77.

44. Emphasis added.

45. Official records reveal that the tributaries called upon the Virginia government for protection several times during the late seventeenth century.

46. As is seen from the list of grievances about the Chickahominys that Cockacoeske presented to officials on June 5, 1678, and a letter she sent to England on June 29, 1678, sustaining her position was not accomplished without bloodshed and resentment.

47. Documentary evidence reveals that the Chiskiacks survived until at least August 1677, at which time they were granted the right to conduct trade in Gloucester County, where they lived. Hening, *Statutes*, 2:411.

48. Hening, *Statutes*, 2:275–77.

49. Queen of Pamunkey (Cockacoeske), The Agrievances of the Queen of Poemunkey and her Sonn Captain John West, June 5, 1678, in PRO, CO 1/42, fol. 177.

50. Cockacoeske, letter to Colonel Francis Moryson, June 29, 1678 in PRO, CO 1/42, fol. 276.

51. Cornelius Dabney, letter to Colonel Francis Moryson, June 29, 1678, in PRO, CO 1/42, fol. 277.

52. Dabney, letter to Colonel Francis Moryson.

53. Thomas Ludwell, letter to Right Honorable, January 30, 1678, in Coventry Papers, vol. 73, Bath 65, fols. 202–3.

54. Ludwell, letter to Right Honorable, January 30, 1678, in Coventry Papers, vol. 73, Bath 65, fols. 202–3. Article 12 of the treaty proved troublesome to colonial officials, as did article 18, which required them to arbitrate disputes among the tributary Indians. That article faced them with a dilemma, for in siding with one tribe they automatically alienated another. Ludwell noted that the Virginia government was obliged not only to settle quarrels among the tributary Indians but also to protect them against warring tribes, something he also found vexing. "Now," Ludwell argued, "we have a warr with those Irachors [Iroquois] but our Indians have not, because the treaty with them at Fort Albany was ordered before our peace was concluded there." Anonymous [Thomas Ludwell], letter to Sir Joseph Williamson, June 8, 1678; Thomas Ludwell, letter to Right Honorable, August 3, 1678, in Coventry Papers, vol. 73, Bath 65, fol. 281.

55. Anonymous [Thomas Ludwell], letter to Sir Joseph Williamson, Secretary of State, in Coventry Papers, vol. 73, Bath 65, unpaginated folio.

56. Thomas Ludwell, letter to "Right Honorable," June 28, 1678, in Coventry Papers, vol. 73, Bath 65, fol. 264.

57. Thomas Ludwell, letter to the "Right Honorable," August 3, 1678, in Coventry Papers, vol. 73, Bath 65, fol. 281.

58. McIlwaine and Kennedy, *House*, 1693–1702, 349; Thomas Story, *A Journal of the Life of Thomas Story* (Newcastle upon Tyne: James and John Wilson, 1747), 162.

59. McIlwaine, *Executive Journals*, 1:79.

60. Louis des Cognets Jr., *English Duplicates of Lost Virginia Records* (Princeton NJ: privately published, 1958), 57; William P. Palmer, ed., *Calendar of Virginia State Papers and Other Manuscripts Preserved in the Capital at Richmond*, 13 vols. (Richmond: Virginia State Library, 1875–93), 1:184–85; Francis Nicholson, letter to his Council, October 22, 1702, in PRO, CO 5/1312, part 1, fol. 318.

"Our Bond of Peace"

Patterns of Intercultural Exchange in the Carolina Piedmont, 1650–1750

JAMES H. MERRELL

Revisiting the Carolina Piedmont and "Our Bond of Peace"

I must confess that it was at first somewhat disconcerting to be invited to revisit something I wrote more than two decades ago, published more than fifteen years past—and have scarcely looked at since. After all, when I first tried to work out the links in this "Bond of Peace," I was fresh out of graduate school, with much yet to learn (even more than I still have to learn) about the historian's craft. Moreover, I long ago left the Southern piedmont and its peoples, both literally and figuratively, as my interests led me to other frontiers and other folks.[1] Meanwhile a wealth of fine scholarship has appeared—probing the piedmont, exploring exchange, and chronicling the entire colonial encounter. It seemed likely that this apprentice scholar's long-ago attempt to stitch together the fabric of exchange in one corner of the colonial South would not stand the test of time.[2]

It was with some relief, then, that upon rereading "Our Bond of Peace" I found it less embarrassing, less dated, than I had feared it might be. The central argument still, in my view, delineates the overall pattern of exchange in that time and place. Native Americans were indeed actors in this drama; they did indeed, in the early going, set colonial men and colonial merchandise into existing structures of belief and behavior. Over time, however, the balance of power shifted from native to newcomer as piedmont peoples came to depend on regular supplies of foreign wares. I believe that this script still captures, with a fair degree of accuracy, the story's plot. Even with two decades more scholarly experience, I would concur with my younger self that "the trade's effects on piedmont societies remained more evolutionary than revolutionary."

Recent scholarship generally supports this interpretation. One line of inquiry vigorously pursued over the past twenty years or so has been piedmont archaeology: native ways of life once only dimly visible have been much more thoroughly uncovered and brought to light. Those lifeways are in accord with the idea that piedmont peoples tended to be conservative in their engagement with a new world of wares. The archaeological evidence suggests that traditional habits of hunting, gathering, and farming endured long after European trade goods found their way into upcountry villages, as did the ancient skills of potters and fletchers. And although natives now might send their dead into the spirit world equipped with glass beads instead of sea shells, a brass kettle instead of a clay pot, a cloth coat instead of a deerskin cloak, and a musket instead of a bow, replacement of one item with another was not symptomatic of fundamental "changes in ritual and ideology." Rather, archaeologists argue, "these changes are better interpreted as adaptive responses within societies that remained, in many respects, resistant to change and that attempted to maintain their traditional cultural systems."[3]

Continuity and *adaptability* have also been watchwords of recent historical treatments of intercultural exchange in the colonial Southeast in particular and colonial North America in general. It turns out that natives well beyond the southern piedmont, experienced and adept in the art of swapping goods with foreigners long before Europeans arrived, continued to dictate trade's terms. The neighboring Cherokees were "shrewd bargainers" in their dealings with colonists, observes Tom Hatley. "The life of the towns was changed but not revolutionized by the presence of traders and trade goods within them."[4] Among Creeks, too, Kathryn Braund notes, established "[n]ative customs and attitudes toward both trade goods and trading partners worked to shape the commercial relations they established with outsiders." Moreover, Braund goes on, "Europeans were forced to respect— and often adopt—the . . . traditions of their Indian trade partners" in order "to meet Creek needs on Creek terms."[5]

Scholars working on even larger canvases concur. Surveying the entire colonial South, James Axtell concludes that "[t]he great majority of these [European trade] items . . . were only pleasing or superior substitutes for functional native-made goods, and their traditional meanings and uses were largely retained."[6] Looking beyond the region to consider all of eastern North America, Daniel K. Richter finds that, while "expanded trade" eventually "reordered Native economies" and "dramatically reshaped Native cultures," initially beads, metal tools, and other objects "fitted seamlessly into existing patterns" and were "integrated into familiar cultural niches."[7] Some dissenting voices stress that trade with Europeans "disastrously affected native religious beliefs" and "wreaked cultural havoc with the life style of American Indians."[8] For the most part, however, the consensus is that, especially in trade's early years, the portrait of exchange that I sketched a generation ago (following in the footsteps of such pathbreaking scholars as Bruce G. Trigger, James Axtell, and Neal Salisbury) is still a fair likeness.[9]

If the advances in scholarship and the development of my own thinking have left the essay's interpretive edifice more or less intact, nonetheless, were I to embark on this project today, I certainly would recast "Our Bond of Peace" in various ways. One revision would be to avoid certain terms and phrases that subtly—and, sometimes, not so subtly—distort the encounter and favor European ways of thinking.[10] True, I did watch my language well enough to avoid some loaded words still in use today like *trinkets* (which adopts a colonial scale of values) and *backcountry* (which views things from Charlestown or Williamsburg rather than from Indian country).[11] And I managed to sidestep the popular but confusing designation *Indian trader*. In common parlance this means a colonist who traded with Indians, but in fact it could denote an Indian involved in exchange or a slave dealer who traded *in* Indians (just as a *deerskin trader* peddled animal hides).[12]

But other misnomers found their way into the essay. *Precontact,* for example, shorthand for the millennia prior to 1492, ignores the fact that during those millennia every native village had extensive *contact* with other Indian towns and tribes, instead perpetuating outmoded ideas about primitive, isolated aboriginal Americans awaiting Columbian "contact." No less distorting is the lingo inherited from European habits of thought about the exchange of material objects. To write, as I did then, of "Cheraw traders . . . conducting business among Catawba River towns," of natives "being choosy customers," of "an Indian [who] took his business elsewhere," is to imply that natives thought of such behavior more or less the way Europeans did, as an enterprise solely of bargaining and haggling, profits and prices. Although other scholars still write of native "consumers" with real or figurative "shopping lists," I would no longer do so, particularly in treating the early stages of colonial contact when, as "Our Bond of Peace" argues, such activities were more than "economic," when natives involved in them were doing more than "business" and were more than "customers."[13]

Pursuing this line of thought still further leads to the word *trade* itself. In recent years some scholars have asserted that any attempt to grasp the natives' point of view must recognize that even talk of *trade* and *trader* distorts this experience. "[T]he exchange of goods is not so easily fenced off into an economic realm . . .," notes Richard White. "[T]he fur trade proper is merely an arbitrary selection from a fuller and quite coherent spectrum of exchange that was embedded in particular social relations."[14] Use of the phrase "'[t]he fur trade . . .,'" Peter Cook agrees, "tends to obscure the great variety of goods and services exchanged between First Nations and colonials. . . . [T]he commonsense meaning of trade does not easily accommodate exchanges occurring in contexts that cannot be imagined as a kind of market."[15] Because "Cherokees did not compartmentalize commercial, personal, and political relationships," observes Hatley, we ought to imagine "exchange in the broadest terms, a realm of transactions in which goods simultaneously built 'bridges' and tore down 'fences' between colonist and mountain villager."[16] And Michael Morris insists that "trade" must not be divorced from "gift-giving"; in native societies these two terms "take on a deeper meaning, which may be lost on the more technologically sophisticated culture," a meaning that "introduces an emotional aspect to a relationship."[17] While "Our Bond of Peace" occasionally glimpsed that broader spectrum and deeper meaning of exchange relations—in its treatment of gifts and trade goods, of diplomacy and kinship ties, for example—if I were today approaching the piedmont, I would go more explicitly and more strenuously against the grain of conventional notions about "trade."

I would also pay more attention to the gendered nature of exchange. Just as I now would scrap the term "business" in the phrase "an Indian took his business elsewhere," so I might well drop "his." I recognized, back then, that Indian women had a role to play as "She-Bed-Fellow" to a colonial trader, weaving that outsider into native kinship networks, teaching him the language, and otherwise easing his passage from foreign to familiar. I did not, however, have the benefit of work that brings to light profound differences between how native men and native women engaged in exchange with colonists.

Among the piedmont peoples' Cherokee neighbors, Theda Perdue finds, men were more quickly and more deeply drawn into European methods and markets, hunting deer and preparing skins for sale; women's exchange experience, largely confined to food and baskets, was more conservative, more traditional, more immune to new and alien notions of buying and selling. In general, she notes, "[w]omen shared" while "men sold"; from that difference "[t]wo economies characterized by very different economic values began to emerge—an agricultural economy of women and a commercial hunting economy of men." One was shaped by a "cooperative ethic," the other by "individualistic pursuits." In the end, Perdue concludes, "[t]rade . . . introduced new ways for Cherokee men and women to relate to each other." Whether the evidence from piedmont towns could sustain a similarly rich treatment there, I would be more alert to glimpses of the place that the variable of gender had in the equation of exchange.[18]

Besides recognizing the gendered and emotional as well as the diplomatic and commercial aspects of intercultural exchange, scholarship over the past two decades has better uncovered its spiritual dimension as well. Here, too, the poverty of piedmont sources might make it hard to reconstruct the religious impact of a copper kettle or a steel knife. But imaginative work by Christopher Miller and George Hamell, by Bruce White and Frederic Gleach, has unearthed how, in the early years of exchange with Europeans, natives fitted both the goods and the men who brought them into a magical mind-set that made these items and these beings powerful and enticing, dangerous and wondrous, sacred and strange. Attention to this subtle, hidden way of thinking and of treating outsiders—whether objects or people—adds much to efforts to recapture what went on when natives and newcomers approached one another, goods in hand. Less clear is how quickly this enchantment wore off, how soon trade goods lost their spiritual character and traders their "other-worldly" status, how rapidly native disenchantment set in.[19]

Whether enchanted or not, the opening seasons of Indian exchange with colonists, scholars now suggest, often witnessed not just the *continuity* in native ways—which I emphasized in "Our Bond of Peace"—but even *improvement* in daily life along with an "efflorescence" of craft and culture—

which I did not. As Richter argues, "[t]he new material things were always in some practical way superior to the old" because they were "lighter, sharper, [and] more durable." From chopping down trees to lighting fires to cooking over those flames, Richter goes on, "[f]or Indian men and women, any number of everyday tasks became much easier." Not only that, but "[n]ew tools and new materials made life . . ., in countless ways, aesthetically richer," whether in beadwork, carving, or other pursuits.[20]

Signs of such developments are scarce in the southern piedmont, but new archaeological finds there suggest one possibility: smoking. Excavations of an upcountry village site suggest that during the late seventeenth century, inhabitants changed their "smoking etiquette." For centuries, piedmont peoples had smoked locally grown tobacco, with use probably restricted to certain rituals conducted by special individuals. Now, a new sort of pipe became common, its shape reminiscent of colonial and European forms, its bowl stuffed, perhaps, with non-native tobacco, "a milder English blend" originally imported from the West Indies. "What was sacred and ritually prescribed behavior," suggest H. Trawick Ward and R. P. Stephen Davis Jr., "became more secular and widespread . . . after 1650." Side by side with time-honored tobacco use by priests for "purification and curing rituals," "smoking was a leisure activity enjoyed by almost everyone." Whether this trend can be considered cultural "efflorescence" is something else again.[21]

The piedmont soil has also yielded traces of another response to the goods that colonists introduced: a shift in social status and its markers. Burials of men who, though relatively young, had acquired (and been interred with) impressive amounts of European wares suggest that a phenomenon seen elsewhere in colonial times might also have come to the upcountry. So-called big men, their position acquired via access to and redistribution of precious European wares, became more common and highly visible figures in Indian country. They might well have challenged traditional leaders whose stature rested on age and lineage, experience and eloquence, skill in conjuring, hunting, or war. Brandishing such highly visible status symbols as iron knives and flintlock pistols, large leather belts and knee breeches, "[t]hese big men," archaeologists conclude, "were young adult males who probably replaced more elder[ly] leaders who had been most influential prior to European contact."[22] First widespread smoking, then a generation gap: sometimes the past does not seem so remote, so foreign after all.

Burials yield new insight into another fundamental feature of Indian life during this period, one that is indeed (fortunately for us) foreign nowadays: the devastation wrought by new diseases. That epidemics visited the piedmont in the very years colonial traders and their packhorses first arrived there in large numbers was well known two decades ago. But excavations in more recent times have turned up grim details of the human and cultural toll exacted by these scourges. What had been towns became cemeteries, so many were the burials. More sobering still, many of the dead were children, their bodies lowered into shallow graves that were left empty of the goods that customarily traveled with the departing spirit as it embarked on its journey to the afterlife. "It almost seems," conclude Ward and Davis, "as if the energy required to maintain traditional mortuary practices"— besides the grave goods, there usually had been burial feasts—"could no longer be mustered."[23]

No less telling of a profound shift in belief and behavior, interments that once had been placed within the confines of the village—even in the floors of houses—now were clustered beyond the town's edge, as if the dead had become dangerous foreigners to be shunned instead of familiar kin to be cherished.[24] It is clear that, while piedmont peoples were indeed remarkable for the persistence of their cultural traditions, new goods and new diseases arrived in the region together and, together, fundamentally and forever altered native life.

From disease and despair to smoking and status, from the multiple meanings hidden in a term like *trade* to the distortion wrought by commonplace words or phrases, the new scholarship has many lessons to teach. It offers handy tools for refashioning—though not, I still maintain, wholly recasting—the interpretive structure I put together in the pages that follow.

One final turn of phrase that entered the scholarly conversation after this essay came out would certainly, were I undertaking the project today, have shaped my thinking as it has shaped so much work over the past fifteen years: *the middle ground*. This phrase, coined by Richard White in his classic account of relations between newcomers and natives in the Great Lakes region, denotes a physical and cultural place where different peoples could come together to forge relationships based on shared pursuits, shared understandings, and shared agendas, whether those agendas were war or peace, trade or sex. "The middle ground," White explains, "is the place in between: in between cultures, peoples, and in between empires and the nonstate world of villages. . . . It is the area between the historical foreground of European invasion and occupation and the background of Indian defeat and retreat."[25] Because neither colonists nor native peoples could dictate the terms of engagement in this region, they had to find ways to get along.

White's book—and especially its evocative title—has had a powerful, pervasive effect on studies of the American encounter.[26] Was the southern piedmont's "Bond of Peace" in fact a species of middle ground? In the adaptations and adjustments that went on in those precincts—especially by colonial traders, especially in the early years—there is a resemblance. But the very phrase *bond of peace* testifies to a relentless European drive for power and control that became a reality much more quickly in the piedmont than it did around the Great Lakes; it took a generation, not a century or more. Another recent student of the colonial South, Martin Quitt, cautions about being too quick with the "middle ground" label. Examining early exchange relations between Powhatans and Virginians "shows how problematic bridging a deep cultural chasm can be," Quitt points out, "how hard it was for . . . two peoples to find a middle ground between their cultures." Along the James River, at least, even thriving intercultural trade taught a "hard lesson . . .: mutual understanding does not necessarily engender mutual respect, tolerance, or civility."[27] I leave it to the reader of "Our Bond of Peace" to decide how far piedmont peoples and their colonial counterparts managed, via trade, to construct something like a middle ground some three centuries ago.

"Our Bond of Peace"
Patterns of Intercultural Exchange in the Carolina Piedmont, 1650–1750

In the winter of 1701 the English explorer John Lawson and several companions visited the lands and peoples lying northwest of Charlestown, South Carolina. While traveling among the Santee Indians one hundred miles from the coast, the party stopped overnight at a Santee hunter's empty hut and, Lawson wrote, "made our selves welcome to what his Cabin afforded, (which is a Thing common) the Indians allowing it practicable to the *English* Traders, to take out of their Houses what they need in their Absence, in Lieu whereof they most commonly leave some small Gratuity of Tobacco,

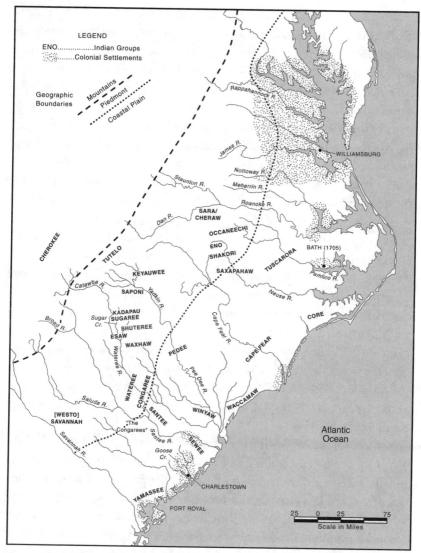

Figure 1. The Carolinas and Virginia, circa 1700.

Paint, Beads, etc." Ten days later a Waxhaw Indian eager to trade intercepted
the travelers on their way north to invite them to his town. "We receiv'd
the Messenger with a great many Ceremonies," Lawson noted in his journal, "acceptable to those sort of Creatures."[28]

As these episodes indicate, Lawson's party was following a code of conduct governing trade relations between Anglo-American colonists and In-

dians in the southern upcountry (fig. 1). The process of drawing up the code's rules and rituals had begun in earnest some fifty years before Lawson passed through, when a handful of trade-minded Virginia colonists turned their sights toward the untapped native populations southwest of the colony.[29] Over the next several decades these men—joined at the end of the century by others from Charlestown—penetrated deeper into the interior. By 1700 contacts with the Indian peoples there had become routine, and piedmont villages from the James River to the Wateree were part of the European trade network, linked to colonial Americans in a relationship that the clergyman and naturalist John Banister in 1679 termed "our Vinculum Pacis"—our bond of peace.[30]

Banister, who was acquainted with the trading community that clustered along the upper James and Appomattox rivers for voyages into the interior, was convinced that the "bond of peace" gave colonists complete control over the Indians. "Since there has been a way layd open for Trade . . .," he asserted, "many Things which they wanted not before because they never had them are by that means become necessary both for their use and ornament."[31] A generation later John Lawson agreed, claiming that the Carolinians were "absolute Masters over the *Indians* . . . within the Circle of their Trade." The Santees, for one, had become "very tractable" by virtue of their proximity to South Carolina and their consequent dependence on European technology.[32]

Yet beneath the Anglo-American boasts lay a more complex story. As Lawson's own conduct among the Santees and Waxhaws illustrated, piedmont Indians still shaped the contours of trade, "allowing" an outsider into their domain only if he behaved in "acceptable" ways. Natives entangled in the web of intercultural commerce did not abruptly abandon their own habits or meekly submit to the dictates of a colonist handing out his wares. Rather, upcountry peoples were active participants in the development of exchange across cultural boundaries, and for many years the pattern of trade looked more Indian than European. If with time the balance of economic and cultural power did indeed tip toward the colonists, the trade's effects on piedmont societies remained more evolutionary than revolutionary.[33]

Colonial traders could not change native ways overnight, in large part because the newcomers confronted a deeply rooted system of aboriginal commerce. Few details of the pre-Columbian trade survive, but it was clearly extensive, involving every group and a wide range of products. Although each village could provide itself with the basic necessities of life, peoples occupying different environments had access to certain highly prized commodities. Easily transportable items such as copper, natural dyes, and mica from the interior or shells from the seacoast composed the bulk of the trade, their passage from one hand to the next aided by interpreters, sign language, symbols, or other methods of surmounting linguistic barriers.[34] Beyond distributing these products over a wide area, aboriginal trade probably served as a vital means of maintaining ties among the independent towns scattered through upland river valleys, bringing different peoples together in a formal setting conducive to cementing peaceful relations. Like the exchange of goods, the exchange of people—as "hostages," adoptees, or marriage partners—symbolically confirmed friendship and trust.[35]

The Indians' trade with colonists emerged from these established forms. Some aboriginal exchange even remained untouched by the arrival of Anglo-Americans, for certain native groups still had access to traditional trade goods that were in great demand elsewhere. John Lawson remarked that coastal Indians gathered shells, along with yaupon plants for brewing "*Indian* Tea," "which they carry a great way into the main Land, to trade with the remote *Indians*, where they are of great Value." In return, people near the mountains collected a root to make red powder for paint. "They have this Scarlet Root in great Esteem," Lawson learned, "and sell it for a very great Price, one to another."[36]

At the same time, however, native traders began making subtle adjustments to the European presence without leaving the familiar confines of aboriginal exchange. Those near Anglo-American settlements manufactured wooden bowls, straw baskets, and clay pipes, traded them for raw deerskins at Indian towns to the west "that perhaps," Lawson speculated, "have greater Plenty of Deer," and returned home to finish dressing the skins before selling them to colonists. Both the products and the methods of exchange were wholly traditional; for generations, Indians in the interior customarily traded deerskins to native peoples of the lowcountry. But European demand for pelts, and perhaps also a declining deer population near colonial plantations, gave this traffic larger dimensions and new meaning.[37]

Eventually the cargoes that nearby Indians ferried to distant towns began to include European products as well as native manufactures. In 1670 Cheraw traders already acquainted with the Virginia men were conducting business among Catawba River towns, and it seems safe to surmise that they were peddling glass beads as well as red roots.[38] By the end of the century there was no longer room for doubt. To his surprise, Lawson met headmen in the piedmont who owned horses that had been spirited away from colonial settlements "by some neighbouring *Indian*, and transported farther into the Country, and sold." Liquor proved more popular than livestock, and groups near the sea introduced it to "the Westward Indians, who never knew what it was, till within very few Years."[39] Many Carolina natives must have gaped at a horse, tasted rum, or tried on a matchcoat before seeing their first European.

However obtained, most of the new wares were readily absorbed into native life. It was easy enough to come up with words for "gun," "powder horn," or "shot bag" and add them to one's vocabulary, or to substitute glass beads for shells, iron pots for clay vessels, metal bells for tortoise-shell rattles, and cloth for furs.[40] If necessary, Indians could also "fix" a foreign object so it suited their needs. Thus Keyauwee fletchers chipped arrowheads from broken bottles, while hunters, upon acquiring a musket, held it as they would a bow, with the left hand far forward, and then took great pains to "set it streight, sometimes shooting away above 100 Loads of Ammunition, before they bring the Gun to shoot according to their Mind."[41]

When they arrived on the scene, colonial traders were set straight in a similar manner. Men poised at the falls of the James River for a trek into the interior had to learn patience while also mastering the rudiments of the native system of communication, for Indians chose to "let us know . . . by grains of Mayze, or small stones, when they will come in, when they shall have any truck for us to go out, or the like."[42] Once he did enter the upcountry, the colonist found himself playing the trading game by native rules. Relying heavily on local guides, most early adventurers were taken along aboriginal trails.[43] Only John Lederer, who explored the far reaches of the piedmont in 1670, neglected to hire a guide; only Lederer ignored Indian directions—and only Lederer became hopelessly lost, wandering for days over "steep and craggy Cliffs," in "a continued Marish over-grown with Reeds," and across "a barren Sandy desert." After he finally staggered back to Virginia he warned anyone brave (or foolish) enough to try retracing his steps that "the way [is] thorow a vast Forest, where you seldom fall into any Road or Path." Those who did follow in Lederer's footsteps, aware that one did not simply "fall into" a trail, heeded native advice and stuck to established routes.[44]

Upon arriving at a piedmont settlement the colonist became a central player in a social drama directed by the townspeople. His welcome and treatment did not depart from earlier practices, for native hosts made no distinction among visitors, the local headman "always entertaining Travellers, either *English*, or *Indian*."[45] Lederer's description of the etiquette of greeting illustrates the passive stance that the wise colonist adopted in the early years of contact. "Being arrived at a Town," he advised, "enter no house until you are invited; and then seem not afraid to be led in pinion'd like a prisoner: for that is a Ceremony they use to friend and enemies without distinction. You must accept of an invitation from the Seniors, before that of young men," he went on, "and refuse nothing that is offered or set afore you: for they are very jealous, and sensible of the least slighting or neglect from strangers, and mindful of Revenge."[46]

If their guest behaved himself, some piedmont peoples offered him a more permanent place in native society. While Lederer was among the Saponis, for example, they wanted to "oblige me to stay amongst them by a Marriage with the Kings or some of their great Mens Daughters." The bewildered greenhorn managed to escape this fate, but his more experienced successors were less skittish. In Lawson's day traders "have commonly their Indian Wives" with whom they lived while among the native inhabitants of the uplands.[47] Here again Indians were treating a colonist like any other visitor, making arrangements designed to place him in the web of kinship that lay at the foundation of native life. Adoption or marriage into this network carried duties and obligations (as well as rights) understood by all in the town. Unfamiliar with relationships based solely on the market, Indians sought to bring colonists to obey the traditional rules governing interpersonal relations. When he took an Indian companion, the trader, to native eyes, accepted local forms of social control.

That Lawson's contemporaries went along with all this is obvious; less clear is just how much they understood of the arrangement's implications. Villagers who welcomed a visiting colonist were acting out behavioral codes that emphasized hospitality to outsiders and the need to establish personal or familial connections to potential trading partners. It appears that their guests continued to consider the economic basis of the relationship paramount. While staying with the Shuterees and other upcountry groups around the turn of the century, for example, the Virginia trader John Evans carefully recorded in his account book payments he made to his "Landlord" and "Landlady" for food and lodging.[48]

Indians who went further and formally accepted a trader into their kinship network invited similar misunderstandings. Colonists leapt at the offer of a mate, but they apparently considered it a shrewd business move more than anything else. "They find these *Indian* girls very serviceable to them," Lawson remarked. "This Correspondence makes them learn the *Indian* Tongue much the sooner," and they enjoy "the Satisfaction of a She-Bed-Fellow" who devoted herself to "dressing their Victuals, and instructing 'em in the Affairs and Customs of the Country. . . . Such a Man gets a great Trade with the Savages."[49] Given the linguistic and economic (not to mention sexual) advantages of these liaisons, a colonial trader would have been a fool to decline the offer.

Thus even men wholeheartedly embracing native hospitality probably knew less than the full story of what they were getting themselves into. Still, outward conformity was better than bumbling ignorance or casual indifference. Whether or not they fully grasped what was going on, colonists heading into the Carolina piedmont at the end of the seventeenth century did so largely on native terms. Just as their journeys were channeled into aboriginal paths, so their encounters with the inhabitants followed cultural pathways set out by their hosts.

An Indian group assimilated people and goods successfully because it was selective in its contacts—both personal and material—with outsiders. Men who failed to respect native customs were given short shrift. "They never frequent a Christian's House that is given to Passion," wrote Lawson, "nor will they ever buy or sell with him, if they can get the same Commodities of any other Person; for they say, such Men are mad Wolves, and no more Men."[50] Similarly, Indian customers chose merchandise most in keeping with established tastes. Many insisted that the colonial trader continue to supply traditional goods like shells.[51] And those willing to consider glass beads instead still wanted them to be a certain size and color. In short, to make a profit a colonist had to mind his manners and work tirelessly to match English goods with Indian preferences.[52]

If efforts to absorb colonists and their wares helped ensure that the early years of intercultural exchange would bring a minimum of disruption to piedmont towns, the products swapped for these goods also promoted adjustment to European intrusion. The principal Indian trade items were baskets, mats, deerskins, and slaves; none marked a radical departure from precontact ways. Piedmont women were accustomed to weaving and dyeing cane baskets or mats, and deer were already a primary source of meat and clothing. Hence the skills for producing these commodities were in place before Europeans arrived.[53]

The colonial demand for Indian slaves entailed equally few dramatic changes in native life, for enslavement of war captives was common in the aboriginal Southeast.[54] Although traders did, as one South Carolina clergyman charged, "excite [Indians] to make War amongst themselves to get Slaves which they give for our European Goods," excitement was in the air already, and it is often difficult to distinguish native from colonial impulses.[55] When Westoes crossed the Santee River to capture people there in 1670, were they after slaves for the colonial trade or victims, as Lederer put it, "to sacrifice to their Idols"? When Santees went off to war against Indians near the mouth of the Winyaw River three decades later, were they bent on settling old scores, acquiring slaves, both, or neither? All that can be known for certain is that the traffic in slaves entailed a large and destructive extension of existing habits, not the creation of an altogether new system for taking and selling human beings.[56]

None of these activities so monopolized the natives' time that the routine subsistence practices that had long sustained Indian Carolina broke down. Hunters still went out after meat to feed their families as well as pelts to sell to colonists. In the spring young men still took time out from the chase and the warpath to plant crops, and women still tended those crops in summer, in winter gathering nuts and other wild plant foods. Moreover, the hunting, planting, and gathering all remained thoroughly grounded in a ceremonial cycle without which, natives believed, life was unthinkable. Elaborate rituals to celebrate the harvest and pray for future bounty continued to occupy the piedmont winter. Hunters supplying food for these ceremonies—and skins for barter—were careful to propitiate the unseen yet powerful forces governing their fortunes. "All the *Indians* hereabouts carefully preserve the Bones of the Flesh they eat," Lawson noted while among the Keyauwees in 1701, "and burn them, as being of Opinion, that if they omitted that Custom, the Game would leave their Country, and they should not be able to maintain themselves by their Hunting."[57]

During the latter half of the seventeenth century, then, inhabitants of the piedmont were able to weave foreigners and their alien wares into the existing cultural fabric without drastically altering its texture or design. Trade was indeed a "bond of peace" that united two cultures in a common enterprise, but only because few colonists dared to challenge native hegemony. Like Lederer, they recognized that they were still guests in a foreign land and therefore had better behave themselves. Lest they forget, news of a friend, relative, or partner killed by Indians somewhere in the interior occasionally reached the coastal settlements to refresh their memory.[58]

Still, the evidence of continuing native control over the trade could not conceal some of the more gradual and more profound effects of participation in the Atlantic economy, effects that existed for a time alongside the signs of control and would eventually replace them.[59] At the most fundamental level, colonists were transforming the very nature of trade in the piedmont. Exchange became more than a means of cementing relations among groups through gifts whose symbolic value outweighed their practical uses. As early as 1670 Lederer, having glimpsed the Indians' education in European methods, was able to capture the transition from one pattern of trade to another. The "remoter Indians," he discovered, were still operating under an older set of rules and therefore "are apt to admire such trinkets . . . as small Looking-glasses, Pictures, Beads and Bracelets of glass, Knives, Sizars, and all manner of gaudy toys and knacks for children." Instead of bartering for these goods, Lederer happily reported, "remoter Indians"—accustomed to considering exchange a form of gift-giving—were content to "purchase them at any rate." Those living near the colonists, on the other hand, had learned enough to demand cloth "and all sorts of edg'd tools" as well as "Guns, Powder and Shot, etc." Moreover, these "neighbour-Indians" would "greedily barter for" European merchandise and "spend time in higgling for further abatements" in price.[60]

Before long, despite the efforts of more experienced native traders to screen "remoter Indians" from direct contact with Europeans and their ways, word still spread to distant towns regarding the range of products available from the English and the accepted means of procuring them. By the 1680s the Virginia trader William Byrd was warning his English suppliers that the commodities they shipped to him must be not only the proper size and color but also the right price.[61] The symbolic significance of exchange had by no means disappeared; it was still a form of diplomacy, and Indians never lost their taste for what colonists considered trinkets. But alongside these older forms arose a demand for tools and weapons, an awareness of the value Anglo-Americans attached to the objects involved, and a willingness to hold out for a better deal.

Indians soon enough learned that driving a hard bargain was the best way to procure the fruits of European technology. Yet the taste of some of these fruits proved more bitter than sweet as natives found themselves unable to assimilate every product as readily as they did a string of beads or a new musket. Liquor, for example, disrupted piedmont existence from the first. Although natives sought to treat alcohol as they did other foreign merchandise and make it fit existing cultural and ceremonial forms, its destructive effects were soon painfully obvious.[62] Drunken Indians crippled themselves by falling into campfires or plunging off cliffs; they crippled each other when, inhibitions lowered by drink, neighbors and kinfolk quarreled, shattering the peace of a community. Natives knew too well that rum was a "poisonous Plant" that could "make People sick," yet still they could not resist it. "They have no Power to refrain this Enemy," Lawson observed, nor could they find an antidote for the poison it injected into their lives.[63]

Hidden by the dramatic, even explosive effects of alcohol was a more general, less visible intoxication with foreign technology that grew with each passing year. The first and most obvious dependence was on European firearms. "They think themselves undrest and not fit to walk abroad," remarked one amused Virginian in 1690 of the piedmont Indians living nearby, "unlesse they have their gun on their shoulder, and their shot-bag by their side."[64] By the end of the century it seemed that no self-respecting warrior anywhere in the southern uplands was without a musket.[65]

Picking up a gun did not transform an Indian into a slave of the marketplace, of course. Men still manufactured and used the old weapons, and some limited their reliance on the colonial trader's return by mending a cracked musket stock themselves or fashioning a new ramrod from the same wood used to make arrow shafts.[66] But these were delaying tactics, not declarations of economic independence. The time, effort, and skill invested in crafting the traditional tools fell off precipitously once European substitutes became readily available.[67] Worse still, among those craftsmen copying their European contemporaries rather than their own ancestors, fixing a gunstock or replacing a ramrod was one thing, repairing a broken hammer, a rusted barrel—or an empty shot pouch—quite another. In time Indians were not just accustomed to a steady influx of certain merchandise, they were dependent upon it. And the Europeans who manufactured the guns and distilled the rum were not oblivious to the fact that commercial addictions ensure a steady market.

The transformation of European wares from luxuries to necessities went hand in hand with the metamorphosis of the colonial trader from the passive, timid observer of John Lederer's day to the confident leading player on the piedmont stage he became after 1700. In the course of their many voyages into the interior colonists were bound to pick up the tricks of the trade. From success and failure alike, Anglo-Americans learned the shortest routes, the friendliest Indians, the choicest phrases, the most popular items.[68] The school was a hard one, but graduation had its rewards. One was simply survival; another was profit; a third was a certain assurance that permitted the outsiders to begin placing their own stamp on the patterns of exchange.

The transgressions seemed harmless enough at first. Sometime around the turn of the eighteenth century, for example, traders apparently stopped waiting for a summons from the interior and began setting out from their homes when they pleased. Colonists had once entered the piedmont for a month or two in late winter and early spring to meet Indians recently returned from the winter hunt; the rest of the year, natives had the interior virtually to themselves. After 1700, however, colonial traders came when they liked and stayed as long as they chose, inaugurating an important change in the cadence of the upcountry.[69]

A visitor from the lowlands who stayed longer among his native hosts quite naturally had more opportunities to bend the rules and more confidence—as he detected the Indians' deepening reliance on the merchandise he brought—that he could get away with it. One built a trading hut near but not in the Indian village, which took him out of the headman's dwelling and placed him both figuratively and literally beyond local control.[70] The natives' reaction to this particular innovation is unknown, but other colonial inventions met stiff resistance. The steelyard, a metal contraption for weighing merchandise, proved a particular point of contention between native and newcomer. Any colonial trader venturing to set up this gadget in an Indian town faced "prodigious trouble," according to one Virginia observer, because of the natives' "resolute stupidity and obstinacy in receiving a new custom . . . for they could not apprehend the power and justice of the stilliard." Nowhere was the subtle tug-of-war for control of intercultural exchange more evident. A piedmont resident accustomed to standards of measurement based on the human body—a string of beads by the arm's length, for example, or rum by the mouthful—had no use for this particular foreign import. He could see if the person measuring an arm's length of roanoke was tall or short, he could judge the size of a customer's mouth and detect a surreptitious swallow or two; he could not understand a device designed, manufactured—and often rigged—by strangers. Colonists exaggerated the justice of the steelyard; they did not exaggerate its symbolic power.[71]

As the tug-of-war went on, the intruders mingled careful attention to established custom with callous breaches of etiquette. During that overnight stay in the vacant Santee dwelling, for example, John Lawson left the requisite gift but merely shrugged when he accidentally burned down part of the building while cooking his dinner. Lederer would have departed in haste if not in panic, as he did on more than one occasion when the situation looked ominous; Lawson sauntered away the next morning, unperturbed. Similarly, at a Catawba village farther up the path, Lawson's party headed straight for the headman's house as custom dictated, but the visitors seemed more amused than alarmed when this Indian, his routine offer of a gift flatly refused, "flew into a violent Passion, to be thus slighted, telling the *Englishmen*, they were good for nothing." Once again a comparison with Lederer's probable reaction to such a rebuke is instructive, for it points clearly to the direction trade was taking.[72]

The line between impolite and abusive is blurred, but with time more and more traders clearly stepped across it. In 1715 David Crawley, a Virginia

trader, maintained that his South Carolina counterparts had launched a
virtual reign of terror in the native Southeast. According to Crawley's in-
dictment, the men from Charlestown robbed their Indian clients, forced
burdeners to carry skins vast distances for a pittance, sent the men off on er-
rands and then raped the women, and beat up anyone who dared to protest
this sort of behavior.[73] Crawley was a competitor, not an impartial judge of
South Carolina's Indian affairs; still, the South Carolina accounts confirm
his claims, and worried officials in Charlestown admitted as much when
they passed laws to put a stop to the traders' crime spree. But measures that
looked stern on paper tended to be feeble hundreds of miles away in Indian
country, and the agents sent to bridge the gap between council chamber
and council house were as likely to be part of the problem as part of the solution. The traders had run amok, and ultimately many of them paid for
their sins with their lives when Yamasee Indians south of Charlestown led
a rebellion against the Carolina trading regime in April 1715. The colony's
traders were the first casualties, but not the last. In less than a month hundreds more colonists were dead, and Indian warriors seemed bent on driving the rest into the sea.[74]

The connection between that smoldering Santee hut in 1701 and the smoldering lowcountry plantations in 1715 seems clear. Certainly most colonists
who gave the Yamasee War's causes much thought blamed the traders, drawing a straight and bloody line from confidence to arrogance through abuses
to uprising. For Yamasees and their neighbors south of the provincial capital, it was indeed almost that simple.[75] Not so for the "mixture of Catabaws,
Sarraws Waterees etc." from the north who—to the shock and dismay of
colonists—joined the fray in late April or early May.[76] For all the evidence
that the tides of trade were turning against the piedmont peoples, that dependence was increasing and the traders getting out of hand, the surviving sources yield few hints that the groups there had yet suffered anything
like the oppression Yamasees endured; the litany of native complaints issuing from South Carolina's southern flank before 1715 had no counterpart
in villages to the north.[77] Given the silence from that direction, it seems
unlikely that many of the colonial traders in these "northern" nations had
yet stepped over the line from boorish to brutal behavior. Why, then, did
piedmont Indians join the rebellion? Once again trade holds the key, but
here the causal connection is more difficult to trace than it is farther south.

Here it was less the South Carolina trader's assaults on Indians than his assaults on Virginians that brought the "mixture" of Indian warriors from the north down on the colony's head.[78]

The first links in the causal chain were forged late in the seventeenth century when South Carolinians finally woke up to the fact that they had little knowledge of—and less influence over—powerful Indian nations in the colony's own backyard. During its first generation of existence Carolina had directed most of its attention south and west, with the result that the colony's experts could speak with more authority about Indians as far as the Mississippi River than about those much beyond the Santee.[79] To remedy this problem the colony looked to trade, a tried and true means of making friends and influencing peoples. Make an Indian nation dependent on us for weapons, the accepted wisdom went, and it is ours, for "whenever that nation . . . shall misbehave themselves towards us, we shall be able whenever we please by abstaineing from supplying them with Ammunition . . . to ruine them."[80] The only flaw in the plan was that the upcountry Indians being targeted did not need South Carolina's trade; they had goods aplenty from Virginians like David Crawley. The men in Charlestown's corridors of power had an answer to that, too: they declared a trade war against their fellow Anglo-Americans. In October 1698 the South Carolina Commons House of Assembly fired the first shot with a resolution "that the Virginians be Prohibitted from Tradeing in This Province." Over the next fifteen years the war raged, its battlefields as disparate as the piedmont's villages and the Privy Council's chambers. Since neither province could gain the upper hand, the threats and skirmishes, the discriminatory laws and "legal" confiscations, the charges and countercharges went on and on.[81]

For the most part the upcountry Indians remained above the fray, reaping the rewards of neutrals in a war zone. The vicious competition for customers probably meant that goods were plentiful and prices lower. It may also be one reason traders as yet were not guilty of many excesses in the contested region; politeness won points, and Indians with an alternative source of supply—who, as Lawson put it, "can get the same Commodities of any other Person"—had to be handled with kid gloves, not an iron fist. At the same time, however, the intercolonial trade war had pernicious, even lethal, consequences for the neutral natives. Trade was the principal lens through which piedmont Indians viewed the colonial world, and battles between one colony and another presented those Indians with a distorted view of that world. Merely by watching and listening to the squabbling in their midst, natives picked up a great deal. They saw the confrontations and confiscations; they heard the war of words that accompanied this war of nerves, as each colonist tried to persuade natives of his own virtues and his competitors' vices.[82] From experience, then, Indians could conclude that Anglo-Americans looked and acted much alike, they pulled the same wonderful things from their packs, but they were deeply divided, and they quarreled with one another like the "mad Wolves" natives found so distasteful. In the spring of 1715, pressed by Yamasee ambassadors urging war, familiar enough with the traders' penchant for straying from the accepted cultural paths to believe those who predicted that such arrogance would lead only to greater abuse, piedmont nations would act on the information gleaned from years of watching Virginia and Carolina men go at each other. The Carolina traders were killed, their Virginia competitors merely detained so that, to the Indians' way of thinking, the vital connection to Virginia remained unbroken. Then upcountry warriors headed down the Wateree River valley, confident that they could go on killing South Carolinians indefinitely with Virginia's bullets.[83]

They were dead wrong. If, as the beleaguered South Carolinians claimed, Virginia traders had indeed "encouraged our Indians to do what they have done and promised to supply them at a much easier rate than our Indian traders did and that they would give them much better treatment," Virginia officials were not prepared to go along with the scheme.[84] No Crown appointee who valued his career would have knowingly handed Indians the wherewithal to kill fellow subjects of Great Britain. If in April 1715 natives did not know that (because the traders, their only source of information, had not told them), they found out soon enough. Upon learning of South Carolina's desperate plight, Lieutenant Governor Alexander Spotswood rushed the stricken colony precious shiploads of men and supplies, slapped an embargo on Virginia's trade with Indians, and met with South Carolina agents to see what more he could do. When ambassadors from the Cheraws and Catawbas visited Williamsburg in October, they must have been startled to find men from the two provinces, seated amicably side by side, awaiting them as they entered the council chamber.[85]

Piedmont Indians had another surprise in store for them. While learning that the two colonies in fact stood shoulder to shoulder, natives were also discovering that South Carolina's old plan to bring Indians to heel by fostering dependence on European trade had worked after all. Piedmont warriors had all but exhausted their supply of weapons in the initial invasion of the lowcountry; what was left they abandoned as they fled homeward after being defeated by colonial forces on June 13.[86] Any hope of getting more from Virginia was dashed by Spotswood's embargo, and by August colonists holed up in Charlestown began to sense that their native foes "want ammunition and are not able to mend their arms."[87] By then upcountry nations, "their necessity of all manner of goods being very great," were already talking about ending the conflict.[88] The Indians' thirst for European wares was painfully obvious in the negotiations with Virginia, discussions in which headmen invariably spoke of "a Peace and a free Trade" in the same breath. In October the Catawba and Cheraw delegates went even further, bluntly admitting that "they cannot live without the assistance of the English."[89] From a "bond of peace," trade had become a cause of war; now trade's absence promised peace again.

Indians, defeated in war and crushed in the vise of trade, could still hope not only for peace, not only for trade, but even for trade "as formerly," meaning as an arm of diplomacy, with low prices for abundant supplies of goods brought by obedient rather than truculent colonists.[90] Colonial authorities had other ideas. Convinced, as the Commons House put it, that Indians "are no longer to be kept in Subjection [unless] the Necessity or Interest obliges them[,] which may be accomplished by . . . making them Dependent for necessaries of all kinds, and in these keep[in]g them bare and unstored," both South Carolina and Virginia launched reform programs.[91] The various provisions were designed to end unsupervised contacts between colonist and Indian by licensing colonial traders, making them post bond for their good behavior, and—in South Carolina's most ambitious move—requiring native traders to do business at designated posts.

Despite the concerted efforts to direct the flow of trade into different channels, the actual system of exchange that rose from the ashes of the war bore a striking resemblance to the earlier version. By 1717 the Carolina-Virginia trade war had picked up where it left off, with colonists using fair means or foul to gain the advantage. The natives, meanwhile, reaped all the benefits of a buyers' market. After the drought came the deluge, as colonists eager to make up for lost time (and lost profits) flooded the interior with merchandise. This meant that Indians, far from pathetic beggars greedily gobbling any crumbs that the victorious Anglo-Americans happened to throw their way, still had the luxury of being choosy customers. If the quality of the powder, the size of the hoes, the shape of the beads, or the asking price of the item was wrong, colonists would hear about it.[92] And if satisfaction was not forthcoming, an Indian took his business elsewhere. South Carolina's grand plan to entice Catawbas to a trade factory at the Congarees and Cheraws to another along the Winyaw enjoyed only limited success: although Indians did show up at the specified sites, to the policymakers' chagrin the natives also continued to trade at home—"as formerly"—or ventured into the lowcountry in search of the right price, the right color, the right size.[93]

While Catawbas and their neighbors took the framework of exchange that had been put together in far-off capitals and bent it into something approximating its earlier shape, while goods poured in and prices dropped, one thing did change after the war: the men who helped Indians ignore the official decrees, who brought the goods and haggled over the prices, now seemed somehow tamer. The events of 1715 remained fresh in the minds of those who had escaped death during that fateful spring, and veterans probably passed their memories along to the next generation. Thomas Brown, who would dominate the Catawba trade in the second quarter of the eighteenth century, got his start in the mid-1720s with stock purchased from John Thompson and William Marr, two old hands who may have thrown in some advice at no extra charge.[94] Brown's chief competitor, John Evans, who set up a base along the Santee River at about the same time, may have been related to the Virginia trader of the same name and would have had some stories of his own to tell.[95]

Heading back into the upcountry with eyes open, ears cocked, and minds filled with chilling tales of what had happened there in 1715, few traders were looking for trouble. Where John Lederer's contemporaries had been ignorant and frightened and John Lawson's experienced and arrogant, Thomas Brown's tended to be experienced and frightened. Their very different relations with native women help measure the dimensions of the change that occurred in the aftermath of the Yamasee War. Lederer ran from the prospect of an arranged marriage; the men of Lawson's day jumped at the chance for the wrong reasons; Thomas Brown and John Evans married native women and formed deep attachments to the offspring of these marriages, attachments that suggest an understanding of Indian ways unheard of in Carolina before 1715.[96] As a confirmation of his status Brown became something of an adviser to the Catawbas. Earlier English visitors had scrupulously, then more casually, sought out the native headman before engaging in trade; now Catawba headmen routinely repaired to Brown's trading post "to form their Councils."[97] Evans went even further, taking on the physical risks—and the social rewards—of accompanying Indian war parties, earning himself the title of "our old Freind and Linguister."[98] The contrast with John Lawson's day could hardly have been greater.

In the 1730s William Byrd II charged that the Carolina traders were "petty rulers," "little tyrants" who "pretend to exercise a dictatorial authority over [Catawbas] . . . and use them with all kinds of oppression."[99] Byrd was either a sore loser or out of touch. Men like Brown and Evans knew too well the fate of tyrants in the native Southeast. They achieved influence by behaving correctly—as kinsman, counselor, or warrior—and then exerting that influence through persuasion, not bullying or brute force. Only in this way could they advance their interests—and save their necks. Brown would never have survived two decades trading among the Catawba River peoples, and Evans twice that, had they been the "petty rulers" their detractors claimed they were.

Indians and colonists so quickly resurrected trade out of the ruins left by the Yamasee War that it is tempting to consider 1715 little more than a bad memory, a brief and unfortunate interruption in the regular rhythms of exchange. Men from Virginia and Carolina—repenting their earlier ignorance and arrogance—rushed back to their piedmont haunts, preached the gospel of commerce with renewed fervor, and converted the Indians once again. It seemed almost too good to be true, and it was. In fact, beneath every peaceful encounter after 1715 lurked the harsh truth that the swift revival of exchange could not hide: although piedmont peoples could still choose where and with whom they would trade, they could no longer choose not to trade at all. Like it or not, Indians were bound to Anglo-America by a chain forged from beads and muskets, kettles and hoes, cloth and powder.

If the chain usually rested fairly lightly on Indian shoulders as the two cultures went about their daily business in the generation following the Yamasee War, it could never be cast off. To remind natives of this, colonists occasionally gave the chain a yank. In a 1727 meeting with the Virginia councilor and trader Nathaniel Harrison, a Sugaree headman reiterated the traditional native understanding of the exchange relationship as a diplomatic tool, a means of confirming friendship. "To shew the kindness we have" for the Virginia people, the Indian said, "we make it our business to kill deer and get skins for their Traders." A set speech, one probably heard by every colonist since Lederer. Once upon a time the response would probably have been a simple nod of assent—not anymore. Harrison scoffed, replying that "we don't look upon that as a particular freindship in you, for . . . I know you are oblig'd to kill deer for the Support of your Women and Children." Underscoring his assessment of their dependent condition, Harrison alluded to the Sugarees' tenuous state of health and reminded their leader of the consequences of being unarmed in a land where slave raids or attacks by roaming Iroquois were a fact of life: "without our freindship in supplying you with Guns, and Amunition you must all starve and what is as bad, become a prey to your Enemies[;] so that the Freindship is from us in trading with and supplying you with these Necessarie Goods, for your support, and Defence."[100]

In time of crisis the insults easily became threats, and the tugs on the chain were harder. When piedmont Indians killed several colonists in the Wateree River valley during the winter of 1737–38, Charlestown rushed to the Catawbas an agent armed with instructions to demand satisfaction. If the headmen proved stubborn, the agent was ordered "to put the Catawba Indians in Mind that when they differed with us and applied to the People of Virginia for a free Trade with them, the People of Virginia knowing in what Manner they had used us . . . refused to trade with them while they were at Enmity with us; . . . and as the same good Understanding remains between us and Virginia, as at that Time[,] so they may expect in Case they disoblige us to be made sensible of the Resentment of both Provinces."[101] Before 1715 the Indians could have considered this sort of talk mere bluff and bluster; it certainly did not conform to the gist of the traders' whispers in those days. Now they knew better: Virginia and Carolina might squabble, but in time of trouble the differences between them evaporated, leaving Anglo-Americans (who had the manufactures) on one side and Indians (who needed them) on the other.

Even as South Carolina was issuing its threats, the chances of piedmont Indians' playing the Virginia card were increasingly remote, for fewer Virginians were bothering to make the trip. William Byrd II could remember the days when fifteen men leading one hundred packhorses had headed into the piedmont; in the 1730s a good year saw only half that many set out, and by midcentury the number was down to a mere handful.[102] South Carolina had won at last, although by then the prize was hardly worth having: piedmont Indian populations had diminished sharply, and there were no longer enough deer in the area to support very many traders—colonial or Indian. The days of the great piedmont deerskin trade were fast drawing to a close.

Long before that happened, however, the trade had brought Indians to toe the Anglo-American line. From masters of the upcountry they had become, like the Santees Lawson had met, "tractable" peoples unable to inspire much fear in anyone able to calculate the power of the trade. In 1733 Byrd's exploring party came across the remains of a recent Indian encampment in the piedmont, a discovery that was "a little shocking to some of the company." Byrd, who knew the score, was unperturbed. "In case they were Catawbas," he observed drily, "the danger would be . . . little from them, because they are too fond of our trade to lose it for the pleasure of shedding a little English blood."[103] At last, John Banister's words had become more reality than dream: commerce had indeed become the Anglo-American "bond of peace."

Acknowledgments

This chapter is a revised and expanded version of a paper delivered at the annual meeting of the American Historical Association in December 1982, and I would like to thank Robert Mitchell, James Axtell, and particularly Neal Salisbury for their comments on that earlier version. Expanded still further, it appears in my *The Indians' New World: Catawbas and Their Neighbors from European Contact through the Era of Removal* (Chapel Hill: University of North Carolina Press, 1989), published for the Institute of Early

American History and Culture; I am grateful to the Institute for permission to publish portions of that work here. Finally, the general thrust of the argument and some of the examples offered here have appeared in "The Indians' New World: The Catawba Experience," *William and Mary Quarterly*, 3rd ser., 41 (1984): 537–65, and "'This Western World': The Evolution of the Piedmont, 1525–1725," in *The Siouan Project: Seasons I and II*, ed. Roy S. Dickens Jr., H. Trawick Ward, and R. P. Stephen Davis Jr., Monograph Series 1 (Chapel Hill: Research Laboratories of Anthropology, University of North Carolina, 1987), 19–27.

Notes

1. See James H. Merrell, *Into the American Woods: Negotiators on the Pennsylvania Frontier* (New York: W. W. Norton, 1999).

2. For some of the scholarship, see Peter C. Mancall and James H. Merrell, eds., *American Encounters: Natives and Newcomers from European Contact to Indian Removal, 1500–1850* (New York: Routledge, 2000); James H. Merrell, "Indian History during the English Colonial Era," in *A Companion to Colonial America*, ed. Daniel Vickers (Malden MA: Blackwell, 2003), 118–37.

3. H. Trawick Ward and R. P. Stephen Davis Jr., *Time before History: The Archaeology of North Carolina* (Chapel Hill: University of North Carolina Press, 1999), 236, 242, 244–46, 251, 254–55, 260; Ward and Davis, *Indian Communities on the Carolina Piedmont, AD 1000 to 1700*, Research Laboratories of Anthropology, The University of North Carolina at Chapel Hill, Monograph No. 2 (Chapel Hill NC: Research Laboratories of Anthropology, 1993), 213–14, 413, 415–18; R. P. Stephen Davis Jr., Patrick C. Livingood, H. Trawick Ward, and Vincas P. Steponaitis, eds., *Excavating Occaneechi Town: Archaeology of an Eighteenth-Century Indian Village in North Carolina*, CD-ROM (Chapel Hill: University of North Carolina Press, 1998), 233 ("adaptive responses"); Edmond A. Boudreaux III, "The Fredricks Site: Social Diversity within a Late Contact Period Siouan Community in North Carolina," in *The Archaeology of Native North Carolina: Papers in Honor of H. Trawick Ward*, ed. Jane M. Eastman, Christopher B. Rodning, and Edmond A. Boudreaux III, Southeastern Archaeological Conference, Special Publication 7 (Biloxi MS: Southeastern Archaeological Conference, 2002), 36–45, esp. 43. (I am grateful to Greg Waselkov for alerting me to this publication.) For additional archaeological work on the piedmont, see David G. Moore, *Catawba Valley Mississippian: Ceramics, Chronology, and Catawba Indians* (Tuscaloosa: University of Alabama Press, 2002).

4. Tom Hatley, *The Dividing Paths: Cherokees and South Carolinians through the Era of Revolution* (New York: Oxford University Press, 1995), 43, 50.

5. Kathryn E. Holland Braund, *Deerskins and Duffels: The Creek Indian Trade with Anglo-America, 1685–1815* (Lincoln: University of Nebraska Press, 1993), 26.

6. James Axtell, *The Indians' New South: Cultural Change in the Colonial Southeast* (Baton Rouge: Louisiana State University Press, 1997), 66.

7. Daniel K. Richter, *Facing East from Indian Country: A Native History of Early America* (Cambridge MA: Harvard University Press, 2001), 41–43.

8. Michael P. Morris, *The Bringing of Wonder: Trade and the Indians of the Southeast, 1700–1783*, Contributions in Comparative Colonial Studies, Number 26 (Westport CT: Greenwood Press, 1999), 7, 75.

9. Bruce G. Trigger, *The Children of Aataentsic: A History of the Huron People to 1660* (Kingston ON: McGill-Queen's University Press, 1976); James Axtell, *The European and the Indian: Essays in the Ethnohistory of Colonial North America* (New York: Oxford University Press, 1981), esp. chapters 5 and 9; Neal Salisbury, *Manitou and Providence: Indians, Europeans, and the Making of New England, 1500–1643* (New York: Oxford University Press, 1982).

10. See James Axtell, "Forked Tongues: Moral Judgments in Indian History," in *After Columbus: Essays in the Ethnohistory of Colonial North America*, ed. James Axtell (New York: Oxford University Press, 1988), 34–44; Merrell, "Indian History," in *Companion to Colonial America*, ed. Vickers, 132.

11. For use of the word *trinkets*, see Ward and Davis, *Indian Communities*, 416, 426; Ward and Davis, *Time before History*, 244. For *backcountry*, see Braund, *Deerskins and Duffels*, xiv, 34, 81; Hatley, *Dividing Paths*, 36, 46; R. P. Stephen Davis Jr., "The Cultural Landscape of the North Carolina Piedmont at Contact," in *The Transformation of the Southeastern Indians, 1540–1760*, ed. Robbie Ethridge and Charles Hudson (Jackson: University Press of Mississippi, 2002), 135; Theda Perdue, *Cherokee Women: Gender and Culture Change, 1700–1835* (Lincoln: University of Nebraska Press, 1998), 72.

12. For continuing use of the term, see Braund, *Deerskins and Duffels*, 81 ("Indian traders"), 82 ("Creek traders" were colonists involved in trade with Creeks).

13. Braund, *Deerskins and Duffels*, xiii, 34, 121; Bruce G. Trigger and William R. Swagerty, "Entertaining Strangers: North America in the Sixteenth Century," in *The Cambridge History of the Native Peoples of the Americas*, ed. Trigger and Wilcomb E. Washburn, vol. I, *North America*, part 1 (New York: Cambridge University Press, 1996), 378.

14. Richard White, *The Middle Ground: Indians, Empires, and Republics in the Great Lakes Region, 1650–1815* (New York: Cambridge University Press, 1991), 94. For the character of this spectrum of exchange in the colonial South, see Daniel H. Usner Jr., *Indians, Settlers, and Slaves in a Frontier Exchange Economy: The Lower Mississippi Valley before 1783* (Chapel Hill: University of North Carolina Press, 1992), Part II.

15. Peter Cook, "Symbolic and Material Exchange in Intercultural Diplomacy: The French and the Hodenosaunee in the Early Eighteenth Century," in *New Faces of the Fur Trade: Selected Papers of the Seventh North American Fur Trade Conference, Halifax, Nova Scotia, 1995*, ed. Jo-Anne Fiske, Susan Sleeper-Smith, and William Wicken (East Lansing: Michigan State University Press, 1998), 75.

16. Hatley, *Dividing Paths*, 44, 51.

17. Morris, *Bringing of Wonder*, 1–2; see also David Murray, *Indian Giving: Economies of*

Power in Indian-White Exchanges (Amherst: University of Massachusetts Press, 2000), and Gregory Waselkov, "Exchange and Interaction since 1500," in *Handbook of North American Indians*, vol. 14, *Southeast*, ed. Raymond D. Fogelson (Washington DC: Smithsonian Institution, 2004). 686–96.

18. Perdue, *Cherokee Women*, 72, 76, 83, 64; see also Hatley, *Dividing Paths,* chap. 5. For intriguing results derived from archaeological research, see Jane M. Eastman, "Mortuary Analysis and Gender: The Response of Siouan Peoples to European Contact," in *Archaeology of Native North Carolina*, ed. Eastman, Rodning, and Boudreaux, 46–56.

19. Christopher L. Miller and George R. Hamell, "A New Perspective on Indian-White Contact: Cultural Symbols and Colonial Trade," *Journal of American History* 73 (1986): 311–28; Bruce M. White, "Encounters with Spirits: Ojibwa and Dakota Theories about the French and Their Merchandise," *Ethnohistory* 41 (1994): 369–405; Frederic W. Gleach, *Powhatan's World and Colonial Virginia: A Conflict of Cultures* (Lincoln: University of Nebraska Press, 1997), 54–60.

20. Richter, *Facing East from Indian Country*, 44–46. See also Braund, *Deerskins and Duffels*, 61, 130.

21. Ward and Davis, *Indian Communities*, 365–68, 414; see also Ward and Davis, *Time before History*, 236–37 (Ward and Davis stress that this is only "an hypothesis"); Boudreaux, "Fredricks Site," in *Archaeology of Native North Carolina*, ed. Eastman, Rodning, and Boudreaux, 39. There is also the possibility of a cultural "efflorescence" in response to the impressive amount of goods either handed out or left behind by sixteenth-century Spaniards, whose intrusions, scholars now believe, went through the Carolina piedmont rather than farther south. However, the archaeological record is not yet sufficient to trace how natives handled these new goods. See Gregory A. Waselkov, "Seventeenth-Century Trade in the Colonial Southeast," *Southeastern Archaeology* 8 (1989): 117–33; Moore, *Catawba Valley Mississippian*, 25–26.

22. Ward and Davis, *Time before History*, 253–54; Ward and Davis, *Indian Communities*, 278, 310–12, 317; Davis et al., *Excavating Occaneechi Town*, 23, 233 (quotation). See Elise M. Brenner, "Sociopolitical Implications of Mortuary Ritual Remains in 17th-Century Native Southern New England," in *The Recovery of Meaning: Historical Archaeology in the Eastern United States*, ed. Mark P. Leone and Parker B. Potter Jr. (Washington DC: Smithsonian Institution Press, 1988), 147–81. A possible contrary development, in which a group of young men might have eschewed European goods, is suggested by Eastman, "Mortuary Analysis and Gender," in *Archaeology of Native North Carolina*, ed. Eastman, Rodning, and Boudreaux, eds., 54.

23. Ward and Davis, *Indian Communities*, 316, 423, 425 (quotation); Ward and Davis, *Time before History*, 253–54, 257–60. Ward and Davis (*Time before History*, 259) stress that such a breakdown in mortuary practices only came at the very end, and then only for children. At Occaneechi Town (occupied around 1680–1710), "deep graves were arduously dug into a stiff subsoil clay, and the dead were laid to rest with full, traditional ceremony." In seasons of terrible social strain, too, at "the last desperate gasp" of one group, "[a]dult graves . . . were placed . . . in deep shaft-and-chamber pits. Burial goods indicate

that these individuals were given their last rites in a traditional manner. Even during the worst of times, the dead were still buried, and more often than not, they too were laid to rest with full ceremony."

24. Ward and Davis, *Time before History*, 242–44, 258–59. Recent archaeological finds also reveal grim evidence of escalating violence in this period: one man's skull showed scalp marks; one woman had a musket ball buried in her leg and perhaps another in her pelvis. Ward and Davis, *Time before History*, 256; Davis et al., *Exploring Occaneechi Town*, 25, 30.

25. White, *Middle Ground*, x; see especially ix–x and 50–53 for his definition of the term.

26. For fuller discussion of its effect, see Merrell, "Indian History," in *Companion to Colonial America*, ed. Vickers, 123–32.

27. Martin H. Quitt, "Trade and Acculturation at Jamestown, 1607–1609: The Limits of Understanding," *William and Mary Quarterly*, 3rd ser., 52 (1995): 227–58, quotations on 228, 244, 258.

28. John Lawson, *A New Voyage to Carolina*, ed. Hugh T. Lefler (Chapel Hill: University of North Carolina Press, 1967), 24, 39.

29. For the growing interest in this southwestern region, see "A Present Description of Virginia" (London, 1649), in *Tracts and Other Papers, Relating Principally to the Origin, Settlement, and Progress of the Colonies in North America*, ed. Peter Force, 4 vols. (Washington DC: Peter Force, 1836–46), 3:8–10, 13; Edward Williams, *Virginia: More especially the South part thereof, Richly and truly valued . . .*, 2nd ed. (London, 1650), 18, 34–37, 12[A]–13; "The Discovery of New Brittaine, 1650," and "Francis Yeardley's Narrative of Excursions into Carolina, 1654," all in *Narratives of Early Carolina, 1650–1708*, ed. Alexander S. Salley (New York: Charles Scribner's Sons, 1911), 1–29.

30. John Banister to Dr. Robert Morison, April 6, 1679, in *John Banister and His Natural History of Virginia, 1678–1692*, ed. Joseph Ewan and Nesta Ewan (Urbana: University of Illinois Press, 1970), 42.

31. Banister to Morison, April 6, 1679. See also John Banister, "Of the Natives," in *Natural History*, ed. Ewan and Ewan, 385.

32. Lawson, *New Voyage*, 10, 23.

33. Students of Indians elsewhere in eastern North America have begun to recognize that natives had an active role in the trade, and some of the themes touched upon here may be pursued in James Axtell, "The English Colonial Impact on Indian Culture," in his *The European and the Indian: Essays in the Ethnohistory of Colonial North America* (New York: Oxford University Press, 1981), 253–65; Francis Jennings, *The Invasion of America: Indians, Colonialism, and the Cant of Conquest* (Chapel Hill: University of North Carolina Press for the Institute of Early American History and Culture, 1975), 85–97; Toby Morantz, "The Fur Trade and the Cree of James Bay," in *Old Trails and New Directions: Papers of the Third North American Fur Trade Conference*, ed. Carol M. Judd and Arthur J. Ray (Toronto: University of Toronto Press, 1980), 39–58; Arthur J. Ray, "Indians as Consumers in the Eighteenth Century," in Judd and Ray, *Old Trails*, 255–71; and Salisbury, *Manitou and Providence*, esp. 47–60, 147–49. Of particular interest for its emphasis on the Indians' un-

derstanding of the trade is Miller and Hamell, "A New Perspective on Indian-White Contact," 311–28. The Southeast has received less attention, but see John Philip Reid, *A Better Kind of Hatchet: Law, Trade, and Diplomacy in the Cherokee Nation during the Early Years of European Contact* (University Park: Pennsylvania State University Press, 1976), and J. Leitch Wright Jr., *The Only Land They Knew: The Tragic Story of the American Indians in the Old South* (New York: Free Press, 1981), esp. 93–96, 106–11, 170–74, 221–23, 227.

34. "True Relation of the Vicissitudes That Attended the Governor Don Hernando de Soto . . . Now Just Given by a Fidalgo of Elvas," in *Narratives of the Career of Hernando de Soto*, ed. Edward G. Bourne, 2 vols. (New York: A. S. Barnes, 1904), 1:50–51, 66–67; Garcilaso de la Vega, El Inca, *The Florida of the Inca*, trans. and ed. John G. Varner and Jeanette J. Varner (Austin: University of Texas Press, 1951), 253–54, 285, 310–11, 316, 323; Francisco Fernandez de Ècija, "Testimonio del Viaje . . ." in Gene Waddell, *Indians of the South Carolina Lowcountry, 1562–1751* (Spartanburg SC: Reprint Company, 1980), 225–27; Joffre Coe, "The Cultural Sequence of the Carolina Piedmont," in *Archeology of Eastern United States*, ed. James B. Griffin (Chicago: University of Chicago Press, 1952), 307, 310–11; James B. Griffin, "Eastern North American Archaeology: A Summary," *Science* 156 (1967): 189; George E. Stuart, "Some Archeological Sites in the Middle Wateree Valley, South Carolina" (master's thesis, George Washington University, 1970), 115, 128; Sharon I. Goad, "Exchange Networks in the Prehistoric Southeastern United States" (PhD diss., University of Georgia, 1978). For means of communication, see Elvas, "True Relation," in Bourne, *De Soto Narratives*, 1:50–51, 54–55, 61, 67; "Relation of the Conquest of Florida by Luys Hernandez de Biedma in the Year 1544 . . ." in Bourne, *De Soto Narratives*, 2:12; Inca, *Florida*, 253–54, 302, 310; "Report of Franciso Fernandez de Ècija," in *The Jamestown Voyages under the First Charter, 1606–1609*, ed. Philip L. Barbour, 2 vols. (London: Published for the Hakluyt Society by Cambridge University Press, 1969), 2:295, 298, 299, 302, 314, 317–18; Lawson, *New Voyage*, 48, 49.

35. Lawson, *New Voyage*, 178; William P. Cumming, ed., *The Discoveries of John Lederer* (Charlottesville: University of Virginia Press, 1958), 33. See also Harold Hickerson, "Fur Trade Colonialism and the North American Indians," *Journal of Ethnic Studies* 1 (1973): 19–21. It is difficult to prove that the exchange of people had pre-Columbian origins. But in the early contact period the natives' readiness, even eagerness, to give the Anglo-Americans "hostages" and the occasional reference to individuals living among other peoples suggest that these habits were already in place. See "Yeardley's Narrative," in Salley, *Narratives of Carolina*, 26, 28; "Discovery of New Brittaine," in Salley, *Narratives of Carolina*, 20; Lawson, *New Voyage*, 57, 63–64.

36. Lawson, *New Voyage*, 98, 218, 174. For the Indian tea, see Charles M. Hudson, ed., *Black Drink: A Native American Tea* (Athens: University of Georgia Press, 1979). The root may have been red puccoon, or bloodroot. See Banister, "Of the Natives," 263, 377 n35.

37. Lawson, *New Voyage*, 217; see also Lawson, *New Voyage*, 64. For the earlier exchange network, see Ècija, "Testimonio," 226.

38. Cumming, *Discoveries of Lederer*, 31. For the Cheraws' early trade with Virginia, see William Byrd, "A Journey to the Land of Eden, Anno 1733," in *The Prose Works of*

William Byrd of Westover: Narratives of a Colonial Virginian, ed. Louis B. Wright (Cambridge: Harvard University Press, 1966), 400; Jack H. Wilson, "Feature Fill, Plant Utilization and Disposal among the Historic Sara Indians" (master's thesis, University of North Carolina, 1977), xiv.

39. Lawson, *New Voyage*, 44, 232; see also 48.

40. For trading vocabularies, see Lawson, *New Voyage*, 233–39; Edward P. Alexander, "An Indian Vocabulary from Fort Christanna, 1716," *Virginia Magazine of History and Biography* 79 (1971): 303–13. For the substitutions, see Liane Navey, "An Introduction to the Mortuary Practices of the Historic Sara" (master's thesis, University of North Carolina, 1982), chap. 4 (beads); Lawson, *New Voyage*, 44–45 (bells), and 46 (iron pot).

41. Lawson, *New Voyage*, 63, 33. William J. Hinke, trans. and ed., "Report of the Journey of Francis Louis Michel from Berne, Switzerland, to Virginia, October 2, 1701–December 1, 1702," *Virginia Magazine of History and Biography* 24 (1916): 42. Archaeologists have found glass arrowheads in South Carolina. See Tommy Charles, "Thoughts and Records from the Survey of Private Collections of Artifacts throughout South Carolina: A Second Report" (Institute of Archeology and Anthropology) *Notebook* 15 (1983): 31.

42. Banister, "Of the Natives," 384.

43. "Discovery of New Brittaine," in Salley, *Narratives of Carolina*, 8–9, 11, 13, 16–18; "John Clayton's Transcript of the Journal of Robert Fallam," in *The First Explorations of the Trans-Allegheny Region by the Virginians, 1650–1674*, ed. Clarence W. Alvord and Lee Bidgood (Cleveland: Arthur H. Clark, 1912), 184, 185, 187, 189; Lawson, *New Voyage*, 31, 37, 39, 48, 61.

44. Cumming, *Discoveries of Lederer*, 20, 30, 32, 38–39.

45. Lawson, *New Voyage*, 34.

46. Cumming, *Discoveries of Lederer*, 41.

47. Cumming, *Discoveries of Lederer*, 23; Lawson, *New Voyage*, 192, 35.

48. John Evans, "Journal of a Virginia[?] Indian Trader in North and South Carolina[?]," n.p., South Caroliniana Library, Columbia.

49. Lawson, *New Voyage*, 35–36, 192.

50. Lawson, *New Voyage*, 210.

51. Cadwallader Jones to Lord Baltimore, February 6, 1681/82, Public Record Office, Colonial Office Papers, ser. 1, vol. 48, 115–16 (microfilm copy, reel 327, Virginia Colonial Records Project, Colonial Williamsburg Archives, Williamsburg, Virginia); William Byrd to Stephanus Van Cortlandt, August 3, 1691, in *The Correspondence of the Three William Byrds of Westover, Virginia, 1684–1776*, ed. Marion Tinling, 2 vols. (Charlottesville: University of Virginia Press, 1977), 1:163; Inventory of Giles Webb, entered February 1713/14, Henrico County (Virginia) Records [Deeds, Wills], 1710–14, part 1, 241 (this and all other Henrico County records cited were consulted on microfilm copies provided by the Virginia State Library, Richmond).

52. Banister, "Of the Natives," 385 (beads). Indians were also particular about the color of cloth and the size of hoes. See Byrd to Perry and Lane, March 29, 1685, 1:30, and Byrd

to Arthur North, June 5, 1685, 1:41 (cloth); Byrd to North[?], March 8, 1686, 1:57 (hoes), all in Tinling, *Byrd Correspondence.*

53. "A Narrative of De Soto's Expedition Based on the Diary of Rodrigo Ranjel . . ." in Bourne, *De Soto Narratives,* 2:102, 104; Inca, *Florida,* 313, 315–16; Banister, "Of the Natives," 384; Lawson, *New Voyage,* 34, 196, 217 (baskets and mats). Ranjel, "Narrative," 2:99; Elvas, "True Relation," 1:66; Lawson, *New Voyage,* 217 (deer).

54. Inca, *Florida,* 329–30. See Theda Perdue, *Slavery and the Evolution of Cherokee Society, 1540–1866* (Knoxville: University of Tennessee Press, 1979), chap. 1.

55. Francis Le Jau to the Secretary, September 15, 1708, in *The Carolina Chronicle of Dr. Francis Le Jau, 1706–1717,* ed. Frank J. Klingberg, University of California Publications in History 53 (Berkeley: University of California Press, 1956), 41.

56. Cumming, *Discoveries of Lederer,* 30; Lawson, *New Voyage,* 30.

57. Lawson, *New Voyage,* 58. For midwinter rituals, see Lawson, *New Voyage,* 34, 39, 42–45, 177. The continuity of subsistence routines is evident throughout Lawson's account.

58. Letter of Abraham Wood to John Richards, August 22, 1674, in Alvord and Bidgood, *First Explorations,* 215–17; Byrd to Thomas Grendon, April 29, 1684, in Tinling, *Byrd Correspondence,* 1:16; Byrd to ?, May 10, 1686, in Tinling, *Byrd Correspondence,* 59; Henrico County Record Book [Deeds and Wills], 1677–92, part 2, 388; Francis Nicholson to the Committee, January 26, 1690/91, CO 5/1306, 43 (Library of Congress transcripts); H. R. McIlwaine et al., eds., *Executive Journals of the Council of Colonial Virginia,* 6 vols. (Richmond: Virginia State Library, 1925–66), 1:254–55.

59. This transition period was even more complex than suggested here. Often the same observers who noted native control of the trade also included in their accounts glimpses of the future, when the tables would be turned. In dividing native from colonial hegemony for analytical purposes, then, to some degree I simplify the shift from one to the other. I am grateful to Neal Salisbury for pointing this out to me.

60. Cumming, *Discoveries of Lederer,* 41–42.

61. Byrd to Perry and Lane, February 2, 1685, in Tinling, *Byrd Correspondence,* 1:29; Byrd to North, June 5, 1685, in Tinling, *Byrd Correspondence,* 1:41; Byrd to North[?], March 8, 1686, in Tinling, *Byrd Correspondence,* 1:57. For the Indian middlemen, see James H. Merrell, "The Indians' New World: The Catawba Experience," *William and Mary Quarterly,* 3rd ser., 41 (1984): 551–52.

62. Lawson, *New Voyage,* 18, 210–11; Robert Beverley, *The History and Present State of Virginia* (1705), ed. Louis B. Wright (Chapel Hill: University of North Carolina Press, 1947), 182. I detail these efforts in "The Indians' New World," 550.

63. Lawson, *New Voyage,* 18, 184, 211–12, 240.

64. Banister, "Of the Natives," 382.

65. Lawson, *New Voyage,* 38.

66. Lawson, *New Voyage,* 107, 175.

67. For the cruder crafts, see Ernest Lewis, "The Sara Indians, 1540–1768: An Ethnoarchaeological Study" (master's thesis, University of North Carolina, 1951), 310; Joffre L. Coe, *The Formative Cultures of the Carolina Piedmont,* Transactions of the Ameri-

can Philosophical Society, n.s. 54, part 5 (Philadelphia: American Philosophical Society, 1964), 49–50; Michael Trinkley and S. Homes Hogue, "The Wachesaw Landing Site: The Last Gasp of the Coastal Waccamaw Indians," *Southern Indian Studies* 31 (1979): 11. In my larger work I also explore the cultural or psychological costs of this loss of craft skills, a loss more difficult to measure from the historical and archaeological record, though one no less important.

68. William Byrd (*Prose Works*) provides the best insight into the culture these men fashioned to survive the rigors of a physical and cultural wilderness. I deal more fully with the traders' acculturation in my study of the Catawbas, *The Indians' New World* (Chapel Hill: University of North Carolina Press, 1989).

69. The evidence for this shift can only be impressionistic. Lederer and some other early explorers did not conform to this timetable (see Alvord and Bidgood, *First Explorations*, passim). But William Byrd's letters from the 1680s suggest that the traders went out in early March and returned home in May. After 1700 traders were reported among the Indians at various times of the year. For pre-1700, see Byrd to Grendon, April 29, 1684, in Tinling, *Byrd Correspondence*, 1:16; Byrd to [Arthur North?], March 3, 1685[/86], in Tinling, *Byrd Correspondence*, 1:57; Byrd to Perry and Lane, March 3, 1685 [/86], in Tinling, *Byrd Correspondence*, 1:58; Byrd to [Addressee Unknown], May 10, 1686, in Tinling, *Byrd Correspondence*, 1:59; Byrd, "Land of Eden," in *Prose Works*, 400; Henrico County Record Book, no. 2, 1678–93 [Deeds, Wills, Settlements of Estates, etc.] (transcript of Henrico County Order Book, 1678–93), 74; Henrico County Record Book [Deeds and Wills], 1677–92, part 2, 487. For the years after 1700, see Lawson, *New Voyage*, 49–50, 60–61; Depositions of Robert Hix and others, enclosed in Edmund Jenings to Board of Trade, October 8, 1709, CO 5/1316, fol. 41 (Library of Congress transcripts, 189–93); Evans Journal, n.p.; "Copy of Bond required of those authorized to trade with the Western Indians," and "Copy of form of passport given to traders with the Western Indians," in *Calendar of Virginia State Papers and Other Manuscripts, 1652–1781, Preserved in the Capitol at Richmond*, ed. William P. Palmer (Richmond VA: R. F. Walker, Superintendent of Public Printing, 1875), 155–56; Louis B. Wright and Marion Tinling, eds., *The Secret Diary of William Byrd of Westover, 1709–1712* (Richmond VA: Dietz Press, 1941), 447–48.

70. Lawson, *New Voyage*, 23.

71. Hugh Jones, *The Present State of Virginia, from Whence Is Inferred a Short View of Maryland and North Carolina*, ed. Richard L. Morton (Chapel Hill: University of North Carolina Press for the Virginia Historical Society, 1956), 57. For Indian standards of measurement, see Lawson, *New Voyage*, 203, 232–33; Stanley Pargellis, ed., "An Account of Indians in Virginia," *William and Mary Quarterly*, 3rd ser., 16 (1959): 231.

72. Lawson, *New Voyage*, 24, 50. For Lederer, see Cumming, *Discoveries of Lederer*, 26, 33.

73. David Crawley to the Lords Commissioners of Trade and Plantations, July 30, 1715, in W. Noel Sainsbury, comp., *Records in the British Public Record Office Relating to South Carolina, 1663–1782*, 36 vols., microfilm ed. (Columbia: South Carolina Archives Department, 1955), 6:110–11.

74. For South Carolina trade and the Yamasee War, see Verner W. Crane, *The Southern Frontier, 1670–1732* (1928; reprint, New York: W. W. Norton, 1981), chaps. 5–7; Reid, *Better Kind of Hatchet*, chaps. 4–7; Wright, *Only Land They Knew*, 121–25.

75. Richard Haan has added to the abuses the ecological pressures generated by colonial settlement among the Yamasees. See Richard L. Haan, "The 'Trade Do's Not Flourish as Formerly': The Ecological Origins of the Yamasee War of 1715," *Ethnohistory* 28 (1981): 341–58.

76. Le Jau to the Secretary, August 23, 1715, in Klingberg, *Carolina Chronicle*, 163; South Carolina Commons House Journals, May 8, 1715, in William Sumner Jenkins, comp., *The Records of the United States of America*, microfilm ed. (Washington DC, 1949), S.C. A.1b, reel 1, unit 4, 398–99.

77. Only one complaint from this region survives, and even it apparently was resolved without bloodshed. See William L. McDowell Jr., ed., *Journals of the Commissioners of the Indian Trade, September 20, 1710–August 29, 1718* (Columbia SC: State Commercial Printing Company, 1955), 33.

78. In my *Indians' New World* I deal in more depth with the complexities of the causal connections summarized here. Included in that greater complexity are the piedmont Indians' experiences as allies of the colonists during the Tuscarora War of 1711–13, experiences that, I believe, served to confirm the impressions of colonial society that these Indians had already gained from the traders.

79. See Crane, *Southern Frontier*, chaps. 1–3, 109–10, 132–33.

80. Lords Proprietors to the Govern[o]r and Councill att Ashley River in Carolina, March 7, 1680/81, in A. S. Salley Jr., indexer, *Records in the British Public Record Office Relating to South Carolina, 1663–1684* (Atlanta GA: Foote and Davies for the Historical Commission of South Carolina, 1928), 116, 118.

81. A. S. Salley Jr., ed., *Journals of the Commons House of Assembly of South Carolina for the Two Sessions of 1698* (Columbia: State Company for the Historical Commission of South Carolina, 1914), 22. For the trade war, see Crane, *Southern Frontier*, 153–57.

82. For example, see the aspersions cast by William Byrd II henceforth.

83. McIlwaine et al., *Executive Journals*, 3:405–6. Just who was among the Indians at the time and who was killed is unclear, though the fact that Indians discriminated against South Carolinians and in favor of Virginians seems clear from this reference and from those cited in note 84.

84. "Extracts of several letters from Carolina relating to the Indian Warr . . ." in William L. Saunders, ed., *The Colonial Records of North Carolina*, 10 vols. (1886–90; reprint, New York: AMS Press, 1968), 2:251. See also Saunders, *Colonial Records*, 2:252–53; McIlwaine et al., *Executive Journals*, 3:405–6; Robert Daniell and others to Spotswood, June 22, 1715, in Palmer, *Calendar of Virginia State Papers*, 181–82; "Memorial from Mr. Kettleby and several merchants trading to Carolina . . . ," in Saunders, *Colonial Records of North Carolina*, 2:201–2.

85. McIlwaine et al., *Executive Journals*, 3:411–12. For the shipments, see McIlwaine et al., *Executive Journals*, 3:402–4; Spotswood to the Lords Commissioners of Trade and Plan-

tations, July 15, 1715, in R. A. Brock, ed., *The Official Letters of Alexander Spotswood, Lieutenant-Governor of the Colony of Virginia, 1710–1722*, Collections of the Virginia Historical Society, n.s. 1 and 2 (Richmond: Virginia Historical Society, 1882–85), 2:119–20.

86. Rev. William Tredwell Bull to the Secretary, August 16, 1715, in Society for the Propagation of the Gospel in Foreign Parts, manuscript A, XI, 58 (microfilm, Library of Congress). See also Le Jau to the Secretary, August 23, 1715, in Klingberg, *Carolina Chronicle*, 163–64; Boston *News-Letter*, July 11, 1715.

87. Le Jau to John Chamberlain[?], August 22, 1715, in Klingberg, *Carolina Chronicle*, 162. See also Memorial from Kettleby, in Saunders, *Colonial Records of North Carolina*, 2:201; Boston *News-Letter*, October 31, 1715.

88. Spotswood to Secretary Stanhope, October 24, 1715, in Brock, *Spotswood Letters*, 2:131. See also McIlwaine et al., *Executive Journals*, 3:406, 412, 422, 447; "Passport to the Southern Indians to come to Virginia to treat for peace and commerce," in Palmer, *Calendar of Virginia State Papers*, 182.

89. McIlwaine et al., *Executive Journals*, 3:406, 412. See also McIlwaine et al., *Executive Journals*, 3:422.

90. McIlwaine et al., *Executive Journals*, 3:422.

91. Commons House Agents to the Lords Commissioners of Trade and Plantations, December 5, 1716, PRO-SC, 6:265. Virginia's law, actually passed in 1714 on the eve of the Yamasee War, was based on the colony's painful experiences with illegal traders during the Tuscarora War. See W. Neil Franklin, ed., "An Act for the Better Regulation of the Indian Trade: Virginia, 1714," *Virginia Magazine of History and Biography* 72 (1964): 141–51; McDowell, *Journals of the Commissioners of the Indian Trade*, 325–29. The best scholarly discussion of South Carolina's postwar reform efforts is in Reid, *Better Kind of Hatchet*, chaps. 8–12.

92. McDowell, *Journals of the Commissioners of the Indian Trade*, 95, 144, 156, 180, 211–12.

93. For the Congarees garrison and the northern trade factory, see McDowell, *Journals of the Commissioners of the Indian Trade*, passim. For the lowcountry trade, see South Carolina Upper House Journals, January 5, 1722, and November 28, 1733, Records of the States, S.C. A.1a, 1/1, 150, and 2/1, 668–69; Thomas Cooper and D. J. McCord, eds., *The Statutes at Large of South Carolina*, vol. 3 (Columbia SC: A. S. Johnston, 1838), 332, 371–72; South Carolina Commons House Journals, September 14–15, 1733, Records of the States, S.C. A.1b, 4/1, 1127, 1129–30; *South-Carolina Gazette*, December 19, 1743.

94. South Carolina Commons House Journals, May 24, 1734, Records of the States, S.C. A.1b, 4/3, 186.

95. Public Treasurer's Accounts, December 9, 1725, Ledger A, 1726, fol. 57, South Carolina Department of Archives and History, Columbia; Evans to Governor James Glen, December 16, 1755, in *Documents Relating to Indian Affairs, 1754–1765*, ed. William L. McDowell Jr. (Columbia: University of South Carolina Press for the South Carolina Department of Archives and History, 1970), 89; Evans to Governor William Henry Lyttelton, September 7, 1759, William Henry Lyttelton Papers, William L. Clements Library, Ann Arbor,

Michigan. A John Evans also served in the Congarees trade factory. See McDowell, *Journals of the Commissioners of the Indian Trade*, 202, 320.

96. Samuel Cole Williams, ed., *Adair's History of the American Indians* (1930; reprint, New York: Promontory Press, 1974), 369; South Carolina Council Journals, April 27, 1748, Records of the States, S.C. E.1p, 3/4, 233.

97. South Carolina Council Journals, July 25, 1744, Records of the States, S.C. E.1p, 2/3, 427.

98. South Carolina Council Journals, May 6, 1760, Records of the States, S.C. E.1p, 8/3, 120; Catawbas to Glen, October 15, 1754, *Indian Affairs Documents*, 14.

99. William Byrd, "History of the Dividing Line betwixt Virginia and North Carolina Run in the Year of Our Lord 1728," in Wright, *Prose Works*, 311.

100. "An Acco[un]t of Nathaniel Harrison's proceedings when he went out . . . to meet with the Cautaubau Indians," enclosed in Lieutenant Governor William Gooch to Board of Trade, September 21, 1727, CO 5/1321, 11 (Library of Congress transcripts, 13–14).

101. J. H. Easterby, ed., *The Journal of the Commons House of Assembly, November 10, 1736–June 7, 1739* (Columbia: Historical Commission of South Carolina, 1951), 488.

102. Byrd, "History," 308.

103. Byrd, "Land of Eden," 393.

Cherokee Women Farmers Hold Their Ground

TOM HATLEY

John Stuart had been working for three years in his new appointment as Superintendent of Indian Affairs for the Southern District when he wrote a long memorandum in 1765 to his superiors at the Colonial Office in London. He struggled to try to bring home something of the reality of the Native American cultures he dealt with daily. "The whole business of Indian life," Stuart began, "is war and hunting."[1] Folios of interoffice correspondence echoing this view of Indian society make up one of the legacies of the British imperial presence in North America. Neither in Stuart's personal explication of the nature of native Southeasterners two hundred years ago nor in these files does the core of the internal Cherokee economy appear. Cherokee agriculture and the women who had charge of it are omitted from the record. Yet farming was as important to the tribal as to the colonial economy, and tribal women were more directly connected to political and economic decision-making than were their colonial counterparts.

Although men took part in it, farming among the Cherokees was largely women's work.[2] And whereas these first Appalachian farmers were changed by their encounter with Euroamerican culture during a three-hundred-year colonial period, the experience of Cherokee agriculture during this time contrasts sharply with the dislocation of the traditional occupations of Cherokee men, brought about by the European demand for peltry and leather. Cherokee agriculture was out of the bounds of colonial trade, at least until the last decades of the eighteenth century, but it was not unchanging. It was becoming even more closely tied to a distinctly female village economic sector. By examining Cherokee farming in some detail, deliberately isolated from its interconnections with trade and hunting, we can gain a new perspective not only on what was happening to the women of the tribe but also on the economic and political conflict faced by native and colonial societies during the century. Inasmuch as the Cherokees had emerged by the late seventeenth century as the largest indigenous people within the Appalachians and a powerful player in the geopolitics of the eighteenth-century South, their story must be included in any history of the region. Native American history—cultural and agricultural—which extends back thousands of years and into the present within the southern mountains, provides an essential reminder of the long time scales and deep prior contexts prefacing the colonial "beginnings" of the region.

A recent parade of unexpected archaeological discoveries has left old assumptions about the antiquity of human occupation in the South—as across the New World—behind. With advent of humanity now more plausibly placed in eastern North America at 20,000 BP (before the present) or more, rather than 10,000 or 15,000 BP, the old fences in our thinking about paleoeconomies, including cultivation whatever its form, also need to be removed. The rough edges of the real history of this time are irretrievably smoothed at such a great distance, but there is no doubt that this deep past was a turbulent one, with humanity providing for itself against the odds of climate change, faunal replacement, and its own political and demographic ups and downs, including tidal waves of ancient migration sweeping through the continent at wide intervals. According to Cherokee religious tradition, their people emerged from the Kituwah mound. While the scientific tradition could be seen at odds with this view, at such a distance of time the distinction between "migration" and "origin" begins to bleed together. At such a distance, myth trumps history.

Myths and stories offer some recent perspectives as well. The Cherokees recalled the mythical female origins of their agriculture in the story of Selu, a woman whose name means "corn." In the legend, Selu and her husband, Kana Ti, or "Lucky Hunter," had two sons. These children became suspicious that their mother was a witch and spied on her through a crack in the cornhouse chinking. "They saw Selu standing in the middle of the room with the basket in front of her on the floor. Leaning over the basket, she rubbed her stomach—so—and the basket was half full of corn. Then she rubbed her armpits—so—and the basket was full to the top with beans. The boys looked at each other and said, 'this will never do; our mother is a witch. If we eat any of that it will poison us.' The sons did kill their mother, but they dragged her body around the circle, and wherever her blood fell on the ground the corn sprang up."[3] Variations on this story could be found among many of the neighbors of the Cherokees.

The myth of Selu, the Corn Mother, testifies to the female symbolic economic identity as well as the real-life practice of corn growing among the Cherokees and their ancestors, and perhaps neighboring predecessor peoples. Archaeological and palynological evidence has suggested, however, that Selu's corn was not the first stage in the development of crop cultivation in the region. Before the arrival of what would become the now-familiar "Thanksgiving feast" foods, there were older agricultures. Generations of crops were sequentially developed in situ or imported into the Appalachians, cultivated, and gradually fitted. The history of farming—a term subject to many definitions—in the region has wellsprings much deeper and much older than the Selu myth.

The agricultural history of the region resembles less a deep channel of tradition than a braided stream, with many meanders, shallow to deep courses, and occasional cut-offs. At greatest remove is the very long formative, figurative *first generation* agriculture—here covering thousands of years—that saw what we familiarly understand as "gathering" rather than "agriculture." During the glacial periods, stability was reduced, and animal migrations, as well as access to plants, reflected great pulses. Where there was continuous canopy cover, there were other opportunities for gathering. While hunting and gathering are linked in our minds as living off the bounty of the land, plant gathering over millennia reshaped the land toward making bounty insurable. They prepared the way for the markers of what are commonly, but too exclusively, understood as farming—annual crop plants. Habitats, crops, techniques were under construction that would provide the remarkable durability of a traditional farming system and which would serve as the launching pad for innovation.

The *second generation*, marked by crop plants identifiable to the modern eye, appeared in the Tennessee River valley and its tributaries, one of the most ancient eastern Amerindian homelands, long before corn. In this second generation came squash, and then gourd; seeds recovered from archaeological sites place the advent of relatives to today's domesticated crops at roughly 3000 or 4000 BP.[4] Some of these varieties and crops arrived in the Appalachians from drier places of origin to the southwest, but increasingly multiple centers of domestication have been suggested. Other cultigens, those less immediately identifiable to modern eyes as foods—sumpweed, sunflower, chenopods (or pigweeds), cresses, maypops, maygrass—were all indigenous eastern domesticates of degree. Once viewed as an "eastern horticultural complex," this agriculture is seen now as representing a "center of agricultural diversity," sharing the world stage with the Near East, Africa, and Asia, and closing in on their antiquity.[5] Writing about the eastern Woodland era, agriculture stands out as exemplifying among other cultural features the highest degree of "temporal and spatial variation" during its precolonial phases.[6] In common with other such centers worldwide, agricultural diversity correlates with native botanical diversity. This is the case in the Southern Appalachian highlands, where plant diversity and endemism are in the highest global rank of temperate zone sites. Obviously such places are rich material in the hands of cultivators of all kinds, rich in potential for both biological diversity and traditional knowledge.[7]

This new perspective is sharpened as we move forward in time. Corn, as the Selu myth and its relatives suggest, remade the landscape. The introduction of corn into the Appalachian region came later, approximately 1500 to 800 BP. Requiring more selectivity and genetic fitting, it came latest of all to the remote mountain country of the Cherokees. Around eight hundred years ago beans joined corn to form the paired staples of "Mississippian" agriculture.[8] The increase in productivity that accompanied corn-and-bean-centered farming, and the dominance of both in myth and field, represents the *third generation* of mountain agriculture, and was not supplanted until colonial times. The twin crops have been linked both to agricultural intensification and an expansion of human population and political control over the same period.[9] Some older, reliable crops seem to have been casualties of the enthusiasm for corn; for example, a cultivated variety of sumpweed, now known only from excavated seeds.[10] Corn growing added a powerful new component to the agriculture of the Appalachian cultivators who preceded the Cherokees, just as it did when introduced to the Old World as a prize of colonization.[11] Its march was not without a few casualties among older crops, and the relatively recent advent and dimension of cornfield agriculture throws much of what came earlier into deeper shadow.

Cherokee corn cultivators, most often women, continually adjusted the new crop to the climatic and soil contours of the narrow river floodplains and isolated terraces where fields were located. Corn cropping required intervals of fallow, and possibly burning for nitrogen recharge, though the inherent fertility of the soils made them a tremendous farming base.[12] New varieties of this crop were introduced through trade and were gradually created in the course of cultivation in individual villages.[13] Such changes beg the question of how active and how passive; biologists may see the change as random selection pressure, but the picture clearly includes intentional intervention. Traditional scientific knowledge is perhaps the best evidence of the latter. Whatever the agency, the net result was more diversified corn-growing in which the productivity of the plant was fine-tuned to highly variable local climatic and soil conditions. Trader James Adair testified in the 1760s to the importance and diversity of this plant among the southeastern tribes: "Corn is their chief produce and main dependence. Of this they have three sorts; [one is] the smaller sort of Indian corn, which usually ripens in two months, from the time it is planted; though it is called by the English the six weeks corn. . . . The second sort is yellow and flinty, which they call 'hommony-corn.' The third is the largest, of a very white and soft grain, termed 'bread corn.'"[14] A critical moment for the third generation of mountain agriculture of the Cherokees was the advent, approximately a thousand years ago, of northern flint corn varieties adapted for cold and for a short growing season.[15] These "new" corn varieties, bred with older tropical varieties, gave enough genetic and physiological diversity to provide some insurance against localized crop failure or pest problems.[16]

Partially in response to these dangers, Cherokee farmers had in the ancient past learned to draw their harvest from beyond the boundaries of what could be reconstructed as recognizably cultivated fields. Thus first generation agriculture remained as central as corn to the colonial-era Cherokee diet. Gathered foods—nuts, fruits, and grasses—made a critical contribution to the Cherokee diet and were almost entirely collected by women.[17] These foods perhaps made up as much as half of the nonmeat portion of the early Cherokee diet in the precontact period.[18] Cherokee gathering, as in many agricultural societies, focused on species growing on the edge of the forest and often in old fields. Not surprisingly, trees provide the most conspicuous, persistent, and persistently overlooked evidence. At an old townsite along the Savannah River, William Bartram described in 1775 a husbanded—or, perhaps more properly, mothered—forest community growing in "ancient cultivated fields." Among the species Bartram listed were persimmon, honey locust, Chickasaw plum, red mulberry, shellbark hickory, and black walnut, and he drew attention to their apparent semidomestication: "Though these are natives of the forest, yet they thrive better, and are more fruitful, in cultivated plantations, and the fruit is in great estimation with the present generation of Indians."[19] Traces of the hands that created the "cultivated plantations" of trees described by Bartram are visible at various points: in the apparent range extensions of the chestnut; in the yard trees, especially persimmons, locusts, and native stone-fruits such as the "Chickasaw" plum; in the scatter of locations for pecan, walnut, and especially thin-shelled hickories like the shellbark hickory. This esteem reflected differences in quality attributable to long attention to these and other quasi-domesticated trees and shrubs bearing high-quality edible fruits and nuts.[20] Field and town edges were in part colonized by such useful "plantations."

Fire also played a role, though the specific cultural and natural histories of fire, especially in the southern Appalachians, have been little investigated until recently. Stereotypes—of "fireproof" wet forests especially in mountain regions—or about Indians as reckless forest arsonists—have been in the way even of asking the question. Always a handmaiden of farming nearly worldwide, fire could reopen regrown old fields and eased replanting. Again following analogous environments and peoples, burning could in some cases enhance yields—or ease collection—of shrub or tree crops such as chestnut in the southern Appalachians. Interviews of Cherokee elders today suggest that such a pattern of burning, in this case targeted (rather than wide scale) low intensity annual burning, did exist for chestnut "orchards," much like piñon in the Southwest.[21]

Fire also played a role in managing rivercane stands, as fire can reinvigorate growth at intervals. Rivercane today snakes unnoticed (or confused with imported bamboo) along berm-edges of rivers raised by flood-deposited silt and sand. Throughout the South canebrakes—large expanses of cane, which much resembled tall grass prairie in the impression made as settlers encountered them—exist as ghosts of themselves. Surviving rivercane strips represent an artifact aboveground, just as certainly as buried pottery is an artifact underground. Ironically, the visual evidence has been less noticed than things buried and out of plain sight. Sacred and diverse in its uses, rivercane, as Sarah Hill evocatively wrote, was used by the Cherokees and other southeastern tribes to weave their world. Cultivated, perhaps, yet Cherokee traditional knowledge today suggests tending and a pattern of management. Whether or not its nearly wheat-sized seeds were consumed by native peoples or by important flocking birds including passenger pigeons or both remains an article of speculation. The pressure of living together on the small flat spots in the southern mountains resulted in a "push and pull" between cornfields and cane. Whether rivercane arrived with human help or worked its own way into the deeper mountain valleys that represent the cold-limit of its range is unknown.

A kind of order was engineered into the landscape; the process of improvement was continuous over thousands of years and into the eighteenth century. In this way the precontact rural landscape of the southern Appalachian hills at the time of Euroamerican settler incursions reflected prior transformation over millennia. The familiar and often quaint terms landscape and farmscape fail to communicate the depth of this transformation. The long-settled valleys of the Cherokees represented what might be labeled agriscapes, landscapes shaped for subsistence, in which field-based farming was only one element.

The agriscape was much more than a handful of crops; it was also a system of cultivation cross-bedded into a broader ecosystem—a designed landscape.[22] The success or failure of Cherokee farming depended on the timing and technology of planting and harvesting, on the way in which fields were tended, and on how the year's harvest was stored, as much as on the weather or productivity of individual seedstocks. A sketch of the workings of the Cherokee agricultural system can be composed from the fragmentary archaeological record and from patchy historical evidence. The southeastern tribes, including the Cherokees, traditionally grew their crop plants in complex mixtures of species, of which Adair provides an account: "They are so interested in having 'multum in parvo' that they plant the corn hills so close, as to thereby choak up the field. They plant their corn in straight rows, putting five or six grains into one hole, about two inches distant—they cover them with clay in the form of a small hill. Each row is a yard asunder, and in the vacant ground they plant pumpkins, water-melons, marsh-mallows, sunflowers, and sundry sorts of beans and peas." Further, Adair notes, they were so slow to hoe that they "let the weeds outgrow the corn."[23] What Adair attributed to laziness was in fact a very different and highly effective kind of cultivation, practiced in African as well as in Amerindian agriculture.[24] Close intercropping of a variety of plants in the Cherokee manner made ecological and agricultural sense and raised crop yields by creating a stable garden "microclimate," inducing a favorable balance of predatory and pest insect species. This system also put nitrogen-fixing plants, such as beans, in proximity to nitrogen-demanding plants, such as corn.[25] Similarly, many of the weeds Adair observed in the garden may have been encouraged and tolerated as supplemental food sources, as "nonweeds," to use an inelegant ecological term, or may have been unrecognized and ancient agricultural features. Maygrass, pokeweed, maypops and chenopods, for example, fall into this category.[26] For the Cherokees, the pattern of planting corn and other crops was partially encoded in the instructions of generation to generation, and even explicitly stated in myth and ritual calendar. For example, the Selu myth instructed the women to work the corn crop only twice; in other traditions, the time of planting was marked.[27]

Against uncertainties of pests or weather, Cherokee women offered subsidies, the most obvious of which was the labor required in watching a field to frighten off predators, whether deer after pumpkins or flocks of Carolina parakeet after peaches. Other elements of their agricultural system, such as planting schedules, were also designed carefully. For example, the Cherokees kept their newly planted corn from becoming a crow's meal by timing planting to coincide with the ripening of wild fruit near the margins of their fields, which served to distract the birds.[28] Ko-ga, or crow, is a common Cherokee family and place name. Language mirrors landscape, and the crow place-names present at Qualla today may reflect something of the arrangement of the land and its inhabitants—whether cultivator or predator—at the edge of memory. Storage of the year's surplus was also essential to the tribe, and it was effectively accomplished in special single-household and communal storehouses. The architecture of corn houses, built of interwoven cane covered with clay daub, was carefully designed to meet this need: "Their corn-houses . . . are raised up upon four Posts, four and some five feet high from the Ground; its Floor is made of round Poles, on which the Corn-worms cannot lodge, but fall through, and thus the Indians preserve their Corn from being destroyed by the Weevils a whole year."[29] Selu's two sons spied on her from holes in the chinking of such a granary. Less obvious than the corncrib but surviving as pots are oil storage jars. Large embossed clay vessels held hickory nut oil through the winter. By engineering effective storage, as well as controllable elements of planting and cultivation, Cherokee agriculture was able to withstand the effects of droughts and pest outbreaks that occasionally translated into famine for individual villages or even larger sections of the tribal territory.[30]

Cherokee farm management techniques extended also into less tangible realms. Magical formulas were applied to stave off inevitable problems; Cherokees blamed severe spring frosts on "a black petty God" of the north wind. This was a trickster god and the priests' best efforts to stop his bad works often failed: "Sometimes at night he sends out cold without wind and blasts the fruit trees and the water and muskmelons and pumpkin vines and the first small corn that we plant called rosripe corn. But he is forced to do it very stealthily."[31] Public morality seems to have been linked in Cherokee religious belief with agricultural as well as other misfortunes. Women played a key role in mediating this interaction by employing and tithing priestly rainmakers and preventing social improprieties that could upset the prospects for a good harvest.[32] Real difficulty came less at the hands of trickster gods than on the heels of war, social strife, or territorial interlopers. The agriscape of the mountain farmers was much more resilient than the social system under the booted heel of war and pestilence.

"Wheat and Flax Only Excepted"

European colonization (and its delayed, though dramatic, invasion of the Appalachian territory of the Cherokees during the late eighteenth century) tested the resiliency of the Cherokee agricultural system in new and unparalleled ways. The period between the Spanish *entradas* of the 1540s and the establishment of the deerskin trade through Charlestown in the 1680s, coupled with intercolonial and intertribal wars late in the seventeenth century, represents a poorly defined gray zone in the life of the tribe. When substantial changes—a possibly catastrophic mortality from Old World diseases *before* Europeans and Africans came into their country, the toll of Indian slave trade, and the damaging breakdown of aboriginal political alliances—created an instability to which the mountains, however remote, conferred no immunity.[33] As the record becomes clearer in the eighteenth century, some of the changes especially in farming appear to have been positive, as in the case of the introduction of sweet potatoes and domestic animals. Yet at the same time Cherokee women moved against the tide of war, depopulation, and political instability.

The selectivity with which the Cherokees accepted new crops allows an important insight not only into the assessment of what the new crops had to offer but also into the psychology of self-reform undertaken by indigenous societies during the late colonial period, which, among the Cherokees, created a *fourth generation* revision of their agriculture. Perhaps more than the first three, this generation began with the diminishment and some loss at the core of what had gone before. Cherokee farming began to intertwine with that of new neighbors. The earliest travel accounts that give any details of Cherokee farming date from the 1740s, and indicate that the Cherokees were already growing and eating sweet potatoes, or *nuna*, that were beginning to replace some native foods such as wild potatoes, *gu-da-ge-wi*.[34] Wild potatoes (*Apios americana*) are actually wild peas with edible starchy tubers and seeds, and were presumably harvested and quasi-domesticated from the beginning of mountain farming. Like sumpweed, wild potatoes are easy to disregard as minor castoffs of dietary history.

It is easy to dismiss this as a footnote to the evolution of mountain farming, except for the fact that one the seven Cherokee clans is commonly called "wild potato," *ani-gu-da-ge-wi* (fig. 1).[35] A genetic cousin of the fabled (and late-coming) *Phaeseolus* bean, some evidence points toward a very early association with human occupation of the region, though conversations with elders today suggest that it has fallen out of use and, to some degree, recognition.[36] As with other dietary mainstays absent from today's menu, wild potatoes, also a nitrogen-fixer, still grow on the floodplain, but unlike corn, on waterlogged heavy-clay soils. When and how the plant fell out of common use is difficult to say, though after the eighteenth century its appearances in outsiders' records are infrequent. Possible explanations can be offered for how a plant, once of both agricultural and cultural importance, could become unfamiliar. Grazing or trampling by increasing domestic animal stocks during the nineteenth century could have reduced abundance. Perhaps the newly arrived sweet potatoes tasted better, or were easier to store and could be propagated in fenced gardens, and pushed the wild potato aside.

The wild potato is a subject of active investigation today into its "new crop" potential.[37] However, wild potatoes perhaps served the dual purposes of feeding and healing its gatherers. Recent research has identified in *Apios* a high and diverse protein content, an anticarcinogenic compound, and

Figure 1. Cherokee Fall Fair exhibit. Clan masks include the wild potato clan, second from left, and canned vegetables, including traditionally gathered Jelico and Slick mushrooms (photo by Roger Haile, courtesy of the Folklife Program of the North Carolina Arts Council).

point to more; "though studies have been conducted on the quality of tuber storage (e.g., as food), very little is known about compounds that could have beneficial effects on humans and animal health." The same comparison can be made for most studies of Cherokee foodways that also had active healing aspects, and the same point about lack of research into all but the most obvious caloric dimensions of Cherokee farming. While there was a distinction between food and medicine, choices about what to gather or not gather involved weighing both sides. Some plants from a European perspective were clearly medicinal, and some of these counted as the pound-for-pound most valuable exports by far during the colonial period—ginseng and Seneca snakeroot. In other cases the distinction from the *outside* breaks down when viewed from *inside* Cherokee understanding in which food and medicine were not separate categories. For instance, corn, a plant clearly in the female domain, was also used medicinally, but has been examined as a food almost exclusively.[38] Corn, rivercane, wild potatoes, and chenopods: each was woven into the landscape managed by Cherokee women to maintain the health of their people.

Without knowing precisely the loss side of the equation represented by the wild potato, the introduction of sweet potatoes likely gave a critical boost to village diets, perhaps comparable to the ancient acquisition of corn. Testifying to the fast-moving and most syncretic period of mountain farming, Bartram listed "those nourishing roots usually called sweet or Spanish potatoes" as one of the four most important foods of the nation.[39] Other crop plants were accepted as well. Archaeological evidence from the very early contact period indicates that southeastern tribes such as the Cherokees were growing at least two introduced fruits, the peach and the watermelon.[40] The Cherokees were quick to grow watermelons, originally an African cultigen. For example, a Chickasaw party raiding near a village during the Cherokee War found "three Cherokees eating watermelon; these they surrounded, one of them they killed and scalped." The peach was another and by the end of the eighteenth century the trees were silent markers of abandoned villages.

The route of these plant exchanges is difficult to trace; sweet potatoes, watermelon, and peaches could have come to the Cherokees through contact with the Spanish in Florida, or refugee tribes such as the Apalachees during the early eighteenth century, and the forced migrations of other tribes like them could have been a conduit for seed or rootstock exchange. The small numbers of African American runaways and traders also may have handed off the crops. In addition, long-range trading networks such as that involving the traffic of yaupon holly (from which the ritual Black Drink was made) from coastal tribes to the "Mountain Indians . . . as the Spanish do with the South Sea tea from Paraguay to Buenos-Aires" operated through the Southeast, continued to funnel new crops with the colonization of the south Atlantic coast.[41] Retracing the apparent route of "Appalachian beans" or black-eyed peas from the Old World, from Africa, to the Creeks and perhaps Cherokees is instructive. These peas were possibly carried by Apalachee refugees or by Creeks (trading and also growing them), quickly arriving in French Louisiana.[42] Very likely all these routes carried the seeds of agricultural change both to and from the southern highlands.

Taste had much to do with it as well, and all the systems and crops we have discussed ended up in the pot. Nutritional approaches to food, as suggested above, offer a more sophisticated understanding of why some old foods were retained and others discarded, but taste is cultural and personal;

what's good for you isn't always good to eat. In this light, the persimmon, an ancient tree crop exceptionally rich in vitamins, made sense as a target for gatherers. And perhaps even more so in the case of nuts, specifically hickory nuts, rich in fatty acids that, among other effects, seem to ameliorate sugar metabolism. We can safely assume that for each "horticultural complex" there existed a cuisine. For example, in *America's First Cuisines* Sophie Coe presents a several-course repast of the diet and culture of Middle America. Perhaps the eastern cuisine was distinctive for "seethed" foods."[43]

Each of these new crops fit the garden (as opposed to field) agriculture of the tribe. The Cherokees cultivated two types of plots: intensive gardens close to the villages and larger fields more distant from their dwellings. The garden plots closely packed around villages slowed William Bartram's way as he entered the town of Whatoga: "The road carried me winding about through their little plantations of Corn, Beans, etc. up to the council house. . . . All before me appeared little plantations . . . divided from each other by narrow strips or borders of grass, which marked the bounds of each one's property, their habitation standing in the midst."[44] More extensive corn crops were planted in outfields that moved around the village margin in a cycle of fallowing and planting. Although these were still domains of the women, men participated in the planting and harvesting of the larger fields, whereas the smaller gardens were completely under women's management.[45] Sweet potatoes again provide a window, this time into the technological dimensions of change. Because of their utility in cultivating corn and sweet potato mounds, wooden and then iron hoes remained the preferred tool of Cherokee agriculture late into the century.[46] Thus the new crops adopted by the tribe were assimilated into the sector of Cherokee agriculture most in the hands of women.

This pattern is even more marked with respect to the adoption of domestic animals, especially the hog. Excavations (many of them carried out prior to the flooding of the former center of the Overhill Cherokee homeland by the Tellico Dam in present east Tennessee) have illuminated the introduction and use of European domestic animals. For instance, at the Cherokee town of Citico on the Little Tennessee River the hog was an important supplementary meat source, second only to white-tailed deer and bear, through the middle and late colonial period. When the provisions of the English garrison at Fort Loudoun, established in the late 1750s in the territory of the western tribal towns, ran low, the commander of the fort wrote to headquarters that, in spite of his request, "The Indians do not care to sell their Hoggs because they had a bad Hunt."[47] The husbandry of pigs in this case allowed a margin of safety for the villages, particularly in the last half of the century when disruptions, such as smallpox outbreaks and warfare with American settlers, became tragically commonplace.[48]

The hogs were being kept by women. The manner of this adoption is clear in a passage from Adair: "Their women and children . . . feed their [pigs] in small pens or enclosures through the crop-season, and chiefly on long pursley, and other wholesome weeds, that their rich fields abound with."[49] Hog pens under the management of women must have become an increasingly common part of the Cherokee farm landscape during the mid-eighteenth century.

Archaeological findings demonstrating the substantial presence of swine among the midcentury Cherokees provide a valuable benchmark for judging the divisions between male and female responses to Cherokee innovations during a rapidly changing time, especially since the observations left by colonists are full of contradictions. For example, James Adair (who, it should be remembered, was attempting to prove that Native Americans were a lost tribe of Israel and thus was hesitant to report pork-eating among the tribes) at first wrote that the opossum and the hog were considered undesirables, but he had to admit that pork raising existed at midcentury. Of the opossum he noted, "Several old men assure us, they formerly reckoned it as filthy uneatable animal as a hog."[50] In the Cherokee language the names for the two animals were synonymous and unflattering: *si-gwa* was the original word for hog and opossum.[51] Chickens were assimilated into the diet during the century as well, but like the hog, the chicken was also marked with some disdain, at least by Cherokee men. Young warriors readying for raids against the upcountry South Carolina settlements promised to honor their towns by "killing swarms of white dung-hill fowls, in their corn fields and asleep."[52]

Although Cherokee males may have felt the same contempt for the domestic animals of whites as for their owners, they were eating more and more of these animals at home. Throughout the eighteenth century the most important contribution by men to the Cherokee diet—the meat of bear, white-tailed deer, and small game animals—declined steadily, offset by the consumption of domestic animals.[53] Perhaps the women's perspective on the desirability of these animals differed from the men's because the domestic animals accepted by the tribe fitted into the garden component of Cherokee subsistence.

Another subsistence choice reflects a similar mix of intercultural and internal politics. Although many Cherokees kept hogs after midcentury, nearly all villagers rejected cattle for reasons of practicality, preference, and prejudice. The absence of cattle in their towns was so conspicuous to one observer in 1762 that he suggested the lack be corrected by "breeding some tame buffaloes."[54] Part of the reason cattle were not accepted was direct and practical: from the female farmer's point of view, cattle posed a danger to garden crops. Further, the Cherokees considered cattle the "deer" of the colonists and therefore viewed these domestic animals as male-culture animals associated with the economic pursuits of men. Because the hog was neither hunted nor herded, it was not in the male domain of Cherokee culture and did not compete, as did the land-demanding colonial stock-raising business, for land or for a share of the leather market with Cherokee hunters. This cultural distinction in the manner in which the Cherokees selected domestic stock makes understandable the rapidity with which the Cherokees accepted another large domestic animal, the horse, which was identified with the male pursuits of hunting and warfare. By the 1760s Adair was able to write: "Almost everyone hath horses, from one to a dozen. . . . [The Cherokees] are skillful jockies, and nice in their choice."[55]

By "everyone" Adair meant Cherokee men. The feelings of women on the stocking of village grounds with horses were mixed, as Adair elsewhere makes clear: "Around this small farm they fasten stakes in the ground, and tie a couple of split hiccory, or white-oak saplings, at proper distances to keep off the horses: though they cannot leap fences, yet many of the old horses will creep through these enclosures, almost as readily as swine, to the great regret of the women, who scold and give them ill names, calling them ugly mad horses, and bidding them go along, and be sure to keep away, otherwise their hearts will hang sharp within them, and set them on to spoil them, if envy and covetousness lead them back . . . [in the outfields]."[56] The fondness of Cherokee men for horses, not entirely shared by women farmers, was bolstered not only by the quest for speed in horse racing but also by the use of horses as draft animals in moving leather long distances to colonial markets and, perhaps late in the century, by the substitution of horse stealing for life-taking in risky traditional warfare. Horse trading and stealing had become the moral equivalent of war.

From the middle decades of the century on, farming and the trade in corn and produce—the most direct economic activities of women—were enhanced by growing new crops and tending domestic animals. These changes may have allowed women new possibilities in selling garden produce and handmade items such as baskets, medicinal herbs, and dried corn both within the tribe and to outside purchasers. Military installations among the Cherokee towns, such as the garrison at Fort Loudoun in the 1750s, as well as Tellico blockhouse at the turn of the nineteenth century, purchased provisions from women.[57] The real gain though was for the entire tribe, since the new crops brought into cultivation substantially boosted the diversity and yield base of Cherokee agriculture. At the same time the particular selections (pigs and sweet potatoes) were also a good bargain in terms of labor demands, relative to tending cattle or small grains introduced by colonists. This gain partly offset the recurrent loss and dislocation of population and the consequent labor scarcity during the early and middle eighteenth century, when the number of Cherokees declined by half, to ten thousand. Judicious innovation thus played a clear role in the rapid evolution of the Cherokee farm economy in the eighteenth century. Women chose the hog and sweet potato, men the horse. These choices would change the terms on which Cherokee society was to meet the acceleration of economic stress and the challenge to the existence of Cherokee culture posed by American aggression late in the century.

One of the most complete and detailed depictions of the state of Cherokee agriculture and the adversity faced by the Cherokee people is owed, ironically, to the colonial and British troops who attempted their destruction during the Cherokee War of 1759–62. The grim staccato prose of James Grant's military reports of his march into the Cherokee hills during the summer of 1761 is part of this record: "July 28: . . . town and country were destroyed. We passed the Sticoe River a second time and proceeded to Tessantee where another poor old man was killed. . . . [In] a few hours this town and the plantation round it were in flames, all the corn cut down and an end put to the back settlements. . . . Fifteen towns and all the plantations in the country have been burnt—above 1,400 acres of corn, beans, pease, etc., destroyed; about 5,000 people including men, women and children drove into the woods and mountains to starve."[58] In targeting the Cherokee cornhouses (one colonial witness called them "astonishing magazines of corn") for destruction the troops had fixed on a conspicuous and critical element in the tribal agriculture, destroying both food and planting seed.[59] Equally damaging but less visible was the disruption caused by consecutive spring campaigns against the Middle Towns at higher elevations, where the narrow window for planting permitted by late spring warming and early frost was missed. The Cherokees did not strongly resist the Grant campaign. They melted away, sidelined by a kind of total war that had no equivalent in their own traditions.

Drought and disease compounded the job of recovery.[60] However, the swiftness of the postwar recovery, which continued until 1776, was remarkable in this light, and testified to the resilience of the female-dominated agriculture. In the wake of the Grant campaign, a newspaper headlined its report "A firm peace is now made with all the Cherokees" and followed this news by stating: "All the Lower Towns . . . are again settled and the Indians replanting these."[61] The peace that followed allowed the tribe to reconstruct its life. In the words of a Moravian missionary, this was the time of "their greatest prosperity in their way."[62] In the campaigns of 1761 and 1776, the provincial soldiers, many of them small farmers, were impressed with their enemies' agricultural accomplishments. Arthur Fairie was an immigrant farmer along on one of the three campaigns, the little known but decisive "Indian War of 1776," launched against the mountain Indians. Fairie had a farmer's eye; he remarked: "Wednesday July 25th, 1776, We were ordered to cut down corn and peach trees, apple trees, etc. . . . After this we were ordered to march, and started, and came along the said Valley to another town called Nowewee; this we plundered and destroyed, corn and all vegetables belonging thereto, abounding much with corn, potatoes, peas and beans. . . . The aforesaid Valley looks very curious on account of its being hemmed in on both sides by mountains, and likewise the fertility of the soil. The Indians made great crops of corn, and indeed of all sorts of serviceable fruits, wheat and flax only excepted."[63]

The reconstruction of farming in the decades after the Grant campaign and the American Revolution testifies to the resilience of Cherokee farming. Even when there was peace, the last years of the eighteenth century were hard times for the tribe, with periodic outbreaks of smallpox and other infectious diseases, often accompanied by famine. Each tragic episode disturbed the life of the farming women and their crops: seed sown too late, harvests interrupted because of a lack of labor, and corn storehouses in need of repair. Despite these pressures, Cherokee farming and Cherokee land provided for the tribe. Relative to other native peoples of the Southeast during the same period, the Cherokees did more than hold their own; they even appear to have gained status, in part because of the contributions of the Cherokees' field crops and agriscape.[64]

The Domestic Politics of Land

Cherokee women originally held higher status than any other women of the major southeastern tribes, which was reflected in the freedom they enjoyed in and out of marriage. "The Cherokee are an exception to all civilized or savage nations, in having no laws against adultery," trader Adair wrote in the 1760s; "they have for a considerable time been under petticoat government and allow their women full liberty to plant their brows with horns as often as they please, without fear of punishment."[65] Like most other southeastern tribes, the Cherokee society was matrilineal; women also had a strong part in tribal warfare, governance, and ritual.[66] The persistence of this relatively strong standing compared with women of other tribes is suggested by the retention of women's role in the Cherokee green corn festival. The son of the first Indian Agent of the state of Tennessee remembered watching the festival in the 1790s and the way women participated: "When the women dance alone, the leader, (a matron) sings (as the others do) and has the shells of terrapins with pebbles, confined to the legs, just above the ankle, with these she makes a singular noise agreeing with the singing."[67] By comparison, in the Chickasaw ritual, recounted forty years before, women played a more passive and submissive role.[68] Similarly, a few Cherokee women retained the status of "beloved woman" and other traditional honorific titles, although the number holding them was sharply diminished by the end of the eighteenth century. If Cherokee women finished the century in a relatively strong position compared with women of neighboring tribes, the difference must be attributed in part to their standing at the beginning.

Cherokee women had, by the same token, both more to lose and less to gain politically and economically as changes eroded the position of the tribe. The issue is complicated by the problem of estimating the original status of women or even of the political organization of the tribe before it became entangled with the colonists. The development of a commercial economy based on hunting has usually been seen as growing from the economic power of women as opposed to men. And intercolonial political negotiations were mainly (in sharp contrast to Cherokee tradition) managed as male-only events. Cherokee women, even if they were present (which was frequently the case), were, like their colonial counterparts, denied a place at the table. The gifts, favors, and political prestige that came to Cherokee men as a result of this system also eroded the political standing of women, at least outside of village arenas.[69]

Considering the colonial Cherokee experience in more detail, especially in terms of women's participation in trade in corn and herbs, in handicrafts, and in other areas of support, a more measured interpretation seems appropriate. Cherokee agriculture, the clearest domain of women, was a conspicuous success in adapting new crops and techniques of cultivation. This success may help explain why Cherokee women fared well compared to other Indian women. The basis for their comparatively strong standing throughout the colonial period is attributable to the persistence of an initially strong place in Cherokee society and to the continued viability of their economic role as the tribal farmers.

After the Treaty of Hopewell in 1785, an era of direct conflict as political equals with American society came to a close. After this point the politics of the tribe began to reflect more clearly the new divisions, which continued the gender and economic tensions of earlier decades. The rift between mixed-blood "progressives" and full-blood "conservatives" was at once political, agricultural, and sexual. In those areas where some families adopted a market-oriented, slave-owning, and paternalistic, male-centered agriculture, the position of women was especially threatened.[70] Two Moravian missionaries observed the results of this process firsthand in 1799, when they visited the household of a mixed-blood named Walker, whom they judged to be "too civilized for the gospel to appear to him in the nature of good news." Walker's behavior toward his wife also disturbed them, and while at his house they observed "clearly how the women among the Indians are oppressed. First we received our meal, then Walker had himself served and after that the young wife breakfasted quite alone."[71]

Among the majority of Cherokee families, however, who were tradition-minded full-bloods scattered throughout the entire tribal area (but concentrated in the Appalachian valleys), large-scale farming based on the colonial model of slave agriculture was not practiced extensively.[72] Instead, the older Cherokee pattern of women's farming remained widespread and offered passive resistance to fundamental changes in both cultivation style and in the status of women. The testimony of another missionary early in the nineteenth century throws light on women at work in this more traditional side of Cherokee society: "Though custom attached the heaviest part of the labor to the women, yet they were cheerful and voluntary in performing it. What others have discovered among the Indians I cannot tell, but though I have been about nineteen years among the Cherokees, I have perceived nothing of that slavish, servile fear, on the part of women, so often spoke of."[73]

The continuing intersection of gender and economic issues within the Cherokee settlements was reflected in the continued hesitation of many Cherokees to accept cattle as part of their farming, although other southeastern tribes had widely adopted them by the end of the eighteenth century. For example, in the 1760s whereas some Creeks and Cherokees kept cattle, "most declined them." But four decades later the situation was changed, at least among the Creeks. In 1799 Moravian missionaries reported: "We saw a number of Creek Indians, who had driven cattle thither for the garrison. The cattle had been made to swim the river and were immediately shot. . . . [The Creeks] were mostly young, with silver rings in their noses and long slits in their ears. . . . One of them had his left eye painted red and the right cheek black and pleased himself not a little with this decoration. Their women were obliged to content themselves outside the house. The Creeks bring much cattle into this region, some of it very fine." And they ended by observing that, instead of cattle, "in the Cherokee country droves of hogs are often bought up and driven out."[74] Some Cherokees did own cattle in the eighteenth century, but the decided cultural preference seems to have been for raising pigs, in consonance with their traditional agricultural pattern.[75]

Apart from the substantial presence of cattle, the cultivation patterns found in backcountry American settlements established late in the eighteenth century bore a superficial resemblance to Cherokee farming. Corn, for example, tended to be the primary cereal crop and was often interplanted with mixtures of beans, pumpkins, and other plants. Similarly, the hoe was at first the dominant instrument of cultivation for most settlers. These perceived similarities fade in light of differences of domestic politics and historical experience. Appalachian agriculture during the late colonial period was the child of remembered ethnic traditions and hardscrabble trial and error and, for the most part, did not benefit from the advice and experience that Native American farmers could have provided had the openness of Appalachian society in the early eighteenth century persisted. The political transformation of the Appalachians during the Revolution, in which Americans initiated their intent toward total political dominance of the region, closed out the earlier promise of exchange.

With the assertion of political dominance by Americans, and in many sections by Cherokee planter elite, even traditional farmers superficially mimicked the farming style of their neighbors. New crops, implements, and farming techniques gradually came into use. Missionaries, interested in making a pitch for agricultural reform, found that women were their best audience.[76] Women's acceptance of the plow reversed an objection, like that made against cattle raising, to an implement strongly associated with male-centered agriculture.[77] In this way the faces of Cherokee farming changed, though the domestic relationships that underlay the pursuit of agriculture were not radically altered in traditional households. Even in areas such as northern Georgia where the Cherokee landscape had undergone an "almost complete recasting" and closely resembled that of the neighboring American farming area, significant differences remained. Instead of single-family dwellings on individual farms, Cherokee farmsteads often had multiple houses and maintained a more extensive garden space.[78] In less "Europeanized" sections of the uplands, the look of the land was more traditional, and the farmstead was still to a large extent a woman's domain.

The Evolving Pattern

Eighteenth-century Cherokee agriculture was one of many possible technical solutions to producing food in the Appalachians. However, it was a deliberate mode of farming the land. Measured by sustainability, it must be judged a success and model, especially for the disposable mountain agriculture economies that came in rapid succession after Removal. This first Appalachian agriculture was able to change during the eighteenth century, the worst of times for the tribe, in a way that preserved its distinctiveness and the continuity of the women's farming tradition that it represented. Yet after its rapid evolution in the eighteenth century, the political and agricultural terms of Cherokee farming began to split as American techniques and settlement patterns began to supplant older indigenous ways. This technical compromise disguised an effort to avoid similar concessions by Cherokee women, who continued to resist the challenges to their traditional role in this arena. Had its integrity as a system of agriculture been maintained, perhaps the basic subsistence problem into which its successor, nineteenth-century Appalachian agriculture, was later to fall—the tight spiral of population growth and economic decline—could have been delayed. Perhaps it might even have granted an alternative solution through the continuing refinement of a tradition of Appalachian farming that was already centuries old. The Cherokees attempted to escape the threat of political dependency by purposeful compromises within their social and cultural life. Yet the issue was not to be one of scale or of technical sophistication in competing agricultural styles. Politics, and not the inherent productivity of traditional Cherokee agriculture, ultimately prevented a test of its potential for the generation of white and black farmers that would occupy lands once held by the tribe. Some solutions, such as the slaveholding accepted by the Cherokee elite, were dramatic and visible. Over generations Cherokee women undertook the redevelopment of their basic economic pursuit and attempted to use farming adaptively. In this way they helped maintain what was possible of their older roles both as women and as Cherokees.

The experience of Native American women is written on the faded margin of the documents we have inherited from the colonial period. Too often this partial record has been read as proof of a "'natural' conservatism, supposed irrationality, and assumed passivity" in the way that Native American women responded to the dramatic events that marked their lives during the colonial period.[79] The same terms—conservatism, passivity, and backwardness—have applied to traditional highland valley agriculture by reformers and critics since the eighteenth century.[80] The truth seems far from that. The highland agriculture practiced by the Cherokees had never been static. A static agriculture could not have achieved resilience in the face of the dramatic cultural stresses met by the Cherokees during the eighteenth century. The collective actions of Cherokee women working as farmers successfully stabilized the foundation of the domestic economy and deflected, though they could not stem, the strong undertow engendered by the depopulation, recurrent warfare, and demands of economic involvement in colonial trade. Agricultural change allowed the villagers a somewhat surer footing against these strong currents during decades when the legitimacy of the Cherokees as an independent political entity, or even in a broader cultural sense as a "people," was directly challenged.

During a century of largely male conflict between colonials and southeastern Indians, perhaps the female awareness of being both farmers and women crossed cultural lines as well. James Adair unselfconsciously suggests this possibility when he recounts that as he was writing his eighteenth-century history while lodged in the South Carolina upcountry, "a Chikkasah female, as great a princess as ever lived among the ancient Peruvians," was at his side. Just after finishing a passage on the design of wooden mortars, Adair wrote, "She bids me not to mark the paper wrong, after the manner of traders; otherwise it will spoil the making of good bread or hommony, and of course will beget the ill will of our white women."[81] It is just as important today not to mark the paper wrong, or spoil the bread, in writing about women's role in Native American agriculture in the southern mountains during the colonial period.

Postscript

The cornfields of the southern Appalachians today, pressed in along river and creek flats, have seen continuous cultivation, though not always of corn, for thousands of years. Much reduced today, cornfields may soon be sought after and photographed as prized historic landscapes. And lingering around the fields, hemmed in along the edges for the last two hundred years are all the bits and pieces of a shattered women's farming world: ancient chestnut roots still sending up sprouts after eighty years of near certain death aboveground, rivercane, wild potatoes, pigweed, thin-shelled hickories, pokeweed, persimmons, walnuts, and maypops.

After the many years since this essay was first published we are able to tell the story with new depth. The emergence of a melded environmental and historical perspective has thrown new light on the history of Cherokees and other peoples of southeastern North America. Old and new questions, however, remain. The most promising field for understanding Native American agriculture has been the most neglected—Indian people themselves. Traditional knowledge has been discounted, though it remains. Cherokee religion teaches that the Cherokee people, *ani-tsi-gi-du-wa-gi*, emerged from the Southern Appalachians. The Cherokees remain, as does their land.

Recent scholarship has also gone far in heeding the admonition of the Chickasaw "princess" to James Adair. Scholars are bringing forward new perspectives on war and hunting, diplomacy and peace, and a fuller view of women's (and men's) roles in farming and gathering. Viewing things from inside as well as outside of indigenous experience animates once ordinary words: potato, crop, farming, opossum. It may even guide the future of a region again under assault, this time affecting Cherokees and newcomers alike, and threatened by globalization, suburbanization, and migration. The history of native agricultural resilience and persistence can provide materials, sometimes admittedly bits and pieces, but still critical elements, with which to construct a bulwark against these forces.

Perhaps a *fifth generation* of mountain farming is possible, a regenerative durable relationship of "agriculture and culture," in Wendell Berry's phrase. The fourth Appalachian agriculture of the Cherokees, a syncretic enterprise, stretches from the colonial period into the twenty-first century just as the farms are disappearing on and off Qualla Boundary, the ancestral homeland of the Eastern Band of Cherokee Indians. This enterprise can bring us together, across disciplines as well as social lines, in rediscovering—and celebrating—the long-unrecognized but still present Cherokee farming tradition. While the age is both post-colonial and post-industrial, no age is ever post-agricultural. The accomplishments of Cherokee farmers in holding on to their land can inspire the shared future of the southern Appalachian land itself.

Notes

This essay is dedicated to Marvin John Taylor (1953–2005) of Qualla Boundary: gatherer, friend, teacher.

1. John Stuart, "Of Indians in General," Colonial Office 323/17/255, June 8, 1764 (microfilm copy, Hunter Library, Western Carolina University, Cullowhee, North Carolina).

This chapter first appeared in *Appalachian Frontiers*, edited by Robert Mitchell (Lexington: University Press of Kentucky, 1991). I am indebted to the University Press of Kentucky for granting permission for me to publish this revised and extended version of my original work, and to Robert Mitchell for his editorial skill and backing at an early stage of my work in this field. I also appreciate the inspired work of my coeditors Gregory Waselkov and Peter Wood, and the insightful comments and perspectives of Lisa Lefler on health and food, Carrie McLachlan on religion, and Tom Belt on Cherokee etymology among others as I revised this chapter. My book *The Dividing Paths* (Oxford: Oxford University Press, 1993) expands, particularly, on political themes in the last part of this chapter.

2. Recent works have greatly extended our understanding of women's roles in Cherokee history. Sarah Hill's *Weaving New Worlds* (Chapel Hill: University of North Carolina Press, 1997) sets new standards for bringing traditional voices into the telling of environmental and social history. See also Theda Perdue, *Cherokee Women* (Lincoln: University of Nebraska Press, 1998), an outstanding work on the subject.

3. James Mooney, *Myths of the Cherokees*, Nineteenth Annual Report, Bureau of American Ethnology (Washington DC: 1900), 242–52.

4. For studies of vegetation change over ten thousand years within the southern Appalachian landscape occupied by the Cherokees, see works by Paul and Hazel Delcourt; also Jefferson Chapman et al., "Man-Land Interaction: 10,000 Years of American Indian Impact on Native Ecosystems in the Lower Little Tennessee River Valley, Eastern Tennessee," *Southeastern Archaeology* 1 (1982): 115–22. For the climate-driven context of southeastern vegetation change over eighteen thousand years, see Thompson Webb III, "The Appearance and Disappearance of Major Vegetational Assemblages: Long-Term Vegetational Dynamics in Eastern North America," *Vegetatio* 69 (1987): 177–87.

5. A generation of new work by ethnobotanists and archaeologists allows new interpretations and understandings, summarized in theory and practice especially in Bruce Smith's *Rivers of Change* (Washington DC: Smithsonian Institution Press, 1992), see p. 268.

6. Kenneth Sassaman and Michael R. Nassaney, "Epilogue," in *Native American Interactions*, ed. Sassaman and Nassaney (Knoxville: University of Tennessee Press, 1996), 342.

7. "Cherokee used a larger number of biological resources than does any other surviving community, and each part of this ecological adaptation deserves serious attention." John Witthoft, "Cherokee Use of Potherbs," *Journal of Cherokee Studies* 2 (1977): 251. New studies follow the link between linguistic diversity and biodiversity, especially among the Klamath-Siskiyou (comparable to the Southern Appalachians as temperate zone centers of plant biodiversity and cultural diversity) in North America.

8. Stephen A. Chomko and Gary W. Crawford, "Plant Husbandry in Prehistoric Eastern North America: New Evidence for Its Development," *American Antiquity* 43 (1978): 408.

9. Gregory A. Waselkov, "Prehistoric Agriculture in the Central Mississippi Valley," *Agricultural History* 51 (1977): 513–18.

10. Richard A. Yarnell, "Domestication of Sunflower and Sumpweed in Eastern North America," in *The Nature and Status of Ethnobotany*, ed. Richard Ford, Anthropological Paper 67 (Ann Arbor: University of Michigan Museum of Anthropology, 1978), 289–301.

11. Fernand Braudel, *Capitalism and Material Life, 1400–1800* (New York: Fontana, 1973), 68–97.

12. See Daniel D. Richter and Daniel Markewitz, *Understanding Soil Change* (Cambridge: Cambridge University Press, 2001), 107–15, for a new analysis of the acid clay soils of the Southern upcountry occupied by the Cherokee lower towns.

13. The complexity of Appalachian environments and the pattern of field-crop evolution engendered by this complexity are suggested by analogy with the diversity of peasant-grown crops in other mountain areas, on which the literature is growing. For a Himalayan example, see Peter T. S. Whiteman, "The Mountain Environment: An Agronomist's Perspective with a Case Study from Jumla, Nepal," *Mountain Research and Development* 5 (1985): 151–62.

14. James Adair, *Adair's History of the American Indians*, ed. Samuel Cole Williams (1775; reprint, Johnson City TN: Watauga Press, 1930), 437.

15. Waselkov, "Prehistoric Agriculture," 515.

16. During approximately the same period a parallel adaptation in Europe was contributing to the slow climb in crop yields for wheat, oats, and rye. See L. T. Evans, "The Natural History of Crop Yield," *American Scientist* 68 (1980): 388–89; B. H. Slicher van Bath, "Eighteenth-Century Agriculture on the Continent of Europe: Evolution or Revolution?" *Agricultural History* 43 (1969): 169–80.

17. See, for example, the case studies in Frances Dahlberg, *Woman the Gatherer* (New Haven CT: Yale University Press, 1981), 1–250.

18. This percentage reflects analogous societies, including central Europe. Better estimation awaits a full reconstruction of agriculture and consumption. Tom Hatley, "The Dividing Path: The Direction of Cherokee Life in the 18th Century" (master's thesis, University of North Carolina, Chapel Hill, 1977), 64.

19. William Bartram, *The Travels of William Bartram*, ed. Mark Van Doren (1791; reprint, New York: Dover, 1955), 57; see also Mark Catesby to Sir Hans Sloane, November 27, 1724 (Sloane Manuscripts, microfilm copy, Library of Congress, Washington DC). Catesby had obtained an "Indian apron made of the bark of wild mulberry" in upcountry South Carolina. Samuel Cole Williams, the Tennessee historian, noted that the Cherokee name for the present site of Knoxville was Mulberry Grove. Samuel Cole Williams, ed., *Lieut. Henry Timberlake's Memoirs, 1756–65* (Johnson City TN: Watauga Press, 1927). The diversity of domesticated protected trees is impressive, even next to the better-documented tree cultivation practiced in Mesoamerica. For comparison, see William J. Folan, L. A. Fletcher, and E. Kintz, "Fruit, Fiber, Bark, and Resin: Social Organization of a Maya Urban Center," *Science* 204 (1979): 697–701. For ethnohistorical evidence pointing toward a similar manipulation and use of arboreal and shrub communities, see Charles W. Spellman, "The Agriculture of the Early North Florida Indians," *Florida Anthropologist* 1 (1948): 44. For subarctic introductions of useful tree species, see Jean M. Black, "Plant Dispersal by Native Americans in the Canadian Subarctic," in *Nature and Status of Ethnobotany*, ed. Ford, 255–63.

20. Roger T. Saucier, "Current Thinking on Riverine Process and Geologic History as Related to Human Settlement in the Southeast," *Geoscience and Man* 12 (1981): 8–10; Chapman et al., "Man-Land Interaction," 118.

21. Personal communication, Thom Alcoze, Northern Arizona University, 2002. Interviews with Cherokee elders point toward what ecologists have suggested all along—a frequent, perhaps three-year, fire interval.

22. The broader context of agriscape has a slightly more restrictive label—cultivated landscape; in William Doolittle, *Cultivated Landscapes of Native North America* (Oxford: Oxford University Press, 2000). Doolittle's book is a monumental encyclopedia of many of the features discussed here, inspired by exciting work in Mesoamerica.

23. Adair, *History*, 438–39.

24. For the African American garden, see Thomas Hatley, "Tending Our Gardens," *Southern Changes* 6 (1984): 18–23.

25. Miguel A. Altieri, D. K. Letourneau, and J. R. Davis, "Developing Sustainable Agroecosystems," *Bioscience* 33 (1983): 45–49.

26. C. Wesley Cowan, "The Prehistoric Use and Distribution of Maygrass in Eastern North America: Cultural and Phytogeographical Implications," in *Nature and Status of Ethnobotany*, ed. Ford, 285; J. C. Chacon and S. R. Gliessman, "Use of the Non-Weed Concept in Traditional Tropical Agroecosystems of Mexico," *Agroecosystems* 8 (1982): 1–11.

27. Mooney, *Myths*, 245.

28. Adair, *History*, 436. In all likelihood this reference is to a second, early summer corn planting.

29. John G. W. De Brahm, *De Brahm's Report of the General Survey in the Southern District of North America*, ed. Louis De Vorsey Jr. (Columbia: University of South Carolina Press, 1971), 110.

30. Droughts occurred periodically, as did food shortages; often disease outbreaks or other social disruptions seemed to be as much a cause as environmental factors. The years of the Cherokee War, 1759–62, saw this convergence of events. See discussion in Thomas Hatley, "The Three Lives of Keowee: Economic Destruction and Reconstruction in Eighteenth-Century Cherokee Villages," in *Powhatan's Mantle: Indians in the Colonial Southeast*, ed. Peter H. Wood, Gregory A. Waselkov and M. Thomas Hatley (1st ed., Lincoln: University of Nebraska Press, 1989).

31. David Corkran, "A Small Postscript on the Ways and Manners of the Indians Called Cherokees," ed. Alexander Longue, *Southern Indian Studies* 11 (1969): 14. The present average length of the growing season in the Cherokee homeland, with over 170 days of frost-free weather, offers the potential for two closely spaced corn crops. James W. Clay et al., *North Carolina Atlas* (Chapel Hill: University of North Carolina Press, 1975), 100.

32. For the roles of women and priests among the Creeks and Cherokees in the religious management of rain and social conduct, see Adair, *History*, 90–93. The precontact (and later) role of the Cherokee "priests" has been the subject of considerable scholarly interest, although the sources are ambiguous and open to radically different interpretations. See

Raymond D. Fogelson, "Who Were the *Ani-Kutani*? An Excursion into Cherokee Historical Thought," *Ethnohistory* 31 (1984): 255–63.

33. Peter H. Wood, "The Changing Population of the Eighteenth-Century South: An
Overview, by Race and Subregion, from 1685 to 1700," this volume; Marvin T. Smith, "Aboriginal Population Movements in the Early Historic Period Interior Southeast," this volume; Charles M. Hudson, "The Genesis of Georgia's Indians," in *Forty Years of Diversity:
Essays on Colonial Georgia*, ed. Harvey H. Jackson and P. Spaulding (Athens: University
of Georgia Press, 1984), 31. Also see the discussion in Henry F. Dobyns, *Their Number Become Thinned* (Knoxville: University of Tennessee Press, 1983).

34. De Brahm, *Report*, 116; Mooney, *Myths*, 492; Antoine Bonnefoy, a Frenchman held
captive by the tribe in 1742, was served sweet potatoes (the first mention of the plant among
the Cherokees) along with traditional foods at his reception into the tribe. "Journal of Antoine Bonnefoy," in *Travels in the American Colonies*, ed. Newton D. Mereness (New York:
Macmillan, 1916), 245. The Catawabas served "Indian potatoes" (very likely a native *Apios*
species) to officers of the Grant expedition in 1762, and it is possible that sweet potatoes
became a substitute for this collected plant food. See Christopher French, "Journal of an
Expedition to South Carolina," *Journal of Cherokee Studies* 2 (1977): 294.

35. William H. Gilbert, *The Eastern Cherokees*, Bureau of American Ethnology, Anthropological Paper 23 (Washington DC: Smithsonian Institution, 1943), 204–5. Carrie
McLachlan and William Anderson pointed me toward basic information on Cherokee
clans—a subject of some debate, with the wild potato clan among the debatable, though
it is recognized today.

36. The distribution of a single other member of the genus *Apios*, the very rare and local
Price's potato-bean, suggests obliquely the invisible hand of even more ancient landscape
dynamics: its major population occurs in riparian openings outside of a rock shelter where
fire may have formerly and quite anciently been decisive in speciation. Cherokee elders consulted informally through the Eastern Band of Cherokee Indians Cultural Resources Office were familiar with the name of the plant, but less so with its actual use.

37. Ironically, Asa Gray pointed to the "wild" state of such promising crop plants as *Apios* as evidence of the lack of agriculture among Native Americans. Researchers frantically
looked at the American wild potato during the Irish potato famine as a blight-resistant substitute. See Hari Krishnan, "Identification of Genistein, an Anti-Carcinogenic Compound,
in the Edible Tubers of American Groundnut," *Crop Science* 38 (1998): 1052.

38. Other plants may have been toxic, as is the commonest Cherokee traditional potherb
in use today, *so-ts-v-na*, or sochan, without correct preparation. Cherokee elders and gatherers consulted did not see it as a risk. Witthoft, "Cherokee Use of Potherbs," 251.

39. William Bartram, "Observations on the Creek and Cherokee Indians," *Transactions
of the American Ethnological Society* 3 (1853): 47.

40. Gregory A. Waselkov and R. Eli Paul, "Frontiers and Archaeology," *North American
Archaeologist* 2 (1980–81): 309–29; *South Carolina Gazette*, July 26–August 2, 1760 (microfilm, Perkins Library, Duke University, Durham, North Carolina).

41. Mark Catesby, *The Natural History of Carolina, Florida, and the Bahama Islands*, 2 vols. (London: 1731–48), 2:57.

42. Personal communication, Gregory Waselkov, 2003. Antoine Simon Le Page du Pratz, *History of Louisiana* (London: T. Becket, 1774), 204–5.

43. Adair, *History*, 437.

44. Bartram, *Travels*, 284.

45. Adair, *History*, 434–37; Bartram, "Observations," 39–40.

46. The plow was introduced during the late eighteenth century but met with strong resistance. Bartram, "Observations," 48.

47. William L. McDowell, ed., *Documents Relating to Indian Affairs*, vol. 3 (Columbia: University of South Carolina Press, 1970), 264.

48. Arthur E. Bogan, "Faunal Remains from the Historic Cherokee Occupation of Citico (40MR7) Monroe County, Tennessee," *Tennessee Archaeologist* 8 (1983): 34; R. D. Newman, "The Acceptance of European Domestic Animals by the 18th Century Cherokee," *Tennessee Anthropologist* 4 (1979): 101.

49. Adair, *History*, 242.

50. Adair, *History*, 17.

51. De Brahm, *Report*, 126. I appreciate Tom Belt's guidance in sorting out the linguistic and cultural tangles related to the history of words for opossum, pig, and wild potatoes.

52. Adair, *History*, 262–63. Cherokee border warfare seems to have been directed against both Euroamerican farmers and their domestic stock. This was the case in an incident on the Broad River in upper South Carolina in which "Hogs and fowles . . . were killed and piled upon the bodies of the murdered. Several cattle were also found dead adjacent and at least 20 head of horses." James Francis to James Glen, October 7, 1754, in McDowell, *Documents*, 3:21.

53. Bogan, "Faunal Remains," 34.

54. Williams, *Timberlake's Memoirs*, 73.

55. Adair, *History*, 242.

56. Adair, *History*, 436.

57. McDowell, *Documents*, 3:346; Samuel Cole Williams, *Early Travels in the Tennessee Country, 1540–1800* (Johnson City TN: Watauga Press, 1928), 485.

58. James Grant, "Journal of Lieutenant-Colonel James Grant, Commanding an Expedition against the Cherokee Indians, June–July 1761," *Florida Historical Quarterly* 12 (1933): 35.

59. Thomas Mante, *History of the Late War in America* (London: 1772), 284.

60. For accounts of the 1759 drought, see the *South Carolina Gazette*, September 29, 1759; "Bethabara Diary," *Records of the Moravians in North Carolina*, ed. Adelaide L. Fries, 7 vols. (Raleigh: North Carolina Historical Commission, 1922–1947), 1:209; Adair, *History*, 266.

61. Reported in the *South Carolina Gazette*, April 22, 1762.

62. Williams, *Early Travels*, 257.

63. Arthur Fairie Journal, Draper Collection, 3VV192–93 (microfilm, Perkins Library, Duke University, Durham, North Carolina).

64. Hudson notes that "of all the Indians of the Southeast, the Cherokees, despite population loss through disease, appear to have been stronger 'vis-à-vis' other Southeastern Indians in the 18th century than they had been in the 16th century." Hudson, "Genesis of Georgia's Indians," 31.

65. Adair, *History*, 152–53; see Charles Hudson, *The Southeastern Indians* (Knoxville: University of Tennessee Press, 1976), 184–86.

66. Theda Perdue, *Cherokee Women*; Perdue, "The Traditional Status of Cherokee Women," *Furman Studies*, n.s., 26 (December 1980): 19–25.

67. William Martin to Lyman C. Draper, December 1, 1842, Draper Collection, 14DD113/26–7.

68. For example, the often cited account in Adair, *History*, 105–17.

69. A classic article by Carol I. Mason points out that the trading economy of the Lower Creeks in some respects reinforced the town status of women, especially when the trade was considered in the context of agriculture: "The removal of men from the villages and towns for very long periods tended to preserve the aboriginal pattern of matrilineal land control and matrilineal descent in spite of the increasing importance of deer hunting to the community. The core of women who remained home in the villages were the agriculturalists, as they had always been, and retained their control over land and the products of the land. Women, therefore, and particularly the matrilineage, served as the thread of cultural continuity from generation to generation and certainly were a powerful force for cultural conservatism." Mason, "Eighteenth-Century Culture Change among the Lower Creeks," *Florida Anthropologist* 16 (1963): 65–81. Although the term conservatism presents some problems in approaching women's historical roles, hinging on whether *conservatism* is open-ended or closed, the process Mason describes was also at work in the Cherokee towns. For an article outlining the long-term success of Iroquois agriculture when measured against trade and hunting, see Thomas R. Wessel, "Agriculture and Iroquois Hegemony in New York, 1610–1779," *Maryland Historian* 1 (1970): 93–94.

70. For detailed discussions of the nineteenth-century development of Cherokee society, see Theda Perdue, *Slavery and the Evolution of Cherokee Society* (Knoxville: University of Tennessee Press, 1979); William G. McLoughlin, *Cherokee Renascence in the New Republic* (Princeton NJ: Princeton University Press, 1986).

71. Williams, *Early Travels*, 492.

72. See the discussion in William G. McLoughlin and W. H. Conser, "The Cherokees in Transition: A Statistical Analysis of the Federal Cherokee Census of 1835," *Journal of American History* 64 (1977): 678–703.

73. Comment by Daniel Butrick, with the American Board of Commissioners for Foreign Missions, quoted in Perdue, "Southeastern Indians and the Cult of True Womanhood," in *Web of Southern Social Relations: Women, Family and Education*, ed. Walter J. Fraser Jr., R. Saunders, and Jon R. Wakelyn (Athens: University of Georgia Press, 1985), 35–52 (citation, 38).

74. Williams, *Early Travels*, 464.

75. The case of Nancy Ward (a mixed-blood progressive and a friend of the American rebels during the Revolution at a time when most tribe members, if they took sides, were with the British) provides a telling exception. She was "rich in stock," and when the American army approaching the Cherokee backtowns asked for provisions, she agreed to have "a parcel driven in." Her choice in political causes as well as agricultural style indicates a torn allegiance to traditional Cherokee values. W. Martin to L. C. Draper, Draper Collection, 14DD113/10.

76. Perdue, "Southeastern Indians and the Cult of True Womanhood," 8.

77. Bartram, "Observations," 48; Mason, "Eighteenth-Century Culture Change," 76.

78. Richard Pillsbury, "The Europeanization of the Cherokee Settlement Landscape Prior to Removal: A Georgia Case Study," *Geoscience and Man* 22 (1983): 59–69. Compare McLoughlin and Conser, "Cherokees in Transition," 701–2; and Douglas C. Wilms, "Cherokee Settlement Patterns in Nineteenth-Century Georgia," *Southeastern Geographer* 14 (1974): 46–53.

79. Mona Etienne and Eleanor Leacock, eds., *Women and Colonization: Anthropological Perspectives* (New York: Bergin and Garvey, 1980), 22.

80. For example, Thomas Jefferson lumped all native agriculture into the following passage: "All the nations of Indians in North America lived in the hunter state, and depended for subsistence on hunting, fishing, and the spontaneous fruits of the earth, and a kind of grain which was planted and gathered by the women, and is now known by the name of Indian corn." Jefferson, *Notes on the State of Virginia*, ed. W. Peden (1787; reprint, Chapel Hill: University of North Carolina Press, 1954), 202.

81. Adair, *History*, 447.

Symbols and Society

Introduction

TOM HATLEY

In his foreword to the 1873 edition of *Antiquities of the Southern Indians*, author Charles Colcock Jones thanked the friends who had helped him assemble a "cabinet" of the "arts and manufactures" of the southern tribespeople. Jones used the contents of this cabinet—"relics" and assorted old papers—to construct his history of Native Americans in the South.[1] In the following five chapters, many of the same objects that found their way into Jones's "cabinet"—pipes, plats and surveys of mounds, maps, honorific titles of address inscribed on treaty documents or recorded in council books—have again been taken down from the felt-lined shelf and, one by one, carefully reexamined. Understood not only as artifacts but also as evidence of perishable historical events, they provide a new perspective on interaction between people and peoples during a specific time in the colonial Southeast. Each reminds us of the complicated psychological scalings, from personal meetings to public rituals, that general labels such as "culture contact" can often conceal. The maps drawn in the clear hand of Chickasaw graphic style; the "earth-dwelling" mounds; and the gender-based grammar of formal diplomatic greeting between the French and the southern tribes all provide glimpses of the elusive connection between symbol and life in the colonial Southeast.

What was understood between natives and colonists through exchanged information—whether for mutual gain or for the darker, one-sided goals of commercial or political advantage—was just as easily misunderstood or even manipulated. Patricia Galloway suggests that the French learned just enough about Choctaw kinship to be counterproductive in the very negotiations they had hoped to sway through alternating expressions of familiarity and power. Choosing to present themselves metaphorically as the fathers of the tribe, the French were received as such by the Choctaws, who "proceeded to treat them as their matrilineal society taught them they should: as kind, indulgent nonrelatives who had no authority over them." In Choctaw society the French would have commanded more real respect—or at least en-

gendered less damaging confusion—by taking on the identity of true Choctaw authority figures, such as uncles on the mother's side.[2] Galloway's essay
suggests the importance of understanding not only what was said at councils but also the unintended "non-verbal leakage"—the gestures and glances
that accompany all human communication. Further, Galloway reminds us
that kinship and gender must be seen as structures of social organization
and also as critical variables in negotiation and other political affairs usually regarded as the domain of Euro-American-style male authority.[3]

Indigenous diplomacy employed the calumet ceremony, part of a ritual
of greeting, to enable individuals from different societies—such as French
officials—to become fictional kin, thereby creating a social basis for negotiation and trade. Ian Brown, in an essay new to this collection, traces the
prehistoric origins of this custom through the numerous archaeological finds
of the red stone bowls of the calumet pipe. The earliest French to reach the
midcontinent, in the late seventeenth century, found calumet ceremonialism
to be rich in symbolism, representing a "laying down of arms" and a symbolic "armor" that protected travelers in a hostile landscape. Peacemaking
has received less attention than war making in the histories, and Brown's
work, about creative rather than destructive energy, ultimately points toward the fragility of the former.[4] However useful the calumet was to the
never numerous French during encounters with potential enemies, their en-
thusiastic embrace of this Native American ceremony quickly dissipated its
symbolic power. Abuse of the ceremony by duplicitous French officials, and
efforts by French colonists to mass-produce the pipes soon undermined the
ritual's sacred character, transforming it "from an inviolable contract to a
formulaic ritual of little real consequence."

While knowledgeable spiritual leaders might, on occasion, address European inquisitiveness about the calumet ceremony and other native beliefs, questions sometimes were not asked or not answered for a reason. For
instance, no evidence of the long residence of the southeastern tribes was
more substantial than the "mounds" scattered across the region. It was convenient for whites interested in undermining native claims of ancient residence in the land to ask tribespeople two questions about them: Did you
build them? Do you know who did? The answer was usually negative on
both counts; possibly for reasons of privacy, politeness, or hostility, tribespeople predictably ended the conversations at this point.

The conclusion the first gentlemen-archaeologists of the nineteenth century provided for themselves was that the original mound-builders—and with them the secrets of the mounds themselves—were long dead and gone, and that the mound-builders had no genetic connection to the tribes that populated the young United States. This interpretation was truer to ideology than to archaeology, and was directly contradicted by indigenous tradition. If the props could be knocked from under contemporary Native Americans' claims to ancient ancestry, their rights to an inheritance of land encompassing the southeastern interior could be weakened and their territories opened to legal "taking." The argument for an extinct American mound-building civilization also conveniently gave scholars, self-conscious about the supposed immaturity of North American culture, something to use in countering the claims to priority of European writers (who were beginning to brag on the great age and importance of Old World creations such as the pyramids). The mound-builder myth persists in the popular mind, and reflects lingering anxieties about Indian "claims" to the land. Archaeologists, however, long ago decided that the mound-builders were not a vanished "race" at all, but the real ancestors of the indigenous southeastern peoples the colonists encountered.[5]

Just as the mound-builders live on in this sense, Vernon J. Knight Jr., suggests that mounds have survived into our time as sacred spaces of Amerindian culture.[6] The reality was in the image—not in the piled dirt—and the image was with the people, a way of seeing that could be protected like a mental "ark of the covenant" and deployed wherever tribal people found themselves. Knight's contention that mound-making represents an unbroken southeastern cultural tradition enduring at least one thousand years will be startling, especially for readers accustomed to thinking of eastern Amerindian cultures as scattered and cut off from their roots. It will, however, be much less so to current practitioners of Native American religion. Inquiring into the survival of the mound image in the Southeast suggests what many tribal people can verify, that these roots remain both strong and deep. Knight's discussion of mound metaphors allows us to begin to bridge the gap separating "prehistoric" transcontinental movements of peoples, ideas, and artistic designs and the life of the colonial—and the present—indigenous Southeast.[7]

The Indian maps made in the colonial Southeast represent a vast summation of meetings and exchanges of information, both intertribal and intercolonial, between far-flung villages and the coastal enclaves of European power. Although some of the maps Greg Waselkov discusses have a distinctive personal content or style (notably the sad disorientation in the autobiographical map drawn by the refugee called Lamhatty), most reflect sharply delineated lines of diplomacy, trade, and alliance. A few are drawn in a "realistic" style as charts of rivers and roads and must have been immediately understandable to the colonial authorities who requested them. Another more stylized group of maps, employing the indigenous circle-mapping style, must have seemed very foreign to the colonials, who augmented them with explanatory legends and notes. In fact, these maps were shipped home to England not only in diplomatic pouches but also in boxes of "curiosities" designed to strike royal patrons' fancy for American exotica.

More than simply cartographic illustrations of the political protocol of the indigenous Southeast, these diverse maps have an energy, an elegance of design, and a language of their own. The coexistence of both "realistic" and "metaphorical" maps produced during the same period suggests that their makers were fluent in two mapping languages and testifies to the diverse regional pathways of communication. The double mapping styles of the colonial-period tribespeople corresponded to the multilingual abilities of native Southeasterners, many of whom included in their linguistic repertory Mobilian, the commercial lingua franca of the lower South. Learning to read maps like these brings home the necessity of becoming literate in the vibrant verbal and nonverbal languages of the Southeast, with their rich symbols and intercultural inflections.

Alongside the "arts and manufactures" lining Charles Colcock Jones's "cabinet" were two human skulls, dug from a "tumulus" or mound near Macon, examples of the casual dehumanizing racism of a time (sadly, not long past) that converted body parts into collectible curiosities.[8] In our concluding chapter, written for this revised edition of *Powhatan's Mantle*, Claudio Saunt documents how the ideology of race, as it developed in the antebellum South, reshaped southeastern Indian communities. By tracing the marriages and inheritances of the Grayson family, from the Creek town of Hilabi, Saunt reveals the increasing intolerance of interracial relationships, and a growing acceptance of a hierarchy of race, by Creek society. His study carries our book beyond the American Revolution, generally considered the end of the colonial era, and on to the period of Indian Removal in the 1830s. As he effectively argues, early federal efforts to impose a "plan of civilization" on southeastern Indians, dismantle their governments, and then forcibly relocate them west of the Mississippi were all acts of a U.S. colonizing policy.[9]

Each of the following essays will inspire questions for which there is increasing interest and audience. After all, some of the oldest and seemingly best-known questions remain the best questions, because the search for the answer is more important than the answer itself. This point is forcefully made throughout the following chapters, where the authors help us see familiar archaeological artifacts and historical documents in an unexpected light and tell their stories in new ways. With these new perspectives on the symbolic life of the southeastern tribes, we can understand the impatience of James Adair when he scorned the European council translators of the eighteenth century, for whom the "golden trophes and figures" of the tribal "talks" were more than "illiterate interpreters can well comprehend, or explain."[10] In the following chapters we are fortunate to be led by able guides and interpreters further down the path of knowledge that some among each generation have followed since the first encounter between colonists and tribespeople in the Southeast.

Notes

1. Charles Colcock Jones Jr., *Antiquities of the Southern Indians, Particularly of the Georgia Tribes* (New York: Appleton, 1873), iv; also in facsimile edition, introduced by Frank T. Schnell Jr. (Tuscaloosa: University of Alabama Press, 1999). Stephen Williams offers modern readers an introduction to the scientific, speculative, and, in some cases, outright fraudulent nineteenth-century students of America's prehistory in *Fantastic Archaeology: The Wild Side of North American Prehistory* (Philadelphia: University of Pennsylvania Press, 1991).

2. For case studies of kinship and gender issues in colonization outside the South, see Mona Etienne and Eleanor Leacock, *Women and Colonization: Anthropological Perspectives* (New York: Praeger, 1980). Many excellent new histories take women's roles seriously, as more than "inclusion." See Nancy Shoemaker, ed., *Negotiators of Change: Historical Perspectives on Native American Women* (New York: Routledge, 1995) for several case studies. Theda Perdue, *Cherokee Women: Gender and Culture Change, 1700–1835* (Lincoln: University of Nebraska Press, 1998) offers the reflections of one historian after many years of research.

3. For a modern reanalysis of southeastern Native American kinship, see Greg Urban and Jason Baird Jackson, "Social Organization," in *Handbook of North American Indians*, vol. 14, *Southeast*, ed. Raymond D. Fogelson (Washington DC: Smithsonian Institution, 2004), 697–706.

4. A new global literature on conflict resolution includes Robert A. Williams Jr., *Linking Arms Together: American Indian Treaty Visions of Law and Peace, 1600–1800* (Oxford: Oxford University Press, 1997); John T. Juricek, ed., *Early American Indian Documents: Treaties and Laws, 1607–1789*, vol. 11, *Georgia Treaties, 1733–1763* (Washington DC: University Publications of America, 1989) and vol. 12, *Georgia and Florida Treaties, 1763–1776* (Washington DC: University Publications of America, 2002).

5. An early study is Cyrus Thomas, "Report on the Mound Explorations of the Bureau of Ethnology," in *Twelfth Annual Report of the Bureau of Ethnology* (Washington DC: Government Printing Office, 1894). Also see two companion volumes by Robert Silverberg, *The Mound Builders of Ancient America: The Archaeology of a Myth* and *The Mound Builders* (New York: New York Graphic Society, 1968; reprint, Athens: Ohio University Press, 1986). See also Roger G. Kennedy's *Hidden Cities: The Discovery and Loss of Ancient American Civilization* (New York: Free Press, 1994).

6. Studies in anthropology and in popular culture increasingly influence research in history. Influential popular works include Edwin Bernbaum, *Sacred Mountains* (Berkeley: University of California Press, 1997). A regional example includes David Lewis Jr. and Ann T. Jordan, *Creek Indian Medicine Ways: The Enduring Power of Mvskoke Religion* (Albuquerque: University of New Mexico Press, 2002). I appreciate the assistance of religious historian Carrie McLachlan in navigating this burgeoning literature. For the legal and political dimensions of sacred place, see Andrew Gulliford, *Sacred Objects and Sacred Places* (Boulder: University Press of Colorado, 2000).

7. For a controversial discussion of ancient Amerindian artistic origins and affinities see Terence Grieder, *Origins of Pre-Columbian Art* (Austin: University of Texas Press, 1982).

8. Jones, *Antiquities of the Southern Indians*, 160–61, pl. IV-A.

9. Similar sentiments have been expressed by Susan A. Miller, *Coacoochee's Bones: A Seminole Saga* (Lawrence: University Press of Kansas, 2003), xii–xiii.

10. Samuel Cole Williams, ed., *Adair's History of the American Indians* (1775; 1930 ed.; reprint, New York: Promontory Press, 1974), 55. The most recent edition is James Adair, *The History of the American Indians*, ed. Kathryn E. Holland Braund (Tuscaloosa: University of Alabama Press, 2005).

"The Chief Who Is Your Father"

Choctaw and French Views of the Diplomatic Relation

PATRICIA GALLOWAY

When anthropologists set out to study a culture-contact situation, the first thing they look for is evidence of acculturation. When the object of historical study is the contact of Europeans with Native Americans, this is also the case, but all too seldom do scholars make any effort to treat both sides equally in the analysis: they apply the methods of anthropology to the Native Americans, the methods of history to the Europeans. As a result, the original inhabitants of the continent are seen as victims rather than as active agents in this drama, and the extended European state becomes the fixed formal stage upon which the natives writhe in the throes of their tribal passions.[1]

For the colonial period, reconstructing the meaning and function of Indian social institutions will always remain more difficult than describing comparable institutions among the Europeans who dealt with the Indians. It is fortunate that at least we can understand the European institutions, for the Indians were certainly acting upon their own view of them, and to understand how Indian institutions responded to contact with Europeans it is indispensable that we discover what the Indians sought to achieve through their response. If the French were clearly attempting to manipulate Choctaw power brokers, the Choctaws were certainly trying to return the favor.

I shall propose a thesis that explores both sides of the diplomatic interface in the same way: Indian as seen by European and European as seen by Indian. I shall argue that in the diplomatic relations between the Choctaws and the French in the eighteenth century, the French colonial governors, conditioned by their own patrilineally biased society and ignoring a Choctaw institution that would have offered them more authority, adopted the metaphorical position of "father" to the Choctaws, and the Choctaws then proceeded to treat them as their matrilineal society taught them they should: as kind, indulgent nonrelatives who had no authority over them. The governors, well aware that the Choctaws could represent a formidable enemy at their gates, were forced to play this role until the end of their regime.

This is a very simple thesis, so simple that at first glance it may seem frivolous. Inevitably, too, less than perfect evidence and a confusion in levels of discourse hamper any effort to document its validity. To make sense of the thesis it will be necessary to reconstruct what each group thought of the other's institutions and, behind that, the reality of the institutions themselves.

Before arguing that the Indians used a certain kinship mechanism for diplomacy, I must show that it is valid to see the external diplomacy of certain ethnic groups having matrilineal descent and tribal social organization as a metaphor for how lineages dealt with one another within that group. Since the example here is a major southern tribe, I shall draw mainly upon what is known of the southeastern Indians to establish this point.

Like most of the southeastern tribes, the Choctaws at contact reckoned kinship matrilineally. John R. Swanton established in his 1931 study that matrilineal descent groups and exogamous moieties made up Choctaw social structure.[2] Fred Eggan then proposed that the Choctaw system of matrilineal descent had reflected the pure Crow pattern before European contact, and Alexander Spoehr carried out work that demonstrated Eggan's thesis.[3]

Within a matriliny the roles of the men must be clearly defined if the group is to maintain stability.[4] The brothers of the women of the lineage hold authority over household and lineage activities and children. They are charged with managing the property of the householders, their sisters, and with assuring the continuity of lineage holdings by approving and arranging marriages for its women. They also maintain the traditions and customs of the tribe as a whole by taking charge of the education of their sisters' sons. And the role of primary authority in the lineage, held by the oldest male, passes regularly to his eldest sister's eldest son rather than to his own, who belongs to a different lineage. This whole complex of patterns granting certain kinds of authority to the maternal uncles of a matriliny is designated by the anthropological term "avunculate," and it constitutes one of the distinctive features of matrilineal societies.

The in-marrying men in this picture, the husbands of the women of the lineage, cannot develop relationships of authority within the lineage without creating unacceptable tensions; besides, as their own sisters' brothers, they enjoy an opportunity to exercise authority within their own lineage. Their role in the conjugal family, then, gives them the opportunity to display affection without authority toward their own children, and they are looked upon by those children as the indulgent parent. Because they also have no important educational responsibilities, the children are not obliged to pay any particular attention to them when it comes to advice about proper conduct within their society. That this role remained extremely well established among the Choctaws was forcefully demonstrated during the nineteenth century when, in an effort to conform to white conventions, the Choctaws enacted legal sanctions against fathers for not supporting their families or serving as the authority figures in them.[5]

Spoehr has noted that an elder male of a lineage might have the same authority over the activities of the lineage as the mother's brother does over her children.[6] This idea can be very fruitful, especially when examined more closely in terms of the structural pose of a sociopolitical system for diplomacy.[7] Gearing has described how the Cherokees arranged themselves for the four main functions of their lives: food procurement, dealing with death and other serious events of life, making corporate political decisions, and making war; the Choctaws ordered their society in much the same ways.[8] Although the structural pose for war sometimes arrogated to itself de facto the conduct of extratribal relations, generally speaking the appropriate mechanism for dealing with such matters throughout the Southeast was the council structure, where mature deliberation was the governing principle in making corporate decisions.

Demonstrating that the heads of the council served as a sort of corporate avunculate for the group they led is not easy, nor would Gearing consider the concept of a council exercising authority at all as valid for the Cherokees, but I believe it can be argued for the post-contact Muskogean groups. In Creek society, for example, the senior male of each matrilineal clan was known as the "clan uncle," and he represented the clan in council and enjoyed great authority in the lineage itself.[9] We can test the validity of an extension of this concept by simply comparing the functions served by the council for the whole group and by the senior male for the lineage. The council was entrusted with weighty matters like the food supply, justice, and negotiation or war with external entities. The senior male of a lineage was supposed to organize the lineage for farming and procuring game, to ensure the defense of a member of the lineage who had behaved unlawfully, and to lead the lineage in pursuing revenge when a member had been killed. At both levels the bearer of responsibility had to display conduct that was wise, deliberative, and authoritative.

It is a bit easier to establish that an extratribal entity was treated by the tribe or tribal subgroup as the lineage treated another lineage. Much has been written about one of the major tools of southeastern Indian diplomacy, the calumet ceremony. Whatever its origin, Donald Blakeslee has argued effectively that it was in use in the Southeast well before the coming of any Europeans; hence, it was a working instrument for intertribal diplomacy that the Europeans encountered and were forced to act as though they accepted—thus accepting by implication the connotations of the ceremony.[10] Apparently the most frequent aboriginal use of the calumet ceremony was cementing trade alliances, but specific evidence shows that among the Chickasaws and the Choctaws the ceremony had been further elaborated to encompass diplomatic alliances through the adoption of a leading man among the potential allies.[11] I want to suggest that this institution was the vehicle through which intertribal diplomatic alliances operated in terms of social structure: the ally nation was "adopted" as a fictive lineage within the tribe. This phenomenon will be discussed in more detail after the development of additional evidence.

The foregoing description of social institutions for diplomacy applies to a society that had already altered considerably from its precontact state. By the early eighteenth century the Muskogean Indians of the Southeast had been adjusting for two hundred years to the new reality of European presence. All over the Southeast the late prehistoric hierarchical chiefdoms that had built towns and ceremonial centers on the bounty of floodplain agriculture had been severely shaken and almost universally shattered by the impact of European diseases during the sixteenth century.[12] In the course of the seventeenth century they mostly reorganized as the "tribes" we know: shifting and resilient groupings of locally autonomous villages, any one of which could stand on its own for subsistence and social requirements, each possessing its local "big man" or chief. In this restructured Indian world, authoritarian institutions had been smashed and abandoned. Instead, kinship and hospitality were the operative forces, blood vengeance the negative sanction.

The French came into contact with the Choctaws for the first time in 1699/1700, when Pierre Le Moyne d'Iberville led the first expeditions to establish a colonial beachhead on the Gulf coast. From the start, as had been the case in all their dealings with Native American tribes, the French presented themselves as "father" to the Choctaws, expecting to play a role toward them analogous to their own notion of a *père de famille*. This notion was of course rooted in the patrilineal traditions of the French, and it is obvious that they expected the analogy to be played out in just this way—they extended it by referring to the Indians as their children.[13] French cultural arrogance precluded any astonishment that the Choctaws should apparently accept this role without objection, and that they did so probably reinforced the French conviction of its suitability. The Choctaws and other Native Americans, of course, were not offended by such an approach, since they were accustomed to conduct diplomacy in terms of fictive kinship. But they must have wondered why the French leaders chose to present themselves as in-marrying affine rather than as mother's brother.

How then must French institutions have looked to the Choctaws? Historians have made a profession of contrasting the authoritarian French regime and its transplanted institutions with the more egalitarian behavior of the English shopkeepers, but they have overlooked the fact that inevitably the perfect scheme of administration planned in France would be altered by local conditions.[14] In isolated Louisiana, which France treated as a stepchild anyway, circumstances reduced the colony's official policies to little more than the strengths and inclinations of its leading personalities, much as the ubiquitous insects and fungus reduced government buildings to the most durable of their constituent materials.

The organization of the Louisiana colony was meant to be the basically authoritarian one of the French military. The general scheme, even under the monopolies of Crozat, Law, and the Company of the Indies, consisted of a governor with authority over the military personnel and in charge of implementing the colony's Indian policy, assisted by a commissary or finance officer who administered funds and supplies of matériel and merchandise. Between them, the governor and commissary were to share in the "general police" of the colony—to see that order was kept and justice done. After 1712 the governor and commissary were assisted in legal administration by the Superior Council, which became the colony's highest court.[15]

What the Indians saw, however, was not this ideal administrative structure, which was incomplete at the colony's earliest shaky beginnings and
which in any case was vitiated by quarrels between the governor and commissary. Instead, they observed something more familiar and understandable: that the real armature of the Louisiana colony for most of its history
was a family, the Le Moynes. The personal self-interest of this band of brothers generally appeared to coincide with the needs of the colony in its early
years, and they controlled it through de facto domination of the governorship even when someone else actually held the position. Le Moyne tenure
of this leading role was so constant over the first twenty years of the colony's
history that it must have been influential in shaping the Choctaw concept
of the function of the governor in the French colony. And fate had it that
the most important of those brothers, Bienville, not only took the trouble
to learn at least some Choctaw but also had no children of his own and exercised influence through his sisters' sons.[16]

The Choctaws thus saw a small tribe, numbering in the hundreds at first
and never larger than several thousand, a fraction of Choctaw numbers. This
tribe claimed to owe allegiance to a "great chief" in the Big Village across
the water, but in Louisiana itself it was led by a war chief, the governor who
controlled the troops, and a peace chief, the commissary general who controlled the goods in the warehouses. These two chiefs often quarreled instead of alternating their authority according to consensus, and although
they eventually acquired a council to help them, they even quarreled with
this council on occasion. The war chief exercised an astonishing life-and-
death authority over his warriors, and since he generally held the balance
of power, this small tribe seemed always to be on a war footing. Yet neither
he nor the peace chief seemed to have great influence over the councils of
the great chief in France and his supplies of merchandise. Impressive as the
prestige goods offered by the French might seem, they were nearly always in
short supply, and the fine quality of the most desirable of them—guns and
ammunition—emphasized the warlike nature of the French tribe.

Just as the Europeans failed to notice the systemic implications of what
they perceived as the anomalous institution of matriliny, so too the Choctaws apparently failed to grasp fully the patricentric bias of the French social fabric. How were they to realize that the meaning of "father" to the
French might differ from their own concept? They met in their villages

only the missionary, who was strangely wedded to his gods; the trader and interpreter, who were more interested in complying with Indian ways than in imposing their own; the officer and soldier, who had a strong interest in Choctaw women and proved appallingly reckless in battle. So far as is known, no Choctaw lived permanently among the French, so no Choctaw saw the full range of commercial or domestic life in the settlements; what they knew of French villages was learned through participation in the annual celebration of alliance at the present giving, with its fine speeches, ceremonies, feasts, and opportunities for trading. The vivid presence of Bienville and his brothers and their sisters' sons, which so powerfully dominated these annual events, must have scotched any Indian suspicion that Frenchmen behaved strangely toward their sons.

These two sets of attitudes and social conventions interacted in diplomacy. Swanton quotes a French description of the Choctaw structural pose for council that gives a basic sketch of the sort of corporate entity the French thought they had to deal with:

> In each village, besides the chief and the war chief, there are two Tascamingoutchy ["made a war chief"] who are like lieutenants of the war chief, and a Tichou-mingo ["assistant chief"] who is like a major. It is he who arranges for all of the ceremonies, the feasts, and the dances. He acts as speaker for the chief, and oversees the warriors and strangers when they smoke. The Tichou-mingo usually become village chiefs. They (the people) are divided into four orders, as follows. [The first are] the head chiefs, village chief, and war chief; the second are the Atacoulitoupa [Hatak-holitopa] or beloved men (hommes de valleur); the third is composed of those whom they call simply tasca or warriors; the fourth and last is atac emittla [hatak imatahali?]. They are those who have not struck blows or who have killed only a woman or a child.[17]

This account mixes several levels of analysis from my point of view. The first part of it deals with the structure of the top levels of village council, biased toward the structural pose for war, while the second describes somewhat incompletely a sorting of the entire population of the group in full council, omitting the women. There seems to be no sense of the several levels of organization, which were lineage, village, and division, and how these levels might have been related through kinship mechanisms. By examining this question we can attempt to establish how the metaphorical avunculate of the Choctaw council functioned in external diplomacy.

Within the lineage, as has been seen, the senior man or men bore the responsibility of authority. We do not know how village headmen or chiefs were chosen, but from accounts of village government we may assume that one of the requirements was the "moral virtuosity" that Gearing describes for the Cherokees.[18] The witness cited above suggests there was some sort of established succession in the village; perhaps the chief chose his *tichoumingo* as a potential successor, and if so there is some evidence that he chose him from his own lineage.[19] It is also clear that the chief and his council were most often older men—the French regularly describe village chiefs as such; many are shown as almost feeble.[20]

The three divisions in the Choctaw nation as encountered by the French—Eastern, Western, and Sixtowns—were very real. Swanton has brought forward evidence that the Sixtowns or Southern division was a different ethnic group; even a century later they spoke a different dialect and wore their ornaments in a distinctively different way.[21] Archaeological evidence suggests that the Eastern and Western divisions may also have represented different ethnic backgrounds.[22] In any case, as *political* divisions they not only were present in 1700 but also were still present and exerting political influence after Removal a century and a half later.[23]

The divisions had already become truly political entities by the time of permanent contact in the late seventeenth century. Although village membership in a division might shift over time, the divisions held steadily to certain territorial loci, based as they were on landholding of a kind by kinship groups.[24] How they were governed is also described in the first part of the passage just quoted; they had a chief who had his functionaries and a council of older men, just as the villages did. The division chief was usually, if not always, a village chief also, and it seems that his functionaries remained the same at both levels.[25] On the division level of the council, however, it is likely that other village chiefs and older men representing lineages filled the places. Full council, as it met for annual ceremonies and other events of moment, such as the conduct of diplomacy, would consist of the entire population of the division, classed as described in the second part of the description in the quote but including women. The office of chief of the whole

nation was a late introduction fostered by the French, and the division remained the operative unit of Choctaw "national" politics.[26]

The French records give little information about Choctaw councils, because except for the traders, whose voices are only rarely heard in the documents, the French were apparently never in the villages (or welcome in the
villages, or in the right village) when such gatherings took place. Possibly,
in a vain search for something like a national council, the senior French
leaders simply overlooked village or divisional ones. There is thus no direct documented observation of a Choctaw council, although there are accounts by Frenchmen who were kept at a distance and given reports of the
progress of a council.[27] From this limited evidence I can say with some assurance that the council strove for consensus and that those who disrupted
it were disapproved of; that everyone present at the council had a chance to
speak; and that the division council made decisions of peace and war, which
were then supposed to be carried out by the chosen war chief.[28] The practice with regard to embassies is less clear, but although we have only secondhand information about embassies to other tribes, there is ample opportunity to observe the embassies sent to treat with the French.

The Choctaws seem to have employed something very like an abbreviated council structure for the direct conduct of diplomatic relations with the
French at the beginning. When Henri de Tonti traveled among the Choctaws and Chickasaws to request their participation in an alliance in 1702,
the Choctaws, after having had several days to consider the matter, sent to
Mobile not one man, but a party consisting of three men and two women.
Tonti's letters suggest strongly that the three men represented the three divisions of the Choctaw nation.[29] As the relationship between the French and
the Choctaws developed, it became the practice for the Choctaws to travel
to Mobile every year to give and collect presents and to trade deerskins. In
this activity the Choctaws seemed to attend by division, sending at a minimum chiefs, officials, and honored men, so that the meetings often took a
month or more, a fact the French governors bitterly lamented.[30] Thus the
Choctaws conducted external diplomacy using in some way all of the persons who made up the council or corporate avunculate. To investigate further the actual conduct of this diplomacy, we must now turn to the details
of diplomatic interaction.

In testing the hypothesis that the Choctaws actually did take the French at their word and treat them as fathers, the overt use of kinship terminology is highly relevant, since, as has been shown, the Choctaws did consciously use the kinship metaphor in diplomacy. There are five terms that appear consistently in the reports of French and Indian speeches: father, child, brother, elder brother, younger brother; and these terms fall into two groups, father-child and brother. I shall examine usages by both of the interacting groups to attempt to determine two things: how the Choctaws applied kinship terms to the French, since we think we understand what the Choctaws meant by them; and how the Choctaws perceived the French as applying kinship terms to them.

French usages are most frequently represented in the written record; the men who wrote the documents were fond of recording their own eloquence. There is no guarantee that what we read is precisely what the Indians heard, but for present purposes we will assume it is. For the Choctaw usages, we are at the mercy of the interpreters, but again we will assume that what we read is what was stated and simply hope in both cases that the aggregate of examples in the sample will correct for error. It will also be necessary to quote examples at some length, since we need to look not only at the use of the words themselves but also at the implications attached to that use.

"Father" and "child," of course, were used by both sides in their transactions to refer to the relationship the French had specified from the beginning, with the "father" term referring to the governor of the colony and the "child" being the Indians. French usages strongly stressed love and kindliness between father and child—precisely what the Choctaws would expect. A speech on behalf of Governor Périer, regarding a promised redress of Choctaw grievances about poor treatment from French traders and delivered by Régis du Roullet in 1729, exemplifies this theme: "You know that the Great Chief is your father and that he carries you all in his heart, that he seeks nothing else than to enrich you and to make you happy and content. . . . Ah! the heart of the Great Chief is deeply grieved. He is greatly pained to think that the French of whom he is the master treat you so ill, you who are his children and his friends."[31] In 1744 Governor Vaudreuil reported a speech of a similar tenor that he gave to the Choctaws at the time of the presents in nominally asking their consent to conclude a Chickasaw peace: "As the Choctaws in these latest wars had acted in concert with us and had always conducted themselves not only as faithful allies but even as children who were extremely attached and perfectly devoted to the Great Chief of the French, their father, I was unwilling to conclude anything without their consent."[32]

More generally, however, the French use of the term was in a context in which the father-child relationship implied the child's obligation to perform requested actions. In presenting the conditions of peace to the Chickasaws in 1744, the interpreter/trader Renochon, representing Vaudreuil, told them "that the great chief of the French, their father, was granting them gladly the peace . . . if they would carry out the conditions . . . that then he would regard them as his children."[33] When Beauchamp went among the Choctaw villages in 1746 to demand retribution for the murder of three Frenchmen, he constantly stressed that he was bringing "the word of M. de Vaudreuil their father"; in reproving the Choctaws for failing to go to war with the Chickasaws as they had promised, he said, "Instead of keeping the word that they had given their father, most of them fell asleep in their cabins."[34] Finally, Governor Kerlérec combined the tenderness theme with that of obligation when he told the Choctaws: "as long as they behaved well, they would always find a father's heart in the Great Chief of all the French."[35]

By contrast, the Choctaws referred to the French "father" exclusively in terms of love and kindness; there is rarely even mention of obligation on the part of the "children." In complaining to their missionary, Father Baudouin, of the haughtiness and cruelty of Governor Périer's minion Régis du Roullet as keeper of the Yowani post warehouse, they expressed their hope of the return of a governor like Bienville: "Frenchmen will come at once who will have the pity of a father for them and whose experience and courage will obtain for them a peace like the one that they enjoyed several years ago."[36] Upon Bienville's return in 1732, he wrote to Maurepas of one of many expressions of confidence from the Choctaws referring to his having armed them in the early days of the colony: "they must regard me as their father since I had set them free of slavery to the English."[37] When Vaudreuil met with Choctaw chiefs to discuss ways of ending the Choctaw civil war in 1749, "Alibamon Mingo addressed all the Choctaws and told them that I had just spoken to them like a father touched by the misfortunes of their nation."[38]

When Kerlérec arrived in the colony to take up the governorship in 1754, the Choctaws made a great thing of adopting him: "Before their departure from the different villages they held general assemblies where it was agreed they would give me the Choctaw names Youlakty Mataha Tchito, anké achoukema, which in our language means King of the Choctaws and greatest of the race of the Youlakta, which is the finest and the oldest; all this ends with anké achoukema, which means a very good father."[39] After this ceremony, Kerlérec proceeded with his plans to weld a southern alliance by trying to persuade the Choctaws to keep peace with the Alabamas, Tallapoosas, and Abihkas, French allies among the Upper Creeks:

> *Since they had adopted me as their father, they ought to listen to my word and my will, which was to see the roads white between the Alabamas and them; that the former having been for a long time our allies and our friends, I ought to regard them likewise as my children, and do everything I could to reestablish tranquillity among them for that reason. . . . The oldest medal chief began to speak, and said to me: "We see clearly, my father, that you love your children, that you are a good father who ought to be listened to . . . henceforth we place our vengeance beneath your feet that you may trample it deeply into the sand."*[40]

There is a rather strange incident in the record that illustrates quite clearly a French failure to understand Choctaw kinship obligation concepts and Choctaw rejection of French assumptions, which I cite here because it makes an idiosyncratic use of the "father" terminology. In 1734 Diron d'Artaguette, commandant at Mobile, went among the Choctaws to dissuade them from trading with the English. In what he apparently thought was a stroke of cleverness, he claimed to have been compelled to see them by a dream: "As I was at home sleeping very soundly I felt a hand pulling me by the foot. I awoke with a start. It was the spirit of your fathers who spoke to me as follows: 'As you are the father of the Choctaws, as you have a good heart for them, and as we see them on the point of falling over a precipice . . . we . . . tell you to go and dissuade them.'"[41] This obviously did not cut much ice with his interlocutors; according to Bienville's report one of the important chiefs remarked drily: "I have neither dreamed nor seen the spirits."[42]

In contrast to "father-child" references, the French made very little use of the "brother" terminology. When they did so, it seemed to be modeled upon the Indian usage, as when Régis du Roullet reproved the Choctaw Red Shoe: "If he wished that hereafter I should regard him as my brother, he ought to tell his warriors to have no dealings with the Chickasaws."[43] The Choctaws, on the other hand, used this terminology often to refer to their relationship with Frenchmen other than the governor. For example, Régis also reported the speech of the man recognized by the French as great chief of the Choctaw nation, who referred to Diron d'Artaguette as "my brother, Mr. Diron, chief of Mobile, who gave me a medal and a big letter of consideration."[44]

After the Natchez massacre of their French garrison in 1729, a Choctaw told Périer, "I am very sorry about the death of our brothers." When told that it was suspected that the Choctaws were part of the conspiracy, the man said he could not believe that, "because of the friendship that we have for our brothers the French."[45] In one instance the "brother" term was further specified. The chief of the Cushtushas, in supporting arguments of Lusser in a Choctaw council in 1730, said "he considered the Frenchman whom he had with him as his elder brother."[46] This term was not unknown in intertribal diplomacy; the Choctaws and the Chickasaws considered the Alabamas a kindred senior to their own, and the Alabamas in one instance referred to their relationship with the Chickasaws as one to younger brothers.[47] Taken in aggregate, these references display a degree of consistency that suggests that the referents of the terms being used were sufficiently similar in the minds of both parties to have been viable and communicative terms for their relationship. But what did these terms mean to the communicating parties? The most revealing contexts for investigating their meaning are those in which the terms are juxtaposed.

The first example, a speech delivered in the presence of Bienville and Diron d'Artaguette by the Choctaw great chief after the present giving in 1736, made a distinction between father and brother on the basis of relative authority: "'Bad messages have often been brought us in which I have placed no faith, and I shall listen only to those that come from you [Bienville], my father. And you, my brother,' he added, speaking to M. Diron, 'I exhort to be more circumspect in the future than you have been, because since you are a chief your words and your actions have more weight than

those of a private person."[48] The chief speaking obviously considered himself a peer of his "brother," whatever his standing vis-à-vis his "father" may
have been.

The Indians of Louisiana were quite aware of the career of Vaudreuil
and his father in Canada before he arrived as governor of Louisiana, and
they were especially impressed with his influence on the ferocious northern Indians. The Chickasaws, proposing to exchange French hostages for
peace, greeted him with a notice of that fact: "All the red men of the North
are your children," they reminded Vaudreuil. "If you wish to regard us as
your children, listen to our word. . . . We love your Frenchmen. We regard
them as our brothers."[49]

Finally, there is a very clear indication of how the kinship terms so far
examined fit into the model of adoption of allies as a fictive tribal lineage.
Indian allies of the French, asked to capture French deserters from the wilderness posts and return them to the French, invariably did so on condition
they not be punished. One such instance in the 1750s involved the Choctaws. Alibamon Mingo's plea for pardon for deserters combines all the kinship terms I have discussed:

> I know well . . . that these Frenchmen have done wrong, but that
> will show the red men so much the more clearly that M. de Vau-
> dreuil, their father, has consideration for their requests. He can easily
> imagine the infinite pain that it would give the Choctaws to see shed
> the blood of people who every day bring them the things they need,
> and that with great difficulty. Furthermore are not these French-
> men, so to speak, our brothers; do we not dwell, as it were, in the
> same cabin? I hope therefore that the great chief of the French will
> not refuse his children the favor that they ask of him.[50]

Not only was it the chiefs lately allied with the French in the Choctaw civil
war who asked for this pardon, but they also accompanied their request with
a present of five deerskins, which another chief described as "a white sign for
us, which shows that the blood of these Frenchmen must not be shed inasmuch as it would be the Choctaw nation that would be the cause of their
death."[51] Thus it seems clear that the Choctaws took this fictive kinship of
alliance seriously. But there may be something even more interesting here.
In this example the Choctaws seem to be trying to avoid the blood guilt of

responsibility for a death. Such blood guilt was a problem, however, only when a member of *another* lineage was killed; it would not be incurred by the death of a sibling; hence, it is just possible that this example indicates that the French "brothers" of the Choctaws were considered classificatory brothers rather than sons of the same father.[52]

How do these usages correspond with kinship terminology among the Choctaws? First there is the caveat that in trying to examine kinship terminology of the Choctaws in the eighteenth century we are trying to hit a moving target: as Eggan proposed and Spoehr tried to prove, the Choctaws were on their way from a prehistoric/early historic Crow pattern to another form under acculturative pressure, and all the variations in this trajectory could be seen in the different Muskogean tribes of the Southeast.[53] Yet the kinship data gathered by researchers, from whatever period, agree very clearly that the only people a man might term his brothers were the sons of his father and those of his father's sister's daughter (see fig. 1).[54] This is the key to the proof of the thesis I am arguing. In no case were any of the descendants of the maternal uncle referred to as "brother," even in "aberrant" schedules. In other words, kin and non-kin were separated terminologically, and a "brother" could fall on the side of the father, as non-kin. Hence the Choctaws, in referring to the governor as their father and his men as their brothers, did intend that these kinship terms be taken to mean what they meant in Choctaw culture.

If this is true, then it is necessary to examine Choctaw-French diplomatic relations in a new light. With the foregoing evidence in mind, it is now time to return to the institution the Choctaws used to establish external alliances. As I have said, the calumet ceremony was the primary instrument of alliance in the native societies of the Southeast and indeed of much of North America. Among the Chickasaws and apparently the Choctaws, however, it had been uniquely institutionalized. The evidence for this comes from a letter from Thomas Nairne written about the Chickasaws in 1708, a letter that emphasizes the analogy between external diplomacy and the conduct of interlineage relations. Nairne explains the function of the calumet ceremony and of the official known as *fanimingo* ("squirrel chief"):

> The Chicasaws Yassaws and other people of these parts have one pretty
> rationable Esteablishment that is that any fameily of a nation who

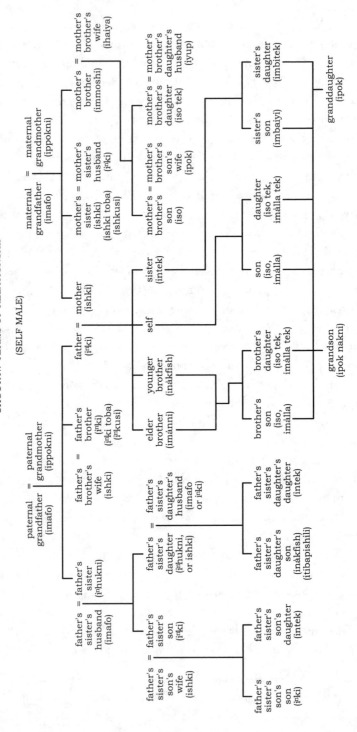

Figure 1. Choctaw terms of relationship, self male, after John R. Swanton, *Source Material for the Social and Ceremonial Life of the Choctaw Indians*, Bureau of American Ethnology Bulletin 103 (Washington DC: Government Printing Office, 1931), 85.

*pleases usually chuse a protector or freind out of another fameily. He
thus chose is generally some growing man of Esteem in the Warrs, they
who chuse & owne him for the head or Chief of their Fameily, pay
him severall little devoirs as visiting him with a present upon their
returnes from hunting saluting him by the name of Chief. Then he
is to protect that Fameily and take care of it's concerns equally with
those of his own. Thus likewise Two nations at peace, each chuse
these protectors in the other, usually send them presents. His buss-
iness is to make up all Breaches between the 2 nations, to keep the
pipes of peace by which at first they contracted Freindship, to devert
the Warriors from any designe against the people they protect, and
Pacifie them by carrying them the Eagle pipe to smoak out of, and
if after all, ar unable to oppose the stream, are to send the people
private intelligence to provide for their own safety.*[55]

Nairne goes on to describe the method by which such a fanimingo was
made, and what he describes is a detailed version of the calumet ceremony
so well known in the Southeast, complete with singing, dancing, "striking
the post," and ritual cleansing of the anointed chief—all of it lasting four
days.[56] This was the same treatment given to La Salle's party by the Quapaws in 1682 and to Iberville by the Bayogoulas in 1700.[57] Evidence that
the Choctaws knew of and participated in such a practice in intertribal relations appears in the lists of chiefs' names reported by the French, which
contain several fanimingos.[58]

The clearest example of the use of the ceremony by the Choctaws to create a French fanimingo for themselves comes in the description we have already seen written by Kerlérec, last French executive governor of the Louisiana colony. But every year at least, at the Mobile present-giving ceremonies
and at other times when the French sent important emissaries to the Choctaws, we hear the long-suffering remark that three or four days were taken
up with the calumet ceremony. If it can be assumed that at least part of the
time the Choctaws were honoring fanimingos, then clearly they were concerned to adopt in this way people they perceived as important French officials and to reiterate the commitment by renewal of the ceremony.

This notion of a revered person who could intercede with his own group
for the group that so honored him explains a lot in the practice of diplomacy
among the Choctaws. For one thing, the description of the duties of the

fanimingo toward those who made him suggests that the ceremony establishes a fictive kinship relation obliging the fanimingo to perform many of the duties within his own group that he would perform if he were the senior male in a lineage that was a subgroup of it—that he would act, in short, as a clan uncle for the adopting group in the councils of his own people.

Since the French had little understanding of the Choctaw practice or its meaning and therefore did not intentionally choose to "make" a fanimingo, it would be hard to establish the existence of a Choctaw fanimingo in Nairne's sense who represented the French.[59] There were instances in which the French presented pipes to southeastern groups—Iberville's presentation of a pipe in the form of a ship comes to mind—but no clear evidence that any French ceremony was ever construed by the Choctaws as honoring one of them as the French fanimingo.[60] It is possible to think that perhaps the Choctaws understood the institution of systematic present giving by the French—which was designed to influence in their favor those chiefs they considered the most important—as creating some sort of obligation similar to the fanimingo institution. Over time the present-giving ceremonies became more and more elaborate, as a special building was erected for the purpose and the French governors banqueted the Choctaw chiefs for days on end, singling out a very few for special recognition with medals and parchment citations.[61] And chiefs especially honored by the French through the presentation of medals, when they ceased to support the French, apparently felt some kind of moral crisis themselves, since in at least two cases such chiefs cast their medals into running water and destroyed or gave away other French presents.[62]

There are tantalizing hints in the literature that the French might have made more use of the fanimingo institution. In 1732 the officer Lusser was invited to extend his stay in the pro-French Concha village by a fanimingo who had given him intelligence about dangerous events in the nation at a crucial time and had agreed to mediate a disturbing quarrel over justice given to the French for a murdered man; a few days later Lusser lectured what must have been another fanimingo at Bouctoucoulou about the faithfulness due to the French.[63] Although it does not show French use of the fanimingo, this incident casts further light upon the role in that the fanimingo of Bouctoucoulou asserted that peace with the Chickasaws, then being blamed by the French for the Natchez revolt, was a desirable end—and

Lusser then says: "He was taking the thing very much to heart, *being calumet chief of this nation.*"[64] Thus the fanimingo probably was a calumet chief, a sort of "secretary of state" of his village or division in that he was the designated fanimingo for all external diplomatic relations with other Indian groups. But it seems that the French never made effective use of this official, perhaps because their patrilineal bias made them incapable of understanding the institution. Instead they chose to adopt via the distribution of medals such division and village chiefs as were useful to them.

Yet the Choctaws for their part did their best to create French fanimingos. How strange it must have seemed to them to so adopt the leading men of the French and to find them insisting upon being considered fathers! It should have been disappointing as well, since as uncles they would have been of the same lineage as the Choctaws, which in this metaphorical context meant of the same tribe. Since only the notion of the fanimingo as "clan uncle of the Choctaws in the councils of the French" would have a clearly institutionalized meaning for the Choctaws, they would have had to fall back on the concept of the father's role in the family and then to graft that onto the fanimingo concept. Yet Kerlérec's adoptive name, "support of the Inholahta [the senior moiety] and a very good father," indicates that the Choctaws were able to assimilate the French obsession to their own institution and profit by it at the same time. In fact the reason the governors attended the meetings in Mobile so assiduously, in spite of seasickness and fever, was that they received considerable presents from the Choctaws.[65] In return the Choctaws hoped that the French governor would send good reports of them and enable them to obtain trade goods from the French king. If the governor insisted upon being considered their father, then they were so much the better off—there was no necessity to obey him where it was inconvenient or dangerous to do so, and among their father's kin they would always be received fondly. Experience with these "father" fanimingos over time must have reinforced the Choctaw belief that this mongrel concept was correct, since the continual shortages of French trade goods argued strongly that their fanimingo's influence in his own group's councils was meager at best, and he continued to flatter and cajole them almost no matter what they did.

Thus there was an ironic truth in the way the fanimingo concept was modified, since in fact the Louisiana governors' influence at the French court *was* inconsiderable. And the Choctaws behaved with essential impunity, as they would toward a father. The French attempt to manipulate Choctaw government and war making through a hierarchical system of presents had guaranteed that nothing would be more expensive or less reliable than assuring the constancy of the Choctaws as allies.[66] Part of this, of course, was due to misunderstanding of the Choctaw notion of war. But some of the problem must be attributed to the French failure to understand what they had gotten themselves into and their insistence that the Choctaws see things as they did. The French never understood that they had become a fictive Choctaw lineage, separate from other Choctaw lineages but included within the same tribe, in spite of the fact that the records are full of Choctaw use of kinship terms with reference to them. Even when the Choctaw divisions fought a civil war over the French failure to take up their lineage duties and avenge themselves on some Choctaw murderers of Frenchmen, the French remained in this instance too afraid of Choctaw numbers to trust the assertion that kin-group vengeance was required.[67] Because they needed the Choctaws more than the Choctaws needed them, the French tried to fulfill Choctaw demands for trade goods and presents even at times when they had not enjoyed adequate reciprocity. Small wonder the Choctaws then assumed that the French governor meant what he said when he insisted upon being accepted as a father: fathers were kind and generous, but they had no authority.

Postscript

Since this paper was first written, others (not necessarily influenced by it) have paid serious attention to Native American diplomatic conventions and how they related to indigenous traditions, among them George Sabo for the Caddo, Richard White for Native groups in the Midwest, Claudio Saunt for the Creeks, and Greg O'Brien for the Choctaws at a later period than I write about here. The essay itself has been well-received and widely cited; I think many others found the concept suggested in it as obvious, once developed, as I found it when the idea first came to me. But in general I think this essay and other such work (of which this volume is an example) emerged when it did because ethnohistory in general was moving toward a less "external" view of the people whose history we write and beginning to seek more nuanced anthropological explanations of Native agency in events. I still feel that the argument is right, and I am looking forward to doing more work on whether Bienville himself understood what was going on well enough to actually have been exploiting Native conventions when he used his sisters' sons in diplomacy.

Notes

1. James Axtell, *The Indian Peoples of Eastern America* (New York: Oxford University Press, 1981), xv. I am happy to say that this situation has ameliorated somewhat due to the efforts of ethnohistorians, but the pendulum may have swung too far, as mainstream American historians have converted Native Americans into rational actors in the market revolution.

2. John R. Swanton, *Source Material for the Social and Ceremonial Life of the Choctaw Indians*, Bureau of American Ethnology Bulletin 103 (Washington DC: Government Printing Office, 1931), 76–90.

3. Fred Eggan, *The American Indian: Perspectives for the Study of Social Change* (New York: Cambridge University Press, 1980), 27–37; Alexander Spoehr, *Changing Kinship Systems*, Field Museum of Natural History Anthropological Series 33, no. 4 (Chicago: Field Museum Press, 1947). Some of these conclusions about kinship evolution and why it took place are now under discussion as anthropologists work toward a more nuanced and historically constructed view of kinship. For my purposes here, however, the general points about matrilineal kinship are secure enough to sustain the argument. For a summary, see Greg Urban, "The Social Organization of the Southeast," in *North American Indian Anthropology: Essays on Society and Culture*, ed. Raymond J. Demallie and Alfonso Ortiz (Norman: University of Oklahoma Press, 1994), 172–93.

4. David M. Schneider, "The Distinctive Features of Matrilineal Descent Groups," in *Matrilineal Kinship*, ed. David M. Schneider and Kathleen Gough (Berkeley: University of California Press, 1966), 1–29.

5. Eggan, *American Indian*, 29.

6. Spoehr, *Kinship Systems*, 201.

7. The notion of "structural pose," which acknowledges that power and influence may be differently distributed depending upon the particular activity, is taken from Fred Gearing, *Priests and Warriors: Social Structures for Cherokee Politics in the Eighteenth Century*, Memoir 93 (Washington DC: American Anthropological Association, 1962).

8. Swanton, *Source Material*, 55–102; Charles Hudson, *The Southeastern Indians* (Knoxville: University of Tennessee Press, 1976), 184–257.

9. John R. Swanton, "Social Organization and Social Usages of the Indians of the Creek Confederacy," in *Forty-Second Annual Report of the Bureau of American Ethnology* (Washington DC: Government Printing Office, 1928), 55–102.

10. Donald J. Blakeslee, "The Origin and Spread of the Calumet Ceremony," *American Antiquity* 46, no. 4 (1981): 759–68.

11. Blakeslee, "Origin and Spread," 765–66. The widespread trade and culture contacts that crisscrossed the Southeast during the Mississippi period had to be supported by some sort of mechanism to make contact possible; whether or not the mechanism was the full-blown calumet ceremony of the eighteenth century is really immaterial. The early date of the Nairne description of the *fanimingo* institution suggests that the underlying model for the mechanism was fictive kinship.

12. Henry Dobyns, *Their Number Become Thinned: Native American Population Dynamics in Eastern North America* (Knoxville: University of Tennessee Press, 1983), 298–334. Dobyns's claims are now seen as rather extreme; a more measured examination of the population issue is in Russell Thornton, *American Indian Holocaust and Survival: A Population History since 1492* (Norman: University of Oklahoma Press, 1987).

13. A typical example (a speech from Governor Périer to the Choctaw chiefs, delivered by Régis du Roullet in 1729): "You know that the Great Chief [i.e., Périer] is your father and that he carries you all in his heart . . . you who are his children and his friends" (Archives des Colonies, ser. C13A [henceforth AC, C13A], vol. 12: fols. 74–74v, Journal of Régis du Roullet). It was not only Indians who were managed from within the framework of a structure derived from the patrilineal family by French colonial elites, it also affected the relations between post commandants and settlers. In 1751 Governor Vaudreuil spoke of the necessity of appointing commandants to posts with settlements who not only had skills in Indian diplomacy, but who also "would be at the same time capable of governing like a good *père de famille* the people who have settled there . . ." (AC, C13A, vol. 35: fol. 86v, Vaudreuil to Rouillé, April 28, 1751).

14. Wilbur Jacobs, *Wilderness Politics and Indian Gifts: The Northern Colonial Frontier, 1748–1763* (1950; reprint, Lincoln: University of Nebraska Press, 1966), 29–45.

15. James D. Hardy Jr., "The Superior Council in Colonial Louisiana," in *Frenchmen and French Ways in the Mississippi Valley*, ed. John Francis McDermott (Urbana: University of Illinois Press, 1969), 87–101.

16. It seems more likely that Bienville's language acquisition was confined to the Choctaw-based Mobilian trade jargon rather than that he actually learned to speak the more complex Choctaw language; it is clear, however, that he understood spoken Choctaw rather well. Bienville had several nephews who served as officers in Louisiana military posts, and several of them were involved in Indian diplomacy. Perhaps the most notable was a son of his sister Jeanne Le Moyne, Gilles Augustin Payen de Chavoy de Noyan (known as "Noyan"), who served as acting governor for Bienville during the Chickasaw campaign of 1736, undertook an important diplomatic mission to the Choctaws for Bienville in 1738, and commanded as king's lieutenant in New Orleans after 1741. Patricia Kay Galloway, ed., *Mississippi Provincial Archives: French Dominion*, vol. 4 (Baton Rouge: Louisiana State University Press, 1984), 96n.

17. Swanton, *Source Material*, 91, quoting from the so-called Anonymous Memoir (Ayer Collection, The Newberry Library); Swanton's parenthetical comments.

18. Gearing, *Priests and Warriors*, 44–46, 66–67.

19. A particularly clear example of this practice seems to emerge in the career of Toupa Oumastabé of Concha. Identified as a "brother" of the important chief Alibamon Mingo of Concha, in 1731 he was an honored man of his village, but by 1746 he was "captain" of Concha. In 1731, when Alibamon Mingo became chief of the Eastern division, he asked that Toupa Oumastabé be given the office of second chief of Concha. Galloway, *Mississippi Provincial Archives*, 4:66, 279.

20. At the beginning of the troubles leading to the Choctaw civil war, the great chief of the nation told Beauchamp that he was "old and no longer in a position to be able to undertake anything" (AC, C13A, 30:231v, Beauchamp's Journal, 1746).

21. Swanton, *Source Material*, 56–57.

22. John Blitz, *An Archaeological Study of the Mississippi Choctaw Indians*, Archaeological Report 16 (Jackson: Mississippi Department of Archives and History, 1985). Blitz's reanalysis of all known collections of Choctaw pottery from archaeological sites shows that there are at least two pottery traditions combined into the Choctaw assemblage.

23. Angie Debo, *The Rise and Fall of the Choctaw Republic* (Norman: University of Oklahoma Press, 1961), 151; Swanton, *Source Material*, 98–97; Arthur H. DeRosier Jr., *The Removal of the Choctaw Indians* (Knoxville: University of Tennessee Press, 1970), 166. I have developed the argument for the ethnogenesis of the Choctaws from confederation of several ethnically different groups in the sixteenth and seventeenth centuries in *Choctaw Genesis 1500–1700* (Lincoln: University of Nebraska Press, 1995).

24. The Eastern, Western, and Sixtowns divisions were on the watersheds of the Tombigbee, Pearl, and Pascagoula rivers, respectively.

25. This was apparently the case; in the documents we never hear of a different set of officials for the district chiefs.

26. Dunbar Rowland and Albert G. Sanders, trans. and eds., *Mississippi Provincial Archives: French Dominion*, 3 vols. (Jackson: Mississippi Department of Archives and History, 1929–32), 1:156; AC, C13A, 14:184, Baudouin to Salmon, November 23, 1732.

27. Such a situation seems to be reflected in the report of the 1745 Concha assembly (AC, C13A, 29:191–92v, Louboey to Maurepas, October 6, 1745). There are many other such examples, but perhaps the most striking is found in Beauchamp's 1746 journal, which reports at length the view of a Frenchman on the outside looking in—with great difficulty—as the Choctaws made the decisions that would eventuate in a civil war (AC, C13A, 30:222–40v).

28. This was true until the ascendancy of Red Shoe in the 1730s. His influence grew beyond that of war chief until he no longer followed the inclinations of the council. Cf. AC, C13A, 14:189v-190, Baudouin to Salmon, November 23, 1732.

29. Patricia Galloway, "Henry de Tonti du village des Chactas, 1702: The Beginning of the French Alliance," in *La Salle and His Legacy*, ed. Patricia Galloway (Jackson: University Press of Mississippi, 1982), 146–75.

30. Kerlérec's complaint in 1754 is typical (AC, C13A, 38:129, Kerlérec to De Machault d'Arnouville, December 18, 1754).

31. AC, C13A, 12:74–74v, Régis du Roullet's Journal, 1729.

32. AC, CI3A, 28:204–204v, Vaudreuil to Maurepas, February 2, 1744.

33. AC, CI3A, 29:197, Louboey to Maurepas, October 6, 1745.

34. AC, CI3A, 30:235v, Beauchamp's Journal, 1746.

35. AC, CI3A, 40:148v, Kerlérec's Memoir on the Indians, December 12, 1758.

36. AC, CI3A, 14:192–192v, Baudouin to Salmon, November 23, 1732.

37. AC, CI3A, 18:158v, Bienville to Maurepas, April 23, 1734.

38. AC, CI3A, 33:20, Vaudreuil to Rouillé, March 3, 1749. Alibamon Mingo was the senior chief of both the Eastern division and the senior moiety, the Inholahta.

39. AC, CI3A, 38:123, Kerlérec to De Machault d'Arnouville, December 18, 1754. The translation Kerlérec offers here is quite correct: *inki* means "father," and *achukma* means "excellent, benevolent." Cyrus Byington, *A Dictionary of the Choctaw Language*, Bureau of American Ethnology Bulletin 46 (Washington DC: Government Printing Office, 1915).

40. AC, CI3A, 38:125v–126.

41. AC, CI3A, 18:194v, Bienville to Maurepas, September 30, 1734. Lest the reader imagine that Bienville invented this ludicrous story to discredit Diron, one can refer to Diron's own much briefer version in AC, CI3A, 19:129–129v, Diron to Maurepas, September 1, 1734.

42. AC, CI3A, 18:195v, Bienville to Maurepas, September 30, 1734.

43. AC, CI3A, 15:206v, Régis du Roullet to Maurepas, 1729–33.

44. AC, CI3A, 12:78v, Régis du Roullet's Journal, 1729.

45. AC, CI3A, 12:39v–40, Périer to Maurepas, March 8, 1730.

46. AC, CI3A, 12:127v, Lusser's Journal, 1730.

47. AC, CI3A, 22:226, Diron d'Artaguette to Maurepas, May 8, 1737.

48. AC, CI3A, 21:141v–142, Bienville to Maurepas, February 10, 1736.

49. AC, CI3A, 28:92–92v, Chickasaw Chiefs to Vaudreuil, August 1743.

50. AC, CI3A, 35:357, Dupumeux to Beauchamp, June 18, 1751.

51. AC, CI3A, 35:358, Dupumeux to Beauchamp, June 18, 1751.

52. Compare the example of the French attempt to have Red Shoe killed during the Choctaw civil war. They found that the only way this could be done without initiating a string of blood revenge killings was to have a kinsman of his own lineage do the deed: AC, CI3A, 30:237v.

53. Fred Eggan, "Historical Changes in the Choctaw Kinship System," *American Anthropologist* 39 (1937): 34–52; Spoehr, *Kinship Systems*.

54. Swanton, *Source Material*, 85, gives a kinship schedule that includes the appropriate Choctaw words.

55. Alexander Moore, ed., *Nairne's Muskhogean Journals: The 1708 Expedition to the Mississippi River* (Jackson: University Press of Mississippi, 1988); text is quoted from the second letter, dated April 12, 1708.

56. Moore, *Nairne's Muskhogean Journals*.

57. For the Quapaw version of the ceremony see Pierre Margry, *Découvertes et établissements des Français dans l'ouest et dans le sud de l'Amérique Septentrionale (1614–1754)* (Paris: Maisonneuve, 1879), 1:553–54, from the narrative of Nicolas de La Salle. For Iberville, see Richebourg Gaillard McWilliams, ed., *Iberville's Gulf Journals* Tuscaloosa: University of

Alabama Press, 1980), 46; in this case the Bayogoulas explicitly told Iberville that he was being made the ally of several mostly Choctaw-related tribes.

58. AC, C13A, 12:89–90v, Régis du Roullet to Maurepas, 1729.

59. Note that in the "Anonymous Memoir" account of Choctaw social organization quoted in note 17, the fanimingo is not even mentioned.

60. McWilliams, *Gulf Journals*, 46.

61. Presents were first given, of course, as soon as Iberville met a new group of Indians, but they were systematized by Bienville and his other brother Châteaugué in the 1720s to create a hierarchical redistributional system in which the great chief received all the presents and was to divide them among lesser chiefs, and so on (for a list, see AC, C13A, 12:90v, Régis du Roullet's Journal, 1729). The first medals were given before 1732, as chiefs with them appear on lists of names by that time (Archives du Service Hydrographique, vol. LX-CII2, no. 14–1, portefeuille 135, document 21, Journal of Régis du Roullet). Kerlérec, who was only the last of the governors to recognize their value for the style of diplomacy developed by the French (AC, C13A, 40:150v-152v, Kerlérec's Memoir on the Indians, 1758), had a large building erected in Mobile to accommodate the present-giving ceremonies (AC, C13A, 37:202v, Bobé Descloseaux to Rouillé, November 27, 1753).

62. In 1729 the so-called great chief of the Choctaws was insulted by Diron d'Artaguette, commander at Mobile, as a result of which "I threw my medal and my big letter into the water" (AC, C13A, 12:79, Régis du Roullet's Journal, 1729). That this was a ceremonial act is suggested by what followed, in that the next day "the Great Chief sent his son to look for his medal and his big letter that he had fished for when he learned of my [Régis's] arrival, but which he had not yet worn. He took it in his hand and holding his fan in the other he came with ceremony to say these words to me: . . . If I threw away my medal it was because my brother, Mr. Diron, sent me word that I was a woman; that he did not wish to see me any more, and because, since I did not get any coat last year, I was ashamed to wear it" (AC, C13A, 12:83v–84, Régis du Roullet's Journal, 1729). The identical procedure occurred for a similar reason in 1746, when Mongoulacha Mingo of Chickasawhay, hearing "that the authority of the medal chiefs was being taken away to be given to the red chiefs . . . made him decide to cut off his medal and throw it into a stream" (AC, C13A, 30:225v, Beauchamp's Journal, 1746). In the sequel, this chief sided with Red Shoe against the French and was put to death by pro-French warriors of his village "for having cut off and thrown away the medal with which he had been decorated for supporting the mission of the Reverend Father Baudouin" (AC, C13A, 32:216, Beauchamp to Maurepas, October 24, 1748). Being the French god's fanimingo was clearly no joke.

63. AC, C13A, 12:108–108v, Lusser to Maurepas, 1730.

64. AC, C13A, 12:109v, Lusser to Maurepas, 1730 (emphasis added).

65. The French documents, most of them either written or vetted by the governors, have little to say about this, but there is plenty of evidence in the form of letters from discontented officers complaining of the profitability of the governorship to show that such presents were given and that they were ample. One of the accusations against Bienville in the 1707–8 investigation of his administration was that he had sold meat brought him by the

Indians "in exchange for the presents that the King gives them" (AC, C13A, 2:256, Abstract of Testimony). Bienville himself remarked rather dryly with reference to the new governor, de l'Epinay: "The governors are ordinarily jealous about giving the presents themselves" (AC, C13A, 5:63, Bienville to Regency Council). This was not unusual or new; it may be recalled that La Salle had nearly been buried by the pelts and other gifts piled on him by the Quapaws in 1682.

66. Richard White, *The Roots of Dependency* (Lincoln: University of Nebraska Press, 1983), 50–51.

67. See Patricia Galloway, "Choctaw Factionalism and Civil War, 1746–1750," *Journal of Mississippi History* 44 (1982): 289–327.

The Calumet Ceremony in the
Southeast as Observed Archaeologically

IAN W. BROWN

There remains no more, except to speak of the Calumet. There is nothing more mysterious or more respected among them. Less honor is paid to the Crowns and scepters of Kings than the Savages bestow upon this. It seems to be the God of peace and of war, the Arbiter of life and of death. It has but to be carried upon one's person, and displayed, to enable one to walk safely through the midst of Enemies— who, in the hottest of the Fight, lay down Their arms when it is shown. For That reason, the Illinois gave me one, to serve as a safeguard among all the Nations through whom I had to pass during my voyage.

Father Jacques Marquette
among the Illinois in 1673

Few material items in historic times have had such singular cultural significance as the calumet. The first Frenchmen in the northern Mississippi valley were amazed at its power, and they soon learned that carrying calumets with them enhanced safety and security. The calumet, or rather the confidence placed in it, had the ability to create peaceful interaction. For intervals of varying duration, the calumet was able to make temporary friends out of potential foes. By the eighteenth century calumet ceremonialism was practiced in many regions of the Southeast, particularly the lower Mississippi valley. The mechanisms as to why, how, and when this institution was adopted have been topics of much debate. There can be no question that the calumet ceremony firmly was embedded in the upper Mississippi valley and Great Lakes regions long before Europeans arrived on the scene.[1] The timing is not so clear for the Southeast, however. One of the principal questions has been whether or not the French were responsible for its introduction and spread into the Southeast, or whether the cultural roots of the calumet ceremony stretch far back into prehistory in this area also. From a review of the historical and archaeological records, I propose that French exploration in the late seventeenth century in large measure promoted the spread of the calumet ceremony into the southern regions of the lower Mississippi valley and, subsequently, to other parts of the Southeast. The main reason for this rapid and widespread diffusion seems to be that the calumet ceremony provided balance in a rapidly changing world.

Calumets: Description and Function

The word "calumet" is believed to derive from a medieval French word *chalemel* (and later *chalumeau*) meaning reed, cane, stem, tube, or pipe (fig. 1).[2] The highly ornamented wands that were often used by the Indians in ceremonial dances intrigued early French adventurers in the Great Lakes and Mississippi valley areas. Because these wands sometimes doubled as stems for pipes, it was unclear to the French whether the calumet was the stem or the bowl of the pipe, or perhaps both.[3] Among Plains Indian tribes, the term calumet usually signified the highly decorated stem, and it is possible that this was the case in the Mississippi valley also.[4] Dumont dit Montigny reported that the calumet was given to the opposite party, while the pipe bowl was retained, which suggests that the Indians did indeed make a distinction between the two parts.[5] From an extensive study of seventeenth- and eighteenth-century calumet ceremonies, Mildred Mott Wedel concluded that French explorers in the Mississippi valley particularly were impressed with the highly polished pipe bowls and, as a result, may have underestimated the significance of the stems. Dancing and much waving of the wands characterize the earliest renditions of the ceremony, but smoking, curiously, is not a prime feature in these accounts.[6]

Robert Hall feels a distinction should be made between the historic development of the round-stem calumet pipe of the Hako type in the Plains and the flat-stem council pipe/sacred pipe of the Eastern Woodlands.[7] With regard to the latter, he believes that the smoking aspect has been important for millennia, its development having come directly out of Hopewellian flat-stemmed atlatl pipes. Jordan Paper also believes ritual smoking was practiced for millennia.[8] He reserves the term "calumet" for elaborate feathered stems similar to those used in the Pawnee Hako, but he groups all of the round-stemmed and flat-stemmed pipes together under the term "Sacred Pipes," including the calumet when the bowl is present.

Father Marquette referred to two types of calumets: one for peace, the other for war. The stem was a two-foot-long, hollow cane that was adorned

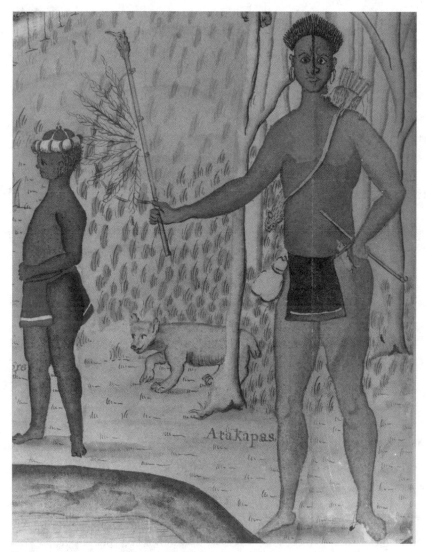

Figure 1. Attakapa Indian with calumet (minus the pipe bowl). Enlargement from "Drawing of Savages of Several Nations, New Orleans, 1735" by Alexandre De Batz (courtesy of the Peabody Museum, Harvard University, photo by Hillel S. Burger, 41-72/20).

with long, colored feathers and the heads or necks of various birds. The pipe itself was made from a red stone that had been polished like marble.[9] Dumont also made mention of a red stone that looked like coral, but added that sometimes a black stone closely resembling marble was used. According to Dumont, the stem measured about 4 ft. (1.2 m) and was painted and adorned with feathers and porcupine quills.[10] The types of birds selected depended on the nature of the calumet. Antoine Simon Le Page du Pratz reported that the Indians used eagle feathers and duck skin for peace calumets, but for the war type they employed flamingo feathers and buzzard skin because of the symbolic association of bald heads with scalping.[11] Nicolas de La Salle reported that the Arkansas Indians also used two pipes in their rendition of the calumet ritual.[12] Among the Omahas calumets were used in pairs, with one representing the female element and the other the male.[13] The calumet itself symbolically represents both male (stem) and female (bowl) genders.[14]

The red stone of the pipe bowls, popularly known as "catlinite," is named after the nineteenth-century artist-adventurer George Catlin. He claimed to have been the first white man to see the famous pipestone quarry in southwest Minnesota, but it is clear that its presence was known long before the nineteenth century.[15] Red pipestone is actually a form of argillite.[16] The term "pipestone" does not appear in petrology texts, but it is well known in archaeological parlance as a nickname for reddish, fine-grained, dense, easily carved lithic materials. Prior to the introduction of iron implements, flint or other hard minerals must have been used to cut and shape this soft stone. Drilling of the bowl and shank of the pipe was done with a chipped flint tool or by rotating a hollow reed between the hands, using sand as an abrasive agent.[17]

Although pipestones often appear to be similar they are actually quite different mineralogically. The red color in pipestone argillites is produced by hematite (Fe_2O_3) content. Colors for pipestone material from the Plains include red, maroon, brown, orange, yellowish orange, gray, green-gray, blue-gray, cream, and white. In addition to Pipestone National Monument in southwestern Minnesota, which is now considered the only true source of catlinite, red pipestone sources include south-central Minnesota, southeastern South Dakota, eastern Kansas, north-central Wisconsin, Ohio, and Arizona.[18] But these are only quarry sources. It is clear that the various pipestone outcrops in Minnesota were gouged by glacial action during the Pleistocene, with sediments having been plucked and transported by fluvial action to regions far to the south. As revealed by a study of red pipestone from various sites in Iowa, James Gundersen and Joseph Tiffany showed that early native populations actually used these glacially and fluvially distributed materials long before the Pipestone National Monument catlinite source was discovered and, subsequently, quarried.[19]

Because of the confusion with the word "catlinite," I use redstone as an adjective in this essay when discussing pipes that are believed to have been involved in calumet rituals, but I should emphasize that redstone pipes in the Plains were not used exclusively in calumet rituals.[20] Such pipes also were employed in other ceremonies, and although redstone was most commonly used as a pipe-bowl material, it also was employed in the manufacture of many other items.[21]

Nicotiana rustica L. is the only type of tobacco known to have been used in the Eastern Woodlands prior to European contact.[22] Interestingly enough, the prehistoric distribution of *N. rustica* L. in the eastern half of North America approximates the distribution of sacred pipes. The plant itself reaches a height of between 1.0 and 1.5 m and has large fleshy leaves with small, pale yellow blossoms. Indians smoked both the leaves and the blossoms of this hardy, self-seeding plant. Although tobacco can be chewed or snuffed, in Native North America it was most commonly smoked. The smoke itself is considered an offering to the spirits. As tobacco is an extremely potent species, particularly in terms of nicotine content, it typically was combined with other plant products prior to smoking. The resulting mixture has become known as "kinnikinnick."

> *In discussing tobacco in Native religion, one is discussing not only varieties of the genus* Nicotiana, *but other substances either mixed with* Nicotiana *or smoked in its place. In North America, these alternatives are, most commonly, the inner bark of certain trees of the genus* Cornus, *such as red osier, the leaves of one of the sumacs* (Rhus glabra) *when they have turned red in autumn, and the leaves of bearberry* (Arctostaphylos uvaursi). *All these plants have an association with red, a color representing blood, the essence of life— the outer bark of red osier is as named, red; sumac leaves turn brilliant red; bearberry has red berries, and the dried leaves are similar to the green of Native dried tobacco leaves. The Algonkian word, "kinnikinnick," is variously applied to a smoking mixture as well as to individual elements.*[23]

Jordan Paper has argued for tobacco being perhaps the first domesticated plant in North America, but the archaeological evidence really does not support this view.[24] There is some evidence to suggest that *N. rustica* may have been around during the Early Woodland period, but the best evidence for its first appearance in the Eastern Woodlands occurs in west-central Illinois at the confluence of the Missouri, Illinois, and Mississippi rivers between the first century BC and the second century AD. Tobacco started to become common on Late Woodland sites in the American Bottom region of Illinois at around AD 300, after which its use remains unbroken through the Mississippi period into historic times.[25] The earliest evidence of the use of *N. rustica* L. among Plains groups comes from a Plains Woodland context in northwestern Iowa that dates to around AD 550.[26] Most researchers believe this species of tobacco probably came directly from Mexico into the Eastern Woodlands, rather than having passed through the Southwest into the Plains.[27] Some scholars have even argued that some form of South American contact may have occurred as the species seems to have originated in the Andean region, but I will leave this puzzle to the archaeobotanists.[28] Since the wild ancestors of tobacco are not indigenous to North America, one thing that is sure is that the plant originally had to have been traded from long distances, on the order of thousands of miles.

Tobacco smoking seems primarily to have been a Late Woodland, Mississippian, and historic phenomenon. It is not clearly understood what earlier Indians may have been smoking in tubular and platform pipes prior to the introduction of tobacco. It has been proposed by some that various hallucinogenic plants may have also been smoked prehistorically, and this may have been the case. Tobacco itself is not one of the true hallucinogens recognized by botanists, but it is important to remember that its active ingredient, the alkaloid nicotine, has been known to induce dramatic psychodynamic effects.[29]

Of critical significance is that throughout prehistory Native Americans primarily smoked tobacco for ritualistic purposes. Secular usage was almost always a rarity.[30] Even though we know that tobacco was around in late prehistoric times in the Southeast, we should not automatically assume that its use was ever commonplace. C. Margaret Scarry, for example, has analyzed plant remains from over two hundred distinct contexts in the Mississippian Moundville polity in Alabama, but has found only one tobacco seed. As might be expected, or hoped, it was associated with a mound (Q) at the Moundville site.[31]

The calumet was always more than just a pipe.[32] In the Plains it became the principal part of a ceremony that made friends out of foes (or at least nominal friends for specific occasions). Trade between sedentary horticulturists and nomadic bison hunters of the Plains stretched back into protohistoric times, if not before. The exchange of garden produce for meat and skins resulted in symbiotic relationships that provided benefits for all, and the resulting exchanges linked up the economies of the Plains, Great Basin, and Plateau culture areas. The constant threat of intertribal warfare, however, posed a serious threat to this kind of trade system. Strife easily could sever the links in such a complex network.[33]

It has been demonstrated that the calumet-pipe bowl form (in clay and in redstone) appeared in the eastern Plains after about AD 1200, but the exact mechanisms as to how or why it developed remain unknown.[34] Robert Hall has argued that the evolution of the calumet pipe can be traced over a four-thousand-year period.[35] Basically this is equivalent to the time when pipes first appeared on North American sites.[36] Although the links between pipe bowl forms are not as well defined as one might hope, Hall's writings certainly offer fascinating insights into prehistoric belief systems. Particularly intriguing is his thesis that the calumet ceremony originated as an adoption ceremony closely associated with a mourning ritual.[37] It is clear, however, that by protohistoric/historic times a prime function of the presenting and smoking of calumets in the Plains was to preserve peace for the period of trade. Under the umbrella of the calumet, groups that normally were mortal enemies could safely complete their transactions.[38] Whether or not this was the reason the calumet spread into the northern Mississippi valley is not known, but it surely is a viable hypothesis.[39]

Between 1665 and 1682, Allouez, Marquette, Joliet, and La Salle encountered the calumet among groups as far south along the Mississippi River as the Natchez Indians.[40] Thus there is the suggestion that the calumet ceremony was practiced by a number of southeastern groups some years prior to French exploration in the late seventeenth century.[41] At this time it seems to have been confined primarily to the western periphery of the Eastern Woodlands, but there is at least one example of its practice by the Apache Indians as early as 1660.[42] There is little indication that the calumet cere-

mony was practiced in the Northeast until well after initial European contact. William Turnbaugh has argued, for example, that the appearance of
the calumet dances among the St. Francis "Abnakis" in the late seventeenth/
early eighteenth centuries represents a nativistic movement.[43] This particular case study serves to highlight his major premise that the use of calumets in the Eastern Woodlands coincided with and expanded during the
period of European contact.[44]

Smoking certainly was common throughout the Northeast in protohistoric times, but it was the presentation of wampum belts, not calumets, that
played a key role in establishing peace for business in this area.[45] Although
the Iroquois did have calumets in the late seventeenth century, they do not
appear to have been as important as they were among groups in the Midwest.[46] Henri de Tonti, for example, was frustrated in his attempt to use
the calumet to bring peace between the Iroquois and the Illinois. Tonti was
wounded in the short battle that erupted, but one of the Iroquois chiefs saw
that he was a Frenchman and his life, consequently, was spared. This chief
"asked loudly what they had meant by striking a Frenchman in that way,
that he must be spared, and drew forth a belt of wampum to staunch the
blood and make a plaster for the wound."[47] Another suggestion of the value
equivalence shared by wampum and calumets is revealed in Henri Joutel's
visit to the Quapaws in 1687 when he recorded wampum bracelets (said to
have come from the Indians of New England) as having been given as part
of the calumet ceremony.[48]

Further indication that calumet presentation in the East represents a
symbolic laying down of arms is suggested in the works of Robert Hall.[49]
Over the years he has marshaled a wealth of data demonstrating a clear association between calumets and weapons such as atlatls and arrows. Father
Jacques Marquette himself reported a mock battle among the Illinois, which
also reveals this connection. He noted that one of the dancers was armed
with real weapons, the other with a calumet, a clear connection between
the weapon and the instrument aimed at preventing its use.[50]

Calumet Ceremonialism in the Southeast

> *Every one, at the outset, takes the Calumet in a respectful manner, and, support-*
> *ing it with both hands, causes it to dance in cadence, keeping good time with the*
> *air of the songs. He makes it execute many differing figures; sometimes he shows*

it to the whole assembly, turning himself from one side to the other. After that, he
who is to begin the Dance appears in the middle of the assembly, and at once con-
tinues this. Sometimes he offers it to the sun, as if he wished the latter to smoke
it; sometimes he inclines it toward the earth; again, he makes it spread its wings,
as if about to fly; at other times, he puts it near the mouths of those present, that
they may smoke. The whole is done in cadence; and this is, as it were, the first
Scene of the Ballet.

Father Jacques Marquette
among the Illinois in 1673

Calumet ceremonialism in the Southeast was but one part of a complex
"meeting ritual." Elaborate processions, lengthy speeches, feasting, gift exchanges, dancing, and ceremonial smoking accompanied historically all
political negotiations, either of an intra- or interpolity nature.[51] Second-
ary features included physical contact in the form of rubbing, the seating
of participants on mats or skins, and the beating of posts coordinated with
the recitation of war heroics. The calumet also established symbolic kinship between prominent leaders of different Indian villages as well as visiting Europeans. Adoption ceremonies often were very important parts of
calumet exchange ceremonies.[52] The etiquette involved in the reception of
two different groups of people was structured tightly, and any departure
from the standard could result in the failure of the meeting.

Although there are examples of calumet ceremonialism among the Creeks
and Chickasaws the finest descriptions of its elaborate nature pertain to
Mississippi valley groups. Examples are from Marquette among the Illinois, Joutel among the Quapaws, and Iberville among the Mugulashas,
Bayogoulas, and Houmas.[53] Iberville's hosting of a delegation of five different groups that visited him on the coast is another fine demonstration of
the ceremony.[54] Excellent descriptions also derive from Bienville's punitive
expedition against the Natchez and Father Charlevoix's and Father Le Petit's visits to this same group.[55]

Significantly, the historical literature makes no mention of the calumet ceremony in sixteenth-century southeastern society. Although abundant archaeological evidence exists for prehistoric smoking in the area, nowhere do the various sixteenth-century Spanish accounts refer to smoking
as part of a meeting ritual.[56] There was an elaborate meeting ritual, to be
sure, as the Hernando de Soto accounts do contain extensive documentation on feasting and gift exchanges.[57] It also has been demonstrated that

lengthy harangues, the stroking and carrying of guests, the recitation of war heroics, symbolic-adoption ceremonies, and the seating of participants on robes or other prepared surfaces were characteristic features of Florida Indian greeting rituals throughout the sixteenth century, but the calumet markedly is absent.[58]

James Springer feels calumet ceremonialism must have existed in the lower Mississippi valley during the sixteenth century and that its absence in the de Soto records is due to the short amount of time spent in the area and the scarcity of cultural information overall.[59] I disagree. The Spanish certainly spent more than enough time in the Southeast to see a calumet performance, if the ritual actually had existed. A number of colleagues have pointed out to me that the Spanish and French encounters with Mississippi valley groups cannot be dealt with in the same manner. De Soto entered the lower Mississippi valley with an immense army and hostile intent, whereas the French adventurers came into it with a canoe or two and all the reason in the world to want peaceful interaction.[60] While admitting that the contact situations were very different, I still believe there was enough Spanish-Indian interaction to have resulted in at least an observance of calumet usage if indeed it existed in the lower Mississippi valley in the mid-sixteenth century. It is also important to remember that "The Sacred Pipe was used for all intertribal relationships, not only peace, but war as well"—all the more reason why de Soto should have observed the calumet ceremony.[61]

Although there is no reference to calumet presentation or smoking as part of early meeting rituals in the Southeast, the playing of a flute-like instrument appears to have served an analogous role among many groups. Robert Hall has argued, quite convincingly, that there is a direct relation among spear throwers, flutes, and pipes in many portions of the Americas, including the Eastern Woodlands.[62] Pánfilo de Narváez observed flutes in use in Florida as early as 1527, they were displayed prominently in a number of contacts made by de Soto in the 1540s, and the English even observed Powhatan playing a flute in initial contacts at the turn of the seventeenth century.[63] Jacques Le Moyne provided a vivid description of its use in a 1564 French encounter with the Timucua Indians.[64] The Spaniard Diego Romero was treated to a procession that involved reed whistles and flutes when he experienced the calumet ceremony among the Apaches in 1660.[65]

At some time between the late sixteenth century and the mid- to late seventeenth century, flute-like instruments disappeared in southeastern meeting rituals and were replaced by calumets. As discussed earlier, it is clear that the calumet ceremony had become well entrenched in the northern and central regions of the Mississippi valley by the time the first French explorers emerged on the scene. French explorers from Marquette on knew the importance of carrying the calumet with them in their travels, and they learned to present it immediately upon meeting new peoples. The French accounts, from Allouez to La Salle, and from Iberville to Le Page du Pratz, are so similar in their descriptions of the meeting ritual that it often is possible for us to observe where mistakes occurred and why participants took offense.

The significance of the calumet as symbolic armor is apparent in the one time that La Salle was without it. In October of 1679 his men took some corn from a deserted Illinois Indian village. He left goods in exchange, but this action apparently was not enough to satisfy the irate inhabitants of this village. Had it not been for the timely arrival of a number of his men bearing a calumet, La Salle's expedition (and his place in history) might have been terminated prematurely. He certainly learned his lesson, as he and his officers seldom failed to have calumets in hand as they visited groups to the south.[66]

I believe that some groups encountered by La Salle in the southern portion of the lower Mississippi valley may not have been familiar with the ritual. For example, the Quinipissa Indians, located near the mouth of the Mississippi, rejected the calumet, an action that came as some surprise to La Salle.[67] Of course, it is impossible to know whether or not their rejection of the calumet is necessarily an indication that they were unaware of its importance. When Iberville arrived along the Gulf coast only seventeen years later, however, there was no question that each group, whether big or small, knew the significance of the calumet as part of the meeting ritual. Iberville and his brother Bienville sang the calumet not only with the Quinipissas but also with the Bayogoulas, the Biloxis, the Chitimachas, the Choctaws, the Houmas, the Mugulashas, the Natchez, the Pascagoulas, and the Washas.[68] Iberville clearly promoted its use. At one point he made carvings on trees of his three ships, along with a depiction of a man carrying a calumet of peace, and when he visited the Bayogoula he presented to the chief a calumet custom-made of iron.[69]

When we got to where my brother was, the chief or captain of the Bayogoula came to the seashore to show me friendliness and courtesy in their fashion, which is, being near you, to come to a stop, pass their hands over their faces and breasts, and then pass their hands over yours, after which they raise them toward the sky, rubbing them together again and embracing again. I did the same thing, having watched it done to the others. They did the same thing to the Annocchy, their friends. After our meeting and amenities on both sides, we went to my brother's tent, to which all the Bayogoula made their way to show friendliness to me and all my men, all embracing one another. I had them smoke, and together we all smoked an iron calumet I had, made in the shape of a ship with the white flag adorned with fleurs-de-lis and ornamented with glass beads. Then [I gave it to them] along with a present of axes, knives, blankets, shirts, glass beads, and other things valued among them, making them understand that with this calumet I was uniting them to the French and that we were from now on one.[70]

It certainly was in the best interests of the French to promote the calumet ceremony, because it provided a measure of predictability. Meeting a new group of Indians always proved to be an uncertain event. Outnumbered and in unfamiliar surroundings the explorers generally felt at a disadvantage, but here in the upper reaches of the Mississippi River the French discovered something that could serve as a flag of truce. It is small wonder that they encouraged the use of the calumet in the Southeast, but were they responsible ultimately for its spread? William Fenton has argued that the French explorers were indeed the mechanism for the appearance of calumet ceremonialism in the lower Mississippi valley.[71] William Turnbaugh and Donald Blakeslee support a historic spread of this institution into the Eastern Woodlands, whereas James Springer and Robert Hall advocate a prehistoric development for the ceremony in this same area.[72] To help resolve this issue, it is appropriate to examine the archaeological evidence.

Archaeological Evidence for Calumet Ceremonialism

The second ["Scene of the Ballet"] *consists of a Combat, carried on to the sound of a kind of drum, which succeeds the songs, or even unites with them, harmonizing very well together. The Dancer makes a sign to some warrior to come to*

take the arms which lie upon the mat, and invites him to fight to the sound of
the drums. The latter approaches, takes up the bow and arrows, and the war-
hatchet, and begins the duel with the other, whose sole defense is the Calumet.
This spectacle is very pleasing, especially as all is done in cadence; for one attacks,
the other defends himself; one strikes blows, the other parries them; one takes to
flight, the other pursues; and then he who was fleeing faces about, and causes his
adversary to flee. This is done so well—with slow and measured steps, and to the
rhythmic sound of the voices and drums—that it might pass for a very fine open-
ing of a Ballet in France.

Father Jacques Marquette
among the Illinois in 1673

A number of southeastern Indian groups, including the Quapaws, Natchez, Tunicas, Choctaws, Chickasaws, Creeks, and Cherokees, are known
to have had pipes with redstone bowls, presumably a reflection of calumet
ceremonialism.[73] An immediate difficulty with any archaeological investigation of calumet ceremonialism is that the very fragile stems, the principal components of symbolism, do not survive. All that remain to reflect the
movements of people, the trade contacts, and the ritual exchanges are the
redstone pipe bowls. Although such pipes have been found in numerous excavations, the meaning of the finds in sociocultural terms is not clear. First
of all, it is not necessarily true that every redstone pipe signifies a calumet.
Although this may have been the case early in the history of calumets, by
the nineteenth century Indians and whites frequently exchanged redstone
pipes and the uses often had become secularized. Whites even manufactured redstone pipes in the nineteenth century to trade to Indians and we
now know that they did so in the early eighteenth century too, at least in Alabama.[74] A total of 375 fragments of red pipestone debitage has been found
at the Old Mobile site (1MB94) and at a nearby Indian house site (1MB147)
in south Alabama, both of which date to the period 1702–11.[75] A very press-
ing concern is that red pipestone was not the only material used for calumet-pipe bowls. As Dumont noted, for example, sometimes a marble-like
black stone was employed.[76] Stone pipes are common occurrences in prehistoric and historic southeastern contexts, but it would be a gross error to
assume that they were all associated with the calumet.

The shapes also must be considered. On the Plains and prairies both el-
bow- and disk-pipe types occur in redstone and are known to have been associated with calumets in historic times, but we do not know if this was also

the case prehistorically. Non-redstone disk and elbow pipes have been found in the Southeast, but it is unclear whether or not these should be considered calumet paraphernalia. Finally, as stated earlier, most disconcerting is Dumont's statement that the calumet was given to the opposite party, while the pipe bowl was retained.[77] This division of the complete object is troublesome, because it is possible that the significance of the bowl may have diminished once it was severed from the stem. As it is impossible to know what value the bowl may have had once it was removed from its ritual usage, it is best to refrain from reading too much into the excavation context of a bowl. Its function may have changed in the interval between when it was used and when it was buried. All that can really be said is that the presence of a redstone pipe bowl on a site suggests that some sort of ceremonial activity had once occurred.

Redstone Platform and Micmac Pipes

Redstone pipes have appeared in archaeological contexts in the Southeast as early as Middle Woodland times, but this material was not utilized to any great degree until after AD 900.[78] The Middle Woodland redstone pipe appears in the platform (or monitor) form and most commonly is found in the upper Mississippi valley and Prairie Peninsula area. It consists of a cylindrical bowl situated on top of a flattened, often arched, tube. Platform pipes made of redstone are rare in the Southeast, but they have turned up as far south as Tennessee.[79] Although of general interest in the history of calumet-pipe use among southeastern Indians, I do not believe platform pipes are of direct significance to the questions as to when and how calumet ceremonialism was introduced to the area.[80] Robert Hall's interpretation that calumet pipes actually developed out of Hopewellian platform pipes is most interesting, but not totally convincing.[81] His exhaustive research has produced a strong hypothesis that symbolic linkages might exist, but because of the long temporal gap between the Middle Woodland and the historic period, the connections must be considered tenuous.

Pipe bowls shaped like vases occasionally occur in redstone, but this form is more typically associated with other types of stone. Vase-shaped pipes generally occur in late prehistoric/early protohistoric contexts.[82] The Micmac pipe form is far more commonly seen in the Eastern Woodlands. Its bowl, which resembles an inverted acorn, occasionally appears on the elbow-type pipe, but the classic Micmac pipe has a very small base that extends little beyond the limits set by the bowl.[83] This pipe is named after the Micmac Indians of Nova Scotia who were recorded as using it (in stone other than redstone) in the late seventeenth or early eighteenth centuries.[84] The type became a common calumet-pipe bowl form in the northern Plains and prairies among groups like the Sauks, Kaskaskias, Potawatomis, Ottawas, Ojibwas, and Blackfeet. The Pawnees also are known to have utilized redstone Micmac pipes.[85]

The earliest firmly dated redstone Micmac pipe that I am aware of is one reported from Kentucky that has a crudely incised "1717" date on its base.[86] The type has been dated to the second Potawatomi occupation (1670–1730) at the Rock Island site in Door County, Michigan.[87] At the Crawford Farm site, a Sauk village on Rock Island, Illinois, these pipes have been dated to the period 1790–1810.[88] Numerous redstone pipes, including eight of the Micmac form, were found at the Guebert site in Randolph County, Illinois. This site supported a Kaskaskia village between 1719 and 1833.[89] Micmac pipes appear to have been most common in the upper Mississippi valley and Great Lakes regions in the eighteenth century. They are very rare in the Southeast and probably are unrelated to calumet ceremonialism. The disk- and elbow-form redstone pipes appear to have the most promise for resolving issues as to when and how calumet ceremonialism entered the Southeast.

Redstone Disk Pipes

There are two types of disk pipes: the "handle disk," which has a forward extension of the base that may have served as a handle, and the "handleless disk," which lacks this appendage. The disk of the handleless type is wider than its handle is long.[90] Often referred to as the "Siouan type" or "Oneota style type," redstone disk pipes have as their center of distribution the Upper Mississippi River and Lower Missouri River regions. They are particularly common in Wisconsin, Iowa, Minnesota, and Missouri where they are a marker for the Oneota culture that flourished between AD 1550 and 1650.[91] In her study of interaction patterns during the Western Fort Ancient period, Penelope Drooker provides a map that shows the distribution of disk pipes in the Eastern Woodlands and Plains.[92] On this map she compares the distribution of redstone disk pipes to those of other colors. Whereas redstone disk pipes tend to have a broad distribution over much of the Midwest and Southeast above the fall line, those made of other types of stones tend to cluster only in four locations: the Fort Ancient region of southern Ohio and northern Kentucky; the Caborn-Welborn region of southwest Indiana, southern Illinois, and adjacent portions of Kentucky; north-central Missouri; and the upper Mississippi valley of southwest Wisconsin, southeast Minnesota, and northeast Iowa.

The zones in figure 3 that outline where redstone disk and elbow pipes are most common are based on Salter's detailed distributional studies of these pipes.[93] He lists these pipes by county, and the boundaries on the map represent my visual interpretation of Salter's data. There can be no question that redstone disk pipes predate the French in the lower Mississippi valley as they were scattered widely in the Southeast on the de Soto time level, if not before.[94] They have been found at most major Mississippian mound sites, such as Moundville, Hiwassee Island, Spiro (perhaps), and Cahokia, and there are distinct clusters of such pipes in northeast Arkansas and the Bootheel of southeast Missouri.[95] The highest frequencies of redstone disk pipes occur in Wisconsin and Missouri, followed by Illinois and Iowa.[96] Redstone disk pipes also have been found in Indiana, Minnesota, and even in Ontario, but for our purposes, in examining the spread of redstone disk pipes into the lower Mississippi valley and the Southeast in general, only those specimens discovered in the southern portions of Missouri and Ohio and points south will be discussed here.[97]

Although central Missouri falls outside the focus of this paper, one cannot discuss redstone disk pipes without at least mentioning the Utz site (23SA2). Excavations at this Oneota site have yielded sixty-three pipes of the disk form. Utz was the primary village of the Missouri Indians when first contacted by Europeans. It definitely was occupied between 1673 and 1728, and possibly as early as 1400, if not before.[98]

To my knowledge, thirty-five redstone disk pipes have been discovered elsewhere in the Southeast. In the northern portion of the lower Mississippi valley, along both sides of the Mississippi River from southeast Missouri to just below Memphis, the redstone disk pipe is a marker for the Armorel phase. Williams believes there is a relationship between this late prehistoric/

protohistoric phase (AD 1500–1700) and Siouan-speaking peoples, and that the distribution of such items as the redstone disk pipe may be indicative of late movements of Siouan populations into the region.[99] Nine redstone disk pipes from seven sites have been recovered in this general area.[100] The Campbell site (23PM5) in southeast Missouri produced a redstone pipe in association with Spanish artifacts that date to circa 1550.[101] One very large redstone disk pipe, bearing a handle, was found in a fragmentary condition on the surface of the McCoy site (23PM21) in Pemiscot County, Missouri. This late Mississippian site has no evidence of trade goods.[102]

Two redstone pipes are reported to have been found by "night diggers" at the Blytheville Mound (3MS5) in Mississippi County, Arkansas, and two additional redstone pipes of the same form were recovered at Upper Nodena (3MS4) in the same county.[103] One of the Upper Nodena pipes accompanied an extended burial (No. 302). Its disk has an incised figure on its surface, probably a conventionalized human form. A surface-collected fragment represents the second pipe from Upper Nodena. All of the Upper Nodena specimens are believed to date between AD 1450 and 1650.[104] The Wildy site (3MS10), another Nodena phase site (with some Parkin phase influences) located in Mississippi County, has yielded fragments of a very large redstone disk pipe.[105] Some artifacts dating to circa AD 1700 also have been found at the site, but the primary occupation appears to have been between AD 1550 and 1650.[106]

A redstone disk pipe (No. 419) also was found in a high-status infant burial at the Nodena phase Walnut Mound (3MS2) in northeast Arkansas. The grave also contained another pipe (of undesignated form), eight pots, two stone discoidals, arrow points, a gorget, a clay reel-shaped object, and gastropod shells. This burial (No. 115) was excavated by the Alabama Museum of Natural History in 1932 and the information provided here was secured from their survey files, courtesy of Stephen Williams.[107] The final redstone disk pipe in this region comes from Site 3SF5, a Mississippian village site (AD 1300–1650) in the Lower St. Francis River basin of eastern Arkansas. A handle disk pipe of redstone was discovered near the right hand of an adult burial at this site (fig. 2a).[108]

A number of other regions in Arkansas have produced redstone disk pipes. In central Arkansas, the Carden Bottoms (3YE14) and Field's Chapel (no number) sites have yielded one and two redstone disk pipes, respec-

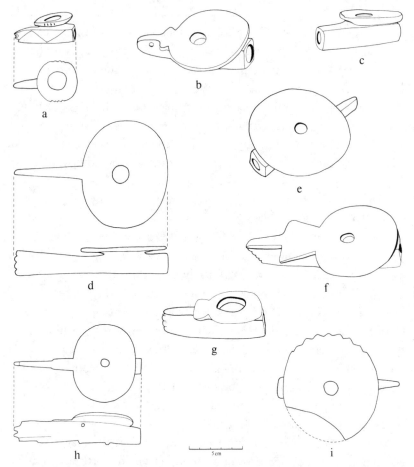

Figure 2. Redstone disk pipes: (a) 3SF5, Arkansas; (b) Kentucky, no provenience; (c) Noel Stone Box Grave Cemetery, Tennessee; (d) Great Tellico, Tennessee; (e) Moundville, Alabama; (f) Seven Mile Island, Alabama; (g) Nacoochee, Georgia; (h) Mohman, Georgia; (i) Spiro, Oklahoma.

tively. Both of these sites are located in Yell County in the Arkansas River valley and are of protohistoric/historic age.[109] Redstone disk pipes also have been reported from Saline and Sevier counties. The Saline County specimen is from the Hughes Mound (3SA11), a multistage Caddoan substructure mound whose date range is not known.[110] The Sevier County pipe came from the Steele Place (no site number), but temporal placement of this site also is unknown.[111]

Considering all the occurrences of redstone disk pipes in Arkansas, it is remarkable that such pipes have not turned up in either Louisiana or Mississippi. The only pipe of the disk form thus far recorded from these two states is a handleless limestone one from a trash pit at the Portland site (22WR542) in Warren County, Mississippi. This site is believed to be a Tunica Indian occupation that dated to the turn of the eighteenth century.[112] An unfinished limestone disk pipe was also found at the Bradley Place (3CF7) in Crittenden County, Arkansas. It occurred in burial association with late Mississippian ceramics. Such pipes are believed to be local copies of redstone prototypes, suggesting that the latter were manufactured elsewhere and subsequently introduced into the Southeast.[113]

Disk pipes overall are quite common at Fort Ancient sites in the Ohio valley. Western Fort Ancient populations had particularly strong interregional ties both with northern Ohio and with Oneota peoples of western Iowa and northern Illinois. They also had strong contacts with people in the central portion of the Mississippi valley.[114] The Madisonville site, located in present Cincinnati, is a premier late Western Fort Ancient period site. Many Oneota-style disk pipes have come from this site, which is suggestive of strong and formal diplomatic relations between the regions. These pipes are often associated with high status male burials.[115] Penelope Drooker dates the Late Fort Ancient Madisonville horizon between 1450 and 1650, but as most of the glass trade beads date to around 1600, it is possible that the disk pipes at Madisonville do not last as late as the mid-seventeenth century.[116] Five redstone pipes were found at Madisonville. At least three of the pipes are of the disk type and two others may have once been of this form. One complete pipe is quite small and bears an engraved weeping-eye symbol on the top of its base. It was found with an adult burial. One of the other redstone disk pipes from Madisonville is reworked from the notched prow of a typical post-1400/1450 Oneota disk pipe. Three additional pieces of shaped red pipestone have also come from this site.[117]

Redstone disk pipes have been found at several other Fort Ancient sites. Two specimens came from Kentucky. One was found at the Hardin site (15GP22) in Greenup County, while another was associated with a burial at the Fox Farm site (15MS1) in Mason County. The Hardin site was occupied between AD 1500 and the early 1600s. Another redstone disk pipe was discovered at the Buffalo site (46PU31), a late seventeenth-century Fort Ancient occupation in Putnam County, West Virginia.[118] Interestingly enough, the fine, large, elaborately shaped red pipestone disk pipes that occur fairly commonly in the Southeast have not been found on Fort Ancient sites.[119] It is possible that the pipe depicted in figure 2b, which is attributed to Kentucky, may have come from a Fort Ancient site.

Although it is out of our region, it should be noted that an Oneota-style redstone disk pipe was found at the mid-sixteenth-century Reed Fort/Richmond Mills site (NYSM #1036), in Ontario County, New York, which is attributable to either the Seneca or Cayuga. Although redstone pipes of the elbow form have been observed in very small numbers in Iroquoian sites in western New York and Ontario, this particular redstone disk pipe is the only one of its kind that has been found deep within Iroquois territory. Interestingly enough, it was ritually killed.[120]

Returning to the Southeast, redstone disk pipes have turned up in some frequency and they generally tend to be finely made. Such pipes are especially common in Tennessee.[121] One reworked specimen was found in mound fill at the Hiwassee Island site in what is believed to be a Dallas phase context.[122] A refuse pit in a single-component Dallas phase village site (40RE89) on the Clinch River in northeast Tennessee yielded a redstone pendant fashioned out of a disk-pipe fragment.[123] A trash pit at Cockrills Bend (40DV36), a Mississippian site located on the Cumberland River in Davidson County near present Nashville, was the context for another redstone disk pipe.[124] At the Noel Stone Box Grave Cemetery (40DV3), also in the vicinity of Nashville, Gates Thruston found a redstone disk pipe (fig. 2c). It is not clear, however, whether the pipe in question was recovered from a stone-box grave or in adjacent earth.[125] It is also possible that it is a fake.[126]

The Great Tellico site (40MR12) in east Tennessee yielded a redstone handle disk pipe from a high-status Dallas phase burial (fig. 2d). Also associated with this adult male (aged between twenty-five and thirty years) were several greenstone celts and chert adzes, conch-shell containers, shell ear pins and beads, and two quivers of arrows. The pipe itself was situated at the knees in a position that suggests a fairly long wooden stem had once been attached to it.[127]

Redstone disk pipes have been found at two sites in Alabama. Moundville, a major Mississippian site on the Black Warrior River, has yielded two specimens. One of the pipes (M-WWA 4) is of the handle disk form (fig. 2e). It was recovered west of Mound W in uncertain context. The other (RHO-235), of undesignated form, was found in village midden.[128] Also in northwest Alabama, but on the Tennessee River, the Seven Mile Island site has produced a redstone disk pipe from a burial (fig. 2f). Three additional disk pipes that were found in nearby burials are made of local limestone. They are similar to the one from the Bradley Place in Arkansas. These pipes presumably pre-date AD 1650 as there were no European trade goods in the graves.[129]

In Georgia a redstone disk pipe was found in a historic Cherokee context. At the Nacoochee site, located at the headwaters of the Chattahoochee River in northwest Georgia, such a pipe was found accompanying an adult burial in a platform mound (fig. 2g). The burial had blue glass beads with it, indicative of a historic context.[130] The Mohman site (9FL 55) in Floyd County, Georgia, also produced a redstone handle disk pipe (fig. 2h). Nineteen burials were found within what appears to have been a charnel house that was located near a mound. The pipe was associated with a partially flexed adult burial that had been laid on its right side, with its skull to the southwest. The body partially had been cremated in place. In addition to the pipe, which was placed at the thighs, grave furniture included a cache of thirty-two small Dallas Triangular points at the knees (probably a quiver), a small greenstone elbow pipe near the lower waist area, a cache of twelve heavily worn drills at the neck, which was covered by a deposit of red ochre, and a small number of shell beads beneath the skull. The cremated chest was covered with mica. This high-status burial is reminiscent of the Great Tellico find mentioned previously. Some iron artifacts have turned up in the Mohman site excavations, suggesting that the site is protohistoric.[131]

Redstone disk pipes also have been found in Oklahoma. One was found at the Spiro site along the Arkansas River in the eastern portion of the state (fig. 2i). This pipe was recovered along with a redstone effigy pipe during the looting of the Craig Mound. Both specimens are believed to be intrusive, however, as neither were found within the central chamber.[132] It also is possible that dealers may have attributed these pipes to Spiro to inflate their value, a common practice of the time.[133]

Although there is evidence for ethnographic usage of redstone disk pipes, it is clear from the archaeological record that they were much more common prehistorically; or suffice to say that more got into the ground prior to the contact period. Many redstone pipes exhibit file or saw marks, thus revealing European influence, but this is not the case for disk pipes. They appear to have been made solely by traditional techniques.[134] In the Oneota culture of the upper Mississippi valley, where redstone disk pipes are most common, they may date as early as AD 1350. At Oneota sites in southern Wisconsin, where such pipes are particularly abundant, most of them seem to date from AD 1400 to about 1650. They were employed in small numbers, however, into the early nineteenth century, as they have turned up in historically utilized war bundles attributed to the Iowas, Omahas, and Osages. They also have been observed among the Sioux on the Pine Ridge Reservation in South Dakota, as well as in Cherokee contexts in Georgia. Obviously such pipes had to have retained important cultural significance long after their main period of distribution.[135]

It is important to note that up to now I have been addressing primarily those redstone disk pipes that have been found in archaeological contexts. Objects observed ethnographically have a somewhat different story to tell. Jordan Paper, for example, has examined sacred pipes in museum collections throughout the country and found that a number of them are of the disk form.[136] In my original article on the subject of calumet pipes I stated that, "Though Catlin depicted many catlinite elbow pipes in his early nineteenth-century travels on the Missouri River, it is significant that he made no mention of the disk pipe."[137] John Ewers was quick to point out that Catlin actually did make mention of such a pipe among the Mandan and that he even illustrated it![138] Catlin revealed that the sacred pipe used by Lone Man during the Okipa Ceremony to fend off the Evil Spirit was clearly a disk pipe.[139] Ewers believed this to be the same pipe that Edward Curtis photographed during the early years of the twentieth century. On this matter I certainly stand corrected, but having said that, I will still stand by the numbers. Although it is clear that the disk pipe was around historically, it tended to be in hidden contexts. It was in no way as visible to Western eyes as the elbow type form yet to be discussed. Disk pipes do not seem to have appeared at rituals to which most nineteenth-century European adventurers were privy.[140]

Penelope Drooker noted that the historic disk pipe "survivors" generally tend to be smaller and much more compact that late prehistoric examples found archaeologically. Handles, for example, tend to be shorter and disks smaller. Also, when the disk shape does occur in late historic archaeological contexts, it is interesting that more often than not limestone is the material of choice. This is true at late prehistoric or protohistoric Orr phase (Ioway) sites on the upper Iowa River, and at Caborn-Welborn phase sites in south-western Indiana and north-central Kentucky of late sixteenth- to early seventeenth-century date.[141] As noted, it has also been observed at the early eighteenth-century Portland site in Mississippi. Drooker especially noted the transitional nature of certain "disk" pipes at Madisonville, most of which are made of local materials. The disk itself is of miniscule proportions and "Some of them may be transitional to later elbow/'calumet' forms."[142]

In the lower Mississippi valley redstone disk pipes definitely predate the French, and this appears to be the case for the Southeast overall. The archaeological evidence already presented reveals them to be a late prehistoric/early protohistoric phenomenon in the Southeast.[143] Their occurrence at Moundville, Hiwassee Island, and Spiro might suggest a somewhat earlier appearance, but at each of these sites the actual context of the pipes is not clear. John Walthall, who has had extensive archaeological experience in both the Midwest and Southeast, has observed that redstone disk pipes found in the Southeast tend to be of much finer quality (in terms of carving and grinding) than those excavated on sites to the north.[144] There are two obvious explanations for this phenomenon: (1) that only the best pipes were traded south; or (2) that redstone was transported into the south primarily in raw form and then fashioned into final shapes by southeastern carvers. It has been noted, however, that unworked redstone is extremely rare on sites beyond the immediate vicinity of the redstone quarries, and I myself know of no evidence for redstone debitage being found on a prehistoric southeastern site.[145] This would seem to suggest that the pipes did indeed arrive in a finished form, but if so, why they should be of such high quality is a question that requires closer scrutiny.

Redstone Elbow Pipes

There are two basic forms of redstone elbow pipes. Those with a handle (known as a prow) are T-shaped, and those that lack a forward projection are L-shaped. Prows can be pointed, squared, rounded, cut at an angle, or hatchet shaped, while bowls range from flaring, to cylindrical, to "Micmac" in shape, and sometimes have carved effigy figures. A ridge or crest often embellishes the shank of these pipes, and perforations in these crests probably once held feathers or other ornaments. In short, a large number of combinations are possible, and seldom are any two elbow pipes alike.[146]

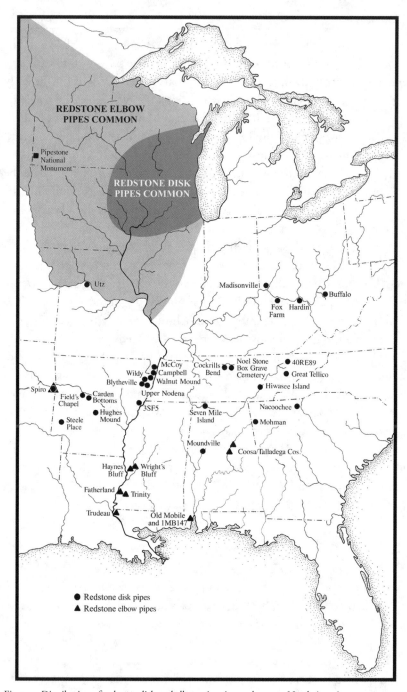

Figure 3. Distribution of redstone disk and elbow pipes in southeastern North America.

The elbow type occurs in about the same frequency as disk pipes in the Southeast, with thirty-three of the former and thirty-five of the latter, but it is not distributed as widely as the disk form (see fig. 3). Redstone elbow pipes are much more common in the Plains and prairies, typically being found in Wisconsin, Minnesota, Iowa, Illinois, and the Dakotas. They also are represented in Idaho, Indiana, Kansas, Manitoba, Michigan, Missouri, Montana, Nebraska, New Mexico, Ohio, Vermont, and Washington.[147] In the Southeast they have been reported from Mississippi, Louisiana, Tennessee, Alabama, Georgia, and Oklahoma, and they have been observed in association with almost all Plains, prairie, and Plateau Indian groups. Catlin reported that every tribe he visited was in possession of at least one redstone pipe, and usually several.[148] His pen-and-ink drawing of the pipes he observed reveals the prominence of the elbow type. It is this form that the French settlers observed when they moved into the lower Mississippi valley, as revealed in the depictions of Le Page du Pratz and Alexandre de Batz (figs. 4 and 5).

Whereas redstone disk pipes are unusually common on Arkansas sites, but absent in Mississippi and Louisiana, the opposite is the case for redstone elbow pipes. In Adams County, Mississippi, the Fatherland site (22AD501), Grand Village of the Natchez Indians, produced a portion of a redstone elbow-pipe bowl. Although the exact provenience is not clear, it probably dates to the historic Natchez phase.[149] To the east of Fatherland, a midden at the Trinity site (22AD783), which dates between AD 1700 and 1730, has yielded several fragments of what is believed to be a redstone pipe.[150]

Haynes Bluff (22WR501), located in the vicinity of Vicksburg in Warren County, Mississippi, has yielded two redstone pipes. Amateurs found one associated with an adult-male burial that was located north of the mounds. It is T-shaped, in that it has a prow in front (fig. 6a). Since two native-made pots, a large brass kettle, sixteen cast brass bells, copper tinklers, and coils of iron also accompanied the burial, the context is clearly historic. The other Haynes Bluff elbow pipe was found on the summit of Mound A associated with the skeleton of an adult male. The pipe is L-shaped and has a large notched perforated crest (fig. 6b). Such holes would have held feathers or other adornments. A gun buried with this individual is of a type that predates AD 1710. Haynes Bluff was occupied by the Tunicas between AD 1699 and 1706, by the Yazoos until AD 1730, and by the Chakchiumas in

Figure 4. Presentation of the calumet from a Chitimacha delegation to Bienville, by Le Page du Pratz (1758, 1: facing p. 105). Note the fan of feathers and the elbow-pipe form of the calumet.

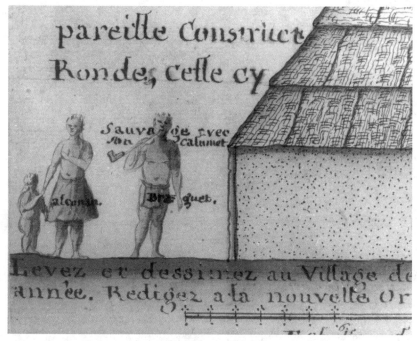

Figure 5. Detail showing redstone elbow pipe from "Temple and Cabin of the Chief, Acolapissa, 1732" by Alexandre de Batz (courtesy of the Peabody Museum, Harvard University, photo by Hillel S. Burger, 41-72/16).

AD 1736, so the pipes must predate 1736. An early eighteenth-century date is reasonable for both specimens.[151]

High on the hills above Haynes Bluff is the Wright's Bluff site (22WR540). A burial excavated by a pothunter at this site yielded an L-shaped redstone elbow pipe with a notched and drilled crest (fig. 6c). Also with the burial of this adult male were parts to seven guns, six large open-mouthed bells, a screwdriver, twenty-two hand wrought nails, a glass bead, and two native-made pots. The burial dates to the early eighteenth century.[152]

In Louisiana, four complete redstone elbow pipes were discovered at the Trudeau site (16WF25), a Tunica Indian site dating from AD 1731 to 1764. Clarence B. Moore illustrated an L-shaped pipe with two perforations in its crest (fig. 6d). Three additional elbow-type pipes, two L-shaped and one T-shaped, are part of the "Tunica Treasure" that was recovered from this site (fig. 6e–g). All three of these specimens have perforated crests, and all of the complete pipes at Trudeau are believed to have been associated with burials.[153] Excavations conducted by the Lower Mississippi Survey of Har-

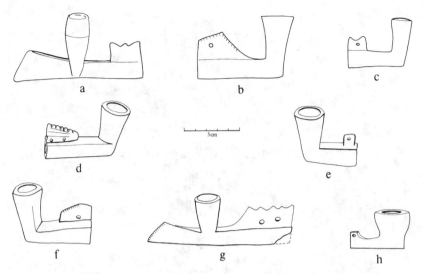

Figure 6. Redstone elbow pipes: (a–b) Haynes Bluff, Mississippi; (c) Wright's Bluff, Mississippi; (d–g) Trudeau, Louisiana; (h) Georgia, no provenience.

vard University resulted in the discovery of part of the prow of a redstone elbow pipe in village midden. This object reveals evidence for aboriginal reuse.[154]

One redstone elbow pipe has been reported from Georgia and at least eight are known from Oklahoma.[155] The strange elbow-form redstone effigy pipe from Spiro is the only excavated example from Oklahoma that possibly could be prehistoric. One very small and unusual redstone elbow pipe has been recorded from Tennessee and four have turned up in excavations conducted in central Alabama.[156] Three of the latter specimens probably were excavated in Coosa County. Two are L-shaped in form and have bowls carved in the shape of a bird-like head (fig. 7, a and b). The larger of these pipes has a prominent crest bearing a single perforation. Its stem tapers to the bowl and contains a pewter liner. The smaller "bird" pipe has a cylindrical stem and a miniscule crest. The remaining Coosa County redstone pipe is T-shaped, with a large prow, a barrel-shaped bowl, and a crest bearing three perforations (fig. 7c). A fourth Alabama redstone elbow pipe, reported to have come from "Old Coosa" in Talladega County, has a small crest and a fractured bowl (fig. 7d). It is part of the Brame Collection.

Prior to 1989, when I first published my calumet ceremony article, there was no known red pipestone debitage in the Southeast, no evidence whatsoever for the working of this material. That picture has changed dramati-

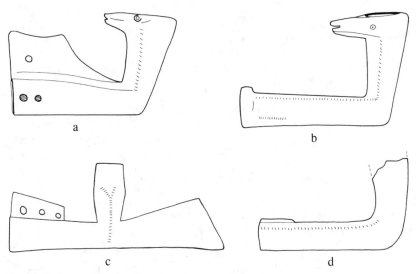

Figure 7. Redstone elbow pipes from Coosa and Talladega counties, Alabama.

cally in the last decade. Two sites in south Alabama have made an immense impact on the archaeological manifestation of the calumet ceremony. At the Old Mobile site (1MB94) and the adjacent Indian site of 1MB147, both of which date from 1702 to 1711, 375 fragments of red pipestone have been found, 248 pieces from 1MB147 and the rest from Old Mobile. What is amazing about the 127 fragments found at Old Mobile is that they were divided between six different structures. This is a clear indication that redstone pipes were made by numerous French colonists and their Indian neighbors at the beginning of the eighteenth century.[157] As I had originally argued that the French were responsible for the spread of the calumet ceremony in the Southeast, I could not have hoped for a more dramatic support of my thesis than the actual manufacture of such objects in considerable numbers at French-related sites.

Eight of the worked pieces of raw red pipestone material from Old Mobile, as well as a whittled bead blank and two sawn pieces from 1MB147 are made from Kansas pipestone. The other artifacts, however, are true catlinite, definitely derived from Pipestone National Monument. The sample includes sixteen fragmentary pipes, two tubular beads, and fifteen pieces of raw material from Old Mobile and one sawn piece of raw material from 1MB147.[158] Knowing now that most of the raw material at Old Mobile and 1MB147 is catlinite, the obvious question is how did it get there? Gregory

Waselkov and James Gundersen make a good case for the bulk of the raw material having come from an expedition led by Pierre-Charles Le Sueur who is known to have been in central Minnesota in mid-1700. By February of 1702 he was on Dauphin Island at the mouth of Mobile Bay, having brought with him a vast quantity of beaver robes and "blue and green earth" from his mines. Although there is no mention of him having actually carried catlinite with him, there is circumstantial evidence that he may have done so. Included in his list of western Sioux bands is the entry, "Hinhanetons—village of the red stone quarry," an indication that he at least knew of this material.[159]

How the Kansas pipestone got to Old Mobile and 1MB147 is another issue. We cannot automatically assume that a French expedition had to have gone to Kansas to get this material, as direct access to this region probably did not occur until the 1720s. Consequently it is possible that the Kansas pipestone may have gotten to south Alabama by indirect means, either having been traded or offered as gifts by western Indians. It is also possible that the Kansas-type pipestone argillite at Old Mobile and 1MB147 may have come from an as yet undetected source that is (or was) located closer to the source of true catlinite. As all of the Kansas pipestone that is known thus far has come from secondarily deposited glacial drift, there may have been an actual mine farther to the north that was the source of the south Alabama finds. If this was the case, Le Sueur may have transported it to Old Mobile too.[160]

It should also be mentioned that various imitations of redstone pipes were made in south Alabama at the turn of the eighteenth century. The residents of Old Mobile, for example, worked green chlorite into a pipe form. Unfortunately, it is difficult if not impossible to track down this rock type to a single source.[161] A clay pipe in imitation of a standard elbow type form was also found at 1MB147. The bowl has the same hexagonal shape of an elbow type redstone pipe and there are pierced holes along the prow, presumably for the insertion of feathers.[162] Finally, on Mound L at the Bottle Creek site (1BA2), a major Pensacola culture mound center in the Mobile-Tensaw Delta, a hematitic sandstone object was found that resembles the prow of a "catlinite" pipe. It is tabular in shape and bears striations from having been sawn. The top is rounded and the bottom and sides appear to have been ground flat. This object is believed to date to the early to mid-eighteenth century.[163]

Only one redstone pipe has been recovered from Florida to date. A fragment of a bowl bearing an engraved human face decoration was found in Pensacola at Santa María de Galve (8ES1354), a Spanish settlement that was occupied between 1698 and 1722. The pipe was probably made at Old Mobile, as an active (and illegal) trade is believed to have occurred between these two settlements at the turn of the eighteenth century.[164]

For the Southeast overall, redstone elbow pipes certainly seem to be more at home in French Louisiana than in regions to the east (see fig. 3). All archaeological evidence thus far suggests that the appearance of redstone elbow pipes in the Southeast was a historic phenomenon. It is true that they occur in prehistoric Oneota cultural contexts, but they certainly were far less popular than the disk shape in late prehistoric times.[165] Almost all redstone elbow pipes in museum collections relate to historic ethnographic groups.[166]

Summary

Redstone elbow and disk pipes clearly have separate independent histories in both the Plains and in the Southeast. In considering just the southeastern finds, not only do the disk and elbow pipes fail to coincide temporally, but they also have distinct geographical distributions. The disk form is distributed over the area much more evenly, while the elbow form is more at home in French Louisiana. In the upper Mississippi valley redstone disk pipes occur between AD 1400 and 1650, and are an especially strong marker for the Oneota culture between AD 1550 and 1650. Redstone elbow pipes occur only between about AD 1650 and 1700 in this area.[167] In the Plains we know that redstone disk pipes continued to be used historically as they are found in war bundles, but for some reason they no longer had an archaeological expression. Why this should be so bears further investigation. In the Southeast redstone disk pipes thus far have not been recorded south of the fall line (see fig. 3), while redstone elbow pipes only have been found below this natural divide. This is a curious spatial pattern that also requires examination. It is probable that this unusual distribution has historical or cultural significance.

The disk form obviously has the greater pedigree in the Southeast as it was dispersed far and wide in late prehistoric/protohistoric times, but we cannot be sure that pipes of this type necessarily indicate calumet ceremonialism. It is clear from historical records that there is indeed a close connection between redstone elbow pipes and calumet ceremonialism, so it is logical to associate these archaeological finds with such activities. However, because the disk and elbow pipes have been shown to have very different temporal and spatial distributions, we cannot automatically assume that the redstone disk pipes also are related to calumet ceremonialism. And yet that does seem to be their usage in more recent times, as disk pipes constitute nineteenth-century sacred bundles of Plains groups like the Iowas and Osages.[168] But there is a gap in the lower Mississippi valley specifically and the Southeast overall in which the disk form phases out and is replaced by the elbow form. The elbow type is clearly historic. In no case does it occur prior to the mid- to late seventeenth century, and as such, I stand by my thesis that it was at that time that calumet ceremonialism entered the Southeast, probably via French adventurers. And at the turn of the eighteenth century it is clear that the settlers at Old Mobile, and their Indian neighbors, were generating redstone pipes for regional distribution, which certainly complicates the situation but also makes it more fascinating.

Conclusions

> The third Scene ["of the Ballet"] consists of a lofty Discourse, delivered by him who holds the Calumet; for, when the Combat is ended without bloodshed, he recounts the battles at which he has been present, the victories that he has won, the names of the Nations, the places, and the Captives whom he has made. And, to reward him, he who presides at the Dance makes him a present of a fine robe of Beaver-skins, or some other article. Then, having received it, he hands the Calumet to another, the latter to a third, and so on with all the others, until every one has done his duty; then the President presents the Calumet itself to the Nation that has been invited to the Ceremony, as a token of the everlasting peace that is to exist between the two peoples.
>
> Father Jacques Marquette
> among the Illinois in 1673

In the seventeenth century the Mississippi valley was an arena of dramatic demographic changes. Diseases were taking their toll, remnant groups were moving vast distances as a result of Iroquois pressure from the north and east, and warfare was a fact of everyday life. Something was needed to create balance. Perhaps that is why the calumet ceremony and its elaborate meeting ritual spread so rapidly in the southern portion of the Mississippi valley. If the foe could not be vanquished, he at least could be tamed, at least for a while, at least to find out why he was there and what it was that he wanted. There were few good things that the French or any other European power brought to the Indians of the lower Mississippi valley, but the calumet ceremony might be the one important exception. Indian groups in the northern regions of the valley prior to French arrival had already adopted it, and most likely it would have passed south quickly in the late seventeenth century with or without the French. Through one of the strange twists of history, however, the French explorers seem to have been in a position to spread a purely native complex of ideas. It benefited the French as well as the Indians, and perhaps that is why it was adopted so fast.

Of course the French could not have taught the Indians the symbolism associated with such a complex ceremony as the calumet, as its roots extend far back into prehistory, but the evidence does seem to suggest that at least some southern groups in the lower Mississippi valley were unfamiliar with the calumet pipe and its ritual prior to French exploration.[169] The learning process, including its incorporation within an already existing highly structured meeting ritual, must have occurred in the late seventeenth century through interaction among native populations. It is possible that the calumet pipe substituted for a flute-like instrument that had deep prehistoric roots in the Southeast. The calumet ceremony played an important role in social relations throughout the early years of the eighteenth century, but it was never infallible, and the French learned not to put too much stock in its performance. Ironically, the French also may have had a hand in the eventual collapse of this institution.

Having once achieved such a paramount role, the ritualized smoking of the calumet pipe was not something to be taken lightly. This is true of the meeting ritual in general. The Indians knew this, but the French conveniently forgot it when it did not fit their purposes. La Salle insulted the Natchez, for example, by not awaiting the "Suns" (chiefs) of several towns who were to sing the calumet with him. Similarly, Cadillac and Bienville refused to smoke the calumet with the Natchez, as did Gravier and Poisson among the Quapaws.[170] The Natchez Indian murder of five Frenchmen in 1716 is believed to have been related to Governor Cadillac's unwillingness to smoke the calumet. His failure to do so was considered a declaration of war.[171] Such slights no doubt diminished the value of the calumet to the Indians in the early eighteenth century. If the calumet no longer made friends out of foes, or at least kept the peace for the period of immediate interaction, it had failed at its purpose. To be successful, all parties had to honor the ritual; otherwise it made little sense for the Indians to continue to abide by a ceremony whose rules had been changed by the intruders.[172] It is also probable that the mass production of calumet pipes at Old Mobile did irreparable damage to the sacred meaning of red pipestone to the Indians of the lower Mississippi valley.[173] The European dishonor in their dealing with the calumet ceremony, when combined with a flood on the market from mass-produced redstone pipes, may have inevitably led to the Indians themselves breaking the rules.[174] And once this happened, the symbolic significance of the calumet ceremony and its ability to make friends out of potential foes slipped into the continuing turmoil of the eighteenth century.

The power of the calumet declined dramatically in the lower Mississippi valley as the region fell under control of European powers, but its significance as an institution continued much longer in the Plains, undoubtedly because of the lag time in the advancing frontier.[175] When Lewis and Clark explored the northern Plains and Plateau between 1804 and 1806, they were well aware of the power of the calumet and of its position within an elaborate ceremony. Wherever they went, whether among the various Siouan groups, the Mandans, the Flatheads, the Shoshones, or even the Clatsops, Lewis and Clark encountered a meeting ritual that varied little, one that was very similar to that observed in the Mississippi valley. It usually consisted of a long procession, often with the visitors carried by their hosts, seated on mats, presented with a lengthy harangue, given a feast and gifts, and offered a calumet to smoke.[176] The only things missing were the body rubbings and the post striking, perhaps southeastern embellishments to the ritual.

As with the French explorers of more than a century earlier, Lewis and Clark appreciated the value of the meeting ritual in accomplishing their goals, and they participated fully in it. Clark even carried a prized ceremonial tomahawk pipe with him on his travels, analogous to Iberville's custom-made iron pipe of a century earlier.[177] A two-year expedition into uncharted land with but a single death from aggression was a remarkable achievement, but it probably would not have been possible without adherence to the rigid structure of the calumet ceremony. The advancing frontier eventually caught up with the Plains tribes, too, and the power of the calumet as a tool of temporary alliance soon faded. The sacred importance of the calumet pipe itself and ritual smoking continue to remain strong, however, highlighting just how important traditional values remain to modern Native Americans.[178]

Postscript

This article was originally published as Ian W. Brown, "The Calumet Ceremony in the Southeast and Its Archaeological Manifestations," *American Antiquity* 54 (1989): 311–31. Since it was written a lot of new literature has appeared on the subject of the calumet ritual and its associated pipes. The two most significant treatises on this subject are Jordan Paper, *Offering Smoke: The Sacred Pipe and Native American Religion* (Moscow: University of Idaho Press, 1988) and Robert L. Hall, *An Archaeology of the Soul: North American Indian Belief and Ritual* (Urbana: University of Illinois Press, 1997). Although released a year before my article was published, Paper's insightful volume unfortunately was not available to me at the time I was writing. Hall's extremely innovative probing of the mind and soul of past Indians basically represents a synthesis of works he had published in the previous two decades, most of which are referenced herein. The 1990s also witnessed a great deal of new research that shed light on past collections, such as Penelope B. Drooker's, "The View from Madisonville: Protohistoric Western Fort Ancient Interaction Patterns," *Memoirs of the Museum of Anthropology* No. 31 (Ann Arbor: University of Michigan, 1997), as well as new excavations that produced more redstone pipes. The most important recent discoveries are those at Old Mobile in south Alabama, a site that has yielded evidence of the working of pipes to trade or offer to Indians, in James N. Gundersen, Gregory A. Waselkov, and Lillian J. K. Pollock, "Pipestone Argillite Artifacts from Old Mobile and Environs," *Historical Archaeology* 36, no. 1 (2002): 105–16. I am grateful to Gregory Waselkov for giving me the opportunity to rethink the subject of archaeology and calumet ceremonialism and for being able to incorporate it into this revised and expanded edition of *Powhatan's Mantle*. I also thank Nancy Lambert-Brown for her help in revising figure 3.

Notes

The four Father Jacques Marquette epigraphs in this chapter are from Jacques Marquette's journal in Reuben Gold Thwaites, ed., The Jesuit Relations and Allied Documents: Travels and Explorations of the Jesuit Missionaries in New France, 1610–1791, *73 vols. (Cleveland: Burrows Brothers, 1896–1901), 59:129, 131; 59:135; 59:135, 137; 59:137, respectively.*

1. Robert L. Hall, "The Evolution of the Calumet-Pipe," in *Prairie Archaeology: Papers in Honor of David A. Baerreis,* ed. Guy E. Gibbon, Publications in Anthropology No. 3 (Minneapolis: University of Minnesota, 1983), 39; Robert L. Hall, *An Archaeology of the Soul: North American Indian Belief and Ritual* (Urbana: University of Illinois Press, 1997); Reuben Gold Thwaites, ed., *Collections of the State Historical Society of Wisconsin,* vol. 11 (Madison WI: Democrat Printing, 1888), 83.

2. Hall, *An Archaeology of the Soul,* 4; Jordan Paper, *Offering Smoke: The Sacred Pipe and Native American Religion* (Moscow: University of Idaho Press, 1988), 12; James W. Springer, "An Ethnohistoric Study of the Smoking Complex in Eastern North America," *Ethnohistory* 28 (1981): 230; Thwaites, ed., *Jesuit Relations,* 65:124–25.

3. Dumont de Montigny, *Mémoires historiques sur la Louisiane,* vol. 1 (Paris: 1753), 189–95 (for the origin of the more common "dit" in Dumont's name, see Jean Delanglez, "A Louisiana Poet-Historian: Dumont *dit* Montigny," *Mid-America* 19 [1937]: 32); Hall, "Evolution of the Calumet-Pipe," 37; Antoine Simon Le Page du Pratz, *Histoire de la Louisiane,* vol. 2 (Paris: 1758), 416–18; Richebourg Gaillard McWilliams, *Fleur de Lys and Calumet* (Baton Rouge: Louisiana State University Press, 1953), 5; A. H. Salter, "Catlinite Calumets: Artifactual Clues to Late Prehistoric and Historic Interactions in Eastern North America," (Honor's thesis, Harvard College, 1977), 8–9; Springer, "An Ethnohistoric Study," 230; John R. Swanton, *Indian Tribes of the Lower Mississippi Valley and Adjacent Coast of the Gulf of Mexico,* Bureau of American Ethnology Bulletin No. 43 (Washington DC: Government Printing Office, 1911), 128–29, 136–38; Thwaites, ed., *Jesuit Relations,* 58:96–99, 59:131.

4. John R. Swanton, *The Indians of the Southeastern United States,* Bureau of American Ethnology Bulletin 137 (Washington DC: Government Printing Office, 1946), 547; C. Wissler, "North American Indians of the Plains," Handbook Series No. 1 (New York: American Museum of Natural History, 1927), 116.

5. Dumont de Montigny, *Mémoires,* 1:194; Swanton, *Indian Tribes of the Lower Mississippi,* 138.

6. Mildred Mott Wedel, personal communication, 1987.

7. Hall, "Evolution of the Calumet-Pipe," 51; Hall, *An Archaeology of the Soul,* 4–5.

8. Paper, *Offering Smoke,* 12.

9. Thwaites, ed., *Jesuit Relations,* 59:130–31.

10. Dumont de Montigny, *Mémoires,* 1:190–91; Swanton, *Indian Tribes of the Lower Mississippi,* 136–37.

11. Le Page du Pratz, *Histoire de la Louisiane,* 2:416–18; Swanton, *Indian Tribes of the Lower Mississippi,* 128–29.

12. Pierre Margry, *Découvertes et établissements des Français, recit de Nicolas de La Salle, 1684* (Paris: 1875), 553; Paper, *Offering Smoke,* 20.

13. Hall, *An Archaeology of the Soul*, 50, 52.

14. Paper, *Offering Smoke*, 39–40, 74, 80.

15. George Catlin, *Letters and Notes on the Manners, Customs, and Condition of the North American Indians*, 2 vols. (New York: Wiley and Putnam, 1841), 2:163–77, pl. 270; Jeffrey P. Brain, "Tunica Treasure," in *Papers of the Peabody Museum of Archaeology and Ethnology*, vol. 71 (Cambridge MA: Peabody Museum, Harvard University, 1979), 248; John C. Ewers, *Indian Art in Pipestone: George Catlin's Portfolio in the British Museum* (London: British Museum Publications and Washington DC: Smithsonian Institution Press, 1979); Ewers, *Plains Indian Sculpture: A Traditional Art from America's Heartland* (Washington DC: Smithsonian Institution Press, 1986), 47; Gundersen et al., "Pipestone Argillite Artifacts," 107; W. R. Hiller, "History and Mythology of the Red Pipestone Quarries," *Minnesota Archaeologist* 5, no. 1 (1939): 11, 13; Paper, *Offering Smoke*, 56, 70–71; George A. West, "Tobacco, Pipes and Smoking Customs of the American Indians," *Bulletin of the Public Museum of the City of Milwaukee*, vol. 17, 2 pts. (Milwaukee: Public Museum of the City of Milwaukee, 1934), 329–30.

16. "Petrologically, pipestones of the upper middlewest and western prairies are soft argillites. An argillite is a specific petrologic name used for a claystone/mudstone shale, consisting of either clay-size mineral fragments, layered-silicate clay or 'clay-like' minerals or both, that has been naturally compacted and slightly heated during subsequent burial under later sediments into a dense (low permeability), sound (non-slacking in water), soft (easily cut with a flake of chert) low-grade metasediment. More intense squeezing and heating might have metamorphosed such a sediment into a very fine-grained red slate. Numerous argillite layers occur within the mile-plus thick Sioux Quartzite of the late Proterozoic Era (Huronian, ca. 1.5–1.7 billion years). These argillite layers can be envisioned as numerous, thin but extensive, mud-puddle deposits that collected during quiescent periods of sedimentation of the cross-bedded, very mature (well weathered), shifting sands that subsequently buried and preserved these former mudstones/claystones." James N. Gundersen and Joseph A. Tiffany, "Nature and Provenance of Red Pipestone from the Wittrock Site (13OB4), Northwest Iowa," *North American Archaeologist* 7, no. 1 (1986): 48.

17. Catlin, *Letters*, 1:234; C. S. Erickson, "Catlinite," *Central States Archaeological Journal* 13 (1966): 135.

18. James N. Gundersen, "'Catlinite' and the Spread of the Calumet Ceremony," *American Antiquity* 58 (1993): 561; Gundersen and Tiffany, "Nature and Provenance of Red Pipestone," 47; Gundersen et al., "Pipestone Argillite Artifacts," 106–7. In a review of my initial article on the calumet ceremony, I was admonished for using the term "catlinite" to classify the multitude of sources that have produced red pipestone argillites (Gundersen, "'Catlinite' and the Spread of the Calumet Ceremony"), and rightly so; the critique is valid. From the work of Gundersen and his associates at Wichita State University, it is clear that the use of "catlinite" in a generic manner confuses more than it clarifies. The term should only be used to classify stone that actually came from Pipestone National Monument. What I failed to do in my initial article is make a distinction between "provenance" and "provenience." I focused on the latter, the contexts for the discovery of pipes, and totally ignored

the former, the sources. By doing so, I missed the opportunity to explore issues relating to control of quarries, trade, and alliance networks. We now know that each of the red pipestone sources has a distinct mineralogical signature. In addition to the above sources, see James N. Gundersen, "Wisconsin Pipestone: A Preliminary Mineralogical Examination," *Wisconsin Archeologist* 68 (1987): 1–21; Gundersen, "Pipestones of the St. Helena Phase," in *The St. Helena Phase: New Data, Fresh Interpretations,* ed. Donald J. Blakeslee (Lincoln NE: J and L Reprint, 1988), 79–97; Gundersen, "The Mineralogical Characterization of Catlinite from its Sole Provenance, Pipestone National Monument, Minnesota,"*Research/Resources Management Report* MWR-17 (Omaha NE: National Park Service, Midwest Region, 1991); Gundersen, "Comments on the Distribution of Pipestone and Pipestone-Bearing Clastics in Kansan Drift, Southeastern Nebraska," *Proceedings of the Nebraska Academy of Science* 92 (1992): 2; Gundersen, "The Mineralogy of Pipestone Artifacts of the Linwood Site (Historic Pawnee) of East Central Nebraska," *Proceedings of the Nebraska Academy of Science* 92 (1992): 3; James L. Murphy, "Comments on the Composition of Catlinite and Ohio Pipestone," *Ohio Archaeologist* 46, no. 1 (1996): 10–11.

19. Gundersen and Tiffany, "Nature and Provenance of Red Pipestone."

20. Paper, *Offering Smoke,* 9, 12, uses the term "Sacred Pipe" for short stem stone pipes that were meant to be used with long wooden stems. He defines them as follows: "The distinguishing characteristic of the Sacred Pipe is that the bowl is separable from the stem and the two parts are kept apart except during ritual use. That the pipe consists of two parts is itself of symbolic importance and signifies to many Native cultures a pipe of religious consequence." Hall, *An Archaeology of the Soul,* 4, 119, prefers the term "calumet pipe" for describing these same pipes, as do I, but having said this, I must add that I recognize that not all calumet pipes had red-colored stone as a bowl material. When it is ambiguous, or actually makes a difference in my discussion, I use the adjective "redstone" to describe the bowl.

21. Joseph D. McGuire, "Pipes and Smoking Customs of the American Aborigines Based on Material in the U.S. National Museum," *Annual Report of the U. S. National Museum for 1897* (Washington DC: Government Printing Office, 1899), 571–84; William A. Turnbaugh, "Cloudblowers and Calumets," in *Plains Indian Seminar in Honor of Dr. John C. Ewers,* ed. George P. Horse Capture and G. Ball (Cody WY: Buffalo Bill Historical Center, 1984), 56.

22. Thomas W. Haberman, "Evidence for Aboriginal Tobaccos in Eastern North America," *American Antiquity* 49 (1984), fig. 1; Hall, "Evolution of the Calumet-Pipe," 40–41; Paper, *Offering Smoke,* 4–5, 8; Thomas J. Riley, Richard Edging, and Jack Rossen, "Cultigens in Prehistoric Eastern North America: Changing Paradigms," *Current Anthropology* 31, no. 5 (1990): 529–30; Alexander Von Gernet, "North American Indigenous *Nicotiana* Use and Tobacco Shamanism: The Early Documentary Record, 1520–1660," in *Tobacco Use by Native North Americans: Sacred Smoke and Silent Killer,* ed. Joseph C. Winter (Norman: University of Oklahoma Press, 2000), 59–80; Gail E. Wagner, "Tobacco in Prehistoric Eastern North America," in Winter, *Tobacco Use,* 185–201; Joseph C. Winter, "Botanical Description of the North American Tobacco Species," in Winter, *Tobacco*

Use, 97–108; Winter, "Introduction to the North American Tobacco Species," in Winter, *Tobacco Use,* 4; and Winter, "Traditional Uses of Tobacco by Native Americans," in Winter, *Tobacco Use,* 14–20.

23. Paper, *Offering Smoke,* 4.

24. Paper, *Offering Smoke,* 6.

25. Riley et al., "Cultigens in Prehistoric Eastern North America," 529; Wagner, "Tobacco in Prehistoric Eastern North America," 185; Winter, "Botanical Description," 4, 108.

26. Haberman, "Evidence for Aboriginal Tobaccos," 283.

27. Gayle Fritz, "Multiple Pathways to Farming in Precontact Eastern North America," *Journal of World Prehistory* 4, no. 4 (1990); Bruce D. Smith, "Prehistoric Plant Husbandry in Eastern North America," in *Rivers of Change: Essays on Early Agriculture in Eastern North America,* ed. Bruce D. Smith (Washington DC: Smithsonian Institution Press, 1992), 291; Wagner, "Tobacco in Prehistoric Eastern North America," 185.

28. Marlene Dobkin de Rios, *Hallucinogens: Cross-Cultural Perspectives* (1984; reprint, Prospect Heights IL: Waveland Press, 1996), 38; James L. Pearson, *Shamanism and the Ancient Mind: A Cognitive Approach to Archaeology* (Walnut Creek CA: Altamira Press, 2002), 162; Riley et al., "Cultigens in Prehistoric Eastern North America," 530.

29. Dobkin de Rios, *Hallucinogens,* 40; Pearson, *Shamanism and the Ancient Mind,* 102, 108–9; Von Gernet, "North American Indigenous *Nicotiana,*" 74.

30. Dobkin de Rios, *Hallucinogens,* 38; Pearson, *Shamanism and the Ancient Mind,* 108.

31. C. Margaret Scarry, "The Use of Plants in Mound-Related Activities at Bottle Creek and Moundville," in *Bottle Creek: A Pensacola Culture Site in South Alabama,* ed. Ian W. Brown (Tuscaloosa: University of Alabama Press, 2003), 128.

32. But having said this, it is important to remember that the pipe is a central feature of the calumet ceremony. "All of these theories as well as others have reversed the development. The Sacred Pipe is not important because of the 'calumet' ritual; rather, the Sacred Pipe is used in the 'calumet' ritual because it is central to all rituals in North America." Paper, *Offering Smoke,* 35.

33. Ian W. Brown, "Contact, Communication, and Exchange: Some Thoughts on the Rapid Movement of Ideas and Objects," in "Raw Materials and Exchange in the Mid-South," ed. Evan Peacock and Samuel O. Brookes, Archaeological Report No. 29 (Jackson: Mississippi Department of Archives and History, 1999), 132–41; John C. Ewers, "The Indian Trade of the Upper Missouri before Lewis and Clark," in *Indian Life on the Upper Missouri,* ed. John C. Ewers, (1954; reprint, Norman: University of Oklahoma Press, 1968), 20–21; Hall, *An Archaeology of the Soul,* 50; James P. Ronda, *Lewis and Clark among the Indians* (Lincoln: University of Nebraska Press, 1984), 49, 75; W. Raymond Wood, "Plains Trade in Prehistoric and Protohistoric Intertribal Relations," in *Anthropology on the Great Plains,* ed. W. Raymond Wood and Margot Liberty (Lincoln: University of Nebraska Press, 1980), 98–109.

34. Donald J. Blakeslee, "The Origin and Spread of the Calumet Ceremony," *American Antiquity* 46 (1981): 759–68; Ewers, *Plains Indian Sculpture,* 34–35; Turnbaugh, "Cloud-blowers and Calumets," 55.

35. Robert L. Hall, "An Anthropocentric Perspective for Eastern United States Prehistory," *American Antiquity* 42 (1977): 499–518; Hall, "Evolution of the Calumet-Pipe," 37–52; Hall, *An Archaeology of the Soul*, 109–23.

36. Paper, *Offering Smoke*, 89–90.

37. Robert L. Hall, "Calumet Ceremonialism, Mourning Ritual, and Mechanisms of Inter-Tribal Trade," in *Mirror and Metaphor: Material and Social Construction of Reality*, ed. Daniel W. Ingersoll Jr. and Gordon Bronitsky (Lanham MD: University Press of America, 1987), 31–42; Hall, *An Archaeology of the Soul*, 5, 50, 81–85.

38. Donald J. Blakeslee, "The Plains Interband Trade System: An Ethnohistoric and Archaeological Investigation" (PhD diss., University of Wisconsin, Milwaukee, 1975); Hall, "Calumet Ceremonialism," 30; Paper, *Offering Smoke*, 34; Wood, "Plains Trade," 98–109.

39. Blakeslee, "The Origin and Spread," 765–66; Springer, "An Ethnohistoric Study," 223–25.

40. Paper, *Offering Smoke*, 18–20.

41. Springer, "An Ethnohistoric Study," 222–23.

42. John L. Kessel, *Kiva, Cross, and Crown: The Pecos Indians and New Mexico, 1540–1840* (Washington DC: National Park Service, U.S. Department of the Interior, 1979), 194–96. See also Hall, *An Archaeology of the Soul*, 81–82; Paper, *Offering Smoke*, 18.

43. William A. Turnbaugh, "Calumet Ceremonialism as a Nativistic Response," *American Antiquity* 44 (1979): 685–91; see also Jacques Le Sueur, "History of the Calumet and of the Dance," *Contributions from the Museum of the American Indian*, vol. 12, no. 5 (New York: Heye Foundation, 1952); Edward S. Rutsch, *Smoking Technology of the Aborigines of the Iroquois Area of New York State* (Cranbury NJ: Associated University Presses, 1973), 105.

44. Turnbaugh, "Cloudblowers and Calumets," 61; personal communication, 1987.

45. On smoking see Springer, "An Ethnohistoric Study," 217–35; William A. Turnbaugh, "Tobacco, Pipes, Smoking and Rituals among the Indians of the Northeast," Quarterly Bulletin of the Archeological Society of Virginia 30 (1975): 59–71; Turnbaugh, "Elements of Nativistic Pipe Ceremonialism in the Post-Contact Northeast," *Pennsylvania Archaeologist* 47, no. 4 (1977): 1–7. On the presentation of wampum belts see Hall, "An Anthropocentric Perspective," 504; McGuire, "Pipes and Smoking Customs," 506–7, 555.

46. Paper, *Offering Smoke*, 24.

47. Tonti in Isaac J. Cox, ed., *The Journeys of René-Robert Cavelier, Sieur de La Salle*, vol. 1 (New York: A. S. Barnes, 1905), 119; Springer, "An Ethnohistoric Study," 227.

48. Pierre Margry, *Mémoires et documents pour servir a l'histoire des origines françaises des pays d'outre-mer, découvertes et établissements des français dans l'ouest et dans le sud de l'Amérique septentrionale (1614–1698)*, vol. 3 (Paris: Maisonneuve, Libraires-éditeurs, 1879–1888), 444–47; Springer, "An Ethnohistoric Study," 217–35.

49. Hall, "An Anthropocentric Perspective," 503; Hall, "Evolution of the Calumet-Pipe," 38; Hall, *An Archaeology of the Soul*, 109–23.

50. Thwaites, ed., *Jesuit Relations*, 59:134–37.

51. Drooker, "View from Madisonville," 57; David H. Dye, "Feasting with the Enemy:

Mississippian Warfare and Prestige-Goods Circulation," in *Native American Interactions: Multiscalar Analyses and Interpretations in the Eastern Woodlands*, ed. Michael S. Nassaney and Kenneth E. Sassaman (Knoxville: University of Tennessee Press, 1995), 296.

52. Drooker, "View from Madisonville," 57; Galloway, this volume; Hall, "Calumet Ceremonialism," 31; Robert L. Hall, "Cahokia Identity and Interaction Models of Cahokia Mississippian," in *Cahokia and the Hinterlands: Middle Mississippian Cultures of the Midwest*, ed. Thomas E. Emerson and R. Barry Lewis (Urbana and Chicago: University of Illinois Press, 1991), 30–31; Hall, *An Archaeology of the Soul*, 5, 81–85; Paper, *Offering Smoke*, 34–35.

53. On the Creeks and Chickasaws see Newton D. Mereness, ed., *Travels in the American Colonies* (New York: Macmillan, 1916), 519–20; Alexander Moore, ed. *Nairne's Muskogean Journals: The 1708 Expedition to the Mississippi River* (Jackson: University Press of Mississippi, 1988); Thomas Nairne, "Capt. Thomas Nairne's Journalls to the Chicasaw and Talapoosies," Additional Ms. 42,559 (London: British Library, 1708); Swanton, "Indians of the Southeastern United States," 546. On the Illinois see Thwaites, ed., *Jesuit Relations*, 59:129–37; on the Quapaws see Margry, *Mémoires et documents*, 3:444–46, and Springer, "An Ethnohistoric Study," 224; on the Mugulashas, Bayogoulas, and Houmas see Richebourg Gaillard McWilliams, trans. and ed., *Iberville's Gulf Journals* (Tuscaloosa: University of Alabama Press, 1981), 58–59, 67–70, and Swanton, "Indian Tribes of the Lower Mississippi," 285–86.

54. Benjamin Franklin French, ed., *Historical Collections of Louisiana and Florida* (New York: J. Sabin and Sons, 1869), 37–41.

55. On Bienville against the Natchez see Swanton, *Indian Tribes of the Lower Mississippi*, 199. On Charlevoix's and Le Petit's visits see Swanton, *Indian Tribes of the Lower Mississippi*, 134–35; Thwaites, ed., *Jesuit Relations*, 68:159–63; for an exhaustive literature search as to where the calumet ceremony was practiced, see McGuire, "Pipes and Smoking Customs," 546–71.

56. McWilliams, *Fleur de Lys and Calumet*, 5; Swanton, *Indians of the Southeastern United States*, 386.

57. Edward G. Bourne, ed., *Narratives of the Career of Hernando de Soto*, 2 vols. (New York: A. S. Barnes, 1904); Lawrence A. Clayton, Vernon J. Knight Jr., and Edward C. Moore, eds. *The De Soto Chronicles: The Expedition of Hernando de Soto to North America in 1539–1543*, 2 vols. (Tuscaloosa: University of Alabama Press, 1993).

58. George E. Lankford III, "Saying Hello to the Timucua," *Mid-America Folklore* 12 (1984): 7–23.

59. Springer, "An Ethnohistoric Study," 226.

60. Dan F. Morse and Vincas P. Steponaitis, personal communications, 1987.

61. Paper, *Offering Smoke*, 37.

62. Hall, "The Evolution of the Calumet-Pipe," 49–51; Hall, *An Archaeology of the Soul*, 109–23.

63. Bourne, *Narratives*, 1:81, 90–91; Lankford, "Saying Hello to the Timucua," 14–15; Swanton, *Indians of the Southeastern United States*, 547.

64. Lankford, "Saying Hello to the Timucua," 13.

65. Kessel, *Kiva, Cross, and Crown*, 195.

66. Cox, *Journeys*, 1:78–79, 136.

67. Cox, *Journeys*, 1:147–48.

68. McWilliams, *Iberville's Gulf Journals*, 46–48, 58–59, 67–68, 78, 87, 121–22, 125.

69. McWilliams, *Iberville's Gulf Journals*, 39, 46, 59.

70. McWilliams, *Iberville's Gulf Journals*, 46.

71. William N. Fenton, *The Iroquois Eagle Dance: An Offshoot of the Calumet Dance*, Bureau of American Ethnology Bulletin No. 156 (Washington DC: Government Printing Office, 1953), 164–65.

72. Blakeslee, "Origin and Spread," 766; Hall, "An Anthropocentric Perspective," 499–518; Hall, "Evolution of the Calumet-Pipe," 37–52; Springer, "An Ethnohistoric Study," 226; Turnbaugh, "Calumet Ceremonialism," 685–91; Turnbaugh, "Cloudblowers and Calumets," 54–72.

73. William Bartram, "Observations on the Creek and Cherokee Indians, by William Bartram 1789, with Prefatory and Supplementary Notes by Ephraim G. Squier," *Transactions of the American Ethnological Society*, vol. 3, pt. 1, article 1 (New York: George P. Putnam, 1853), 12; Mereness, *Travels*, 519; James Mooney, "Myths of the Cherokee," *Bureau of American Ethnology, Annual Report, 1897–1898*, pt. 1 (Washington DC: Government Printing Office, 1900), 485; John R. Swanton, "An Early Account of the Choctaw Indians," *Memoirs of the American Anthropological Association*, vol. 5, no. 2 (Lancaster PA: New Era Printing, 1918), 67; Swanton, *Indians of the Southeastern United States*, 546; Gregory A. Waselkov and Kathryn E. Holland Braund, ed., *William Bartram on the Southeastern Indians* (Lincoln: University of Nebraska Press, 1995); Samuel Cole Williams, ed., *Lieut. Henry Timberlake's Memoirs, 1756–1765* (1927; reprint, Marietta GA: Continental Book, 1948).

74. Ewers, *Plains Indian Sculpture*, 12; William Henry Holmes, *Handbook of Aboriginal American Antiquities*, Bureau of American Ethnology Bulletin No. 60, pt. 1 (Washington DC: Government Printing Office, 1919), 262–64; McGuire, "Pipes and Smoking Customs," 576–77; Paper, *Offering Smoke*, 94–97; Salter, "Catlinite Calumets," 124, 150; Turnbaugh, "Cloudblowers and Calumets," 54–58; West, "Tobacco, Pipes and Smoking Customs," 327–28.

75. Gundersen et al., "Pipestone Argillite Artifacts," 106; Gregory A. Waselkov, "Old Mobile Archaeology," Archaeology Booklet No. 1 (Mobile: University of South Alabama, Center for Archaeological Studies, 1999), 41–43.

76. Dumont de Montigny, *Mémoires*, 1:190–91; Swanton, *Indian Tribes of the Lower Mississippi*, 137.

77. Dumont de Montigny, *Mémoires*, 1:194.

78. John S. Sigstad, "The Catlinite Age and Distribution Project," *Museum Graphic*, vol. 20, no. 3 (1968): 4–5.

79. A catlinite pipe of this form from Marshall County, Tennessee, was displayed in the Gates P. Thruston exhibit at the Tennessee State Museum, Nashville, in the late 1980s.

80. Salter, "Catlinite Calumets," 121; West, "Tobacco, Pipes and Smoking Customs," 383.

81. Hall, "Evolution of the Calumet-Pipe," 42–51; Hall, *An Archaeology of the Soul*, 120; Paper, *Offering Smoke*, 90–91, also believes in the direct historical continuity between the monitor pipe and the "Sacred Pipe."

82. Drooker, "View from Madisonville," 62; John Witthoft, Harry Schoff, and Charles F. Wray, "Micmac Pipes, Vase-Shaped Pipes, and Calumets," *Pennsylvania Archaeologist* 23, nos. 3–4 (1953): 94.

83. Eli Lilly, *Prehistoric Antiquities of Indiana* (Indianapolis: Indiana Historical Society, 1937), 193; McGuire, "Pipes and Smoking Customs," 479–87; Salter, "Catlinite Calumets," 107–8; George A. West, "The Aboriginal Pipes of Wisconsin," *Wisconsin Archeologist* 4, nos. 3–4 (1905): 92–97. Witthoft et al., "Micmac Pipes."

84. Turnbaugh, "Cloudblowers and Calumets," 63; West, "Aboriginal Pipes of Wisconsin," 93. Paper, *Offering Smoke*, 69–70, 86, prefers to call this the keel type of pipe, but the Micmac name is so engrained in the literature that I see no need to revise it here.

85. John C. Ewers, *Blackfoot Indian Pipes and Pipemaking*, Bureau of American Ethnology Bulletin No. 186 (64) (Washington DC: Government Printing Office, 1963), 39–42; Ewers, *Plains Indian Sculpture*, 50; Ronald J. Mason, "Rock Island: Historical Indian Archaeology in the Northern Lake Michigan Basin," Midcontinental Journal of Archaeology Special Paper No. 6 (Kent OH: Kent State University, 1986), 158, 160–63; Salter, "Catlinite Calumets," 111; Waldo R. Wedel, *An Introduction to Pawnee Archaeology*, Bureau of American Ethnology Bulletin No. 112 (Washington DC: U.S. Government Printing Office, 1936), pl. 8j.

86. McGuire, "Pipes and Smoking Customs," 485–86, fig. 107.

87. Mason, "Rock Island," pl. 14.8, numbers 7, 11, pl. 14.9, number 9.

88. Marshall McKusick and C. Slack, "Historic Sauk Indian Art and Technology," *Journal of the Iowa Archeological Society* 12, no. 1 (1962): 2, pl. 3.

89. Mary Elizabeth Good, "Guebert Site: An 18th Century Historic Kaskaskia Indian Village in Randolph County, Illinois," *Memoir* no. 2 (Wood River IL: Central States Archaeological Societies, 1972), fig. 17, pl. 18a, e.

90. Paper, *Offering Smoke*, 70, 72, 87, 92–93; Salter, "Catlinite Calumets," 56–57; West, "Tobacco, Pipes and Smoking Customs," 205–12.

91. Henry W. Hamilton, "Tobacco Pipes of the Missouri Indians," *Memoir* no. 5 (Columbia: Missouri Archaeological Society, 1967), 13, 20; Fletcher Jolly III, "A Catlinite Disk Pipe and Associated Vessels from Lowland Eastern Arkansas," *Arkansas Archeologist* 14 (1973): 5; Lilly, *Prehistoric Antiquities of Indiana*, 194; McGuire, "Pipes and Smoking Customs," 487–88; O. L. Rice Jr., "A Catlinite Disk Pipe Find: Salvage Archaeology at 40MR12," *Central States Archaeological Journal* 21 (1974): 166; Salter, "Catlinite Calumets," 57; Turnbaugh, "Cloudblowers and Calumets," 63; West, "Tobacco, Pipes and Smoking Customs," 206; Gordon R. Willey, *An Introduction to American Archaeology: North and Middle America* (Englewood Cliffs NJ: Prentice-Hall, 1966), 310; Stephen Williams, "Ar-

morel: A Very Late Phase in the Lower Mississippi Valley," *Southeastern Archaeological Conference Bulletin* 22 (1980): 105–10.

92. Drooker, "View from Madisonville," fig. 8-29.

93. Salter, "Catlinite Calumets."

94. Jolly, "A Catlinite Disk Pipe," 1–12.

95. On the Mississippian mound sites see Jeffrey P. Brain and Philip Phillips, *Shell Gorgets: Styles of the Late Prehistoric and Protohistoric Southeast* (Cambridge MA: Peabody Museum Press, Harvard University, 1996), 384; "Catlinite" does not appear in the American Bottom region of Illinois, however, until the fourteenth century at the earliest, but more likely not until the sixteenth or seventeenth centuries, well after Cahokia's heyday; Thomas E. Emerson and Randall E. Hughes, "De-Mything the Cahokia Catlinite Trade," *Plains Anthropologist* 46, no. 176 (2001): 149–61; Thomas E. Emerson, Randall E. Hughes, Mary R. Hynes, and Sarah U. Wisseman, "The Sourcing and Interpretation of Cahokia-Style Figurines in the Trans-Mississippi South and Southeast," *American Antiquity* 68 (2003): 289.

96. Salter, "Catlinite Calumets," table 5.

97. W. A. Fox, "*Thaniba Wakondagi* among the Ontario Iroquois," *Canadian Journal of Archaeology* 26 (2002): 130–51.

98. Carl H. Chapman, *The Archaeology of Missouri, II* (Columbia: University of Missouri Press, 1980), figs. 6, 9d–e; Ewers, *Plains Indian Sculpture*, 38–39, fig. 9; Hamilton, "Tobacco Pipes of the Missouri Indians," 13; Dale R. Henning, "Development and Interrelationships of Oneota Culture in the Lower Missouri River Valley," *Missouri Archaeologist* 32 (1970): 143; Jolly, "A Catlinite Disk Pipe," 4, 10; Salter, "Catlinite Calumets," 63, 65.

99. Williams, "Armorel," 106, 108–9, fig. 2g.

100. Dan F. Morse and Phyllis A. Morse, *Archaeology of the Central Mississippi Valley* (New York: Academic Press, 1983), 277; Dan F. Morse, personal communication, 1987.

101. Dan F. Morse, personal communication, 1987.

102. Jolly, "A Catlinite Disk Pipe," 7; Williams, "Armorel," fig. 2g.

103. Dan F. Morse, personal communication, 1987. The euphemism "night diggers" refers to looters, unethical pillagers of the past who sneak onto the property of others to dig under cover of darkness.

104. Dan F. Morse, ed., "Nodena: An Account of 75 Years of Archeological Investigation in Southeast Mississippi County, Arkansas," Research Series No. 4 (Fayetteville: Arkansas Archeological Survey, 1973), 36, 70, 83; Dan F. Morse, personal communication, 1987; Morse and Morse, *Archaeology*, 277–78, fig. 13.3b; Williams, "Armorel," 109.

105. Jolly, "A Catlinite Disk Pipe," 7.

106. Dan F. Morse, personal communication, 1987.

107. Stephen Williams, personal communication, 1987.

108. Jolly, "A Catlinite Disk Pipe," fig. 3.

109. Jolly, "A Catlinite Disk Pipe," 7.

110. Jolly, "A Catlinite Disk Pipe," 7–8; Salter, "Catlinite Calumets," table 5; West, "Tobacco, Pipes and Smoking Customs," 215.

111. Jolly, "A Catlinite Disk Pipe," 8.

112. Jeffrey P. Brain, "Tunica Archaeology," *Papers of the Peabody Museum of Archaeology and Ethnology*, vol. 78 (Cambridge MA: Peabody Museum, Harvard University, 1988), 249–52; Ian W. Brown, "The Portland Site (22-M-12), an Early Eighteenth Century Historic Site in Warren County, Mississippi," *Mississippi Archaeology* 11, no. 1 (1976): 2–11; Brown, "Early 18th Century French-Indian Culture Contact in the Yazoo Bluffs Region of the Lower Mississippi Valley," (PhD diss., Brown University, 1979), 757, pl. 63.

113. Jolly, "A Catlinite Disk Pipe," 6–7.

114. Drooker, "View from Madisonville," 283–337; Penelope B. Drooker, "The Ohio Valley, 1550–1750: Patterns of Sociopolitical Coalescence and Dispersal," in *The Transformation of the Southeastern Indians, 1540–1760*, ed. Robbie Ethridge and Charles Hudson (Jackson: University Press of Mississippi, 2002), 120.

115. Drooker, "View from Madisonville," 303–9, 331–32, table 7-18, figs. 6-20, 7-5a, 7-6, 7-30; Drooker, "Ohio Valley, 1550–1750," 119–20.

116. Drooker, "Ohio Valley, 1550–1750," 121–22; Penelope B. Drooker and C. Wesley Cowan, "Transformation of the Fort Ancient Cultures of the Central Ohio Valley," in *Societies in Eclipse: Archaeology of the Eastern Woodlands Indians, AD 1400–1700*, ed. David S. Brose, C. Wesley Cowan, and Robert C. Mainfort Jr. (Washington DC: Smithsonian Institution Press, 2001), fig. 8.2.

117. Drooker, "View from Madisonville," 153, 232, 270, 305, figs. 6-20, 7-6, 8-25a.

118. Drooker, "View from Madisonville," 304–5, table 4-3, fig. 8-28; Lee H. Hanson Jr., "The Buffalo Site, a Late Seventeenth Century Indian Village Site (46PU31) in Putnam County, West Virginia," Report of Archaeological Investigations No. 5 (Morgantown: West Virginia Geological Survey, 1975), 81; W. E. Sharp, "Fort Ancient Farmers," in *Kentucky Archaeology*, ed. R. Barry Lewis (Lexington: University Press of Kentucky, 1996), 169–73.

119. Drooker, "View from Madisonville," 304.

120. Drooker, "View from Madisonville," 46; Hamilton, "Tobacco Pipes of the Missouri Indians," 24, fig. 15a; Rutsch, *Smoking Technology*, 104–5; Witthoft et al., "Micmac Pipes," 92, 102. An artifact that has been "ritually killed" is complete but broken, presumably to release the object's spirit prior to burial.

121. Salter, "Catlinite Calumets," table 5; Gates P. Thruston, *The Antiquities of Tennessee and the Adjacent States and the State of Aboriginal Society in the Scale of Civilization Represented by Them: A Series of Historical and Ethnological Studies* (Cincinnati OH: Robert Clarke, 1890), fig. 100.

122. Thomas M. N. Lewis and Madeline Kneberg, *Hiwassee Island: An Archaeological Account of Four Tennessee Indian Peoples* (Knoxville: University of Tennessee Press, 1946), 119, pl. 70c.

123. Jolly, "A Catlinite Disk Pipe," 7; Victor P. Hood and Donald B. Ball, "Rejoinder to Rich and Jolly's 'A Catlinite Pendant from East Tennessee,'" *Tennessee Archaeologist* 30 (1974): 132–37; Jack Rich and Fletcher Jolly III, "A Catlinite Pendant from East Tennessee," *Tennessee Archaeologist* 29 (1973): 58–62; Jack Rich and Fletcher Jolly III, "Reply to Hood and Ball's Rejoinder of 'A Catlinite Pendant from East Tennessee,'" *Tennessee Archaeologist* 31 (1975): 2–10.

124. John T. Dowd and John B. Broster, "Cockrills Bend Site 17c," *Journal*, vol. 1 (Nashville TN: Southeastern Indian Antiquities Survey, 1972): 17, fig. 9.

125. Jolly, "A Catlinite Disk Pipe," 7; Thruston, *Antiquities of Tennessee*, fig. 99.

126. Dan F. Morse, personal communication, 1987.

127. Jolly, "A Catlinite Disk Pipe," 7; Rice, "A Catlinite Disk Pipe Find," fig. 98.

128. Emma Lila Fundaburk and Mary Douglass Foreman, *Sun Circles and Human Hands* (Luverne AL, 1957), 36; Jolly, "A Catlinite Disk Pipe," 6; Vernon J. Knight Jr., personal communication, 1987; W. Phillip Krebs, Polly Futato, Eugene M. Futato and Vernon J. Knight Jr., "Ten Thousand Years of Alabama Prehistory: A Pictorial Resume," *Bulletin* No. 8 (Tuscaloosa: Alabama State Museum of Natural History, 1986), 62; Robert O. Mellown, *The Art of the Alabama Indians* (Tuscaloosa: University of Alabama Art Gallery, 1976), fig. 67; Salter, "Catlinite Calumets," table 5; Gregory Waselkov, personal communication, 1986; Williams, "Armorel," 109.

129. Fletcher Jolly III, "Evidence of Aboriginal Trade in Late Prehistoric Times," *Journal of Alabama Archaeology* 15, no. 2 (1969): 41, 43, fig. 1; Jolly, "A Catlinite Disk Pipe," 6–7.

130. George G. Heye, Fredrick W. Hodge, and G. H. Pepper, "The Nacoochee Mound in Georgia," *Contributions from the Museum of the American Indian* 4, no. 3 (New York: Heye Foundation, 1918), 5, 39–40, 77, pls. 14a, 49a; Salter, "Catlinite Calumets," 62–63, fig. 6a.

131. David J. Hally and John A. Walthall, personal communications, 1987.

132. Henry W. Hamilton, "The Spiro Mound," *Missouri Archaeologist* 14 (1952): 39, 90–91, pl. 22a; Hamilton, "Tobacco Pipes of the Missouri Indians," 24, fig. 15b; Salter, "Catlinite Calumets," 63.

133. Jeffrey P. Brain and Dan F. Morse, personal communications, 1987.

134. Jolly, "A Catlinite Disk Pipe," 4–5; West, "Tobacco, Pipes and Smoking Customs," 207.

135. Drooker, "View from Madisonville," 57, 62, fig. 3-8; W. Green, "Examining Protohistoric Depopulation in the Upper Midwest," *Wisconsin Archeologist* 74, nos. 1–4 (1993): 300; Heye et al., "Nacoochee Mound in Georgia," 5, 39–40, 77, pls. 14a, 49a; Jolly, "A Catlinite Disk Pipe," 5; Lilly, *Prehistoric Antiquities of Indiana*, 194; R. A. Murray, "A Brief Survey of the Pipes and Smoking Customs of the Indians of the Northern Plains," *Minnesota Archaeologist* 24, no. 1 (1962): 9–10; Paper, *Offering Smoke*, 87, 128, 133, 136; Salter, "Catlinite Calumets," table 5; West, "Tobacco, Pipes and Smoking Customs," 207, 212–16, pl. 152, figs. 1–2, pl. 153.

136. Paper, *Offering Smoke*, 121–40.

137. Brown, "Calumet Ceremony in the Southeast," 326.

138. Letter from John C. Ewers to Ian W. Brown, dated July 6, 1989, author's files.

139. Ewers, *Plains Indian Sculpture*, 180–81, fig. 177.

140. Ewers, "Letter to Brown," shared some interesting thoughts on what he believed to be the principal symbolic differences between disk and elbow pipes: "It is interesting that your findings suggest that the disk pipe is older and more widespread than the elbow pipe was in early historic times. Yet it has survived longest as a well-documented ceremonial pipe,

long after the calumet ceremony disappeared. I wonder if, even in relatively early historic times the two types may have had quite different, but equally important symbolic importance to the Indians who used them? The elbow for intertribal or intercultural meetings; the disk for ceremonies intended to bring supernatural blessings upon the maintenance of the solidarity of the in-group itself. Certainly that is what the disk pipe turned out [to] symbolize among several plains tribes during the 19th century, and among the Gros Ventres and Arapaho to this day, as their tribal medicines—comparable in importance during the 19th century to the sacred arrows of the Cheyenne and the Taime of the Kiowa as tribal medicines." This is a very important observation.

141. On the Orr phase sites see Drooker, "View from Madisonville," 62; see also Mildred Mott Wedel, "Oneota Sites on the Upper Iowa River," *Missouri Archaeologist* 21, nos. 2–4 (1959): fig. 11; West, "Tobacco, Pipes and Smoking Customs," pl. 259. On the Caborn-Welborn phase sites see Drooker, "View from Madisonville," 62, 304; Drooker, "Ohio Valley, 1550–1750," 119, 121; Warren K. Moorehead, "A Narrative of Explorations in New Mexico, Arizona, Indiana, etc.," *Bulletin* No. 3 (Andover MA: Phillips Academy Department of Archaeology, 1906), fig. 23.

142. Drooker, "View from Madisonville," 304.

143. Jolly, "A Catlinite Disk Pipe," 7; Morse and Morse, *Archaeology*, 277–78.

144. John Walthall, personal communication, 1987.

145. Turnbaugh, "Cloudblowers and Calumets," 56.

146. Salter, "Catlinite Calumets," 81, 85, 107; Turnbaugh, "Cloudblowers and Calumets," 60. For a discussion of basic elbow pipe forms, see Ewers, *Plains Indian Sculpture*, 50–51; Paper, *Offering Smoke*, 68–69.

147. Paper, *Offering Smoke*, 84–86; Salter, "Catlinite Calumets," 74, 122, table 9.

148. Catlin, *Letters*, 1:234–35, pl. 98.

149. Robert S. Neitzel, "Archeology of the Fatherland Site: The Grand Village of the Natchez," *Anthropological Papers*, vol. 51, pt. 1 (New York: American Museum of Natural History, 1965): 16, 49, pl. 13k.

150. Ian W. Brown, "Natchez Indian Archaeology: Culture Change and Stability in the Lower Mississippi Valley," Archaeological Report No. 15 (Jackson: Mississippi Department of Archives and History, 1985): 172, fig. 112e–g.

151. Jeffrey P. Brain, "The Archaeology of the Tunica (cont'd): Trial on the Yazoo," *National Geographic Society Research Report of Investigations Conducted by the Lower Mississippi Survey, Summer 1974, NGS Grant no. 1340* (in Lower Mississippi Survey files, Peabody Museum, Harvard University, Cambridge MA, 1975), fig. 7; Brain, "Tunica Treasure," 248; Brain, "Tunica Archaeology," 201–2, 209–11, 217, table 49, figs. 162, 166.

152. Brown, "Early 18th Century," 222, 758.

153. Jeffrey P. Brain, "From the Words of the Living: The Indian Speaks," in *Clues to America's Past*, ed. R. L. Breeden (Washington DC: National Geographic Society, 1976), 81; Brain, "Tunica Treasure," 248; Brain, "Tunica Archaeology," 66–67, fig. 56; Clarence B. Moore, "Some Aboriginal Sites on Mississippi River," *Journal of the Academy of Natural Sciences of Philadelphia* 14 (1911): fig. 1.

154. Brain, "Tunica Archaeology," table 4, fig. 60a.

155. For the pipe from Georgia see E. A. Barber, "Catlinite: Its Antiquity as a Material for Tobacco Pipes," *American Naturalist* 17 (1883): fig. 4; Salter, "Catlinite Calumets," table 9. For the pipes from Oklahoma see Robert E. Bell, "Protohistoric Wichita," in *Prehistory of Oklahoma*, ed. Robert E. Bell (Orlando FL: Academic Press, 1984), 373; Hamilton, "Spiro Mound," pl. 22.B; Salter, "Catlinite Calumets," table 9; West, "Tobacco, Pipes and Smoking Customs," pl. 116, fig. 3, pl. 184, figs. 2–7, pl. 209, fig. 1.

156. West, "Aboriginal Pipes of Wisconsin," pl. 204, fig. 2.

157. Gundersen et al., "Pipestone Argillite Artifacts," 106, table 1; Diane E. Silvia, "Indian and French Interaction in Colonial Louisiana during the Early Eighteenth Century" (PhD diss., Tulane University, 2000), 218–40; Gregory A. Waselkov, "Archaeological Survey Locates Blacksmith Site," *The Old Mobile Project Newsletter* No. 3 (Mobile: University of South Alabama, 1990), 1–2; Waselkov, "Archaeology at the French Colonial Site of Old Mobile (Phase I: 1989–1991)," *Anthropological Monograph* No. 1 (Mobile: University of South Alabama, 1991), 94–96; Waselkov, "Pipestone from Far Afield," *The Old Mobile Project Newsletter* No. 8 (Mobile: University of South Alabama, 1993), 3; Waselkov, "Pensacola-Mobile Trade," *The Old Mobile Project Newsletter* No. 10 (Mobile: University of South Alabama, 1994), 2–3; Waselkov, "Old Mobile Archaeology," 41–43.

158. Gundersen et al., "Pipestone Argillite Artifacts," 110–11.

159. Gundersen et al., 113–14; Waselkov, "Old Mobile Archaeology," 42.

160. Gundersen et al., "Pipestone Argillite Artifacts," 114.

161. Gundersen et al., 112–13.

162. Silvia, "Indian and French Interaction," 221, fig. 82.

163. Silvia, "Indian and French Interaction," 278, fig. 109; Diane E. Silvia, "Historic Aboriginal Reuse of a Mississippian Mound, Mound L at Bottle Creek," in *Bottle Creek, a Pensacola Culture Site in South Alabama*, ed. Ian W. Brown (Tuscaloosa: University of Alabama Press, 2003), 96.

164. Jerry Nielsen, Neal Robison, and Ernest Seckinger, *Archeological Investigations of Underground Electrical Utilities and Fort San Carlos de Austria, Site 8ES1354, Naval Air Station, Pensacola, Florida* (Mobile AL: U.S. Army Corps of Engineers, Mobile District, 1992); Waselkov, "Pensacola-Mobile Trade"; Waselkov, "Old Mobile Archaeology," 42.

165. Hamilton, "Tobacco Pipes of the Missouri Indians," 9; Wedel, "Oneota Sites on the Upper Iowa River," 54–57, fig. 11.

166. Paper, *Offering Smoke*, 121–40; Salter, "Catlinite Calumets," 74, 81.

167. Drooker, "View from Madisonville," fig. 3-8.

168. Drooker, "View from Madisonville," 57; Paper, *Offering Smoke*, 87, 128, 133; West, "Tobacco, Pipes and Smoking Customs," 212–16.

169. Hall, *An Archaeology of the Soul*; Paper, *Offering Smoke*.

170. Swanton, *Indian Tribes of the Lower Mississippi*, 193, 199, 218–19; Thwaites, ed., *Jesuit Relations*, 65:120–21, and 67:248–53.

171. Patricia Galloway, "Colonial Period Transformations in the Mississippi Valley: Disintegration, Alliance, Confederation, Playoff," in *The Transformation of the Southeastern*

Indians, 1540–1760, ed. Robbie Ethridge and Charles Hudson (Jackson: University Press of Mississippi, 2002), 245.

172. Paper, *Offering Smoke*, 22.

173. "The decline of the calumet ceremony in the Southeast from an inviolable contract to a formulaic ritual of little real consequence to either party may have been hastened by the infusion of dozens, perhaps hundreds, of calumets into the region via Old Mobile. If every household in the French town and nearby Indian villages had access to red pipestone, as is indicated by the archaeological data, how could a material previously possessed exclusively by a tribe's political and spiritual leaders retain its sacred character? When red pipestone calumets became items of popular culture, their symbolic power quickly dissipated. By around 1720 French colonists had lost interest in a now-ineffective ceremony, and importation of red pipestone to Louisiana essentially ended." Gundersen et al., "Pipestone Argillite Artifacts," 115.

174. Pierre F. X. Charlevoix, *History and General Description of New France*, trans. and ed. John Gilmary Shea, vol. 6 (London: Francis Edwards, 1902), 85–86; Jean Delanglez, *The French Jesuits in Lower Louisiana (1700–1763)* (New Orleans: Loyola University Press, 1935), 253; French, *Historical Collections*, 123–24; Dunbar Rowland and Albert G. Sanders, trans. and eds., *Mississippi Provincial Archives, 1729–1740, French Dominion*, vol. 1 (Jackson: Mississippi Department of Archives and History, 1927): 99; Swanton, *Indian Tribes of the Lower Mississippi*, 136; Thwaites, ed., *Jesuit Relations*, 68:174–75.

175. As emphasized in Paper, *Offering Smoke*, 1–3, 113–14, the importance of ritual smoking continues among Plains groups and many other Native Americans even up to the present.

176. Bernard De Voto, ed., *The Journals of Lewis and Clark* (Boston: Houghton Mifflin; Cambridge: Riverside Press, 1953), 38–39, 185–86, 191, 233, 251; Ronda, *Lewis and Clark among the Indians*, 187; Reuben Gold Thwaites, ed., *Original Journals of the Lewis and Clark Expedition, 1804–1806*, 3 vols. (New York: Dodd, Mead, 1904–5), 1:214–15, 3:362.

177. Ronda, *Lewis and Clark among the Indians*, 118, 176.

178. Paper, *Offering Smoke*, 101–14.

Symbolism of Mississippian Mounds

VERNON JAMES KNIGHT JR.

At least three centuries separate the prehistoric Mississippian cultures from the best ethnographic descriptions of their descendants, the historic southeastern Indians. The transformation that took place across this span seems so thoroughgoing that students of Mississippian culture often hesitate to use analogies based on southeastern ethnographic and ethnohistorical materials. Although dramatic changes occurred over this interim, spotty documentary and archaeological records make it hard to determine the precise nature of these changes. But much of the result can be summed up by the term "deculturation"—a loss of cultural elements, including, it is assumed, much of the richness and detail of Mississippian mythology, beliefs, and ceremonialism. The obscurity of historical processes leading to this deculturation has lent Mississippian culture a mystique that is not shared by other very late prehistoric cultures of the New World.

One of the cultural elements long assumed to have been lost during this transformation was the platform mound, a hallmark of Mississippian culture. When questioned about the origin of the mounds that dotted the region, historic southeastern Indians sometimes claimed these monuments were built by long-vanished people of whom they had no knowledge. Much was made of this, of course, by proponents of various "lost tribe" theories who imagined a superior race of mound-builders preceding that of the "red Indians." Even once it was established as fact that the southeastern Indians' ancestors had indeed built the mounds—and in the not too distant past—the nature and symbolism of Mississippian platform mounds still remained largely a mystery.

A few ethnologists, however, have noticed certain features in southeastern Indian ritual that seem relevant to the problem of Mississippian platform mounds. It appears, in fact, that although Indians of the historic era were no longer building large mounds, the beliefs underlying the practice survived. When viewed at the level of symbolism the problem dissolves, and the "loss" of platform mound ceremonialism can be seen as merely a change of emphasis within an unbroken ritual tradition. The primary aim of this chapter is to demonstrate briefly the extent of mound-related symbolism in historic southeastern Indian language, folklore, and ritual practice. These elements do not directly explain all the observed archaeological details concerning Mississippian platform mounds, as no one would expect them to, but they do give us a foothold in beginning to understand one element of the Mississippian belief system. We can begin with some lexical data.

An eighteenth-century Muskogee-language term for the large prehistoric Mississippi-period mounds scattered throughout the Creek country of Alabama and Georgia was *ekvn-like*, a compound that translates literally as "earth placed" or "earth sitting."[1] Since *liketv* also denotes placement in the sense of "dwelling" or "residence," a freer translation might be "earth dwelling." *Ekvnv*, meaning "earth" or "world," provides the root of the first part of the compound. This root word also appears in Muskogee terms for cave, mountain, hill, earthquake, and other features and properties of the physical world.[2]

A Yuchi term for mound has parallel associations. This is *ɟaetshine(ha)*, literally "land sitting," from a root connoting "earth" or "mountain."[3] Here, though, the reference is not to large Mississippi-period earthworks. Instead, it is apparently the term applied to the small ceremonial mounds still used in Yuchi square grounds.

In both of these southeastern languages, artificial mounds are conceived metaphorically as "earth sitting." This is more than just a descriptive phrase. The "earth" invoked here is the cosmological world concept, the earth island, an idea highly charged with symbolic associations in native southeastern belief systems. As this suggests, mound constructions may be understood in one sense as icons. It can be shown that artificial mounds among the historic southeastern Indians operated as conventional world symbols.

Artificial mounds occasionally figure in Muskogee origin myths, in contexts that illuminate their symbolic significance. This body of folklore shows that traditional knowledge concerning large earthworks persisted well into the modern era.[4] Mounds appear primarily in Muskogee myths associated with the towns of the Kasihta and Coweta. In one version, Kasihta warriors encounter and subsequently kill certain survivors of a vanquished enemy town. The survivors are found to be in mourning for their dead kinsmen, and they are engaged in building earthen mounds. From the context, the mounds are apparently intended, at least partly, for the burial of the dead.[5] The Kasihtas themselves also construct large mounds in the texts of at least two myths. The mounds are built to invoke supernatural assistance and protection and to provide a locus for purification ritual before battle. Black drink, the ritual emetic tea, is taken on the summit. The mounds are described as being hollow or as having a central chamber, in which people assemble to fast and purify themselves.[6] During a mythical attack by Cherokees, Coweta warriors hidden within a ceremonial mound surprise their assailants as they "pour up from the bowels of the earth" to defeat the Cherokees.[7]

This imagery of people emerging from a hollow in a mound is analogous to several Muskogee texts in which ancestors issue from underground. A Tukabatchee example compares this emergence to ants pouring out of the earth, presumably from an anthill, which substitutes for the mound in the Kasihta example.[8] In some cases this ancestral point of origin has an association with mountains, but in a text recorded by Benjamin Hawkins the mountains are replaced by two artificial mounds, supposed to be in the forks of the Red River.[9]

Several of John Swanton's Muskogee informants identified the place where the ancestors came up out of the ground as "the navel of the earth," a metaphor invoking the connection between the navel and birth or fertility.[10] There is a further connection between the "navel of the earth" and death. According to some Muskogee sources, the eventual fate of the Indians is judged to be a return into the earth at this place, just as each individual human body returns to the ground at death.[11] Additional light on this metaphor is gained from a nineteenth-century Chickasaw source. One of Henry Schoolcraft's informants noted that the Chickasaw term current for the old Mississippian mounds in their country signified "navels." "They thought that the Mississippi was the center of the earth, and those mounds were as the navel of a man in the center of his body."[12]

The motif of a great mound with a hollow chamber in its center appears again in Choctaw origin and migration mythology. In accounts collected by Henry Halbert, the large platform mound at Nanih Waiya in Winston County, Mississippi, was considered the *ishki chito*, the "great mother," of the Choctaw tribe. "In the very center of the mound, they say, ages ago, the

Great Spirit created the first Choctaws, and through a hole or cave, they crawled forth into the light of day."[13] David Bushnell collected a southern Choctaw version that adds that men emerged out of the mound together with grasshoppers and that certain men remaining inside were transformed into ants.[14] This parallels the Tukabatchee myth in respect to ants as underground dwellers that emerge to colonize the earth.

A much different account is the Choctaw migration myth recorded by Gideon Lincecum, in which the Nanih Waiya mound appears as a cultural construction erected by the Choctaws at the end of their wanderings. In the Lincecum myth the term applied to the large platform mound is *yokni chishinto*, literally "earth elevated in the shape of a mound," where again *yokni* expresses the native earth concept with a variety of connotations. One of the most remarkable accounts in southeastern Indian traditional lore is Lincecum's detailed description of the building of a large quadrilateral, multistage platform mound. The Lincecum myth also discusses the building of the smaller conical mound at the Nanih Waiya site, supposed to be erected as a foundation for the sacred pole. The larger platform mound is again represented as possessing a central chamber, as in the Choctaw creation myths collected by Halbert and Bushnell. But here, since this is a mortuary mound, the chamber harbors not living progenitors but the ancestral dead. The mound has been erected by the Choctaws for the placating of ancestral spirits and, at the same time, for the spiritual renewal of the living. As a symbolic manifestation of world renewal, the mound surfaces are replanted with trees after the mound is completed.[15]

Cherokee tradition repeats some of these images. The Cherokees conceived the Nikwasi Mound at Franklin, North Carolina, as having a central chamber inhabited by powerful spirits called the Immortals, who could pour forth by the hundreds to assist humans in battle. The symbolic equivalence of mound and sacred mountain is implicit in the belief that the Immortals possessed another lodge beneath Pilot Knob. Collapsed Cherokee townhouses of the historic era were ritually buried beneath a mantle of earth and clay, and the Cherokees believed that the large Mississippian mound in the town of Toqua, in east Tennessee, had been built in this manner.[16]

Large earth mounds, then, of recognizable Mississippian-like form and structure, were far from ignored or forgotten among the historic southeastern Indians. Linguistic and traditional material from Muskogee, Yuchi,

Chickasaw, Choctaw, and Cherokee sources yields a reasonably coherent picture of mounds as symbols. Mounds possess symbolic associations with autochthony, the underworld, birth, fertility, death, burial, the placation of spirits, emergence, purification, and supernatural protection. They are metaphorical mountains, anthills, navels, or womb-like "earth mother" representations. All are related ideas of native southeastern belief, and they find objective expression in the artificial mound as an earth or world icon.

The constructions invoked in each of the sources cited so far are all large earthworks. Some appear to be purely mythological images, whereas others have real referents, some of which can be identified today as Mississippi-period platform mounds. They differ greatly in scale from the smaller ceremonial earth mounds constructed in modern times within the square grounds of the Muskogees, Oklahoma Seminoles, and Yuchis. These small ceremonial mounds nevertheless are connected historically and developmentally to earlier, much larger earthworks. This connection will be shown presently, but first it is worth considering the nature and significance of small earthworks as observed ethnographically.

This brings us to the concept of *tadjo*, the Muskogee and Oklahoma Seminole name for ceremonial square-ground mounds. These mounds, including the Yuchi equivalents, are rebuilt each year in connection with a purification rite, the sweeping of the square ground. Yuchi examples, and perhaps Muskogee and Seminole versions as well, appear to be made up partly of dirt from square ground sweepings and partly of fresh dirt dug up nearby. In each case the new mound covers the remnant of the mound built the previous year. The mounds serve as a focal point in certain dances performed during the green corn ceremony. These are the buffalo dance and war dances among the Muskogees and Seminoles, in which the dance leader or singer may stand on the mound. Among the Yuchis the mound figures mainly in the dance-related ceremony called "jumping the mound." These mounds are distinct from other small mounds formed by successive ash piles from the annually renewed sacred fires.[17]

Other uses of the term tadjo show the significance of the connection between mounds and purification by sweeping. The low ridge formed around the square ground from repeated sweepings is also called tadjo in Muskogee and Seminole contexts.[18] The term may also refer to the circular area surrounding the ball pole at some Muskogee square grounds. This again is an area purified each year by sweeping, resulting in a low circular ridge around the margin, and sometimes a low central mound on which stands the ball pole, a "world tree" symbol.[19]

Some of these uses of the term tadjo appear to refer to a place or to structural components of the square ground, but the term may also refer to the substance "swept dirt."[20] This connotation of substance appears in the phrase "mound of tadjo," referring to the ceremonial mound.[21] In all cases, however, the emphasis is clearly on the symbolically polluted earth removed from an area to be purified and subsequently deposited in an accretional earth construction.

No other information is available concerning the detailed symbolic meanings of tadjos and their Yuchi equivalents. Nevertheless some essential features are apparent that have definite counterparts in the large constructions appearing in southeastern traditional sources and potential counterparts in Mississippian constructions. Tadjos are accretional objects, ritually constructed and ritually employed. They involve the symbolic manipulation of earth in the creation of an objective focus for purification. This occurs within the broader context of communal ceremonies directed to world renewal and agriculture.

Evidence can now be summarized in support of the contention that tadjo-type constructions of the modern era are lineal descendants of large platform mounds. First, not all reported tadjo constructions are as small as the ones seen at modern square grounds in Oklahoma. Swanton described and illustrated a tadjo at an abandoned nineteenth-century Tukabatchee square ground in Oklahoma that is comparable in size to some Mississippian mound stages. This was a platform four feet high and, estimating from Swanton's photograph, perhaps thirty feet in diameter. According to Swanton, the mound was the site of the Tukabatchee buffalo dance and war dances.[22] There are no apparent tadjo-like constructions mentioned in the earlier eighteenth-century source materials on the Muskogees, but they definitely used substructure mounds, as did the Cherokees. In the Chattahoochee valley town of Apalachicola, abandoned by approximately 1755, Bartram observed that both the square ground and the rotunda had been elevated on low substructure mounds (fig. 1).[23]

The account of John Howard Payne, describing the Tukabatchee green corn ceremony in Alabama in 1835, provides a documentary bridge between

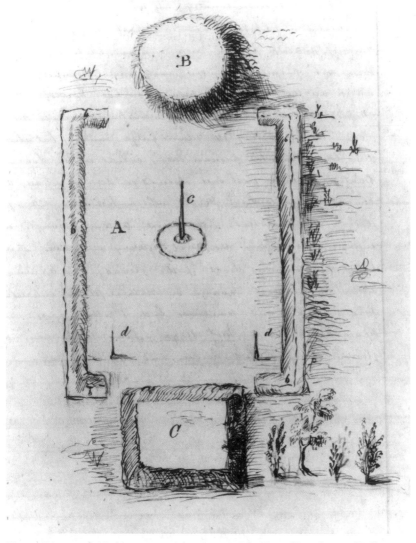

Figure 1. Diagram of a Muskogee ceremonial center, 1789. John Howard Payne's copy of William Bartram's "A view of the Antient Chunky Yard" (The Historical Society of Pennsylvania).

the addition of earth mantles to large pyramidal mounds and the more recent tadjos. Payne describes two mounds at Tukabatchee. One, perhaps both, still exists at the site, and the larger mound of the two is a typical truncated pyramid begun probably in Late Mississippi (Shine II phase) times. Payne observed the uses of these mounds during the ceremonies, but more important, he noticed that both were renewed before the observances. The large mound, used as a dance platform during the "gun dance," had been given a new coat of earth scraped from the adjacent square ground. Here then is rather stunning testimony documenting Creek mound construction in the nineteenth century, involving the addition of an earth mantle (albeit a thin one) to a genuine Mississippian platform mound. The ritual context, more-over, is unambiguous. The symbolism is that of world renewal and purifi-cation within the framework of communal green corn ceremonialism. The mantle was composed of tadjo in the sense of that term as a substance.[24]

What, then, is the significance in this context of timber buildings on Mississippian mound summits? Two observations may help clarify this is-sue. First, numerous well-documented Mississippian mound stage surfaces never supported a structure of any type. At the Mississippi-period Cemo-chechobee site in Georgia, for example, only four (or possibly five) of ten mantle surfaces in Mound B supported structures, and none of the five man-tle surfaces in Mound A yielded any evidence of a structure.[25] Second, the high degree of diversity seen in summit structure types and inferred activi-ties (contrasted with the homogeneity of mound structure) suggests the in-volvement of several kinds of social groups, or Mississippian institutional domains, in summit use.

This suggests that the symbolism of mound-building ritual and of the mound as an icon may be viewed as analytically independent of the wide variety of summit uses, whether sacred or secular, potentially sponsored by a corresponding variety of social domains in Mississippian culture. The plat-form mound and its fundamental symbolic associations may be interpreted as an expression of a broad-based communal cult type, oriented to earth, fertility, and purification, whereas summit use seems clearly the product of several more restricted orders of social organization and ritual.[26]

As Antonio Waring surmised in the 1940s, purification by the addition of blanket mantles is a dominant theme in the ritual of platform mound construction.[27] The complete sealing of earlier constructions by mantle ad-dition appears to be a kind of burial symbolism, sometimes complete with summit offerings resembling grave goods. It is no contradiction to say that it is also a kind of world renewal symbolism, since the burial of old surfaces effects renewal.[28]

These are the most conspicuous images identifiable in Mississippian platform mound ceremonialism. Other formal characteristics of Mississippian mounds may also be appropriate to their interpretation as manipulable earth symbols. The "earth island" as a cosmological entity among the southeastern Indians was normally conceived as flat-surfaced and as manifesting four world directions. A Muskogee source conceives of the earth as both flat and square, dropping off on four sides.[29] The quadrilaterality and flat-topped configuration of most Mississippian mounds may express this image concretely in an appropriate medium, earth. Even earthen ramps, a common feature of Mississippian platform mounds, may have symbolic significance, with possible affinities to the symbolism of "rain roads" and related pathways to the middle of world center icons in the Plains and the Southwest. Such world centers are called "mother earth navels" in the Rio Grande pueblo area, and they are replanted in renewal rituals.[30] These features recall Muskogee and Chickasaw sources connecting mounds with navels, and the traditional Choctaw replanting of Nanih Waiya mound.

Several of the objective characteristics of Mississippi-period platform mounds thus are also seen to be consistent with the image of the mound as an earth icon in later southeastern Indian belief. It seems justifiable, in light of the evidence for continuity, to claim that these are manifestations of an unbroken southeastern ritual tradition. This tradition employs earth mounds, either figuratively or actually, as earth icons in communal world renewal ceremonialism. Such a ritual tradition evidently predates Mississippian culture, and it survives in the green corn ceremonialism of the displaced southeastern tribes of Oklahoma.

Postscript

This paper was originally written in 1985, presented that year at the Southeastern Archaeological Conference in Birmingham. Many of the ideas herein had their origins in my dissertation research, inspired in turn by the experience of excavating Mississippian mounds on the Chattahoochee River in 1977–78.[31] Some of the basic notions in this paper first were aired briefly in another paper published in *American Antiquity* in 1986. However, the earlier article was about Mississippian religious organization, not symbolism, so my comments about meanings were left unelaborated.[32] Seeing that the former paper was well received, I felt the need to present a more fully documented essay on the symbolic significance of Mississippian mounds. The result is what you see here.

A motivating factor in writing the paper was that the few discussions of Mississippian mound building in the 1970s were thoroughly bound up with the ecological functionalism so dominant in archaeological theory at that time. Mounds, in this perspective, were seen as devices for legitimizing leadership by concentrating labor in pubic works. In an adaptationist framework, mounds were reminders of hierarchical power differences, and mound building reinforced important economic ties and social integration within the political unit. The mounds themselves were most often referred to inaccurately as "temple mounds," redundant earthen substructures for public buildings at ceremonial centers. There was little talk of meanings. Like all functionalist accounts, this was unsatisfying in that it failed to account for the specificity of the forms encountered. Many of the details I felt were most interesting about these monuments still needed examination. I was convinced that headway could be made by the strategy of "upstreaming" from historic southeastern Indian beliefs and practices. The late 1970s–early 1980s was a period during which there were growing dissatisfactions with eco-functional explanations in archaeology, and a growing awareness among archaeologists that all material culture was, to use a catch phrase of the day, "meaningfully constituted."

In general it is gratifying that the basic ideas—that Mississippian mounds were icons, that they symbolized the earth island and related concepts, that their construction can be considered as a ritual practice, that this ritual was communal in scale, and that these practices were a form of world-renewal ceremony—seem to have found wide acceptance, or at least they have been periodically cited.

A number of developments have occurred since the paper was written. Some of the notions examined in the paper have been extended backward in time, to cover pre-Mississippian earthen mounds in the Southeast as well. For example my own subsequent work suggests that Middle Woodland platform mounds reveal the same emphasis on world renewal as their later Mississippian flat-topped counterparts. I concluded, "The entire history of platform mound building in the Southeast may be seen as a conservative, long-term complex of world-renewal ritual." Beyond this, Robert Hall, in his book *An Archaeology of the Soul: North American Indian Belief and Ritual* (Urbana: University of Illinois Press, 1997), claims that Hopewellian dome-shaped burial mounds of the Middle Woodland expressed a combination of world renewal and spirit adoption ceremonies. And Jon Gibson claims that even mounds as old as the Archaic may embody Earth Island symbolism.[33] Such observations as these hint at the possibility of a uniform symbolic core underlying the whole spectrum of earth mound building in the Southeast, from its beginnings in the Middle Archaic through to its present expressions. For my part I am not prepared to defend any such claim. It is highly problematic to extend the "upstreaming" method quite that far upstream, but such speculations clearly are legitimate grist for the mill.

The critical reader should be aware of a further issue that has arisen. This chapter makes reference to a portion of a Choctaw migration myth, concerning the mounds at Nanih Waiya, recorded by Gideon Lincecum. At the urging of one of the editors, the original chapter included a verbatim extract from Lincecum's account as an appendix. Since then, Patricia Galloway's excellent treatment of Choctaw history included a strident critique of Lincecum, calling him "an accomplished con artist" and his account of Choctaw mythology as unreliable "claptrap." Galloway feels that everything in the Lincecum account that is not to be found in other versions of the Choctaw origin myth is suspect. Certainly the narrative in question, together with the man's published autobiography, were composed when Lincecum was approaching old age, decades after his residence with the Choctaws, and certainly they possess a storytelling quality and embellishments in keeping with an old man's reminiscences. There is no doubt about that. But at the same time I hesitate, without further evidence, to cast Lincecum aside as a puffed-up liar, à la Rafinesque.[34] Although Galloway fails to mention that Lincecum was a respected contributor to the natural sciences in his later years, she has raised an important red flag.[35] Perhaps the jury may be considered still out.[36]

Notes

1. A different Muskogee term glossed as "mound," *ekvn-hvlwuce*, is given in R. M. Loughridge and David M. Hodge, *English and Muskogee Dictionary* (1890; reprint, Ocmulgee OK: Baptist Home Mission Board, 1964), 120. There is no evidence, however, that this term was applied to artificial constructions. It seems properly to mean "hillock" or,

literally, "little mountain." The symbol *v* is pronounced in English as *u* in "but." The symbol *c* is pronounced as *ch*.

2. Benjamin Hawkins, "A Sketch of the Creek Country in the Years 1798 and 1799," *Georgia Historical Collections* 3, no. 1 (1848): 39; Loughridge and Hodge, *Dictionary*, 120, 157.

3. W. L. Ballard, "English-Yuchi Lexicon," undated typescript, Columbus Museum of Arts and Sciences, Columbus, Georgia. The symbol ¿ is a glottal stop.

4. Early authorities such as Bartram, Swan, and Hawkins state or imply a degree of ignorance on the part of Muskogee informants concerning the origin of particular mounds or mound groups. The specific mounds in question were perhaps centuries old at the time of these inquiries and seem to have possessed no immediate ritual importance to the local inhabitants, hence these statements. This should not be interpreted, however, as indicating that the Muskogees of the period were not acquainted with the ritual significance of mound construction. In fact there is substantial evidence of such knowledge.

5. John R. Swanton, "Social Organization and Social Usages of the Indians of the Creek Confederacy," in *Forty-Second Annual Report of the Bureau of American Ethnology* (Washington DC: Government Printing Office, 1928), 57.

6. These are activities normally appropriate for the structures of Creek ceremonial grounds.

7. Swanton, "Social Organization," 54–57.

8. Swanton, "Social Organization," 65.

9. Swanton, "Social Organization," 52, 53; Hawkins, "Sketch," 81–83.

10. Swanton, "Social Organization," 52, 63–64.

11. Swanton, "Social Organization," 77.

12. Henry Rowe Schoolcraft, *Historical and Statistical Information Respecting the History, Condition, and Prospects of the Indian Tribes of the United States*, 6 vols. (Philadelphia: Lippincott, 1851–57), 1:311.

13. Henry S. Halbert, "The Choctaw Creation Legend," *Publications of the Mississippi Historical Society* 4 (1901): 293. A description of the Nanih Waiya site is provided by Calvin S. Brown, *Archeology of Mississippi* (University: Mississippi Geological Survey, 1926), 24–28.

14. David I. Bushnell Jr., "Myths of the Louisiana Choctaw," *American Anthropologist* n.s., 12 (1910): 527. Robert L. Hall, "The Cultural Background of Mississippian Symbolism" (unpublished typescript in possession of the author, 1984), 44, sees a distant connection between this and Aztec origin accounts featuring a "grasshopper hill" (Chapultepec, in modern Mexico City) possessing an opening leading to underground caverns.

15. Gideon Lincecum, "Choctaw Traditions about Their Settlement in Mississippi and the Origin of Their Mounds," *Publications of the Mississippi Historical Society* 8 (1904): 21–42. Cf. the shorter Cherokee account of mound construction and consecration in James Mooney, "Myths of the Cherokee," in *Nineteenth Annual Report of the Bureau of American Ethnology*, pt. 1 (Washington DC: Government Printing Office, 1900), 395–96, 501–2; Cyrus Byington, *A Dictionary of the Choctaw Language*, Bureau of American Ethnology Bulletin 46 (Washington DC: Government Printing Office, 1915), 107, 367.

16. Mooney, "Myths of the Cherokee," 330, 336–37, 477; William C. Sturtevant, "Louis-Philippe on Cherokee Architecture and Clothing in 1797," *Journal of Cherokee Studies* 3 (1978): 200.

17. James H. Howard, *Shawnee! The Ceremonialism of a Native American Tribe and Its Cultural Background* (Athens: Ohio University Press, 1981), 113, 141, 146; Swanton, "Social Organization," 219.

18. Swanton, "Social Organization," 190; Howard, *Shawnee!*, 111.

19. Albert S. Gatschet, *A Migration Legend of the Creek Indians*, Brinton's Library of Aboriginal American Literature, 1, no. 4 (Philadelphia, 1884), 176; Swanton, "Social Organization," 60, 266.

20. See Loughridge and Hodge, *Dictionary*, 199.

21. Swanton, "Social Organization," figs. 35, 54.

22. John R. Swanton, "The Interpretation of Aboriginal Mounds by Means of Creek Indian Customs," in *Smithsonian Institution, Annual Report for 1927*, 498; Swanton, "Social Organization," 219, pl. 5a.

23. Frances Harper, ed., *The Travels of William Bartram*, naturalist's edition (New Haven CT: Yale University Press, 1958); William Bartram, "Observations on the Creek and Cherokee Indians," *American Ethnological Society Transactions* 3, no. 1 (1853): 52.

24. John R. Swanton, "The Green Corn Dance," *Chronicles of Oklahoma* 10 (1932): 170–95; Vernon James Knight Jr., *Tukabatchee: Archaeological Investigations at an Historic Creek Town, 1984*, Report of Investigations 45 (Moundville: University of Alabama, Office of Archaeological Research, 1985).

25. Frank T. Schnell, Vernon James Knight Jr., and Gail S. Schnell, *Cemochechobee: Archaeology of a Mississippian Ceremonial Center on the Chattahoochee River* (Gainesville: University Press of Florida, 1981).

26. Vernon James Knight Jr., "The Institutional Organization of Mississippian Religion," *American Antiquity* 51 (1986): 675–87.

27. Antonio J. Waring Jr., "The Southern Cult and Muskhogean Ceremonial," in *Waring Papers*, ed. Stephen Williams, Peabody Museum Papers 58 (Cambridge MA: Peabody Museum, Harvard University, 1968), 58. Citing Lewis and Kneberg's account of Hiwassee Island mound construction, Waring concluded that "the sealing off of the old structure was more important than the purely architectural consideration of creating an imposing temple foundation."

28. Vernon James Knight Jr., "Mississippian Ritual" (PhD diss., University of Florida, 1981); Knight, "Institutional Organization."

29. John R. Swanton, "Religious Beliefs and Medicinal Practices of the Creek Indians," in *Forty-Second Annual Report of the Bureau of American Ethnology* (Washington DC: Government Printing Office, 1928), 477.

30. Robert L. Hall, "Medicine Wheels, Sun Circles, and the Magic of World Center Shrines," *Plains Anthropologist* 30 (1985): 181–93.

31. Knight, "Mississippian Ritual"; Schnell et al., *Cemochechobee.*

32. Knight, "Institutional Organization."

33. Robert L. Hall, *An Archaeology of the Soul: North American Indian Belief and Ritual*. (Urbana: University of Illinois Press, 1997), 168 and passim; Vernon James Knight Jr., "Feasting and the Emergence of Platform Mound Ceremonialism in the Eastern United States," in *Feasts: Archeological and Ethnographic Perspectives on Food, Politics, and Power*, ed. Michael Dietler and Brian Hayden (Washington DC: Smithsonian Institution Press, 2001), 312; Jon L. Gibson, *The Ancient Mounds of Poverty Point: Place of Rings* (Gainesville: University Press of Florida, 2000), 186.

34. Charles Boewe, ed., *Profiles of Rafinesque* (Knoxville: University of Tennessee Press, 2003).

35. See the editors' introductions to Gideon Lincecum, "Autobiography of Gideon Lincecum," *Publications of the Mississippi Historical Society* 8 (1904): 443–519, and Gideon Lincecum, *Pushmataha: A Choctaw Leader and His People*, with a new introduction by Greg O'Brien (Tuscaloosa: University of Alabama Press, 2004).

36. Patricia K. Galloway, *Choctaw Genesis: 1500–1700* (Lincoln: University of Nebraska Press, 1995), 332–33; Lincecum, "Choctaw Traditions."

Indian Maps of the Colonial Southeast

GREGORY A. WASELKOV

Drawing maps was within the competence of every adult southeastern Indian of the colonial period. Early colonizers, such as Captain John Smith, John Lawson, Pierre Le Moyne d'Iberville, and René-Robert Cavelier, Sieur de La Salle, found native North Americans to be proficient cartographers whose geographical knowledge greatly expedited the first European explorations of the region. For a century and a half, information imparted by means of ephemeral maps scratched in the sand or in the cold ashes of an abandoned campfire, sketched with charcoal on bark, or painted on deerskin was incorporated directly into French and English maps, usually enhancing their accuracy. Once this fact is appreciated, one can no longer share the astonishment of Governor James Glen of South Carolina, who in 1754 wrote, "I have not rested satisfied with a verbal Discription of the Country from the Indians but have often made them trace the Rivers on the Floor with Chalk, and also on Paper, and it is surprizing how near they approach to our best Maps."[1] Although the governor might not have conceded or even realized the fact, the information contained in Glen's best maps of the interior Southeast was originally derived in large part from Indians.

Christopher Columbus first discovered the existence of an indigenous mapmaking tradition among the American Indians when, on his fourth voyage in 1502, he waylaid a Mayan trading canoe carrying an old man who drew charts of the Honduran coast.[2] From the English colony at Jamestown, established in 1607, came the earliest records of southeastern Indian maps. The Powhatan Algonquians spontaneously produced maps on at least three occasions, ranging in scope from a simple one showing the course of the James River to an ambitious map depicting their place at the center of a flat world, with England represented by a pile of sticks near the edge.[3] Only rarely, however, did European explorers express any interest in Indian cosmography; their curiosity generally was limited to the locations of rivers, paths, and settlements. When traveling through totally unfamiliar terrain, this sort of geographical information proved invaluable to numer-

ous Englishmen and Frenchmen seeking new lands to exploit. As a consequence, Indians sometimes withheld such information. According to John
Lawson, "I have put a Pen and Ink into a Savage's Hand, and he has drawn
me the Rivers, Bays, and other Parts of a Country, which afterwards I have
found to agree with a great deal of Nicety: But you must be very much in
their Favour, otherwise they will never make these Discoveries to you; especially, if it be in their own Quarters."[4] Lawson evidently lost their favor because of his encroachments on Indian lands while serving as surveyor-gen-
eral of the North Carolina colony, for he was the first Englishman killed in
the Tuscarora War of 1711.

But on the whole, geographically uninformed Europeans seldom were
disappointed in their hundreds of requests for Indian maps.[5] Unfortunately,
few of these maps now are extant, even as transcripts. G. Malcolm Lewis
has suggested that Europeans were primarily interested in the information
content, which could be incorporated directly into their own manuscript
and printed maps, and had little regard for the ethnographic value of original Indian maps as artifacts.[6] Of the six southeastern maps discussed in this
essay, five survive in the form of contemporary transcripts and the sixth is
an English manuscript map with a considerable Indian contribution. Powhatan's Mantle, a large decorated deerskin artifact, while not a geographical map in the strict sense, does share several important features with Indian maps and so is included here. The discussion that follows is limited
to a comparison of these few remaining examples of southeastern Indian
cartography, followed by a brief historical commentary and detailed place-
name analysis of each map.

Given the present rarity of colonial-period Indian maps, the very existence of these six suggests that they may be in some way atypical or at least
not necessarily representative of the entire range of maps produced by Indians of the Southeast. Such an inference seems justified when one considers the origins of the maps and the intentions of the mapmakers, insofar as
they are known or can be deduced.

Francis Nicholson, who served as governor in Maryland, Virginia, and
South Carolina, seems to have been responsible—directly or indirectly—
for collecting and preserving four of the surviving maps. The earliest map
in this group was drawn by Lawrence van den Bosh in 1694, incorporating information "on the left Side of Messacippi River, which discription I

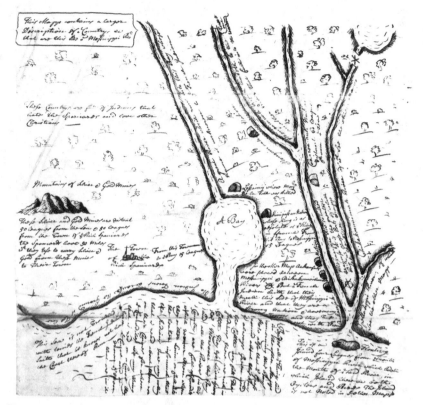

Figure 1. Van den Bosh/French Indian map, 1694 (photo courtesy of Edward E. Ayer Collection, The Newberry Library, Chicago).

lately reced. of the French Indian" (fig. 1). Soon after his arrival in Maryland, Nicholson, the newly appointed royal governor, requested a copy from van den Bosh, who seems to have obtained his information from either an Illinois or a Shawnee Indian, maybe a member of the Shawnee band that had settled near van den Bosh's home the previous year. In 1698 Nicholson interviewed a different band of Shawnees from a village on the Savannah River and persuaded one of the Indians (with the assistance of a Frenchman who lived with them) to draw "a rude draught of the route to the nearest French settlements, and by the Mississippi to the gulf."[7] That map no longer exists, so we cannot assess its accuracy, but Nicholson was impressed by its general agreement with Father Louis Hennepin's map of the region.[8] This is of particular interest in light of Nicholson's 1699 letter to Governor Black of South Carolina, whom he urged to interrogate

Figure 2. Lamhatty map, 1708 (courtesy of Virginia Historical Society, Richmond).

"Indians which you can rely upon, and lett them draw out the Country as Hennepin says one of the Shauanee Indians did for him for I think at least 400 leagues wch he found to be true."[9] The expansion of French trade and settlements in the Mississippi valley during the late seventeenth and early eighteenth centuries worried Nicholson, and he took every opportunity to learn more about the inhabitants and routes through what he termed "the Western inland frontier."[10]

The second surviving map, drawn early in 1708, depicts the travels of the Tawasa Indian Lamhatty during his captivity, from the Florida Gulf coast to Virginia (fig. 2). Colonel John Walker, who kept the Indian in servitude for a few months, sent Lamhatty's original map to Governor Jennings of Virginia. In so doing Walker may have been continuing a practice endorsed by Francis Nicholson, who had actively solicited Indian maps while governor from 1698 to 1705. However that may be, colonial officials

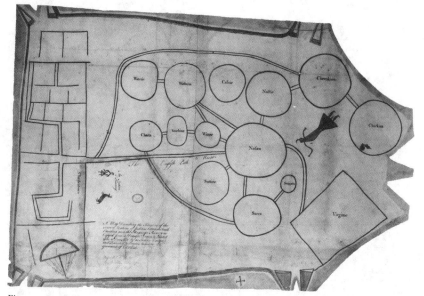

Figure 3. English copy of a Catawba deerskin map, circa 1721 (courtesy of the British Public Record Office).

preserved a contemporary copy of the map, a brief Tawasa vocabulary, and two accompanying letters.

The next two maps, in chronological sequence, are copies of painted deerskin originals presented to Nicholson after he was appointed governor of South Carolina in 1720. One details the distribution of the predominantly Siouan-speaking tribes of the South Carolina piedmont, some of which were probably loosely confederated by this time and collectively known to the English as Catawbas (fig. 3). Headmen of the Catawbas were among those Indian leaders summoned to meet the new colonial governor upon his arrival in Charlestown in 1721, so Nicholson probably received the original deerskin map sometime in that year. A second deerskin map, with extensive notations in Chickasaw, probably came into Nicholson's possession during a meeting and exchange of presents in 1723 at a Chickasaw camp near the Savannah River (fig. 4). Two years later, this most diligent collector and solicitor of southeastern Indian maps returned to England for the last time.

The final set of surviving maps exists in the form of two copies drafted by Alexandre de Batz at New Orleans in 1737, during a lull in the long war between the French and the Chickasaws. Like the two maps just described, these originally had been painted on skins. One, referred to here

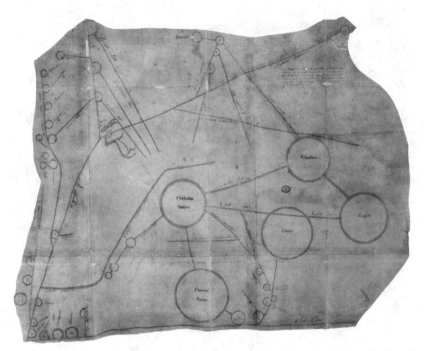

Figure 4. English copy of a Chickasaw deerskin map, circa 1723 (courtesy of the British Public Record Office).

as the Chickasaw/Alabama map, portrays the geographical disposition of Chickasaw allies and enemies as explained to an Alabama Indian emissary sent to the Chickasaws by the French (fig. 5). The other map is a plan of the Chickasaw villages, drawn by the same Alabama headman acting as a spy in anticipation of a renewed French attack (fig. 6).

Our sample of six maps can be divided, for discussion, into two groups reflecting the different intentions of their makers. In the van den Bosh/French Indian, Lamhatty, and Alabama maps, the primary concern was to convey information about the landscape by attempting to delineate river courses, networks of paths, locations of mountain ranges, and placement of villages, all in proper spatial relationship to one another. European colonists most frequently requested this type of Indian map, which could be directly transferred to printed form, occasionally with attributions to Indian sources.[11] This also was the commonest sort drawn by the native Southeasterners for their own use. Undoubtedly Baron de Lahontan's 1703 description of the northeastern Indians is applicable to the Southeast as well:

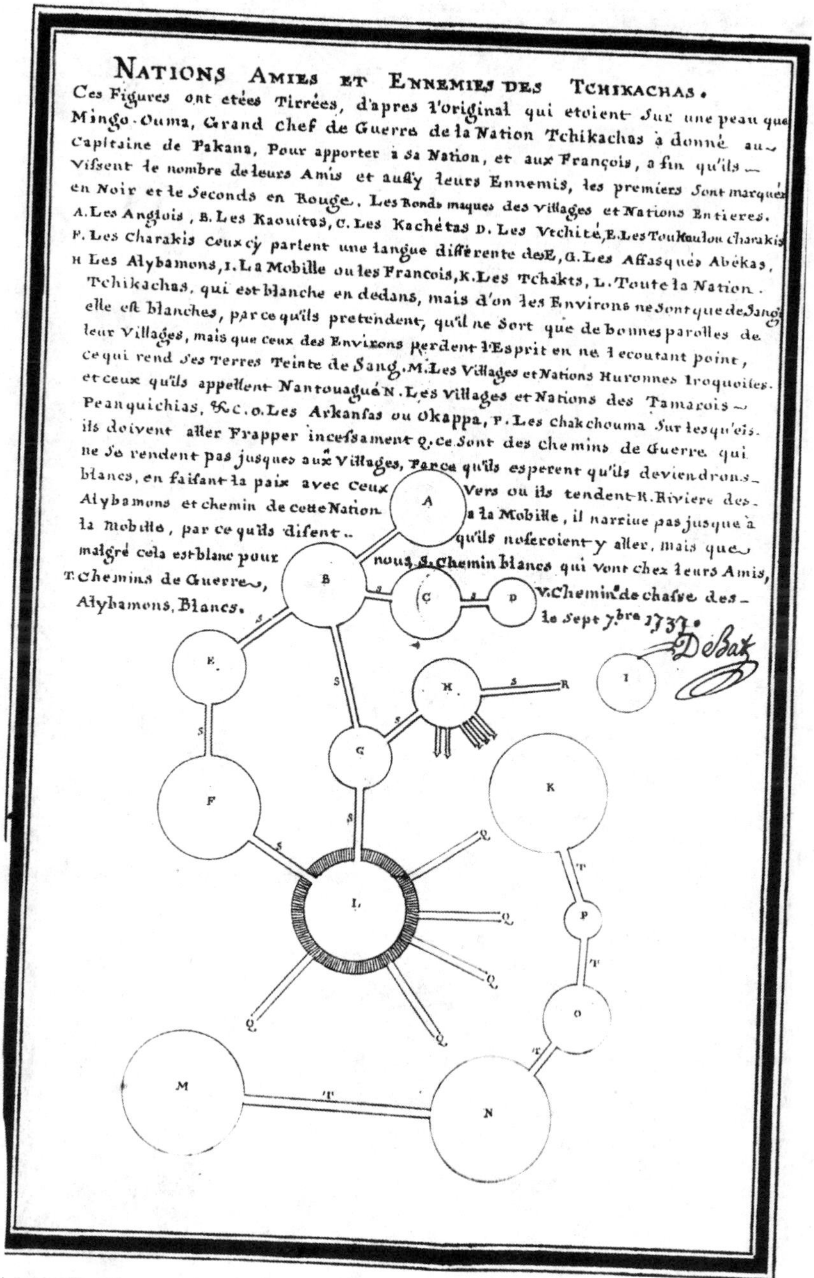

Figure 5. French copy of a Chickasaw/Alabama map, 1737 (courtesy of the Centre des Archives d'Outre-mer).

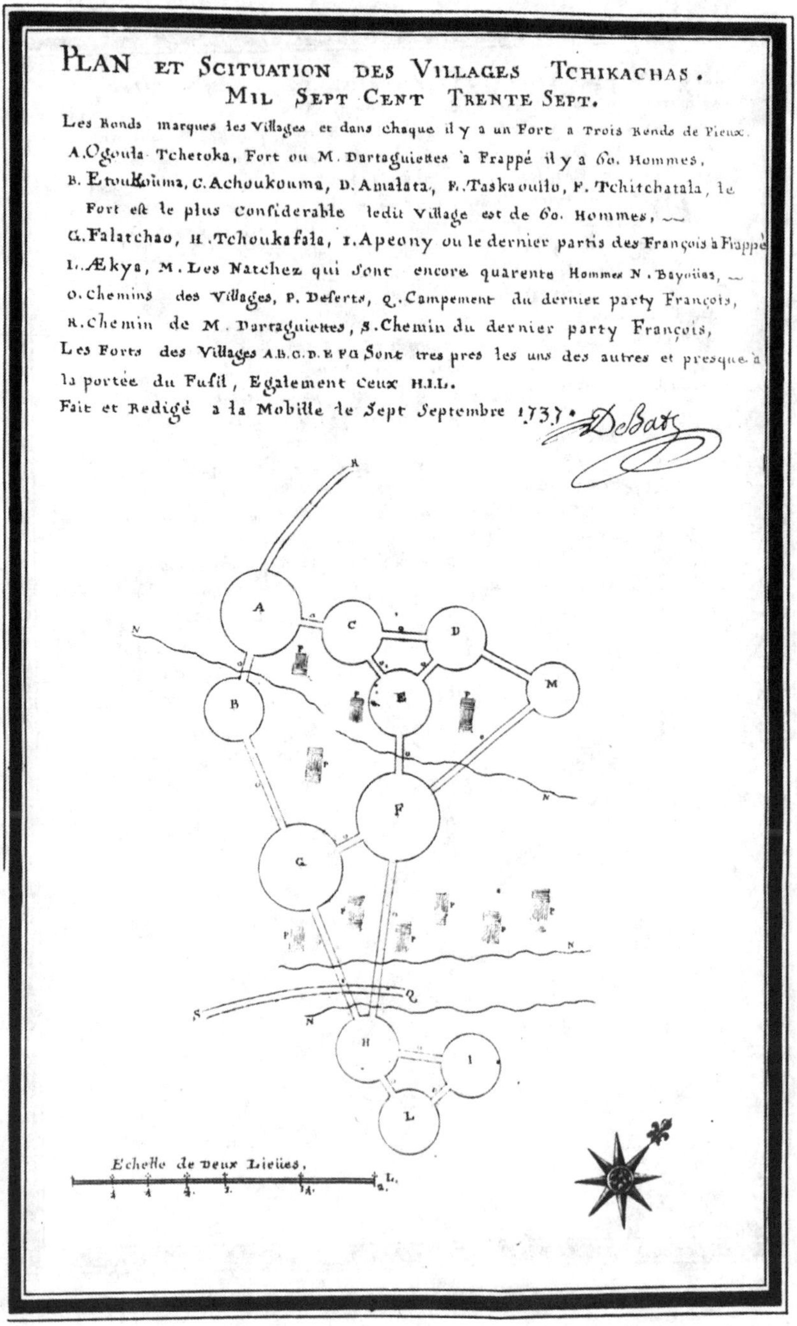

PLAN ET SCITUATION DES VILLAGES TCHIKACHAS.
MIL SEPT CENT TRENTE SEPT.

Les Ronds marques les Villages et dans chaque il y a un Fort a Trois Ronds de Pieux.
A. Ogoula Tchetoka, Fort ou M. Dartaguietes 'a Frappé il y a 60. Hommes,
B. Etoukouma, C. Achoukouma, D. Amalata, E. Taskouilo, F. Tchitchatala, le
Fort est le plus Considerable ledit Village est de 60. Hommes, ~
G. Falatchao, H. Tchoukafala, I. Apeony ou le dernier partis des François à Frappé
L. Ækya, M. Les Natchez qui Sont encore quarente Hommes N. Bayouïes, ~
O. Chemins des Villages, P. Deferts, Q. Campement du dernier party François,
R. Chemin de M. Dartaguietes, S. Chemin du dernier party François,
Les Forts des Villages A.B.C.D.E F.G Sont tres pres les uns des autres et presque a
la portée du Fufil, Egalement Ceux H.I.L.
Fait et Redigé a la Mobille le Sept Septembre 1737. DeBat

A C D
M
B E
F
G
H I
L

Echelle de Deux Lieües.

Figure 6. French copy of an Alabama Indian map, 1737 (courtesy of the Centre des Archives d'Outre-mer).

They draw the most exact Maps imaginable of the Countries they're acquainted with, for there's nothing wanting in them but the Longitude and Latitude of Places: They set down the True North according to the Pole Star; the Ports, Harbours, Rivers, Creeks and Coasts of the Lakes; the Roads, Mountains, Wood, Marshes, Meadows, etc. counting the distances by Journeys and Half-Journeys of the Warriors and allowing to every Journey Five Leagues. The sechorographical Maps are drawn upon the Rind of your Birch Tree; and when the Old Men hold a Council about War or Hunting, they're always sure to consult them.[12]

Although the Catawba, Chickasaw, and Chickasaw/Alabama maps also contain considerable geographical detail, their main function was to portray social and political relationships. Such a shift in the mapmakers' perspective required a new set of conventions to represent their social world, a set that differed from the more familiar conventions used to represent the southeastern landscape. Social distance (based, for example, on the degree of kin relatedness between social groups) and political distance (the degree of cooperation between groups, or the extent of control over groups) could be effectively mapped, but only by replacing absolute measures of Euclidean distance with a flexible, topological view of space. Topological distortion is especially evident in the Catawba and Chickasaw/Alabama examples, where distance scale and orientation to cardinal points vary continuously as one moves from place to place within each map.

Actually, topological distortion of physical space occurs in all the maps (and for that matter in contemporary European maps of the region). Although the evidence to support such an assertion is sparse, we may suppose that most southeastern Indians in the early eighteenth century were intimately familiar with a fairly small region. Lamhatty, for example, drew the Tawasa homeland, the area best known to him, more accurately, in greater detail, and to a larger scale than the rest of his map. He also made numerous errors in locating river courses and confluences once he was carried beyond his own territory. De Soto found an equally limited range of geographical knowledge among the Indians during his traverse of the Southeast in the mid-sixteenth century. Presumably the "catchment area" or home territory, the region of daily subsistence activities and closest kin ties, was as closely circumscribed for most native southeasterners as it was for Lamhatty, who unfortunately was the only one to leave us a visual depiction of his small world. Thus the distortion found in this individual type of map is attributable largely to cumulative errors by those who attempted to portray the physical landscape of areas about which they had only superficial knowledge.[13]

In contrast to the apparent geographical parochialism of Lamhatty's personal depiction is the Chickasaw deerskin map, an extraordinarily comprehensive view of what could be termed the "Greater Southeast." This map was drafted by a Chickasaw headman who probably had access to information accumulated by other tribe members. In other words, the great breadth of geographical knowledge indicated by this map, ranging as it does from Texas and Kansas in the west to New York and Florida in the east, may represent the *collective* knowledge of the Chickasaws in 1723, even if no individual Chickasaw had ever traveled so widely. This possibility also applies to the similar Catawba and Chickasaw/Alabama maps, which likewise were drawn by headmen.

These three maps have a number of important features in common, the interpretation of which can provide insights concerning the southeastern Indians' organization of their social environment and how they perceived their world. One obviously significant characteristic is the maze of paths and rivers carefully detailed on each map and connecting many of the other map elements. Rivers and trails, distinguished only in the captions, merge to form communication networks that define the limits of mapped space, which is otherwise unbounded. Rivers arise and flow to their outlets within the confines of the maps, and paths end at the most distant villages or tribal domains. These are self-contained worlds.

They are also ethnocentric worlds. In each case the cartographer has placed his native group near the map center with paths radiating outward from the focus of attention. This results in a concentric, hierarchical organization of social space; the mapmaker's village or tribe occupies the exclusive innermost position, and all others are relegated to outlying rings. On the Catawba map, small Siouan groups occupy the inner ring surrounding the centrally located Nasaws, who dominated the Catawba confederacy, while the English colonies and non-Siouan Cherokees and Chickasaws compose the outer ring. In this manner the Catawba headman expressed

social and psychological reality schematically by his manipulation of topological space.

The use of circles to represent human social groups, from the level of villages to entire tribal confederacies, is the single most widely shared symbolic feature of southeastern Indian maps (the exception being the Europeanized van den Bosh/French Indian map). In this context the circle, one
of the basic symbolic forms in the Southeast since prehistoric times, probably represents the social cohesion of the group, mirroring the village plan
common to many southeastern native societies of the period.[14] An early example of the same symbolic use of circles can be seen on the deerskin artifact attributed to Powhatan and dating to about 1608 (frontispiece). Here
thirty-four solid circles or roundlets, apparently representing all the separate
chiefdoms at least nominally under Powhatan's control, are arranged in the
familiar concentric pattern around three central figures, one of which may
represent Powhatan himself (placed in an egocentric rather than an ethnocentric position). The distribution of roundlets is essentially symmetrical,
suggesting that there was no attempt to show the actual geographical distribution of the tributary chiefdoms. In its symbolic content and organization, this decorated "mantle" differs little from the later Catawba, Chickasaw, and Chickasaw/Alabama maps. The Catawba mapmaker expanded
the metaphor of the social circle when he drew, for contrast, a rectangular
grid plan of Charlestown and a square representing Virginia. This dichot-
omy carries the clear message that Indians were alike in being circular people; the English were square. Other symbolic oppositions, either implied or
explicit, occur throughout these documents. In the concentric structure of
some maps we see an inherent opposition between us and them, the center
and the fringes of each worldview. In other cases color draws the distinction, as in the use of black paint to indicate allies and red to identify enemies on the Chickasaw/Alabama map. Here too trails appear to end before
reaching a circle, signifying a "broken" path traveled only by war parties
and distinguished from the continuous roads of peace.

By recognizing and attempting to interpret the symbolic content of the
maps we begin to understand that they are indeed political documents,
graphic depictions of the balance of power among the southeastern Indians. Consider the Chickasaw map of 1723 and the Chickasaw/Alabama map
of 1737. Despite the fourteen years that separate the two maps and the dif-

ferent audiences they were intended for (the first Governor Nicholson of English South Carolina and the other Governor Bienville of French Louisiana), the message remained essentially the same. The long war against the French and their numerous Indian allies left the Chickasaws nearly surrounded by enemies and increasingly dependent upon the distant English. But whether one's viewpoint was friendly Charlestown or hostile Nouvelle-Orléans, the Chickasaws remained a significant political entity in the region. They knew, as their maps clearly illustrated, that they still occupied a critical position at the center of the southeastern trading network. Paths interrupted by war translated to paths unusable for trade or hunting, a fact the Chickasaws found equally useful whether in requesting continued aid from the English or in peace negotiations with the French.

The Catawba headman, in his map, made a similar plea that the English recognize the Catawbas as a significant political and economic force, despite their small numbers, by virtue of their strategic location astride the crossroads of the principal trading paths from Virginia to South Carolina and from there to the numerically and economically more important Cherokees and Chickasaws. The Spanish, French, and English had long manipulated their own maps of the Southeast to propound comparable political statements, such as when each laid claim to the other's colony by extending the titles "Florida," "Louisiane," and "South Carolina" across the entire region. So they should have had little difficulty grasping the central messages carried by Indian maps and achieved through the deliberate selection and studied arrangement of symbols.

Other sorts of information included in symbolic form in these maps may not have been so readily understood by the Europeans. Both the French and the English tended to view the southeastern Indians as comprising a discrete number of autonomous tribal societies with fixed membership and relatively stable territorial boundaries, thus imposing a conformity to European notions of social and political order. Anthropologists and ethnohistorians have long understood that Native American societies held shifting views of social boundaries and inclusiveness, some evidence of which can be seen in the Indian maps. James Merrell has pointed out with regard to the Catawba map, for example, "Though colonial records had virtually ceased to mention them, Nassaws, Sugarees, Waterees, Cheraws, Saxapahaws and others still populated the mapmaker's world. Independent groups bounded by circles and linked to each other—and to Virginia and Charles Town—by paths, these entities represented the reality of Indian life as the natives saw it. 'Catawba' was nowhere to be found."[15] Other instances abound. On the earlier of the two Chickasaw maps, the rubric "Creeks" subsumed a wide range of ethnic diversity. On the later map that term was elaborated, perhaps by the Alabama Indian collaborator, who separately depicted the component polities of the Creek confederacy. Lamhatty, whether by design or because of his confusion, seems to have employed the same circular map symbol for individual villages (in Tawasa country) and related clusters of villages (in the Creek country). The visual similarity between the Alabama map of Chickasaw villages and the other maps of larger social and political groups presents the clearest evidence that the circles on these maps represent social units of significance to Indians in the particular context in which each map was drawn. They do not necessarily correspond to the "tribes" conceptualized by European colonists.

Another notable feature of the three social/political maps, and one whose meaning may have been obscure to the European recipients, is the scaling evident in the sizes of the numerous circles. Since this seems unlikely to have been selected at random, what relationships *were* specified on the basis of relative circle size? G. Malcolm Lewis has suggested that the Indians employed a range of different-sized circles as a proportional technique for showing differences in tribal populations.[16] Because we are fortunate enough to have population estimates nearly contemporaneous with the Catawba and Chickasaw maps, Lewis's idea can be explored.

First consider the 1723 Chickasaw deerskin map with its forty-three circles. Governor Bienville wrote a report a few years after the map was drawn listing the number of gunmen (a frequently used term indicating those men and boys capable of acting as warriors or hunters—about a quarter of the population) for twenty-two of the groups mentioned on the map.[17] In addition, a comparable Cherokee gunmen estimate is available from a 1721 census.[18] When these proxy population data for the twenty-three societies are compared with circle diameters on the map (fig. 7), two distinct clusters can be observed. Nineteen groups, each with fewer than 1,000 gunmen, are represented by a series of smaller circles, but within this cluster circle size does not correlate accurately with population size. A cluster of larger circles representing the more populous groups—the Creeks (2,500),

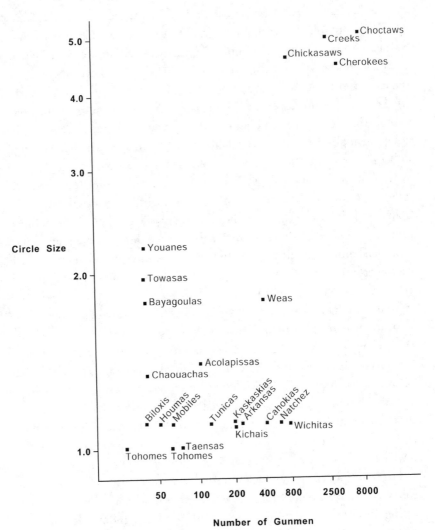

Figure 7. Comparison of map circle size and population size for twenty-three groups shown on the Chickasaw deerskin map of circa 1723.

Cherokees (3,510), and Choctaws (8,000)—also includes, somewhat incongruously at first glance, the Chickasaws, with only 800 gunmen. And among these four, the Chickasaw circle is proportionally the largest in relation to population. Evidently population alone does not adequately explain the Chickasaw mapmaker's intentions. These are more clearly understood when we recall the ethnocentric perspective common to all of these maps.

In the social environment of the Chickasaws in 1723 there were at least two types of societies: an exclusive group of numerically, militarily, politically, or economically dominant societies (which naturally included the Chickasaws as well as the English) and another including the rest of the southeastern tribes, relatively insignificant by comparison.[19]

Similar concerns shaped the Catawba mapmaker's world. According to a 1720 census, the seven Catawba villages (probably corresponding to the circles labeled Nasaw, Nustie, Casuie, Wiapie, Suttirie, Succa, and Saxippaha) contained 1,470 persons.[20] When circle size is again correlated with population, this time there does seem to be a proportional relationship, at least when comparing the Catawbas with other Siouan tribes, the smaller Wasmissas and the even less populous Charras. However, the correlation breaks down in the case of the Chickasaws and particularly the Cherokees, who had almost eight times the population of the Catawbas but were represented by only one-quarter of the encircled area. Catawba ethnocentrism led to the exaggeration of those map features most significant to the mapmaker and the reduction of peripheral elements, a distortion commonplace in the cartographic views of most cultures.

This consideration of the half-dozen surviving southeastern Indian maps brings us to the inescapable conclusion that, though every one of these documents is a representation of geographical reality, reality is perceived from culturally determined points of view. The messages encoded in visual form on these maps are only partially decipherable because our ignorance of this lost world is so great. But we can appreciate, through an imperfect understanding of these unusual and remarkable maps, the multidimensional complexity of the Southeast in the colonial era.

Postscript

I have made only minor changes to the foregoing essay. After a passage of numerous years, I think it still accurately summarizes what we know about Indian mapmaking in the colonial Southeast. In the detailed map descriptions that follow, however, I have corrected and augmented extensively. The seven artifacts/documents at the heart of this chapter carry a truly impressive amount of information, the decipherment of which can carry a re-

searcher into nearly every corner of the voluminous and ever-growing literature on the colonial Southeast. I do not doubt there is much more to
learn from them.

One of the most satisfying recent developments is the appearance of several landmark reference works on Native American mapmaking that place
these maps in a context of broader cartographic traditions. Most important of these is a comprehensive overview of that huge topic by geographer
G. Malcolm Lewis, published in 1998 by the University of Chicago Press
in volume two, book three of its encyclopedic series, *The History of Cartography*.[21] Lewis pioneered the systematic study of traditional Native American maps, which generally had been admired for their aesthetics, while
simultaneously considered sadly deficient in geographical content and cartographic sophistication. In other words, to most modern eyes they seemed
picturesque relics but, at best, naive maps. Through his publications Lewis
has encouraged many researchers (including me) to acknowledge and set
aside counterproductive ethnocentric biases, and to undertake thoroughgoing ethnographic, historical, ethnohistorical, and cartographic assess-
ments of each document's cultural context of creation and use. This chapter, in both its original and revised states, has benefited in many ways from
Lewis's inspiration, his critical editorial eye, and his unrivaled knowledge
of the field.

A flurry of research in the 1990s broadened the corpus of maps of the
Southeast drawn by Indians during the colonial period, revealing the existence of three original maps, two on skin and one on paper, from the northern and western peripheries of the region. One, drawn in ink on paper in
1755 by Chegeree, who may have been a Miami (or Twightwee) Indian, depicts the entire length of the Ohio River and many of its tributaries, associated Indian and European settlements, and paths.[22] Another, painted in
black and red on (deer?) skin, portrays rivers, towns, and trails of the Wabash valley and adjacent areas. Malcolm Lewis thinks a Piankashaw Indian
made it in 1775 during negotiations with Wabash Land Company representatives at Vincennes.[23] Both are reminiscent of the circa 1723 Chickasaw
map in their symbolism and topological geometries.

The third original is a painted bison skin curated by the Musée de l'Homme
in Paris. Brightly painted in blue, red, green, and black on a beautifully
tanned hide, the complex motif consists of three segments: at the center are

two calumets, a lunar disc, and a solar disc; along one long edge, a group
of warriors attacks an Indian town; on the opposite edge, a line of men and
women dance near three clusters of conical houses and a fourth group of
European-style buildings. Above the native houses are three Quapaw town
names and the word "ACKANSAS," the Illinois name for the Quapaw. A sinu-
ous line connects activities on the two sides of the hide, thereby conveying
a sense of mapped space. Judge Morris Arnold interprets this painted skin
as a record of a successful Quapaw attack on the Chickasaws, and the subsequent victory dance at their three villages, sometime in the 1740s. He further identifies the cluster of European-style buildings as a representation of
Arkansas Post, a French fort near the mouth of the Arkansas River. If Arnold has interpreted the cartographic elements correctly, this is the oldest
extant original of a southeastern Indian map.[24]

Several researchers have sought the conceptual origins of social/politi-
cal "circle maps" among the archaeological artifacts and settlements of prehistoric eastern North America.[25] There are suggestive visual similarities
between these maps and site plans of some of the famous Ohio Hopewell
earthworks, with their enormous circular, rectangular, and octagonal em-
bankments linked by long, paired ridges of earth.[26] Yet we still know little
about the significance of the earthwork shapes, and their ancient dates—
some thirteen centuries prior to the earliest historic Indian map—should
give pause to those who would argue for analogous (or even homologous)
symbolic values.

Apart from the Hopewell resemblance, remarkably few examples of the
"linked circles" motif have been identified in the prehistoric artwork of
eastern North America. Petroglyphs, pictographs, and mud glyphs (rock
carvings, rock paintings, and sketches on the walls of muddy caves, respectively), mostly postdating AD 1000, offer no obvious parallels.[27] One shell
artifact, an engraved marine shell cup from the Mississippi-period Spiro
site in eastern Oklahoma, has been proposed as a prehistoric map. Two
matching fragments of this partially preserved cup carry "concentric cross-
in-circle motifs in a connected grid," a design that, like the Ohio Hopewell
earthworks, does generally resemble the historic circle maps.[28] Robert H.
Lafferty III not only postulates a formal similarity between shell design
and map style but also goes so far as to overlay the engraved pattern on a
modern map of major Mississippian population centers, equating two of

the cross-in-circle elements with the large prehistoric mound sites at Cahokia and Lake George.[29]

Lafferty's identification of the Spiro shell engraving as a circle map has been deemed "plausible" and "intriguing" by several writers, but I suspect it is incorrect.[30] Even if we set aside problems of scale and circle identification there is good reason to think that the Spiro shell design is not a social/political map of the sort used by Indians of the colonial Southeast.[31] The "concentric cross-in-circle motifs in a connected grid" also appear on pottery excavated at the site of Moundville, in northern Alabama, and other important Mississippian towns, where the design has been called Moundville Engraved, *variety Hemphill*.[32] On those pots, other associated iconography indicates a cosmological interpretation—the circles as cosmic centers, not earthly places. Mississippian iconography, in general, depicts a mythic, archetypal universe, not everyday reality.[33] Although the apparent similarity of the Spiro shell engraving and historic circle maps unravels upon close scrutiny, I do not doubt that the Indians of the Southeast created circle maps, route maps, and probably other sorts of cartographic images long before the colonial period. Those native mapping traditions were well established and widespread by the eighteenth century, which suggests deep temporal origins, even in the absence of archaeological evidence to trace their development. During the colonial period Indian maps were ephemera, done on materials that seldom last long, except when curated (contrary to Indian expectations) in an archive or a museum. Evidence of prehistoric mapping may turn up someday, but we should not be surprised at its apparent absence from the archaeological record.

Most exciting of all the recent developments in Native American cartographic studies is a revival of interest in toponymy, or the study of place names, a subject largely out of favor with academics for most of the mid-twentieth century. Drawing inspiration from Keith Basso's elegant account of Western Apache place name usage in his book *Wisdom Sits in Places*, anthropologists and Indians alike are renewing efforts to record, map, and understand the American landscape as lived by native peoples. This challenging task is proving most feasible in the North American Arctic, Northwest Coast, and Southwest, where indigenous languages still thrive.[34] In the Southeast, formidable obstacles would impede a systematic mapping of sacred and secular places in the region for any particular period, historical or modern. Of course the Indian-drafted maps described in this chapter offer an intriguing starting point, but their place name content is unfortunately quite small, limited almost entirely to "tribal," village, river, and path names. Only the circa 1723 Chickasaw map, with its (now) ambiguous phrase, "Elav Chickasau au abbe," suggests the kinds of descriptive event names that must have once blanketed the landscape.[35] Yet our uncertainty over the precise translation of that phrase highlights the near impossibility of deciphering with confidence those words or phrases written down by English, French, or Spanish speakers centuries before modern linguists developed technical conventions of orthography. Colonial-era interlocutors often struggled mightily to convey sounds heard in Chickasaw, Tawasa, or Catawba speech, but simply not present in spoken English. Such transcriptions are bound to contain errors and ambiguities, many of them irresolvable today. Only in cases of place names recorded in more recent times, and subject to interpretation by native speakers, can we be certain of their meanings. Nevertheless I do not mean to be entirely discouraging. A great number of place names have already been collected and translated, and a useful (though not comprehensive) map of the region, circa 1750 for instance, might be recreated that reflects the perspectives of the Indians that inhabited the colonial Southeast.[36]

Powhatan's Mantle, circa 1608

Title: "Powhatan's Mantle" [four sewn deerskins ornamented with shell beads, reported to have belonged to the Virginia Algonquian chief, Powhatan]

Size: 235 cm × 160 cm

Original: Tradescant Collection, Ashmolean Museum, Oxford.

Reproductions:[37]

Description: This ethnographic artifact consists of four tanned deerskins pieced together with sinew thread and decorated with thirty-seven figures made from numerous small marine shell beads sewn individually onto the garment.[38] The figures include a centrally placed human in front view flanked by two animals shown in profile. The animal on the right, generally interpreted as a white-tailed deer, has cloven hooves, a short, thin tail, and large ears, while the other animal has paws with five digits, a long tail, and rela-

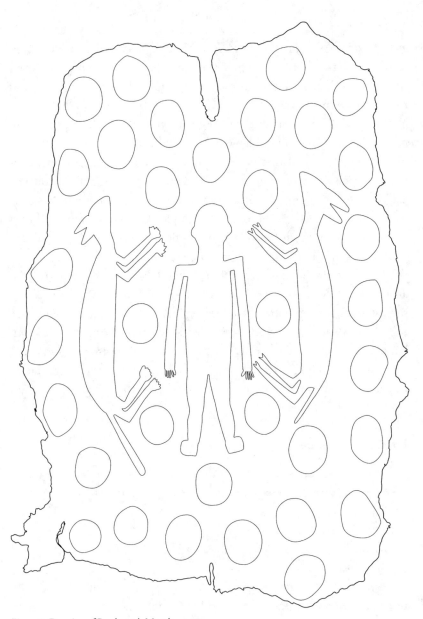

Figure 8. Drawing of Powhatan's Mantle.

tively small ears—perhaps a mountain lion. The remaining thirty-four design elements are spirally formed roundlets or discs placed in approximate
symmetry on either side of the midline. Many of the shell beads have fallen
away, leaving only thread holes to mark the original locations of two entire
roundlets and the hind legs and tails of the two animals.

This object has been considered for a very long time to be an item of
clothing, a cloak or mantle, associated with Powhatan. In 1638 a visitor to
a private museum in Lambeth, England reported seeing "the robe of the
King of Virginia" among curiosities collected by the two John Tradescants,
elder and younger.[39] An entry in a 1656 catalogue of the Tradescant collection describes an item, which is probably this same Mantle, as "Pohatan,
King of Virginia's habit all embroidered with shells, or Roanoke." Elements
of the Tradescant collection were purchased by Elias Ashmole in 1659 and
donated twenty years later as part of the Ashmolean collection to Oxford
University, where Powhatan's Mantle resides today.[40]

The younger Tradescant visited Virginia in 1637 and may have procured
the Mantle then.[41] An equally circumstantial argument for derivation can
be traced through the earliest Virginia colonial documents. Late in 1608
Captain Christopher Newport, at the behest of the Virginia Company of
London, staged a farcical "coronation" ceremony for Powhatan. Since Powhatan apparently viewed the bestowal of a scarlet robe and copper crown
as a gift from King James I deserving of reciprocity, "he gave his old shoes
and his mantle to Captain Newport." Newport sailed for England in December and arrived there by mid-January 1609. On March 5 of that year
the Spanish ambassador, Don Pedro de Zúñiga, wrote to King Philip III
that Powhatan "has sent a gift to this king," meaning James I of England.[42]
This unspecified gift could have included the mantle presented to Newport, although it seems unlikely that a present intended for the king would
then have found its way to the Tradescants.

Whatever the artifact's ultimate origin, it has until recently been thought
an undoubted southern Algonquian garment of the type described in 1624
by Captain John Smith: "The better sort use large mantels of Deare skins,
not much differing in fashion from the Irish mantels. Some imbrodered with
white beads, some with Copper, other painted after their manner."[43] Ethnohistorian Christian Feest has challenged this consensus view, however,
with an insightful reevaluation of Virginia Algonquian clothing and other

leather artifacts. In two perceptive articles, published in 1983 and 1992, he effectively discredited the "mantle" identification and offered an alternative function. In essence, Feest argues that true Virginia Algonquian mantles were smaller, fringed skins worn horizontally and tied over one shoulder— substantially different from the oversized, cloak-like Ashmolean specimen, with its vertically oriented decoration.[44] He also undermines the one historical reference that best seems to support an identification of Powhatan's Mantle as a true mantle. The annual report for 1639 on the English Jesuit mission in Maryland includes a passage that, on first glance, appears to describe Algonquian use of items precisely like Powhatan's Mantle as clothing. "The only peculiarity by which you can distinguish a chief from the common people is some badge; either a collar made of a rude jewel, or a belt, or a cloak, oftentimes ornamented with shells in circular rows."[45] Yet as Feest points out, this report was compiled in London, not Maryland, where observations of the object identified as "Powhatan's Mantle"—by that time present in the Tradescants' museum for at least a year—could have influenced the writer's interpretation.

Rather than a cloak or mantle, Feest thinks the artifact is ritual paraphernalia (possibly acquired as loot by English colonists during the years of warfare after 1622) from a Virginia Algonquian temple, where chiefly families kept the remains of their dead relatives.[46] Powhatan's matrilineal chiefly family maintained such a structure. According to John Smith, "A mile from Orapakes in a thicket of wood hee hath a house in which he keepeth his kind of Treasure, as skinnes, copper, pearle, and beades, which he storeth up against the time of his death and buriall. Here also is his store of red paint for ointment, and bowes and arrowes. This house is 50 or 60 yards in length, frequented only by Priestes. At the 4 corners of this house stand 4 Images as Sentinels, one of a Dragon, another a Beare, the 3 like a Leopard and the fourth like a giantlike man, all made evillfavordly, according to their best workmanship."[47] In support of the notion that Powhatan's Mantle once functioned in Pamunkey chiefly burial ritual, Feest cites a description of a comparable skin used in an analogous way later in the seventeenth century at the funeral of "Princess Eliz. Sonam, Sole-Daughter and Heir Apparent of Ann Sonam, a converted Queen of Maryland: It is a Doe Skin fixed upon a round Hoop near a Yard in Diameter, adorned with their Shellmoney, viz. *Roanoke* Silver and *Peak* Gold, with some rude Lines and Colours, probably designed as the Arms."[48]

Considering the uncertain history and debatable function of "Powhatan's Mantle," we should also question its attribution to Powhatan, although a less specific chiefly association seems probable. We can also accept that the decorative shell bead patterns, in addition to their aesthetic function, once carried considerable symbolic import. The central human figure and flanking feline seem to echo Smith's "Leopard and . . . a giantlike man" adorning Powhatan's family temple at Orapakes, even though we do not know their significance in Virginia Algonquian cosmography.[49]

Randolph Turner first suggested that the thirty-four roundlets may have had a more mundane political meaning, representing the social districts under Powhatan's control.[50] Turner based his supposition on a 1612 reference by William Strachey, who noted that Powhatan's "petty Weroances in all, may be in nomber, about three or fower and thirty, all which have their precincts, and bowndes, proper."[51] Strachey went on to enumerate thirty-two werowances from the area of the James and York rivers. His list, however, includes both greater and lesser werowances, corresponding to about twenty-four districts in a limited area, evidently the core of the chiefdom and the extent of Powhatan's absolute control.[52] Beyond that core area, Powhatan claimed as many as thirty-six districts subject, in some degree, to his influence, which may coincide more closely to Strachey's description of the geographic limits of Powhatan's power than does his list of werowances.[53] The "Mantle" so long attributed to that paramount chief could be interpreted not as a statement of absolute control over a circumscribed region, but as a claim to broad hegemony over a core area plus an incompletely consolidated periphery.

Van den Bosh/French Indian Map, 1694

Title: Discription of ye Countryes that are this side ye Messacippi River
Size: 37 cm × 32 cm
Original: Ayer Collection no. 59, The Newberry Library, Chicago.
Reproductions:[54]
Description: This manuscript map is accompanied by a letter (both copies of lost originals) from Lawrence van den Bosh to Governor Francis Nicholson of Maryland, dated "From North Sassifrix, ye 19th Day of October

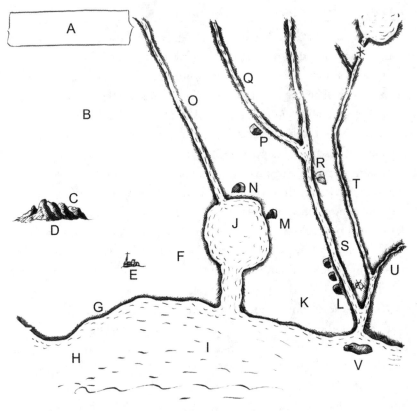

Figure 9. Keyed drawing of the van den Bosh/French Indian map.

1694." Van den Bosh has been identified as Laurent van den Boschk, an ordained Anglican priest from the Carolinas, who later resided in North Sassafras Parish, Cecil County, Maryland, near the falls of the Susquehanna River.[55] The letter states that he obtained his information "on the left Side of Messacippi River, which discription I lately reced. of the French Indian." The identity of this Indian remains unknown, but it is interesting to note that "Wittowees, Twistwees and naked Indians" (i.e., Miamis and other western Indians) encouraged by the French, raided the Maryland colony at the falls of the Susquehanna and Potomac rivers during the 1690s.[56] Probably more relevant is the appearance of the Frenchman Martin Chartier and a band of Shawnees in Maryland in 1692. By the following year these Indians were settled on the south bank of the lower Elk River in Cecil County, not far from van den Bosh's residence. Before 1690 they had lived near the French outpost at Starved Rock (Fort St. Louis on the Illinois River), which was La Salle and Tonti's base for western and southern exploration.[57] The accompanying letter reads as follows:

Copy of a Letter to Collo Nicholson Govr of Maryland

Sr

I intended at first to Send this Map to yor Excy by Collo Hermans, but in that Regard being Disapointed of my purpose I gave it to Mr Hensbys [?], who forgott to carry it to yor Excy, in fine Mr Robinson was pleased to take it and to promise that he would deliver it unto yor Excy wch if he hath done 'tis well if not I send now again to yor Excy (by Mr Tarkington) a copy of the Same Mapp and a larger description of the Countrys River ec that are on the left Side of Messacippi River, which discription I lately reced of the French Indian. If this Labour of Mine hath the happiness to please yor Excy I will rejoice for it and I shall think my Pains not to have been Spent in vain In ye mean while I am & will Remain

Yor Excy ec
Lawrence Vanden Bosh
From North Sassifrix
ye 19th Day of Octobr
1694

Key to map notations:

A. This Mapp contains a larger Discription of ye Countrys ec that are this side ye Messicippi Rivr

B. These Countrys are full of Indians that hate the Spaniards and love other Christians

C. Mountains of Silver & Gold Mines

D. These Silver and Gold Mines are distant 50 leagues from the Sea & 50 leagues from the Town of ye Rich Spaniards the Spaniards have 50 Miles [Mules?] wch they use to carry Silver & Gold from these Mines to their Town

E. The Town of the Rich Spaniards

F. From this Town to ye Bay 15 leagues

G. No Indian Towns because the Ground is Too low

H. This Sea is not Troubled with winds the French Indian Saith that he knows not how the Coast thereof Runs

I. Besides all ye Things Said in the other Mapp concerning this Bay Note also that ye Grass round about this Bay is always Green and the Cattle very fatt The Indians there are rich in Cattle They use Silver Spoons &c Moreover this Bay and all the Rivers in this Country are full of Crocodiles which devour Men when they either Swim or fall into the Water insomuch that the Indians dare cary nothing that is read about them nor on their Canoes for when ye Crocodiles See any thing that is red on a Canoe they turn ye Canoe and so drown ye Men that are in it

J. A Bay

K. In the other Map Ackansahs were placed between Messacippi & Chikakomaimah Rivers But ye French Indian Saith that they dwell this Side of Messicippi River and that they are a Strong Nation & have many Towns and they Trade not with ye French

L. Ackansah Nation

M. Kinipiseau Nation whose King is as absolute as ye King in France From this Bay to Messicippi 15 leagues

N. Lessainy where Monsr De la Sale was killed

O. A great River which runs into this Bay whose name is unknown to ye French Indian

P. Mongoin nah Nation

Q. Mongoin nah River leadeth to the Towne [?] another River that fall in to the western one

R. Coa-roa-auh Nation distant 60 leagues from ye Sea

S. Messacippi Rivr so called because it is the greatest Rivr in those Parts of islands see the other Mapp

T. Chikakomaimah River of wch See the other Mapp

U. Ipellasippi River; of which See the other Mapp

V. This is a Floating Island four leagues from ye mouth of Messicippi River which hideth the Mouth of ye Said River, in which Island there be both Oysters and Birds The Island is not Noted in ye other Mapp

Compared with seventeenth-century European maps of the Southeast, this has the most accurate rendering of the lower Mississippi valley, superseded only by Delisle's influential *Carte du Mexique et de la Floride*, published in 1703, that incorporated the discoveries of Iberville and Bienville.[58]

According to van den Bosh's map legend, this enhanced accuracy is largely attributable to the "French Indian" who contributed, apparently to a significant extent, to the drafting and captions. There are a few parallels to Louis Hennepin's 1683 map and other derivations of the La Salle era explorations.[59] The "Silver and Gold Mines" (D), usually referred to as the "Mines St. Barbe" (Santa Bárbara) in the Spanish province of Nueva Vizcaya (New Biscay, now in the state of Chihuahua, Mexico), and the provincial capital of Monterrey (perhaps "The Town of the Rich Spaniards" [E]) are all present, although much farther from Galveston Bay and the Gulf of Mexico than the map informants imagined.[60] But Hennepin misplaced most of the Indian groups and had a muddled notion of the river systems of the lower valley. Van den Bosh, with his "French Indian" collaborator, accurately portrayed Galveston Bay (J), the Trinity River (O), and the villages of the Cenis ("Lessainy," N) near where La Salle was murdered in 1687. The Cenis were the Hasinais, a confederacy of Caddoan speakers.[61] The map legends indicate some confusion over the correct location of the Ackansah (L), the Illinois Algonquian name for the Quapaws, whose villages were situated near the mouth of the Arkansas River.[62] Kinipiseau (M) was La Salle's name for the Mugulashas, who occupied the west bank of the Mississippi River above the present site of New Orleans.[63]

The schematic description of the Mississippi River (S) includes what appears to be one fanciful detail: the "Floating Islands" (V) at the mouth. In fact, this not only alludes to the driftwood and other debris that collected around the channel's unique "mud lumps," obscuring the entrance for early navigators, but also refers directly to the amazing floating islands of swamp vegetation that are sometimes dislodged by spring flooding and drift back and forth for weeks on the tides at the edge of the Gulf.[64] The Chikakomaimah River (T) has been depicted in correct relationship to the main river if it is in fact the Yazoo, but its name and position suggest it may be related to de Soto's "Chucagua," which La Salle thought "is different from the Mississippi and . . . goes along side by side with it."[65] The Ipellasippi River (U), shown as a tributary of the Yazoo, is presumably the Big Black River, which actually flows into the Mississippi separately.

Farther upstream (R) are found the Koroas (Coa-roa-auh).[66] One puzzling feature of this map is the presence of the Mongoin nah Nation (P) and Mongoin nah River (Q) branching westward from the Mississippi. This name certainly refers to the Moingwena division of the Illinois, who lived on the Des Moines River in eastern Iowa from at least as early as 1673 to about 1700.[67] The inclusion of an upper Mississippi valley tribe and river in this schematic map of the lower valley suggests that the Moingwenas were of particular significance to the mapmakers. Van den Bosh's "French Indian" collaborator might have been a Moingwena Illinois; some Illinois had accompanied La Salle on his explorations of the Mississippi River valley, and one could have joined (by marriage, for instance) the Shawnee band at Starved Rock before their move to Maryland.

Note that if (Q) does refer to the Des Moines River, then the mention of another river nearby "that fall in to the western one" would be a logical reference to the neighboring Nebraska River, which descends into the Missouri. Alternatively, if (Q) represents a rough approximation of the Missouri or the Arkansas, then "the western one" might refer to the much more distant Colorado, already known vaguely by rumor among the English colonists to flow toward the Pacific. The entire map can be seen as an early English attempt to make sense of a century's accumulation of imperfect, and often misleading, geographical accounts concerning the midcontinent, with the help of an Indian informant who had some direct experience with the region.

Lamhatty Map, 1708

Title: Mr. Robert Beverley's Acct. of Lamhatty

Size: 30 cm × 27 cm

Original: Lee Family Papers (MS 1, L51, fol. 677), Virginia Historical Society, Richmond.

Reproductions:[68]

Description: This manuscript map is a contemporary copy of an original drawn in 1708 by Lamhatty, a Tawasa Indian, and annotated by Robert Beverley and Lt. Colonel John Walker of King and Queen County, Virginia. In a letter of January 16, Walker informed Governor Edmund Jennings concerning this "Strange Indian."

> *On Saturday, ye 3d of Janr Instant an Indian came naked of armes into one of ye houses of the upper Inhabitants in this County, upon which the people there tied him by ye arm & brought him to me,*

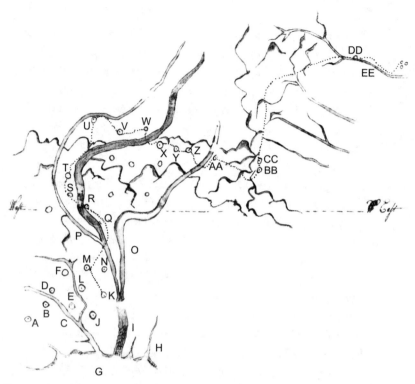

Figure 10. Keyed drawing of Lamhatty's map.

they got to my house with him on ye day following, at first I put him in Irons and would have brought him to yor: Honr, but the extremity of ye weather prevented any passage over Yorke River. After three days finding him of a seeming good humour, I let him at liberty about the house where he still continues; I got ye Interpreter and a tuscarora Indian to talk with him, he at all times seemd verey inclinable to be understood, and was verey forward to talk, but neither of them could understand him.

What I have learnt from him in this long acquintance is thus he calls his name Lamhátty, and his town Towása near which there were nine other nations of Indians confederates with his Town, under distinct names for ye particular, but all under the common name of Towása's, which are described by those O's on ye North side the East and West line; those O's on ye South side ye sd. line with severall others which he sayes are there, have also their particular names,

*but all under the common name of Tuscaróras he says, that not far
from their Town is great falls, and a little below that a great salt
water [lak]e, whose waves he describes to tumble and roar like a sea
he sayes He was taken prisoner 9 months agoe; that he was 3 months
in carrying to Telapoúsa where they made him work in ye groun
That there they use canoes that he was 2 mo. in carrying through ye
6 next Towns, and one month in passing from ye 6th from Telapoúsa to ye 7th, where he was sold, vizt. Sowanóuka They in a short
time took him out a hunting, vizt. 6 men 2 women & 3 children,
along ye ledge of Lower mountains, (as he at first described to us by
heaps of dirt tho' his geography has not made him hit it right in this
draught) Whence he run away from them and in 9 dayes time came
to ye house by Robert Powells where he was taken and brought to me
He sayes that ye first time ye Tuscaróras made warr, they swept off
3 of their nations clear and ye next time 4 more, and ye other three
run away The map is all his own drawing which I thought might
be satisfaction to your honr to send, ye red line denotes his march,
ye black lines, ye Rivers, & ye shaded lines ye mountains, which he
describes to be vastly big among some of those Indian Towns, for
ye rest I must referr yor Honr: to ye map; he seems very desirous to
stay, if I might have yor: Honrs: leave to keep him.*[69]

On the reverse of the surviving manuscript map is an account of Lamhatty's experiences written by Robert Beverley, which essentially corrobo-
rates Walker's relation and adds some significant details.

*Lamhatty an Indian of Towása of 26 years of age comeing naked
& unarmed into the upper inhabitants on the north side of Mattapany in very bad weather in ye Xt. mass hollidays anno 1707 gives
this accot.*

*The foregoeing year ye Tusckaróras made war on ye Towasas &
destroyed 3 of theyr nations (the whole consisting of ten) haveing
disposed of theyr prisoners they returned again, & in ye Spring of
ye year 1707: they swept away 4 nations more, the other 3 fled, not
to be heard of. 'twas at this second comeing that they took Lamhatty & in 6 weeks time they caryed him to Apeikah from thence in*

a week more to Jäbon, from thence in 5 days to tellapoúsa (where they use canoes) where they made him worke in ye Ground between 3 & 4 months. then they carryed him by easy Journeys in 6 weeks time to Oppónys from thence they were a month crossing ye mountains to Souanoúka: where they sold him A party of ye Souanoúka's comeing a hunting Northward under the foot of ye mountains took him with them, there were of ye Souanoúkas, 6 men 2 women & 3 children, he continewed with them about 6 weeks, & they pitched theyr Camp on ye branches of Rapahan: River where they pierce ye mountains, then he ran away from them keeping his course E b S & E S E. Crossing 3 branches of Rapahan: River & thrice crossing Mattapany till he fell in upon Andrew Clarks house which he went up to & Surendered himselfe to ye people they being frightned Seized upon him violently & tyed him tho he made no manner of Resistence but Shed tears & Shewed them how his hands were galled and Swelled by being tyed before; whereupon they used him gentler & tyed ye string onely by one arme till they brought him before Lt. Collo. Walker of King & Queen County where is at Liberty & Stays verry Contentedly but noe body can yet be found that understands his language.

Postscript [torn] after some of his Country folks were found servants [torn] he was Sometimes ill used by Walker, became verry melancholly often fasting & crying Several days together Sometimes useing little Conjurations & when Warme weather came he went away & was never more heard of.[70]

Key to map notations:

A. Poúhke

B. Tomoóka

C. Sowoólla·Oubab·

E. Aulédly [or Anlédly]

E. Ephíppick

F. Ogolaúghoos

G. Ouquodky, Saltwater Lake or Sea, Bay of Florida

H. Alatám

I. [*torn*]hbly Netúckqua [or Uetúckqua]

J. Sowoólla

K. Towása

L. Choctóuh

M. Socsoóky

N. Susenpáh

O. Chauctoúbab·

P. Sayénte Alatám Oúbab

Q. Wichise

R. Apéicah·

S. Jäbon·

T. Alabáchehah

U. Tellapoúsa

V. Tockhoúsa

W. Cheeawoóle

X. Caweta

Y. Awhíssie

Z. Oŭquáney

AA. Oukfúsky

BB. Sowanoúka

CC. Poehússa

DD. R. Powels

EE. Matapani R.

The following discussion agrees generally, although not in every respect, with the interpretations of David Bushnell and John Swanton concerning these accounts, the map notations, and a sixty-word Tawasa vocabulary on the reverse of Walker's letter.[71] As Swanton discovered, there are a number of errors in Walker and Beverley's accounts. For instance, the Tawasa villages are represented on the map by circles on the south (not north) side of the east-west line. Second, the English were misled by the Tuscarora interpreter, who, although admittedly unable to understand the Tawasa language, claimed that his people had made war on the Tawasas and that they occupied the numerous towns Lamhatty visited during his captivity, towns actually inhabited by Upper and Lower Creeks. Recent writers occasionally still accept the self-serving interpreter's story.[72]

The identity of the Tawasas has puzzled ethnohistorians ever since Bushnell discovered Lamhatty's map in 1908. Lamhatty's homeland lay along the Florida Gulf coast (G, Ouquodky), apparently around the Chipola (C) and west of the Apalachicola (I) and Ochlockonee (H) rivers, a region originally occupied by the Chacatos (known later to the French as Chatots). Two Spanish missions were established among the Chacatos in 1674, and shortly afterward the Franciscans built Sabacola Mission, at the confluence of the Chattahoochee (P) and Flint (O) rivers. Those missionaries soon encountered armed resistance and were forced from the region, accompanied by some Chacato converts who resettled among the Apalachees farther east.[73]

The Tawasas lived far beyond the reach of either Franciscan missionaries or Spanish troops at that time. They may have descended from the Tuasi chiefdom traversed by the de Soto expedition somewhere in east-central Alabama in 1540, but the first certain mention of them occurs in Spanish records in 1675 as the village and "province" of Toâssa situated in that same general location, near the confluence of the Coosa and Alabama rivers.[74] In the aftermath of their rebellion that year, many Chacatos found refuge with the Tawasas, far to the north and safe from Spanish retribution. Numerous Christian Chacatos remained among the Tawasas eleven years later when Marcos Delgado visited the region.[75] By 1695, however, some event turned the other central Alabama tribes against the Tawasas, who then sought refuge themselves when a "cacique of Tabassa and his people appeared on the borders of Apalachee province requesting permission to settle."[76] The Tawasas relocated to northwest Florida, near their old acquaintances, the Chacatos, who saw an opportunity to repay a twenty-year-old debt of hospitality. There they remained, west of Apalachee, unconverted and outside the Spanish mission system, until Creek-English raids in 1706–7 dispersed their towns, carrying some (like Lamhatty) into slavery in the English colonies and propelling the rest westward to a haven near French colonial Mobile.

Beginning in 1685, the Florida missions increasingly became targets of English-inspired slave raids by Creeks, Yamasees, and Yuchis from the north. Three raids by the Creeks in 1702–4 (including one led by Colonel James Moore of South Carolina) effectively destroyed the Timucuan and Apalachee missions in northern Florida, resulting in the killing, dispersal, or enslavement of most of the resident Indian population. Creek attacks of 1706 and

1707 on Tawasa villages in former Chacato country were a continuation of the protracted slaving wars instigated by the Carolinians.

In fact, the Tawasa confederation by 1706 seems to have consisted primarily of refugees from the provinces of Apalachee and Timucua attacked in preceding years. Choctóuh (L) was certainly a Chacato village, perhaps a remnant of San Carlos de Chacatos in Apalachee. Sowoólla (J) probably was a group of refugees from Sabacola, later known as the Sawokli village of the Lower Creeks, and Tomoóka (B) may have been a Timucua village.[77] Three others town names (D, E, and F) resemble those of missions destroyed earlier (although the latter may refer to the Yuchis).[78] The number of similarities suggests that Lamhatty's "Tawasa" towns constituted a short-lived confederation of refugee Tawasas, Timucuans, Apalachees, and Chacatos who had sought mutual protection but were soon dispersed again by the Creeks. Between July and September of 1706, after the first raid mentioned by Lamhatty, bands of surviving Chacatos and Tawasas made their way to Mobile, where they received French protection.[79]

During his captivity, Lamhatty was taken to a number of Creek towns indicated on his map. Bushnell and Swanton both assumed that the map notations refer to specific towns, but some of them actually seem to be names of more inclusive social groupings (just as Lamhatty alternatively applied the name "Towása" to his village and to the ten-town confederacy). During the late seventeenth and early eighteenth centuries, the English, Spanish, and French consistently referred to groups such as the Alabamas, Tallapoosas, Coosas or Abekas, Apalachicolas, and Ocheses; only later did the terms Upper Creek and Lower Creek come into vogue as a reflection of increasing political centralization in the course of the eighteenth century.[80] Considered in this light, Lamhatty's Creek "town" names can be correlated with the following intermediate-sized polities: Apéicah· (R) and Jäbon· (S) (Abekas and Jiape, or Hillabees, on the Coosa River), Alabáchehah (T, Alabamas [?] on the upper Alabama River), Tellapoúsa (U, Tallapoosas on the lower Tallapoosa River), Tockhoúsa (V, Coosas on the Coosa River), Caweta (X, Cowetas on the Ocmulgee River), Awhíssie (Y) and Oŭquáney (Z) (Ocheses and Oconees on the Oconee River).[81] A list of Creek "nations" or villages dating from 1700 includes a number of comparable names (i.e., Apicales, Alebamons, Ouacoussas, Choualles, and Couitas).[82]

Lamhatty's detailed geographical knowledge seems to have been limited to the immediate vicinity of the Tawasa towns and adjacent Gulf coast. This is apparent from his river locations and names, which seem accurate in the southern reaches but become progressively distorted north of the east-west line. Based on our knowledge of Creek town locations at that period, Lamhatty inaccurately connected the Tallapoosa (west of U) and Ocmulgee (Q) rivers with the Chattahoochee (P), and the Oconee (east of Z) with the Flint (O). Thus Lamhatty's map consists of two reasonably comprehensible north and south halves that have been inaccurately melded along the "east-west" line. These errors are readily attributable to the enslaved Lamhatty's understandable disorientation in unfamiliar country, where he frequently crossed rivers that he mistakenly equated with those flowing through Tawasa territory. Swanton failed to grasp this point, even going so far as to claim that the Wichise River (Q) was the Chattahoochee, although the name Ochese Creek is known to have referred to the Ocmulgee River, the location of the Cowetas (X) in 1707.[83]

Lamhatty was traded by his Creek captors to one of the Shawnee towns (BB) on the upper Savannah River.[84] He soon escaped and made his way to the English settlements on the Mattaponi River (EE), but others of his tribe may have been among the Indian slaves brought into Charlestown by the Savannahs in 1707.[85] The appearance of other Tawasas kept as "servants" on neighboring Virginia plantations resolved Lamhatty's ambiguous status. No longer a "Strange Indian," he received treatment his English captors deemed appropriate for a slave.[86] As Robert Beverley noted, Lamhatty endured the cruelty of his English master for a time before wandering off into the forest, "& was never more heard of."

Catawba Deerskin Map, circa 1721 (English Copies)

Titles: (Copy 1) This Map describing the Scituation of the Several Nations of Indians to the N. W. of South Carolina was coppyed from a Draught drawn & painted on a Deer Skin by an Indian Cacique and presented to Francis Nicholson Esqr. Governour of South Carolina by whom it is most humbly Dedicated To His Royal Highness George Prince of Wales [above a crown with three plumes and a banner inscribed "ICH DIES"]

(Copy 2) A Map Describing the Situation of the several Nations of Indians between South Carolina and the Massisipi River; was Copyed from

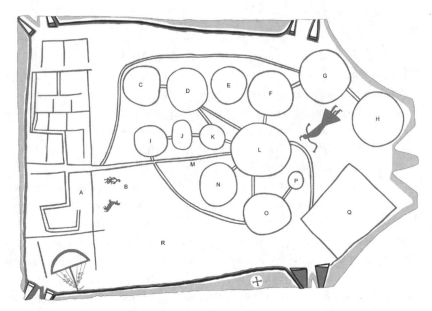

Figure 11. Keyed drawing of the Catawba deerskin map.

a Draught Drawn & Painted upon a Deer Skin by an Indian Cacique; and Presented to Francis Nicholson Esqr. Governour of Carolina.

Size: (1 and 2) 112 cm × 81 cm

Originals: (1) Additional MS 4723 (formerly, Sloane MS 4723), British Library, London, England. (2) Colonial Office 700, North American Colonies, General no. 6 (1), Map Room, Public Record Office (PRO), The National Archives, Kew, London, England.

Reproductions: (1)[87] (2)[88]

Description: Two copies exist of a lost original, which, as the titles indicate, was painted on a deerskin. Both copies were redrawn in red pigment outlined with black ink on paper cut in the shape of deerskins; they are quite similar, so a single description will serve, with discrepancies noted as necessary.

The central features are thirteen irregular circles labeled with Indian names and connected by an intricate network of double lines representing paths. Along the left edge of the map is "Charlestown," with its rectangular street grid and a ship in harbor with pennants flying. In the lower right corner is a large rectangle labeled "Virginie." The deerskin is bounded on the top, left, and bottom by a solid red line. Below the bottom line, set apart from the other map elements, is a Greek cross. At the corners are pairs of isosceles triangles (truncated and partly colored red on the PRO copy), presumably representing deer hooves. In addition to the titles (which differ between the copies, as already noted), there are two other interesting features. One is a large female (?) figure shaded entirely in red, with a feather (?) in her hair, arms outstretched, wearing a skirt and having what appears to be a tail or a dangling belt. The other consists of a pair of figures, a male in hunting frock carrying a musket facing a buck, and the caption "An Indian a Hunting."

Key to map notations:

A. Charlestown
B. An Indian a Hunting
C. Waterie
D. Wasmisa
E. Casuie
F. Nustie
G. Cherrikies
H. Chickisa
I. Charra
J. Youchine
K. Wiapie
L. Nasaw
M. The English Path to Nasaw
N. Suttirie
O. Succa
P. Saxippaha
Q. Virginie
R. [*titles*; see above]

Governor Francis Nicholson obtained the original deerskin map sometime between his arrival in Charlestown on May 29, 1721, and his departure for London on May 17, 1725. As was customary upon the appointment of a new colonial governor, Indian leaders from each of the major tribes were summoned in 1721 to meet Nicholson. Among these were Creeks and Cherokees, "as also the Catawba: A Head man out of each Town of each Nation to come down."[89] Nicholson probably took this opportunity to solicit a map from "an Indian Cacique," who is generally thought to have been from one of the South Carolina piedmont tribes that were clearly of principal interest to the mapmaker. The British Library copy (1) may have been among the "several curiosities" from South Carolina that Nicholson presented to the Prince of Wales soon after his return to England.[90]

Several of the names on the map are readily recognizable: Charlestown (A), Virginia (Q), Cherokees (G), and Chickasaws (H). The others refer to the numerous small tribes situated in the South Carolina piedmont in the 1720s. Collectively known to the English as Catawbas, these predominantly Siouan-speaking peoples settled near one another for mutual protection and may have been loosely confederated by this time. A 1715 census, taken just before the Yamasee War, lists seven villages of "Catapaws," one "Sarow" town, and four "Waccomassus" settlements in this region.[91] William Byrd noted in his diary in 1728 that "about three-score Miles more [from Crane Creek, North Carolina] bring you to the first Town of the Catawbas, call'd Nauvasa, situated on the banks of Santee river. Besides this Town there are five Others belonging to the same Nation, lying all on the same Stream, within a Distance of 20 miles."[92]

Byrd's "Nauvasa" corresponds to Nasaw (L), the largest circle and evidently the mapmaker's focus of interest. From this point paths radiate to the neighboring piedmont Indians and to the English colonies. According to James Merrell, "Prior to the Yamassee War colonists . . . [labeled] Indians in the Catawba/Wateree River valley Esaws, Catawbas, and Usherees, using none of these terms in a consistent manner. . . . By 1715 even Esaw/Usheree disappeared, to emerge later as 'Nassaw,' a principal town of the 'Catawba' Nation. Catawba itself had become the common term, though it remained unclear exactly what peoples this word included."[93]

Nustie (F) is equivalent to "Neustee," one of six Catawba towns mentioned in 1754.[94] Succa (O) and Suttirie (N) represent two tribal groups whose similar names caused much confusion among the English. The Succas (also known as the Shoccories, and perhaps including the Sugerees, Sugarees, Sughas or Tansequas) and the Suttiries (Sutarees, Satarees, Shuterees) established villages near the Nasaws in the early eighteenth century, and together they formed the nucleus of the Catawbas.[95]

Most of the other groups portrayed on the map eventually were assimilated by the Catawbas, but precisely when is not known. The Saxippahas
(P) (Sasapahaes, Saxapahaws, Saxabahaws, Sissipahaws) formed a separate
political entity at least as late as 1717, though they eventually sought greater
security by coalescing with the Catawbas.[96] Likewise, the Charras (I) (or
Saras, Saraws, Charraws, Cheraws) maintained a distinct identity and separate landholdings until at least 1738; before that they cooperated with the
Catawbas in negotiations with the English.[97]

The Wateries (C) (or Waterees) occupied a single large town and, according to James Adair, spoke a "Dialect" different from the "Katahba."[98]
Another linguistically distinct people were the Casuies (E) (Coosoes, Kussoes, Coosahs), who originally lived in coastal South Carolina before moving northward to join the Catawbas.[99]

Wasmisa (D) may refer to the Waccamaws (Wassamassaws, Washam-
saws, Wassamèsāh; cf. Wackamaws).[100] This group was closely associated
with the Pedees from 1716 to 1755, the Waccamaws being the more populous
of the two. In 1727 they inhabited a village one-half mile from the Catawbas.[101] The remnant of a third tribe, the Wawees, apparently was affiliated
with the Waccamaws and Pedees in 1716.[102] This group might conceivably
be the Wiapies (K) shown on the map near Wasmisa. "Weaipee Town" is
referred to in a 1741 list of headmen receiving commissions from the English, but by 1756 the "Weyappees" had merged with the Nasaws.[103]

The final group, identified on the map as Youchine (J), may be a band of
Yuchis who temporarily joined the Catawbas. James Mooney pointed out
that the Catawba word "nieya" (meaning "people" or "Indians") was often
abbreviated to "nie" or "ye" (as in "Kataba nie," or "Virginie" on this map).[104]
I know of no independent historical reference to Yuchis living near or with
the Catawbas in the 1720s, although some may have taken refuge there when
they fled their Savannah River towns during the Yamasee War.[105]

Although this map may appear schematic, placement of Indian groups
and paths was done precisely, reflecting the mapmaker's detailed geographical knowledge of the South Carolina piedmont. If the map is turned so that
Charlestown (A) is to the lower right and Virginia (Q) is at the top (i.e.,
to the north), the viewer can more easily compare the deerskin map with
two approximately contemporary English maps, the War Map of 1715 and
Colonel Bull's map of 1738.[106] All three show the English Path to Nasaw

(M) or the Catawba Path (running from Charlestown up the east side of the Wateree River to Nasaw, by way of the Charras), the Occaneechi Path (from Virginia to Nasaw), and the Cherokee Path (from Charlestown to the Cherokees, following the Savannah River, and on to the Chickasaws). (Incidentally, the British Library copy [1] has an additional path connecting Wasmisa [D] and Charra [I] that is lacking in the PRO version [2]. Another difference is the placement of the path from Suttirie [N], which leads directly to Nasaw [L] in the PRO version but intersects the Nasaw [L]-Succa [O] path on the other copy.)

An important difference between the Indian and English maps is the Indian's use of a variable distance scale, which allowed him to include such far-off groups as the Cherokees, Chickasaws, and Virginians while simultaneously depicting the relative locations of the piedmont societies. Nine of these Indian groups (D, E, F, J, K, L, N, O, and P) probably occupied a tightly circumscribed area around the Catawba River, the Wateries (C) being situated farther south and the Charras (I) to the southeast. Thus the mapmaker accurately conveyed the proper spatial ordering of map elements by manipulating distance, which permitted him to provide a great deal of information regarding the Siouan groups as well as providing a regional perspective, all within the irregular confines of a deerskin.

Chickasaw Deerskin Map, circa 1723 (English Copy)

Title: A Map Describing the Situation of the several Nations of Indians between South Carolina and the Massisipi River; was Copyed from a Draught Drawn upon a Deer Skin by an Indian Cacique and Presented to Francis Nicholson Esqr. Governour of Carolina[107]

Size: 145 cm × 114 cm

Original: Colonial Office 700, North American Colonies, General no. 6 (2), Map Room, Public Record Office, The National Archives, Kew, London, England.

Reproductions:[108]

Description: The history of this map is similar to that of the Catawba map. Sometime during his tenure as governor of South Carolina, Francis Nicholson obtained the deerskin original, now lost. This document is a copy on deerskin-shaped paper with red painted elements, most outlined in black

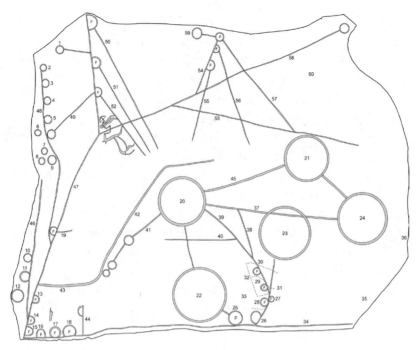

Figure 12. Keyed drawing of the Chickasaw deerskin map.

ink. As with the Catawba map, the ethnicity of the mapmaker is not specified in Nicholson's map title, but it can be inferred with reasonable certainty from the map's content.

Several of the map notations include words that are western Muskogean in origin (e.g., *Ucau*, "water"; *Humer*, "red").[109] This language group consists of several dialects of Choctaw and Chickasaw, considered by many linguists to be two distinct, though very similar, languages.[110] In addition, a trade jargon known as Mobilian developed in the Southeast (apparently during the historic period) to facilitate intercultural contact, and both Chickasaw and Choctaw contributed to this pidgin.[111] Judging from the western Muskogean word list on the map, and particularly the map's longest phrase ("Elav Chickasau au abbe"), the mapmaker can be identified—with considerable confidence—as a Chickasaw speaker.[112]

During Nicholson's residency in Charlestown, the Chickasaws were at war with the French until early in 1725 and maintained close trade ties with the English. The Choctaws seem to have had no direct contact with the South Carolina government from before the 1715 Yamasee War until late in 1725, after Nicholson's departure for England. In 1723 a small band of Chickasaws settled near Savannah Town at the invitation of the English and in September met with Nicholson, with whom "presents were exchanged."[113] A reasonable surmise is that this map was among the Chickasaw gifts to the governor. The map organization also suggests a Chickasaw perspective. That group is placed at the center of the map (20) with paths and river routes radiating from the "Chickasaw Nation." Also, numerous tribes with the letter "F" next to their names (denoting alliance with the French) encircle the Chickasaws, a fact they probably wanted emphasized to the English.

This map presents many interpretive challenges, primarily because the orthography is so unusual. The Englishman who transcribed the Chickasaw place names seems to have done so with great care, although the copyist introduced several errors, such as "n" for "u" at the end of "Yausan" (43), and "u" for "n" in the middles of "Commaucerilau" (3), "Causau" (5), and "Tausau" (27). Some of the tribal names seem to be unique to this map and a few remain unidentified.[114]

Key to map notations:

1. Sauhau
2. Vossulau
3. Commaucerilau
4. Pauneasau
5. Causau
6. Carenahish
7. Sovuasau
8. Vauhu
9. Tovocolau
10. Kejos
11. Katulaucheu
12. Notauku
13. Nauchee (F)
14. Tunecau (F)
15. Humau (F)
16. Sovuasau (F)
17. Oakculapesar (F)

18. Biuculau (F)
19. Ucaupau (F)
20. Chickasaw Nation
21. Charikee
22. Choctau Nation
23. Creeks
24. English
25. Noe India (F)
26. Came in the Indian War
27. Tausau (F)
28. Movele (F)
29. Tume (F)
30. Tume (F)
31. Chocktau Benelee
32. Elav Chickasau au abbe
33. Appaulachee
34. Salt Water
35. Pansecula
36. St. Augustine
37. Creek and English Path
38. Tongolickau Oakhinnau
39. Shaterrau Oakhinnau
40. Tyannacau Oakhinnau
41. Chockchumau Path
42. Chickasau Oakhinnau
43. Yausan Oakhinnau
44. Hoppe Oakhinnau
45. Charikee Path
46. Ucau Humer Oakhinnau
47. Massasippe River
48. Ucau Humer Oakhinnau
49. Ussaule Path
50. Pavuaule Path
51. Cow' a-keer Path
52. Cuscuskeer Path
53. Ta[s?]canuck Oakhinnau

54. Yoltenno Oakhinnau
55. Yoltenno Path
56. Chickabou Path
57. Kenocolu Path
58. Senottova Oakhinnau
59. Yaumeer
60. [*title; see above*]

Beginning with the large circles in the center, the locations of the Chickasaws (20), Cherokees (21), Choctaws (22), and Creeks (23) are clearly marked. To the south and southeast are the Gulf of Mexico (34), Spanish Pensacola (35), St. Augustine (36), and the English colony of South Carolina (24), the latter symbolized by a circle instead of a rectangle or town grid, as seen on the Catawba map of circa 1721. The Savannah River Path to the Cherokees, also shown on the Catawba map, is unlabeled here (between 21 and 24), but the Upper Trading Path (37) and the Cherokee-Chickasaw Path (45) are both indicated.[115]

The rivers in this area are recognizable from their relative locations, although the meanings of the names given them are obscure. John Dyson has identified Tyannacau Oakhinnau (40) as the Yanica River, now known as Tibbee or Line Creek, a physically unassuming but historically significant stream that divided Chickasaw and Choctaw territories. Shaterrau Oakhinnau (39) is the much larger Tombigbee River. Tongolickau Oakhinnau (38) is probably a garbled Chickasaw variant of Tuscaloosa, the colonial era designation of the Black Warrior River, distinct from the unlabeled Alabama River emanating from the Creeks' homeland.[116] Interestingly, in every case "river" is written "Oakhinnau" (*okhina'*, from *oka'* ["water"] + *hina'* ["road"]), to emphasize navigability for canoe travel, instead of the more general Chickasaw term *abookoshi'*.[117]

Shown in considerable detail is the area near French Mobile, where Bienville resettled several refugee tribes—including the Apalachees (33) who fled from Florida in 1704—among the towns of the native Mobilians (28) and Tomés (29, 30).[118] Curiously, and significantly, neither French colonial Mobile nor New Orleans appears on this map. East of the Mobile Indians, and across their eponymous bay and river, were the Taensas (27), who arrived in 1715 from Louisiana. Those who "came in the Indian War" (26) may refer to the Tawasas, Lamhatty's relatives, and the Chacatos who fled westward as refugees from Creek slaving raids of 1706 and 1707. Alternatively if "the Indian War" means the Yamasee War of 1715, those who came could be the poorly documented band of Yamasees who reportedly settled south of Mobile for some years.[119] The identity of "Noe India" (25) is not known, although the Choctaw town of Yowani occupies this spot, far to the southeast of the other Choctaw towns, on the 1733 de Crenay map.[120] Four dotted lines crisscross the area, seemingly indicating either trails or tribal territory boundaries. Most interesting of all are two phrases, neither one associated with a tribal circle, that seem to be Chickasaw place names. Paralleling the lower Tombigbee River, immediately west of the Tomé villages, is a long phrase (32) that may translate as "where a different one killed a Chickasaw," or alternatively as "where, while escorting the Chickasaws, they murdered them." Both interpretations suggest that some violence was inflicted on Chickasaws in this vicinity, northwest of French Mobile. An event of that sort did occur at the end of February 1705, when the Choctaws killed thirty or more Chickasaw headmen who had traveled to Mobile for negotiations with French officials. The Chickasaw delegation had been escorted as far as the main Choctaw village by twenty-five French troops commanded by Pierre Dugué Boisbriant. As the massacre began the soldiers tried to intervene, but withdrew when Boisbriant was wounded. The Chickasaws long remembered this treachery, although by 1723 this would have been just one of many injustices the Chickasaws felt they had endured at the hands of the Choctaws and the French.[121]

The small tribes situated around Mobile were frequent targets of Chickasaw attacks during this period. The shorter phrase, "Chocktau Benelee" (*Chahta'* ["Choctaw"] + *Biniili'* ["settlement(s)"]) (31), is written east of the Mobile-Tensaw delta, next to a bracket pointed at the dotted line (trail?) that runs past both Tomé towns.[122] The Tomés were Choctaw speakers who interacted routinely with their Choctaw-proper kin to the northwest.[123]

Leading southwest from the Chickasaw towns was the Natchez Trace (41), which crossed Chakchiuma, Koroa, Ofogoula, and Yazoo lands. The adjacent river is the Yazoo (43), known as the Chickasaw River (42) in its upper reaches.[124] The lower Mississippi River (47) tribes include the Natchez (13), Tunicas (14), Houmas (15), Chawashas (16, placed too far upstream), Acolapissas (17), and Bayagoulas (18).[125] A small red pointing hand, of unknown significance, was drawn just above 16 and 17. "Hoppe Oakhinnau" (44) probably refers to the Pearl River, where the Biloxis were situated.[126]

Along the left edge of the deerskin, the Chickasaw headman portrayed three Caddoan tribes identifiable as the Nadacos or Anadarkos (12, part of the Hasinai Confederacy, with villages on the Neches River), the Kadoha-dachos (11), and the Kichais (10), both on the Red River (46).[127] Farther up the Mississippi River were the Arkansas or Quapaws (19) at the mouth of the Arkansas River (48, labeled the same as 46). In the upper reaches of the Arkansas are shown divisions of the Wichitas, including the Touacaras or Tawakonis (9), the Tawehash or Taovayas (6, 7, and 8), and the Panias-sas (4).[128] "Causau" may be the Kansas (5), although they should be located north of the Wichitas.[129] Farther west, onto the Great Plains, were the Co-manches, apparently designated "Commaucerilau" (3).[130] The meaning of "Vossulau" (2) remains a mystery. Jean-Baptiste Bénard de La Harpe dis-covered that the Chickasaws were personally acquainted with at least some of these tribes during his visit to a Tawakoni village in 1719. A week after his arrival, a lone Chickasaw appeared with trade goods, apparently acting as a middleman for either French or English traders.[131]

To the east are shown three paths leading to French-allied tribes. From north to south, these are the Peoria (cf. Peoualen) Path (50) to the upper Il-linois River, the Cahokia Path (51) to the St. Louis area, and the Kaskaskia Path (52) to southern Illinois.[132] An armed warrior leading a horse appears on the Kaskaskia Path, perhaps symbolizing an attack by the Chickasaws on the Kaskaskias. The "Ussaule Path" (49) probably corresponds to the path followed by Dutisné in 1719 when he traveled overland from Kaskaskia to the Osages.[133] "Sauhau" (1) are the Sioux, who were already known to the French by a similar name.[134]

The Ohio River (58) is named for the Senecas, situated in western New York.[135] Branching to the southeast is the Tennessee River (53; the name is only partly legible because of a crease in the manuscript). On the Wabash River (54) are three more French allies, with paths leading to each tribe from the southeast. "Yoltenno" (55) is probably equivalent to Ouyatenon or Wea.[136] Chickabou (56) may derive from Kickapoo.[137] I do not recog-nize "Kenocolu" (57). The Miamis may be represented by the term "Yau-meer" (59).[138]

Thomas Hatley described this map as the "first unified cartographic depiction of the now familiar southeastern 'region.'"[139] It covers an even larger area encompassing approximately 700,000 square miles, from southeastern Texas (12), western Kansas (3), and southern Minnesota (1) on the west to northeastern Florida (36) and western New York (the circle at the end of 58) on the east.[140] The range and depth of this unnamed Chickasaw headman's cartographic knowledge was extraordinary; undoubtedly much of the map's significance remained beyond the grasp of Nicholson or any of his European contemporaries.

Chickasaw/Alabama Map, 1737 (French Copy)

Title: Nations Amies et Ennemies des Tchikachas [Nations Friendly and Hostile to the Chickasaws]

Size: 51 cm × 35 cm

Original: Archives des Colonies, ser. C13A, vol. 22, fol. 67, Centre des Archives d'Outre-Mer, Archives Nationales, Aix-en-Provence, France.[141]

Reproductions:[142]

Description: In 1730 the Chickasaws offered protection to about two hundred Natchez Indians who were the object of a French war of extermination, thereby involving themselves in a protracted war against the French and their Choctaw allies. After receiving repeated rebuffs to French demands for surrender of the Natchez refugees, Governor Bienville launched a two-pronged attack on the Chickasaws. Owing to poor communication, the northern force of four hundred men (consisting of Illinois regular troops and militia and Miami, Iroquois, and Kaskaskia warriors) led by Major Pierre d'Artaguette arrived at the Chickasaw towns before the main army. D'Artaguette's force was utterly defeated on March 25, 1736, and most of the captured Frenchmen were subsequently burned alive. Bienville's army of six hundred French troops and six hundred Choctaws did not reach the Chickasaw villages until the following day. This second attack also failed, and they were compelled to retreat.[143] It was to gain the release of two French captives and to produce a map of the Chickasaw villages that the Captain of Pakana, an Alabama war leader, visited Chickasaw country in June 1737 as an emissary on behalf of the French. While there he met with Mingo Ouma, a Chickasaw war leader from the village of Ogoula Chitoka, who professed respect for the French and a desire for peace. To the Captain of Pakana, Mingo Ouma proposed that the Alabamas and Chickasaws join forces to kill the remaining Natchez and then destroy the Chakchiumas.[144] He also, according to the map legend, presented the Alabamas and the French with this map painted on a skin.

The surviving copy, redrawn and transcribed by the engineer and drafts-man Alexandre de Batz, was sent to France.[145] The caption translates as follows:

> *These figures were taken from the original which were on a skin that Mingo Ouma, great war chief of the Chickasaw Nation, gave to the Captain of Pakana to take to his Nation and to the French, in order that they might see the number of their friends and also their enemies; the former are indicated in black and the second in red. The circles denote villages and entire nations.*

A. The English
B. The Cowetas ["Kaouitas"]
C. The Kasihtas ["Kachetas"]
D. The Yuchis ["Utchite"]
E. The Tugaloo Cherokees ["Toukouloo Charakis"]
F. The Cherokees ["Charakis"] who speak a different language than E
G. The Okfuskee Abekas ["Affasques Abekas"]
H. The Alabamas ["Alybamons"]
 I. Mobile, or the French
K. The Choctaws ["Tchakts"]
L. The whole Chickasaw ["Tchikachas"] Nation, which is white within, but the space surrounding it [shown as a shaded ring] is of noth-ing but blood. It is white because they claim that only good words come from their villages, but those of the surrounding country lose their minds by not listening to them at all, and this stains their lands with blood.
M. The Huron ["Huronnes"] and Iroquois ["Iroquoises"] villages and nations and those they call Nantouague
N. The villages and nations of the Tamaroas ["Tamarois"], Piankashaws ["Peanquichias"], etc.

O. The Arkansas or Quapaws ["Okappa"]

P. The Chakchiumas ["Chakkchouma"], whom they are going to attack at once

Q. These are warpaths that do not go as far as the villages, because they hope that they will become white when they [the Chickasaws] make peace with those toward whom they lead.

R. River of the Alabamas ["Alybamons"] and the path from that nation to Mobile. It does not go as far as Mobile because they say they would not dare to go there, but in spite of that it is white for us

S. White paths that lead to their friends

T. War paths

V. Hunting paths of the Alabamas ["Alybamons"], white. 7th of September, 1737, De Batz.

In the original, the band around L and the "broken paths" were drawn in red. Only a few names on this map present any interpretive difficulties. The English (A), Lower Creeks (B, C) and Yuchis (D), Cherokees (F), the French (I), Choctaws (K), Chickasaws (L), Arkansas (O), and Chakchiumas (P) are all clearly recognizable. "Toukoulou Charakis" (E) refers to Tugaloo, an important Lower Cherokee town. "Affasques Abekas" (G) stood for the Okfuskees situated on the upper Tallapoosa River, part of the Abeka division of Upper Creeks.

Among their northern enemies were the Hurons (M), more commonly known to the English as Wyandots in the eighteenth century, and the "Nantouague" (M), which was a southern synonym for Iroquois (cf. "Nottawagees").[146] "Tamarois" (N) apparently signified not simply the Tamaroas but all of the Illinois tribes, just as the Piankashaws (N) represented the Miami tribes.[147] In its depiction of such far-flung native societies, this 1737 Chickasaw/Alabama map nearly matches the geographical coverage of the Chickasaw map drawn fourteen years earlier.

Patricia Galloway has suggested that both of the maps copied by de Batz were originally drawn by the Captain of Pakana, in support of which she cites a letter from Diron d'Artaguette to Maurepas dated October 24, 1737, which mentions "the explanations that the Captain of Pakana has made himself and from which he has drawn the two maps enclosed herewith which I take liberty of sending you with an albino deerskin, which was sent to me

for a present as an unexampled rarity."[148] There is little doubt that this and
the following map are the same two to which d'Artaguette refers, and Galloway is almost certainly correct regarding the origin of the Chickasaw villages map, discussed herein. But her case is much weaker that an Alabama
Indian drew the original of this map. In addition to the explicit statement
found in the de Batz legend, that the map was given to the Captain of Pakana
by Mingo Ouma, the document contains some internal evidence of having
been drawn by a Chickasaw. For instance, the central figure and focus of the
map is the circle representing the Chickasaws, following a structural con-
vention found repeatedly in Indian maps, whereby each mapmaker placed
his own tribe in a position of importance at or near the middle. And like
the 1723 Chickasaw deerskin map presented to the English, this map emphasizes the plight of the Chickasaws, nearly surrounded by their French-
inspired enemies. The theme is similar, although the earlier map carried
far more informational content. The Alabama headman may have altered
the Chickasaw original somewhat (possibly by the addition of the Alabama
Hunting Paths [V]), but the map appears to have been drawn predominantly from a Chickasaw perspective.

Even though Bienville rejected Mingo Ouma's peace overture, the Chickasaw's imagery was not lost on the French. At a conference with the southern tribes in 1754, Governor Kerlérec echoed Mingo Ouma's words with
his proclamation that "the French desire nothing so much as to see *all the
roads white* forever and a firm peace between the red men."[149]

Alabama Map, 1737 (French Copy)

Title: Plan et Scituation des Villages Tchikachas. Mil Sept Cent Trente
Sept [Plan and Situation of the Chickasaw Villages, 1737]
Size: 51 cm × 35 cm
Original: Archives des Colonies, ser. C13A, vol. 22, fol. 68, Centre des Ar-
chives d'Outre-Mer, Archives Nationales, Aix-en-Provence, France.
Reproductions:[150]
Description: Like the previous map, this one was redrafted from an In-
dian original by Alexandre de Batz and sent to France in 1737 as plans were
being made for a second major offensive against the Chickasaws. Patricia
Galloway has determined that the Captain of Pakana, an Alabama head-

man who visited the Chickasaws during July 1737, undoubtedly produced the original of this map.[151]

At the end of his report on his spying mission, the Captain of Pakana told the French, "There is nothing left for me to do but to tell you about what their situation and their forces are, according to what I saw myself. I was in ten villages and I saw the one of the Natchez, which made the eleventh. The Chickasaws told me that there were two other forts. I do not know if they were lying but I did not see them. In each village there is a fort with three rows of posts and no earth between."[152] This closely accords with the map legend translated here:

The circles indicate the villages and in each one there is a fort with three rows of posts.

A. Ogoula Tchetoka, fort where M. d'Artaguette attacked; there are 60 men.
B. Etoukouma
C. Achoukouma
D. Amalata
E. Taskaouilo
F. Tchitchatala; the fort is the most important, the said village is of 60 men.
G. Falatchao
H. Tchoukafala
I. Apeony, where the last party of Frenchmen attacked
L. Aekya
M. The Natchez, who still have forty men
N. Bayous
O. Paths between the villages
P. Fields ["Deserts"][153]
Q. Encampment of the last French party
R. M. d'Artaguette's Road
S. Road of the last French party

The forts of the villages A, B, C, D, E, F, G are very near each other and almost within musket range. Likewise those designated H, I, L. Prepared and drawn up at Mobile, September 7, 1737. De Batz[154]

Table 1.

Captain of Pakana	De Crenay	Adair
A. Ogoula Tchetoka	Ongoulastoga	
B. Etoukouma		
C. Achoukouma	Chochouma	
D. Amalata		Amalahta
E. Taskaouilo	Tascaolou	Tuskawillao
F. Tchitchatala	Tchichatala	Shatara
G. Falatchao	Falatchao	Phalacheho
H. Tchoukafala	Tchoukaffala	Chookka Pharaah
I. Apeony	Apeony	
L. Aekya	Aekeia	Hykehah
	Tchikoulechasto	
		Yaneka
		Chookheereso
M. Les Natchez		Nanne Hamgeh

Most of these village names are found on de Crenay's Map of 1733 and in the English trader James Adair's description of his life with the Chickasaws.[155] This map is unique in its identification of field locations in relation to village sites, data that should be of considerable value to archaeologists studying Chickasaw settlement patterns.[156] De Batz presumably added these as well as the scale and north arrow, neither of which may be very reliable. But there is a general agreement between topographical descriptions of the 1736 battlefields and the Captain of Pakana's village and stream placements. According to Governor Bienville, their Choctaw guides marched the French army "here and there in the woods as if to lead us to the large prairie where is the main part of the Chickasaw and Natchez villages led us at last to a prairie which is possibly a league in circumference in the middle of which we saw three small villages situated in a triangle on the crest of a hill at the foot of which an almost dry stream was flowing. This small prairie is only a league distant from the large one and is separated from it by a wood," all of which coincides closely in detail with the Alabama map.[157]

Acknowledgments

Sarah Mattics masterfully created the interpretive graphics for this chapter. I am most grateful to Chester DePratter, John Dyson, Patricia Galloway, Ives Goddard, John Hann, Tom Hatley, Jim Knight, G. Malcolm Lewis, Brad Raymond Lieb, James Merrell, Pamela Munro, Mark Seeman, and Peter Wood for commenting on or offering assistance with this chapter. Any faults are entirely my responsibility.

Notes

1. William L. McDowell Jr., ed., *Documents Relating to Indian Affairs, May 21, 1750–August 7, 1754* (Columbia: South Carolina Archives Department, 1958), 536.

2. Justin Winsor, *Christopher Columbus* (Boston: Houghton Mifflin, 1891), 442; cited in Louis De Vorsey, "Amerindian Contributions to the Mapping of North America: A Preliminary View," *Imago Mundi* 30 (1978): 71; Louis De Vorsey Jr., "American Indians and the Early Mapping of the Southeast," in William P. Cumming, *The Southeast in Early Maps*, 3rd ed., revised and enlarged by Louis De Vorsey Jr. (Chapel Hill: University of North Carolina Press, 1998), 65–66.

3. Edward Arber, ed., *Capt. John Smith, Works (1608–1631)* (Birmingham: English Scholar's Library, 1884), 55, 124, 339; Philip L. Barbour, ed., *The Jamestown Voyages under the First Charter, 1606–1609*, Hakluyt Society, 2nd ser., vols. 136–37 (Cambridge: University Press for the Society, 1969), 82, 84; G. Malcolm Lewis, "The Indigenous Maps and Mapping of North American Indians," *Map Collector* 9 (1979): 25–26.

4. John Lawson, *A New Voyage to Carolina*, ed. Hugh T. Lefler (Chapel Hill: University of North Carolina Press, 1967), 214.

5. For excellent general reviews of native North American mapmaking, see De Vorsey, "Amerindian Contributions," 71–78; G. Malcolm Lewis, "Indian Maps," in *Old Trails and New Directions*, ed. Carol M. Judd and Arthur J. Ray (Toronto: University of Toronto Press, 1980), 9–23; Lewis, "Indian Maps: Their Place in the History of Plains Cartography," *Great Plains Quarterly* 4 (1984): 91–108; cf. Catherine Delano Smith, "Cartography in the Prehistoric Period in the Old World," in *The History of Cartography*, vol. 1, ed. J. B. Harley and David Woodward (Chicago: University of Chicago Press, 1987), 54–101.

6. Lewis, "Indigenous Maps," 25, 32; Lewis, "Indian Maps," 12.

7. Verner W. Crane, "The Tennessee River as the Road to Carolina: The Beginnings of Exploration and Trade," *Mississippi Valley Historical Review* 3 (1916): 11.

8. Verner W. Crane, *The Southern Frontier, 1670–1732*, ed. Peter H. Wood (New York: W. W. Norton, 1981), 60–61.

9. Lewis, "Indian Maps," 14.

10. *Great Britain, Public Record Office, Calendar of State Papers Colonial Series, America and West Indies* (hereafter cited as PRO, *Calendar*), vol. 14, *January, 1693–14 May, 1696* (London: Her Majesty's Stationery Office, 1903), 518.

11. Usually the attributions are anonymous. For example, Thomas Kitchin's 1760 map of the Cherokee country carries the legend, "Engrav'd from an Indian Draught," reproduced in Gregory A. Waselkov, "Indian Maps of the Colonial Southeast: Archaeological Implications and Prospects," in *Cartographic Encounters: Perspectives on Native American Mapmaking and Map Use*, ed. G. Malcolm Lewis (Chicago: University of Chicago Press,

1998), 206. Knowledge of the most distant Indian villages shown on John Smith's 1612 map of Virginia was obtained "by relation," as were the captions shown in blue on the Velasco map of 1611. See Barbour, *Jamestown Voyages*, following 374; C. A. Weslager, *The English on the Delaware: 1610–1682* (New Brunswick NJ: Rutgers University Press, 1967), 11–13. For a consideration of unattributed uses of Indian maps, see G. Malcolm Lewis, "Indicators of Unacknowledged Assimilation from Amerindian Maps on Euro-American Maps of North America," *Imago Mundi* 38 (1986): 9–34.

12. Cited in De Vorsey, "Amerindian Contributions," 76.

13. G. Malcolm Lewis has made the point that, in the absence of reasonably precise surveys, the content of Euro-American as well as native maps was topological, with outlines, dimensions, and directions inserted almost independent of the superimposed map graticules. See his "Changing National Perspectives and the Mapping of the Great Lakes between 1755 and 1795," *Cartographica* 17 (1980), fig. 9. See also James H. Merrell, "Natives in a New World: The Catawba Indians of Carolina, 1650–1800" (PhD diss., Johns Hopkins University, 1982), 20.

14. Charles M. Hudson, *The Southeastern Indians* (Knoxville: University of Tennessee Press, 1976), 155–56; Jon Muller, "Serpents and Dancers: Art of the Mud Glyph Cave," in *The Prehistoric Native American Art of Mud Glyph Cave*, ed. Charles H. Faulkner (Knoxville: University of Tennessee Press, 1986), 36–80.

15. Merrell, "Natives in a New World," 190.

16. Lewis, "Indian Maps," 14–15.

17. Dunbar Rowland and A. G. Sanders, trans. and eds., *Mississippi Provincial Archives: French Dominion*, 3 vols. (Jackson: Mississippi Department of Archives and History, 1927–32), 3:526–39.

18. Gary C. Goodwin, *Cherokees in Transition: A Study of Changing Culture and Environment prior to 1775*, Research Paper 181 (Chicago: University of Chicago, Department of Geography, 1977), 109.

19. Jon Muller, "Southeastern Interaction and Integration," in *Great Towns and Regional Polities in the Prehistoric American Southwest and Southeast*, ed. Jill E. Neitzel (Albuquerque: University of New Mexico Press, 1999), 144–48, considers how the structure and integration of communities depicted on these Indian maps might reflect the nature of antecedent prehistoric societies.

20. PRO, *Calendar*, vol. 31, *January, 1719 to February, 1720* (London: His Majesty's Stationery Office, 1933), 302.

21. G. Malcolm Lewis, "Maps, Mapmaking, and Map Use by Native North Americans," in *The History of Cartography*, vol. 2, book 3, *Cartography in the Traditional African, American, Arctic, Australian, and Pacific Societies*, ed. David Woodward and G. Malcolm Lewis (Chicago: University of Chicago Press, 1998), 51–182; also see Lewis, *Cartographic Encounters*; Mark Warhus, *Another America: Native American Maps and the History of Our Land* (New York: St. Martin's Press, 1997); De Vorsey, "American Indians and the Early Mapping of the Southeast," 65–98.

22. Warhus, *Another America*, 109–13.

23. Lewis, "Maps, Mapmaking, and Map Use," 90–93; G. Malcolm Lewis, "An Early Map on Skin of the Area Later to become Indiana and Illinois," *British Library Journal* 22, no. 1 (Spring 1996), 66–87, reprinted under the same title in *Images and Icons of the New World: Essays on American Cartography*, ed. Karen Severud Cook (London: The British Library, 1996), 66–87.

24. Lewis, "Maps, Mapmaking, and Map Use," 117, pl. 6; George P. Horse Capture, "Gallery of Hides," in *Robes of Splendor: Native American Painted Buffalo Hides* (New York: New Press, 1993), 136–37; Gilles Havard, *Empire et métissages: Indiens et Français dans le Pays d'en Haut, 1660–1715* (Sillery QC: Septentrion, 2003), inside front and back covers, 571; Morris S. Arnold, "Eighteenth-Century Arkansas Illustrated: A Map within an Indian Painting?" in Lewis, *Cartographic Encounters*, 187–204; Arnold, *The Rumble of a Distant Drum* (Fayetteville: University of Arkansas Press, 2000), 63–76.

25. These have been labeled "sociogram"-style maps by Patricia Galloway, "Debriefing Explorers: Amerindian Information in the Delisles' Mapping of the Southeast," in Lewis, *Cartographic Encounters*, 231–237, and her *Choctaw Genesis, 1500–1700* (Lincoln: University of Nebraska Press, 1995), 224–27.

26. James A. Marshall, "An Atlas of American Indian Geometry," *Ohio Archaeologist* 37, no. 2 (Spring 1987): 36–49; Bradley T. Lepper, "The Archaeology of the Newark Earthworks," in *Ancient Earthen Enclosures of the Eastern Woodlands*, ed. Robert C. Mainfort Jr. and Lynne P. Sullivan (Gainesville: University Press of Florida, 1998), 114–34.

27. For example, Carol Diaz-Granados and James R. Duncan, *The Petroglyphs and Pictographs of Missouri* (Tuscaloosa: University of Alabama Press, 2000); Charles H. Faulkner, ed., *The Prehistoric Native American Art of Mud Glyph Cave* (Knoxville: University of Tennessee Press, 1986); George Sabo III and Deborah Sabo, *Rock Art in Arkansas* (Fayetteville: Arkansas Archeological Survey, 2005).

28. Philip Phillips and James A. Brown, *Pre-Columbian Shell Engravings from the Craig Mound at Spiro, Oklahoma*, part 1 (Cambridge: Harvard University, Peabody Museum of Archaeology and Ethnology, 1978), pl. 122.3.

29. Robert H. Lafferty III, "Prehistoric Exchange in the Lower Mississippi Valley," in *Prehistoric Exchange Systems in North America*, ed. Timothy G. Baugh and Jonathon E. Ericson (New York: Plenum Press, 1994), 201–5.

30. G. Malcolm Lewis, "Recent and Current Encounters," in Lewis, *Cartographic Encounters*, 78; Muller, "Southeastern Interaction and Integration," 147.

31. Lafferty flattened a paper tracing of the shell design, disregarding the distortion caused by transferring the tracing from a three-dimensional shell. He then scaled his overlay by measuring the modern-map distance between the two "identified" circles on the shell. On the resultant overlay none of the other six shell circles correspond to important Mississippian town sites.

32. Clarence B. Moore, "Certain Aboriginal Remains of the Black Warrior Valley," *Journal of the Academy of Natural Sciences of Philadelphia* 13 (1905): 169; Moore, "Moundville Revisited," *Journal of the Academy of Natural Sciences of Philadelphia* 13 (1907): 347; Vincas

P. Steponaitis, *Ceramics, Chronology, and Community Patterns: An Archaeological Study at Moundville* (New York: Academic Press, 1983), figs. 52s, 63h.

33. Vernon James Knight Jr., James A. Brown, and George E. Lankford, "On the Subject Matter of Southeastern Ceremonial Complex Art," *Southeastern Archaeology* 20, no. 2 (Winter 2001): 137–39.

34. Keith H. Basso, *Wisdom Sits in Places: Landscape and Language among the Western Apache* (Albuquerque: University of New Mexico Press, 1996); Steven Feld and Keith H. Basso, eds., *Senses of Place* (Santa Fe: School of American Research, 1996); for a wonderful result of this reawakened interest in place, see Keith Thor Carlson, *A Stó:lō Coast Salish Historical Atlas* (Vancouver BC: Douglas and McIntyre, 2001).

35. See note 112.

36. For example, Patricia O. Afable and Madison S. Beeler, "Place-Names," in *Handbook of North American Indians*, vol. 17, *Languages*, ed. Ives Goddard (Washington DC: Smithsonian Institution, 1996), 185–99; Karen M. Booker, Charles M. Hudson, and Robert L. Rankin, "Place Name Identification and Multilingualism in the Sixteenth-Century Southeast," *Ethnohistory* 39, no. 4 (1992): 399–451; William A. Read, "Louisiana Place-Names of Indian Origin," *Louisiana State University and Agricultural and Mechanical College, University Bulletin*, n.s. 19, no. 2 (1927); Read, "Florida Place-Names of Indian Origin and Seminole Personal Names," *Louisiana State University, University Studies* 11 (1934); Read, *Indian Place Names in Alabama*, rev. ed. by James B. McMillan (Tuscaloosa: University of Alabama Press, 1984); Read, "Indian Stream Names in Georgia," *International Journal of American Linguistics* 15, no. 2 (1949): 128–32; Read, "Indian Stream Names in Georgia, II" *International Journal of American Linguistics* 16, no. 4 (1950): 203–7; Ovid Vickers, "Mississippi Choctaw Names and Naming: A Diachronic View," *Names* 31, no. 2 (1983): 117–22; Amos J. Wright Jr., *Historic Indian Towns in Alabama, 1540–1838* (Tuscaloosa: University of Alabama Press, 2003). Recent research by John Dyson on the 1723 Chickasaw map demonstrates the value of this approach; John P. Dyson, "Chickasaw Village Names from Contact to Removal: 1540–1835," *Mississippi Archaeology* 38 (2003): 95–134.

37. Edward B. Tylor, "Notes on Powhatan's Mantle, Preserved in the Ashmolean Museum, Oxford," *Internationales Archiv für Ethnographie* 1 (1888): pl. xx (colored engraving); David I. Bushnell Jr., "Virginia—from Early Records," *American Anthropologist* 9 (1907): pl. v (photograph); Christian F. Feest, "Virginia Algonquians," in *Handbook of North American Indians*, vol. 15, *Northeast*, ed. Bruce G. Trigger (Washington DC: Smithsonian Institution, 1978), 261 (photograph); Feest, "Powhatan's Mantle," in *Tradescant's Rarities*, ed. Arthur MacGregor (Oxford: Clarendon Press, 1983), pls. VI and VIII (photographs of obverse and reverse), fig. 19 (outline drawing).

38. The shells are a species of Marginella, a taxonomically challenging group of beach snails. Tylor, "Notes," 217, identified them as *M. nivosa*, a Caribbean species. Feest, "Powhatan's Mantle," 132, favors *M. [Prunum] roscida*, a Virginia coastal species. Gary Coovert and Helen Rountree identify them as fossil shells, *Prunum limatulum*; Helen C. Rountree, "The Powhatans and Other Woodland Indians as Travelers," in *Powhatan Foreign*

Relations, 1500–1722, ed. Helen C. Rountree (Charlottesville: University of Virginia Press, 1993), 238 n117.

39. Arthur MacGregor, "The Tradescants as Collectors of Rarities," in MacGregor, *Tradescant's Rarities,* 21; Feest, "Powhatan's Mantle," 135.

40. John Tradescant, *Musaeum Tradescantium* (London: John Grismond and Nathanael Brooke, 1656), 47; Bushnell, "Virginia," 38.

41. Arthur, "The Tradescants, Gardeners and Botanists," in MacGregor, *Tradescant's Rarities,* 11; Christian F. Feest, "Virginia Indian Miscellany II," *Archiv für Volkerkunde* 21 (1967): 10.

42. Barbour, *Jamestown Voyages,* 414, 257.

43. Philip L. Barbour, ed., *The Complete Works of Captain John Smith (1580–1631),* 3 vols. (Chapel Hill: University of North Carolina Press, 1986), 2:115.

44. Feest, "Powhatan's Mantle," 133–35.

45. Anonymous, "Extracts from the Annual Letters of the English Province of the Society of Jesus," in *Narratives of Early Maryland, 1633–1684,* ed. Clayton C. Hall, (New York: Charles Scribner's Sons, 1910), 125.

46. Feest, "Powhatan's Mantle," 135.

47. Barbour, *The Complete Works,* 1:173–74.

48. Christian F. Feest, "North America in the European *Wunderkammer* before 1750," *Archiv für Volkerkunde* 46 (1992): 82.

49. Feest, "Powhatan's Mantle," 135.

50. E. Randolph Turner III, "An Archaeological and Ethnohistorical Study on the Evolution of Rank Societies in the Virginia Coastal Plain" (PhD diss., Pennsylvania State University, 1976), 133.

51. William Strachey, *The Historie of Travell into Virginia Britania,* ed. Louis B. Wright and Virginia Freund (London: Hakluyt Society, 1953), 63.

52. Strachey, *Virginia Britania,* 63–69; Turner, "Virginia Coastal Plain," 134; Stephen R. Potter, "An Ethnohistorical Examination of Indian Groups in Northumberland County, Virginia: 1608–1719" (master's thesis, University of North Carolina, 1976), 18–24; Potter, *Commoners, Tribute, and Chiefs: The Development of Algonquian Culture in the Potomac Valley* (Charlottesville: University of Virginia Press, 1993), 19, 177.

53. Barbour, *Jamestown Voyages,* 374; Susan M. Kingsbury, ed., *The Records of the Virginia Company of London,* 4 vols. (Washington DC: Government Printing Office, 1933), 3:708; Bushnell, "Virginia," 32.

54. William P. Cumming et al., eds., *The Exploration of North America, 1630–1776* (New York: G. P. Putnam's Sons, 1974), 151, fig. 226 (photograph) (note that parts of the legend are incorrectly transcribed in the editors' caption); G. Malcolm Lewis, "Frontier Encounters in the Field: 1511–1925," in Lewis, *Cartographic Encounters,* 20 (photograph); Lewis, "Maps, Mapmaking, and Map Use by Native North Americans," in *History of Cartography* 2, no. 3: 97 (photograph).

55. Lewis, "Indian Maps," 14.

56. PRO, *Calendar,* vol. 15, *1696–1697* (London: Her Majesty's Stationery Office, 1904),

420; William A. Hunter, "The Historic Role of the Susquehannocks," in *Susquehannock Miscellany*, ed. John Witthoft and W. Fred Kinsey (Harrisburg: Pennsylvania Historical and Museum Commission, 1959), 17; a letter to Governor Nicholson from Lawrence van den Bosh accompanying Ayer MS map 59, quoted courtesy of the Edward E. Ayer Collection, The Newberry Library, Chicago.

57. Barry C. Kent, *Susquehanna's Indians*, Anthropological Series 6 (Harrisburg: Pennsylvania Historical and Museum Commission, 1984), 79; Charles Callender, "Shawnee," in Trigger, *Handbook*, 630.

58. Cumming, *Southeast in Early Maps*, 193–95; for the Delisles' manuscript progression toward this published state, see Galloway, "Debriefing Explorers," 233–57.

59. Sara J. Tucker, *Indian Villages of the Illinois Country, Part I (Atlas)*, Scientific Papers 2 (Springfield: Illinois State Museum, 1942).

60. David J. Weber, *The Spanish Frontier in North America* (New Haven CT: Yale University Press, 1992), 78, 151.

61. John R. Swanton, *The Indian Tribes of North America*, Bureau of American Ethnology Bulletin 145 (Washington DC: Government Printing Office, 1952), 316.

62. Henri Joutel, *A Journal of the Last Voyage Perform'd by Monsr. de la Sale* (London: A. Bell, 1714), 155; Swanton, *Indian Tribes*, 213–14.

63. Richebourg G. McWilliams, ed., *Iberville's Gulf Journals* (Tuscaloosa: University of Alabama Press, 1981), 87–89; Swanton, *Indian Tribes*, 208–9.

64. Richebourg G. McWilliams, "Iberville at the Birdfoot Subdelta: Final Discovery of the Mississippi River," in *Frenchmen and French Ways in the Mississippi Valley*, ed. John F. McDermott (Urbana: University of Illinois Press, 1969); Peter H. Wood, "La Salle: Discovery of a Lost Explorer," *American Historical Review* 89 (1984): 305; Edwin Way Teale, *North with the Spring* (New York: Dodd, Mead, 1951), 76–82.

65. LeMaire, *Carte Nouvelle de la Louisiane* (Paris, 1714); Swanton, *Indian Tribes*, 188; La Salle quoted in Wood, "La Salle," 309.

66. McWilliams, *Gulf Journals*, 72–75; Swanton, *Indian Tribes*, 188.

67. Charles Callender, "Illinois," in Trigger, *Handbook*, 673; J. Joseph Bauxar, "History of the Illinois Area," in Trigger, *Handbook*, 595; also see Guillaume Delisle's maps of 1703 and 1718 illustrated by Cumming, *Southeast in Early Maps*, pls. 43, 47.

68. David I. Bushnell, "The Account of Lamhatty," *American Anthropologist* 10 (1908): pl. xxxv (facsimile drawing); John R. Swanton, "The Tawasa Language," *American Anthropologist* 31 (1929): 441, map 1 (facsimile drawing); Rainer Vollmar, *Indianische Karten Nordamerikas* (Berlin: Dietrich Reimer Verlag, 1981), 48 (facsimile drawing); Gregory A. Waselkov, "Lamhatty's Map," *Southern Exposure* 16, no. 2 (1988): 23 (photograph); Warhus, *Another America*, 75 (photograph); Cumming, *Southeast in Early Maps*, pl. 43a (photograph); Lewis, "Maps, Mapmaking, and Map Use," 98 (photograph).

69. Swanton, "Tawasa Language," 437.

70. Bushnell, "Account of Lamhatty," 568–69. Reprinted with permission from the collections of the Virginia Historical Society, MS 1, L51, fol. 677.

71. Bushnell, "Account of Lamhatty," 568–74; Swanton, "Tawasa Language," 435–53;

Ives Goddard, Patricia Galloway, Marvin D. Jeter, Gregory A. Waselkov, and John E. Worth, "Small Tribes of the Western Southeast," in *Handbook of North American Indians*, vol. 14, *Southeast*, ed. Raymond D. Fogelson (Washington DC: Smithsonian Institution, 2004), 186–87.

72. Cumming, *Early Maps*, 199; J. Leitch Wright Jr., *The Only Land They Knew* (New York: Free Press), 143, 146; Thomas C. Parramore, "The Tuscarora Ascendancy," *North Carolina Historical Review* 59 (1982): 307–26; De Vorsey, "American Indians and the Early Mapping of the Southeast," 86, map 146; Alan Gallay, *The Indian Slave Trade: The Rise of the English Empire in the American South, 1670–1717* (New Haven CT: Yale University Press, 2002), 307. Ives Goddard accepts Walker's north-south directions and interprets the unlabeled circles north of the east-west line as abandoned Tawasa settlements. The number of those unlabeled circles (six) does not agree, however, with Walker's statement that there were ten settlements in the Tawasa confederacy, which are in fact labeled and shown in the correct number south of the east-west line. Ives Goddard, "The Indigenous Languages of the Southeast," *Anthropological Linguistics* 47 (2005): 10.

73. John H. Hann, *Apalachee: The Land between the Rivers* (Gainesville: University Press of Florida, 1988), 184–85.

74. Rodrigo Rangel, "Account of the Northern Conquest and Discovery of Hernando de Soto," in *The De Soto Chronicles: The Expedition of Hernando de Soto to North America in 1539–1543*, ed. Lawrence A. Clayton, Vernon James Knight Jr., and Edward C. Moore, 2 vols. (Tuscaloosa: University of Alabama Press, 1993), 1:285; Lucy L. Wenhold, *A Seventeenth Century Letter of Gabriel Díaz Vara Calderón, Bishop of Cuba, Describing the Indians and Indian Missions of Florida*, Smithsonian Miscellaneous Collections 95, No. 16 (Washington DC: Government Printing Office, 1936), 10.

75. Mark F. Boyd, "The Expedition of Marcos Delgado from Apalache to the Upper Creek Country in 1686," *Florida Historical Quarterly* 16 (1937): 14; John R. Swanton, *Early History of the Creek Indians and Their Neighbors*, Bureau of American Ethnology Bulletin 73 (Washington DC: Government Printing Office, 1922), 137–39.

76. Irving A. Leonard, ed., *Spanish Approach to Pensacola, 1689–1693* (Albuquerque: Quivira Society, 1939), 221, 261, 280, 307; John H. Hann, "Florida's Terra Incognita," *Florida Anthropologist* 41 (1988): 64, 92–103; Gregory A. Waselkov and Bonnie L. Gums, *Plantation Archaeology at Rivière aux Chiens, ca. 1725–1848*, Center for Archaeological Studies, Archaeological Monograph 7 (Mobile: University of South Alabama, 2000), 31–32.

According to Swanton's analysis of the Tawasa vocabulary accompanying Walker's 1708 letter, Lamhatty spoke a Timucuan language, which suggests that older and stronger ties may have drawn the Tawasas to Florida; see Swanton, "Tawasa Language," 451–53; Mary R. Haas, "Southeastern Languages," in *The Languages of Native America*, ed. Lyle Campbell and Marianne Mithun (Austin: University of Texas Press, 1979), 319; James M. Crawford, "Timucua and Yuchi: Two Language Isolates of the Southeast," in Campbell and Mithun, *Languages of Native America*, 333; Julian Granberry, *A Grammar and Dictionary of the Timucua Language*, 3rd ed. (Tuscaloosa: University of Alabama Press, 1993), 3, 7–11; Goddard, "Indigenous Languages," 10–11.

77. Swanton, *Early History*, 141.

78. For Asilédly, cf. San Miguel de Asile in Jerald T. Milanich, "The Western Timucua: Patterns of Acculturation and Change," in *Tacachale*, ed. Jerald Milanich and Samuel Procter (Gainesville: University Press of Florida, 1978), 64, 66; for Ephíppick, cf. Santa Cathalina de Afuica, in Mark F. Boyd, Hale G. Smith, and John W. Griffin, *Here They Once Stood: The Tragic End of the Apalachee Missions* (Gainesville: University Press of Florida, 1951), 11; for Ogolaúghoos, cf. San Joseph de Ocuia, in B. Calvin Jones, "Colonel James Moore and the Destruction of the Apalachee Missions in 1704," Florida Division of Archives, History and Records Management, Bureau of Historic Sites and Properties Bulletin 2 (1972): 25. Alternatively, Ogolaúghoos may be an attempt to render Ogolaúghees, an approximation of the Shawnee name for the Yuchis, according to Jason Baird Jackson, "Yuchi," in Fogelson, *Handbook*, 426, 428.

79. Swanton, *Early History*, 134–38; Rowland and Sanders, *Mississippi Provincial Archives*, 2:25; Jay Higginbotham, *Old Mobile: Fort Louis de la Louisiane, 1702–1711* (Mobile AL: Museum of the City of Mobile, 1977), 288 n1; George E. Lankford, "Ethnohistory: A Documentary Study of Native American Life in the Lower Tombigbee Valley," in *Cultural Resources Reconnaissance Study of the Black Warrior Tombigbee System Corridor, Alabama*, ed. Eugene Wilson (Mobile: University of South Alabama, 1983), 50, 60.

80. Gregory A. Waselkov and John W. Cottier, "European Perceptions of Eastern Muskogean Ethnicity," in *Proceedings of the Tenth Annual Meeting of the French Colonial Historical Society*, ed. Philip Boucher (Lanham MD: University Press of America, 1985), 23–45.

81. Christian F. Feest, "Creek Towns in 1725," *Ethnologische Zeitschrift* (Zurich) 1 (1974): 173.

82. Vernon J. Knight and Sherrée L. Adams, "A Voyage to the Mobile and Tomeh in 1700, with Notes on the Interior of Alabama," *Ethnohistory* 28 (1981): 181.

83. Swanton, "Tawasa Language," 443. On the name Ochese Creek, see Verner W. Crane, "The Origin of the Name of the Creek Indians," *Mississippi Valley Historical Review* 5 (1918): 340; Swanton, *Early History*, 215; Carol A. I. Mason, "The Archaeology of Ocmulgee Old Fields, Macon, Georgia" (PhD diss., University of Michigan, 1963), 231.

84. See Edward Crisp's map of 1711, illustrated by Cumming, *Southeast in Early Maps*, pl. 44; Swanton, "Tawasa Language," 446; John R. Swanton, *The Indians of the Southeastern United States*, Bureau of American Ethnology Bulletin 145 (Washington DC: Government Printing Office, 1946), 184–86.

85. William R. Snell, "Indian Slavery in Colonial South Carolina, 1671–1795" (PhD diss., University of Alabama, 1972), 126.

86. Gallay, *Indian Slave Trade*, 307–8.

87. Justin Winsor, ed., *Narrative and Critical History of America* (New York: Houghton Mifflin, 1887), 349 (crude facsimile drawing); R. H. Gabriel, ed., *The Pageant of America*, 2 vols. (New Haven CT: Yale University Press, 1929), 2:22 (facsimile drawing); Douglas S. Brown, *The Catawba Indians: The People of the River* (Columbia: University of South Carolina Press, 1966), following p. 32 (facsimile drawing); J. Ralph Randolph, *British Travelers among the Southern Indians, 1660–1763* (Norman: University of Oklahoma Press, 1973),

following p. 112 (photograph); Hudson, *Southeastern Indians*, 271 (photograph); Vollmar, *Indianische Karten*, 51 (photograph); Merrell, "Natives in a New World," fig. 2 (facsimile drawing); William Graves, ed., *Historical Atlas of the United States* (Washington DC: National Geographic Society, 1993), 39 (color photograph); Warhus, *Another America*, 78 (color photograph); Lewis, "Maps, Mapmaking, and Map Use," pl. 4 (color photograph).

88. M. Thomas Hatley III, "The Dividing Path: The Direction of Cherokee Life in the Eighteenth Century" (master's thesis, University of North Carolina, 1977), map 4 (photo copy); James H. Merrell, *The Indians' New World: Catawbas and Their Neighbors from European Contact through the Era of Removal* (Chapel Hill: University of North Carolina Press, 1989), 93 (photograph); Julia E. Hammett, "Interregional Patterns of Land Use and Plant Management in Native North America," in *People, Plants, and Landscapes: Studies in Paleoethnobotany*, ed. Kristen J. Gremillion (Tuscaloosa: University of Alabama Press, 1997), 196 (photograph); Galloway, "Debriefing Explorers," 225 (photograph); Cumming, *Southeast in Early Maps*, pl. 48e (photograph).

89. A. S. Salley, ed., *Journal of His Majesty's Council for South Carolina: May 29, 1721–June 10, 1721* (Atlanta: Foote and Davies, 1930), 18; PRO, *Calendar*, vol. 32, *March, 1720 to December, 1721* (London: His Majesty's Stationery Office, 1933), 336.

90. Bruce T. McCully, "Governor Francis Nicholson, Patron *par Excellence* of Religion and Learning in Colonial America," *William and Mary Quarterly* 39 (1982): 330–31. G. Malcolm Lewis has argued for a 1720 date for this and the following map on the grounds that the governor is referred to in the map legends as "Francis Nicholson Esqr." and he was purportedly knighted in that year. In this Lewis is mistaken, since Nicholson was never rewarded with knighthood as has commonly been supposed. See Lewis, "Indian Maps," 21 n18; Leonard W. Labaree, "Francis Nicholson," *Dictionary of American Biography* (New York: Scribner's, 1934), 7:501.

The manuscript copy of the Catawba map dedicated to the Prince of Wales became part of Sir Hans Sloane's private museum (Sloan MS 4723), one of the founding collections of the British Museum. According to the British Library Acquisitions Catalogue, Dr. Matthew Maty, Under Librarian of the British Museum, catalogued this item on December 24, 1762. Marjorie Caygill, "Sloane's Will and the Establishment of the British Museum," in *Sir Hans Sloane: Collector, Scientist, Antiquary, Founding Father of the British Museum*, ed. Arthur MacGregor (London: British Museum Press, 1994), 54, 68.

91. Chapman J. Milling, *Red Carolinians* (Columbia: University of South Carolina Press, 1969), 222; PRO, *Calendar*, 32:302.

92. William Byrd, *Histories of the Dividing Line betwixt Virginia and North Carolina* (New York: Dover, 1967), 300.

93. Merrell, "Natives in a New World," 189; also see James Mooney, *The Siouan Tribes of the East*, Bureau of Ethnology Bulletin 22 (Washington DC: Government Printing Office, 1894), 68–69; Blair A. Rudes, Thomas J. Blumer, and J. Alan May, "Catawba and Neighboring Groups," in Fogelson, *Handbook*, 315; Goddard, "Indigenous Languages," 20–21.

94. Milling, *Red Carolinians*, 247; Rudes, Blumer, and May, "Catawba," 316.

95. On the Succas see Mooney, *Siouan Tribes*, 62; Lawson, *New Voyage*, 61; Merrell, *In-*

dians' New World, 94–95; Verne E. Chatelain, The Defenses of Spanish Florida, 1565–1763, Publication 511 (Washington DC: Carnegie Institute of Washington, 1941), map 8; Rudes, et al., "Catawba," 317; Goddard, "Indigenous Languages," 26. On the Sittiries see Lawson, New Voyage, 49; Frank G. Speck, "Siouan Tribes of the Carolinas as Known from Catawba, Tutelo, and Documentary Sources," American Anthropologist 37 (1935): 218; Merrell, "Natives in a New World," 85, 251; Wayne C. Temple, Indian Villages of the Illinois Country, Part II (Atlas Supplement), Scientific Papers 2 (1) (Springfield: Illinois State Museum, 1975): pl. LXVII; Rudes, et al., "Catawba," 317; Goddard, "Indigenous Languages," 27.

96. Swanton, Indian Tribes, 84; McDowell, Journals, 163; Merrell, Indians' New World, 94; Rudes, et al., "Catawba," 317.

97. Mooney, Siouan Tribes, 60; PRO, Calendar, vol. 34, 1724–1725 (London: His Majesty's Stationery Office, 1936), 281; William L. McDowell Jr., ed., Journals of the Commissioners of the Indian Trade, September 30, 1710–August 29, 1718 (Columbia: South Carolina Archives Department, 1955), 163; Merrell, "Natives in a New World," 14, 115, 215, 309; Rudes, et al., "Catawba," 316; Goddard, "Indigenous Languages," 21.

98. On the Wateries see Mooney, Siouan Tribes, 81; Speck, "Documentary Sources," 221; Milling, Red Carolinians, 225. James Adair, The History of the American Indians (1775; reprint, New York: Johnson Reprint, 1968), 235–36; Rudes, et al., "Catawba," 317; Goddard, "Indigenous Languages," 27.

99. Adair, History, 235–68; McDowell, Journals, 112, 114; Gene Waddell, Indians of the South Carolina Low Country, 1562–1751 (Spartanburg SC: Reprint Company, 1980), 267; Gene Waddell, "Cusabo," in Fogelson, Handbook, 254–64; Goddard, "Indigenous Languages," 22–23. Merrell in Indians' New World, 110, errs in equating the coastal Coosahs with the like-named Muskogean Coosas of the Creek Confederacy.

100. Adair, History, 61; Mooney, Siouan Tribes, 77; McDowell, Journals, 80, 96, 111, 218; Milling, Red Carolinians, 226; Waddell, Indians, 341; Rudes, et al., "Catawba," 317.

101. Merrell, "Natives in a New World," 312.

102. McDowell, Journals, 96.

103. The Public Accounts of John Hammerton, Esqr., Secretary of the Province, Inventories LL, 1744–46, 1-57. South Carolina Department of Archives and History, Columbia; John (?) Evans, "Cuttahbaws Nation. men fit for war 204 In ye year 1756," Dalhousie Muniments, General John Forbes Papers, Document 2/104 (microfilm copy in the South Carolina Department of Archives and History, Columbia), cited in Merrell, Indians' New World, 320 n51; perhaps synonymous with Keyauwee, judging from Rudes, et al., "Catawba," 316.

104. Mooney, Siouan Tribes, 69.

105. I am grateful to Chester DePratter for this suggestion.

106. Winsor, Critical History, 346; Chatelain, Defenses, map 8.

107. In Cumming, Southeast in Early Maps, 221, editor Louis De Vorsey claims that I "omitted the phrase '& Painted' from the title information found on the map," but that phrase is not present in the title.

108. Hatley, "Dividing Path," map 3 (facsimile drawing); G. Malcolm Lewis, "Trav-

elling in Uncharted Territory," in *Tales from the Map Room: Fact and Fiction about Maps and Their Makers*, ed. Peter Barber and Christopher Board (London: BBC Books, 1993), 41; Hammett, "Interregional Patterns of Land Use," 198 (photograph); Galloway, "Debriefing Explorers," 226 (photograph); Warhus, *Another America*, 103 (photograph); Lewis, "Maps, Mapmaking, and Map Use," 100; Gregory A. Waselkov, "Exchange and Interaction since 1500," in Fogelson, *Handbook*, 691.

109. See Albert Gallatin, *A Synopsis of the Indian Tribes of North America*, Transactions and Collections 2 (Philadelphia: American Antiquarian Society, 1836), 307–67; Cyrus Byington, *A Dictionary of the Choctaw Language*, Bureau of American Ethnology Bulletin 46 (Washington DC: Government Printing Office, 1915).

110. Mary R. Haas, "The Classification of the Muskogean Languages," in *Language, Culture and Personality*, ed. Leslie Spier et al. (Menasha WI: Sapir Memorial Publishing Fund, 1941), 54–55; James M. Crawford, "Southeastern Indian Languages," in *Studies in Southeastern Indian Languages*, ed. James M. Crawford (Athens: University of Georgia Press, 1975), 26; Pamela Munro and Catherine Willmond, *Chickasaw: An Analytical Dictionary* (Norman: University of Oklahoma Press, 1994).

111. James M. Crawford, *The Mobilian Trade Language* (Knoxville: University of Tennessee Press, 1978); Emanuel J. Drechsel, *Mobilian Jargon: Linguistic and Sociohistorical Aspects of a Native American Pidgin* (Oxford: Clarendon Press, 1997).

112. In response to my request for assistance regarding the meaning of this phrase, Ives Goddard (personal communication, June 25, 2003) initially posited a reconstitution of this Subject-Object-Verb phrase as *Ila Chikashsha aa-abi'* ("different" [a nominalized form of *ila'*] + "Chickasaw" + locative prefix + "kill"), which Pamela Munro (personal communication, June 25, 2003) interpreted alternatively as "A different one kills a Chickasaw there" (as a sentence), or "where a different one killed a Chickasaw" (as a place name). John Dyson thinks "Elav" could be interpreted differently. He suggests the entire phrase might be *Ilawiit Chikashsha aa-abi'*, with *Ilawiit* meaning "leading" or "escorting" (based on those meanings of the verb *ilawiili* in modern Choctaw, and hypothesizing an earlier similar form in Chickasaw three hundred years ago). Thus, the phrase would translate "where, while escorting the Chickasaws, they murdered them" (John P. Dyson, personal communications, July 6, 2003, and April 1, 2004). Munro is unconvinced (personal communication, July 10, 2003) and still favors Goddard's version, although she acknowledges that neither is certain. I thoroughly enjoyed watching e-mails fly across the country as Munro, Goddard, and Dyson debated the meaning of this phrase, and I greatly appreciate their generous insights to this linguistic puzzle. Their multiple possible interpretations exemplify the uncertainties and ambiguities surrounding nearly all transcriptions made in the eighteenth and early nineteenth centuries before the development of modern standardized linguistic orthographies.

Abi commonly formed part of the given names of Chickasaw warriors in the strife-ridden eighteenth century. According to James Adair, *The History of the American Indians* (London: Edward and Charles Dilly, 1775), 192:

> They crown a warrior, who has killed a distinguished enemy, with the name, Ya-

nasabe, "the buffalo-killer;" Yanasa is a buffalo, compounded of Yah, the divine essence, and Asa, "there, or here is," as formerly mentioned: the Abe is their constant war-period, signifying, by their rhetorical figure "one who kills another." It signifies also to murder a person, or beat him severely. This proper name signifies, the prosperous killer, or destroyer of the buffalo, or strong man. . . . Abi appears in 104 of the 108 male war names John Swanton recorded from Chickasaw speakers early in the twentieth century; John R. Swanton, "Social and Religious Beliefs and Usages of the Chickasaw Indians," in *Forty-Fourth Annual Report of the Bureau of American Ethnology, 1926–1927* (Washington DC: Government Printing Office, 1928), 188–89.

113. In January 1723, the Choctaws, incited by a French offer for bounties on Chickasaw scalps, carried out a massive raid on their southernmost towns, destroying several towns and killing or enslaving four hundred Chickasaws. This disaster prompted a general consolidation of Chickasaw towns northward, and a migration of others to the Savannah River; see Crane, *Southern Frontier*, 273–74; PRO, *Calendar*, vol. 33, *1722–1723* (London: His Majesty's Stationery Office, 1934), 352; Adair, *History*, 377–78; Rowland and Sanders, *Mississippi Provincial Archives*, 3:343; Jean-Baptiste Bénard de La Harpe, *The Historical Journal of the Establishment of the French in Louisiana*, trans. Joan Cain and Virginia Koenig, ed. Glenn R. Conrad (Lafayette: University of Southwestern Louisiana, 1971), 160.

114. The copyist may have been William Hammerton, secretary to the colony, according to G. Malcolm Lewis, "Maps, Mapmaking, and Map Use," 101.

115. John H. Goff, "The Path to Oakfuskee," *Georgia Historical Quarterly* 39 (1955): 1–86, 152–71.

116. On Tyannacau Oakhinnau see Dyson, "Chickasaw Village Names," 102, 131. On Shaterrau Oakhinnau see Dyson, "Chickasaw Village Names," 104, 132, who interprets this more specifically as the upper Tombigbee. On Tongolickau Oakhinnau see Swanton, *Early History*, pl. 5.

117. Munro and Willmond, *Chickasaw*, 7, 107, 267.

118. Lankford, "Lower Tombigbee Valley," 52–58.

119. Swanton, *Early History*, 106; Peter J. Hamilton, *Colonial Mobile*, rev. ed. (1910), ed. Charles G. Summersell (Tuscaloosa: University of Alabama Press, 1976), 111, 113; Demarigny, "Carte particulière d'une partie de la Louisianne, par les Srs. Broutin, de Vergés, ingénieurs & Saucier dessinateur, 1743," G4010 1743 D4 Vault, Geography and Map Division, Library of Congress, Washington DC. I am indebted to Robert Myers for bringing this map, with its Yamasee village notation south of Mobile, to my attention.

120. Rowland and Sanders, *Mississippi Provincial Archives*, 1:116.

121. See note 112. Bénard de La Harpe, *Historical Journal*, 49–50; Richebourg Gaillard McWilliams, trans. and ed., *Fleur de Lys and Calumet, Being the Pénicaut Narrative of French Adventure in Louisiana* (Tuscaloosa: University of Alabama Press, 1988), 73–76.

122. Munro and Willmond, *Chickasaw*, 65; John P. Dyson, personal communication, January 28, 2004.

123. Waselkov and Gums, *Plantation Archaeology*, 20, 36–37.

124. William E. Myer, "Indian Trails of the Southeast," in *Forty-Second Annual Report*

of the Bureau of American Ethnology (Washington DC: Government Printing Office, 1928), pl. 15. Albert S. Gatschet, *A Migration Legend of the Creek Indians*, 2 vols. (Philadelphia: D. G. Brinton, 1884), 1:91; cf. Swanton, *Early History*, pl. 5.

125. Swanton, *Indians of the Southeastern United States*, 204.

126. Compare the French pronunciations of *"Hoppe* Oakhinnau" and "Rivière *aux Perles*"; Swanton, *Early History*, pl. 5. "Hoppe" may, alternatively, be a corruption of "Houspé," used in 1699 to refer to the Ofos; see Jean Delanglez, "Documents: Tonti Letters," *Mid-America* 21 (October 1939): 228 n30.

127. On the Nadacos see Swanton, *Indian Tribes*, 315; McWilliams, *Gulf Journals*, 154. On the Kadohadachos and Kichais see Mildred M. Wedel, "J.-B. Bénard, Sieur de La Harpe: Visitor to the Wichitas in 1719," *Great Plains Journal* 10 (1971), La Harpe's map of 1725; Wedel, *La Harpe's 1719 Post on Red River and Nearby Caddo Settlements*, Texas Memorial Museum Bulletin 30 (Austin: University of Texas, 1978); Douglas R. Parks, "Kitsai," in *Handbook of North American Indians*, vol. 13, *Plains*, ed. Raymond J. DeMallie (Washington DC: Smithsonian Institution, 2001), 571; J. Daniel Rogers and George Sabo III, "Caddo," in Fogelson, *Handbook*, 630.

128. John R. Swanton, *Source Material on the History and Ethnology of the Caddo Indians*, Bureau of American Ethnology Bulletin 132 (Washington DC: Government Printing Office, 1942), 58; Mildred M. Wedel, "Claude-Charles Dutisné: A Review of His 1719 Journeys, Part II," *Great Plains Journal* 12 (1973): 157; Wedel, "The Ethnohistoric Approach to Plains Caddoan Origins," *Nebraska History* 60 (1979): 186; Wedel, "Visitor to the Wichitas," 45; W. W. Newcomb and T. N. Campbell, "Southern Plains Ethnohistory," in *Pathways to Plains Prehistory*, ed. D. G. Wyckoff and J. L. Hofman, Memoir 3 (Norman: Oklahoma Anthropological Society, 1982), 36; William W. Newcomb Jr., "Wichita," in DeMallie, *Handbook*, 565.

129. Garrick A. Bailey and Gloria A. Young, "Kansa," in DeMallie, *Handbook*, 474–75.

130. Thomas W. Kavanagh, "Comanche," in DeMallie, *Handbook*, 902; Gary Clayton Anderson, *The Indian Southwest, 1580–1830: Ethnogenesis and Reinvention* (Norman: University of Oklahoma Press, 1999), 150.

131. John Dyson has suggested "Vossulau" may be "Wosola'," the Wichita name for the Siouan-speaking Missouris and Otoes; John P. Dyson, "Early Chickasaw Encounters with the Native Other: A Map of Trade, Diplomacy, and Warfare," presentation at the annual meeting of the American Society for Ethnohistory (Chicago IL: 2004). On the Chickasaw trader among the Tawakonis, see Pierre Margry, *Découvertes et établissements des Français dans l'ouest et dans le sud de l'Amérique Septentrionale (1679–1754)*, 6 vols. (Paris: Maisonneuve et Ch. LeClerc, 1888), 6:297; also see Tanner's chapter in this volume.

132. Callender, "Illinois," 673, 680. All three paths were still in use thirty years later, since they appear again on a map drawn for the English around 1755 by Chegeree, probably a Miami Indian; for a photograph of Chegeree's map, see Warhus, *Another America*, 110.

133. Wedel, "Visitor to the Wichitas," La Harpe's map, ca. 1725; Garrick A. Bailey, "Osage," in DeMallie, *Handbook*, 494.

134. Raymond J. DeMallie, "Sioux until 1850," in DeMallie, *Handbook*, 749–50.

135. Thomas S. Abler and Elisabeth Tooker, "Seneca," in Trigger, *Handbook*, 516.

136. Charles Callender, "Miami," in Trigger, *Handbook*, 689; Rowland and Sanders, *Mississippi Provincial Archives*, 3:534.

137. Charles Callender, Richard K. Pope, and Susan M. Pope, "Kickapoo," in Trigger, *Handbook*, 662.

138. Compare "Yaumeer" with the traditional name, "Meearmeear"; C. C. Trowbridge, *Meearmeear Traditions*, ed. Vernon Kinietz, Occasional Contributions 7 (Ann Arbor: University of Michigan Museum of Anthropology, 1938); Callender, "Miami," 688.

139. Hatley, "Dividing Path," 52–53.

140. G. Malcolm Lewis superimposed meridians of longitude and parallels of latitude on this Chickasaw map, anchored at river sources or confluences and some irrefutable place names, and found distances compressed and angular distortion increasing away from the map center; "this central area is not necessarily represented in greater detail (the information content thereabouts is no more than in some other parts of the map) but is shown large and relatively undistorted in relation to the rest. Radially away from it in each direction, though least so to the south, directional distortion increases, area diminishes, and shape becomes increasingly deformed. The forty-five-degree clockwise rotation of the Red and Arkansas Rivers in relation to the Mississippi River and the excessively straight representation of the eastern Gulf Coast close to and parallel with one of the flanks of the skin were doubtless due to peripheral constraints imposed by the shape and size of the deerskin." Lewis, "Maps, Mapmaking, and Map Use," 100–101; Lewis, "Travelling in Uncharted Territory," 40–41.

141. Lewis, "Maps, Mapmaking, and Map Use," 104, reports "an unsigned manuscript copy in L'atlas Moreau de Saint Méry (F3 290 12), Directions des Archives de France, Aix-en-Provence."

142. Baron Marc de Villiers, "Note sur deux cartes dessinées par les Chickachas en 1737," *Journal de la Société des Américanistes* 13 (1921): pl. 1; Patricia D. Woods, *French-Indian Relations on the Southern Frontier, 1699–1762* (Ann Arbor MI: UMI Research Press, 1980), illus. 4, p. 133 (facsimile drawing); Vollmar, *Indianische Karten*, 56 (photograph); Patricia Kay Galloway, ed., *Mississippi Provincial Archives: French Dominion*, vols. 4–5 (Baton Rouge: Louisiana State University Press, 1984), vol. 4, facing p. 142 (photograph); Robert H. Lafferty III, "Prehistoric Exchange in the Lower Mississippi Valley," 203 (drawing); Lewis, "Maps, Mapmaking, and Map Use," 104 (photograph); Gregory A. Waselkov, "Indian Maps of the Colonial Southeast," in Lewis, *Cartographic Encounters*, 208 (photograph); Jon Muller, "Southeastern Interaction and Integration," 148 (drawing).

143. Arrell M. Gibson, *The Chickasaws* (Norman: University of Oklahoma Press, 1971), 48–53; Joseph L. Peyser, "The Chickasaw Wars of 1736 and 1740: French Military Drawings and Plans Document the Struggle for the Lower Mississippi," *Journal of Mississippi History* 44 (1982): 5–6.

144. Rowland and Sanders, *Mississippi Provincial Archives*, 3:703; Galloway, *Mississippi Provincial Archives*, 4:149–51.

145. David I. Bushnell Jr., *Drawings by A. DeBatz in Louisiana, 1732–1735*, Smithsonian Miscellaneous Collections 80, No. 5 (Washington DC: Government Printing Office, 1927): 1–2; Samuel Wilson Jr., "Ignace François Broutin," in *Frenchmen and French Ways in the Mississippi Valley*, ed. John F. McDermott (Urbana: University of Illinois Press, 1969), 250, 279.

146. William N. Fenton, "Northern Iroquoian Culture Patterns," in Trigger, *Handbook*, 320.

147. Callender, "Illinois," 673–80; Callender, "Miami," 681–89.

148. Galloway, *Mississippi Provincial Archives*, 4:150, caption facing p. 142; Rowland and Sanders, *Mississippi Provincial Archives*, 1:308; Galloway has suggested (personal communication, 1986) that the maps were copied by de Batz at a distribution of presents to Alabama and other Indian allies held about September 7, 1737, in Mobile and attended by the Captain of Pakana. Diron d'Artaguette probably then sent the copies to France, followed or accompanied by a letter critical of Bienville's inefficiency in pursuing the Chickasaw War, which had led to the death of Diron's brother Pierre.

149. Italics added; Galloway, *Mississippi Provincial Archives*, 5:146–47. Also see Adair, *History*, 159.

150. Marc de Villiers, "Deux Cartes," pl. 11; Woods, *French-Indian Relations*, illus. 3, p. 131 (facsimile drawing); Vollmar, *Indianische Karten*, 55 (photograph); Galloway, *Mississippi Provincial Archives*, vol. 4, facing p. 154 (photograph); James R. Atkinson, "The Ackia and Ogoula Tchetoka Chickasaw Village Locations in 1736 during the French-Chickasaw War," *Mississippi Archaeology* 20 (1985): fig. 5 (photograph); Gregory A. Waselkov, "Changing Strategies of Indian Field Location in the Early Historic Southeast," in *Peoples, Plants, and Landscapes: Studies in Paleoethnobotany*, ed. Kristen J. Gremillion (Tuscaloosa: University of Alabama Press, 1997), 181 (photograph); Warhus, *Another America*, 108 (photograph); Lewis, "Maps, Mapmaking, and Map Use," 102 (photograph); Waselkov, "Indian Maps of the Colonial Southeast: Archaeological Implications and Prospects," 215 (photograph); Muller, "Southeastern Interaction and Integration," 145 (drawing).

151. Galloway, *Mississippi Provincial Archives*, 4:154 n27.

152. Galloway, *Mississippi Provincial Archives*, 4:150.

153. John F. McDermott, *A Glossary of Mississippi Valley French, 1673–1850*, Studies in Language and Literature 12 (St. Louis: Washington University, 1941), 66.

154. This translation is corrected from Rowland and Sanders, *Mississippi Provincial Archives*, 1:357.

155. Swanton, *Early History*, pl. 5; Adair, *History*, 225, 353–54; also see John R. Swanton, "Social and Religious Beliefs and Usages of the Chickasaw Indians," in *Forty-Fourth Annual Report of the Bureau of American Ethnology* (Washington DC: Government Printing Office, 1928); Bernard Romans, *A Concise Natural History of East and West Florida* (New York, 1775); Daniel H. Usner Jr., "Frontier Exchange in the Lower Mississippi Valley: Race Relations and Economic Life in Colonial Louisiana, 1699–1783" (PhD diss., Duke University, 1981), 77.

156. Waselkov, "Changing Strategies," 179–94; Waselkov, "Indian Maps of the Colonial Southeast," 214, 220 n31.

157. Rowland and Sanders, *Mississippi Provincial Archives*, 1:304; see Atkinson, "Chickasaw Village Locations in 1736," 61–70. However, the three small prairie villages are evidently labeled incorrectly on this map; see James R. Atkinson, *Splendid Land, Splendid People: The Chickasaw Indians to Removal* (Tuscaloosa: University of Alabama Press, 2004), note in fig. 6.

The Graysons' Dilemma

A Creek Family Confronts the Science of Race

CLAUDIO SAUNT

Whether exploring the foundations of patriarchy in seventeenth-century Virginia, the dynamics of the southern campaign in revolutionary America, or the making of white supremacy in the Jim Crow era, historians of the South position race at the center of their narratives.[1] Historians of the native South, however, grant race only a limited role in their accounts of Indian history. They have investigated the origins of racism in native America yet have minimized its impact on everyday social interactions, local economies, and community politics.[2] In short, the historiography implicitly suggests that the Indians' adoption of an ideology of race had little effect on their communities.[3]

The absence of race in literature on southern Indians may reflect disciplinary conventions rather than the daily realities of the South's native peoples. Ethnohistorians hold as a central tenet that Indians should not be written about as if they were white or black Americans, and they contend that the themes of colonial history and the practices of colonists should not be transferred wholesale to native America.[4] Those who write about the Southeast therefore emphasize the ways in which Native Americans drew on ancient Mississippian traditions, but rarely do they trace the impact of Mississippian traditions of a more recent age, namely racism in all of its many manifestations. Indians, deeply influenced by patterns established many centuries ago, seem immune from changes taking place in their own lifetimes.[5]

It would surely be folly to suggest that the central theme of southern Indian history is "the problem of race control," as U. B. Phillips once remarked of southern history more generally.[6] Yet southeastern Indians were Indian *and* southern. They lived in the same region as their colonial counterparts, their economy was closely linked to the larger regional and Atlantic market, and they married into white and black southern families. Biologically, culturally, socially, and economically, they had a number of commonalities with other southerners, even if, to be sure, they differed in significant ways. Their dual identity as part of the colonial South yet apart from the southern colonies is absent from most histories. Although the central theme of southern Indian history may not be the problem of race control, race in fact played a far larger role in native communities than scholars have yet realized.

The pervasiveness of race in the lives of Indians reached a peak in the early nineteenth century. This period is traditionally considered part of the antebellum South, but for Native Americans, it more properly belongs to the colonial era. The United States forcefully introduced American cultural practices into Indian communities, dismantled their governments, and appropriated their land. In short, for vast areas of the South, the colonial era ends not with the American Revolution but with Removal, when southern states displaced the Five Tribes and when the federal government relocated its colonial subjects and policies west of the Mississippi. In the decades leading up to Removal, race structured all aspects of the relationship between Indians and colonists. It gave logic to U.S. colonial policy, affected the daily actions of the government's Indian agents, and validated ordinary Americans' contempt for native peoples. In turn, it shaped the actions of Indians themselves.

The contours of this period may be roughly sketched by scouring the reports of Indian agents for passages that shed light on everyday life in the native South. But the full impact of race is perhaps better captured by exploring the story of a single family, the Graysons. From the 1780s to the present, this family has struggled to reconcile its Creek, Scottish, and African ancestry with the racial hierarchy born in the colonial South. The Graysons faced a particularly trying time in the nineteenth century, when the ascendancy of race culminated in the emergence of scientific racism. Their story illustrates that race and scientific racism reshaped Indian communities in profound and terrible ways.

The Graysons trace their New World origins to the late 1700s, when Sinnugee, a Creek woman, took as her husband Robert Grierson (later changed to Grayson), a recent Scottish immigrant and deerskin trader who set up shop in Hilabi, a Creek town once located a few miles northeast of present Alexander City, Alabama. The historical record reveals almost nothing about Sinnugee but that she belonged to the Spanalgee or "Spanish" clan, created by Creeks to account for women who emigrated from Spanish Florida.[7] (Immigrant men were adopted into existing matrilineal clans.) Given that people directly from Iberia were unlikely to end up in the Creek nation, Sinnugee or her mother were very probably part African, European, and Native American, like so many other Floridians.

Sinnugee and Robert had at least six children. Raised in Hilabi, the children met a remarkably diverse group of people. Most residents were born and raised in the Creek Nation by Creek parents, but some were Scottish immigrants, like Robert Grierson and his fellow trader Thomas Scott.[8] Others came from Africa by way of Georgia, South Carolina, or Florida. Two such newcomers arrived in Hilabi in August 1788, after fleeing 225 miles from their owner, Captain Martín Palao of Pensacola. In Hilabi, they joined a growing population of fugitives, including at least one other of Palao's slaves.[9]

Like Robert Grierson, immigrants, both black and white, frequently married locally, and Hilabi therefore counted among its residents a number of people contemptuously called "half breeds" by white Americans. One North Carolinian, a U.S. Indian agent, singled out Auwillaugee by such a name, although he noted approvingly that she owned seventy head of cattle.[10] By the agent's logic, Sinnugee might have warranted the same designation, yet the agent called Sinnugee an Indian, for he was blind to the frequent marriages between Native Americans and African Americans.[11]

Still other immigrants were African or European American but had lived so long in the Creek Nation that they all but became native Creeks. John Eades's son Daniel surely fit this description. Born in Wilkes County, Georgia, in 1770, Daniel was kidnapped at the impressionable age of nine by a party of Creeks. Fourteen years after this traumatic event, John hopefully reported that his son was held "captive" in Hilabi. Yet Daniel, then age twenty-three, was scarcely a prisoner. He had adopted a new identity and now answered to the name Saucy Jack.[12]

Although the Graysons lived in this diverse and mixed community, they also knew racial stratification. In the 1790s, Robert owned forty black slaves, and by 1812, he owned twice that number.[13] The slaves produced cotton and tended to their master's three hundred cattle.[14] Robert does not appear to have driven his slaves as hard as cotton planters elsewhere in the South, for none of his visitors reported seeing the great wealth that might be expected of a master of so many men and women.[15] Nevertheless, Robert's constant business disputes in the 1810s over the title of slaves suggests that his slaves were property more than kin, sent to market or to the field according to the balance of his account book.[16]

Given the diverse and mixed population in Hilabi and the Graysons' proximity to a number of black slaves, it is not surprising that as a young adult their daughter Katy developed a sexual relationship with a man of African descent. By the early 1810s, Katy and her partner had two children, John and Annie.[17] At the time interracial relationships in the southern states were at best bitterly tolerated, and more frequently, they were met with violence, especially those involving black men and white women.[18] In the Creek Nation, by contrast, the heterogeneous population and the comparatively minor investment in race slavery gave residents little reason to condemn Katy's actions.

If race had remained unimportant in Indian communities, Katy and her partner might have continued to raise their family together, without regard to ancestry, skin color, or any other measure of racial difference. Such was not to be the case. In the second and third decade of the 1800s, the tensions between Hilabi's diverse community and its residents who were experimenting with plantation agriculture rose significantly. Several forces aggravated these tensions, including the outbreak of a Creek civil war in 1813, the constant pressure on the nation to cede lands to the United States, and the spread of cotton agriculture into the Deep South. At the same time American scientists began taking measurements of racial differences in an effort to explain the origins of the most salient characteristic of the United States, the hierarchy of races. The new American fascination with the science of race had a counterpart in the native Southeast, where Indians also began searching for ways to explain the hierarchy of races. With the emerging scientific discourse on inferior races emanating from America's learned halls and with a similar effort underway in Indian communities, the Graysons, linked to Africa by ancestry, marriage, and economics, found it expedient to clarify their family's relationship with dark-skinned people. They could either reject their African relatives and embrace the science of race, or embrace their African relatives and reject the racial ideology sweeping the South.

All through the 1700s leading American scientists and philosophers had believed that Africans, Europeans, and Indians were merely different varieties of a single species. Two pieces of evidence strongly supported their position. The first rested on simple observation. A species could not produce fertile offspring with another species, scholars believed, and everyone knew that in the Americas people of all sorts were multiplying rapidly. In fact, the terms to describe these offspring—mulatto, mestizo, zambo, quadroon, octoroon, and so on—proliferated as fast as humans themselves. Clearly, the reasoning went, Africans, Europeans, and Indians must be different varieties of a single, unified species. The second piece of evidence seemed equally unassailable. Species were said to be by definition immutable and primordial. Unless there were multiple creations of humans at the beginning of time, every person had to belong to the same species. Were there multiple creations? Genesis, the foundational text of natural history, strongly suggested not.[19]

Despite this belief in the unity of humankind, Americans could still be virulently prejudiced. "The blacks may be of the same species, for the mixed progeny will breed," conceded one author in the *Southern Literary Journal* in 1835. "But they are an inferior variety of the animal, man."[20] Yet belief in the unity of humankind led some influential white Americans to formulate policies that held out the possibility of amalgamation. "You will become one people with us," Thomas Jefferson told an Indian audience; "your blood will mix with ours; and will spread with ours over this great island."[21] In the early 1800s, however, belief in the unity of humankind began to crumble under the attack of scientists.

Samuel George Morton, perhaps the country's leading natural scientist, did more than anyone else to advance the science of race. In the 1830s he set about collecting and measuring skulls, eventually amassing 867 crania from around the world, a collection that the Swiss scientist Louis Agassiz deemed alone worth a visit to America.[22] Morton's enormous collection and his meticulous measurements yielded a magnum opus in 1839, *Crania Americana*, a detailed study of the size and shape of hundreds of Native American skulls. The work did two things: by measuring skull size, it established a hierarchy of races, with whites at the top and Indians and blacks at the bottom; and by comparing ancient and modern skulls, it demonstrated the permanency of the differences between Africans, Indians, and Europeans.[23]

Morton's work gave race a new scientific legitimacy, and by illustrating permanent differences across great spans of time, it undermined the very foundations of environmentalism.

These rarified scientific debates about human difference may seem far removed from the Graysons, but Indians could not ignore the growing hostility toward their presence in the United States, nor could they avoid the unwelcome attention of natural scientists. In fact the debates waged in learned journals were far more meaningful to Indians than they were to most other North Americans. "[W]e are convinced that the only method to protract the existence of that people, as a distinct race, is to send them into the wilderness," concluded one scientific racist, Charles Caldwell.[24] T. Hartley Crawford, the commissioner of Indian affairs who would oversee the Creeks' removal from the Southeast, echoed Caldwell's conclusions. "It is late in the Indian's day," he asserted, "and his sun, it is feared, will soon set. . . . The only atmosphere through which it can much longer light his way, is west of the great river."[25] In some cases, the impact of science's new obsession was felt even more directly. Morton's *Crania Americana* included a full-page engraving of the skull of Athlaha Ficksa, reportedly "a full-blood chief of the Creek nation." A veteran of the 1836 Creek War, Athlaha Ficksa died in 1837 in Mobile, where a navy doctor removed his head, cleaned it of flesh, and mailed it to Morton's Philadelphia laboratory. Morton judged it a "remarkably fine head," and carefully measured its "parietal diameter," "inter-mastoid arch," and "occipito-frontal arch."[26] Athlaha Ficksa had served in war alongside five Graysons; in this nation of some 22,000 people, the Graysons surely knew him, if not personally then by reputation.[27] The removal of his head must have alarmed and disgusted Creeks throughout the nation.

Morton had other Creek skulls in his collection. Item number 441 in his catalogue had once belonged to a "Creek Warrior of Alabama," and no. 751 had belonged to a "Creek woman from Georgia." No. 408 reputedly came from a Choctaw Indian, but Morton observed that "the skull strongly indicates a mixture of the Negro," a remark that indicated the direction of scientific racism.[28] The next decade would see a new obsession with "hybridity," the mixing of peoples, a phenomenon understood to have measurable and lamentable consequences. One 1842 article would carry the title,

"The Mulatto a Hybrid—Probable Extermination of the Two Races if the Whites and Blacks Are Allowed to Intermarry."[29]

It would be satisfying to assume that Creeks ignored the poor science and apologies for slavery that emanated from America's centers of learning. It might even be expected that they passionately despised the propaganda of their colonizers. Yet Creeks could not escape the South, with its racial hierarchies and vast slave plantations. Nor could they avoid recognizing the racial hierarchy that was taking root in their own nation. In fact some Creeks not only shared the beliefs of scientific racists but also in a sense even anticipated their arguments. Like white Southerners, southeastern Indians developed stories to explain the origins of the racial hierarchy that was so evident in the South.

Naturalists such as Samuel George Morton provided the scientific evidence to overturn the long-held belief in the unity of humankind, but this belief did not rest solely on observation of the physical world. It was also grounded in faith, for Genesis stated clearly that humans were descended from Adam and Eve. This conflict between religion and science embarrassed a number of naturalists. Some sidestepped the issue by denying that their theories conflicted with the Bible. The races, distinct and immutable, surely existed, they said, but their origins remained a mystery. Others, by contrast, took glee in rejecting the historical validity of Adam and Eve's travails.[30] Surprisingly, despite their great investment in slavery, white Southerners never rejected the biblical doctrine of the unity of humankind. They were unwilling to commit heresy, even if that heresy made slavery unassailable on scientific grounds. Their rejection of separate creations did not rest solely on a foundation of piety, for they well knew that the Bible also offered ample evidence in defense of slavery.[31] With less investment in the Bible, however, a southern people who fancied themselves masters and not slaves would have fully embraced the notion of separate creations, thereby dissolving the tension between foundational beliefs and empirical observation.

As Southerners with little interest in the stories of Genesis, the Creeks were just such a people. Their willingness to believe in separate creations suggests that by the early nineteenth century they understood Indians, Europeans, and Africans to be intrinsically different. In the eighteenth century, Creeks did not bother to account for the existence of Africans and Europeans.[32] When by the 1760s they began mentioning Europeans and Africans in their narratives, they frequently did not specify how these newcomers came to be, but when they did, they spoke of a single creation. Both "red and White Men spring from the same God," one Creek said in 1765, suggesting that they were born in a single creation, although his ambiguous statement allowed for multiple creations as well.[33] In 1793 a Seminole leader was similarly vague about the specifics of creation. (The Seminoles were culturally affiliated with the Creeks.) "I was told the great water divided the world in seven parts, and this part (America) was given to the *red people*," he said. "And when the white people first came to this part," he continued, "the red people was afraid of the white people."[34] That same year, a Creek leader named White Lieutenant offered more detail. All "the people in the world" were descended from a single couple, his forefathers had learned from the Spanish.[35] Here was the doctrine of unity, stated explicitly.

In considering these examples, it must be taken into account that Creeks were speaking to a white audience in a politically charged atmosphere. White Lieutenant and others flattered their listeners by telling them what they wanted to hear. Hence all of these early origin stories mirror the accounts in Genesis, and all of them seem to be in the tradition of a single Edenic creation. It is all the more striking, then, that in 1818 and twice more in 1823–24, Seminoles recounted stories of *separate* creations. Neamathla's story, told to the governor of Florida in 1823 or 1824, is the most complete of these narratives. God made a white man first, Neamathla explained. Displeased with his "pale and weak" creation, he made another, but this one was too black. "The Great Spirit liked the black man less than the white," Neamathla reportedly said, "and he shoved him aside to make room for another trial." Then he made his favorite creation, "the red man." Neamathla explained that the "Great Spirit" set three boxes on earth and allowed the white man as his first creation to choose his fate. The white man opened the boxes and selected "pens, and ink, and paper, and compasses." When the black man stepped forward to make his choice, the Great Spirit said, "I do not like you," and ordered him to stand aside. The red man then selected "tomahawks, knives, war clubs, traps, and such things as are useful in war and hunting." The black man took what was left: "axes and hoes, with buckets to carry water in, and long whips for driving oxen." Neamathla concluded that "the negro must work for both the red and white man, and it has been so ever since."[36] With its description of "pale and weak" white men, of a god who worked according to trial and error, and of separate creations, this was hardly a tale to flatter a white audience. (In 1842, one Creek would recount a similar story to a visitor in Indian Territory.)[37]

The racial content of these stories cannot be attributed merely to the presence of a white audience, for Creeks and Seminoles spoke of separate creations at a time when only a mere handful of whites shared their views.[38] Why had Indians taken up the belief of separate creations and of immutable and distinct races? The racial climate in the South had much to do with the formation of their views. Unburdened by Christian dogma, they adopted their stories to explain what they saw and thought to be true, not unlike scientists such as Samuel George Morton. In the South, where skin color was closely correlated with status, they concluded that Africans must indeed be a different sort of human. White Americans saw the same social world and developed an entire science to justify its existence, but despite their deep-seated and vicious prejudices, they could not so easily dismiss the tenets of Christianity. (Their struggles to reconcile faith and what they believed to be the natural world resembled those of educated Europeans in the age of Copernicus or Galileo.) Ironically, Africans also may have contributed to the emergence of a Creek belief in separate creations. There are African precedents for Neamathla's story that date back to 1698, and some folklorists believe that the long history of cultural convergence between blacks and Indians in the Southeast gave rise to accounts of separate origins.[39]

Influenced by both whites and Africans, Indians also drew on their own traditions and experiences. One scholar suggests that color symbolism in the native Southeast, where red and white were commonly understood to be opposites, gradually took on racial connotations.[40] Others have noted that southeastern Indians frequently dismissed all outsiders as nonhumans.[41] It is not difficult to see how this disdain for others might have led to the conviction that plantation slaves were separate and distinct beings. Whatever the underlying precedents, the Indian belief in separate creations anticipated the direction of America's scientific racists. Although many Indians surely rejected the principle that Indians, blacks, and whites existed in a natural hierarchy, but even so, they may have occasionally harbored doubts about the essential unity of humankind. Perhaps blacks were inferior; perhaps whites were more naturally gifted at studious pursuits; perhaps the admixture of white blood did hold the only chance of long-term survival for

Indian peoples. These thoughts, no matter how briefly entertained, would have weighed heavily on families such as the Graysons.

Just how heavily is illustrated by Katy's actions. Sometime in the late 1810s, Katy and her African partner parted ways. It is impossibly to say why for certain: she abandoned him because of the increasingly hostile racial climate or simply because she grew to dislike him; she was abandoned by him for similar reasons; he was sold out of the Creek Nation; or maybe he simply died. Yet the timing of her actions suggests that race played a critical role. In the second decade of the nineteenth century, when both white and Indian Southerners began to propose that racial differences were permanent and unchanging, Creeks such as Katy could not fail to see the implications for their families. The emerging science of racial difference in the native Southeast, as Neamathla's story illustrates, predicted and even prescribed the permanent degradation of people of African ancestry. Few Indians would have willingly consigned themselves and their families to such a fate.

Katy's subsequent transformation into a slaveholder further suggests that her separation from her black partner was likely linked to the deteriorating racial climate at the time. In 1817 Katy's father Robert made her a generous gift of slaves out of "natural love and affection" and for her "better support and maintainance." These sentimental reasons were perhaps outweighed by Robert's desire to make "all other bonds and deeds null, and void," for he was involved in a series of lawsuits and desperately wished to clear the title to his slaves. Katy received Will; Dy; Ian; James and his wife Venus, and their children, Sam, Robin, Amanda, Will, Hector, Mary, Ann; and Abigail and her children, Judy, Kit, and John.[42] Robert's gift to Katy made her dependent on the degradation of blacks and, intentionally or not, illustrated a simple choice—be a mother to black Creeks or a master of black slaves. Katy took the message to heart, and as if to emphasize the point, soon after separating from her black partner, she married Johnnie Benson (Tulwa Tustanagee), half Creek and half European.[43]

The details of Katy and Johnnie's early life together remain unknown except that they continued to live in Hilabi. Katy's daughter Annie unfortunately disappears altogether from the record.[44] And her son John appears only rarely. At age nineteen, he was living in a separate residence a few miles from his mother.[45] John and Katy's proximity to each other suggests that they continued to keep in contact, but John must have looked at his mother's family with some bitterness. The only black Creeks now allowed in Katy's family were slaves, fourteen of them by 1832.[46]

Katy's new marriage did not solve the problem of race for the Graysons. Soon after she and her African partner separated, her brother William began a relationship with Judah, a slave who belonged to his father Robert. In 1819 Judah gave birth to their first child, William Jr.[47] The displeasure of William's family became manifest in 1823, when Robert died. The Creek Nation appointed William McIntosh, a Grayson family friend, to oversee the disposal of the property. Each of Robert's children received a share of slaves except for William. William was mentioned only once in the disposition of the estate: Robert's daughter Elizabeth, the settlement read, "may loan or bestow to Wm Grayson the negro woman Judy and her son William, at her pleasure."[48] The phrase—whether originating from patriarch Robert or from William McIntosh—cut two ways. It placed the ownership of William's partner and child in the hands of his sister, and at the same time it called attention to the reason for his exclusion from his father's estate.

Two years later, William McIntosh's son Chilly would codify in writing a Creek law seemingly aimed at William and Judah. "If any of our people have children and Negros and either of the children should take a Negro as a husband or wife," wrote Chilly, "and should said child have a property given to it by his parent the property shall be taken from them and divide among the rest of the children." The law's conclusion left little room for ambiguity: "It is a disgrace to our Nation for our people to marry a Negro." McIntosh's code further degraded Africans by stipulating that Indians who killed "negros" need suffer no punishment if they "pay the owner the value."[49] By conflating Negroes and slaves, McIntosh made it clear that African ancestry was indelibly associated with bondage. Yet William ignored the hostility, as was visible to all at the time of his father's death. Judah was then pregnant with their second child, Emma. By 1830 they would have five children.

As both masters and companions of Africans, the Graysons could not escape the growing presence of race in the Creek Nation. "I do not like you," the Great Spirit had said to the first African. By nature, dark people were laborers, meant to aspire to nothing more than clearing fields, planting crops, and hauling water for their masters. Encouraged by the Great Spirit and by America's leading scientists, Creeks increasingly tried to subjugate black people, if not eliminate them entirely from the Nation.

The hostility toward Africans explains in part why Creeks attacked the Grayson plantations a number of times in the early 1820s.[50] In one such raid in 1823, nine Grayson slaves bore the brunt of the violence. They may have fallen victim to a law that forbade slaves from holding property. Lawmakers "may do as they please" with the confiscated property, according to the act.[51] Each Grayson slave lost hundreds of dollars of goods, ranging from moccasins and pantaloons to rings and broaches. William's partner Judah suffered $128 in damages.[52] Her neighbor Dick lost nearly eight hundred dollars of goods, including a pair of "fine shoes," a fiddle, and a fur hat.[53] Two years later Creek warriors caught William visiting Judah on Elizabeth's plantation. Judah was pregnant with another child, Henderson—or perhaps had recently given birth. The warriors bound and flogged William and "carried away and Kill.d every thing on the plantation of any value."[54]

At the same time Creeks targeted slaves elsewhere in the nation. In 1826 a Baptist missionary reported that one of the most powerful politicians in the Creek nation had threatened blacks who attended prayer meetings with "the direst penalties."[55] Apparently the threat was serious, for into the following year congregations of slaves had to meet on the sly or not at all.[56] Then in 1828 as many as thirty Creeks broke into a prayer meeting at Withington Station, on the border of Georgia and Alabama, and bound and tied the black participants. They led the worshippers one by one to a post in the yard and beat them.[57] According to one account, a twelve-year-old girl was forced to witness the proceedings. Later, the warriors pulled her dress over her head, flogged, and sexually molested her.[58] When missionaries asked for justice, one Creek leader asked "if it were worth while to shed blood for a *few old negroes*." One of the slaves' owners expressed satisfaction at the punishment meted out, regretting only that her other slave women had escaped.[59] Prayer meetings continued, but in secret and in fear.[60] These hostilities marked Judah and other slaves as outsiders, unwelcome in the Creek Nation even as the lowliest laborers.

Around the nation, dark-skinned Creeks recognized the growing uncertainty of their status in the nation and the increasing importance of complexion. As early as 1823, a few Creeks of African ancestry took steps to reaffirm their freedom. Sakay Randall got a number of Creek leaders to declare

in writing that she was "free from Slavery or servitude to any person whatever togeather with all the Issue of her body." Careful to attend to the interests of her children, Sakay clearly feared for the future of black Creeks in
the nation. Alex and Sampson Perryman went before the local Indian agent
that same year to secure written confirmation that they were "born free and
ever since have been so."[61] Although free since birth, they evidently believed
that the hostile climate of the 1820s placed their status in jeopardy.

Most Graysons were preoccupied with protecting the value of their human property. Losing title to slaves, Robert once wrote, was "the next thing
to Death."[62] William, however, had other concerns. By 1835 he and Judah
had seven children. After purchasing Judah from his sister sometime before that date William went before Creek leaders and declared that he was
freeing Judah and her children "from motives of humanity and benevo-
lence and for faithful services tendered."[63] William and Judah would live
together until his death in 1861.

William and Katy's families followed divergent paths in the nineteenth
century. In each generation, the majority of William's descendants married
dark-skinned people, while Katy's chose light-skinned partners, reflecting
the different opportunities in marriage available to each side. As a result,
Katy and Johnnie Benson's descendants were relatively fair-skinned. Grandson George Washington Grayson, for example, had "exceedingly red hair"
and was "quite white in complexion."[64] William and Judah's grandson Eli,
by contrast, was visibly "Indian mixed with black."[65] The physical differences reflected and perpetuated the ideology of race and served as the key
for the unequal distribution of resources in the native South throughout
the nineteenth century. The result of this inequality is captured by a simple
comparison, the probate records of George Washington and Eli Grayson.
When George Washington Grayson died in 1920, he possessed thirteen lots
in Eufala, Oklahoma, valued at $2,234, and personal property amounting
to $6,000, for a total of $8,234. When his cousin Eli died in 1931, he owned
a John Deere wagon, a dun horse, a saddle and bridle, a pair of spurs, one
jersey cow, and 120 acres of farmland in Oktaha, Oklahoma. A few years
later, Eli's land was seized for debt.[66]

The story of the Grayson family illustrates how powerfully race shaped
southeastern Indian communities. It is especially revealing because of the

choices made by Katy and William, but even for native families without such dramatic moments in their past, race was a constant presence in their lives. Every Southerner recognized that light-skinned Indians fared better than those with dark complexions in the United States, and these inequalities, visible to everyone in the form of material wealth, were partially replicated in the native South, where they correlated with differences in education, economic practice, and political alliance. Light skin produced privilege; it also was produced by privileged people who had the choice to marry white Americans or Native Americans of European descent. In this way, race affected all Indians, not just those with African ancestry.

The choices Indians made based on skin color were at times based on hard calculation and dictated by the desire to survive. At other times the choices surely crossed into the realm of unreason and reflected a deep-seated prejudice against Africans, or, in the case of some light-skinned Indians, an aversion toward "full-bloods," to use Samuel George Morton's term. In either case, it is clear that race played an important, if often silent, role in manifold daily interactions in the native Southeast. Southeastern Indians bear the mantle of ancient as well as more recent Southerners.

Notes

1. Kathleen M. Brown, *Good Wives, Nasty Wenches, and Anxious Patriarchs: Gender, Race, and Power in Colonial Virginia* (Chapel Hill: University of North Carolina Press, 1996); Sylvia R. Frey, *Water from the Rock: Black Resistance in a Revolutionary Age* (Princeton NJ: Princeton University Press, 1991); Jane Dailey, Glenda Gilmore, and Bryant Simon, eds., *Jumpin' Jim Crow: Southern Politics from Civil War to Civil Rights* (Princeton NJ: Princeton University Press, 2000).

2. A number of articles investigate the origins of racism among southeastern Indians, but book-length studies on the South's native peoples rarely integrate race into their narratives. Two exceptions are Theda Perdue, *Slavery and the Evolution of Cherokee Society, 1540–1866* (Knoxville: University of Tennessee Press, 1979); and Claudio Saunt, *A New Order of Things: Property, Power, and the Transformation of the Creek Indians, 1733–1816* (New York: Cambridge University Press, 1999). On the origins of racism, see William S. Willis, "Divide and Rule: Red, White, and Black in the Southeast," *Journal of Negro History* 48 (July 1963): 157–76; William G. McLoughlin, "Red Indians, Black Slavery and White Racism: America's Slaveholding Indians," *American Quarterly* 26 (October 1974): 366–83; James H. Merrell, "The Racial Education of the Catawba Indians," *Journal of Southern History* 50 (August 1984): 363–84; Kathryn E. Holland Braund, "The Creek Indians, Blacks, and

Slavery," *Journal of Southern History* 57 (November 1991): 601–37; and Nancy Shoemaker, "How Indians Got to Be Red," *American Historical Review* 102 (June 1997): 625–44.

3. For a statement on the unimportance of race in southeastern Indian societies, see Theda Perdue, *"Mixed Blood" Indians: Racial Construction in the Early South* (Athens: University of Georgia Press, 2003).

4. The discipline of ethnohistory has generated its own set of thematic and methodological concerns different from those of traditional southern history. These concerns are addressed in a number of edited books, including Donald L. Fixico, ed., *Rethinking American Indian History* (Albuquerque: University of New Mexico Press, 1997); Devon Mihesuah, ed., *Natives and Academics: Researching and Writing about American Indians* (Lincoln: University of Nebraska Press, 1998); Russell Thornton, ed., *Studying Native America: Problems and Prospects* (Madison: University of Wisconsin Press, 1998); and Nancy Shoemaker, ed., *Clearing a Path: Theorizing the Past in Native American Studies* (New York: Routledge, 2002).

5. See, for example, James Taylor Carson, *Searching for the Bright Path: The Mississippi Choctaws from Prehistory to Removal* (Lincoln: University of Nebraska Press, 1999).

6. Ulrich B. Phillips, "The Central Theme of Southern History," *American Historical Review* 34 (1928): 31.

7. Journal of Benjamin Hawkins, December 11, 1796, in *Letters, Journals, and Writings of Benjamin Hawkins*, ed. C. L. Grant (Savannah: Beehive Press, 1980), (hereinafter LBH), 1:15; Jack Martin to the author, August 4, 1999.

8. "At a Congress of the Principal Chiefs and Warriors of the Upper Creek Nation," October 29, 1771, P. K. Yonge Library of Florida History, University of Florida (hereinafter PKY), Lockey Collection, Public Records Office, Colonial Office 5/589.

9. Arturo O'Neill to Estevan Miró, October 28, 1788, Papeles Procedentes de Cuba (hereinafter PC), leg. 38, 555, reel 191, PKY; Martin Palao and Josef Monroy to Arturo O'Neill, November 23, 1788, PC, leg. 38, 600, reel 191, PKY.

10. Benjamin Hawkins, "A sketch of the Creek Country in the years 1798 and 1799," LBH, 1:301.

11. Hawkins, "A sketch of the Creek Country in the years 1798 and 1799," LBH, 1:301.

12. Affidavit of John Eades, October 30, 1793, in J. E. Hays, ed., "Creek Indian Letters, Talks, and Treaties, 1705–1839," (Georgia Department of Archives and History, [hereinafter GDAH]), 1:349.

13. Journal of Benjamin Hawkins, December 11, 1796, *Letters of Benjamin Hawkins, 1796–1806: Collections of the Georgia Historical Society*, vol. 9, (Savannah: Georgia Historical Society, 1916), 31; Statement made by John Winslett, April 13, 1832, Letters Received, Office of Indian Affairs, frames 337–40, reel 236, M-234, National Archives (hereinafter NA).

14. Hawkins, "A sketch of the Creek Country in the years 1798 and 1799," LBH, 1:301.

15. Oddly, in 1796 Grayson hired Indian women to pick his cotton crop. Benjamin Hawkins, an Indian agent, reported that Grayson's farm outside Hilabi was a mere thirty acres. Journal of Benjamin Hawkins, December 9–10, 1796, *Letters of Benjamin Hawkins, 1796–1806*, 29–30.

16. Henry Walker v. Robert Grierson, 1817, Jasper County Superior Court Case Files, 179-1-1, GDAH; Robert Grierson v. James Black, 1818, Jasper County Superior Court Case Files, 179-1-1, GDAH.

17. Claim no. 1184, John Grayson, Records Relating to Loyal Creek Claims, 1869–1870, box 12, entry 687, RG 75, NA.

18. Martha Hodes suggests that there was a surprising degree of tolerance for interracial relationships in the South before the Civil War, but her anecdotal evidence must be treated as exceptional rather than normal. Martha Hodes, *White Women, Black Men: Illicit Sex in the Nineteenth-Century South* (New Haven CT: Yale University Press, 1997).

19. John C. Greene, "Some Early Speculations on the Origin of Human Races," *American Anthropologist* 56 (1954): 31–41; Reginald Horsman, *Race and Manifest Destiny: The Origins of American Racial Anglo-Saxonism* (Cambridge MA: Harvard University Press, 1981); William Stanton, *The Leopard's Spots: Scientific Attitudes toward Race in America, 1815–59* (Chicago: University of Chicago Press, 1960); Robert E. Bieder, *Science Encounters the Indian, 1820–1880: The Early Years of American Ethnology* (Norman: University of Oklahoma Press, 1986). For the sixteenth and seventeenth centuries, see Lee Eldridge Huddleston, *Origins of the American Indians: European Concepts, 1492–1729* (Austin: University of Texas Press, 1967).

20. Quoted in Horsman, *Race and Manifest Destiny*, 141.

21. Quoted in Horsman, *Race and Manifest Destiny*, 108. The classic work on environmentalism and Indian policy is Bernard W. Sheehan, *Seeds of Extinction: Jeffersonian Philanthropy and the American Indian* (Chapel Hill: University of North Carolina Press, 1973).

22. Samuel George Morton, *Catalogue of Skulls of Man and the Inferior Animals*, 3rd ed. (Philadelphia, 1849); Stanton, *The Leopard's Spots*, 102.

23. For an examination of Morton's flawed science, see Stephen Jay Gould, *The Mismeasure of Man* (New York: Norton, 1981), 82–104.

24. Charles Caldwell, *Thoughts on the Original Unity of the Human Race* (New York: E. Bliss, 1830; 2nd ed., 1852), 82.

25. T. Hartley Crawford to B. F. Butler, January 9, 1837, *The New American State Papers* [no editor listed] (Wilmington DE: Scholarly Resources, 1972), 9:550.

26. Samuel George Morton, *Crania Americana* (Philadelphia: J. Dobson, 1839), 170.

27. Five Graysons served in the Creek War of 1836. Index to Compiled Service Records of Volunteer Soldiers Who Served during Indian Wars and Disturbances, 1815–1858, M629, NA.

28. Skull no. 441 could possibly have belonged to Athlaha Ficksa, but Morton indicated that it had a different provenance. Morton, *Catalogue of Skulls of Man and the Inferior Animals*.

29. Stanton, *The Leopard's Spots*, 66–67.

30. Stanton, *The Leopard's Spots*, 120, 142.

31. Stanton, *The Leopard's Spots*, 194.

32. Talk of Creek leaders, June 11, 1735, *Colonial Records of the State of Georgia*, ed. Kenneth Coleman and Milton Ready (Athens: University of Georgia Press, 1982), 20:381–87.

33. "At a Congress held at the Fort of Picolata in the Province of East Florida . . .," December 9, 1765, Public Records Office, Colonial Office 5/548, in Writers' Program. Florida. British Colonial Office Records, 2:574, PKY.

34. Mr. Payne to James Seagrove, May 23, 1793, *American State Papers: Indian Affairs*, [no editor listed] (Washington DC, 1832), 1:392.

35. A talk from the White Lieutenant of the Ofuskees to his Friend and Brother, and also his Father, the Governor of New Orleans, November 9, 1793, no. 212, in *McGillivray of the Creeks*, ed. John Walton Caughey (Norman: University of Oklahoma Press, 1938).

36. John R. Swanton, *Myths and Tales of the Southeastern Indians* (1929; reprint, Norman: University of Oklahoma Press, 1995), 74–75; Alan Dundes, "Washington Irving's Version of the Seminole Origin of Races," *Ethnohistory* 9 (1962): 257–64; William C. Sturtevant, "Seminole Myths of the Origin of Races," *Ethnohistory* 10 (1963): 80–86.

37. Grant Foreman, ed., *A Traveler in Indian Territory: The Journal of Ethan Allen Hitchcock, Late Major-General in the United States Army* (Cedar Rapids IA: Torch Press, 1930), 125–27. For another version of this origin story, see Augustus W. Loomis, *Scenes in the Indian Country* (Philadelphia: Presbyterian Board of Publication, 1859), 54–57.

38. For an examination of the motives behind Indian recountings of stories about the origins of the races, see William G. McLoughlin and Walter H. Conser Jr., "'The First Man Was Red'—Cherokee Responses to the Debate over Indian Origins, 1760–1860," *American Quarterly* 41 (1989): 243–64.

39. William G. McLoughlin, "A Note on African Sources of American Racial Myths," *Journal of American Folklore* 89 (1976): 331–35; Alan Dundes, "African Tales among the North American Indians," in *Mother Wit from the Laughing Barrel*, ed. Dundes (1973; reprint, Jackson: University Press of Mississippi, 1990), 114–25.

40. Shoemaker, "How Indians Got to Be Red," 625–44.

41. Merrell, "The Racial Education of the Catawba Indians," 363–84.

42. Statement of Robert Grierson, February 10, 1817, Records of Conveyance, book A–D, County Courthouse, Montgomery County AL; Journal of John Crowell, Alabama Department of Archives and History, Montgomery.

43. G. W. Grayson, *A Creek Warrior for the Confederacy: The Autobiography of Chief G. W. Grayson*, ed. W. David Baird (Norman: University of Oklahoma Press, 1988), 21–25.

44. There is a small possibility that Annie Grayson is the "unknown woman from Ketchapataka" so identified in a massive Barnett family tree compiled in 1936 by Sim L. Liles of Sapulpa, Oklahoma, and now in the archives of the Oklahoma Historical Society, Oklahoma City.

45. Creek Land Location Register, vol. 4, Creek Lands, Creek Removal Records, entry 287, RG 75, NA.

46. 1832 Census of Creek Indians, T-275, NA.

47. Self Emigration Claims of Creek Indians, February 7, 1874, Letters Received, Office of Indian Affairs, frames 243–48, reel 235, M-234, NA.

48. Journal of John Crowell, Alabama Department of Archives and History, Montgomery.

49. Copy of laws of the Creek Nation, January 7, 1825, box 6, folder 22, doc. 1, Keith Read Collection, Hargrett Rare Book and Manuscript Library, University of Georgia, Athens.

50. Elizabeth Grierson v. Hillabee Indians, box 10, 1st series, no. 24, Creek Removal Records, entry 300, RG 75, NA; McIntosh Party Claims, frames 808–11 reel 27, Office of Indian Affairs (hereafter, OIA), Special Files, M-574, NA.

51. The law was first recorded in 1825 but may have been in force even earlier. Copy of laws of the Creek Nation, January 7, 1825, box 6, folder 22, doc. 1, Keith Read Collection, Hargrett Rare Book and Manuscript Library, University of Georgia, Athens.

52. McIntosh Party Claims, frames 1121–22, reel 27, OIA Special Files, M-574, NA; Claimants' accounts, December 1825, LR, OIA, frames 776–77, reel 220, M-234, NA.

53. Dick Grayson v. the Creek Nation, box 10, 1st series, no. 20, Creek Removal Records, entry 300, RG 75, NA.

54. John C. Webb, assee. of E. Grierson v. the Creek Nation, May 23, 1832, box 10, 1st series, no. 36, Creek Removal Records, entry 300, RG 75, NA.

55. Lee Compere to Dr. Bolles, September 31, 1826, FM-98, American Indian Correspondence: The Presbyterian Historical Society Collection of Missionaries' Letters, 1833–1893 (hereinafter PHS) (microfilm; Philadelphia PA).

56. Lee Compere, Withington Journal, September 1, 1827 to February 28, 1828, FM-98, PHS.

57. Lee Compere to Lucius Bolles, May 19, 1828, FM-98, PHS.

58. Lee Compere to Thomas McKenney, May 20, 1828, LR, OIA, frames 703–7, reel 221, M-234, NA.

59. Lee Compere, Withington Journal, March 1828, FM-98, PHS.

60. Lee Compere, Withington Journal, March 1828, FM-98, PHS.

61. Journal of John Crowell, Alabama Department of Archives and History, Montgomery.

62. Robert Grierson to David Mitchell, November 29, 1820, box 6, folder 20, doc. 3, Keith Read Collection, Hargrett Rare Book and Manuscript Library, University of Georgia, Athens.

63. Council Minutes of the Creek Nation West, 1831–1835, Creek Indian Memorial Association Archives, Roll 1, frame 234/235, Oklahoma Historical Society, Oklahoma City.

64. Grayson, A Creek Warrior, 45.

65. Interview with Wilma Moore and Ruth Woods, June 10, 2000, Oktaha, Oklahoma.

66. Edmond Grayson, Individual Indian Case File, entry 346, RG 75, NA-Fort Worth.

The Contributors

Ian Brown is Professor of Anthropology at the University of Alabama and Curator of Gulf Coast Archaeology at the Alabama Museum of Natural History. He has published widely on the history of archaeology, prehistoric Indian culture history, settlement patterns, ceremonialism, ceramics, and various aspects of trade and technology, especially regarding the use of salt by Indian populations. Most of his research has been in the lower Mississippi valley, on the southwest coast of Louisiana, and in the Mobile-Tensaw delta of Alabama, where he has excavated many prehistoric and historic sites.

A specialist on early Spanish American frontiers and borderlands, **Amy Turner Bushnell** has published two monographs, *The King's Coffer: Proprietors of the Spanish Florida Treasury* (1981) and *Situado and Sabana: Spain's Support System for the Presidio and Mission Provinces of Florida* (1994), plus numerous articles and book chapters. Retired from the College of Charleston, she holds courtesy appointments at Brown University and the John Carter Brown Library, where she is preparing an exhibition and catalogue of the Library's early Florida holdings.

Kathleen DuVal is an assistant professor of history at the University of North Carolina, Chapel Hill. Previously she was a postdoctoral fellow at the McNeil Center for Early American Studies at the University of Pennsylvania. She is the author of several articles and a book on the colonial Arkansas River valley, *The Native Ground*, (2006).

Patricia Galloway has a BA in French from Millsaps College, master's and PhD in comparative literature from the University of North Carolina–Chapel Hill, and PhD in anthropology from the University of North Carolina–Chapel Hill as well. In the 1970s she worked on archaeological sites in Europe and supported humanities-oriented computing in the University of London. From 1979 to 2000 she worked at the Mississippi Department of

Archives and History, carrying out documentary editing and editing *Mississippi Archaeology*; as a result, she developed an interest in colonial-period ethnohistory. Having also created the electronic records program for the state of Mississippi, she went in 2000 to the School of Information, University of Texas–Austin, where she teaches courses on digital archives.

Tom Hatley is the Sequoyah Distinguished Professor in Cherokee Studies at Western Carolina University. He has worked and written in the field of environment and culture in sustainable development for twenty-five years and is the author of *The Dividing Paths: Cherokees and South Carolinians through the Era of Revolution* and co-author of *Uncertainty on a Himalayan Scale*. He lives in Asheville, North Carolina.

Vernon James Knight is Professor of Anthropology at the University of Alabama. He holds graduate degrees from the University of Toronto and the University of Florida. His research interests include ethnohistorical approaches to the archaeology of southeastern North America and the Caribbean.

Martha W. McCartney, an independent researcher, is a consultant to the Colonial Williamsburg Foundation and for a decade was project historian for the National Park Service's Jamestown Archaeological Assessment. She is the author of three books and has received five historic preservation awards. Her special interest is seventeenth-century Virginia history.

James H. Merrell, Lucy Maynard Salmon Professor of History at Vassar College, is the author of *The Indians' New World: Catawbas and Their Neighbors from European Contact through the Era of Removal* (1989), and *Into the American Woods: Negotiators on the Pennsylvania Frontier* (1999).

Stephen R. Potter, regional archeologist with the National Park Service for the National Capital Region, has overseen excavations on deeply buried prehistoric sites, African American slave sites, and Civil War battlefields. He is the author of *Commoners, Tribute, and Chiefs: The Development of Algonquian Culture in the Potomac Valley* and co-editor of *Archaeological Perspectives on the American Civil War* as well as the author of numerous articles and chapters on a variety of topics. His research interests include both the prehistoric and historic archaeology of the eastern United States, the seventeenth-century Chesapeake frontier, the southern Algonquian Indians, and the archaeology and history of the American Civil War.

Claudio Saunt teaches American Indian and early American history at the University of Georgia. He is the author of *A New Order of Things: Property, Power, and the Transformation of the Creek Indians, 1733–1816* and recently completed a book on the Grayson family from the eighteenth to the twentieth centuries, published by Oxford University Press in 2005.

Marvin T. Smith is Professor of Anthropology at Valdosta State University. He is the author of *Archaeology of Aboriginal Culture Change in the Interior Southeast: Depopulation during the Early Historic Period* (1987), *Coosa: The Rise and Fall of a Southeastern Mississippian Chiefdom* (2000), and more than seventy other scholarly publications. He received the C. B. Moore Award for excellence in southeastern archaeology in 1992.

Helen Hornbeck Tanner, Senior Research Fellow at The Newberry Library, Chicago, developed an interest in communication routes as a student of Spanish Borderlands history at the University of Florida and the University of Michigan. She expanded her research to include Indian people of the Middle West as an expert witness in litigation before the Indian Claims Commission and other state and federal courts. She is the author of *Zéspedes in East Florida, 1784-90* (Coral Gables: University of Miami Press, 1963; Gainesville: University Press of Florida, 1989), and editor of the *Atlas of Great Lakes Indian History* (Norman: University of Oklahoma Press, 1987), and *The Settling of North America: An Atlas* (New York: Macmillan, 1995).

Daniel Usner is the Holland M. McTyeire Professor of History at Vanderbilt University. His forthcoming book, *A Frontier History of Mississippi*, will be published by Indiana University Press in its Trans-Appalachian Frontier series.

Gregory A. Waselkov is Professor of Anthropology at the University of South Alabama and director of the Center for Archaeological Studies. His research interests embrace prehistoric shell middens, the archaeology of

French colonialism in North America, and the archaeology and ethnohistory of the Creek Indians in the colonial South. He has recently completed a book on Creek métis, Fort Mims, and the Redstick War of 1813-14, to be published by the University of Alabama Press in 2006.

Peter H. Wood is a graduate of Harvard and Oxford who teaches early American history and Native American history at Duke University. He has a longstanding interest in race relations in the early South, as seen in his books *Black Majority* and *Strange New Land*. He is a lead author for a major college-level American history text entitled *Created Equal*, and his most recent book, *Weathering the Storm: An Exploration of Winslow Homer's "Gulf Stream,"* was published by the University of Georgia Press in 2004.

Index

Page references in *italics* indicate a figure, illustration, or table.